THE OFFICIAL®

2015
BLACKBOOK PRICE GUIDE TO UNITED STATES COINS

FIFTY-THIRD EDITION

BY MARC HUDGEONS, N.L.G.
& TOM HUDGEONS, JR.
& TOM HUDGEONS, SR.

HOUSE OF COLLECTIBLES

RANDOM HOUSE REFERENCE • NEW YORK

House of Collectibles and colophon are registered trademarks of Random House, Inc.

RANDOM HOUSE is a registered trademark of Random House LLC.

Please address inquiries about electronic licensing of any products for use on a network, in software, or on CD-ROM to the Subsidiary Rights Department, Random House Audio Publishing Group, fax 212-572-6003.

This book is available for special discounts for bulk purchases for sales promotions or premiums. Special editions, including personalized covers, excerpts of existing books, and corporate imprints, can be created in large quantities for special needs. For more information, write to Random House LLC, Special Markets/ Premium Sales, 1745 Broadway, MD 3-1, New York, NY 10019 or e-mail specialmarkets@randomhouse.com.

Visit the Random House Web site:
www.randomhouse.com

ISBN: 978-0-375-72350-6

ISSN: 0193-9610

Printed in the United States of America

10 9 8 7 6 5 4 3 2 1

Fifty-Third Edition: June 2014

CONTENTS

OFFICIAL BOARD OF CONTRIBUTORS

We would like to thank the following contributors for sharing their professional expertise and experiences in the field of United States Coins.

The American Numismatic Association, Colorado Springs, CO, for the "Official ANA Grading" section.

Scott Barman for his article "Using Technology to Enhance Your Collecting Experience." Scott is a collector and author of the Coin Collectors Blog (coinsblog.ws). He is also President of the Montgomery County Coin Club (montgomerycoinclub.org) and President of the Maryland State Numismatic Society (mdstatenumisassn.org). After more than thirty years in the computer and information security industry, Scott recently started Having-Fun Collectibles to serve collectors in multiple markets.

Tom Bilotta, President of Carlisle Development Corporation in Carlisle, MA, for his article "Numismatic Inventory Software" as well as the coin listing information from Carlisle's Collector's Assistant Software.

The late **Dale Cade** for his timeless article on the history of "Civil War Tokens." Dale was well-known for his expertise in this field and has been inducted into the Civil War Token Society's Hall of Fame. He was a prolific author in their *Civil War Token Journal* and tirelessly worked to spark interest in the field.

Tom Culhane, for the Market Review as well as his pricing expertise throughout the book. Tom is a coin dealer since 1979 and operates his coin store, The Elusive Spondulix, at 954 Stuyvesant Avenue, Union, NJ 07083 as well as the website www.rarecoin.com. Tom was also a grading consultant who spent more than ten years working with the two major grading services, PCGS and NGC, along with grading for Stacks, the New York auction firm. He is a member of several numismatic organizations and an authorized dealer with the major grading services for more than twenty-five years.

Mike Ellis for his article "Errors and Varieties" as well as for the extremely valuable information he provided for the "Expert Tips on Buying and Selling Coins," "How and When to Conserve Coins," and "The American Numismatic Association" chapters. Mike has been a professional numismatist for over twenty years, serving as an authenticator, grader, researcher, teacher, and writer. He is an honorary life member of the Combined Organizations of Numismatic Error Collectors of America (CONECA) and a Life Member of the American Numismatic Association (ANA). For his devotion to and love of the hobby, Mike has received every award CONECA has to offer, including induction into their Hall of Fame.

John Ostendorf and the Civil War Tokens Society for their assistance with our chapter on Civil War Tokens. John Ostendorf is the Secretary of the Civil War Token Society and has written numerous articles for the *CWTS Journal*. He is also the author of *Civil War Store Cards of Cincinnati* and the chairman of the Committee to revise the Civil War Token Store Card book. He has received several awards from the CWTS recognizing his research and contributions, including induction into the CWTS Hall of Fame.

Michael White at The Department of the Treasury, United States Mint, Washington, DC, for photographs and mintage figures.

INTRODUCTION

By Tom Culhane

Welcome to the 2015 edition of *The Official Blackbook Price Guide to United States Coins.* This comprehensive guide book contains the latest pricing information on all U.S. coins starting with pre-Federal colonial issues. You will find all U.S. Mint issues up to the present day as well as coins issued for daily commerce, special commemoratives, and bullion-related series. Keep your newly updated *Blackbook* within arm's reach to enhance your leisure time hobby of collecting while learning the history behind America's coins.

This is my eighteenth consecutive introductory article for *The Official Blackbook.* Reexamining certain trends and events from my time in the hobby will hopefully give you some insights into evolving happenings and some reoccurring situations in the coin hobby. Back at the turn of the millennium gold was under $300 an ounce and now at the start of 2014 spot is $900 higher. Presently gold is quite a bit cheaper than in our last *Blackbook* so the entire gold section had to be refigured at $400 an ounce lower. Go back a bit further to twenty-five years ago and coin collectors were amazed at the broad scope of dazzling quality specimens offered in the Pittman and Eliasberg collections.

The year 2013 saw the cognoscenti of gem material marvel at the sale of Mr. Newman's superb early U.S. type coins through Heritage Auctions of Dallas, Texas, which included a $1.53 million price on a 1796 quarter. The year also included more coins breaking the million-dollar barrier than at any time in the past. Two recognized stars of U.S. numismatics both exceeded the seven-figure mark by more than tripling it in 2013. The Class 1 1804 dollar brought $3,877,500 in a Heritage auction and the famed 1913 Liberty nickel was also sold by the same firm for $3,172,500. Yet, none of the fabled rarities sold throughout the year would exceed the $10,016,875 price tag that the 1794 $1.00 PCGS Specimen 66 (CAC concurring with its green label) achieved at a Stacks Bowers auction. It was back in 1998 when the auction firm of Sotheby's generated hobby headlines promoting a coin sale with 65 cents face value estimated to bring a million dollars. The eighteen half cents and fifty-six large cents, which included a 1796 half cent with pole in NGC MS 65 Red boggled people's minds thinking those coins in total might approach that seven-figure level.

The passing of years has certainly changed what dollar levels coins and other items bring. After Black Monday's October 19, 1987, Dow Jones drop of 508 points to 1738, industry analysts were left wondering if the decline would continue down below 1500 or possibly skyrocket up to the unthinkable 2500 level. With the DJIA breaking 16,500 near the end of 2013, is it any wonder that trophy coins now seem to warrant six- and seven-figure prices at an increasingly quick pace?

Back in 1998 while coin collectors were learning of a new Ike Dollar Commemorative planned for the near future; the hobby was watching high rolling businessmen such as Bruce McNall forming a coin investment fund with Merrill Lynch. That one, unfortunately, ended with Merrill Lynch having to put up $37 million to end the deal as McNall entered into a bankruptcy of a couple of hundred million dollars. Another coin investment fund of that time failed to pan out when a then-prominent Ohio coin dealer was brought in to evaluate 169 coins sold to an Ohio Funeral Directors contract fund, bringing the attention of the Ohio Attorney General's Office, which sued the seller. The fund included the ex-Eliasberg specimen of the 1834 proof $5.00 gold piece at $225,000 and the ex-Amon Carter example of the 1875 $10 gold eagle in AU 55 at $75,000. Most of today's newsworthy coins seem to sell to individuals rather than consortiums or investment funds.

When searching for that special rare coin you have been pursuing, perhaps my recent experience at the Whitman fall Baltimore coin show will illustrate one reason for keeping this *Blackbook* handy. I was attempting to buy examples of scarcer coins I seldom encounter, hopefully an 1802 half cent in good 4 or 6 along with any date large cent from the 1840s in choice MS 63 condition with red and brown color. I had a buying sign at my table as well as a handout given to most of the U.S. dealers with a table at that show. I wasn't certain of what I would need to pay to acquire one of the large cents but thought I might mention an offer of 20 to 25% over the wholesale buy sheet prices to start negotiations. I was aware any knowledgeable dealer (besides who else would have one in inventory?) would want near or above where the retail guides such as the *Blackbook* list these coins. In actuality it did not make much of a difference what I thought a reasonable price would have been since I was not offered nor could I even locate a single large cent from the 1840s in MS 63 R&B at that major coin convention, never mind the several that I hoped to pick up.

No doubt, the Baltimore show ranks up there with the ANA, Central States, or any commercial show such as Ed Aleo's Bay State Show in Massachusetts; so not locating a coin that is listed in various guides at less than $1,000 indicates how difficult the hunt for truly scarce numismatic items can be. Finding the 1802 half cent was virtually as futile with not a single example being available. Interestingly, the 1802 half cent is a coin that back in 1999 was assumed to be valued at $400 and in 2013 at about $700. If you had made a serious effort to purchase them whenever they were available over those fifteen years you would have likely bought some very desirable coins, but I doubt that you would have been able to come up with a half dozen problem-free Good 4 or 6 coins in that extended time period. Again we are not talking about the readily available mass produced mint and proof sets of our present time but the thrill of the hunt in trying to collect classic American rarities. So understanding the need to refer to a guide book of U.S. coins, this *Blackbook* is the ideal handy tool that will help you judge values on all U.S. coins rather than relying on Internet quotes on common bullion-related issues. This *Blackbook* will also prove its mettle if it happens that your collecting focus is on those modern issues, as the updated pricing information in those sections will prove.

Much of the overall growth of the modern collector market that has occurred since the rise of the Internet might be credited to Harvey Stack of the venerable NYC auction firm Stacks Bowers, since he initially proposed the fifty state quarter program to Congress. Millions of people became very interested in the designs of the series. One hundred or even several hundred years into the future the magnitude of that idea will be appreciated by many more millions of collectors yet unborn. The strength of the modern coin market can be illustrated by comparing the modern silver eagle with the classic Morgan dollar. The Morgan dollar was mass produced for twenty-six years from 1878 to 1904, along with the 1921 coins; our government melted over one hundred million of these coins with millions of others well circulated as tools of commerce.

The silver eagle by 2013, also in its 27th year of production, saw its all-time high mintage exceeding 40 million by November, surpassing the previous mint total of 39, 86,500 sold in 2011. The years 2010 and 2012 saw issues of 34,661,500 and 33,742,500, respectively, so is it any wonder with mintage figures this lofty why promoters aren't heading to the coin show circuit looking to fill orders for Morgan silver dollars in quantity? They can simply offer the eagles displaying the exceptional eye-appealing quality that ensures virtually no returns based on condition. The modern coin buyers continue to be enthralled with these one-ounce beauties, and the occasional variations in striking and lower mintage special issues sparks the notion that opportunities continue in this series.

The year 2013 was the fiftieth of minting Kennedy half dollars, which replaced the Franklin design after a mere twenty-five year run. The 1964 introduction of the Kennedy design provided a real spark in reviving interest in collecting coins. With today's halves only being sold to collectors at premium prices, we are witnessing a corresponding waning of that interest among the general public. While design changes during the past ten years have brought back some interest in the cent and nickel, it now takes 105 and 75 years of coinage to complete these sets. A daunting task for most casual collectors. While the reverse design changes continue with the National Park theme on quarters, the Roosevelt dime that has been around since 1946 remains an uninspiring, little-collected series.

The Presidential dollar series is perhaps the most depressing of all modern issues now that the coins are no longer issued to the public at face value. A look through the *Blackbook* will hopefully stimulate your interest in an underappreciated series. Take the uncirculated Liberty head or "Mercury" dime from the 1940s as a possibility. It was minted in .900 silver during the Second World War with $1.50 of intrinsic bullion value; collectors are able to purchase them for less than $10, which is about the same price as they were back in the mid-1970s.

Let's briefly examine one of the most popular classic American coins, the Walking Liberty half dollar. A "short set" of these consists of the twenty dates and mints from 1941 to 1947-D. Fifteen years ago a gem set would generally run just under $4500 with an Unc 60 set bringing $675, whereas the 2014 edition of the *Blackbook* shows these totaling $5500 and $1000. Obviously an increase in cost, but no consideration is given in this quick mention to the value of the dollar during this time frame. A popular earlier half, the 1830s Bust examples in extra fine condition, essentially all tripled in value during the same time. Currently one of the modern series, the $5.00 gold commemoratives begun in 1986, shows that of the twenty-seven issues in proof condition nearly all (twenty-five to be precise) are now valued strictly as bullion items.

This new *2015 Blackbook* is full of such interesting data and even includes a few non-coins: to wit, the so-called Wilson dollars of 1920. These have shown tremendous price increases in Gem BU 65 condition with silver strikes now valued at $3750 vs. their 1997 price of $350, as well as the copper medals in similar grade listing at $4000 up from the 1997 value of $465. Time and thought spent with your *Blackbook* analyzing pricing information will make you a more astute buyer and likely contribute to your enjoyment when looking at coins.

Interest in the U.S. Territorial issues of the Philippines steadily picks up as many collectors enjoy the comradeship with fellow hobbyists building their registry set collections on the PCGS and NGC websites. Many history buffs and fans of artistic coinage happily pursue the large number of affordable U.S. Philippine coins. Students and followers of WW II are intrigued by the military stories behind our territorial ally of some seventy years ago. Japan hit the Philippines the day after Pearl Harbor and it is quite accurate to say Manila was one of the most devastated cities in the world by the end of the Second World War. Generally low survival rates of mint state Philippine coins means some great rarities exist, namely the 1906-S peso and the newly added to the *Blackbook,* 1903-S fifty centavos. If one of the two listed examples of the 1903-S were to reach the active present market it would have to be considered a possible six-figure coin and thus become the second USPI coin to reach that level.

Last year's introductory article reported on the unique 1907 (P) peso PCGS Proof 64 in .800 silver bringing $189,750 at a Lyn Knight auction. While these prices are certainly higher than when I first added the Philippine section to the *Blackbook* fifteen years ago, they pale in comparison to any other area of U.S. numismatics. Remember, these coins were minted in the U.S. when the archipelago was part of our country. The Wilson dollars as mentioned above are listed in the Commemorative Medals section of the *Blackbook* and are actively sought by USPI collectors as they were struck to mark the opening of the U.S. Branch Mint in Manila. The Philippine coin series truly remains a virgin area of U.S. numismatics in terms of valuing the scarcer pieces.

One of the most interesting stories dealing with "coins" in 2013 was the rising awareness, value, and use of the new Bitcoins being "mined" on the Internet. It gives rise to a furthering move toward a cashless society that futurists expected years ago. Monetary transactions are taking place as banks and their fees are removed from the equation. Whether or not Bitcoins will ever be successfully marketed with an actual physical representation of a coin has yet to be determined. What collector at heart wouldn't like a Bitcoin for a type set of 21st century numismatics?

Other esoteric areas of numismatics warranted some notice, including the purchase of a carved nickel for over $24,000 by Chris Dempsey of Erie, Pa. Mr. Dempsey set the new high-water mark for an artistic double-sided carved Buffalo nickel designed by "Bo" Hughes, a noted Depression era carver. As I explained in last year's edition, "Hoboken" nickels attracted notoriety during the First World War as they proliferated in the NJ waterfront city of Hoboken as America's doughboys shipped out. Some amazing carvings are now being done by today's artists who generally offer their wares on the Internet.

We hope this *Blackbook of U.S. Coins* remains at your side throughout the year while pursuing your coin hobby.

Tom Culhane, a coin dealer since 1979, operates his coin store, The Elusive Spondulix, at 954 Stuyvesant Avenue, Union, NJ 07083 and the web site www.rarecoin.com. He was also a grading consultant who spent more than ten years working with the two major grading services, PCGS and NGC, along with grading for Stacks, the New York auction firm. The television program Jeopardy! has consulted with Culhane to verify numismatic questions. He is a member of several numismatic organizations and an authorized dealer with the major grading services for more than twenty-five years. Culhane became a grading consultant on Irish and Philippine coins in 2013 for the new Wings firm. Culhane has successfully proposed designs for two U.S. Commemorative postage stamps: Irish Immigration and the James Cagney issue. He currently has two additional ideas under consideration by the postal committee: a 350th anniversary stamp for New Jersey and a proposal to honor Saint Patrick's Day on a U.S. Commemorative stamp.

THE HOBOKEN NICKELS OF THE GREAT WAR

By Tom Culhane

As we have now reached the 100th anniversary of the first issuance of the Buffalo or Indian Head nickel, an iconic American design, this is an ideal time to examine the folk art tradition of carving designs into the coins which began shortly after their initial release. 1913 marked the official end of the U.S.-Philipppine War though periodic hostilities continued right up through the late 1930s as mentioned in accounts of New Jersey's Medal of Honor recipient John Basilone's life. America's next war would see the introduction of the popular prank of passing carved Buffalo nickels come into being. Back in the late 1990s I took notice of the occasional newspaper articles announcing the death of aged WWI veterans. In the early 2000s, Alfred Pugh, the last surviving WWI combat wounded American soldier, passed away at the advanced age of 108.

Five years ago in February 2008, Henry Landis, an Army recruit for two months at the war's end, who hadn't served overseas, also died at 108; having been one of the last two WWI veterans. Thus, Fred Buckles, 107 at the time became the final U.S. WWI vet still living and he would eventually reach the impressive age of 109. Buckles had enlisted in the U.S. Army in April 1917 and served as an ambulance driver in France. Amazingly, he also survived three years as a Japanese prisoner of war after being captured in 1941 while employed as a civilian with a Philippine shipping company.

More than three million of the WWI veterans who served overseas passed through my town of birth, Hoboken, NJ, which was the prime port of embarkation for the American Expeditionary Forces. Almost 300,000 troops also departed from Newport News, VA, while other port cities notably Boston, Baltimore, and Philadelphia primarily shipped military equipment and supplies.

At the turn of the 20th century, Hoboken was known by the nickname of "Little Bremen" because of its large German immigrant population. The German-American piers of the Hamburg-American line and North German Lloyd shipping were taken over by the Federal Government to free up the Hoboken waterfront for troop movements. All the German ships docked in Hoboken and other American ports were taken over by the U.S. government. They converted these ships for our use if they hadn't been too severely damaged at the last minute by the German crews on board. A total of 91 merchant ships were seized throughout the nation. The Germans in Hoboken were taken into custody and sent to internment camps until the end of the war, as were the crews of the 91 seized ships.

The mile square city of Hoboken is across the Hudson River from Manhattan, just north of Jersey City on whose riverfront the Black Tan Explosion of July 30, 1916 occurred. Germany was blamed for the attack and fined $50 million in 1939 which was finally paid in 1979. Movie fans can recall a mental image of Hoboken from the acclaimed 1954 Oscar winning picture filmed there, *On the Waterfront*. The city is recognized as the birthplace of baseball and Frank Sinatra. At the outbreak of America's involvement in the Great War's fighting Hoboken had 237 bars along with a number of back house social clubs serving liquor. President Woodrow Wilson several times bade farewell to departing troops from the balcony of the Clam Broth House, a popular bar, as they boarded transport ships at the pier right across the street.

The doughboys of WWI drilled at camps around the country including Camp Merritt, NJ in parts of what became Tenafly, Cresskill, Bergenfield, and Dumont, NJ. Oftentimes to pass the idle periods in military camps, some of the soldiers picked up the new hobby of carving designs into the new Buffalo nickels which proved to be an interesting diversion. Nickel carving was just a small segment of what can be classified as trench art. While appreciated today by a wide number of collectors as novelties and folk art, the nickels were considered debased at the time and thus worthless as money. When the troops left military training camps they were transported by train to Hoboken to ship out. It was the last bit of liberty these servicemen would enjoy in the U.S. and a good many stopped at one or more of those 237 bars. For laughs the soldiers passed carved nickels which often featured a rendition of the Kaiser or some other alteration onto Hoboken bartenders.

Even into the 1950s and early 1960s, some of the bar owners kept a mug full of the carved nickels behind the bar as a lesson to watch the money they were handling. Back in the late teens when the soldiers were crowding into the Hoboken bars, the owners were expected to keep the carved nickels and accept the loss, yet a fair number of them managed to get passed back to customers, usually out of state New Yorkers who had taken the ferry over and may have had a few too many to notice the altered coins. It became commonplace for the "unsporting" bar owners or bartenders afraid of being blamed for taking the coins to pass them on to the tipsy New Yorkers. This happened to enough drinkers that New York newspapers warned their readers to be wary of getting stuck with a handful of the now infamous Hoboken nickels. Disappointed bar owners might wind up with 40 or 50 carved nickels in a week and at that time there weren't any aficionados of these folk art carvings who might redeem the lost nickels. The joking soldiers enjoyed their final days stateside enough that eventually the Federal Government attempted to close all the bars in the waterfront city and bring prohibition to Hoboken.

As the First World War progressed, the Meuse-Argonne Offensive began on September 26, 1918. This attack on the German lines lasted 47 days—America's longest battle up to that point in history. During the assault, General Pershing promised the troops,

"By Christmas you'll be in heaven, hell, or Hoboken!." Many of those troops did not live to return to Hoboken, such as Matthew Juan, an under draft age rodeo performer who enlisted. Being a Native American, he would have been exempt from serving since Indians were not considered American citizens. Although he survived the sinking of his transport ship by a German sub, he nevertheless wound up as the first Native American, as well as the first soldier from Arizona, to be killed in the Great War.

Of the more than two million soldiers who did return to Hoboken, a good many did manage to start their celebrations back in those same Hoboken bars with some newly carved nickels for old times' sake. Other veterans had their Hoboken nickels gold plated while in France and held onto them for years as good luck pocket pieces.

It was a somber day in Hoboken, NJ on May 23, 1921, when President Warren G. Harding addressed the crowds to witness the return of 5,212 bodies of American soldiers, sailors, marines, and nurses for burial. In an age before most people had radio the president's speech was recorded and Victor Record sales throughout the nation let Americans hear the respectful words he spoke at this most solemn occasion. All proceeds from the record sales were donated to the American Red Cross. Most in the Hoboken crowd wore a poppy sent from France on the ship as a symbol of respect for the deceased heroes.

While today's coin collectors like to refer to carved nickels as Hobo nickels and associate them with the Depression of the 1930s, there was an earlier group of men we should remember and honor who had a few laughs with their Hoboken nickels before going off to fight in the Great War.

USING TECHNOLOGY TO ENHANCE YOUR COLLECTING EXPERIENCE

By Scott Barman

When I started collecting coins in the early 1970s, it was still possible to find silver coins and other older coins in pocket change. In fact, it was after being paid several Indian Head cents for delivering newspapers that I became interested in collecting coins. After gathering coins from collecting payments for delivering newspapers, I started to look through my father's pocket change looking for coins to insert into my folders.

Collecting today has advanced far beyond the way I started. To find out more about those Indian Head cents I bought a reference book. To buy or sell coins, I had to travel to a dealer. While there is nothing wrong with dealers, I did not have one in my neighborhood and that made it a difficult proposition. Today, collectors can go online and use their favorite search engine to find information about the coin they found or the coin someone wants to sell them.

Prior to the arrival of the World Wide Web, those of us with access to what was then called the ARPAnet could access simple email lists and a bulletin board–like system called Usenet. Usenet was a distributed messaging system similar to today's online forums except that the articles were distributed to each computer with access. When it was conceived in 1979, computing power and the architecture of the Internet made it easier to distribute the articles in bulk, sometimes overnight, rather than accessing them across the network as we do today.

Among the first technology breakthroughs that helped

collectors were the invention of the simple database and spreadsheet programs. Collectors would use these programs to create databases and spreadsheets to track their collection. These would become the basis for inventory programs that would see their popularity rise in the late part of the last century.

Newcomers to the technologies of the Internet and mobile computing might look at these beginnings as ancient times, but it set the tone for the future of adding technology to enhance the collecting experience. The first breakthrough in expanding the information available was the invention of the World Wide Web.

Sir Tim Berners-Lee and Belgian computer scientist Robert Cailliau, while working at CERN, the European Organization for Nuclear Research, invented the concept of the Web. Using the power of technology offered by the Internet, the Web has brought a new way of delivering information from those who have it to those who want it. In numismatics, it allowed people to build sites that not only deliver information, but also enhance the ways for collectors to communicate with each other.

The initial impact of the Web was the ability for collectors to buy and sell coins anywhere in the country and then around the world. First, the online auction site eBay made it easy to bring buyers and sellers together from the comfort of a computer. Dealers, seeing the successes of collectors shopping on eBay joined the online auction site and then began developing their own online presences to sell directly to collectors.

In the computing industry, we look at the growth in the capability of technology in terms of "Moore's Law." Named for Intel Corporation co-founder Gordon E. Moore, Moore's Law says that the capabilities of technology double every two years. While Moore was talking about the growth of the microprocessors that are the brains behind the computers, there has been a growth in the capabilities of the computers that make them wonderful tools to enhance your collecting experience.

Online Price Guides

The perpetual question from collectors, investors, and those with passing interest is "What does the coin cost?" While paper books are wonderful references and can be more convenient than electronic alternatives, books have the problem of being static from one year to another. To answer the collecting public's desire for more information, one of the first online services for collectors has been online price guides.

Price guides are as varied as their publishers. Some publishers offer their price guides for the retail market available for free while long-time publishers of price guides provide paid online services for their data. Which is best for you depends on your collecting goals.

News and Blogs

Finding numismatic news and information used to be limited to the weekly and monthly publications sent to us via the postal service. Collectors were tied to publishing schedules, causing news to travel slowly. With the ease of producing a well-designed website and hiring writers to look for stories that would be of interest to collectors, there are now websites dedicated to delivering numismatic community news.

While there are many sources, sites that are dedicated to providing frequent updates to news that would of interest to numismatists, collectors, and those with a passing interest are as follows:

- *Coin Collecting News* (coincollectingnews.org)
- *Coin Update* (coinupdate.com)
- *Coin News* (coinnews.net)
- *Coin Week* (coinweek.com)

These sites provide various ways for readers to keep up to date with new articles. Some offer a daily email notice while others offer RSS (Rich Site Summary or Really Simple Syndication) feeds. An RSS feed is a special file accessed from the Web that will tell you when new information is available.

As RSS feeds proliferate and their function has expanded, web browsers have been either dropping support for reading RSS feeds (like Apple's Safari) or have not added enhancements (Microsoft's Internet Explorer and Mozilla Firefox), making it difficult to keep up with the news. Two good stand-alone replacements to use at your computer are Sharp-Reader for Windows (sharpreader.net) and NetNewsWire for the Mac (netnewswireapp.com). Both programs have won many industry awards.

Last year, the popular Google shut down its Reader service that provided Web-based access to subscribe to RSS feeds. Reader also had the advantage of being a central repository that allowed other programs to repackage the feeds so the user could read them in more friendly formats. Since the shutdown of the Reader service, there have been others that have stepped into the void. Here is a sample of services that you can choose from:

Web-Only Resources

• AOL Reader (reader.aol.com) is a Web-based service that was started shortly before Google announced the end of the Reader service. It has gained a following for having a plain, no-nonsense but solid working interface that has satisfied some of the people who have switched to the service.

• The Old Reader (theoldreader.com) is a Web-based service that looks and acts like Google's old Reader service. The author of the service makes it clear that this was not an accident.

Web and Mobile Apps

• Feedly (feedly.com) is a Web-based service that is nearly a drop-in replacement for Reader. Feedly has its own apps for iOS devices (iPhone and iPad), Android, and Kindle Fire but interfaces with many other apps to use its data. See www.feedly.com/apps.html for the list of apps that can read Feedly saved feeds.

• FeedBin (feedbin.me) is a paid service that also has support for many mobile apps. The advantage of using a paid service over a free service is that the paid service comes with support and without advertisements.

• NetVibes (netvibes.com) is an all-inclusive dashboard to manage your Web-based reading. It is free for users but has paid accounts for businesses to monitor trends on the Web. Being a paid service, NetVibes also creates its own "apps" that help cultivate news and information from the Internet and deliver it to your NetVibes account.

• Reeder 2 (reederapp.com) is a no-frills reading app for iOS (iPhone and iPad) that integrates with other services. Reeder started as an iOS interface with Google Reader but had to evolve when Reader was discontinued. Reeder is a paid app with a different version for the iPhone and iPad.

Mash-up Services

Mash-up services combine information from multiple resources to provide a single interface as if it came from a single resource. Mash-up services are usually free to the user but rely on advertising for revenues.

• Digg Reader (digg.com/reader) is a new service from the long-time mash-up system Digg. Digg's new Reader app and service will allow users to create their own mash-ups from selected news feeds rather than create mash-ups on what you read, which is what the Digg service does.

• Flipboard (flipboard.com) is a popular service that turns your interests into an electronic magazine. Users can create their own virtual magazine based on who they follow on Twitter, from RSS feeds, or from various channels that are managed by Flipboard or one of their partners. Flipboard is available for iOS, Android, Windows Phone, and BlackBerry.

This does not mean you have to give up your subscription to the magazines that you have been reading for many years. Rather, you can supplement your collecting news reading at their websites:

• *COINage* (coinagemag.com)

• *Coin World* (coinworld.com), whose current edition can be read online (see the "Digital Edition" section on the website to register for a free account).

• *Coin World neXt* (weekly.coinworld.com) is a weekly electronic publication that focuses on one area of numismatics that strives to bring unique information not available from other sources.

• Krause Publication's Numismaster (numismaster.com), which includes articles from *Numismatic News, World Coin News, Coins,* and *Bank Note Reporter.* In 2014, Krause began to expand online delivery by adding email-only editions to subscribers.

Aside from many specialty websites (you can use a search engine to find information on just about any numismatic topic), there are bloggers dedicated to writing and discussing numismatic information. A blog, which is derived from the term "web log," is the writing of someone with information or an opinion based on the blog's subject manner.

The difference between a blog and a news-based website is that the blog writer, also called a blogger, is not limited to reporting the news. Some bloggers will analyze the news or other issues that affect the numismatic community. Bloggers provide another view into the news, collecting, the numismatic community, and the hobby that adds to the richness of the online information.

Mobile Computing

While there have been ways to carry the Internet in your pocket since the late 1990s, the release of the Apple iPhone and the software that runs the phone (iOS) paved the way for creating a new vehicle to view data on the go. With the addition of the Android system and now the new Windows Mobile phones, tablets, and other mobile devices, the possibilities are endless.

The basic use for a smart mobile phone is to use the built-in browser to explore information on the Web. While many websites may not be enhanced for a mobile display, the browsers have the ability to zoom in to the page so it can be read on the smaller screen. Sites that provide an enhanced display for mobile devices may not provide a lot of information in that format, but it is packaged for the collector on the go.

Two examples of mobile-enhanced websites you may want to bookmark are for the top two grading services: Numismatic Guarantee Corporation (NGC@m.ngccoin.com) and the Professional Coin Grading Service (PCGS@m.pcgs.com). Both sites will allow you to enter label information from their holders to help you determine whether the coin is genuine or otherwise. NGC also has the NGC Coin Explorer to give you more information about coins, and PCGS offers the ability to track your grading order. Having access to both websites helps when attending coin shows.

A key area of mobile computing is apps. Apps, short for applications, are programs designed to run on the mobile device that are capable of doing more than what can be done on a website. App markets are a new industry that was pioneered by Apple for its iPhone, iPod Touch, and iPad devices. Google has introduced Google Play for the Android market and Microsoft opened the Windows Store (windows.

microsoft.com/en-us/windows-8/apps) for desktop, tablet, and phones running Windows 8.

Since apps are new, there are not many good apps for collectors. Most of the currently available apps that can be found are for Apple's devices. Starter lists of apps are as follows:

• Coin World (iPad)—Brings *Coin World* magazine and its website to the iPad. Included is the "Making the Grade" section with pictures of coins in various state of preservation to help you grade your coins.

• CoinFlation (iPhone, iPod Touch, Android)—the mobile companion to coinflation.com. Find out what the metal values of your coins are worth based on the most up-to-date spot prices.

• Eyenote (iPhone, iPod Touch)—this free iOS application from the U.S. Bureau of Engraving and Printing is designed to allow the visually impaired to identify U.S. paper currency. The app limits the identification to Series 1996 and later currency.

• Money Reader (iPhone, iPod Touch)—this app was created to help the visually impaired use their mobile phones to identify paper currency. Not only does this work for U.S. small size currency, but for many currencies around the world, including the euro, British pound, Canadian dollar, and Australian dollar. You can find out more about Money Reader and other apps for the visually impaired at looktel.com.

• NGC Coin Details (iPhone)—Brings the NGC mobile website to your phone as an app offering more options, including the ability to scan label bar codes to look up information about a coin in an NGC holder.

• Numis (iPhone, iPod Touch, Android)—this is the official app to read *The Numismatist*, the monthly journal of the American Numismatic Association. ANA membership is required.

• Numis HD (iPad)—the official iPad app to read *The Numismatist*, the monthly journal of the American Numismatic Association. ANA membership is required.

• Photograde (iPhone, iPod Touch, iPad, Android)—Brings all of the images from PCGS Photograde Online (pcgs.com/photograde) to your mobile device. Since the detailed images that would be used to help you examine your coins are very big, it will save download time, and you can save money by transmitting the images only once to your device.

As the use of mobile devices grows and the collector community talks about its needs, more apps will be developed to satisfy the market.

E-books

Amazon.com, probably the most successful electronic commerce (e-commerce) website, pioneered this era of electronic books (e-books) with the invention of the Kindle. Amazon designed the Kindle so that it would use a standard that it controlled so that you can gain access to the books and information sold on Amazon.com. The Kindle family of e-book readers was the first of the current era of tablets and has been successful in moving the publishing industry to make books available for users of e-readers.

Electronic books are the future of publishing, which can be seen by the phenomenal increase in e-book sales in the last few years. People of all ages are now turning to e-books to enable them to carry libraries with them when they are on the go. Schools and colleges are now turning to e-books to allow students to purchase the most current information they need to support their learning.

As more publishers are providing access to their titles electronically, e-books are key to providing the next generation of collectors, numismatists, and researchers with information in a manner that suits their lives.

E-books are not limited to current editions. There are a number of out-of-print books online that can be downloaded legally without cost. These are books whose copyright has expired and that have been scanned either through Google's book project (books.google.com) or the Internet Archive Books project (archive.org/details/text).

There are a lot of gems hidden in the archives. One of those gems is *Domestic and Foreign Coins Manufactured by the Mints of the United States 1792–1965*. Produced by the U.S. Mint and printed by the Government Printing Office, this book has the statistics about every coin manufactured by the Mint from the information published in annual reports. It is a great history reference into the Mint.

Another advantage of e-book readers is that if you find something interesting that is in Portable Document Format (PDF), it can be saved on the e-book reader to be used as a reference. If you find an article on a website, you can have it available on your e-reader to read later. If you can create a PDF copy of a webpage, that can also be saved to read later on your e-reader.

Although each of the devices has its own online book-store where you can buy e-books, Amazon and Barnes & Noble have apps that run on many devices that will read books bought at their stores. The Kindle app can run on your computer as well as your iOS, Android, BlackBerry, and Widows phones and tablets. If you buy most of your books from Amazon.com, then a Kindle is the best choice, but the Kindle is very restrictive on the number of devices on which you can read the book.

Family readers can benefit from the Nook by Barnes & Noble, where several household members can share an ac-count. The Barnes & Noble Nook app can allow readers to read books bought at bn.com to be read on iPhones, iPads, Android devices, and Windows phones and tablets. These options make the best e-reader a matter of personal prefer-ence without limiting access to the best electronic reading experience.

Social Media

It has taken a while for the numismatic community to begin to embrace social media. Some say that the demo-graphic that uses social media tends to be younger than the average collector. While that may be true, there is a growing online community using social media to talk about collect-ing. Three of the most well-known social media services are Facebook, Twitter, and Pinterest.

Facebook (facebook.com) was not the inventor of social media on the Web, but it has been the most successful be-cause of its ability to adapt to new services. Facebook has made it easy for people of all ages to be social online. Not many collectors have embraced Facebook or they have reserved their Facebook activities to maintaining relation-ships with friends, relatives, and colleagues. Facebook's very public issues with privacy may have collectors think-ing about their use of Facebook and restricting what they share.

Twitter (twitter.com) is called a micro-blogging service. A Twitter message can be no longer than 140 characters in length, making brevity a necessity. Twitter is good for short comments and sending links to interesting information to your followers. Similar to making "friends" on Facebook, on

Twitter you follow a user's messages, called Tweets. Bloggers use Twitter to announce when content is available. Others use Twitter to point to interesting articles for their followers to read.

Some people can get confused by Twitter's fast pace. The thing to remember about Twitter is that it is a snapshot in time. If you are not reading Twitter during the workday, do not worry. Much of the information will be available in the media or should not be much of a concern. Pick interesting people to follow and you might want to consider looking back on their timeline to see if they had anything interesting to say.

Pinterest (pinterest.com) is the new social media service that calls itself a "Virtual Pinboard." Think of Pinterest as the Twitter for pictures. While you can post pointers to images on Twitter, Pinterest is all about pictures. One of the best things about the numismatic community that is growing on Pinterest is the ability to find interesting pictures around the Web and post them to Pinterest. The Pinterest mobile apps will also allow you to take pictures with your mobile device and upload them to a board you set up for others to see. All three services have mobile apps for both the Apple and Android devices.

Additionally, those interested in creating online photo albums and photo journals can look into photo blogging services like Yahoo's Flickr (flickr.com), Photobucket (photobucket.com), and Google's Picasa (picasa.google.com). All three have apps for the Apple devices, while only Photobucket and Picasa have apps for Android. Users of Apple iOS devices can use iCloud to share pictures of their collection.

Buying and Selling Online

Although eBay opened the online world to coin buying and selling, it is not the only place for a collector to search for coins. Dealers the world over have embraced online selling and have created e-commerce websites to sell to more people than those in their local area. Their embracing the Web and e-commerce also provides the collector with a wide variety of purchasing options and a way to expand their collections from the comfort of their computers.

A primary option for purchasing current collectibles would be from the manufacturer. For United States coins, that would be the U.S. Mint (usmint.gov). The U.S. Mint will always offer the latest collectibles and continue to offer some from years past as long as it has the inventory to do so. Most coins must be sold in the year that they are minted, so plan your purchases accordingly or plan to buy your collectible on the secondary market.

The U.S. Mint is not the only mint that sells to the public online. Coins from the Royal Canadian Mint (mint.ca), Royal Mint (royalmint.com), Perth Mint (perthmint.com.au), New Zealand Mint (nzmint.com), and many others can be purchased directly from the source. There are dealers who represent these mints in the United States that offer online ordering with domestic shipping, thus saving costs and customs hassles.

Auctions

Auctions are the oldest type of marketplace, dating back over 2,500 years, with some auction houses in Europe having been in business since the 18th century. As with most businesses, online and mobile technologies have made it easier to participate in auctions from anywhere in the world.

The excitement behind online auctions goes beyond eBay. Traditional auction houses are now moving auctions online as active platforms rather than just as an entry point for absentee bids to floor auctions. Some hold exclusively online auctions while others have found ways to do live bidding online to extend the auction floor to anywhere in the world.

The auction business has seen the growth of a few types of businesses, ranging from ones that fully embrace technology to those that use it as an extension of their traditional business models. Large auction houses like Heritage Auctions (ha.com) have fully embraced the technology and offer exclusively online auctions along with their live auctions that open with pre-bidding online. Heritage has invested a lot into its site, which includes an extensive auction archive with full catalog details and information that makes it a numismatic resource on top of the auctions. Heritage has won awards for Web-based services.

Another evolution in the auction business is the transformation from the telephone to exclusively Web-based, online bidding. One of the first in that transition was Teletrade (teletrade.com), which used to be telephone bidding but now is exclusively online. Others, like David Lawrence Rare Coins (davidlawrence. com), have followed using the exclusively online auction model to make it easier for sellers to consign to the auction and bidders to purchase nice collect-ibles. As a result, other auction companies have expanded their online auction services, making it easier to consign and participate in auctions regardless of where they are being held.

Some dealers have found that sponsoring online auc-tions can profitably help them sell inventory and reach a clientele beyond their hometowns. Using the services from companies like Proxibid (proxibid.com) and Live Auction-eers (liveauctioneers.com) to host their auction and provide transaction support, dealers can take the consignments they obtain locally and offer them to a broader audience to help sellers get the best price for their items.

For the collectors bidding on these auctions, technology gives them access to numismatic items that they would normally not see because of not being able to attend an auction.

Looking into the Future

The first stop on looking into the future is with education. With the number of colleges moving toward online educa-tion, there is a lot of software that can support extending education beyond the classroom. Organizations that have education as part of their missions, like the ANA, can expand their education mission to including people online. Classes can be held exclusively online or in conjunction with events like their Summer Seminar or their national conventions.

Next look into the future would be to use the multimedia capabilities that are available to expand education to create virtual clubs. Virtual clubs can be formed around a collecting interest and have international participation from members. Imagine forming a club for enthusiasts of silver bullion coins with members from Canada, Europe, and Asia.

Other technologies could be cataloging coins by just tak-ing a picture, voice-activated searching for coin information, and possibly coin grading using your mobile phone. The possibilities are endless!

Your Security Online

When looking at the tools to use to enhance your collect-ing experience, remember that scammers and other crimi-nals are using the same tools in their activities. Although the technology is helpful, it is not mature enough to trust to keep you safe. Rather than hope that technology will be safe, there are a few guidelines that you should follow to ensure your safety and security:

1. Make sure your software is up to date. Whether you have an Apple or Windows computer, you should learn how the make sure to update the software on those devices. Updating your software means more than updating the operating system (Windows, OS X, Android, or iOS), it also means updating the apps so that their bugs cannot be used against you. This includes your browser, which is probably the most used program on your computer.

2. Run an anti-virus and anti-malware program. Malware is "malicious software" that would do harm to your computer. This attack would install malware on your system through your browser. Some service providers offer a free download of an anti-virus program. Take advantage of that offer! If you want a good basic anti-virus program try the AVG Anti-Virus Free Edition (free.avg.com). It is not as full featured as others, but it provides good protection.

3. Once you install your anti-virus program, make sure you keep it up to date! Keeping it up to date means that you download the information about new attacks from the manufacturers of the anti-virus program. Threats are constantly changing and you need to keep up to date. If you are using old information, it is like leaving holes in your defenses for the attackers to get through. Make sure the software is updated. Also, pay for the yearly service to keep it updated. Think of it as an insurance policy for your critical data!

4. Desktop and laptop computer systems now come with built-in protections that you should learn how to turn on. If you do not have a relative or friend who can help you, electronic stores provide services to help teach you and set up these features. It is worth spending the time and money for these services to protect your computer from being attacked.

5. Think about what you are doing before you click that link. If you receive a random link in email even from someone you know, contact that person to make sure they sent the link and are not victims of a cyber-attack. If you receive a link in a text message saying that your bank needs for you to verify your account, do not click the link but call your bank and ask if it is a legitimate request—likely it is not.

6. If you do not know what it is, do not investigate; just delete or ignore the message. Email with attachments, links in tweets, and online forum posts can contain links to sites

that are ready to infect your system. If there is any doubt, just throw it out!

7. Know how to tell when a site is legitimate by looking at the visual cues. Does the website's address (URL) look right? If you are supposed to be at your bank's website, is there anything else other than the bank's address? Sometimes scammers in another country will make their addresses look like your bank's address (e.g., yourbank.com.cn, providing your bank is not in China). Remember, the number one and lower-case "l" (letter el) look similar and so does an upper case "O" and zero.

8. Just because there is a lock on your browser does not mean the website is secured. It means that the communications between your browser and the server are secured. The same rules for checking the visual cues (above) apply. If there are any errors when trying to begin what you think is a secure session, you should not trust the connection; instead, contact the company you are trying to do business with. Also, look for the clues for sites that are using enhanced security. When you connect to a website that is using the enhanced security, you should see a green lock or other signal that says that your browser confirmed the site you are connected to uses the enhanced security standards and can be trusted.

9. Although Wi-Fi hotspots are convenient, they are also convenient to the scammer. Most Wi-Fi hotspots are not secure and anyone can connect. If you do not have to enter a password to access the Wi-Fi hotspot, it is the network equivalent of standing on a street corner and broadcasting your personal information for anyone to hear. Using a direct connection, such as the cellular data connection on your mobile device, is safer than using an unsecured Wi-Fi hotspot.

10. Speaking of Wi-Fi, if you have a wireless network at home you should learn how to properly set it up or get help. Even security professionals who do this for a living often find setting up Wi-Fi networks difficult so do not be afraid of asking for help!

11. Protect your personal information. Understand the information you are being asked to provide and give only what is needed to complete the transaction. For example, there is no reason for anyone to require your social security number for any online transaction. Only fill out the required fields in checkout forms. If there are any questions, find the site's privacy policy and make sure you understand how your personal information will be stored and used.

12. Only use safe payment options like credit cards or a third-party proxy like PayPal (paypal.com). Credit cards are the safest option because the issuers will help if something goes wrong such as a product not being delivered or someone using your card without your permission. Never send cash through the mail or use a money-wiring service, because you do not have any recourse if something should go wrong.

Regardless of what you do, keep a record of your online transactions. You should save as much information as possible until the transaction is completed and you are satisfied that everything is in order. Save online receipts by saving the web receipt to a file or keep a printed copy. Save copies of email and write down all telephone call information during the transaction. Keep this information and verify the transaction on your credit card statement as soon as it arrives. Also, make sure there are not any unauthorized charges. If there are any problems or questions, call the financial institution that issued the credit card immediately.

If you want to learn more about staying safe online, the National Cyber Security Alliance (NCSA) maintains a website (staysafeonline.org) with a lot of good information. NCSA is a consortium of major technology vendors and the U.S. Department of Homeland Security that works hard to keep that site up to date with the latest information. It also sponsors Cyber Security Awareness Month every October to remind everyone that while there is a lot of good in cyberspace you do have to be careful.

Scott Barman is a collector and author of the Coin Collectors Blog (coinsblog.ws). He is also President of the Montgomery County Coin Club (montgomerycoinclub.org) and President of the Maryland State Numismatic Society (mdstatenumisassn.org). After more than thirty years in the computer and information security industry, Scott recently started Having-Fun Collectibles to serve collectors in more markets than just numismatics because collecting should be fun. When not out searching for different and interesting collectibles he can be found with his wife and two puggles while they check out his pocket change.

CURRENT TECHNOLOGY TRENDS FOR COIN AND PAPER MONEY COLLECTORS

By Tom Bilotta
Carlisle Development Corporation

The trend toward computing platforms other than the traditional desktop PC has continued to accelerate. Tablet computers such as the iPad and its Windows-based competitors have exploded in use and are now commonly used for functions previously performed on traditional PCs. Microsoft has now entered this market with the new Surface tablet and Windows 8 RT. Smartphones and e-book readers also continue to become more useful and will play an increased role in collector applications. In 2014, the Android platform also gained significant market share.

The year 2014 has seen the emergence of some applications (apps) for numismatists on the iPhone and iPad. These apps go beyond the functionality of simple browsers accessing Web content to fully functional mobile applications. Initial applications have focused on educational information such as coin identification and grading. Also some applications to educate young numismatists have appeared in the app store; 2015 should bring continued growth in numismatic offerings on mobile platforms.

COIN COLLECTING IN RETIREMENT

The demographics of coin collectors continue to show a long-term trend toward older coin collectors. Currently, the average age of serious coin collectors is probably in excess of 55. Collectors nearing or in retirement have specific needs regarding their coin collections. Paramount in their minds is planning for eventual disposition of their collection in a manner that benefits their family. They also face different challenges in order to continue to enjoy the pursuit of coin collecting, sometimes with reduced funding and/or the need to begin to liquidate some portions of the collection. A new website (www.coincollecting retirement.com) addresses many of the issues faced by such collectors.

BULLION VALUATION AND ANALYSIS

Over the past several years, the volatility of spot bullion prices has sparked collector interest in understanding the bullion value of their collection. Collectors of gold and silver coins have experience with the complex relationship between bullion and numismatic values. Often numismatic premiums diminish as bullion values rise. This has increased the importance of understanding the bullion value in your collection as well as its impact on the overall value of your collection and projected cost to purchase new items.

PORTABLE COMPUTING

Portable computing has much to offer, especially when supported by access to your data via the Internet. For collectors, use of portable devices is in its infancy. Most available collector-oriented applications are primarily Internet browsers, often enhanced to present content optimally on the mobile device. There are very few numismatic software applications available on these devices that go beyond viewing Web content.

One of the challenges of mobile computing particular to the coin collecting market is the basic demographic. The average age of coin collectors is quite high, and many collectors suffer from eyesight limitations. On home PCs this can be addressed by very affordable, large-screen monitors. Small mobile devices tend to use small fonts to allow maximum content. In the future, flexible, expandable screens may help address this issue.

CLOUD COMPUTING

The real benefits of mobile devices for collectors will be realized when user data may be maintained in the cloud and accessed anywhere. In such an environment, a collector could maintain his collection on his PC at home and access it from his cell phone or tablet while attending a show or traveling by airplane. The collector's ability to work with his collection would not be limited to time spent at home. Synchronization of data would be automatic. It is expected that during 2015, cloud computing will find its way into core applications intended to assist collectors in working with their collections.

Cloud Computing—Security

There are a number of issues to be resolved before these benefits are attainable. One of the major ones is security. There are daily reports of security breaches on the Internet. These affect governments, major financial institutions, and corporations and individuals alike. The willingness of collectors to place their sensitive collection data in the cloud will depend on their confidence in the security of their data. It is clear that today we do not understand enough about Internet security to build truly robust and impenetrable defenses. Even major institutions such as the Defense Department are "hacked."

Cloud Computing—Applications Availability

Another issue is the development of collector applications software intended to exploit mobile computing. Such software has to present the capabilities of robust PC-based collectibles software optimized for the smaller viewing area and touch interface of the mobile device. These applications must also perform well in the more limited resource environments available on mobile devices.

The smaller screen areas of mobile devices make it more difficult to present a large amount of information on one screen as well as manipulate it for analytical purposes. Mobile devices currently address this by allowing the user to employ virtual pages that are larger than the device and that can be accessed by simple hand motions.

Cloud Computing—Standards

Several major corporations are setting up resources for cloud computing; these include Apple, Google, and Microsoft. It remains to be seen how these environments will interact. Ideally for the user, data would be seamlessly shared between these environments. A user on a Windows-based PC at home should be able to access data without regard to the specifics of the servers on which it is maintained. The same user should be able to access the same data on an iPhone at a remote location.

Cloud Computing—Reliability of Access

Early users of cloud computing have experienced significant periods during which their data was not accessible. This unreliability will be an impediment to widespread dependence on the cloud. Cloud infrastructure must approach the uptime of other utilities such as your telephone and electric power, which are expected to be up and running very close to 100% of the time. This will require substantial buildup of infrastructure that is not commonly employed for Internet computing currently. Redundant data centers and communications paths will be required throughout the entire network.

CHOOSING THE RIGHT PORTABLE DEVICE FOR YOU

The choice of a portable device is a personal one and is driven by your typical usage, physical limitations, and other considerations. Many users will employ multiple portable devices for different purposes. Many coin collectors are older and would have difficulty with the small screen size and keys on an e-reader or smartphone and would be better served by a traditional laptop or tablet computer. If you find an affordable e-reader or tablet computer that provides adequate viewing quality for you, it will likely be a very convenient choice for all sorts of Internet activity associated with your collecting pursuits.

THE INTERNET

As in recent years, Internet activity by collectors continues to grow. The trend toward cloud computing is one of the newest growth areas of Internet activity.

COIN COLLECTING SOFTWARE

Coin collecting software that runs on your own computer avoids the problems of Internet catalogs and provides you with rich functionality to work with your collection.

Collectors who adopt computer inventory programs increase their enjoyment of collecting, provide the needed documentation to protect their collection, gain insight into the value of their collection, and better prepare their families to deal with their collection if the need arises.

In order to exploit the power that computers bring to collecting, the collector must acquire a base level of knowledge sufficient to harness this capability in a safe and productive manner. The remainder of this article will focus on some of the more important points of using numismatic inventory software.

Coin & Paper Money Inventory Software

One of the first applications of a computer is to organize a collection. This activity requires cataloging what you have, deciding how it will be grouped, and determining what kind of reports you will need. Reports will assist you in defining your collecting objectives, tracking value, and assuring that your collection is adequately protected and insured.

Organizing Your Collection with Coin & Paper Money Inventory Software

Collectors of coins and currency fall into several categories. There is the serious coin collector who enjoys the hobby and pursues personally defined collecting objectives. Accumulators retain many of the coins that they receive in normal commerce and build up large quantities of unsorted coins. Investors use coin collecting to build portfolios intended to produce profits. Inheritors receive a coin collection or accumulation from their families and must decide how they will handle a potentially valuable asset.

All of these collectors have a common need to catalog their items and understand their value. Most collectors also have accumulated many items with a very wide range of values.

A modern inventory program can adapt to meet the needs of all types of users from novice collectors to experienced experts. It will incorporate a comprehensive database of coin and/or paper money to assist users in identifying and defining their collections as well as a flexible set of functionality to enable them to organize their collections in a manner consistent with their collection methodology.

Most collectors will want to organize their collections into several groupings. The collector will want to create collections that mirror their physical collection. For example, someone with coin albums of common series such as Mercury dimes, statehood quarters, or Buffalo nickels will want to have software albums organized in similar fashion. Other coins might be grouped into coins for sale, duplicates, partial collections for other family members, or any other categorization that suits the collector.

Using Your Time Wisely

When using computer software to catalog a coin or paper money collection it is important to use it in a manner consistent with your purposes and that will enhance your enjoyment. You should spend your time, therefore, working with the portions of your collection in which you have the most interest or where the primary financial value exists.

For example, if you are collecting a complete set of Mercury dimes, you may wish to scan an image of each individual piece so that you can print picture catalogs of your collection. For these coins, you might choose to enter in complete information including purchase price, source, certification information, origin, etc. For this type of grouping you will also likely want to include coins that you don't have that are required to complete your collection, enabling you to generate want lists. This will also assist you in identifying the cost to complete your collection and planning your approach.

For large quantities of relatively inexpensive items or coins worth only bullion content and where you have no particular collecting interest, you might choose to only enter a single line item and not bother to take the time to list each coin individually. For example, if you have several hundred silver Washington quarters in circulated condition from the 1950s and 1960s you might enter a single line item 225 Washington Quarters with a date range and average value. In this way, large accumulations can be tracked with minimum effort and your attention can be focused on your real collecting interests. Your coin inventory program should adapt to all of these possible approaches to organizing your collection.

Evaluating Coin & Paper Money Inventory Software

The quality of the software that you purchase will greatly impact the success of your efforts.

One of the most important parts of a coin inventory program

is the database. The database contains standard information about coins and paper money and saves the user from having to type this information manually. The greater the amount of information in the standard database, the easier the task of data entry. A modern coin collecting program at a minimum should include coin type, date, mint mark, denomination, and variety. Comprehensive programs, such as those made by Carlisle Development Corporation, also include such information as designer/engraver, coinage metal, size, weight, edge, and mintage. The organization of the database should reflect commonly used groupings and thereby provide users with guidance in organizing their collections.

Some inventory programs include current market values. It is important that these are updated frequently and produced by reliable sources. Coin values should evolve to include areas of high market interest. For example, over the past year, the market interest in high grade recent coin issues has become very high. It is also important to allow the user the ability to extend the database to include items that are not listed. These may be specialized varieties, private mint products, or other coin-related collectibles.

Ability to share data with other programs and people is also very important. Most computerized collectors are connected to the Internet and will want to share some information with other collectors and dealers. The ability to export listings in common text readable formats for transmission over the Internet or for input into a word processor or spreadsheet is of great value in buying and selling coins and paper money.

Carlisle Development's inventory software, Collector's Assistant, provides a comprehensive database of all coins ever minted by the United States Mint. This includes all type coins by date and mint mark, bullion coins, sets, old and new commemoratives. Recent additions to the database are the 50 states circulating quarters and the new Sacagawea Dollar. Coin values are licensed from Coin World, Inc., an industry leader in providing coin valuations. Quarterly updates are available by subscription, allowing collectors to maintain trends of their values. Carlisle Development's Currency Collector's Assistant has a complete database based on *Friedberg's Paper Money of the United States,* 19th Edition. This database includes all U.S. paper money, including Confederate notes and Encased postage stamps. A relationship with CDN, publisher of the *Greensheet,* makes value information available to the paper money collector in electronic format.

For collectors of ancient coins, Carlisle offers an add-on database containing color images of several hundred ancient coins and a specialized interface containing data-entry fields appropriate for ancient coins. For example, the date field can handle and sort mixed AD/BC dates and has long fields for obverse and reverse inscriptions. The most recent additions to Carlisle Development's databases include the Euro Coin Database and World Currency Database.

Report Generation

Once you have entered your coin collection into an inventory program, the most important function will become its ability to generate a wide array of reports and/or exports for informational purposes.

You will probably want to have a detailed listing, identifying items, their value, and where they are stored for insurance purposes. You will want to generate partial lists of your collections for sales and trading. You may want to generate labels to aide in identifying your coins. You may want to look at your collection in different ways, such as sorted by value or metal content or collection completeness.

One common need of coin collectors is the printing of inserts for 2" flips. Once coins have been cataloged, computer software can allow you to produce customized flip inserts in a standard format of your own design.

Report generation is the subset of an inventory program that produces the listings that you view on the screen, print on paper, or export to other computer applications. Its flexibility will greatly impact its utility. For example, you may want to generate two listings of coins that you have for sale, one that includes your cost and target price (your copy) and one that does not include this information for general distribution to prospective buyers.

At various times, you will probably want to be able to list any subset of the information fields, filter based on a wide array of parameters, and sort using different criteria.

As mentioned at the beginning of this article, report generation may be used to output PDF files, which may be viewed using a portable device such as an e-book reader.

Other Functionality You Should
Expect from Your Inventory Software

Inventory software should be able to store all of the information in which a collector is interested. Specific fields will vary based on collector interest and purpose. Some will require detailed certification and descriptive information, others comprehensive purchase and sales history. Some collectors will want to have comprehensive recording of storage location and insurance information. Modern programs provide sufficient information fields to meet all of these needs.

Backup and restore functionality should allow users to easily protect the data they have meticulously entered. History charting enables the user to track the changes in value of a part of collection over time.

Good software must be easy to use and supported by context-sensitive help that provides users with detailed instructions in a "how-to" format on all of the basic functions that they will wish to perform.

Availability of Timely Updates

Once you have taken the time to catalog your collection in a computer program, you will want to preserve your investment by having access to database updates incorporating information on new coin releases as well as changes in value. Your supplier of inventory software should have a timely program for availability of annual database and value updates.

Educational Software for Collectors

Adding significantly to your enjoyment of collections are electronic information sources that exploit the power of the computer to present you with high-quality information in an easily accessible format. These programs can provide comprehensive knowledge of all aspects of coin collecting, detailed information on grading coins, and specialized information such as collecting coin varieties.

COIN GRADING

Most coin collectors will want to be able to grade their coins, at least to an approximate grade. This enables them to have an understanding of value as well as identify coins that might be appropriate for certification. Coin grading skill is built up through time and experience.

The Grading Assistant offered by Carlisle Development is based on the official *Grading Guide of the American Numismatic Association,* now published by Whitman Publishing. It enables the user to view side-by-side images of their own coins along with various grades from the ANA grading set. These images are supported by detailed descriptions of the wear points for each grade. Using software such as the Grading Assistant, users can develop their skill in grading coins and establish approximate grades for their collections.

VARIETY COLLECTING

The collecting of coin varieties is an exciting area of the hobby currently experiencing some growth. Varieties are the result of differences in the minting process or dies that produce design differences and/or errors. These include such effects as doubling of some of features or letters, extra pieces of metal on the coin surface, and die breaks. Variety collecting requires the collector to identify subtle differences in coin designs.

The Morgan dollar series is one of the most commonly collected and is categorized by many varieties. Carlisle Development offers a *Top 100 Morgan Dollar* CD, based on the book written by Michael Fey and Jeff Oxman. This work provides pictures, identification information, and values for the most sought after and valuable Morgan dollar varieties. It provides a spectacular set of high-quality pictures to assist you in identifying these coins and also the full text and information provided in this work.

BULLION ANALYSIS

The increase in bullion prices has made understanding of bullion value much more important and significantly impacts the cost of acquiring new items. Carlisle Development offers the Bullion Analyzer to assist collectors in understanding bullion values and their impact on your collecting pursuits.

MOBILE APPLICATIONS FOR NUMISMATISTS

During 2013, Carlisle Development introduced its flagship Collector's Assistant in the Apple app store. Collector's Assistant Mobile allows users to view and edit their collection data on iPhones and iPads, and share it with their PCs if desired. This joins Carlisle's existing two apps, the Coin Identification/Mint Mark Locator and Top 100 Morgan Varieties. Both tools are available at the Apple app store (visit www .carlisledevelopment.com\mobileapps.html for a link to the app store). The Coin Identification/Mint Mark Locator assists a collector in identifying U.S. coin types and also locating the mint mark. It covers all coins from 1793–present and includes basic numismatic data. The Top 100 Morgan Varieties provides high-resolution images and supporting numismatic data to assist collectors in identifying more valuable Morgan dollar varieties.

GENERAL EDUCATIONAL WORKS ON COLLECTING

There is much to learn about coin collecting, whether it is technical knowledge such as grading and authentication or practical knowledge such as buying and selling coins, attending trade shows, or participating in auctions. Educational computer software offers advantages over printed works in that the contents may be searched and indexed allowing the user to rapidly retrieve valuable information.

Carlisle Development offers the *Coin Collector's Survival Manual, Sixth Edition*, an interactive edition of the work by Scott Travers. This work provides a set of information that every collector of coins should have. The entire contents of this book are provided in a searchable, interactive format. This allows the user to easily locate information based on word searching, topics, illustrations, bookmarks, a table of contents, or index. The most recent edition of this work, released in 2008, contains the contents of *How to Make Money in Coins Right Now*, covering such topics as cracking-out coins for upgrade and premium coins. In addition to the contents of the book, a set of high-quality grading images has been included for such topics as identifying MS-63, MS-65, MS-67 coins and toning. An interactive grading calculator brings to life the grading methods described in the book.

WELL-DESIGNED COMPUTER SOFTWARE WILL ADD TO YOUR ENJOYMENT OF COLLECTING

Carlisle Development Corporation publishes the most comprehensive line of collector software available, especially regarding coins and paper money.

Central to Carlisle's product line is the Collector's Assistant, the most advanced and comprehensive collection software available. It is sold in a variety of configurations to serve collectors of over thirty collectible types from autographs to toys. Most extensive is support for coins and paper money. The Collector's Assistant family includes:

- United States Coin Database—complete listings of all U.S. coinage from 1793 to the present. The 50 State quarter program and the Presidents Dollar program are recent additions. This also includes Colonial and Hawaiian coinage.

- World Coin Database—A listing of over 5,000 coin types from over forty-five countries, which may be extended by the user. Also includes comprehensive listings of Canada, Australia, Euro coinage, and world bullion gold and silver coins.

- Ancient Coin Database—includes several thousand listings of Byzantine, Judaic, Roman, and Greek coinage along with several hundred images. Data entry screens are optimized for ancient coin collectors and include long fields for inscriptions and preloaded choice lists of rulers, ancient denominations, towns, mints, and others.

- United States Currency Database—A complete listing of all United States currency based on *Friedberg's 18th Edition, Paper Money of the United States.* This also includes 120 high-quality color images of early U.S. currency.

To learn more about Carlisle Development's product line, visit our website at www.carlisledevelopment.com. You will find current product information and may also place orders. You can reach us by e-mail at support@carlisledevelopment.com or by phone at 800–219–0257.

EXPERT TIPS ON BUYING AND SELLING COINS

Intelligent coin buying is the key to building a good collection at reasonable cost. Today, with the added confusion of split grading, slider grading, and other devious practices of some coin sellers, it is more necessary than ever to be a skilled buyer.

In the interest of supplementing the coin pricing and identification in this book with practical advice on astute buying, the editor presents the following article. It reviews major pitfalls to which an uninformed buyer might succumb and gives specific suggestions on getting the most for your money when buying coins.

The editor wishes to state clearly that the exposure of questionable practices by some coin sellers, as detailed below, is not intended as a general indictment of the coin trade. The vast majority of professional coin dealers are ethical and try to please. Moreover, it can be safely stated that if the hobbyist restricts his buying exclusively to well-established coin dealers, he runs very little risk.

UNSATISFACTORY SOURCES OF COINS

Unsatisfactory sources of coins—those entailing a higher than necessary degree of risk—include flea markets, antiques shops, garage sales, private parties who are unknown to you, auction sales in which coins are offered along with non-numismatic merchandise and advertisements in magazines and newspapers published for a general readership rather than for coin collectors and never buy a coin off television. This advice is given to benefit the non-expert buyer and especially the beginner. Advanced collectors with full confidence in their coin buying skills will sometimes shop these sources to find possible bargains.

MAIL-ORDER ADS IN NATIONAL MAGAZINES

The sharp rise in coin values during 1979 and 1980 encouraged many promoters to deal in coins. (Promoters are persons who aren't coin dealers in the accepted sense of the term, but who utilize coins for large-scale mail-order promotions.) The objective, nearly always, is to sell coins to buyers of limited knowledge and thereby succeed in promising more, and charging more, than would a legitimate professional coin dealer. Undoubtedly such promotions are extremely successful judging from the number of such ads that appear regularly.

Here are some examples of the headlines they use:

"Genuine Silver Dollars Struck by the U.S. Mint . . ."

"Real John F. Kennedy Silver Half Dollars . . ."

"Cased Set of U.S. Mint Morgan Dollars . . ."

"Unbelievable But True: U.S. Silver Dollars at Only $21.95 . . ."

The ads look impressive and sound impressive. They show enlargements of the merchandise. They quote facts and figures, often with historical data. They present a variety of guarantees about the coins, and there is no misrepresentation in those guarantees. You do receive genuine coins struck by the U.S. Mint. They really are 90% silver if you order Morgan or Peace dollars. But the price you pay is from twice to three times as much as if you bought from a *real* coin dealer. In the legitimate coin trade, the coins sold via these ads are looked upon as "junk coins." They command a very small premium over their silver bullion value. They are not only the most common dates but are usually in miserable condition.

To lend credibility, the promoters will normally use a company name that gives the appearance of being that of a full-time coin dealer. There is nothing illegal in doing this, but it does contribute to the misleading nature of such ads.

Let's examine some of the specific methods used in today's ever-increasing deceptive coin ads. You will soon see why coins, especially U.S. silver coins, have become a favorite of mail-order promoters: They can be "hyped" in a most convincing manner, without making statements that are patently false. Thus, the advertisers skirt around—though narrowly—allegations of mail fraud. (Fraud cannot be alleged on the basis of price, as a merchant is free to charge what he pleases for whatever he sells.)

1. *Creating the impression that the coins offered originate from a hidden or sequestered cache not previously available to the public.* This is accomplished by the use of such phrases as, "Just found, 2,367 specimens," or "Now released to the public . . ." The assertion that they were "just found" is not wholly inaccurate, however. The advertiser has, more than likely, located a dealer who could supply wholesale quantities of junk coins. The coins themselves were never lost or hidden. "Now released to the public" has nothing to do with official government release or release by a court. It simply means the advertiser is selling them.

In a very few isolated cases, in which mail fraud charges were brought, ads have gone beyond this kind of assertion by innuendo. They actually stated that the coins were from secret government stockpiles. One of them wove an elaborate tale of silver dollars being taken to special storage locations by the army during World War I. Such an event never occurred, and that is the basic difference between prosecutable and non-prosecutable ads. If an advertiser merely hints at something, but does not state it as fact, he is usually within the law.

2. *Leading the potential customer to believe the coins are scarcer or more valuable than they really are.* This is done via numerous techniques. Among the favorites is to compare the advertiser's selling price against prices for other coins of the same series. An ad offering Morgan dollars for $27.50 may call attention to the fact that "some Morgan dollars have sold for $20,000, $50,000, and more." Yes, they have. They are the rare, desirable dates in UNC, not the common, circulated coins you receive from the advertiser.

When half dollars are offered, it will be said that "you just can't find them in circulation any longer." It's entirely true that Walking Liberty halves, Franklins, and the lone 90% silver Kennedy half (1964) cannot be found in day-to-day circulation. But coin dealers have them by the roll and sell them for less than you will pay through such an ad. The fact that these coins are not found in circulation is not an indication of rarity. Many coins carrying very little premium value over their face value cannot be found in day-to-day circulation.

3. *Emphatic guarantee that the coins are genuine.* On this point the advertiser can speak with no fear of legal repercussion. His coins are genuine and nobody can say otherwise. But, even where absolute truth is involved, it can be—and is—presented in such a manner as to give a false impression. By strongly stressing the coins' authenticity, the message is conveyed that many non-authentic specimens exist and that you run a risk in buying from someone else. Such is far from the case. Any large coin dealer can sell you quantities of perfectly genuine Morgan dollars, Peace dollars, or any other coins you want.

4. *Implication that the coins offered are in some respect "special," as opposed to specimens of the same coins available at coin shops.* This presents an obvious difficulty for the advertiser, as his coins are just the opposite of special: usually heavily circulated, often with actual damage such as nicks, gouges, etc. It is not, however, insurmountable. The advertiser can keep silent about the condition of his coins and present them as some sort of special government issue. Usually this is done by selling them in quantities of four or five and referring to them as "U.S. Mint Sets," "Government Mint Sets," or something similar. The uninformed reader believes he is ordering a set assembled and packaged by the Mint. The Mint *does* assemble and package sets, as everyone knows. But it had no part in these! Assembling and packaging was done by the advertiser. Regardless of how attractive the box or case may be, it is not of official nature and lends absolutely nothing to the value. Prior to 1999 the Mint had never issued cased or boxed sets in which all the coins were of the same denomination. In these hard-sell sets you will find such combinations as two Morgan dollars and two Peace dollars, four Morgan dollars, or three half dollars. Dates are a purely random selection. And, we repeat, the coins are in well-worn, circulated condition.

5. *Failure to state actual silver content.* This falls under the heading of deception by silence. The potential customer is left to draw his own conclusions and the advertiser knows full well that those conclusions will be wrong, provided, of course, that the ad is worded in such a way that it lends itself to incorrect conclusions. Typically this sort of advertiser is selling Kennedy halves dated from 1965 to 1970. During these years the Kennedy half contained some silver but not very much—just 40% (after 1970 it contained no silver at all). Its silver content was less than one half that of 50-cent pieces struck prior to 1965. In fact, it was even less than the silver content of pre-1965 quarters. Very few individuals, aside from coin hobbyists, are aware of this reduction of silver content in half dollars from 1965 to 1970. When *silver* coins are advertised they automatically think in terms of 90% silver. Yet the advertiser is legally within his rights in referring to 40% silver coins as silver. As the 40% silver coins look nearly identical to their 90% silver predecessors, few purchasers will suspect they've overpaid—until they have them appraised.

6. *Creation of gimmicked names for coins.* By calling a coin something different than its traditional numismatic name, it is made to seem more unusual or special. Everyone is familiar with Kennedy half dollars but what about "Kennedy Silver Eagles"? This is a promoter's name for the Kennedy half, used in an effort to glamorize it. It is highly inappropriate. Recently the market has been flooded with coins claiming to be "first strikes," "early releases," etc. – they almost never are. Be very wary of such claims.

7. *False references.* Advertisements of this type are sometimes accompanied by doubtful or fairly obvious fake references on the advertiser's behalf. Taking his cue from legitimate coin dealers, whose ads nearly always refer to their membership in coin organizations and often carry other easily verifiable references as well, he feels he must present similar assurances of his background and reliability. Since he has nothing too convincing to offer in the way of genuine references, he manufactures them. He invents the name of a mythical coin organization, of which he is either a member in good standing, an officer, or perhaps even president. If he chooses not to go quite that far, as he might be caught in the deception, he can take a less volatile course and claim membership in "leading coin collector and dealer organizations" without, of course, naming them. This is just like the ads for questionable diet aids that say, "Tests at a leading eastern university have shown . . ." No one is likely to check all 500 or more eastern universities, or enter into a debate about which ones are leading, or what they may be leading *in*. Of the various other unsatisfactory sources of coins, the dangers they present should be fairly obvious.

RECOMMENDED SOURCES OF COINS

As a general rule, coin purchasing should be confined to the following sources:

1. Professional coin dealers who sell coins at a shop and/or by mail order.

2. Auction sales conducted by professional coin dealers or auction houses making a specialty of coins.

3. Shows and conventions for coin collectors.

4. Respectable and knowledgeable dealers, auctions, and collectors on the internet.

Another acceptable source, though unavailable to many coin hobbyists, is the fellow collector with duplicate or surplus specimens to sell or trade. This source is acceptable only if the individual is known to you, as transactions with strangers can result in problems.

If a coin shop is located in your area, this is the best place to begin buying. By examining the many coins offered in a shop you will become familiar with grading standards. Later you may wish to try buying at auction. When buying from dealers, be sure to do business only with reputable parties. Be wary of rare coins offered at bargain prices, as they could be counterfeits or improperly graded. Some bargain coins are specimens that have been amateurishly cleaned and are not considered desirable by collectors. The best "bargains" are popular coins in good condition, offered at fair prices.

The dangers of buying from sources other than these are over graded and consequently overpriced coins; non-graded and likewise overpriced coins; coins that have been doctored, "whizzed," chemically treated, artificially toned, repaired or otherwise altered. You must always be on the lookout for counterfeits as well. Buying from the legitimate, recommended sources greatly reduces but does not absolutely eliminate these risks. The buyer himself is the ultimate safeguard, if he has a reasonably thorough working knowledge of coins and the coin market. In this respect experience is the best teacher, but it can sometimes be costly to learn from bad coin buying experiences.

COIN BUYING GUIDELINES

Smart coin buyers follow certain basic strategies or rules. They will not buy a rare coin that they know little or nothing about. They will do some checking first. Has the coin been frequently counterfeited? Are counterfeits recorded of that particular date and mint mark? What are the specific grading standards? What key portions of the design should be examined under magnification to detect evidence of circulation wear?

The smart coin buyer may be either a hobbyist collecting mainly for the sport of it, or an investor. In either case he learns not just about coins but the workings of the coin trade: its dealers and auctioneers and their methods of doing business. It's essential to keep up to date always, as the coin market is a continual hotbed of activity.

When buying from the recommended sources there is relatively little danger of fakes, doctored coins, or other obviously unwanted material. If such a coin does slip through and escape the vigilance of an ethical professional dealer, you are protected by his guarantee of authenticity. It is highly unlikely that you will ever be "stuck" with a counterfeit, doctored, or otherwise misrepresented coin bought from a well established professional.

Merely avoiding fakes is, however, not the sole object of intelligent coin buying. It is, in fact, a rather minor element in the overall picture. Getting the absolute most for your money in terms of properly graded coins at fair prices is the prime consideration. Here the responsibility shifts from seller to buyer. It is the dealer's responsibility not to sell fakes or misidentified coins. But it is the *buyer's* responsibility to make certain of getting the best deal by comparing prices and condition grades of coins offered by different dealers. Quite often you *can* save by comparison shopping, even after your incidental expenses are tabulated. The unique nature of the coin market makes this possible.

Prices do vary from one dealer to another on many coins. That is precisely the reason—or at least one of the primary reasons—for the *Blackbook.* If you could determine a coin's value merely by checking one dealer's price, or even a few dealers' prices, there would be minimal need for a published price guide. The editors review prices charged by hundreds of dealers to arrive at the median or average market prices that are listed in the *Blackbook.* Prices are matched condition grade by condition grade, from UNC down the line. The results are often little short of astounding. One dealer may be asking $50 for a coin priced at $30 by another. And there are sure to be numerous other offerings of the coin at $35, $40, $45, and various midpoint sums.

It is important to understand why prices vary and how you can utilize this situation to your advantage.

Some readers will remark, at this juncture, that prices vary because of inaccurate grading.

It is unquestionably true that personal applications of the grading standards do contribute to price differences. What one dealer sees as an AU-55 is AU-50 or AU-58 to another, with a corresponding difference in price. It is one reason for non-uniform prices. *It is not the only one.*

Obviously the lower-priced specimens are not always those to buy. Smart numismatic buying calls for knowing when to take bargains and when to bypass them. Low price could result from something directly concerning the coins. Or it may be tied to matters having nothing to do with the coin or coins. A dealer could be oversupplied, or he may be offering coins in which he does not normally deal and wants to move them quickly. He may have a cash flow imbalance and need to raise funds, in which case he has probably reduced most of his prices. He may be pricing a coin low because he made a fortunate purchase in which the coin cost him very little. In all of these cases—and examples of all can be found regularly in the coin trade—the lower than normal price is not a reflection upon the coin's quality or desirability. These coins, if properly graded, are well worth buying. They do save you some money and cause no problems.

Personal circumstances of the dealer are, to one degree or another, reflected in the prices of most of his coins. A dealer cannot very well charge $1,000 for a 1948 Lincoln cent just because he needs the money. The traffic would not bear it. But within reasonable bounds a dealer's pricing structure for his stock reflects his circumstances. If the dealer has substantial operating costs to meet, such as shop rent and employee salaries, his overall pricing structure will reflect this. Yet his prices are not likely to be too much higher than the average, as this class of dealer is intent on quick turnover. Also, there is a certain degree of competitiveness between dealers, particularly those whose advertisements run in the same periodicals. Unfortunately, this competitiveness can be carried to extremes by some dealers, resulting in "bargains" that are sometimes over graded.

Condition has always played a major role in coin prices. Even in the hobby's early, far less sophisticated days, collectors would pay more for a bright, shiny uncirculated coin than for the same coin in worn condition. The undeniable difference in value and desirability of coins in different condition grades led gradually to adoption of grading standards. In a sense, grading standards are comparable to the "scale of one to ten." Some circulated coins show more wear than others, so it is not sufficient to merely call a coin circulated. Even among uncirculated coins, or UNCs, there can be differences in condition and desirability. While UNCs show no circulation wear, the majority do have tiny hairlike or lintlike scratches on both surfaces. You will not see these on casual examination, only if you look closely or, in some cases, only if a magnifying lens is used. These are the "average" UNCs. Uncirculated coins having very few surface abrasions are scarcer, and many buyers are willing to pay extra for them. This increases their market value. Rarely an uncirculated coin has no surface abrasions. It is then regarded as Mint State Perfect, for which the designation on the grading scale is MS-70. A correctly graded specimen in MS-70 will sell higher than any other grade of condition, sometimes much higher.

Buyer beware: in recent years third party grading services have been encapsulating tens of thousands, more likely hundreds of thousands. Be absolutely certain that the coin is perfect. Any mark on a coin prevents it from being MS70. True MS70s are extremely rare. Do not buy such a coin without being convinced yourself that the coin is indeed perfect. The vast majority (95% or more) of coins graded MS-70 or PF-70 are not! The coin must be perfect no matter who or what tells you otherwise.

COIN GRADING

10 Points of Basic Coin Grading

1. Lighting: There is only one acceptable source of lighting when grading coins! That is a 60-100 watt incandescent bulb. Do not use halogen, florescent or natural lighting.

2. Handling: Always handle coins carefully by the edge and over a soft surface.

3. Optics: For standard coin grading a 7x ("x" = power), Hastings triplet loupe (magnifier) is the preferred method.

4. Luster: To properly grade coins, it is mandatory that you know how to identify original mint luster or the lack thereof. Luster is thousands of microscopic lines that reflect line in a unique way that can never be duplicated on a struck coin that had the original luster removed. This unique reflection is best illustrated by the effect that originated the term "cartwheel" on silver dollars.

5. Three sides to a coin: Always remember there are 3 sides to every coin. The third side, or edge, is to be taken into consideration when giving a coin its grade.

6. Be aware of the things that are bad on a coin: Many things can affect the grade of a coin in a negative way. The bad things most often encountered are PVC residue (see number 8), scratches, corrosion, built-up dirt, carbon spots (a form of corrosion), "hairline" scratches, heavy rim and edge dings, cleaning, surface residue and counting wheel marks which appear as small to large patches of "hairlines."

7. You might as well learn to identify various die varieties: Since you are already closely examining the coin, you might as well learn to identify significant die varieties. These die varieties may include but are not limited to doubled dies, misplaced dates, repunched dates, overmintmarks and repunched mintmarks. Spotting these varieties almost always increases the value of a coin from a minimal amount to a large amount.

8. Coin storage: Always return a coin, once graded, to a chemically inert form of storage be it short or long term. The best form of storage is mylar, a form of plastic that does not contain polyvinalchloride (PVC) as do most forms of traditional plastics.

9. So why use a reputable third party grading service? There are many levels of numismatic knowledge ranging from none to that of being an experienced and veteran numismatist. For those who do not fall into the later category a grading service is beneficial because it can confirm or deny authenticity and provide a subjective grade normally accepted in the open market of coin collectors and dealers for a nominal fee.

10. So why bother grading a coin if it is already in a "slab?" It is true; professional coin graders are human too!

Actually, there are many reasons with the most important one being: "Buy the coin because you like it." To do this, you want to protect yourself from buying or selling coins that have been graded and encapsulated (slabbed) by fly-by-night grading services with little or no grading experience. Coin grading is subjective. While most coins from most reputable grading services are graded within a point or two of what any other professional grader would grade it, that one or two points can mean a lot of money. You just might find something that was missed or that you would hate to find later. And, you just might find something that would increase its value. It works both ways!

For learning how to grade and for reference when in doubt, the book is: *The Official Grading Standards for United States Coins.* (Available from most numismatic supply and book dealers and directly from the publisher, Whitman Publishing, LLC.)

The grading guidelines used for U.S. coins are those adopted by the American Numismatic Association and are included in summarized format in this book. Any U.S. coin can be graded by these guidelines, from the very oldest obsolete types to those in current production. The principle behind the grading guidelines is simple.

A coin's design always has certain vulnerable areas. Some parts of the design are more highly raised than others. These show wear the quickest. Likewise, some of the engraved lines are shallower than others and more quickly obliterated with day-to-day handling. By carefully examining a coin and checking these vulnerable areas, one can determine if the coin grades circulated or uncirculated. If it grades circulated, its vulnerable areas will also establish its specific grade, by the amount of wear they've absorbed. Anyone can learn to grade coins, but the process does call for patience, good lighting, a magnifying lens, and objectivity. Objectivity is essential. There is always a natural tendency to believe one's coins are a shade better than they really are. This is true even of a collector who has no intention of selling and takes no particular interest in resale potential. It applies to a greater degree when the person doing the grading has intentions of selling.

Values, as you will see in this book, often jump sharply from one grade to the next higher grade. The difference in price between an AU-55 and MS-60 specimen is not 10% or 20%. It is more often 100%, 200%, or more, depending on the coin, its scarcity, age, and other considerations. Hundreds, or even thousands, of dollars can be riding on the clarity of one tiny portion of its design. Even when a coin is not really rare or expensive, it will be worth quite a bit more in the higher grades of condition than in the lower.

While grading as practiced today is very precise and scientific compared to numismatics' early years, it is not foolproof. The human element still comes into play to some degree. So do situations not specifically accounted for in the grading guidelines. The human element is the great intangible. Two or three persons of equal competency may grade a coin identically. A dozen are not likely to. Someone will believe, honestly and without motive, that the coin is a grade higher or lower than the others consider it. The person who grades it differently is not necessarily careless. He may, in fact, be the most careful observer in the group. His close attention has revealed something overlooked by the rest. Obviously one must use proper lighting and take the time to closely examine the coin. It cannot be done in 3 to 5 seconds or less with the naked eye and achieve any kind of consistency, especially when considering the explosion of all the MS and PF-70 modern coins currently on the market.

Some coins invite variations in grading, for any of various reasons. These include circulated and uncirculated specimens as well as coins that appear to fall directly on the borderline between these categories. What makes certain coins more difficult to grade than others? First we have the coins, usually very old ones, that have not followed the normal patterns of wear. For reasons not always satisfactorily explained, the more vulnerable portions of their designs show less wear than other areas. By strict adherence to the established ANA standards they would grade in the higher ranks of circulated condition. A truly objective grader would hesitate to place them here. He would drop them down a bit, though just how far to drop is, in cases of this nature, mostly a matter of opinion.

Then there are coins that can be matched up easily with their proper condition grade as far as wear is concerned, but that have problems not related to wear. The ANA guidelines apply to circulation wear or its absence *only*. There are no provisions under these guidelines for grading coins with rim nicks, bruises, discoloration, oxidization, porosity, or any other defect not related to circulation wear. Such coins, which are encountered frequently, are treated in different ways by different dealers. Many will grade the coin for wear, then insert a note calling attention to its defect. Some will just grade the coin a little lower and let it go at that.

SLIDER GRADING

According to the ANA grading guidelines, a coin that does not fully meet the requirements for a grading level must be dropped down to the next lower category. If a coin cannot squeeze by as an AU-55 it has to be called AU-50, with the corresponding inevitable difference in retail value. As the guidelines are hardly enforceable by law, however, they are bent at will by anyone who wishes to do so. One of the by-products is so-called *slider grading,* which has become widespread. The use of slider grading is so commonplace today that some of its critics of a few years ago are adopting it. Coin dealers have an entirely logical reason for doing so. Even if a certain dealer is personally opposed to slider grading, he is in effect placing himself at a disadvantage by declining to utilize it. If his fellow dealers are slider grading their coins, his will seem inferior by comparison. His MS-60 price will be the same as another dealer charges for MS-62. Many customers, looking simply at price and the claim made for condition, will order the MS-62. So slider grading is done defensively just as much as offensively.

A slider grade is any grade outside of the accepted guidelines. It is an unofficial grade that exists in the seller's eye and that he hopes will exist in the purchaser's when he examines the coin. It is unofficial because there are no published guidelines for it. Presumably an AU-52 coin is a shade nicer than AU-50, but grading of this sort is very subjective. A great deal of personal opinion comes into play, and that is directly contrary to the purpose of grading standards. They were established to remove personal opinion as much as possible from coin grading. It is certainly understandable that anyone, whether dealer or collector, would be reluctant to grade a coin AU-50 when it seems finer than most specimens of that grade. Under the present guidelines, however, there is no alternative provision for such coins. However one may feel about slider grade coins, one thing is certain: If you pay a premium for them, you take a risk. A dealer who buys your coin collection at some future time will not pay extra for your sliders. He will pay no more than for specimens in the next lower condition ranking.

PUTTING YOUR COIN BUYING KNOWLEDGE TO WORK

General Suggestions (whether buying in person at a coin shop or by other means):

1. Deal with someone in whom you can have confidence. The fact that a dealer has been in the business a long period of time may not be an absolute guarantee of his reliability, but it is definitely a point in his favor. Is he a member of coin collector or coin dealer organizations? You do not have to ask about this to find out. If he does hold membership in good standing in any of the more prestigious organizations, that fact will be prominently displayed in his ads, in his sales literature, and on the walls of his shop. The leading organization for coin dealers is the PNG, or Professional Numismatists' Guild. Its members are carefully screened and must, after gaining admittance, comply with its code of ethics. Complaints against PNG members *are* investigated. Those that cannot be easily resolved are brought before an arbitration panel. You are on the safest possible ground when dealing with a PNG member. As the PNG is rather a select group, however, your local dealer may not be a member. This in itself should not make him suspect. One of the requirements of PNG membership is to carry at least $100,000 retail value in coins, and many dealers simply do not maintain that large an inventory. Is your dealer an American Numismatic Association member? Local Chamber of Commerce?

2. Don't expect the impossible, either in a dealer or his coins. The dealers are in business to make a profit and they could not do this by offering bargains on every coin they sell. Treat the dealers fairly. Look at things from their point of view. For example, a long "layaway" on an expensive coin may not be in the dealer's best interest. The dealers will go out of their way for established customers, but, even then, they cannot be expected to place themselves at a disadvantage.

BUYING IN PERSON AT A COIN SHOP

1. Plan your visits in advance. Don't shop in a rush or on the spur of the moment. Give yourself time to look, think, examine, and decide.

2. Before entering the shop have a clear idea of the specific coins, or at least the type of coins, you want to see. If more than a few dates and mint marks are involved, do not trust it all to memory. Write a list.

3. Look at everything that interests you before deciding to buy anything.

4. When shopping for rarities, bring along your own magnifier. A small one with attached flashlight is the most serviceable. You may not be able to conduct really in-depth examinations in a shop, but you'll learn more with a magnifier than without one. Don't be reticent about using it. The dealers will not be insulted.

5. If the shop has more than one specimen of the coin that interests you, ask to see them all. Even if all are graded identically and priced identically, you may discover that one seems a shade nicer than the rest.

6. If this is your first visit to the shop, you will want to give some attention to whether or not the shop inspires confidence. An experienced collector tends to get different vibrations from each shop, to the point where he can form an opinion almost immediately—sometimes before entering. Some coin shops give the distinct impression of being more professional than others. And that impression is usually correct! There are various points on which this can be judged. Do all coins, with the exception of bullion items, have their prices marked on the holder? Is the price accompanied by a statement of condition grade? Are the holders, and the style of notations on them, fairly uniform from coin to coin? If the coins are housed in various kinds of holders, with notations that seem to have been made by a dozen different people, they are most likely remnants from the stocks of other dealers or so-called "odd lots." Their condition grades should have been verified and they should have been transferred to uniform holders before being placed on sale. Since the shopkeeper failed to do this, he probably knows very little about their actual condition grades. He merely took the previous owners' word for it. Does the shopkeeper impress you as a person with intimate knowledge of coins? He need not love coins, as his business is selling them and not collecting them. But he should appear to regard them a little higher than "just merchandise." He ought to be appreciative of and perhaps even enthusiastic over the finer aspects of a rare coin. Under no circumstances should he treat coins as if he cares nothing about them, such as by handling them roughly or sloppily or touching their surfaces with his fingers.

7. Buying in person gives you an opportunity to converse with the dealer, and this can have its advantages. Upon expressing interest in a coin you may discover that the dealer offers a verbal discount from the market price—even without asking for one. If this does not occur, you do, of course, have the right to at least hint at the matter. Just a modest savings can often turn a borderline item into a sound purchase. Don't get a reputation for asking for a discount on every coin you buy. Let the circumstances guide you and be diplomatic. You are always in a better position to receive a discount when purchasing a number of coins at the same time. Dealers like volume buyers. Never say, "Will you take $300 for this?" or anything that could be construed as making the dealer an offer. The dealers make offers when they buy from the public and the right to make an offer is something they like to reserve for themselves. You can broach the subject in a more subtle fashion. Instead of mentioning what you would be willing to give for the coins, ask if there is a savings ("savings" is a much better word than "discount") on large purchases. If you pay in cash, you have a better bargaining position as you're saving the dealer the time required in collecting the funds. That is the essence of reasonable discounts: playing fair; not becoming a nuisance; and being willing to accept a small consideration even if just 5%. At least with the small discounts you are, or should be, getting good coins. If anyone is willing to discount a coin by 50%, you can be virtually certain it is a problem item.

BUYING BY MAIL ORDER

There is no reason to shun mail orders. Most coin dealing is done by mail. There are at least a dozen mail-order coin dealers for every one who operates a shop. Your local shop may not specialize in your type of coins, but in dealing by mail you can reach any coin dealer in the country and obtain virtually any coin you may want.

Consider the following before doing any mail-order buying:

1. Compare ads and prices, compare descriptions, compare everything from one ad to another running in the same publication. Look for evidence of the advertiser's professional standing, such as PNG membership. Read his terms of sale. There should be an unqualified guarantee of authenticity plus a guarantee of satisfaction. If you are not satisfied with your purchase for any reason, you should have the option of returning it within a specific time period. This time period should be stated in the dealer's terms of sale. It will usually be ten days or two weeks. It should likewise be clearly stated that if you do choose to return the coins, you can receive a full refund or credit as *you* prefer (not as the dealer prefers). Full refund means the sum paid for the coins, with postage and registration fees deducted. Few dealers will refund postage charges. Consequently, when you return a shipment you are paying the postage both ways.

2. Send a small trial order if you haven't previously done business with the advertiser. This will give you an opportunity to judge his grading accuracy and see just what sort of coins he supplies. You will also discover how prompt and attentive he is. The results of this trial order should give a fairly good idea of what you can expect from that dealer when placing larger orders.

3. Do not Xerox an ad and circle numbers. Write out your order, simply and plainly. Mention the publication and issue date. The dealer probably has different ads running in different publications.

4. Give second choices only if this is necessary to qualify for a discount. Otherwise don't. Most dealers will send you your first choice if it's still available. Some will send the second choice, even if they do still have your first choice. This is called "stock balancing." If they have two remaining specimens of your first choice, and twenty of your second choice, they would much prefer sending you the second choice. Only a relatively small proportion of dealers will ignore your wishes in this manner, but our suggestion still applies: no second choices if you can avoid them. To speed things up, make payment by money order or credit card. A personal check may delay shipment by as much as three weeks.

5. Examine the coins as soon as possible upon receiving

them. If a return is necessary, this must be done promptly to be fair to the dealer. Most likely you will not be permitted to remove a coin from its protective holder to examine it. The coins will be in clear mylar (an inert plastic) holders known as "flips" or "flipettes," with a staple at the top. The staple must be in place for a return to be honored. While this may seem harsh, it is necessary as a way for the dealer to protect himself against unscrupulous collectors who could switch coins on him. These individuals could replace a high-grade coin with one of a lower grade from their collection and return the lower-grade specimen, asking for a refund.

In the unlikely event you receive a coin in a holder that does not permit satisfactory examination, the best course is to simply return it. In making your examination be fair to yourself and to the dealer. Should you have the least doubt about its authenticity, submit the coin to the American Numismatic Association for its opinion and inform the dealer of your action. If the ANA finds the coin to be fake or doctored, you can return it even if the grace period for returns has expired. Under these circumstances many dealers will reimburse you for the ANA's expertizing cost. Chances are, however, that you will never receive a suspect coin.

6. Do not file a complaint against the dealer unless he is clearly in violation of his printed "terms of sale." When it is absolutely necessary to do so, a report of the transaction may be forwarded to the organizations in which he maintains membership, as well as the publications in which he advertises. But even if you place hundreds of mail orders, it is unlikely that the need will ever arise to register a formal complaint against a dealer.

BUYING AT AUCTION SALES

The volume of collector coins sold at auction is enormous. Auction buying is preferred by many collectors, as the opportunity exists to buy coins at somewhat less than their book values.

Not everything sold by auction is a bargain, however, and the auction house's "terms of sale" allow you far less latitude in making returns. Still, auction buying in the present day entails considerably less risk than it traditionally did. A generation ago, or even more recently, everything sold at auction was strictly "as is." Nothing could be returned for any reason whatsoever, even if grossly misdescribed or counterfeit. Today, almost all coin auctioneers will take back a fake or doctored coin, and some will take returns of those that have been incorrectly graded or otherwise misdescribed. This varies somewhat from one auction firm to another.

There are two types of auction sales: mail sales, in which all bidding is conducted by mail or phone, and so-called "floor" sales, which have in-person bidding. Even at floor sales, however, one is permitted to make an absentee bid if he cannot personally attend. When an absentee bid is successful, the bidder is notified by mail.

You have just as good a chance of being successful with an absentee bid as if you were present. The reputable auction houses will not bill you for the full amount of your bid if there was weak bidding on the coin. If you placed a bid of $500 and no one else offered more than $200, you would be billed only for an amount sufficient to beat the $200 bid. This would in most cases be $225. At some auctions, though, an automatic "buyer's premium" or surcharge in the amount of 10% is added to the price. In the example just given you would be paying a total of $247.50 plus charges for shipping. Sales at which bids are accepted exclusively by mail and phone do not, as a rule, utilize the buyer's premium. Check the terms of sale to be sure, as this obviously makes a difference in the amounts you should bid.

Whether the auction is a mail or floor sale, there will be a printed list of its contents available for those who may be interested in bidding. This list is circulated well in advance of the sale date to give everyone ample time to study it and plan their bidding. The list may appear as a full-page or multipage advertisement in one of the numismatic magazines or newspapers. It may be issued in the form of a handsome catalog with photos, sent to clients on the auctioneer's mailing list (and available to nonclients at a small charge). In any event, it will be accompanied by a set of regulations for those participating in the sale, and a bidsheet on which prospective buyers can enter their bids. The bidsheet will mention the sale's closing date. Bids received after the closing date, or after the start of vocal bidding in a floor sale, are ineligible.

Here is some advice for auction buying:

1. Find an auctioneer who specializes in your kind of coins and order a subscription to his catalogs. Regardless of the type of coins you collect, there are some auctioneers who handle them more regularly than others and these are the catalogs you should be receiving. Subscribing brings you the catalogs as early as possible and you also receive the list of "prices realized" following each sale. This in itself is extremely useful. It shows the prices actually paid for each coin, and it shows you the coins that failed to draw any bids or were removed from the sale for other reasons. You can utilize this information when placing bids in future sales conducted by the same auction house.

2. Read the entire catalog or list before filling out your bidsheet. Make a photocopy of the blank bidsheet in case you decide to make changes in your bids.

3. Determine whether the prices shown in the catalog are book values, estimated selling prices, or "minimum bids." In some sales you will encounter a mixture of all three, which can become confusing. Sometimes no prices at all will be shown. When estimated selling prices (sometimes called "estimated retail value") are used, you are usually safe in assuming that the majority will sell slightly below those figures. Some will sell for more and others for a good deal less, but most are likely to go for about 10% under the estimates. Once the buyer's premium is added, assuming one is used, they hit right around the auctioneer's estimate. This pattern maintains because a large number of bidders at any given auction will bid predictably by the percentage method. When the auctioneer states $100 as an estimated selling price or estimated retail value, they will bid $90. If the auctioneer states $200, many will bid $175 or some figure in that general neighborhood. This gives them the feeling of obtaining a bargain, though of course it hardly remains a bargain when the buyer's 10% surcharge is added. Such a bid is high enough in most instances to stand a very good chance of success. Those who bid 50% or 60% of the estimates are not really intent on being successful. They would rather lose a coin than pay anything near the normal retail price for it. Occasionally a few of their bids will come through if the sale turns out disappointingly. There will also be some bidders at every sale who bid above the estimate as a way of annihilating the competition. Needless to say, this can be an expensive way of acquiring coins.

If minimum bids are used, no bid lower than the sum stated will be entertained. In any sale in which all the lots are provided with minimum bids, a large number will sell right at the minimum or just fractionally above it, such as $55 for a lot carrying a $50 minimum bid. Minimum bid requirements tend to have a negative psychological influence on many bidders. They feel that if the stated price is satisfactory to the auctioneer and the coin's owner, the coin cannot be worth very much more. In actual fact, many lots with minimum bids are worth considerably more than the sums indicated, and you can sometimes get excellent buys at a "minimum bids" sale. It all depends on the specific nature of the sale and who is running it.

4. The auctioneers frequently stress advantages in bidding early, assuming you are placing an absentee bid. There is, in fact, more logic in bidding late, as long as you can be sure of making the deadline. An early bid is likely to be disclosed to other prospective bidders, who thereby have the opportunity to exceed it. A late bid may give competitors no time to react.

5. If you're interested in bidding on a coin that is not pictured in the catalog, ask the auction house for a photo of it. In most cases they will supply a photo if your request arrives early. There may be a token charge for the photo, but if you can get a photo, it's far preferable to bidding on a coin you have not seen. If you live close enough to the auction house, make a personal visit to examine any coins in the sale. In nearly all sales the coins will be available for inspection as soon as the catalog is circulated.

6. While the "terms of sale" will not vary too drastically from one auction house to the next, it is still advisable to read them thoroughly. If the words "all coins guaranteed genuine and may be returned for full refund if proven otherwise" are not included, this is not a sale in which you should be participating. In some mail sales—never in floor sales—you will find this statement: "no bids reduced." This means you pay the full amount of your bid if you win the coin, even if the next highest bid is considerably less. If you bid the fair market value or somewhat below, you can safely place bids in such a sale.

7. If the buyer's premium of 10% is being used, automatically reduce all your bids by 10%, but always bid in round numbers. A bid of $61 or $33.25 will not be accepted.

8. When bidding in person, always have your catalog open to the page showing the coin being sold at the moment. It is very easy to confuse one lot number with another and place a bid on the wrong coin. Once your bid has been acknowledged by the auctioneer, do not leave your hand up, as in the excitement this may be misinterpreted as a further bid—and you will be bidding against yourself. Always listen carefully to see if you have the high bid. Do not be led by the competitive spirit of a floor sale to bid higher than you had intended. Show no emotion whatsoever during bidding or at the conclusion of bidding. One of the basic strategies of auction bidding is to draw no attention to yourself.

The previous advice should help to better explain coin buying in its various phases. Space limitations have prevented us from covering some of the more specialized aspects of buying, and we have purposely refrained from mentioning things that should be apparent to everyone.

SELLING COINS TO A DEALER

All coin dealers buy from the public. They must replenish their stock, and the public is a much more economical source of supply than buying from other dealers. Damaged, very worn, or common coins are worthless to a dealer. So, too, usually, are sets in which the "key" coins are missing. If you have a large collection or several valuable coins to sell, it might be wise to check the pages of coin publications for addresses of dealers handling major properties, rather than selling to a local shop.

Visit a coin show or convention. There you will find many dealers at one time and you will experience the thrill of an active trading market in coins. You will find schedules of conventions and meetings of regional coin clubs listed in various numismatic publications.

To find your local coin dealer, check the "Yellow Pages" under *"Coin Dealers."*

Coin collecting offers infinite possibilities as an enjoyable hobby or profitable investment. It need not be complex or problem-laden. But anyone who buys and sells coins—even for the most modest sums—owes it to himself to learn how to buy and sell wisely.

HOW AND WHEN TO CONSERVE COINS

Reprinted with Permission, J.T. Stanton

Cleaning coins is a very controversial subject, and there is no general agreement on whether or not cleaning should be done or, if it is to be done, how best to go about it. The ANA takes no position on whether or not coins should be cleaned, except to say that if you don't know what you are doing, don't do anything! However, since you are likely to encounter more than a few cleaned coins in your collecting experience, some general comments on cleaning coins might be of help.

Dipping

The most common form of cleaning is *dipping*, which involves immersing a coin in a solution that is, in fact, a form of dilute acid. The acid reacts with the oxidation (such as toning) on the surface of the coin faster than it reacts with the relatively stable metal of the coin's surface, thereby removing the oxidation with no apparent effect on the metal. However, some small amount of metal is indeed removed from the surface with each immersion, so that after repeated dippings, the coin begins to lose its luster, which was a function of the original surface imparted to the coin by the die. To familiarize yourself with the effects of dipping, you might try taking a common BU silver coin (such as a 1964 quarter) and dipping it over and over until its luster starts to fade. You might even try leaving it in the solution overnight.

If you do use a dip, remember that the surface of the coin will be stripped bare by it, removing any invisible oxidation that may have been protecting the coin from further oxidation. A dipped coin should be rinsed very thoroughly in warm running water. Then, if you are willing to go to the trouble, the coin should be dipped in denatured alcohol or a solvent such as *Dissolve* and allowed to air dry. This removes the water from the surface of the coin and prevents spotting. Be sure to read the instructions for the use of these products carefully before using.

To slow down the reaction of the dip and thus allow you to control the process better through a series of very fast dips until the desired result is achieved, you might try diluting the solution further with distilled water in a ratio of two parts dip to one part water. Commercial dips sold outside of coin shops tend to be very strong, and should be cut 1-to-1 or avoided entirely. Finally, be aware that particles of metal will be suspended in used dip, and it is possible to accidentally plate a coin of one metal with another metal from coins previously dipped in that solution. Separate jars, carefully labeled, should be maintained for each alloy.

Ultrasonic Cleaners

Ultrasonic cleaners with distilled water and a little detergent can be used to remove heavily impacted dirt from a coin, as well as coral encrustation from sea-salvaged coins. Used in connection with a dip, they can be very effective in removing heavy tarnish, but the reaction will take place faster than you think, so be very careful not to leave a coin in too long.

Olive Oil

Pure olive oil can be very effective in cleaning copper or bronze coins or medals, but for some reason it does not work very well on brass and copper-nickel and sometimes turns them dark. Place a single item in a small, covered jar with just enough oil in it to cover the coin and let it sit for 24 hours. Do not place more than one item in the same oil at the same time, as they will tend to darken unevenly. After 24 hours, check the coin for any discoloration and then, if the coin was only lightly dirty or spotted to begin with, wipe it clean with a very soft cloth (such as an old cotton T-shirt). Since the oil must be removed in this way, this method is not recommended for Mint State or Proof coins.

If you are satisfied with the results, finish removing all the oil, give the coin an alcohol or solvent bath, and place it in a holder. Coins that are heavily coated with verdigris or any other sort of green film may need to remain in the oil for 48 to 72 hours, while those with hard green spots may need to soak for a week. On the latter, it sometimes helps if you gently poke at the green spots with the crushed end of a toothpick after two or three days and then continue the treatment. Red corrosion can sometimes (but usually not) be removed by using the same treatment over a two-to-three week period. In any event, be sure to visually inspect the coin every day for signs of damage, as the coin this method might end up worse than it started. Do not wipe the oil off until you are reasonably certain that the dirt or verdigris has been loosened, as the wiping action will tend to lightly polish the coin. Other than this, there seems to be no serious side effects from repeated treatments.

Abrasives

Cleaning with an abrasive such as baking soda, scouring powder or a pencil eraser scratches the surface of a coin, and should never be attempted with a collectible coin. However, you might try this with a few common cents from your pocket, just to familiarize yourself with the results.

Ivory Soap

The safest cleaner is plain old Ivory soap, applied gently by hand and rinsed as described above.

Before using any of these methods, be sure to experiment first with a few common coins to acquaint yourself with the techniques and the associated problems.

In conclusion remember: When in doubt, don't!

HOW TO STORE COINS

Reprinted with Permission, J.T. Stanton

The best place to store coins is in an arid climate, such as Arizona. Lacking this possibility, you should try to store your coins in a climate-controlled environment featuring low humidity and a constant temperature. Low temperatures can cause condensation when the coins are brought out of storage and actually cause a breakdown of tin or *white metal* alloys. High temperatures can cause a deterioration of the plastics in some of the coin holders commonly in use today, with resultant damage to the coins in them.

PVC – Polyvinyl Chloride

A lot has been said over the years about polyvinyl chloride (PVC) holders and the damage they can cause. PVC consists of several types of vinyl mixed with a plasticizer that has a chlorine base. So long as the mixture retains its original form, it cannot harm your coin. However, if the mixture breaks down and the plasticizer begins to leak out of the PVC onto your coin (or bank note), the chlorine will immediately begin to attack the surface. On copper or copper-nickel coins a green *slime* will begin to form on the holder. In time, the chlorine will actually eat its way into the coin. On silver coins the reaction is the same, though it takes longer.

(Should you find this green film developing on any of your coins, remove it with a long bath in a solvent such as *Dissolve,* following the instructions on the container. Do not remove the coins from the holder until you are ready to bathe them, however, as the film may dry out and become harder to remove.)

PVC tends to break down under various combinations of heat,

humidity and pressure, with heat being the fastest acting stimulus. Pressure alone can also break it down, however. A stack of PVC flips squeezed into a box usually becomes tacky with age. A single PVC flip left by itself in a cool, dry place will usually not break down.

In summary, PVC holders are not inappropriate for short-term uses such as the display or sale of a coin. ANA uses oversized, high-quality PVC flips for internal handling of coins, combined with polyethylene sleeves for further protection of the coins. However, the long-term effects of PVC are still under study, and if such products are to be used the collector should inspect his collection at least every six months for signs of deterioration and damage.

Mylar Flips

Mylar is an excellent substance for coin storage products, since it does not have any of the plasticizers found in PVC. However, this also tends to make it somewhat stiffer than PVC, so for years the main use of mylar was the thin liner of cardboard 2x2s. These adequately protect the coin so long as the relatively brittle mylar does not crack, or is not torn by the staple from another holder. Even so, mylar 2x2s are a good, easy and inexpensive way of storing moderately priced coins that are not going to be handled a lot. For further protection, you might try placing a 2x2 coin envelope between each holder to protect the mylar from staples.

Recently a new type of mylar flip has come on the market. Although these are stiffer and a little harder to keep bent at the fold than the vinyl flips, they are still easy to use and possibly even a bit clearer than the vinyl flips. Whether the mylar flips will ever replace the vinyl flips remains to be seen, but for now it would seem they are indeed safer to use.

Acetate Flips

Acetate flips were in use some years ago, but as acetate is even more brittle than mylar, the SE flips tended to crack at the fold or where the two sheets of plastic were bonded together at the edge. Safe enough for careful use in collectors' hands, acetate flips with heavy coins in them seldom survived a trip through the mail.

Koin-Tains

One very successful application of a type of acetate is in Koin-Tains, where cast triacetate is extruded by dies into shells that fit over either side of the coin and grip it by the edge. Since the shells bow outward, the surface of the coin cannot be damaged by the holder, and if properly assembled, the overlapping edges of the shells form a near-airtight seal that keeps moisture and air pollution out. Conversely, they will also keep small amounts of moisture or whatever in the holder, so it is best (if possible) to package your coins in an air-conditioned room or at least on a dry day.

One slight drawback of Koin-Tains is that you cannot write on the holder, so it must be placed in a second holder. If you do not need to be able to see the coin, a plain paper 2x2 envelope works well. If you do wish to be able to see the coin at a glance, placing it in a flip or stapling it into a larger 2x2 will do.

Another slight problem is that presently Koin-Tains are only made to fit U.S. cents, nickels, dimes, quarters, halves and silver dollars, plus foreign crowns, though the 5-cent size will also work for half eagles and the dime size will also work for copper-nickel 3-cent pieces and quarter eagles. A coin placed in an oversized Koin-Tain will slide around inside it just like a coin in a flip or paper envelope. Until such time as Koin-Tains are available to fit obsolete sizes, odd-sized coins should be placed in polyethylene sleeves and then placed inside flips or envelopes for long-term storage. When they are available in the sizes you need, however, Koin-Tains are possibly the best type of protection you can buy.

Lucite Holders

Lucute plastic, such as that found in Capital Plastics holders, is another safe material for a coin holder. Properly assembled, a holder of this sort should be virtually airtight, and it would be hard to damage the coin in it short of dropping an anvil on it. The only drawback here is that U.S. coins vary slightly in diameter from year to year and mint to mint, with the result that you might risk damaging the edge of one coin to get it in the holder while another coin might rattle around loose in the same holder.

PUBLICATIONS

Coin World (weekly)
Amos Press
PO Box 150
Sidney, OH 45365-0150
1-800-253-4555

COINage Magazine (monthly)
4880 Market Street
Ventura, CA 93003
805-644-3824

COINS Magazine (monthly), *Numismatic News* (weekly),
    and *Coin Prices* (bi-monthly)
Krause Publications
700 East State Street
Iola, WI 54945-0001
Subscriber Services—1-800-258-0929; Krause Pub. website—
    http.//www.krause.com;   *Numismatic   News*   e-mail—
    numismatic_news@krause.com

First Strike (quarterly), and the *Numismatist* (monthly)
ANA
818 North Cascade Avenue
Colorado Springs, CO 80903-3729
719-632-2646; Fax 719-634-4085

ERRORS AND VARIETIES

Freaks, FIDOs, and Oddities: If you were once active in the hobby this is what you once referred to mint errors and varieties as. If you are new to the hobby these are terms you are likely to think of when referring to perhaps the most fascinating and exciting segment of the hobby. No matter what the case, these terms are inaccurate but they do paint a rather accurate picture of what you are likely to encounter when exploring this arena of the hobby. Actually they are known as Mint Errors and Die Varieties and there is no doubt throughout the hobby they remain the fastest growing segment of the hobby and now enjoy the largest value increases as well.

It is our belief that most readers of this section will be either novices or experienced collectors who desire to know more about this subject, so this chapter is being written in laymen's terms. Errors and varieties are, by far, the most complicated area of numismatics. Do not be discouraged. The learning curve is large and once you grasp the basic definitions of error and variety coinage causes and effects you will be well armed to begin your own search.

It is best to divide error and variety coinage into three primary categories: planchet errors; die errors (or die varieties); and striking errors. This is known as the P-D-S System and was created by Alan Herbert of Krause Publications, the first secretary of the Combined Organizations of Numismatic Error Collectors of America (CONECA), the only numismatic specialty club devoted exclusively to the study of error *and* variety coinage.

PLANCHET ERRORS

As the name suggests, planchet errors occur on or in a blank or a planchet. Until a planchet is struck, it is not a coin! Planchet errors occur *before* a coin is struck but can account for some very odd-looking struck coins.

Blank—Also known as a type I planchet. A blank is a round disk of metal punched from a long strip rolled for the proper thickness of an intended denomination. It will have a rough edge that appears to be sheared on the entire edge because it is! (Note: All coins have three sides: the obverse, the reverse and the edge.) Blanks are not intended to be struck, though they sometimes are.

Left: Lincoln cent blank.

Right: Lincoln cent planchet (planchet is smaller in diameter).

Planchet—Also known as a type II planchet. These are blanks that have gone through an upset mill that eliminates the rough edge and creates a raised rim to allow for a better design transfer from the die to the planchet and to protect the design from wear. It also makes coins easier to stack.

Improper Alloy Mix—An improper alloy mix is as the name suggests and appears as streaks on coins, such as yellow streaks on copper cents or entire coins of the wrong color. It can also appear as laminations (or fl akes and peels on a coin's surface).

Partial Plated and Unplated—Beginning in 1982, the Lincoln cent composition was changed to a planchet primarily composed of zinc, with a copper plate. Planchets dated 1982 to date with only part of the copper plating are partial plated. Consequently, if no plating is present, they are "unplated."

1985D Lincoln cent partial plated.

A defective planchet showing what is referred to as a "blow hole."

Defective Planchet—Most often resembles a ragged clip planchet (see *Incomplete Planchets*) and sometimes appears as a broken or split planchet. This is caused by an improper alloy mix or bubbles and/or foreign materials trapped in the metal.

1967 Kennedy half dollar with lamination.

Lamination—Appears as flakes or peels on a coin's surface and is due to an improper alloy mix or debris and/or air trapped in the metal. This is very common on Wartime nickels and Wheat cents.

Shield Nickel broken planchet.

Split or Broken Planchet—Can be viewed as an advanced lamination. Split planchets are planchets split or broken through the center as in a clamshell or creme cookie, and broken planchets are those split in two pieces like a "lovers' heart" pendant. Broken planchets are ready to break before being struck but usually break after they are struck. More complete explanations of split planchets follow.

1945 Lincoln cent split planchet before strke.

Split Planchet Before Strike—In this case a planchet split in two before being struck, as the term would suggest. They are usually of normal diameter but are very thin. They are struck on both the obverse and reverse but much of the design is usually light with multitudes of striation lines visible on both sides.

A nice example of both pieces of a
split planchet after strike from a private mint.

Split Planchet After Strike—In this case a planchet was ready to split before it was struck but waited until after it was struck before splitting in two. These are usually of normal diameter; one side, however, will be fully struck showing no striations while the other side will have only a ghost of some design and be heavily striated. These are usually not as valuable as the split panchet before strike unless both pieces remain together as a set.

Split Planchet, Hinged—A normally struck coin that is ready to split but is still together on a small portion of the coin. These resemble open clamshells and are often affectionately referred to as "clamshell splits" or simply "clamshells."

Incomplete Planchets—More commonly referred to as "clipped planchets." There are several types of incomplete planchets and so, for simplicity's sake, they follow as independent definitions and will be referred to as "clips."

Rim Clip—Just a tiny portion of the planchet missing on the rim. May be straight or curved but is usually indistinguishable as to which.

1945 Lincoln cent curved clip.

Curved Clip—Larger than a simple rim clip, usually with 2% or more of the planchet missing from the rim inward forming an inward curve.

Straight Clip—Larger than a simple rim clip, usually with 2% or more of the planchet missing from the rim inward forming a straight or very straight outward bowed edge on the affected area.

Jefferson nickel with ragged clip.

Ragged Clip—A portion of the planchet from the rim inward missing, usually in a fairly straight line but having a very jagged edge on the affected area. If the line is very irregular in shape and comes signifi cantly into the planchet it is known as a defective planchet rather than a ragged clip.

Crescent Clip—More than 50% (by weight) of the planchet missing from the rim inward forming a large crescent-shaped curve, much like the image found on old outhouse doors!

1968D Lincoln cent with incomplete clip.

Incomplete Clip—This is somewhat more diffi cult to describe and more rare than any of the above clips. An incomplete clip is found on otherwise normal appearing coins forming long, rim-to-rim, incused curves in the same location on both the obverse and reverse of a planchet or coin. This is caused by an incomplete punch overlapping another punch from the metal strip when punching blanks.

1945P Jefferson nickel elliptical clip.

Elliptical Clip—A planchet or coin that appears oval in shape, much like a football. This is another rare type of clip and is created much like an incomplete clip except the overlapping punch was complete. A crescent clip and an elliptical clip are often formed at the same time when an incomplete clip fi nally breaks apart and both pieces are struck. If you have an incomplete clipped coin that appears ready to break apart do not break it apart thinking you will create an elliptical and a crescent clip. These pieces must separate before they are struck to qualify! If you do break apart an incomplete clip you have just damaged your valuable error coin, thereby diminishing its value significantly!

Disk Clip—This is a rim clip that usually goes undetected and, though they are minute as far as clips go, they are very scarce. For the most part they can only be positively identifi ed on copper nickel clad coinage. For identifi cation one must examine the edge of the coin where a *step* or *dip* will appear in the copper core. Look at all your copper nickel clad proof coins to try to fi nd one of these; proof planchet and striking errors are rare as a general rule, and this may be your best opportunity to fi nd a genuine, premium touting error on a proof coin.

1970 Lincoln cent with assay clip.

Assay Clip—Probably the most rare clip of them all. This is a clip that usually appears as if somebody cut a piece out of the coin. In effect that is what happened—it happened however, to a planchet before the coin was struck.

A nice corner clip error from a private mint.

Corner Clip—Nearly as rare as assay clips, corner clips are literally the corner of a metal strip! It is only possible, therefore, to have four corner clips from a metal strip from which blanks are punched. Obviously few of these ever happen!

Incomplete Cladding—A copper nickel coin that for one reason or another was struck while missing some of the outer clad layer on either the obverse or reverse or both. These appear as having large copper areas on the surface(s). These should not be confused with sintered planchets (see next).

Sintered Planchets—Before planchets are struck they are given a bath. This bath takes place in a giant vat where thousands, even millions, of other planchets preceded them. In effect, a sintered planchet is a planchet that took a bath in dirty bath water! If a vat has typically been used to clean copper planchets, then a load of white metal coins is dumped in the same solution, the result is often one of the copper adhering to the surface of the white metal, much like electroplating. Genuine sintered planchets, though very scarce, command little premium as the effect is easily duplicated outside the mint and few people are able to authenticate them. A good example would be a Jefferson nickel, normal in all respects except that it looks like it was struck on a copper planchet.

Wrong Stock—A coin, usually copper nickel clad, that was struck on a planchet of normal diameter that was punched from metal strip rolled to the thickness intended for another denomination. These will appear normal in most respects but will either weigh too light or too heavy. The classic example of this is the 1970-D Washington quarter, which was struck on dime stock, or planchets that were punched from metal strip that was rolled to the intended thickness of the Roosevelt dime.

Kennedy half struck on a nickel planchet. This is a "wrong metal" error.

Wrong Metal—A coin struck on a planchet created for another denomination or foreign planchet. These will almost never be perfectly round and are most desirable when the planchet used is of a different color than the intended planchet. For example, a Jefferson nickel struck on a cent planchet.

These are among the most popular of all error types and command sharp premiums. Throughout the years the U.S. Mint has contracted to strike coins for many foreign nations, and sometimes these foreign planchets get stuck in the "tote bins" used to transport planchets to the coining presses. The same thing happens with the wrong denominations for U.S. coins. On U.S. coins this can occur only on planchets that are smaller than the denomination being struck. For example: a nickel on a cent planchet, a cent on a dime planchet, a nickel on a quarter planchet, or a quarter on a dime planchet. These can also be classified as *striking errors*.

Susan B. Anthony dollar struck fragment.

Fragments—A coin struck on an irregular-shaped piece (usually just a scrap) of metal. These pieces must be die struck on both sides. If struck on one side only they are simply laminations that peeled out of the surface of a coin. Fragments are quite rare and are usually found when turning a mint bag inside out and checking the bottom seam!

A classic struck bowtie clip from a private mint.

Bowtie—Actually a form of fragment but included because of its high premium and desirability. A bowtie is simply a piece of already punched metal strip (once punched it becomes known as webbing) that happens to find its way into the coining presses. They are roughly bowtie shaped, hence the name.

Lincoln cent thin planchet.

Thick or Thin Planchets—A coin or planchet that is unusually thick or thin. This is caused by the rolling machine that rolls each metal strip to its proper thickness. It is not enough that a coin *looks* thick or thin, it must weigh more or less than the Mint's tolerable weight.

WRONG STOCK PLANCHET ERROR WEIGHTS

Occasionally the wrong thickness strip (stock) is inadvertently run under the gang punches in the blanking process and the result is a thicker (or thinner) than normal planchet for that particular denomination.

This has occurred primarily with the advent of the clad

coinage, but "wrong stock" silver errors are also known and are eagerly sought after. In order to tell whether or not a "thick" or "thin" error may be a "Wrong Stock" planchet error, we are listing here the weight ranges for the various possible combinations of Clad WSP errors.

Any that fall outside these brackets are probably on planchets that were punched from stock that was rolled to the improper thickness (+ or –), and should not be considered as true "Wrong Stock Planchet" errors.

The possible (not just the known) combinations of Clad WSP errors and weights are:

Dime on quarter stock	46.56	to	48.46 gr.
Dime on half dollar stock	48.65	to	61.05 gr.
Dime on dollar stock	75.8	to	78.9 gr.
Quarter on dime stock	63.31	to	65.71 gr.
Quarter on half dollar stock	98.43	to	102.43 gr.
Quarter on dollar stock	139.65	to	145.25 gr.
Half on dime stock	100.12	to	104.12 gr.
Half on quarter stock	135.98	to	141.58 gr.
Half on dollar stock	221.35	to	230.25 gr.
Dollar on dime stock	155.12	to	161.52 gr.
Dollar on quarter stock	210.78	to	219.48 gr.
Dollar on half dollar stock	265.85	to	276.65 gr.

STRIKING ERRORS

As the class designation suggests, striking errors occur during the actual minting (or striking) of a coin. Overall this group presents the most spectacular errors.

Washington quarter die trial strike.

Die Trial Strikes— Also known as die adjustment strikes and low pressure strikes. This may be a misnomer as there are several ways this could occur, the least common cause being that which the name implies. They can occur when a press is coming to a halt with a planchet seated between the dies, when adjusting the pressure of a strike to allow for proper design relief, when setting vertical and horizontal alignment, and, most often, when a planchet is intentionally left between dies to prevent clashing of the dies while maintenance, routine or otherwise, is being performed on the press. These can be identifi ed as having very weak to no reeding, and very light to almost no design elements, with the strongest toward the center of the coin. As is the case with all errors and varieties, authentication by a specialist is highly recommended.

Washington quarter struck through duct tape.

1978 Eisenhower dollar struck through heavy debris.

Strike Through—This occurs when any foreign substance gets struck into the surface of a coin. Debris composed of tiny metal shavings and thick grease or wax is the usual culprit but it could be anything from a piece of string to a piece of cloth or even a staple! Just recently it was realized that not all, but most, of the coins sold as having been struck through cloth are actually struck through duct tape! One only has to look at mint equipment to realize the enormous quantity of duct tape used and compare many of these struck through errors to realize the unique "weave" pattern as that belonging to duct tape!

1993 Lincoln cent broadstrike.

Broadstrike—A broadstrike is a coin that was struck without the retaining collar in place. The collar is actually the third die and it is what forms reeding on reeded edge coins. Broadstrikes are always larger in diameter than the coin was intended to be—sometimes just barely and sometimes much larger. The larger it is the more desirable. They are sometimes nearly round but they are usually slightly out of round. There are two types of broadstrikes: centered and uncentered. The centered broadstrikes are struck nearly perfectly in the center and, of course, the off-center broadstrikes are not centered. As long as all the design elements remain on the coin it is a broadstrike. If design elements (including the denticles) around the edge are missing, it is then considered an off-center strike.

1920 off-center strike Buffalo nickel.

Off-Center Strikes—As the name implies, these are coins that were struck off center and, naturally, out of collar. These are not to be confused with misaligned die strikes, which are covered under die errors. Some of the obverse and reverse design elements (including denticles when included as part of the design) must be missing. This usually occurs when a planchet does not rest in its proper position inside the press. The most desirable off-center strikes are those that are approximately 40–80% (measured by observing the unstruck portion of the planchet) off center and include a full date. Off-center strikes on obsolete series are very much in demand as well.

The Off Center Coin Position Guide

BLANK PLANCHET

11:00 12:00 1:00 2:00 3:00 4:00 5:00 6:00 7:00 8:00 9:00 10:00

COURTESY
THE ERROR COIN ENCYCLOPEDIA

by Arnold Margolis

This private mint token clearly exhibits what a Lincoln cent would look like double struck and rotated in collar. The reverse of this piece looks nothing like a Lincoln cent.

Double and Multiple Struck—A coin that is struck more than once. Because there are several types, for simplicity's sake they are listed individually below. "Double" and "multiple" are interchangeable on all, with multiple meaning anything more than two strikes. Also note that the most desirable of any of the following are the double or multiple strikes that exhibit more than one date. It may be the same year, but if it is there more than once it is more desirable.

Double Struck in Collar—A coin that was not ejected after having been struck or an already struck coin that found its way back into the coin press and was struck again. To positively identify this rare error type some rotation between strikes must take place.

Susan B. Anthony dollar double struck out of collar.

Double Struck out of Collar—Usually a coin that was struck once normally, in collar, but did not eject properly, receiving a second strike off center. Both strikes can be off center as well.

Flip-over Double and Multiple Struck—All of the above rules apply with one exception; one of the strikes must have occurred after the coin fl ipped over in the coining press. This type of double strike exhibits an obverse and a reverse strike on both sides and is much more scarce than typical double and multiple strike coins. Also, a fl ip-over can occur in or out of collar.

Wrong Metal—Debatable as to whether this falls in this category or that of a planchet error. See the defi nition under "Planchet Errors."

Double Denomination—Unquestionably (as of the time of this writing) the most desirable of all error types. This, too, is debatable as to what heading it should fall under—planchet

Lincoln cent struck on an already struck Roosevelt dime.
This is a double denomination error.

or striking error—but since it involves a previously struck and different denomination than that intended it is placed here. A double denomination is a coin that was struck with two different denomination dies! Of course that also means it is double struck. Examples are cents struck on already struck dimes, nickels struck on already struck cents, and Eisenhower dollars struck on already struck Kennedy halves! The same rule of planchet and die sizes for wrong metal strikes applies to double denominations. They are affectionately referred to as 6-cent, 11-cent, etc., pieces.

1972 Lincoln cent with indent.

Indent—An indent is a depression in the surface of a struck coin caused by an overlapping planchet present during the strike. This depression is usually adjoining the rim and will have no design elements present in the depression. The coin will usually be almost perfectly round except at the outermost edges of the indent. A full indent is caused when one planchet is lying squarely on top of another at the time of the strike. In rare cases, coins may be fully indented with a planchet of smaller size intended for another denomination.

Brockage—Very similar to an indent with the difference being the coin was indented by an already struck coin as opposed to a planchet. As with the indent, brockages may be

Lincoln cent brockage.

1990 Lincoln cent with partial brockage.

full or partial but the indent exhibits incused mirror images of the coin that caused the brockage. The larger the affected area the more desirable the brockage. Additionally, each subsequent strike spreads and weakens the brockage. Early strike brockages that show nearly perfect mirror images are by far the most desirable.

Lincoln cent counterbrockage.

Counterbrockage—Simply put, this is a brockage created by an already brockaged coin.

1975D Lincoln cent capped die strike.

Edge view of Lincoln cent capped die strike.

Die Cap—A coin stuck to a hammer die (the die that moves the most and is not below the collar) that has received several strikes and is spreading enough to creep up the sides of the hammer die. This often resembles a bottle cap (and is sometimes referred to as such) or a thimble. The image of a normally struck coin appears on the inside bottom while usually nothing appears on the outside bottom.

Capped Die Strike—This is actually a late-stage brockage but in order for it to be a late-stage brockage a capped die is created on the hammer die. In other words, this is yet another type of strike through error.

Clad Layer Errors—Like many other errors described in this chapter, clad layer errors have different causes and effects. Copper nickel planchets and coins that are missing one or both of the outer layers due to improper bonding to the copper core are clad layer errors. Again, for simplicity's sake, we will individually defi ne the different types you may encounter. Also, again, it is debatable as to which classifi cation these actually belong—striking or planchet.

Missing Clad Layer, Split Before Strike—These are coins that appear thin and are primarily nickel on one side and copper on the other, but exhibit an otherwise normal strike, though it may be a little weak.

Missing Clad Layer, After Strike—Coins that appear to be thin and primarily nickel on one side and copper on the other. The nickel side will appear normal. The copper side will have many striations and little to no design detail.

Washington quarter missing clad layer (the nickel layer itself).

Missing Clad Layer (the nickel layer itself)—These, too, can be struck before or after they split from the planchet. One that was struck before splitting will appear to be all nickel and will be normal on one side and striated with little detail on the other. Those struck after they split will be almost paper thin and weakly struck on both sides. These nickel layers struck on both sides are very rare as they are so delicate they rarely survive.

A nice example of an edge strike.

Edge Strike—A very rare and desirable striking error created when a planchet is standing rather than lying between the dies and is quickly ejected by the pressure of the strike before it can get folded. These coins display small struck areas on the edge directly opposite of one another and are usually slightly bent.

Lincoln cent fold-over strike.

Fold-over Strike—Rare, though not as rare as a true edge strike, but probably more desirable. Created when a planchet is standing rather than lying between dies while being struck. However, unlike an edge strike, they did not get ejected immediately and were subsequently folded over and struck. They are usually struck slightly off center with the fold itself being off center and very much resembling a piece of bread folded over for a sandwich. Additionally, in recent years, many of the more exotic items, which have been known to not be possible without help, have been minted. These items are still under investigation and one would be wise to exercise caution in purchasing these items as well.

Saddle Strike—This is basically a double-struck off-center coin with the following exception—it can only be produced in a dual or quad press, that is, a press with two or four die pairs and a single collar device with two or four holes corresponding to the die pairs. Differing from typical off-center double strikes, these are buckled in the middle and resemble an equestrian (horse) saddle, hence the name.

Edge view of a partial collar strike on a Nevada state quarter.

Partial Collar Strike—These occur when the anvil or bottom die fails to rise fully above the planchet, restricting outward metal fl ow. For that area of the coin above the collar the diameter will increase, giving the edge a flanged or "lipped" appearance. These may be full or tilted with the full partial collars bringing a slightly higher premium.

Lincoln cent mated pair.

Caution—Caution—Caution

Most of these planchet and striking errors are regularly fabricated either for the fun of it or intentionally to swindle innocent victims out of their hard-earned money. Some of them are quite good. Authentication should be considered mandatory on all of the more expensive and exotic error types!

DIE ERRORS

Die errors were not placed between the planchet and striking errors because they are really very different in that all planchet and striking errors are unique while die errors are recurring. From the moment the event causing the variety occurs each subsequent strike will show the same error until it is effaced in some way or the die is retired. In other words, this section could just as easily have been titled Die Varieties because that is what this section is all about. In the last several years die varieties have exploded in popularity, and most collectors now collect varieties of some kind, be they doubled dies, re-punched or over mint marks, or misplaced dates. Many collect all of them. With communications what they are today it has become much easier to locate all the pieces needed for completing a date and mint set of your favorite series, and in order to continue collecting in one's favorite series one naturally begins collecting by variety. With the explosion of information on die varieties collectors should be kept happy in their own series for many years! Besides, looking for die varieties, even in your pocket change, is, well, downright fun!

Before engaging in any dialogue regarding value, let us cover the basic definitions of the terms you are most likely to encounter when collecting die errors. Following you will find two sets of definitions. The first set is associated with true die errors and it is considered debatable as to what classification—striking or die—its entries belong. The second set of definitions is labeled Die Varieties and comprises those terms that specialists normally think of and refer to when discussing, writing about, researching, or lecturing on die varieties. Although both sets belong under the heading of Die Errors, we are separating the two because the entries in the first set, though they are recurring, tend to "grow" or get bigger or longer, whichever the case may be, with continued strikes.

True Die Errors

Major Die Break (or "CUD")—This is exactly what it sounds like—a major break in the die. Not all dies are perfect and many do break with the repeated pressure applied during the striking process. When the most blatant major die breaks are encountered they resemble a cow's "cud," hence the most frequently encountered term for this highly collect-

D Lincoln cent major die break (or "CUD").

ible and prized error type. In order for a die break to qualify as a major die break the break must show definite separation taking place on the die. This may show as a piece of the die missing, in which case there will be a raised blank spot on the surface of the coin usually exhibiting weak design details in the same area on the opposite (opposite meaning obverse or reverse) side of the coin. It may also show as a portion of the coin being separated from the rest by a heavy line (die crack), with this separated portion being raised above the rest of the coin. This is known as a retained major die break or retained CUD. In almost all instances this major die break, full or retained, adjoins the rim and comes into the fields and design elements on the coin.

Split Die Strike—Actually another form of major die break but different because, rather than displaying a long curved break, it mostly splits the surface of the coin in two with a heavy, solid line down the middle of the surface. This is not to be confused with a rim-to-rim die crack, which is a very thin line with no rise in either half's surface. Split die strikes are quite rare and highly prized.

S Jefferson nickel with die crack.

Die Crack—A thin raised line on the surface of a coin that is the result of the die beginning to break. With repeated strikes die cracks can and do eventually turn into major die breaks. However, die cracks are very common and usually command little or no premium. They are most often used as die markers to assist in identifying other known varieties.

A die chip in the word "Liberty" of a Lincoln cent. It does not matter where but these are enthusiastically collected as "BIE" errors.

Die Chip—Literally a chip out of a die or a tiny piece of a die broken out. They show as a small, raised area on the surface of a coin and this area usually has somewhat ragged looking boundaries. Die chips, much like die cracks, are often used as die markers in identifying other die varieties on the same coin. There are, however, several subclasses of die chips which are widely collected, though they do not command much of a premium. The perfect example would be "BIE" errors, which are nothing more than die chips located somewhere between the letters of "Liberty" on a Lincoln cent.

Interesting die gouges on the reverse of a 1953-S Roosevelt dime.

Die Gouge—This is actually damage to the die but shows on each struck coin after the damage occurred. It may be a sharp, angular, raised area on the surface of the coin. Depending on size and severity these can command a modest premium but, again, are usually used to identify other die varieties.

Clashed Dies or Die Clash—This is the result of two dies coming together without a planchet between them. This transfers a partial impression from die to die. In other words, part of the reverse die images now show on the obverse and vice versa. The infamous "Prisoner cents" are a classic ex-

Shield nickel with clashed die.

ample of clashed dies. Prisoner cents are Lincoln Memorial cents that have the columns of the Memorial clashed both in front of Lincoln's face and behind his head, giving the impression of "prison bars." As a general rule clashed dies do not carry much of a premium. There are exceptions, however. The "Prisoner cents" carry a small premium and strong die clashes showing signifi cant design transfers also carry a small premium. When the date also transfers, leaving a date on both the obverse and the reverse, they carry an even higher premium. Strong clashes on proof coins of the 20th century command a substantial premium.

Broken Collar Die Break—Also known as a collar break or collar cud. Keep in mind that the collar is actually the third die used in the modern minting process; therefore, it can break and exhibit similar properties to that of major die breaks on obverse and reverse dies. Of course there usually are no design elements involved (at least not on U.S. coins of the 20th century). These appear as normal coins except they will be out of round only on the affected area of the edge, which shows as a lump of extra metal on the edge. These are quite scarce and command a decent premium.

Rotated Die—This is the result of improperly installed dies or loose, moving dies. On U.S. coins the die alignment should be such that when you fl ip a coin vertically the design is supposed to be in the upright position. If it is not, then one or both of the dies is rotated from its normal position in the coining press. Rotated dies are quite common on pre–20thcentury U.S. coinage so they command little or no premium. Rotation is measured in degrees either clockwise or counterclockwise, and rotation of less than 15 degrees on 20thcentury coinage is still common. However, there are some reported examples with signifi cant rotation, such as the 1988-P Kennedy half dollar with 180-degree rotated dies, which are worth a decent and sometimes hefty premium.

Die Polish Errors—This is a very common type of die error encountered on virtually all denominations and design types. Sometimes it is necessary for the Mint to remove a die to "stone" (polish) off added undesirable elements such as a die clash. When this is done the polish lines appear as raised scratches on the surface of a coin and more often than not some of the intended design elements are missing. As previously mentioned these are very common and usually command no premium at all. With die-hard die variety enthusiasts they never command a premium. There are, however, exceptions that are noteworthy. The infamous 1937-D "3-legged Buffalo" is such an example. While hardcore die variety specialists do not acknowledge this as a major premium coin because they know what it is—die polishing—the hobby in general has embraced this coin largely because of its endearing nickname and the widespread publicity and marketing it has received. Other examples would be the "No FG" Kennedy half dollars and the "No V.D.B." (post-1917 only) Lincoln cent varieties. Again, because they are such common error types, hard-core specialists usually will pay no premium for such coins, but the hobby in general often does. It pays to educate yourself.

Die Varieties

As previously stated, these are still die errors but have been separated here because they are the die error (die variety) types that are receiving all the hoopla in the hobby these days. These are the coins that often make headlines and are now dominating new research in the hobby. The doubled die is unquestionably the most popular and the most prominent of this group and will be cited last so that we may give you a brief explanation of the different classes of doubled dies immediately following the definition.

Repunched Mint Mark (RPM)—One of the hottest areas of the market because of the variety type desirability and the affordability of most RPMs. Until 1985 for proof coinage and 1990 for circulating coinage the mint mark was hand punched into all the working dies. More often than not a single blow of the punch did not result in suffi cient relief so a second or more blows were necessary. If the punch was not placed in the perfect location for a second blow doubling of the mint mark was the result. In a few rare instances secondary mint marks are completely separate from the primary mint mark and these command substantially higher pre miums than typical RPMs. Examples of this would be CONECA's 1956-D Lincoln cent RPM#8, which is completely separate way south of the primary mint mark, and CONECA's 1942-S Lincoln cent RPM#12, which is completely separate west of the primary mint mark.

1941-S Winged Liberty (Mercury) dime with repunched mint mark (CONECA RPM #1). Photo courtesy of J. T. Stanton

1945-D Winged Liberty (Mercury) dime with repunched mint mark, though this one is normal over horizontal! Photo courtesy of J. T. Stanton

1950-S over D mintmark Roosevelt dime listed as FS-10-1950S-501.

Over Mint Mark (OMM)—The same as a repunched mint mark (RPM) only this involves two different punches with different mint marks. One mint mark is punched on a die and then a different mint mark is also punched on the same die. The most well-know examples would be the 1944-D/S Lincoln cent and the 1954-S/D Jefferson nickel. OMMs are very popular and typically command a substantial premium. Keep in mind that until 1996 all die preparation was done in Philadelphia so the mystery of "How could this happen?" is not so unimaginable.

Dual Mint Mark (DMM)—Many specialists are seeing this and asking "What?!!!" As of this writing this term and acronym are not widely accepted and, in fact are largely unheard of in the hobby. It is included here to alert you to a new and sure to be valuable variety type. This term was conceived by noted author and variety specialist Ken Potter, keeper of the Variety Coin Register, in late 1997 upon the discovery of a 1956 Lincoln cent that sports mint marks from both Denver and San Francisco. It is true! The variety appears to be a normal 1956-D Lincoln cent in every respect except it has an "S" mint mark punched below and between the "1" and the "9" of the date! This was a year when San Francisco produced no circulating coinage, yet the "S" mint mark is there! It differs from a typical OMM in that the mint marks are totally separate. In 1999 a 1980-D Lincoln cent was confirmed to have both a "D" and a separate "S" mint mark!

1844 Seated dime with an excellent repunched date.
Photo courtesy of J. T. Stanton

Repunched Date (RPD)—Repunched dates occur much the same way RPMs and OMMs do. Up to and including 1908 at least one digit (the last in the date) was punched into working dies by hand. This could involve a logo punch with one, two, three, or all four of the digits in the date. Again, in order for subsequent punches to be unnoticeable, perfect alignment was a must. This did not always happen, with the result being some digits showing doubling or tripling or even more. RPDs are quite common from the earliest days of the United States right up to and including 1908, appearing in most years from virtually every denomination. This does not mean, however, that they do not command a premium, as most do. This premium can be small to exorbitant! The general rule of thumb is the more noticeable the repunching the more desirable the piece, therefore the higher the premium. Scarcity of certain RPDs is also a big factor when determining a value. Generally, the older the coin (from pre-1909) the more likely you are to encounter an RPD variety.

1868 Indian Head cent with digits in the denticles—an MPD.
Photo courtesy of J. T. Stanton

Misplaced Date (MPD)—These are, in effect, repunched dates, the major difference being they are digits punched in areas not normally associated with digit placement. In other words, digits punched in the die but not touching the date! Currently there are many hundreds of known MPD varieties and the list continues to grow almost daily! All the rules apply as those for RPDs but the digits may be found almost anywhere within a half inch or so of the date. Digits may be found in the denticles or on other design elements. Sometimes these digits are punched more than once. In fact, there is an 1870 Indian Head cent that has no less than 11 digits punched in the denticles—the exact number of visible digits is still being debated! This term was fi rst coined by Larry Steve, noted author, specialist, and fi rst president of the Flying Eagle and Indian Cent Collectors Society, in about 1990. The organization is affectionately referred to as "The Fly-In Club." Most MPDs command some kind of premium, with many bringing substantial premiums. It is important to note that some MPDs are found on dates and denominations where only one die is known to have been used; therefore, all the coins of that date and denomination display the variety; although these coins have no premium for the variety they are still likely to be valuable coins-sdue to their low mintage. MPDs are extremely popular and widely sought, though in-depth research has really just begun.

Overdates—Overdates are just as the name implies— one date over or under another. These are probably the most de-

1849 Seated Liberty half dime overdate. Notice the 9 is punched over an 8 or a 6; specialists don't always agree as to which. Photo courtesy of J. T. Stanton

sirable of die varieties across the board in numismatics and have been collected for a long time, even though until recently all the causes had not been understood. There are three ways this is known to occur. One digit may be hand punched over another on a die. This is the most common type of overdate and many exist, especially from the early 19th century. Another way is by one gang punch, with all the digits placed in one punching device, punched over another date on a die. This is more scarce than the previous type of overdate but many examples do exist, mostly from the latter part of the 19th century. There are some known instances where both the above were created on dates in a series where only one die was used so, again, the variety itself commands no premium but the coin sure does due to its scarcity. The fi nal cause for overdates leads us right into the hottest area of die variety collecting today—doubled dies. They are the result of Class III (design hub) doubling where a hub of one date received a hubbing of another date. These are rare instances that always bring substantial premiums. These are the cause of most, if not all, 20th-century overdates and will be discussed in more detail in the next section. Examples of this type of overdate are the 1943/2-P Jefferson nickel and the 1942/1 (both Philadelphia and Denver) Winged Liberty (Mercury) dimes.

Doubled Dies—The following defi nitions and descriptions are taken almost verbatim from a special four-page fl yer written by Don Bonser and printed by J. T. Stanton Publishing. It is presented here because of the simplicity and brevity of the respective defi nitions and descriptions, as this is a very diffi cult area to grasp. Take the time to learn this, as doubled die collecting is very rewarding and popular! Post-discussion and comments are by this chapter's author. The result of an error in the hubbing process that causes doubling of some element(s) of a coin's design, doubled dies should not be confused with double strikes. A word of caution: Do not confuse true doubled dies with common, virtually uncollectible machine doubling (also known as strike doubling and ejection doubling, as well as other similar terms). True doubled dies show distinct, rounded doubled images most often with some separation and/or split serifs. Strike or machine doubling is caused (primarily) by a die being loose in the coining press and shows on struck coins as a flat, shelflike doubling (with "sheer" lines usually visible under magnification on the "shelves"). Doubled dies can range from fairly common to very rare. Each individual one (doubled die) is created under a separate circumstance. Most are scarce to very scarce. Following are the (most widely accepted) classes and causes of doubled dies.

Class I, Rotated Hub Doubling—This occurs when different hubbings result in a slight (to major) rotation about the center of the die being hubbed. Doubling is slight near the center of the die (and coins struck from it) and increases toward the edge. Doubling is more or less uniform. The best known examples are the major 1955 and 1972 doubled die cents.

1943 Lincoln cent with strong Class VI doubled die obverse. Photo courtesy of J. T. Stanton	1966 Washington quarter with very strong doubled die reverse. Photo courtesy of J. T. Stanton

Class II, Distorted Hub Doubling—This kind of doubling occurs when a hub that has been used to prepare a particular die is also employed for producing many other dies before being returned for use with the earlier one. During the interim while the hub is hubbing many more dies, its metal fatigues and, literally, "spreads out." Doubling results because the hub's design, when it is used to force its image into the die, is actually in a slightly different location each time. A simple analogy may help you to understand this better. What hap-

1997 Doubled Ear Lincoln cent.
Is it a doubled die or not?
Specialists can't agree!

Close-up of the 1997
Doubled Ear Lincoln cent.
Photos courtesy of John A. Wexler

pens when a pencil eraser is pushed into a hard surface? It spreads out. The same occurs, although to a lesser degree, to a hub as it is used to prepare die after die.

Class III, Design Hub Doubling—This results from differing hub designs being used on the same die. This kind of doubling causes overdates, large over small dates, and small over large dates (to name a few). It also caused the 1878 7 over 8 tailfeathers Morgan dollar varieties.

1994 Lincoln cent showing an excellent class IV doubled die reverse and listed as FS-01-1994-801 and DDR-001.

Class IV, Offset Hub Doubling—This is, by far, one of the rarest forms of doubling on United States coins. Out of over

2,000 listed doubled dies, under 30 are the result of this form of doubling. Ironically, though, both the well-known 1983 (doubled die reverse) and 1984 (doubled die obverse with doubled ear) Lincoln cent doubled dies are Class IV varieties. This kind of doubling occurs when a die, already having been hubbed properly, is hubbed again but is centered improperly under the hub. In other words, the die is somewhat displaced from its original position, but not rotated about this position. Doubling is offset in the same direction across the die and is uniform.

1983 Lincoln cent doubled die obverse listed as FS-01-1983-101 and DDO-001.

Class V, Pivoted Hub Doubling—This is very similar to rotated hub doubling (Class I) except the "pivot point" between hubbings is near the rim of the coin. Design elements farthest from the pivot point will be doubled most obviously, while those closer to it (the pivot point) will be doubled only slightly, if at all. The 1995 Lincoln cent—Die 1, still fresh in the mind of the entire hobby, is an example of pivoted hub doubling with the pivot point (area of least doubling) being around 3 o'clock on the obverse.

Class VI, Distended Hub Doubling—This form of doubling is unique in that there is little to no separation of images on coins produced by dies with this sort of doubling. As hubs are used, their raised design elements flatten out slightly. The design imparted by such a hub will not penetrate as far into a die and the die will produce coins showing designs that are thicker than normal. (The 1943 Lincoln cent with a super fat date is perhaps the most shining example of this form of doubling.)

Class VII, Modified Hub Doubling—This name arises from use of a hub that has had some undesirable part of design ground off, rather than wasting an otherwise useable hub. On occasion, the unwanted portion of design is not ground off completely and all dies prepared by this hub will produce coins showing doubling of a specifi c design element. Examples include 1970 cents of all mints with the remainder of a high or low 70 showing near the date (and a 1963-D cent that shows portions of a 3 whose design never was used, under the primary 3 in the date).

Class VIII, Tilted Hub Doubling—This form of doubling is not included in the aforementioned flyer and is still hotly contested as to whether it is even another class of doubled die. However, most specialists agree that it is, and, if so, it is the rarest known form of hub doubling, as less than a handful of doubled dies are listed with this classifi cation. It is included here because of the signifi cance of those varieties listed with this classification.

This class is defined pretty much the way it sounds and supposedly involves a tilted hub. When we say tilted hub we mean tilted (either the the hub itself or the die being hubbed) in the hubbing press, not the coining press. Remember, the hubbing press is the press that "squeezes" the impression from the hubs to the dies, in effect striking the dies. Supposedly, again, the hub or die is tilted as the result of an uneven cut on the hub or die blank or from some debris or foreign object lodged in the hubbing press so as to not allow for firm, square seating of the die blank being "squeezed." Squeezing is the Mint's term for striking. Many specialists consider the rare Indian cent 1891 doubled die obverse (Fivaz/Stanton #FS-010.87 and Snow #S-3) to be this class of doubled die, as the doubling is easily visible on the word "Of" and slightly on the word "Liberty" but hardly anywhere else.

So there you have it—simple (as simple as can be anyway) and concise defi nitions of the types, causes, and classes of doubled dies normally accepted today. However, in 1996 the U.S. Mint introduced a new hubbing press that is supposed to bring about suffi cient relief on working dies with just one squeeze, thereby eliminating the possibility of doubled dies. Prior to installation of these new hubbing presses one squeeze was never enough, which is why so many doubled dies are known to exist. This new single-squeeze hubbing press has already sparked controversy in the numismatic community with the discovery of a doubled ear 1997 Lincoln cent. First reported by Iowa collector Larry Philbrick, the coin remains mired in controversy, as most specialists believe it to be a Class IV or VIII doubled die while some of the most respected specialists do not agree that it is a doubled die at all. And, indeed, the Mint itself has declared it not to be a doubled die, referring to it mostly as an unfinished die. The Mint claims the area in question (Lincoln's ear) is on all cent dies after the single squeeze and is always, except in this case, stoned or ground off before being used. Specialists who agree with it being a doubled die say, "Show me some other dies with this effect," while those who abide by the Mint's explanation still do not understand fully exactly what the Mint is trying to say! Needless to say, many specialists are lobbying for yet another classification of doubled dies, one that is created with a single hubbing! Stay tuned. . . .

As was stated at the beginning of this chapter, the study of error and variety coinage is very complex, requiring years of study to understand the causes and effects of certain anomalies in the die making and minting process. Obviously this chapter is greatly condensed and multitudes of fine references have been published on the subject—none of them, however, have been or will ever be complete! Also, because of the complexity of the subject and the length of time involved in fully explaining the die making and minting process, we have not even begun to explain the process. This requires a freestanding reference of which several are available and referenced as recommended reading at the end of this chapter.

Additionally, we have largely confined our discussion to those types most normally encountered on coins that have been manufactured using fairly modern equipment. This fairly modern equipment dates back to the mid-19th century but, hey, "If it ain't broke, why fix it?" as the saying goes. This is one area, in our opinion, where the government got it right a long time ago and only minor tweaking has been required since! For example, prior to the installation of this "modern" equipment, coins were hand struck using a giant, awkward screw press. Because each coin was handled by hand very few of the striking errors made it out of the Mint, so you are not as likely to encounter them as all the others discussed in this chapter. As for die varieties, the methods used to manufacture dies has changed as well and would require yet another chapter on the early die-making practice. However, so you are aware of them, early die varieties have been cataloged for nearly as long as the coins themselves have been in existence, and most design types and denominations have excellent references available for the cataloging of their varieties. It was easy to do this with the early coinage as far fewer dies were produced. For example, there was but one original obverse die produced for the 1844 half cent, yet there was somewhere in the neighborhood of 9,000 obverse dies for the 1994-D Lincoln cent alone. Common sense should tell you it is much easier to catalog the half cent varieties than it is to catalog the Lincoln cent, yet collecting Lincoln cents by variety is easily one of the most active areas in the hobby today! Below are listed some of the design types not discussed (as well as many that were) in this chapter along with the name of the cataloging system(s) used and a sample number from each system; this way you may at least be familiar with what you are reading when you encounter them elsewhere.

What the Numbers Mean
Half Cents—Cohen, Munson & Munde—**CMM1**
    —Cohen—**Cohen 1, Cohen PO 1, SR 2,** etc.
    —Breen—**Breen 1**
Large Cents—Sheldon—**Sheldon 1**
    —Newcomb—**Newcomb 1**
Flying Eagle & Indian Cents—Snow—**S-1**
    —FINDERS Report (Larry Steve)—**FND-001**
Two Cents—Leone—**Leone 65P-3o1r**
    —Flynn—**KF-P12-RPD**
Half Dimes (Bust)—Valentine—**V-1**
    (Seated)—Valentine—**V-1**
    —Logan & McCloskey—**LM-1**
Shield Nickels—Fletcher—**F-01**
    Liberty & Shield Nickels—Peters & Mohon—**PM 01.1**
Dimes (Bust)—Davis—**Davis 1**
    —Hilt—Davis, Logan, McCloskey and Subjack
    Variety—**Hilt 7F**
Dimes (Seated)—Ahwash—**Ahwash 1**
    —Greer—**Greer No. 101**
Quarters (Bust)—Browning—**Browning 1**
Quarters (Seated)—Briggs—**Obverse 2-B**
Half Dollars (Flowing Hair & Bust)—Overton—**O-101**
Half Dollars (Seated)—Beistle—**Beistle 2-B**
Dollars (Flowing Hair & Bust)—Bolender-**B-1**
    —Haseltine—**H-1**
    —Bowers-Borckardt—**BB-251**

Dollars (Seated Liberty)—Breen—**Breen 5438**
   —Bowers-Borckardt—**BB-1**
Dollars (Trade)—Breen—**Breen 5796**
   —Bowers-Borckardt—**BB-1**
Dollars (Morgan & Peace)—Van Allen & Mallis—**VAM#1**
Gold (just about any)—Breen—**Breen 1B** or **Breen 6328**
20th-Century Die Varieties (some of which include those of
   series for the 19th century as well):
  Doubled Dies—CONECA—**CONECA DDO#1 & 1-O-I**
   —Wexler—**Wexler DDO-001**
   —Potter—**Potter VCR#1/DDO#1**
  RPMs & OMMs—CONECA—**CONECA RPM#1**
   —Wexler—**Wexler RPM-001**
   —Potter—**Potter VCR#1/RPM**
Miscellaneous Varieties—
  Fivaz/Stanton—**FS#023**
"From the Cherrypickers"—**Guide to Rare Die Varieties
  Series**

It should be noted here that the Wexler numbers are also those of the National Collectors Association of Die Doubling (NCADD).

THE COMBINED ORGANIZATIONS OF NUMISMATIC ERROR COLLECTORS OF AMERICA (CONECA)

In the early part of 1983 there were two signifi cant national error collecting clubs—Collectors of Numismatic Errors (CONE) and Numismatic Error Collectors of America (NECA). By mid-year the two organizations had merged, forming CONECA, the only numismatic specialty club devoted exclusively to the study and advancement of error and variety collecting. Since that time the organization has consistently forged the future of the error and variety hobby using its motto "Knowledge Through Education" as its guiding beacon.

The club supplies members with Errorscope, an award-winning publication, on a bi-monthly basis. Errorscope is full of educational and informative articles including splendid detailed photographs. Also included in each issue is an error and variety auction (in which only members participate), which often consists of more than 800 lots. The auctions offer one of the best sources available anywhere for members to add to their collections or sell their duplicates.

Also included with CONECA membership is perhaps the finest error and variety reference library in existence today. All members have to do to borrow from it is pay shipping both ways on what they borrow. As if that is not enough, the club also offers the fun and sometimes rewarding fund-raiser known as Winner's Windfall where members have an opportunity to win error and variety coins worth sometimes in excess of $500!

For the last several years the club has been aggressively publishing photo attribution guides for die varieties on 20thcentury coins. It is the goal of the club to not stop this trend until all 20th-century coinage is covered in these guides.

The club has always offered an authentication, examination, and attribution service but the one in place today rivals anything ever available anywhere. For just $2.50 per coin for members ($5 for nonmembers), plus shipping and insurance, members receive confident, accurate attributions of their 20th-century die varieties. And, if a submission is a new listing (previously unreported die variety), the member also receives an 8½ x 11 certificate, complete with photographs, the new number, and a complete description of the variety that is suitable for framing. All this for no extra charge!

The pinnacle of each calendar year, after having already been a force at many major coin shows throughout the year, is the group's annual Errorama, usually held in conjunction with the American Numismatic Association's Anniversary Convention. Errorama features many of the nation's top error and variety dealers; the majority of the fi nest researchers; educational and fellowship events; the club's annual business meeting, which members are encouraged to attend; an annual cherrypicking contest; and the anxiously awaited, well-received, well-attended, and hottest party in town—The Annual Awards Banquet. Here the club's most dedicated volunteers are recognized for their hard work amid camaraderie that is perhaps unrivaled in the hobby! The event is always casual and includes a fantastic dinner. CONECA believes hobbies are supposed to be fun so it also believes in having fun.

Membership is currently $25 per year for regular members and only $10 per year for YNs (under age 18). There is also a first-class mailing option, which is highly recommended if you plan to actively participate in any club activities or events. This option costs $12.50 extra, with foreign postage extra as well. For more details and a membership application send a large, self-addressed, stamped envelope (LSASE) to: Paul Funaiole 35 Leavitt Lane Glenburn, ME 04401-1013 or visit the club's Web site at http://conecaonline.org.

Not yet a member of the world's greatest error-variety coin club?

Become a CONECA Member

The Combined Organizations of Numismatic Error Collectors of America

MEMBERSHIP TYPE:		YEAR(s) 1yr / 2yr	
Adult		$25.00 / $50.00	
*Young Member (UNDER 18) Membership only with Online access to *Errorscope		$7.50 / $15.00	
* Young Member (UNDER 18) Membership with Online access and Hard Copy of *Errorscope		$17.50 / $35.00	
Family Membership. (Each paid member within a family membership will be entitled to all club privileges; however, the family will receive just one copy of the club publication)		$12.50 / $25.00	
Club Organizations (Receives NO online access but will receive a copy of *Errorscope)		$25.00 / $50.00	
**Life Membership (Under age of 55)		$750.00	
**Life Membership (Age 55 or older)		$650.00	
MAILING OPTIONS:			
Bulk Rate for *Errorscope:		FREE	
First Class for *Errorscope:		$12.50 / $25.00	
Foreign Members. Please consult with the Membership Coordinator for current postage of the *Errorscope to your location. (this is in addition to your dues)		$	
Donations to CONECA: YN Programs General Fund Publishing Fund		$	
*(Errorscope is published bi-monthly) TOTAL SUBMITTED TO CONECA:		$	

Name: _____

Address: _____

City/State/Zip: _____

Email Address: _____

Phone Number: _____

Username: _____

Password: _____

Date of Birth: _____

Parental Consent: (for YN's) _____

Referred By: (optional) _____

*YN and Life membership applications must include date of birth
**Qualification for Life Memberships are available after one year of regular membership

Your membership is subject to the rules and regulations set forth in the CONECA Constitution and By-Laws

This membership application can be downloaded from the CONECA website at:

http://conecaonline.org/join.html

The CONECA website also has the option of using *PayPal* for payment

Make your check or money order payable to *CONECA* and send to:

**Rachel Irish – CONECA Membership Coordinator
101 W. Prairie Center #323
Hayden, ID 83835**

MRirish5@roadrunner.com

Note: Username and Password will provide you access to the CONECA 'members only' area. (Your information will NOT be provided to others).

Mike Ellis has been a professional numismatist for over 20 years serving as an authenticator, grader, researcher, teacher and writer. He is an honorary life member of the Combined Organizations of Numismatic Error Collectors of America (CONECA), the only organization devoted exclusively to errors and varieties where he has served as President twice as long as anyone else. Mike is also a Life Member of the American Numismatic Association (ANA), the largest coin collecting organization in the United States, where he currently serves on the Board of Governors and continues to teach at the ANA's annual Summer Seminar. For his devotion to and love of the hobby he has received every award CONECA has to offer, including induction into their Hall of Fame. From the ANA he has received the Glenn Smedley Award and a Presidential Award. Ellis continues to teach and write while serving as a consumer advocate to the numismatic community.

OTHER SPECIALTY CLUBS AND ORGANIZATIONS

Whereas CONECA may be the only specialty club devoted exclusively to the study of error and variety coinage, there are many clubs and organizations that specialize in a particular denomination and/or series of U.S. coinage that regularly feature error and variety articles in their publications also. Below is a partial list of them, their area of specialization, and an address you may write to for more information.

Barber Coin Collectors
Society (BCCS)
Eileen Ribar
2053 Edith Place
Merrick, NY 11566
All Barber Design Coinage

Early American Coppers
Box 3497
Lake Worth, FL 33465
Large & Half Cents

John Reich Collectors Society
Stephen Crain
Box 1680
Windham, ME 04062
U.S. Bust Coinage

Flying Eagle & Indian Cent
Collectors Society
(The Fly-In Club)
c/o Eagle Eye Rare Coins
Box 559
Sandwich, IL 60548
Phone 866-323-2646
website: www.fl y-inclub.org
Flying Eagle & Indian Cents

Society of Silver Dollar
Collectors (SSDC)
Box 42112
Greenboro, NC 27425
U.S. Silver Dollars

Bust Half Nut Club
PO Box 4875
Margate, FL 33063
Bust Halves

The National Collectors Association
of Die Doubling
c/o John Bordner
PO Box 15
Lykens, PA 17048-0015
**Doubled Dies, RPMs, and
OMMs**

Liberty Seated Collectors Club
Box 6114
Vernon Hills, IL 60061
Liberty Seated Coinage

RECOMMENDED ERROR- AND
VARIETY-RELATED READING

As has been stated many times throughout this book and especially in this chapter, there is currently a wealth of information available to the error and variety enthusiast. Although it is impossible to list it all here, many of the best are given here for your consideration. Keep in mind that all of the specialty organizations listed previously publish excellent club journals that you should also consider. One should not forget *all* of the recommended publications listed elsewhere in this book as well. Each of them contains error- and variety-related articles and information in each issue, and most of them have regular error- and variety-related columns.

Periodicals

Errorscope
c/o Paul Funaiole
35 Leavitt Lane
Glenburn, ME 04401-1013

Published six times per year, this is the offi cial publication of CONECA and the only periodical devoted exclusively to the study of error *and* variety coinage. This is also the address to write for information on membership in CONECA, or you can visit CONECA's offi cial website for an application form and lots of information on error and variety coinage at www.conecaonline.org.

Cherrypickers' News
PO Box 15487
Savannah, GA 31416-2187

Edited and published six times per year by J. T. Stanton; this publication has historically been full of quality photographs of recent and not-so-recent fi nds. It also features the only price guide available for a Fivaz/Stanton variety 1 coin. Though this publication has been on hiatus for the past couple of years, it is scheduled to make a return.

Error Trends Coin Magazine
PO Box 158
Oceanside, NY 11572-0158

An excellent source of information on error coinage, it usually includes some variety information as well. Each monthly issue also contains error coin pricing information.

Books

The Official Price Guide to Mint Errors, Sixth Edition, by Alan Herbert. This is perhaps the best, all-inclusive reference on the subject, with much more information than just pricing. As far as pricing goes, this book is undoubtedly the most up-to-date book with error coin values but is somewhat out of date due to the sharp, seemingly unending rise in error coin values.

The Cherrypickers' Guide to Rare Die Varieties, Fourth Edition, by Bill Fivaz, J. T. Stanton, and Mike Ellis. One of the best selling books in the entire hobby! A must-have reference for all variety enthusiasts: 320_ pages and 1,000_ photographs!

The Error Coin Encyclopedia, Second Edition, by Arnold

Margolis. One of the two best books available on the subject of error coinage. Loaded with photographs and pricing information, this book takes you through the entire minting process.

The Modern Minting Process, and *U.S. Minting Errors and Varieties,* by Dr. James Wiles. Contains two correspondence courses from the ANA School of Numismatics with over 34 color photographs and hundreds more in black and white. Available only through the American Numismatic Association but one of the best references on the subject today!

Other

Note: Most of the following and the aforementioned books are available through most numismatic book and supply dealers including *Coin World* and the American Numismatic Association's *Money Market* catalog.

The Washington Quarter Dollar Book: An Attribution and Pricing Guide (*1942–1945*), *Volume Two,* by James Wiles, Ph.D.

The Washington Quarter Dollar Book: An Attribution and Pricing Guide (*1946–1954*), *Volume Three,* by James Wiles, Ph.D.

The Jefferson Nickel RPM Book: An Attribution and Pricing Guide, by James Wiles, Ph.D.

The Hot 50 Morgan Dollar Varieties, (50 Exciting New Varieties That Supplement the "Top 100"), by Jeff Oxman.

Treasure Hunting Walking Liberty Half Dollars, by Kevin Flynn and Brian Raines.

The Flying Eagle & Indian Cent Attribution Guide, 2nd Edition, Volume 1 (*1856–1858*), by Richard E. Snow.

The Flying Eagle & Indian Cent Attribution Guide, 2nd Edition, Volume 2 (*1859–1869*), by Richard E. Snow.

The Flying Eagle & Indian Cent Attribution Guide, 2nd Edition, Volume 6 (*1900–1909*), by Richard E. Snow.

Treasure Hunting Mercury Dimes, by John A. Wexler and Kevin Flynn.

The Authoritative Reference on Three-Cent Nickels, by Kevin Flynn and Edward Fletcher.

Treasure Hunting Liberty Head Nickels, by Kevin Flynn and Bill Van Note.

The Washington Quarter Dollar Book: An Attribution and Pricing Guide (*1932–1941*), by James Wiles, Ph.D.

Treasure Hunting Buffalo Nickels, by John A. Wexler, Ron Pope, and Kevin Flynn.

The Complete Price Guide and Cross Reference to Lincoln Cent Mint Mark Varieties, by Brian Allen and John A. Wexler.

The RPM Book, Second Edition: Lincoln Cents, by James Wiles, Ph.D.

Flying Eagle and Indian Cent Die Varieties, by Larry R. Steve and Kevin J. Flynn.

The Fly-In Club Attribution Files, by Rick Snow.

A Buyer's and Enthusiast's Guide to Flying Eagle and Indian Cents, by Q. David Bowers.

The Complete Guide to Lincoln Cents, by David W. Lange.

Longacre's Two-Cent Piece—1864 Attribution Guide, by Frank Leone.

The Shield Five Cent Series, by Edward L. Fletcher, Jr.

The Complete Guide to Shield and Liberty Head Nickels, by Gloria Peters and Cindy Mohon.

Federal Half Dimes, by Russell J. Logan and John W. McCloskey.

The Complete Guide to Liberty Seated Half Dimes, by Al Blythe.

The Complete Guide to Liberty Seated Dimes, by Brian Greer.

The Best of the Washington Quarter Doubled Dies, by John A. Wexler and Kevin Flynn.

The Comprehensive Encyclopedia of United States Liberty Seated Quarters, by Larry Briggs.

The Complete Guide to Barber Quarters, 2nd Edition, by David Lawrence.

The Complete Guide to Barber Halves, by David Lawrence.

The Kennedy Half Dollar Book, by James Wiles, Ph.D.

The Top 100 Morgan Dollar Varieties: The VAM Keys, by Michael S. Fey, Ph.D., and Jeff Oxman.

The Comprehensive Catalog and Encyclopedia of Morgan and Peace Silver Dollars, 4th Edition, by Leroy C. Van Allen and A. George Mallis.

The 1878 Morgan Dollar 8-TF Attribution System, by Jeff Oxman and Les Hartnett.

The 1878 Morgan Dollar 7/8-TF Attribution Guide, by Jeff Oxman and Les Hartnett.

The RPM Book, by John A. Wexler and Tom Miller.

Two Dates Are Better Than One: A Collector's Guide to Misplaced Dates, by Kevin Flynn.

Walter Breen's Encyclopedia of United States Half Cents— 1793–1857, by Walter Breen.

Walter Breen's Complete Encyclopedia of U.S. and Colonial Coins, by Walter Breen.

Bill Fivaz's Counterfeit Detection Guide, by Bill Fivaz. *Encyclopedia of Doubled Dies, Volumes I and II,* by John A. Wexler.

Cherrypickers' News 1996 Yearbook, by J. T. Stanton.

Cherrypickers' News 1997 Yearbook, by J. T. Stanton.

Cherrypickers' News 1998/99 Yearbook, by J. T. Stanton and Mike Ellis.

Joja Jemz Reprints, by J. T. Stanton and Bill Fivaz.

The Lincoln Cent Doubled Die, by John A. Wexler.

WHERE TO BUY AND SELL ERROR AND VARIETY COINAGE

There are many good places to buy and sell error and variety coinage but it may be easiest to fi nd one dealer who is honest, fair, friendly, and encouraging. If you locate that one dealer, even though he may not have what you are looking for nor want everything you have to offer, he can and usually will point you in the "right" direction. Good error and variety dealers enjoy their occupation as much as the collectors they are dealing with.

Currently, the best place to buy and sell error and variety coinage is through CONECA's auction or via the Internet. The eBay site has been a fantastic place to sell striking errors!

ERROR AND VARIETY VALUES

Error and variety coins are among the most difficult of all to assign value to. The number of variables involved in assigning value goes way beyond that of normal coins. Keep in mind that planchet and striking errors are unique—no two are ever just alike! Imagine the implications of that statement. It is possible to supply a very simple and basic generic error type value guide, but it has been impossible, at least to date, to formulate such a price guide and maintain it with any accuracy. Many factors contribute to this dilemma. One of the largest obstacles is the fact that there are no known specific numbers of error types available. Error and variety collecting is a recent phenomena that is very much experiencing growing pains! One of the truly fascinating aspects governing the error and variety hobby is the fact that supply, demand, and desirability are the only governing aspects. In other words, most purchase a coin because they like the coin and not because they believe it will net them lots of money in the future (though at present most should buy for this reason because of the lack of availability!).

As for pricing of die varieties, the equation becomes only a little easier. There are thousands of well-documented, well-publicized die varieties, many of which have been actively sought and highly prized by collectors for years. Value information for these varieties is readily available in many price guides, including the guide found in this book. It is listed with all the normal coins. But what about the thousands more that are not listed anywhere? Again, availability and demand are the key factors. Hints as to relative scarcity and demand found in works about specifi c varieties or series may be used to formulate your own value. Additionally, specialists are regularly confronted with estimate requests and those who actively buy, sell, and trade these varieties should be considered the number one source for this information. However, don't rely on one; ask several. Then you may average out their estimates for a pretty good idea of what is fair for your coin. Several other factors must be considered also: Demand, grade, and known availability are but a few.

The values are for basic, no frills, 20th-century planchet and striking errors. As with all coin pricing guides, values are subject to change with market conditions. The values are for super common and/or undated coins that are most often encountered. With the tremendous increase in popularity of these errors it would be ludicrous to establish prices here for the more glamorous error types as their value continues to spiral upward.

Basic Error Coin Prices

With the extended and increased popularity of error and variety coinage values are mostly spiraling upward even for the most common striking errors. It will likely be many years from now before any kind of true, established value guide can be published. However, through the use of modern technology and instant updating capabilities, there is one company attempting such an endeavor. Through the use of state-ofthe-art software, NumisExpert is making valiant strides and is highly recommended for maintaining organized details and values of your numismatic collection. You may contact the company on the Internet by visiting www.coinweblisting.com. At present, it is believed it will be the first to accomplish the task in a reliable and affordable manner.

THE AMERICAN NUMISMATIC ASSOCIATION

HISTORY

Most of today's coin collectors probably know that there is an American Numismatic Association (ANA), the largest organization of coin collectors in the United States. However, many may not realize that the Association is more than 120 years old.

DR. GEORGE F. HEATH, FOUNDER OF ANA.

AMERICAN NUMISMATIC ASSOCIATION HEADQUARTERS IN COLORADO SPRINGS FEATURES A MUSEUM AND A REFERENCE LIBRARY, BOTH OPEN TO THE PUBLIC.

An educational, nonprofit organization, the American Numismatic Association invites and welcomes to membership all persons who have an interest in numismatics—whether they collect coins, paper money, tokens, or medals—whether advanced collectors or those noncollectors only generally interested in the subject. Members, located in every state of the Union and in many other countries, total nearly 30,000.

A factor that deterred the Association's development during its first three-quarters of a century was the geographic dispersal of its functional offices: the executive secretary was in Phoenix, Arizona; the treasurer in Washington, D.C.; the editor in Chicago, Illinois; and the librarian in Lincoln, Nebraska. None of the staff was full-time or received pay, and most operated out of their homes or private offices. Obviously, this situation limited and hampered communication and made for inefficient operation in general.

Since 1967 ANA operations have been centered in Colorado Springs, Colorado, and in 1982 the building was expanded to almost twice its original size. In 2001 the Edward C. Rochette Money Museum and Library were expanded and completely renovated. Museum exhibits will soon be online at www.money.org A board of governors, which establishes policy in determining all bylaws and regulations, is elected from the membership on a regular basis and serves without pay. Implementing established policy in Colorado Springs is a full-time salaried professional staff that includes an executive director, editor, librarian, curator, and assistants and clerical staff.

The principal objectives of the Association are the advancement of numismatic knowledge and better relations among numismatists. Collectors will find the annual membership dues low compared to the tremendous value to be found in the prestige and services that membership offers.

The ANA does not buy or sell coins. Its revenue comes from membership dues and is supplemented by gifts, bequests, and contributions. It receives no operating funds from any governmental body. Any net income from various activities is used on behalf of its members and for the advancement of the hobby.

When the ANA was organized in October 1891, Dr. George F. Heath, the motivating force, was honored with membership No. 1. Member No. 1,000 was admitted in March 1908; No. 10,000 in March 1944; No. 50,000 in August 1963;

and No. 100,000 in August 1979. Of course, the passing of time has taken its toll, and today's membership is slightly less than a third of the total number enrolled during the Association's more than 100 years.

An important date in the history of ANA is May 9, 1912, when it was granted a federal charter by the U.S. Congress. Signed by President Taft, the act gave the charter a fifty-year life. A congressional amendment dated April 10, 1962, allowed for an increase in the number of ANA board members and perpetuated the charter indefinitely. One of very few such charters ever granted, it has given the Association prestige and has been a stabilizing influence on its management.

DUES

Collectors under the age of twenty-three are encouraged in the hobby by lower membership dues, special exhibit classes and programs at conventions, and other educational programs.

Classes of membership are as follows: **Regular**—adults twenty-three years of age and older (eligible for all benefits, including receipt of *Numismatist Magazine*); **Club**—nonprofit numismatic organizations (entitled to all benefits); **Junior**—twenty-two years of age and younger (entitled to all benefits but cannot hold office); and **Life Member**—corresponding to Regular members but a one-time fee is paid for lifetime membership. Memberships are not transferrable from one person to another, and member numbers are never reassigned.

There are several different types of membership available. Please contact the ANA for more information.

American Numismatic Association
818 North Cascade Avenue
Colorado Springs, Colorado 80903-3279 U.S.A.

General: 800-367-9723
Membership: 800-514-2646
Local Phone: 719-632-2646
website address: www.money.org

NUMISMATIST

Numismatist, the Association's monthly magazine, is actually older than the ANA itself, having been started by Dr. Heath in 1888 (September–October) and published privately through 1910. It did, however, cooperate with and champion the cause of the Association—before and after its organization. In 1910 the vice president of ANA, W.W.C. Wilson of Montreal, purchased the magazine from publisher Farran Zerbe and gifted it to the Association, which has continued its publication without interruption.

Numismatist continues to be the official publication and voice of the Association. It contains well-illustrated articles about various phases of collecting, identifying, and caring for coins, tokens, medals, and paper money. Included are news items regarding Association activities, new issues of coins, medals, and paper money, and developments within the hobby. *Numismatist* is now available online at www.money .org and the association is aggressively improving the content found on the website with plans to make it the number one numismatic resource on the internet.

The advertising pages of the magazine are open only to ANA members, who must agree to abide by a strict "Code of Ethics." Members receive the magazine as one of the advantages of membership.

LIBRARY SERVICES

Aside from the magazine, one of the earliest services offered to ANA members was the use of a circulating numismatic library, which has grown to be the world's largest facility of its kind. The library houses more than 25,000 books and more than 22,000 periodicals and convention catalogs, the majority of which are loaned by mail to members and are available to non-members for use in the Colorado Springs headquarters.

The library's resource center maintains and loans numismatic videos and other programs to members and clubs for their meeting programs. These items cover many different phases of numismatics and are available without cost except for shipping charges.

FLORENCE SCHOOK SCHOOL OF NUMISMATICS

Nowhere on the planet can you get a better education on numismatics than the ANA's Florence Schook School of Numismatics. From talks by guest specialists and luminaries at all of the ANA shows to the programs you can borrow from the library to the fairly extensive correspondence course and live testing certificate program to the Summer Seminar, nothing compares

SUMMER SEMINAR
The best education in Numismatics—period.

For many, Summer Seminar is a life-changing event. It has catapulted the careers of many of the nation's most successful numismatic collectors, authors and dealers, and guided young numismatists to become hobby leaders.

Now celebrating more than 45 years, the annual Summer Seminar features a lineup of classes to meet virtually every collector's needs, including ancients, paper money, counterfeit detection, grading, the Civil War, digital photography, hobo nickels, medals, tokens, and more. Students meet and learn from the hobby's most prominent scholars, rising young stars and successful business leaders.

Additionally, the camaraderie is second to none as well with a midweek benefit auction that is a blast to the available tours to the Lunar Lounge with a dead-on view of Pike's Peak on Colorado College grounds; you will make many new lifetime friends, including many of the instructors. There is simply nothing like it!

THE UNITED STATES MINT

For sixteen years following the Declaration of Independence, this country still relied upon British and other foreign coinage. This was not only unsatisfactory but objectionable to many citizens, as Britain's coins bore the likeness of the not-too-popular George III. In 1791 Congress approved the establishment of a federal Mint. Presses for milling were purchased, designers and die cutters hired. But the question remained whether to fashion U.S. coinage after Britain's or devise an entirely new series with different denominations. After much debate the latter plan was adopted, with the dollar (named for Thalers of the Dutch, who were not our enemies) as the chief currency unit and our coinage based upon divisions or multiples of it. The metal standard was fixed at 15 parts silver to one part gold. When finalized on April 2, 1792, the Mint Act provided for coins in values of $10, $5, $2.50, $1, 50¢, 25¢, 10¢, 5¢, 1¢, and ½¢. The 1¢ and ½¢ were of copper; other denominations, up to $1, silver; those over $1, gold. The $5 piece was regarded as the equivalent to Britain's pound sterling, the 25¢ to the British shilling, while the ½¢ was the counterpart to Britain's farthing or "fourthling" (¼ part of a British penny). It may seem odd that necessity was felt for a coin valued under one cent, but at this remote period even the penny had considerable buying power and fractional pricing of goods was common—apples at 1¢ each or 5½¢ per half dozen, for example. If such a coin was not available, the situation would have invited an onslaught of merchant tokens.

Philadelphia was selected as home for the first Mint building, whose cornerstone was laid July 21, 1792. George Washington, then serving as president, contributed silverware from which the first federal coins were struck—a few half dimes or half dismes as they were called (5¢ pieces). Proceeding cautiously, the Mint's first purchase of metal was six pounds of copper. This was used for cents and half cents, delivered to the Treasurer of the United States in 1793. The following year a deposit of $80,715.73½ worth of French silver coins was made to the Mint by the state of Maryland, to be melted down and used for coinage. They yielded a quantity of 1794-dated dollars and half dollars. Gold was not obtained until 1795 when a Boston merchant turned over $2,276.72 in ingots, which were quickly transformed (apparently along with gold from other sources) into 744 Half Eagles ($5 pieces). Later that year 400 Eagles ($10) were produced. By the close of the year 1800 the Mint had milled $2,534,000 worth of coins and succeeded in distributing them throughout the then-inhabited regions of the country, as far west as Michigan and Missouri.

HOW U.S. COINS
ARE MINTED

THE COIN ALLOY CONTENT

In the coinage process, the first step is to prepare the alloy to be used. Except for nickels and 1-cent pieces, the alloys formerly (1964 and earlier) used in the coining of U.S. coins were as follows:

Silver coins—90% silver and 10% copper
5-cent pieces—75% copper and 25% nickel
1-cent pieces—95% copper and 5% zinc

The cents of 1943 consisted of steel coated with zinc; and the nickels of 1942–45 consisted of 35% silver, 56% copper, and 9% manganese. In 1982 the cent was changed to a zinc interior with copper coating.

WHAT ARE THE NEW CLAD COINS MADE OF?

1971 to date—cupro-nickel dollars and half dollars
1965 to date—quarters and dimes: the outer surfaces are 75% copper and 25% nickel, and the inner core is 100% copper
1965–70—half dollars: the outer surface is 80% silver and 20% copper; the inner core is 21% silver and 79% copper; the overall silver content of the coin is 40%

When clad coinage was introduced in 1965, the designs then in use were retained: the Roosevelt dime, Washington quarter, and Kennedy half. (The United States was not at that time minting dollar coins.) The only alteration since then was for the special 1976 bicentennial designs.

Because of the ever-increasing demand for coinage, the Mint introduced new time-saving steps in its coin minting. Raw metal is cast into giant ingots eighteen feet long, sixteen inches wide, and six inches thick, weighing 6,600 pounds. Previously, they had weighed 400 pounds and were sixteen times smaller in measurement. The ingot is rolled red hot and scaled to remove imperfections. It's then ready for the coins to be stamped; no longer are blanks made and annealed (heated). The excess metal that's left behind is used to make new ingots in a continuous, never-ending process. The new coins are electronically scanned, counted, and automatically bagged. These facilities are in use at the new, ultra-modern Mint in Philadelphia. It has a production capacity of eight billion coins per year and is open to the public, featuring interesting displays and guided tours.

HOW PROOF COINS ARE MINTED

1. Perfect planchets are picked out.
2. They are washed with a solution of cream of tartar.
3. They are washed again and alcohol dipped.
4. The dies for making proof coins receive a special polishing for mirrorlike finish.
5. The planchets are then milled.
6. The coins are minted by special hydraulic presses at a much slower rate than regular coins. The fine lines are much more visible on a proof coin.

Minting: From Metal to Coins

1. Casting

2. Rolled   Rolled again (18–22 times)

3. Blanks punched out of strip

4. Annealed (softened) in gas flame

5. Tumbled (Polished)   Washed   Centrifugally dried

6. Raised edge formed

7. Coins weighed

8. Obverse die   Reverse die   Reeded (milled) and stamped

9. Final coins counted and bagged

MINT MARKS

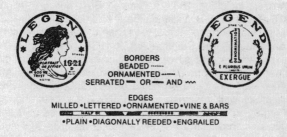

BORDERS
BEADED ·······
ORNAMENTED ·······
SERRATED ━ OR ━ AND ～～

EDGES
MILLED •LETTERED •ORNAMENTED •VINE & BARS

•PLAIN •DIAGONALLY REEDED •ENGRAILED

HISTORY OF MINT MARKS
(Courtesy of *Coin World*)

A mint mark on a United States coin is a small letter (or letters) placed on the field (the flat, featureless areas surrounding the designs and lettering) of the coin to show which Mint manufactured it. (Mint marks appear on either the obverse or reverse.) Mint marks have been used for almost as long as coins have been struck.

From 1793 to 1838, the only U.S. Mint in operation was located at Philadelphia; thus, there was no need to distinguish it by a mint mark. That changed when three Branch Mints were authorized by the Act of March 3, 1835: in Charlotte, NC; Dahlonega, GA; and New Orleans, LA.

In order to distinguish which Mint struck a particular coin, mint marks were introduced on coins struck at the Branch Mints. The Philadelphia Mint, however, continued to strike coins without mint marks.

As new Branch Mints were authorized and opened, new

mint marks were introduced. There have been eight different mint marks used since the United States began striking coins in 1792.

With one four-year exception, U.S. coins struck at the Philadelphia Mint bore no mint marks until 1979. A P mint mark was used on the Jefferson, Wartime 5-cent coins, struck from 1942 to 1945 in a silver alloy. The P mint mark on these issues was designed to distinguish the silver alloy issues from regular copper-nickel 5-cent coins.

In most cases, the mint marks were applied to the reverse sides of U.S. coins until 1968. There are a few exceptions, however, including 1838-O Capped Bust half dollars and 1916-D and 1916-S Walking Liberty half dollars.

Mint marks have not always been used, even at the Branch Mints. The Coinage Act of 1965, which authorized the replacement of silver coinage with copper-nickel clad coinage, also approved the dropping of mint marks. Mint marks were not used on coins dated 1965 through 1967. The move was designed to help alleviate a coin shortage by removing the distinction between coins struck at Branch Mints and those struck in Philadelphia so collectors could not determine which were the more limited strikes.

With the announcement on January 4, 1968, that mint marks would return to coins, Mint Director Eva Adams made a major change in mint mark application. To achieve uniformity, she directed that all mint marks be placed on the obverse. She continued the practice of not placing mint marks on coins struck at the Philadelphia Mint.

A coining facility was opened at the West Point Silver Bullion Depository in 1975, initially to strike cents (and in later years, quarter dollars). These coins are indistinguishable from Philadelphia Mint coins, since they bear no mint mark.

At the same time (mid-1970s into the 1980s), some coins struck at the San Francisco Assay Office were produced without mint marks, primarily to prevent collectors from hoarding the S mint coins.

Major changes were made in mint mark policy beginning in 1979. Anthony dollars struck at the Philadelphia Mint were given a P mint mark. The list of coins to bear the P mint mark grew in 1980, when all other Philadelphia denominations but the 1-cent coin received the new mint mark.

A new mint mark, "W," was belatedly established in September 1983, when the West Point Bullion Depository (now the West Point Mint) began striking 1984-dated $10 Gold Eagles commemorating the Los Angeles Olympic Games. As noted, the West Point facility had been striking coins for circulation without mint marks. Production of circulating coinage (strictly cents by this time) at West Point continued without the addition of a W mint mark.

The W mint mark has been used on various commemorative and bullion coins since then, as well as a 1996-W Roosevelt dime included in the 1996 Uncirculated Mint set as a commemoration of the 50th anniversary of the design. However, no coins struck for circulation have borne a W mint mark.

WHY ARE MINT MARKS IMPORTANT?

Collectors determine a coin's value by examining its date, mint mark, and condition. The most important criterion in determining a coin's value is its condition. However, determining the Mint that struck the coin is extremely important in arriving at its value. That's because the coin may be struck in large quantities at one Mint and very small quantities at another. Consider the 1914 and 1914-D Lincoln cents: more than 75 million examples were struck at Philadelphia (with no mint mark) but only 1.193 million have a little D mark below its date.

MINT MARKS TODAY

Let's examine our current pocket change or coins that collectors may find in today's circulating coinage.

Lincoln cents, 1909–96, have used two mint marks (but have been struck at four Mints). Collectors will find a little "D" for the Denver Mint or "S" for the San Francisco Mint, located directly beneath the date.

Jefferson 5-cent coins, 1938–96, have used three mint marks, in three different locations. Denver and San Francisco coins struck from 1938–42, and from 1946–64, feature the D or S on the reverse, to the right of the representation of Monticello. The mint marks were enlarged and moved to above the dome of Monticello on the wartime alloy coins of 1942–45, and as noted, a P mint mark was used for the first time. The D and S mint marks have appeared on the obverse, just below the last numeral of the date, since 1968, and the P mint mark has appeared in the same location since 1980.

Roosevelt dimes, 1946–96, have used four mint marks

since their introduction. The Denver and San Francisco dimes of 1946–64 bear a D or S mint mark on the reverse, to the lower left of the torch. The mint mark was moved to the obverse in 1968, to just above the last numeral in the date, where it remains today. The P was added in 1980, and the W was used on special 1996-W dimes sold to collectors.

Washington quarter dollars, 1932–96, have used three mint marks. Denver and San Francisco quarters struck from 1932–64 bear the D or S mint mark on the reverse, between the wreath and the denomination QUARTER DOLLAR. The mint marks were moved to the obverse in 1968, to behind Washington's queue. The P was added in 1980.

Kennedy half dollars, 1964–96, have used three mint marks. A D mint mark was used on the reverse of Denver Mint coins in 1964, just above the L in HALF. It's the only such Kennedy half dollar to bear a mint mark on the reverse. The D and S mint marks were moved to the obverse in 1968, right below the bust of Kennedy and above the date on the obverse side of the coin. The P was added in 1980.

MINTS AND THEIR MINT MARKS

By separate Acts of Congress, the government has established Mints in different parts of the country.

1. **"P"** **PHILADELPHIA,** *Pennsylvania*—1973 to date—No mint mark. Until 1973, coins minted at Philadelphia did not carry mint marks, except for the silver-content nickels of 1942–45.
2. **"C"** **CHARLOTTE,** *North Carolina*—gold coins only, 1838–61.
3. **"CC"** **CARSON CITY,** *Nevada*—1870–93.
4. **"D"** **DAHLONEGA,** *Georgia*—gold coins only, 1838–61.
5. **"D"** **DENVER,** *Colorado*—1906 to date.
6. **"O"** **NEW ORLEANS,** *Louisiana*—1838–61 and 1879–1909.
7. **"S"** **SAN FRANCISCO,** *California*—1854–1955 and 1968 to date.
8. **"W"** **WEST POINT,** *New York*—1976 to date, used for special issues only.

ABOUT THE PRICES
IN THIS BOOK

Prices shown in this book represent the current *retail* selling prices at press time. In the first column of each listing, a current *average buying price* is also indicated. This is the price at which coin dealers are buying from the public. Readers should understand that the actual prices charged or paid by any given dealer (there are more than 12,000 coin dealers in the United States) can vary somewhat. Higher grade coins will usually command a higher price based on a percentage of the value listed for the particular grade. Additional factors that will also affect what a dealer is willing to pay for a coin are: 1) how many other coins like yours the dealer has in his inventory; 2) how long it will take for the dealer to sell your coin; 3) whether or not the dealer is buying your coin for his own investment; 4) the rarity of the date or mint mark of your coin. Hence, the *Blackbook* is presented merely as a guide to the average buying and selling prices.

Prices are shown for each coin in various condition grades. It is of utmost importance that a coin be accurately graded before a value can be placed on it. So-called slider grades, such as MS-62, are not included in this book because of space limitations and the difficulties of gathering reliable information on their values. Nor are split grade coins included (such as AU-55/MS-60), but with some simple mathematics their values can be estimated, based on the prices shown.

When a price is omitted, there is not enough reliable pricing information available. This is usually because the coin, in that particular condition grade, is seldom sold publicly. However, this should not lead to the assumption that all such coins are more valuable than those for which prices are indicated. This is not necessarily the case.

For some scarce coins that are not regularly sold, an example will be given of a specific auction sale result, along with the year in which the sale occurred. These are given purely in the interest of supplying some tangible pricing information, but *may not* (especially in the case of older prices) accurately reflect the price that would be obtained for the same coin if sold today.

When a coin is said to be "unique," this indicates that only one single specimen is recorded to exist. It does not preclude the possibility that other specimens, which have escaped the notice of numismatists, might exist.

Prices are given for the major or traditionally acknowledged die varieties, for coins on which die varieties occurred. Many additional die varieties will be noticed in dealers' and auctioneers' literature. The collector status of many of these "minor" die varieties—that is, whether they deserve to be recognized as separate varieties—is a point on which no general agreement has been, or is likely to be, reached. It is important, however, to note, whether discussing major or minor die varieties, that the market values of such coins are not automatically higher than those of the normal die type. Nor can it always be assumed that the variety is scarcer than the normal die type. However, make no mistake about it; many of these varieties do carry substantial premiums.

In the case of common date silver and gold coins of the late 19th and 20th centuries, it must be borne in mind that the values (for buying or selling) are influenced by the current value of the metal they contain. Most coin shops display the current "spot" prices for silver and gold bullion.

HOW TO USE THIS BOOK

Listings are provided in this book for all coins of the U.S. Mint plus colonial coins and several other groups of coins (please consult index).

Each listing carries the following information:

Denomination of coin.

Date (this is the date appearing on the coin, which is not necessarily the year in which it was actually manufactured).

Mintage (quantity manufactured by the Mint). In some cases this information is not available. In others, the totals announced by the Mint may not be entirely accurate. This is particularly true of coins dating before 1830.

Average Buying Price (A.B.P.). This is the price at which dealers are buying the coin in the first condition grade listed. Buying prices can vary somewhat from one dealer to another.

Current Retail Value. In various grades of condition, the price columns following the A.B.P. (or Average Buying Price) show retail prices being charged by dealers. Prices for each coin are given in various grades of condition. Check the column head, then refer to the grading guide if you have any doubt about the condition of your coin. Be sure you have correctly identified your coin and its condition. If the date is missing from your coin, it qualifies only as a "type filler" (that is, a "type" coin in low-grade condition), and its value will be lower than the price shown for a coin of that series.

OFFICIAL ANA
GRADING SYSTEM

The descriptions of coin grades given in this book are intended for use in determining the relative condition of coins in various states of preservation. The terms and standards are based on the commonly accepted practices of experienced dealers and collectors. Use of these standards is recommended by the American Numismatic Association to avoid misunderstandings during transaction, cataloging, and advertising.

The method of grading described in this book should be referred to as the Official ANA Grading System. When grading by these standards, care must be taken to adhere to the standard wording, abbreviations, and numbers used in this text.

When a coin first begins to show signs of handling, abrasion, or light wear, only the highest parts of the design are affected. Evidence that such a coin is not Uncirculated can be seen by carefully examining the high spots for signs of a slight change in color, surface texture, or sharpness of fine details.

In early stages of wear the highest points of design become slightly rounded or flattened, and the very fine details begin to merge together in small spots.

After a coin has been in circulation for a short time, the entire design and surface will show light wear. Many of the high parts will lose their sharpness, and most of the original mint luster will begin to wear, except in recessed areas.

Further circulation will reduce the sharpness and relief of the entire design. High points then begin to merge with the next lower parts of the design.

After the protective rim is worn away the entire surface becomes flat, and most of the details blend together or become partially merged with the surface.

It should be understood that because of the nature of the minting process, some coins will be found that do not conform exactly with the standard definitions of wear as given in this text. Specific points of wear may vary slightly. Information given in the notes at the end of some sections does not cover all exceptions, but is a guide to the most frequently encountered varieties.

Also, the amount of mint luster (for the highest several grades) is intended more as a visual guide than as a fixed quantity. The percentage of visible mint luster described in the text is the *minimum* allowance amount, and a higher percentage can usually be expected. Luster is not always brilliant and may be evident, although sometimes dull or discolored.

A *Choice* coin in any condition is one with an attractive, above average surface relatively free from nicks or bag marks. A *Typical* coin may have more noticeable minor surface blemishes.

In all cases, a coin in lower condition must be assumed to include all the wear features of the next higher grade in addition to its own distinguishing points of wear.

Remarks concerning the visibility of certain features refer to the *maximum* allowable amount of wear for those features.

Note: The official ANA Grading System used in this book is with the permission of the American Numismatic Association.

RECORD KEEPING

For your convenience, we suggest you use the following record-keeping system to note condition of your coin in the checklist box.

ABOUT GOOD ◨	FINE ⊟	UNCIRCULATED ◩
GOOD ◪	VERY FINE ⊡	PROOF ■
VERY GOOD ⊠	EXTREMELY FINE ⊠	

GRADING ABBREVIATIONS

Corresponding numbers may be used with any of these descriptions.

PROOF-70	Perfect Proof	Perf. Proof	Proof-70
PROOF-65	Choice Proof	Ch. Proof	Proof-65
PROOF-60	Proof	Proof	Proof-60
MS-70	Perfect Uncirculated	Perf. Unc.	Unc.-70
MS-65	Choice Uncirculated	Ch. Unc.	Unc.-65

MS-60	Uncirculated	Unc.	Unc.-60
AU-55	Choice About Uncirculated	Ch. Abt. Unc.	Ch. AU
AU-50	About Uncirculated	Abt. Unc.	AU
EF-45	Choice Extremely Fine	Ch. Ex. Fine	Ch. EF
EF-40	Extremely Fine	Ex. Fine	EF
VF-30	Choice Very Fine	Ch. V. Fine	Ch. VF
VF-20	Very Fine	V. Fine	VF
F-12	Fine	Fine	F
VG-8	Very Good	V. Good	VG
G-4	Good	Good	G
AG-3	About Good	Abt. Good	AG

PROOF COINS

The mirrorlike surface of a brilliant proof coin is much more susceptible to damage than are the surfaces of an Uncirculated coin. For this reason, proof coins that have been cleaned often show a series of fine hairlines or minute striations. (It should be noted that, when collecting coins, *under no circumstances should any effort be made to clean coins*. Their value is likely to be reduced by such an attempt.) Also, careless handling has resulted in certain proofs acquiring marks, nicks, and scratches.

Some proofs, particularly 19th-century issues, have "lint marks." When a proof die was wiped with an oily rag, sometimes threads, bits of hair, lint, and so on would remain. When a coin was struck from such a die, an incuse or recessed impression of the debris would appear on the piece. Lint marks visible to the unaided eye should be specifically mentioned in a description.

Proofs are divided into the following classifications:

Proof-70 (Perfect Proof). A Proof-70 or Perfect Proof is a coin with no hairlines, handling marks, or other defects—in other words, a flawless coin. Such a coin may be brilliant or may have natural toning.

Proof-65 (Choice Proof). Proof-65 or Choice Proof refers to a proof that may show some fine hairlines, usually from friction-type cleaning or friction-type drying or rubbing after dipping. To the unaided eye, a Proof-65 or a Choice Proof will appear to be virtually perfect. However, 5× magnification will reveal some minute lines. Such hairlines are best seen under strong incandescent light.

Proof-60 (Proof). Proof-60 refers to a proof with some scattered handling marks and hairlines that will be visible to the unaided eye.

Impaired Proofs; Other Comments. If a proof has been excessively cleaned, has any marks, scratches, dents, or other defects, it is described as an impaired proof. If the coin has seen extensive wear, then it will be graded one of the lesser grades—Proof-55, Proof-45, or whatever. It is not logical to describe a slightly worn proof as AU (Almost Uncirculated) for it never was "Uncirculated" to begin with, in the sense that Uncirculated describes a top-grade normal production strike. So, the term Impaired Proof is appropriate. It is best to describe fully such a coin, examples being: "Proof with extensive hairlines and scuffing," or "Proof with numerous nicks and scratches in the field," or "Proof-55, with light wear on the higher surfaces."

UNCIRCULATED COINS

The term "Uncirculated," interchangeable with "Mint State," refers to a coin that has never seen circulation. Such a piece has no wear of any kind. A coin as bright as the time it was minted or with very light natural toning can be described as "Brilliant Uncirculated." A coin that has natural toning can be described as "Toned Circulated." Except in the instance of copper coins, the presence or absence of light toning does not affect an Uncirculated coin's grade. Indeed, among silver coins, attractive natural toning often results in the coin bringing a premium price.

The quality of luster or "mint bloom" on an Uncirculated coin is an essential element in correctly grading the piece and has a bearing on its value. Luster may in time become dull, frosty, spotted, or discolored. Unattractive luster will normally lower the grade.

With the exception of certain Special Mint Sets made in recent years for collectors, Uncirculated or normal production strike coins were produced on high-speed presses, stored in bags together with other coins, run through counting machines, and in other ways handled without regard to numismatic posterity. As a result, it is the rule and not the exception for an Uncirculated coin to have bag marks and evidence of coin-to-coin contact, although the piece might not have seen actual commercial circulation. The amount of such marks will depend upon the coin's size. Differences in criteria in this regard are given in the individual sections under grading descriptions for different denominations and types.

Uncirculated coins can be divided into three major categories:

MS-70 (Perfect Uncirculated). MS-70 or Perfect Uncirculated is the finest quality available. Such a coin under 4× magnification will show no bag marks, lines, or other evidence of handling or contact with other coins.

A brilliant coin may be described as "MS-70 Brilliant" or "Perfect Brilliant Uncirculated." A lightly toned nickel or silver coin may be described as "MS-70 Toned" or "Perfect Toned Uncirculated." Or, in the case of particularly attractive or unusual toning, additional adjectives may be in order such as "Perfect Uncirculated with Attractive Iridescent Toning Around the Borders."

Copper and bronze coins: To qualify as MS-70 or Perfect Uncirculated, a copper or bronze coin must have its full luster and natural surface color, and may not be toned brown, olive, or any other color. (Coins with toned surfaces that are otherwise perfect should be described as MS-65, as the following text indicates.)

MS-65 (Choice Uncirculated). This refers to an above average Uncirculated coin that may be brilliant or toned (and described accordingly) and that has fewer bag marks than usual, scattered occasional bag marks on the surface, or perhaps one or two very light rim marks.

MS-60 (Uncirculated). MS-60 or Uncirculated (typical Uncirculated without any other adjectives) refers to a coin that has a moderate number of bag marks on its surface. Also present may be a few minor edge nicks and marks, although not of a serious nature. Unusually deep bag marks, nicks, and the like must be described separately. A coin may be either brilliant or toned.

Striking and Minting Peculiarities on Uncirculated Coins

Certain early U.S. gold and silver coins have Mint-caused planchet or adjustment marks, a series of parallel striations. If these are visible to the naked eye, they should be described adjectivally in addition to the numerical or regular descriptive grade: for example: "MS-60 with Adjustment Marks," or "MS-65 with Adjustment Marks," or "Perfect Uncirculated with Very Light Adjustment Marks," or something similar.

If an Uncirculated coin exhibits weakness due to striking or die wear, or unusual (for the variety) die wear, this must be adjectivally mentioned in addition to the grade. Examples are: "MS-60 Lightly Struck," "Choice Uncirculated Lightly Struck," and "MS-70 Lightly Struck."

CIRCULATED COINS

Once again, as a coin enters circulation it begins to show signs of wear. As time goes on the coin becomes more and more worn until, after a period of many decades, only a few features may be left.

Dr. William H. Sheldon devised a numerical scale to indicate degrees of wear. According to this scale, a coin in Condition 1, or "Basal State," is barely recognizable. At the opposite end, a coin touched by even the slightest trace of wear (below MS-60) cannot be called Uncirculated.

While numbers from 1 through 59 are continuous, it has been found practical to designate specific intermediate numbers to define grades. Hence, this text uses the following descriptions and their numerical equivalents:

AU-55 (Choice About Uncirculated). Only a small trace of wear is visible on the highest points of the coin. As is the case with the other grades here, specific information is listed in the following text under the various types, for wear often occurs in different spots on different designs.

AU-50 (About Uncirculated). With traces of wear on nearly all of the highest areas. At least half of the original mint luster is present.

EF-45 (Choice Extremely Fine). With light overall wear on the coin's highest points. All design details are very sharp. Mint luster is usually seen only in protected areas of the coin's surface such as between the star points and in the letter spaces.

EF-40 (Extremely Fine). With only slight wear but more extensive than the preceding, still with excellent sharpness. Traces of mint luster may still show.

VF-30 (Choice Very Fine). With light, even wear on the surface; design details on the highest points lightly worn, but with all lettering and major features sharp.

VF-20 (Very Fine). As preceding but with moderate wear on highest parts.

F-12 (Fine). Moderate to considerable even wear. Entire design is bold. All lettering, including the word LIBERTY (on coins with this feature on the shield or headband), visible, but with some weaknesses.

VG-8 (Very Good). Well worn. Most fine details such as hair strands, leaf details, and so on are worn nearly smooth.

The word LIBERTY, if on a shield or headband, is only partially visible.

G-4 (Good). Heavily worn. Major designs visible, but with faintness in areas. Head of Liberty, wreath, and other major features visible in outline form without center detail.

AG-3 (About Good). Very heavily worn with portions of the lettering, date, and legends being worn smooth. The date barely readable.

Note: The exact descriptions of circulated grades vary widely from issue to issue. It is essential to refer to the specific text when grading any coin.

SPLIT AND INTERMEDIATE GRADES

It is often the case that because of the peculiarities of striking or a coin's design, one side of the coin will grade differently from the other. When this is the case, a diagonal mark is used to separate the two. For example, a coin with an AU-50 obverse and a Choice Extremely Fine-45 reverse can be described as AU/EF or, alternately, 50/45.

The ANA standard numerical scale is divided into the following steps: 3, 4, 8, 12, 20, 30, 40, 45, 50, 55, 60, 65, and 70. Most advanced collectors and dealers find that the gradations from AG-3 through Choice AU-55 are sufficient to describe nearly every coin showing wear. The use of intermediate grade levels such as EF-42, EF-43, and so on is not encouraged. Grading is not that precise, and using such finely split intermediate grades is imparting a degree of accuracy that probably will not be able to be verified by other numismatists. As such, it is discouraged.

A split or intermediate grade, such as that between VF-30 and EF-40, should be called Choice VF-35 rather than VF-EF or About EF.

An exception to intermediate grades can be found among Mint State coins, coins grading from MS-60 through MS-70. Among Mint State coins there are fewer variables. Wear is not a factor; the considerations are the amount of bag marks and surface blemishes. While it is good numismatic practice to adhere to the numerical classifications of 60, 65, and 70, it is permissible to use intermediate grades.

In all instances, the adjectival description must be of the next lower grade. For example, a standard grade for a coin is MS-60 or Uncirculated Typical. The next major category is MS-65 or Uncirculated Choice. A coin that is felt to grade, for example, MS-64, must be described as "MS-64 Uncirculated Typical." It may not be described as Choice Uncirculated, for the minimum definition of Choice Uncirculated is MS-65. Likewise, an MS-69 coin must be described as MS-69 Uncirculated Choice. It is not permissible to use Uncirculated Perfect for any coin that is any degree less than MS-70.

The ANA Grading System considers it to be good numismatic practice to adhere to the standard 60, 65, and 70 numerical designations. Experienced numismatists can generally agree on whether a given coin is MS-60 or MS-65. However, not even the most advanced numismatists can necessarily agree on whether a coin is MS-62 or MS-63; the distinction is simply too minute to permit accuracy. In all instances, it is recommended that intermediate grades be avoided, and if there is any doubt, the lowest standard grade should be used. The use of plus or minus signs is also not accepted practice.

SMALL CENTS—INDIAN HEAD
1859–1909

MINT STATE (*Absolutely no trace of wear.*)

MS-70 (Perfect Uncirculated)
A flawless coin exactly as it was minted, with no trace of wear or injury. Must have full mint luster and brilliance of light toning. Any unusual die or planchet traits must be described.

MS-65 (Choice Uncirculated)
No trace of wear; nearly as perfect as MS-70 except for some small blemish. Has full mint luster but may be unevenly toned or lightly fingermarked. A few barely noticeable nicks or marks may be present.

MS-60 (Uncirculated)
A strictly Uncirculated coin with no trace of wear, but with blemishes more obvious than for MS-65. May lack full mint luster, and surface may be dull or spotted. Check points for signs of abrasion: hair above ear; curl to right of ribbon; bow knot.

ABOUT UNCIRCULATED (*Small trace of wear visible on highest points.*)

AU-55 (Choice About Uncirculated)
OBVERSE: Only a trace of wear shows on the hair above the ear.
REVERSE: A trace of wear shows on the bow knot. Three-quarters of the mint luster is still present.

AU-50 (About Uncirculated)
OBVERSE: Traces of wear show on the hair above ear and curl to right of ribbon.
REVERSE: Traces of wear show on the leaves and bow knot. Half of the mint luster is still present.

EXTREMELY FINE (*Very light wear on only the highest points.*)

EF-45 (Choice Extremely Fine)
OBVERSE: Wear shows on hair above ear, curl to right of ribbon, and on the ribbon end. All of the diamond design and letters in LIBERTY are very plain.
REVERSE: High points of the leaves and bow are lightly worn. Traces of mint luster still show.

EF-40 (Extremely Fine)
OBVERSE: Feathers well defined and LIBERTY is bold. Wear shows on hair above ear, curl to right of ribbon, and on the ribbon end. Most of the diamond design shows plainly.
REVERSE: High points of the leaves and bow are worn.

VERY FINE (*Light to moderate even wear. All major features are sharp.*)

VF-30 (Choice Very Fine)
OBVERSE: Small flat spots of wear on tips of feathers, ribbons, and hair ends. Hair still shows half of details. LIBERTY slightly worn but all letters are sharp.
REVERSE: Leaves and bow worn but fully detailed.

VF-20 (Very Fine)
OBVERSE: Headdress shows considerable flatness. Nearly half of the details still show in hair and on ribbon. Head slightly worn but bold. LIBERTY is worn but all letters are complete.
REVERSE: Leaves and bow are almost fully detailed.

FINE (*Moderate to heavy even wear. Entire design clear and bold.*)

F-12 (Fine)
OBVERSE: One-quarter of details show in the hair. Ribbon is worn smooth. LIBERTY shows clearly with no letters missing.
REVERSE: Some details visible in the wreath and bow. Tops of leaves are worn smooth.

REVERSE   OBVERSE   REVERSE
(without shield, 1859)   (with shield, 1860–1909)

VERY GOOD (*Well worn. Design clear but flat and lacking details.*)

VG-8 (Very Good)
OBVERSE: Outline of feather ends shows but some are smooth. Legend and date are visible. At least three letters in LIBERTY show clearly, but any combination of two full letters and parts of two others are sufficient.
REVERSE: Slight detail in wreath shows, but the top is worn smooth. Very little outline showing in the bow.

GOOD (*Heavily worn. Design and legend visible but faint in spots.*)

G-4 (Good)
OBVERSE: Entire design well worn with very little detail remaining. Legend and date are weak but visible.
REVERSE: Wreath is worn flat but completely outlined. Bow merges with wreath.

ABOUT GOOD (*Outlined design. Parts of date and legend worn smooth.*)

AG-3 (About Good)
OBVERSE: Head is outlined with nearly all details worn away. Legend and date readable but very weak and merging into rim.
REVERSE: Entire design partially worn away. Bow is merged with the wreath.

SMALL CENTS—LINCOLN 1909 TO DATE

MINT STATE (*Absolutely no trace of wear.*)

MS-70 (Perfect Uncirculated)
A flawless coin exactly as it was minted, with no trace of wear or injury. Must have full mint luster and brilliance of light toning. Any unusual die or planchet traits must be described.

MS-65 (Choice Uncirculated)
No trace of wear; nearly as perfect as MS-70 except for some small blemish. Has full mint luster but may be unevenly toned or lightly fingermarked. A few barely noticeable nicks or marks may be present.

MS-60 (Uncirculated)
A strictly Uncirculated coin with no trace of wear, but with blemishes more obvious than for MS-65. May lack full mint luster, and surface may be dull or spotted. Check points for signs of abrasion: high points of cheek and jaw; tips of wheat stalks.

ABOUT UNCIRCULATED (*Small trace of wear visible on highest points.*)

AU-55 (Choice About Uncirculated)
OBVERSE: Only a trace of wear shows on the highest point of the jaw.
REVERSE: A trace of wear on the top of wheat stalks. Almost all of the mint luster is still present.

AU-50 (About Uncirculated)
OBVERSE: Traces of wear show on the cheek and jaw.
REVERSE: Traces of wear show on the wheat stalks. Three-quarters of the mint luster is still present.

EXTREMELY FINE (*Very light wear on only the highest points.*)

EF-45 (Choice Extremely Fine)
OBVERSE: Slight wear shows on hair above ear, on the cheek, and at the jaw.

REVERSE
(wheatline, 1909–1958)

OBVERSE

REVERSE
(memorial, 1959–date)

REVERSE: High points of wheat stalks are lightly worn, but each line is clearly defined. Half of the mint luster still shows.

EF-40 (Extremely Fine)
OBVERSE: Wear shows on hair above ear, on the cheek, and on the jaw.
REVERSE: High points of wheat stalks are worn, but each line is clearly defined. Traces of mint luster still show.

VERY FINE (*Light to moderate even wear. All major features are sharp.*)

VF-30 (Choice Very Fine)
OBVERSE: There are small flat spots of wear on cheek and jaw. Hair still shows details. Ear and bow tie slightly worn but show clearly.
REVERSE: Lines in wheat stalks are lightly worn but fully detailed.

VF-20 (Very Fine)
OBVERSE: Head shows considerable flatness. Nearly all the details still show in hair and on the face. Ear and bow tie worn but bold.
REVERSE: Lines in wheat stalks are worn but plain and without weak spots.

FINE (*Moderate to heavy even wear. Entire design clear and bold.*)

F-12 (Fine)
OBVERSE: Some details show in the hair. Cheek and jaw are worn nearly smooth. LIBERTY shows clearly with no letters missing. The ear and bow tie are visible.
REVERSE: Most details are visible in the stalks. Top wheat lines are worn but separated.

VERY GOOD (*Well worn. Design clear but flat and lacking details.*)

VG-8 (Very Good)
OBVERSE: Outline of hair shows but most details are smooth.

Cheek and jaw are smooth. More than half of bow tie is visible. Legend and date are clear.

REVERSE: Wheat shows some details and about half of the lines at the top.

GOOD (*Heavily worn. Design and legend visible but faint in spots.*)

G-4 (Good)

OBVERSE: Entire design well worn with very little detail remaining. Legend and date are weak but visible.

REVERSE: Wheat is worn nearly flat but is completely outlined. Some grains are visible.

ABOUT GOOD (*Outlined design. Parts of date and legend worn smooth.*)

AG-3 (About Good)

OBVERSE: Head is outlined with nearly all details worn away. Legend and date readable but very weak and merging into rim.

REVERSE: Entire design partially worn away. Parts of wheat and motto merged with the wreath.

Note: The Memorial cents from 1959 to date can be graded by using the obverse descriptions.

The following characteristic traits will assist in grading but must not be confused with actual wear on the coins:

Matte proof cents of 1909 through 1916 are often spotted or stained.

Branch Mint cents of the 1920s are usually not as sharply struck as later dates.

Many of the early dates of Lincoln cents are weakly struck either on the obverse or the reverse, especially the following dates: 1911D, 1914D, 1917D, 1918D, 1921, 1922D, 1923, 1924, 1927D, 1927S, and 1929D.

1922 "plain" is weakly struck at the head, has a small I and joined RT in LIBERTY. Sometimes the wheat heads are weak on the reverse.

1924D usually has a weak mint mark.

1931S is sometimes unevenly struck.

1936 proof cents: early strikes are less brilliant than those made later that year.

1955 doubled die: hair details are less sharp than most cents of the period.

NICKEL FIVE CENTS—
LIBERTY HEAD 1883–1912

MINT STATE (*Absolutely no trace of wear.*)

MS-70 (Perfect Uncirculated)
A flawless coin exactly as it was minted, with no trace of wear or injury. Must have full mint luster but this may range from brilliant to frosty. Any unusual die or striking traits must be described.

MS-65 (Choice Uncirculated)
No trace of wear; nearly as perfect as MS-70 except for some small weakness or blemish. Has full mint luster but may be unevenly toned, frosty, or lightly fingermarked. A few barely noticeable nicks or marks may be present.

MS-60 (Uncirculated)
A strictly Uncirculated coin with no trace of wear, but with blemishes more obvious than for MS-65. May lack full mint luster, and surface may be dull or spotted. Check points for signs of abrasion: high points of hair left of ear and at forehead, corn ears at bottom of wreath.

ABOUT UNCIRCULATED (*Small trace of wear visible on highest points.*)

AU-55 (Choice About Uncirculated)
OBVERSE: Only a trace of wear shows on the highest points of hair left of ear.
REVERSE: A trace of wear shows on corn ears. Half of the mint luster is still present.

AU-50 (About Uncirculated)
OBVERSE: Traces of wear show on hair left of ear and at forehead.
REVERSE: Traces of wear show on the wreath and on corn ears. Part of the mint luster is still present.

EXTREMELY FINE (*Very light wear on only the highest points.*)

EF-45 (Choice Extremely Fine)

OBVERSE: Slight wear shows on high points of hair from forehead to the ear.

REVERSE: High points of wreath are lightly worn. Lines in corn are clearly defined. Traces of mint luster may still show.

EF-40 (Extremely Fine)

OBVERSE: Wear shows on hair from forehead to ear, on the cheek, and on curls.

REVERSE: High points of wreath are worn, but each line is clearly defined. Corn shows some wear.

VERY FINE (*Light to moderate even wear. All major features are sharp.*)

VF-20 (Choice Very Fine)

OBVERSE: Three-quarters of hair details show. The coronet has full bold lettering.

REVERSE: Leaves are worn but most of the ribs are visible. Some of the lines in the corn are clear unless weakly struck.

VF-20 (Very Fine)

OBVERSE: Over half the details still show in hair and curls. Head worn but bold. Every letter on coronet is plainly visible.

REVERSE: Leaves are worn but some of the ribs are visible. Most details in the wreath are clear unless weakly struck.

FINE (*Moderate to heavy even wear. Entire design clear and bold.*)

F-12 (Fine)

OBVERSE: Some details show in curls and hair at top of head. All letters of LIBERTY are visible.

REVERSE: Some details visible in wreath. Letters in the motto are worn but clear.

VERY GOOD (*Well worn. Design clear but flat and lacking details.*)

VG-8 (Very Good)

OBVERSE: Bottom edge of coronet, and most hair details,

OBVERSE   "NO CENTS" REVERSE   REVERSE

are worn smooth. At least three letters in LIBERTY are clear. Rim is complete.

REVERSE: Wreath shows only bold outline. Some letters in the motto are very weak. Rim is complete.

GOOD (*Heavily worn. Design and legend visible but faint in spots.*)

G-4 (Good)
OBVERSE: Entire design well worn with very little detail remaining. Stars and date are weak but visible.

REVERSE: Wreath is worn flat and not completely outlined. Legend and motto are worn nearly smooth.

ABOUT GOOD (*Outlined design. Parts of date and legend worn smooth.*)

AG-3 (About Good)
OBVERSE: Head is outlined with nearly all details worn away. Date readable but very weak and merging into rim.

REVERSE: Entire design partially worn away.

Note: The 1912D, 1912S and 1883 "no cents" variety are often weakly struck.

NICKEL FIVE CENTS— BUFFALO 1913–1938

MINT STATE (*Absolutely no trace of wear.*)

MS-70 (Perfect Uncirculated)
A flawless coin exactly as it was minted, with no trace of wear or injury. Must have full mint luster. Any unusual die or striking traits must be described.

MS-65 (Choice Uncirculated)
No trace of wear; nearly as perfect as MS-70 except for some small weakness or blemish. Has full mint luster but may be unevenly toned or lightly fingermarked. A few barely noticeable nicks or marks may be present.

MS-60 (Uncirculated)

A strictly Uncirculated coin with no trace of wear, but with blemishes more obvious than for MS-65. May lack full mint luster and surface may be dull or spotted. Check points for signs of abrasion: high points of Indian's cheek; upper front leg, hip, tip of tail. Shallow or weak spots in the relief are usually caused by improper striking and not wear.

ABOUT UNCIRCULATED (*Small trace of wear visible on highest points.*)

AU-55 (Choice About Uncirculated)

OBVERSE: Only a trace of wear shows on high point of cheek.
REVERSE: A trace of wear shows on the hip. Half of the mint luster is still present.

AU-50 (About Uncirculated)

OBVERSE: Traces of wear show on hair above and to left of forehead, and at the cheekbone.
REVERSE: Traces of wear show on tail, hip, and hair above and around the horn. Traces of mint luster still show.

EXTREMELY FINE (*Very light wear on only the highest points.*)

EF-45 (Choice Extremely Fine)

OBVERSE: Slight wear shows on the hair above the braid. There is a trace of wear on the temple and hair near cheekbone.
REVERSE: High points of hip and thigh are lightly worn. The horn and tip of tail are sharp and nearly complete.

EF-40 (Extremely Fine)

OBVERSE: Hair and face are lightly worn but well defined and bold. Slight wear shows on lines of hair braid.
REVERSE: Horn and end of tail are worn but all details are visible.

VERY FINE (*Light to moderate even wear. All major features are sharp.*)

VF-30 (Choice Very Fine)

OBVERSE: Hair shows nearly full details. Feathers and braid are worn but sharp.
REVERSE: Head, front leg, and hip are worn. Tail shows plainly. Horn is worn but full.

VF-20 (Very Fine)

OBVERSE: Hair and cheek show considerable flatness, but all details are clear. Feathers still show partial detail.

REVERSE: Hair on head is worn. Tail and point of horn are visible.

FINE (*Moderate to considerable even wear. Entire design clear and bold.*)

F-12 (Fine)

OBVERSE: Three-quarters of details show in hair and braid. LIBERTY is plain but merging with rim.

REVERSE: Major details visible along the back. Horn and tail are smooth but three-quarters visible.

VERY GOOD (*Well worn. Design clear but flat and lacking details.*)

VG-8 (Very Good)

OBVERSE: Outline of hair is visible at temple and near cheekbone. LIBERTY merges with rim. Date is clear.

REVERSE: Some detail shows in head. Lettering is all clear. Horn is worn nearly flat but is partially visible.

GOOD (*Heavily worn. Design and legend visible but faint in spots.*)

G-4 (Good)

OBVERSE: Entire design well worn with very little detail remaining in central part. LIBERTY is weak and merged with rim.

REVERSE: Buffalo is nearly flat but is well outlined. Horn does not show. Legend is weak but readable. Rim worn to tops of letters.

ABOUT GOOD (*Outlined design. Parts of date and legend worn smooth.*)

AG-3 (About Good)

OBVERSE: Design is outlined with nearly all details worn away. Date and motto partially readable but very weak and merging into rim.

OBVERSE

REVERSE

REVERSE: Entire design partially worn away. Rim is merged with the letters.

Note: Buffalo nickels were often weakly struck and lack details even on Uncirculated specimens. The following dates are usually unevenly struck with weak spots in the details:
1913S I and II, 1917D, 1917S, 1918D, 1918S, 1919S, 1920D, 1920S, 1921S, 1923S, 1924D, 1924S, 1925D, 1925S, 1926D, 1926S, 1927D, 1927S, 1928D, 1928S, 1929D, 1931S, 1934D, and 1935D.
1913 through 1916 matte proof coins are sometimes spotted or stained.

NICKEL FIVE CENTS—
JEFFERSON 1938 TO DATE

MINT STATE (*Absolutely no trace of wear.*)

MS-70 (Perfect Uncirculated)
A flawless coin exactly as it was minted, with no trace of wear or injury. Must have full mint luster and brilliance. Any unusual striking or planchet traits must be described.

MS-65 (Choice Uncirculated)
No trace of wear; nearly as perfect as MS-70 except for some small weakness or blemish. Has full mint luster but may be unevenly toned or lightly fingermarked. A few barely noticeable nicks or marks may be present.

MS-60 (Uncirculated)
A strictly Uncirculated coin with no trace of wear, but with weaknesses and blemishes more obvious than for MS-65. May lack full mint luster, and surface may be dull or spotted. Check points for signs of abrasion: cheekbone and high points of hair, triangular roof above pillars. Shallow or weak spots in the relief, particularly in the steps below pillars, are usually caused by improper striking and not wear.

ABOUT UNCIRCULATED (*Small trace of wear visible on highest points.*)

AU-55 (Choice About Uncirculated)
OBVERSE: Only a trace of wear shows on cheekbone.
REVERSE: A trace of wear shows on the beam above pillars. Three-quarters of the mint luster is still present.

AU-50 (About Uncirculated)
OBVERSE: Traces of wear show on cheekbone and high points of hair.
REVERSE: Traces of wear show on the beam and triangular roof above pillars. Half of the mint luster is still present.

EXTREMELY FINE (*Very light wear on only the highest points.*)

EF-45 (Choice Extremely Fine)
OBVERSE: Slight wear shows on cheekbone and central portion of hair. There is a trace of wear at bottom of the bust.
REVERSE: High points of the triangular roof and beam are lightly worn. Traces of mint luster still show.

EF-40 (Extremely Fine)
OBVERSE: Hair is lightly worn but well defined and bold. Slight wear shows on cheekbone and bottom of the bust. High points of hair are worn but show all details.
REVERSE: Triangular roof and beam are worn but all details are visible.

VERY FINE (*Light to moderate even wear. All major features are sharp.*)

VF-30 (Choice Very Fine)
OBVERSE: Hair worn but shows nearly full details. Cheek line and bottom of bust are worn but sharp.
REVERSE: Triangular roof and beam worn nearly flat. Most of the pillar lines show plainly.

OBVERSE

"WARTIME"
REVERSE 1942–1945

REVERSE

VF-20 (Very Fine)

OBVERSE: Cheek line shows considerable flatness. Over half the hairlines are clear. Parts of the details still show in collar.

REVERSE: Pillars are worn but clearly defined. Triangular roof is partially visible.

FINE (*Moderate to heavy even wear. Entire design clear and bold.*)

F-12 (Fine)

OBVERSE: Some details show in hair around face. Cheek line and collar plain but very weak.

REVERSE: Some details visible in pillars. Triangular roof is very smooth and indistinct.

VERY GOOD (*Well worn. Design clear but flat and lacking details.*)

VG-8 (Very Good)

OBVERSE: Cheek line is visible but parts are worn smooth. Collar is weak but visible. Only a few hairlines show separations.

REVERSE: Slight details show throughout building. The arch is worn away. Pillars are weak but visible.

GOOD (*Heavily worn. Design and legend visible but faint in spots.*)

G-4 (Good)

OBVERSE: Entire design well worn with very little detail remaining. Motto is weak and merged with rim.

REVERSE: Building is nearly flat but is well outlined. Pillars are worn flat. Rim worn to tops of letters.

ABOUT GOOD (*Outlined design. Parts of date and legend worn smooth.*)

AG-3 (About Good)

OBVERSE: Design is outlined with nearly all details worn away. Date and legend readable but very weak and merging into rim.

REVERSE: Entire design partially worn away. Rim is merged with the letters.

Note: Jefferson nickels are frequently seen weakly struck, and with the horizontal step lines joined even on Uncirculated specimens. Many of the 1950 and 1955 nickels are unevenly struck with weak spots in the details.

DIMES—BARBER 1892–1916

MINT STATE (*Absolutely no trace of wear.*)

MS-70 (Perfect Uncirculated)
A flawless coin exactly as it was minted, with no trace of wear or injury. Must have full mint luster and brilliance or light toning. Any unusual die or striking traits must be described.

MS-65 (Choice Uncirculated)
No trace of wear; nearly as perfect as MS-70 except for some small blemish. Has full mint luster but may be unevenly toned or lightly fingermarked. A few barely noticeable nicks or marks may be present.

MS-60 (Uncirculated)
A strictly Uncirculated coin with no trace of wear, but with blemishes more obvious than for MS-65. May lack full mint luster, and surface may be dull, spotted, or heavily toned. Check points for signs of abrasion: high points of cheek and hair below LIBERTY; ribbon bow and tips of leaves.

ABOUT UNCIRCULATED (*Small trace of wear visible on highest points.*)

AU-55 (Choice About Uncirculated)
OBVERSE: Only a trace of wear shows on highest points of hair below LIBERTY.
REVERSE: A trace of wear shows on ribbon bow, wheat grains, and leaf near O. Three-quarters of the mint luster is still present.

OBVERSE

REVERSE

AU-50 (About Uncirculated)
OBVERSE: Traces of wear show on cheek, top of forehead, and hair below LIBERTY.
REVERSE: Traces of wear show on ribbon bow, wheat grains, and tips of leaves. Half of the mint luster is still present.

EXTREMELY FINE (*Very light wear on only the highest points.*)

EF-45 (Choice Extremely Fine)
OBVERSE: Slight wear shows on high points of upper leaves, cheek, and hair above forehead. LIBERTY is sharp and band edges are bold.
REVERSE: High points of the wreath and bow lightly worn. Lines in leaves are clearly defined. Part of the mint luster is still present.

EF-40 (Extremely Fine)
OBVERSE: Light wear shows on leaves, cheek, cap, and hair above forehead. LIBERTY is sharp and band edges are clear.
REVERSE: High points of wreath and bow are worn, but all details are clearly defined. Traces of mint luster may still show.

VERY FINE (*Light to moderate even wear. All major features are sharp.*)

VF-30 (Choice Very Fine)
OBVERSE: Wear spots show on leaves, cap, hair, and cheek. Bottom row of leaves is weak but has some visible details. LIBERTY and band are complete.
REVERSE: Wear shows on the two bottom leaves but most details are visible. Nearly all the details in the ribbon bow and corn kernels are clear.

VF-20 (Very Fine)
OBVERSE: Over half the details still show in leaves. Hair worn but bold. Every letter in LIBERTY is visible.
REVERSE: The ribbon is worn, but some details are visible. Half the details in leaves are clear. Bottom leaves and upper stalks show wear spots.

FINE (*Moderate to heavy even wear. Entire design clear and bold.*)

F-12 (Fine)
OBVERSE: Some details show in hair, cap, and facial features. All letters in LIBERTY are weak but visible. Upper row of leaves is outlined, but bottom row is worn smooth.
REVERSE: Some details in the lower leaf clusters are plainly visible. Bow is outlined but flat. Letters in legend are worn but clear.

VERY GOOD (*Well worn. Design clear but flat and lacking details.*)

VG-8 (Very Good)
OBVERSE: Entire head weak, and most of the details in the face are worn smooth. Three letters in LIBERTY are clear. Rim is complete.
REVERSE: Wreath shows only a small amount of detail. Corn and grain are flat. Some of the bow is very weak.

GOOD (*Heavily worn. Design and legend visible but faint in spots.*)

G-4 (Good)
OBVERSE: Entire design well worn with very little detail remaining. Legend is weak but visible. LIBERTY is worn away.
REVERSE: Wreath is worn flat but is completely outlined. Corn and grains are worn nearly smooth.

ABOUT GOOD (*Outlined design. Parts of date and legend worn smooth.*)

AG-3 (About Good)
OBVERSE: Head is outlined with nearly all details worn away. Date readable but partially worn away. Legend merging into rim.
REVERSE: Entire wreath partially worn away and merging into rim.

DIMES—MERCURY 1916–1945

MINT STATE (*Absolutely no trace of wear.*)

MS-70 (Perfect Uncirculated)
A flawless coin exactly as it was minted, with no trace of wear or injury. Must have full mint luster and brilliance or light toning. Any unusual die or striking traits must be described.

MS-65 (Choice Uncirculated)
No trace of wear; nearly as perfect as MS-70 except for some small blemish. Has full mint luster but may be unevenly toned or lightly fingermarked. A few barely noticeable nicks or marks may be present.

MS-60 (Uncirculated)
A strictly Uncirculated coin with no trace of wear, but with blemishes more obvious than for MS-65. May lack full mint

OBVERSE

REVERSE

luster, and surface may be dull, spotted, or heavily toned. Check points for signs of abrasion: high points of hair and in front of ear, diagonal bands on fasces.

ABOUT UNCIRCULATED (*Small trace of wear visible on highest points.*)

AU-55 (Choice About Uncirculated)
OBVERSE: Only a trace of wear shows on highest points of hair above forehead and in front of ear.
REVERSE: A trace of wear shows on the horizontal and diagonal fasces bands. Three-quarters of the mint luster is still present.

AU-50 (About Uncirculated)
OBVERSE: Traces of wear show on hair along face, above forehead, and in front of ear.
REVERSE: Traces of wear show on the fasces bands but edges are sharply defined. Half of the mint luster is still present.

EXTREMELY FINE (*Very light wear on only the highest points.*)

EF-45 (Choice Extremely Fine)
OBVERSE: Slight wear shows on high points of feathers and at hair line. Hair along face is sharp and detailed.
REVERSE: High points of the diagonal fasces bands are lightly worn. Horizontal lines are clearly defined but not fully separated. Part of the mint luster is still present.

EF-40 (Extremely Fine)
OBVERSE: Wear shows on high points of feathers, hair, and at neck line.
REVERSE: High points of fasces bands are worn, but all details are clearly defined and partially separated. Traces of mint luster may still show.

VERY FINE (*Light to moderate even wear. All major features are sharp.*)

VF-30 (Choice Very Fine)
OBVERSE: Wear spots on hair along face, cheek, and neck line. Feathers are weak but have nearly full details.

REVERSE: Wear shows on the two diagonal bands but most details are visible. All vertical lines are sharp. All details in the branch are clear.

VF-20 (Very Fine)
OBVERSE: Three-quarters of the details still show in feathers. Hair worn but bold. Some details in hair braid are visible.
REVERSE: Wear shows on the two diagonal bands but most details are visible. All vertical lines are sharp. All details in the branch are clear.

FINE (*Moderate to considerable even wear. Entire design clear and bold.*)

F-12 (Fine)
OBVERSE: Some details show in hair. All feathers are weak but partially visible. Hair braid is nearly worn away.
REVERSE: Vertical lines are all visible but lack sharpness. Diagonal bands show on fasces but one is worn smooth at midpoint.

VERY GOOD (*Well worn. Design clear but flat and lacking details.*)

VG-8 (Very Good)
OBVERSE: Entire head is weak, and most details in the wing are worn smooth. All letters and date are clear. Rim is complete.
REVERSE: About half the vertical lines in the fasces are visible. Rim is complete.

GOOD (*Heavily worn. Design and legend visible but faint in spots.*)

G-4 (Good)
OBVERSE: Entire design well worn with very little detail remaining. Legend and date are weak but visible. Rim is visible.
REVERSE: Fasces is worn nearly flat but is completely outlined. Sticks and bands are worn smooth.

ABOUT GOOD (*Outlined design. Parts of date and legend worn smooth.*)

AG-3 (About Good)
OBVERSE: Head is outlined with nearly all details worn away. Date readable but worn. Legend merging into rim.
REVERSE: Entire design partially worn away. Rim worn half way into the legend.

Note: Coins of this design are sometimes weakly struck in spots, particularly in the lines and horizontal bands of the fasces.

The following dates are usually found poorly struck and lacking full details regardless of condition: 1916D, 1918S, 1921, 1921D, 1925D, 1925S, 1926S, 1927D, and 1927S.

1920 and 1920D usually show the zero joined to the rim.

1921 usually has a weakly struck date, especially the last two digits.

1923 often has the bottom of the three weakly struck and joined to the rim.

1945 is rarely seen with full cross bands on the fasces.

DIMES—ROOSEVELT
1946 TO DATE

MINT STATE (*Absolutely no trace of wear.*)

MS-70 (Perfect Uncirculated)
A flawless coin exactly as it was minted, with no trace of wear or injury. Must have full mint luster and brilliance or light toning. Any unusual striking traits must be described.

MS-65 (Choice Uncirculated)
No trace of wear; nearly as perfect as MS-70 except for some small blemish. Has full mint luster but may be unevenly toned or lightly fingermarked. A few barely noticeable nicks or marks may be present.

MS-60 (Uncirculated)
A strictly Uncirculated coin with no trace of wear, but with blemishes more obvious than for MS-65. Has full mint luster, but surface may be dull, spotted, or toned. Check points for

OBVERSE

REVERSE

signs of abrasion: high points of cheek and hair above ear, tops of leaves and details in flame.

ABOUT UNCIRCULATED (*Small trace of wear visible on highest points.*)

AU-55 (Choice About Uncirculated)
OBVERSE: Only a trace of wear shows on highest points of hair above ear.
REVERSE: A trace of wear shows on highest spots of the flame. Three-quarters of the mint luster is still present.

AU-50 (About Uncirculated)
OBVERSE: Traces of wear show on hair above ear.
REVERSE: Traces of wear show on flame but details are sharply defined. Half of the mint luster is still present.

EXTREMELY FINE (*Very light wear on only the highest points.*)

EF-45 (Choice Extremely Fine)
OBVERSE: Slight wear shows on high points of hair above ear. Ear is sharp and detailed.
REVERSE: High points of flame are lightly worn. Torch lines are clearly defined and fully separated. Part of the mint luster is still present.

EF-40 (Extremely Fine)
OBVERSE: Wear shows on high points of hair and at cheek line. Ear shows slight wear on the upper tip.
REVERSE: High points of flame, torch and leaves are worn, but all details are clearly defined and partially separated. Traces of mint luster may still show.

VERY FINE (*Light to moderate even wear. All major features are sharp.*)

VF-30 (Choice Very Fine)
OBVERSE: Wear spots show on hair, ear, cheek, and chin. Hair lines are weak but have nearly full visible details.
REVERSE: Wear shows on flame but some details are visible. All vertical lines are plain. Most details in the torch and leaves are clear.

VF-20 (Very Fine)
OBVERSE: Three-quarters of the details still show in hair. Face worn but bold. Some details in the ear are visible.
REVERSE: Wear shows on the flame but a few lines are visible. All torch lines are worn but bold. Most details in leaves are clear.

FINE (*Moderate to heavy even wear. Entire design clear and bold.*)

F-12 (Fine)
OBVERSE: Half the details show in hair. All of the face is

weak but boldly visible. Half of inner edge of ear is worn away.

REVERSE: Vertical lines are all visible, but horizontal bands are worn smooth. Leaves show some detail. Flame is nearly smooth.

VERY GOOD (*Well worn. Design clear but flat and lacking details.*)

VG-8 (Very Good)
OBVERSE: Entire head is weak, and most of the details in hair and ear are worn smooth. All letters and date are clear. Rim is complete.

REVERSE: About half the outer vertical lines in torch are visible. Flame is only outlined. Leaves show very little detail. Rim is complete.

Good (*Heavily worn. Design and legend visible but faint in spots.*)

G-4 (Good)
OBVERSE: Entire design well worn with very little detail remaining. Ear is completely outlined. Legend and date are weak but visible. Rim is visible.

REVERSE: Torch is worn nearly flat but is completely outlined. Leaves are worn smooth. Legend is all visible.

ABOUT GOOD (*Outlined design. Parts of date and legend worn smooth.*)

AG-3 (About Good)
OBVERSE: Head is outlined with nearly all details worn away. Date readable but worn. Legend merging into rim.

REVERSE: Entire design partially worn away. Rim merges into the legend.

QUARTERS—BARBER
1892–1916

MINT STATE (*Absolutely no trace of wear.*)

MS-70 (Perfect Uncirculated)
A flawless coin exactly as it was minted, with no trace of

wear or injury. Must have full mint luster and brilliance or light toning. Any unusual die or striking traits must be described.

MS-65 (Choice Uncirculated)
No trace of wear; nearly as perfect as MS-70 except for some small blemishes. Has full mint luster but may be unevenly toned or lightly fingermarked. A few barely noticeable nicks or marks may be present.

MS-60 (Uncirculated)
A strictly Uncirculated coin with no trace of wear, but with blemishes more obvious than for MS-65. May lack full mint luster, and surface may be dull, spotted, or heavily toned. Check points for signs of abrasion: high points of cheek and hair below LIBERTY, eagle's head and tips of tail and wings.

ABOUT UNCIRCULATED (*Small trace of wear visible on highest points.*)

AU-55 (Choice About Uncirculated)
OBVERSE: Only a trace of wear shows on highest points of hair below BER in LIBERTY.
REVERSE: A trace of wear shows on head, tip of tail, and tips of wings. Three-quarters of the mint luster is still present.

AU-50 (About Uncirculated)
OBVERSE: Traces of wear show on cheek, tips of leaves, and hair below LIBERTY.
REVERSE: Traces of wear show on head, neck, tail, and tips of wings. Half of the mint luster is still present.

EXTREMELY FINE (*Very light wear on only the highest points.*)

EF-45 (Choice Extremely Fine)
OBVERSE: Slight wear shows on high points of upper leaves, cheek, and hair above forehead. LIBERTY is sharp and band edges are bold.
REVERSE: High points of head, neck, wings, and talons lightly worn. Lines in center tail feathers are clearly defined. Part of the mint luster is still present.

OBVERSE

REVERSE

EF-40 (Extremely Fine)

OBVERSE: Light wear shows on leaves, cheek, cap, and hair above forehead. LIBERTY is sharp and band edges are clear.

REVERSE: High points of head, neck, wings, and tail are lightly worn, but all details are clearly defined. Leaves show trace of wear at edges. Traces of mint luster may still show.

VERY FINE (*Light to moderate even wear. All major features are sharp.*)

VF-30 (Choice Very Fine)

OBVERSE: Wear spots show on leaves, cap, hair, and cheek. Bottom row of leaves is weak but has some visible details. LIBERTY and band are complete. Folds in cap are distinct.

REVERSE: Wear shows on shield but all details are visible. Most of the details in neck and tail are clear. Motto is complete.

VF-20 (Very Fine)

OBVERSE: Over half the details still show in leaves. Hair and ribbon worn but bold. Every letter in LIBERTY is visible.

REVERSE: The shield is worn, but most details are visible. Half the details in feathers are clear. Wings and legs show wear spots. Motto is clear.

FINE (*Moderate to heavy even wear. Entire design clear and bold.*)

F-12 (Fine)

OBVERSE: Some details show in hair, cap, and facial features. All letters in LIBERTY are weak but visible. Upper row of leaves is outlined, but bottom row is worn nearly smooth. Rim is full and bold.

REVERSE: Half of the feathers are plainly visible. Wear spots show in center of neck, motto, and arrows. Horizontal shield lines are merged; vertical lines are separated. Letters in legend are worn but clear.

VERY GOOD (*Well worn. Design clear but flat and lacking details.*)

VG-8 (Very Good)

OBVERSE: Entire head weak, and most details in face are worn smooth. Three letters in LIBERTY are clear. Rim is complete.

REVERSE: Eagle shows only a small amount of detail. Arrows and leaves are flat. Most of the shield is very weak. Part of the eye is visible.

GOOD (*Heavily worn. Design and legend visible but faint in spots.*)

G-4 (Good)
OBVERSE: Entire design well worn with very little detail remaining. Legend is weak but visible. LIBERTY is worn away.
REVERSE: Eagle worn flat but is completely outlined. Ribbon worn nearly smooth. Legend weak but visible. Rim worn to tops of letters.

ABOUT GOOD (*Outlined design. Parts of date and legend worn smooth.*)

AG-3 (About Good)
OBVERSE: Head is outlined with nearly all details worn away. Date readable but partially worn away. Legend merging into rim.
REVERSE: Entire design partially worn away and legend merges with rim.

QUARTERS—LIBERTY STANDING, VARIETY I 1916–1917
LIBERTY STANDING, VARIETY II 1917–1924

MINT STATE (*Absolutely no trace of wear.*)

MS-70 (Perfect Uncirculated)
A flawless coin exactly as it was minted, with no trace of wear or injury. Must have full mint luster and brilliance or light toning. Head details* (see p. 146) are an important part of this grade and must be specifically designated. Any other unusual die or striking traits must be described.

MS-65 (Choice Uncirculated)
No trace of wear; nearly as perfect as MS-70 except for some small blemish. Has full mint luster but may be unevenly toned or lightly fingermarked, may be weakly struck in one small spot. A few barely noticeable nicks or marks may be present. Head details may be incomplete.

| OBVERSE | TYPE I REVERSE | TYPE II REVERSE |

MS-60 (Uncirculated)

A strictly Uncirculated coin with no trace of wear, but with blemishes more obvious than for MS-65. May lack full mint luster, and surface may be dull, spotted, or heavily toned. One or two small spots may be weakly struck. Head details* (see p. 146) may be incomplete. Check points for signs of abrasion: mail covering breast, knee, high points of gown and shield; high points of eagle's breast and wings. Coins of this design frequently show weakly struck spots and usually lack full head details.

ABOUT UNCIRCULATED (*Small trace of wear visible on highest points.*)

AU-55 (Choice About Uncirculated)

OBVERSE: Only a trace of wear shows on highest points of mail covering breast, inner shield, and right knee.
REVERSE: A trace of wear shows on breast and edges of wings. Three-quarters of the mint luster is still present.

AU-50 (About Uncirculated)

OBVERSE: Traces of wear show on breast, knee, and high points of inner shield.
REVERSE: Traces of wear show on edges of wings and at center of breast. All of the tail feathers are visible. Half of the mint luster is still present.

EXTREMELY FINE (*Very light wear on only the highest points.*)

EF-45 (Choice Extremely Fine)

OBVERSE: Light wear spots show on upper right leg and knee. Nearly all of the gown lines are clearly visible. Shield details are bold. Breast is lightly worn and may show small flat spot.
REVERSE: Small flat spots show on high points of breast and on front wing edges. Tail feathers have nearly full details. Part of the mint luster is still present.

EF-40 (Extremely Fine)
OBVERSE: Wear shows on breast and right leg above and below knee. Most of the gown lines are visible. Shield details are bold. Breast is well rounded but has small flat spot.
REVERSE: High points of eagle are lightly worn. Central part of edge on right wing is well worn. Traces of mint luster may still show.

VERY FINE (*Light to moderate even wear. All major features are sharp.*)

VF-30 (Choice Very Fine)
OBVERSE: Wear spots show on breast, shield, and leg. Right leg is rounded but worn from above knee to ankle. Gown line crossing thigh is partially visible. Half of mail covering breast can be seen. Circle around inner shield is complete.
REVERSE: Breast and leg are worn but clearly separated, with some feathers visible between them. Feather ends and folds are visible in right wing.

VF-20 (Very Fine)
OBVERSE: Right leg is worn flat in central parts. Wear spots show on head, breast, shield, and foot. Beads on outer shield are visible, but those next to body are weak. Inner circle of shield is complete.
REVERSE: Entire eagle is lightly worn but most major details are visible. Breast and edge of right wing are worn flat. Top tail feathers are complete.

FINE (*Moderate to considerable even wear. Entire design clear and bold.*)

F-12 (Fine)
OBVERSE: Gown details worn but show clearly across body. Left leg is lightly worn. Right leg nearly flat and toe is worn. Breast worn but some mail is visible. Date may show some weakness at top. Rim is full. Outer edge of shield is complete.
REVERSE: Breast is worn almost smooth. Half of the wing feathers are visible, although well worn in spots. The rim is full.

VERY GOOD (*Well worn. Design clear but flat and lacking details.*)

VG-8 (Very Good)
OBVERSE: Entire design is weak, and most details in gown are worn smooth. All letters and date are clear but tops of numerals may be flat. Rim is complete. Drape across breast is partially outlined.
REVERSE: About one-third of the feathers are visible and large feathers at ends of wings are well separated. Eye is visible. Rim is full and all letters are clear.

GOOD (*Heavily worn. Design and legend visible but faint in spots.*)

G-4 (Good)
OBVERSE: Entire design well worn with very little detail remaining. Legend and date are weak but visible. Top of date may be worn flat. Rim is complete.
REVERSE: Eagle worn nearly flat but is completely outlined. Lettering and stars worn but clearly visible. Rim worn to tops of legend.

ABOUT GOOD (*Outlined design. Parts of date and legend worn smooth.*)

AG-3 (About Good)
OBVERSE: Figure is outlined with nearly all details worn away. Legend visible but half worn away and may merge with rim. Date weak and readable.
REVERSE: Entire design partially worn away. Some letters merging into rim.

Note: Coins of this design are sometimes weakly struck in spots, particularly at Liberty's head, breast, knee, and shield and on the eagle's breast and wings.
   *Specimens with "full head" must show the following details: Three well-defined leaves in hair; complete hairline along brow and across face; small indentation at ear. Coins of any grade other than MS-70 can be assumed to lack full head details unless the amount of visible features is specifically designated.

QUARTERS—WASHINGTON
1932 TO DATE

MINT STATE (*Absolutely no trace of wear.*)

MS-70 (Perfect Uncirculated)
A flawless coin exactly as it was minted, with no trace of wear or injury. Must have full mint luster and brilliance or light toning. Any unusual striking traits must be described.

OBVERSE

REVERSE

MS-65 (Choice Uncirculated)
No trace of wear; nearly as perfect as MS-70 except for some small blemishes. Has full mint luster but may be unevenly toned or lightly fingermarked. A few barely noticeable nicks or marks may be present.

MS-60 (Uncirculated)
A strictly Uncirculated coin with no trace of wear, but with blemishes more obvious than for MS-65. May lack full mint luster, and surface may be dull, spotted, or heavily toned. Check points for signs of abrasion: high points of cheek and hair in front and back of ear, tops of legs, and details in breast feathers.

ABOUT UNCIRCULATED (*Small trace of wear visible on highest points.*)

AU-55 (Choice About Uncirculated)
OBVERSE: Only a trace of wear shows on highest points of hair in front and in back of ear.
REVERSE: A trace of wear shows on highest spots of breast feathers. Nearly all of the mint luster is still present.

AU-50 (About Uncirculated)
OBVERSE: Traces of wear show on hair in front and in back of ear.
REVERSE: Traces of wear show on legs and breast feathers. Three-quarters of the mint luster is still present.

EXTREMELY FINE (*Light wear on most of the highest points.*)

EF-45 (Choice Extremely Fine)
OBVERSE: Slight wear shows on high points of hair around ear and along hairline up to crown. Hairlines are sharp and detailed.
REVERSE: High points of legs are lightly worn. Breast feathers are worn but clearly defined and fully separated. Half of the mint luster is still present.

EF-40 (Extremely Fine)
OBVERSE: Wear shows on high points of hair around and at hairline up to crown.

REVERSE: High points of breast, legs, and claws are lightly worn, but all details are clearly defined and partially separated. Part of the mint luster is still present.

VERY FINE (*Light to moderate even wear. All major features are sharp.*)

VF-30 (Choice Very Fine)

OBVERSE: Wear spots show on hair at forehead and ear, cheek, and jaw. Hairlines are weak but have nearly full visible details.

REVERSE: Wear shows on breast but a few feathers are visible. Legs are worn smooth. Most details in the wings are clear.

FINE (*Moderate to considerable even wear. Entire design clear and bold.*)

F-12 (Fine)

OBVERSE: Details show only at back of hair. Motto is weak but clearly visible. Part of cheek edge is worn away.

REVERSE: Feathers in breast and legs are worn smooth. Leaves show some detail. Parts of wings are nearly smooth.

VERY GOOD (*Well worn. Design clear but flat and lacking details.*)

VG-8 (Very Good)

OBVERSE: Entire head is weak, and most details in hair are worn smooth. All letters and date are clear. Rim is complete.

REVERSE: About half of the wing feathers are visible. Breast and legs only outlined. Leaves show very little detail. Rim is complete.

GOOD (*Heavily worn. Design and legend visible but faint in spots.*)

G-4 (Good)

OBVERSE: Hair is well worn with very little detail remaining. Half of motto is readable. LIBERTY and date are weak but visible. Rim merges with letters.

REVERSE: Eagle is worn nearly flat but is completely outlined. Leaves, breast, and legs are worn smooth. Legend is all visible but merges with rim.

ABOUT GOOD (*Outlined design. Parts of date and legend worn smooth.*)

AG-3 (About Good)

OBVERSE: Head is outlined with nearly all details worn away. Date readable but worn. Traces of motto are visible. Legend merging into rim.

REVERSE: Entire design partially worn away. Rim merges into legend.

Note: The obverse motto is always weak on coins of 1932 and early issues of 1934.

The reverse rim and lettering has a tendency to be very weak particularly on coins dated 1934D, 1935D and S, 1936D and S, 1937D and S (especially), 1938D and S, 1939D, and 1940D.

HALF DOLLARS—BARBER
1892–1915

MINT STATE (*Absolutely no trace of wear.*)

MS-70 (Perfect Uncirculated)
A flawless coin exactly as it was minted, with no trace of wear or injury. Must have full mint luster and brilliance or light toning. Any unusual die or striking traits must be described.

MS-65 (Choice Uncirculated)
No trace of wear; nearly as perfect as MS-70 except for some small blemish. Has full mint luster but may be unevenly toned or lightly fingermarked. A few barely noticeable nicks or marks may be present.

MS-60 (Uncirculated)
A strictly Uncirculated coin with no trace of wear, but with blemishes more obvious than for MS-65. May lack full mint luster, and surface may be dull, spotted, or heavily toned. Check points for signs of abrasion: high points of cheek and hair below LIBERTY, eagle's head and tips of tail and wings.

OBVERSE

REVERSE

ABOUT UNCIRCULATED (*Small trace of wear visible on highest points.*)

AU-55 (Choice About Uncirculated)
OBVERSE: Only a trace of wear shows on highest points of hair below BER in LIBERTY.
REVERSE: A trace of wear shows on head, tip of tail, and tips of wings. Three-quarters of the mint luster is still present.

AU-50 (About Uncirculated)
OBVERSE: Traces of wear show on cheek, tips of leaves, and hair below LIBERTY.
REVERSE: Traces of wear show on head, neck, tail, and tips of wings. Half of the mint luster is still present.

EXTREMELY FINE (*Very light wear on only the highest points.*)

EF-45 (Choice Extremely Fine)
OBVERSE: Slight wear shows on high points of upper leaves, cheek, and hair above forehead. LIBERTY is sharp and band edges are bold.
REVERSE: High points of head, neck, wings, and talons lightly worn. Lines in reverse center tail feathers are clearly defined. Part of the mint luster is still present.

EF-40 (Extremely Fine)
OBVERSE: Light wear shows on leaves, cheek, cap, and hair above forehead. LIBERTY is sharp and band edges are clear.
REVERSE: High points of head, neck, wings, and tail are lightly worn, but all details are clearly defined. Leaves show trace of wear at edges. Traces of mint luster may still show.

VERY FINE (*Light to moderate even wear. All major features are sharp.*)

VF-30 (Choice Very Fine)
OBVERSE: Wear spots show on leaves, cap, hair, and cheek. Bottom row of leaves is weak but has some visible details. LIBERTY and band are complete. Folds in cap are distinct.
REVERSE: Wear shows on shield but all details are visible. Most of the details in neck and tail are clear. Motto is complete.

VF-20 (Very Fine)
OBVERSE: Over half the details still show in leaves. Hair and ribbon worn but bold. Every letter in LIBERTY is visible. Bottom folds in cap are full.
REVERSE: Shield is worn, but all details are visible. Half the details in feathers are clear. Wings, tail, and legs show small wear spots. Motto is clear.

FINE (*Moderate to considerable even wear. Entire design clear and bold.*)

F-12 (Fine)
OBVERSE: Some details show in hair, cap, and facial features. All letters in LIBERTY are weak but visible. Upper row of leaves is outlined, but bottom row is worn nearly smooth. Rim is full and bold.
REVERSE: Half the feathers are plainly visible. Wear spots show in center of neck, motto, and arrows. Horizontal shield lines are merged; vertical lines are separated. Letters in legend are worn but clear.

VERY GOOD (*Well worn. Design clear but flat and lacking details.*)

VG-8 (Very Good)
OBVERSE: Entire head weak, and most details in face are heavily worn. Three letters in LIBERTY are clear. Rim is complete.
REVERSE: Eagle shows only a small amount of detail. Arrows and leaves are flat. Most of shield is very weak. Parts of eye and motto visible.

GOOD (*Heavily worn. Design and legend visible but faint in spots.*)

G-4 (Good)
OBVERSE: Entire design well worn with very little detail remaining. Legend and date weak but visible. LIBERTY is worn away.
REVERSE: Eagle worn flat but is completely outlined. Ribbon worn nearly smooth. Legend weak but visible. Rim worn to tops of letters.

ABOUT GOOD (*Outlined design. Parts of date and legend worn smooth.*)

AG-3 (About Good)
OBVERSE: Head is outlined with nearly all details worn away. Date readable but partially worn away. Legend merging into rim.
REVERSE: Entire design partially worn away and legend merges with rim.

HALF DOLLARS—LIBERTY WALKING 1916–1947

MINT STATE (*Absolutely no trace of wear.*)

MS-70 (Perfect Uncirculated)
A flawless coin exactly as it was minted, with no trace of wear or injury. Must have full mint luster and brilliance or light toning. Any unusual die or striking traits must be described.

MS-65 (Choice Uncirculated)
No trace of wear; nearly as perfect as MS-70 except for some small blemishes. Has full mint luster but may be unevenly toned or lightly fingermarked. May be weakly struck in one or two small spots. A few minute nicks or marks may be present.

MS-60 (Uncirculated)
A strictly Uncirculated coin with no trace of wear, but with blemishes more obvious than for MS-65. May lack full mint luster, and surface may be dull, spotted, or heavily toned. A few small spots may be weakly struck. Check points for signs of abrasion: hair above temple, right arm, left breast; high points of eagle's head, breast, legs, and wings. Coins of this design frequently show weakly struck spots and usually lack full head and hand details.

ABOUT UNCIRCULATED (*Small trace of wear visible on highest points.*)

OBVERSE

REVERSE

AU-55 (Choice About Uncirculated)

OBVERSE: Only a trace of wear shows on highest points of head, breast, and right arm.

REVERSE: A trace of wear shows on left leg between breast and left wing. Three-quarters of the mint luster is still present.

AU-50 (About Uncirculated)

OBVERSE: Traces of wear show on head, breast, arms, and left leg.

REVERSE: Traces of wear show on high points of wings and at center of head. All leg feathers are visible. Half of the mint luster is still present.

EXTREMELY FINE (*Very light wear on only the highest points.*)

EF-45 (Choice Extremely Fine)

OBVERSE: Light wear spots show on head, breast, arms, left leg, and foot. Nearly all gown lines are clearly visible. Sandal details are bold and complete. Knee is lightly worn but full and rounded.

REVERSE: Small flat spots show on high points of breast and legs. Wing feathers have nearly full details. Part of the mint luster is still present.

EF-40 (Extremely Fine)

OBVERSE: Wear shows on head, breast, arms, and left leg. Nearly all gown lines are visible. Sandal details are complete. Breast and knee are nearly flat.

REVERSE: High points of eagle are lightly worn. Half the breast and leg feathers are visible. Central part of feathers below neck is well worn. Traces of mint luster may still show.

VERY FINE (*Light to moderate even wear. All major features are sharp.*)

VF-30 (Choice Very Fine)

OBVERSE: Wear spots on head, breast, arms, and legs. Left leg is rounded but worn from above knee to ankle. Gown line crossing body is partially visible. Knee is flat. Outline of breast can be seen.

REVERSE: Breast and legs are moderately worn but clearly separated, with some feathers visible in right wing. Pupil in eye is visible.

VF-20 (Very Fine)

OBVERSE: Left leg is worn nearly flat. Wear spots show on head, breast, arms, and foot. Lines on skirt are visible, but may be weak on coins before 1921. Breast is outlined.

REVERSE: Entire eagle is lightly worn but most major details are visible. Breast, central part of legs, and top edge of right wing are worn flat.

FINE (*Moderate to considerable even wear. Entire design clear and bold.*)

F-12 (Fine)
OBVERSE: Gown stripes worn but show clearly, except for coins before 1921, where only half are visible. Right leg is lightly worn. Left leg nearly flat and sandal is worn but visible. Center of body worn but some of the gown is visible. Outer edge of rim is complete.
REVERSE: Breast is worn smooth. Half the wing feathers are visible, although well worn in spots. Top two layers of feathers are visible in left wing. Rim is full.

VERY GOOD (*Well worn. Design clear but flat and lacking details.*)

VG-8 (Very Good)
OBVERSE: Entire design is weak; most details in gown are worn smooth except for coins after 1921, where half the stripes must show. All letters and date are clear but top of motto may be weak. Rim is complete. Drapery across body is partially visible.
REVERSE: About one-third of the feathers are visible, and large feathers at ends of wings are well separated. Eye is visible. Rim is full and all letters are clear.

GOOD (*Heavily worn. Design and legend visible but faint in spots.*)

G-4 (Good)
OBVERSE: Entire design well worn with very little detail remaining. Legend and date weak but visible. Top of date may be worn flat. Rim is flat but nearly complete.
REVERSE: Eagle worn nearly flat but is completely outlined. Lettering and motto worn but clearly visible.

ABOUT GOOD (*Outlined design. Parts of date and legend worn smooth.*)

AG-3 (About Good)
OBVERSE: Figure is outlined with nearly all details worn away. Legend visible but half worn away. Date weak but readable. Rim merges with lettering.
REVERSE: Entire design partially worn away. Letters merge with rim.

Note: Coins of this design are sometimes weakly struck in spots, particularly at Liberty's head, hand holding branch, and drapery lines of dress, and on the eagle's leg feathers.

HALF DOLLARS—FRANKLIN
1948–1963

MINT STATE (*Absolutely no trace of wear.*)

MS-70 (Perfect Uncirculated)
A flawless coin exactly as it was minted, with no trace of wear or injury. Must have full mint luster and brilliance or light toning. Any unusual striking traits must be described.

MS-65 (Choice Uncirculated)
No trace of wear; nearly as perfect as MS-70 except for some small blemishes. Has full mint luster but may be unevenly toned or lightly fingermarked. A few barely noticeable nicks or marks may be present.

MS-60 (Uncirculated)
A strictly Uncirculated coin with no trace of wear, but with blemishes more obvious than for MS-65. May lack full mint luster, and surface may be dull, spotted, or heavily toned. Check points for signs of abrasion: high points of cheek, shoulder, and hair left of ear; straps around beam, lines, and lettering on bell.

ABOUT UNCIRCULATED (*Small trace of wear visible on highest points.*)

AU-55 (Choice About Uncirculated)
OBVERSE: Only a trace of wear shows on highest spots of cheek and hair left of ear.

OBVERSE

REVERSE

REVERSE: A trace of wear shows on highest points of lettering on bell. Nearly all of the mint luster is still present.

AU-50 (About Uncirculated)
OBVERSE: Traces of wear show on cheek and hair on shoulder and left of ear.

REVERSE: Traces of wear show on bell at lettering and along ridges at bottom. Three-quarters of the mint luster is still present.

EXTREMELY FINE (*Very light wear on only the highest points.*)

EF-45 (Choice Extremely Fine)
OBVERSE: Slight wear shows on cheek and high points of hair behind ear and along shoulder. Hairlines at back of head are sharp and detailed.

REVERSE: High points of straps on beam are lightly worn. Lines at bottom of bell are worn but clearly defined and separated. Lettering on bell is very weak at center. Half of the mint luster is still present.

EF-40 (Extremely Fine)
OBVERSE: Wear shows on high points of cheek and hair behind ear and at shoulder.

REVERSE: High points of beam straps and lines along bottom of bell are lightly worn, but details are clearly defined and partially separated. Lettering on bell is worn away at center. Part of the mint luster is still present.

VERY FINE (*Light to moderate even wear. All major features are sharp.*)

VF-30 (Choice Very Fine)
OBVERSE: Wear spots show on hair at shoulder and behind ear, on cheek and jaw. Hairlines are weak but have nearly full visible details.

REVERSE: Wear shows on bell lettering but some of the details are visible. Straps on beam are plain. Half of line details at bottom are worn smooth.

VF-20 (Very Fine)
OBVERSE: Three-quarters of the lines still show in hair. Cheek lightly worn but bold. Some hair details around the ear are visible.

REVERSE: Wear shows on beam but most details are visible. Bell is worn but bold. Lines across bottom of bell are flat near crack.

Fine (*Moderate to considerable even wear. Entire design clear and bold.*)

F-12 (Fine)
OBVERSE: Hair details show only at back and side of head. Designer's initials weak but clearly visible. Part of cheek is worn flat.
REVERSE: Most of lines at bottom of bell are worn smooth. Parts of straps on beam are nearly smooth. Rim is full.

VERY GOOD (*Well worn. Design clear but flat and lacking details.*)

VG-8 (Very Good)
OBVERSE: Entire head is weak, and most details in hair from temple to ear are worn smooth. All letters and date are bold. Ear and designer's initial are visible. Rim is complete.

HALF DOLLARS—KENNEDY 1964 TO DATE

MINT STATE (*Absolutely no trace of wear.*)

MS-70 (Perfect Uncirculated)
A flawless coin exactly as it was minted, with no trace of wear or injury. Must have full mint luster and brilliance or light toning. Any unusual striking traits must be described.

MS-65 (Choice Uncirculated)
No trace of wear; nearly as perfect as MS-70 except for some small blemish. Has full mint luster but may be unevenly toned or lightly fingermarked. A few barely noticeable nicks or marks may be present.

MS-60 (Uncirculated)
A strictly Uncirculated coin with no trace of wear, but with blemishes more obvious than for MS-65. Has full mint luster, but surface may be dull, spotted, or heavily toned. Check points for signs of abrasion: high points of cheek and jawbone, center of neck, hair below part, bundle of arrows, center tail feather, right wing tip.

OBVERSE

REVERSE

ABOUT UNCIRCULATED (*Small trace of wear visible on highest points.*)

AU-55 (Choice About Uncirculated)
OBVERSE: Only a trace of wear shows on highest points of cheek, jawbone, and hair below part.
REVERSE: A trace of wear shows on central tail feather. Nearly all of the mint luster is still present.

EXTREMELY FINE (*Very light wear on only the highest points.*)

EF-40 (Extremely Fine)
OBVERSE: Slight wear shows on cheek, along jawbone, and on high points of hair below part. Hairlines are sharp and detailed.
REVERSE: High points of arrows and right wing tip are lightly worn. Central tail feathers are worn but clearly defined and fully separated. Three-quarters of the mint luster is still present.

VERY FINE (*Light to moderate even wear. All major features are sharp.*)

VF-30 (Choice Very Fine)
OBVERSE: Wear spots show on hair below part and along cheek and jaw. Hairlines are weak but have nearly full visible details.
REVERSE: Wear shows on arrow points but some details are visible. All central tail feathers are plain. Wing tips are lightly worn.

DOLLARS—MORGAN
1878–1921

MINT STATE (*Absolutely no trace of wear.*)

MS-70 (Perfect Uncirculated)
A flawless coin exactly as it was minted, with no trace of wear or injury. Must have full mint luster and brilliance or light toning. Any unusual striking traits must be described.

MS-65 (Choice Uncirculated)
No trace of wear; nearly as perfect as MS-70 except for a few minute bag marks or surface marks. Has full mint luster but may be unevenly toned. Any unusual striking traits must be described.

MS-60 (Uncirculated)
A strictly Uncirculated coin with no trace of wear, but with bag marks and other abrasions more obvious than for MS-65. May have a few small rim marks and weakly struck spots. Has full mint luster but may lack brilliance, and surface may be spotted or heavily toned. For these coins, bag abrasions and scuff marks are considered different from circulation wear. Full mint luster and lack of any wear are necessary to distinguish MS-60 from AU-55. Check points for signs of wear: hair above eye and ear, edges of cotton leaves and blossoms, high upper fold of cap, high points of eagle's breast, and tops of legs. Weakly struck spots are common and should not be confused with actual wear.

ABOUT UNCIRCULATED (*Small trace of wear visible on highest points.*)

AU-55 (Choice About Uncirculated)
OBVERSE: Slight trace of wear shows on hair above ear and eye, edges of cotton leaves, and high upper fold of cap. Luster fading from cheek.
REVERSE: Slight trace of wear shows on breast, tops of legs,

OBVERSE

REVERSE

and talons. Most of the mint luster is still present, although marred by light bag marks and surface abrasions.

AU-50 (About Uncirculated)
OBVERSE: Traces of wear show on hair above eye and ear, edges of cotton leaves, and high upper fold of cap. Partial detail visible on tops of cotton blossoms. Luster gone from cheek.
REVERSE: There are traces of wear on breast, tops of legs, wing tips, and talons. Three-quarters of the mint luster is still present. Surface abrasions and bag marks are more noticeable than for AU-55.

EXTREMELY FINE (*Very light wear on only the highest points.*)

EF-45 (Choice Extremely Fine)
OBVERSE: Slight wear on hair above date, forehead, and ear. Lines in hair well detailed and sharp. Slight flat spots on edges of cotton leaves. Minute signs of wear on cheek.
REVERSE: High points of breast are lightly worn. Tops of legs and right wing tip show wear. Talons are slightly flat. Half of the mint luster is still present.

EF-40 (Extremely Fine)
OBVERSE: Wear shows on hair above date, forehead, and ear. Lines in hair well detailed. Flat spots visible on edges of cotton leaves. Cheek lightly worn.
REVERSE: Almost all feathers gone from breast. Tops of legs, wing tips, and feathers on head show wear. Talons are flat. Partial mint luster is visible.

VERY FINE (*Light to moderate even wear. All major features are sharp.*)

VF-30 (Choice Very Fine)
OBVERSE: Wear shows on high points of hair from forehead to ear. Some strands visible in hair above ear. There are smooth areas on cotton leaves and at top of cotton blossoms.
REVERSE: Wear shows on leaves of wreath and tips of wings. Only a few feathers visible on breast and head.

VF-20 (Very Fine)
OBVERSE: Smooth spots visible on hair from forehead to ear. Cotton leaves heavily worn but separated. Wheat grains show wear.
REVERSE: Some leaves on wreath are well worn. Breast is smooth, and only a few feathers show on head. Tips of wings are weak but lines are complete.

FINE (*Moderate to heavy even wear. Entire design clear and bold.*)

F-12 (Fine)
OBVERSE: Hairline along face is clearly defined. Lower two cotton leaves smooth but distinct from cap. Some wheat grains merging. Cotton blossoms flat but the two lines in each show clearly.
REVERSE: One-quarter of eagle's right wing and edge of left wing are smooth. Head, neck, and breast are flat and merging. Tail feathers slightly worn. Top leaves in wreath show heavy wear.

VERY GOOD (*Well worn. Design clear but flat and lacking details.*)

VG-8 (Very Good)
OBVERSE: Most details in hair are worn smooth. All letters and date are clear. Cotton blossoms flat and leaves merging in spots. Hair of eagle's right wing and one-third of left wing are smooth. All leaves in wreath are worn. Rim is complete.

GOOD (*Heavily worn. Design and legend visible but faint in spots.*)

G-4 (Good)
OBVERSE: Hair is well worn with very little detail remaining. Date, letters, and design clearly outlined. Rim is full.
REVERSE: Eagle is worn nearly flat but is completely outlined. Design elements smooth but visible. Legend is all visible; rim is full.

ABOUT GOOD (*Outlined design. Parts of date and legend worn smooth.*)

AG-3 (About Good)
OBVERSE: Head is outlined with nearly all details worn away. Date readable but worn. Legend merging into rim.
REVERSE: Entire design partially worn away. Rim merges into legend.

Note: Some of these dollars have a prooflike surface; this should be mentioned in any description of such pieces.

Portions of the design are often weakly struck, especially on the hair above the ear and on the eagle's breast.

DOLLARS—PEACE 1921–1935

MINT STATE (*Absolutely no trace of wear.*)

MS-70 (Perfect Uncirculated)
A flawless coin exactly as it was minted, with no trace of wear or injury. Must have full mint luster or light toning. Any unusual striking traits must be described.

MS-65 (Choice Uncirculated)
No trace of wear; nearly as perfect as MS-70 except for a few minute bag marks or surface marks. Has full mint luster but may be unevenly toned.

MS-60 (Uncirculated)
A strictly Uncirculated coin with no trace of wear, but with bag marks and other abrasions more obvious than for MS-65. May have a few small rim mars, and may be weakly struck. Has full mint luster but may lack brilliance, and surface may be spotted or heavily toned. For these coins, bag abrasions and scuff marks are considered different from circulation wear. Full mint luster and lack of any wear are necessary to distinguish MS-60 from AU-55. Check points for signs of wear: high points of cheek and hair, high points of feathers on right wing and leg. Weakly struck spots are common and should not be confused with actual wear.

ABOUT UNCIRCULATED (*Small trace of wear visible on highest points.*)

OBVERSE

REVERSE

AU-55 (Choice About Uncirculated)
OBVERSE: Trace of wear shows on hair over ear and above forehead. Slight wear visible on cheek.
REVERSE: High points of feathers on right wing show a trace of wear. Most of the mint luster is still present, although marred by light bag marks and surface abrasions.

AU-50 (About Uncirculated)
OBVERSE: Traces of wear visible on neck and hair over ear and above forehead. Cheek shows slight wear.
REVERSE: Traces of wear show on head and high points of feathers on right wing. Three-quarters of the mint luster is still present. Surface abrasions and bag marks are more noticeable than for AU-55.

EXTREMELY FINE (*Very light wear on only the highest points.*)

EF-45 (Choice Extremely Fine)
OBVERSE: Hair around face shows slight wear, but most hair strands are visible. Lower edge of neck lightly worn.
REVERSE: Top of neck and head behind eye show slight wear. Central wing and leg feathers lightly worn. Half of the mint luster is still present.

EF-40 (Extremely Fine)
OBVERSE: Slight flattening visible on high points of hair; most hair strands clearly separated. Entire face and lower edge of neck lightly worn.
REVERSE: Wear shows on head behind eye and top of neck. Some flat spots visible on central wing and leg feathers. Partial mint luster is visible.

DOLLARS—EISENHOWER
1971–1978

MINT STATE (*Absolutely no trace of wear.*)
MS-70 (Perfect Uncirculated)
A flawless coin exactly as it was minted, with no trace of

wear or injury. Must have full mint luster and brilliance or light toning. Any unusual striking traits must be described.

MS-65 (Choice Uncirculated)

No trace of wear; nearly as perfect as MS-70 except for some small blemish. Has full mint luster but may be unevenly toned or lightly fingermarked. A few minute nicks or marks may be present.

MS-60 (Uncirculated)

A strictly Uncirculated coin with no trace of wear, but with blemishes more obvious than for MS-65. Has full mint luster, but surface may be dull, spotted, or heavily toned. Check points for signs of abrasion: high points of cheek and jawbone, center of neck, edge of bust, head, high points of ridges and feathers in wings and legs.

ABOUT UNCIRCULATED (*Small trace of wear visible on highest points.*)

AU-55 (Choice About Uncirculated)

OBVERSE: Only a trace of wear shows on highest points of jawbone and at center of neck.
REVERSE: A trace of wear shows on high points of feathers in wings and legs. Nearly all of the mint luster is still present.

EXTREMELY FINE (*Very light wear on only the highest points.*)

EF-45 (Choice Extremely Fine)

OBVERSE: Slight wear shows on cheek, along jawbone, and on high points at edge of bust. Hairlines are sharp and detailed.
REVERSE: High points of head, legs, and wing ridges are lightly worn. Central feathers are all clearly defined. Three-quarters of the mint luster is still present.

VERY FINE (*Light to moderate even wear. All major features are sharp.*)

VF-30 (Choice Very Fine)

OBVERSE: Wear spots show on hair below part and along cheek and jaw. Hairlines are weak but have nearly full visible details. Slight wear shows at center of neck and along edge of bust.

OBVERSE

REVERSE

REVERSE: Wear shows on head and feathers in wings and legs but all details are visible. All central tail feathers are plain. Wing and leg ridges are lightly worn.

GOLD DOLLARS—TYPE I
1849–1854

MINT STATE (*Absolutely no trace of wear.*)

MS-70 (Perfect Uncirculated)
A flawless coin exactly as it was minted, with no trace of wear or injury. Must have full mint luster and brilliance. Any unusual die or planchet traits must be described.

MS-65 (Choice Uncirculated)
No trace of wear; nearly as perfect as MS-70 except for some small blemish. Has full mint luster and brilliance but may show slight discoloration. A few barely noticeable nicks or marks may be present.

MS-60 (Uncirculated)
A strictly Uncirculated coin with no trace of wear, but with blemishes more obvious than for MS-65. May lack full mint luster and brilliance. Check points for signs of abrasion: hair near coronet; tips of leaves.

ABOUT UNCIRCULATED (*Small trace of wear visible on highest points.*)

AU-55 (Choice About Uncirculated)
OBVERSE: There is a trace of wear at upper hairline below coronet.
REVERSE: Trace of wear visible on tips of leaves. Three-quarters of the mint luster is still present.

AU-50 (About Uncirculated)
OBVERSE: There is a trace of wear on hairlines near coronet and below the ear.
REVERSE: Trace of wear visible on tips of leaves. Half of the mint luster is still present.

EXTREMELY FINE (*Very light wear on only the highest points.*)

OBVERSE

REVERSE

EF-45 (Choice Extremely Fine)
OBVERSE: Slight wear shows on highest wave of hair, hair-line, and below ear. All major details are sharp. Beads at top of coronet are well defined.
REVERSE: Leaves show visible wear at tips, but central details are clearly defined. Traces of mint luster will show.

VERY FINE (*Light to moderate even wear. All major features are sharp.*)

VF-30 (Choice Very Fine)
OBVERSE: Beads on top of coronet are well defined. LIBERTY is complete. Hair around face and neck slightly worn but strands fully separated. Star centers show some details.
REVERSE: There is light even wear on legend and date. Some details show in center of leaves.

VF-20 (Very Fine)
OBVERSE: Beads at top of coronet are partially separated. LIBERTY is complete. Hair around face and neck noticeably worn but well outlined. Some star centers show details.
REVERSE: There is light even wear on legend and date. Only traces of leaf ribs are visible. Bow knot is flat on high point.

FINE (*Moderate to heavy even wear. Entire design clear and bold.*)

F-12 (Fine)
OBVERSE: LIBERTY is complete but weak. Ear lobe is visible. Hairlines and beads on coronet are worn smooth. Stars are clearly outlined, but centers are flat.
REVERSE: Legend within wreath is worn and weak in spots. Leaves and wreath are well outlined. Rim is full and edge beveled.

VERY GOOD (*Well worn. Design clear but flat and lacking details.*)

VG-8 (Very Good)
OBVERSE: Only the outline of hair is visible. Four letters in LIBERTY are clear.

REVERSE: Only the outline of leaves is visible. Legend and numeral are worn and very weak.

GOOD (*Heavily worn. Design and legend visible but faint in spots*).

G-4 (Good)
OBVERSE: Head is outlined with nearly all details worn away. Stars are weak. Full rim shows.
REVERSE: Date and legend well worn but readable. Leaves are outlined. Full rim shows.

Note: The gold dollars struck at Charlotte and Dahlonega are crude compared to those of the Philadelphia Mint. Frequently they have rough edges, and the die work appears to be generally inferior. In grading coins from these Branch Mints, consideration must be given to these factors.

QUARTER EAGLES— CORONET HEAD 1840–1907

MINT STATE (*Absolutely no trace of wear.*)

MS-70 (Perfect Uncirculated)
A flawless coin exactly as it was minted, with no trace of wear or injury. Must have full mint luster and brilliance. Any unusual die or planchet traits must be described.

MS-65 (Choice Uncirculated)
No trace of wear; nearly as perfect as MS-70 except for some small blemish. Has full mint luster and brilliance but may show slight discoloration. A few barely noticeable nicks or marks may be present.

MS-60 (Uncirculated)
A strictly Uncirculated coin with no trace of wear, but with blemishes more obvious than for MS-65. May lack full mint luster and brilliance. Check points for signs of abrasion: tip of coronet, hair, wings, claws.

ABOUT UNCIRCULATED (*Small trace of wear visible on highest points.*)

OBVERSE   REVERSE

AU-55 (Choice About Uncirculated)
OBVERSE: There is a trace of wear on tip of coronet and above eye.
REVERSE: Trace of wear visible on wing tips. Three-quarters of the mint luster is still present.

AU-50 (About Uncirculated)
OBVERSE: There is a trace of wear on coronet and on hair above ear, eye, and forehead.
REVERSE: Trace of wear visible on wing tips, below eye, and on claw. Half of the mint luster is still present.

EXTREMELY FINE (*Very light wear on only the highest points.*)

EF-45 (Choice Extremely Fine)
OBVERSE: There is light wear on coronet, and on hair above ear, eye, forelocks, and top of head.
REVERSE: Light wear shows on edges and tips of wings, on neck, below eye, and on claws. Part of the mint luster is still present.

EF-40 (Extremely Fine)
OBVERSE: Light wear shows on coronet, hair above ear and eye, on forelocks, and on cheek. All major details sharp.
REVERSE: Light wear shows on edges and tips of wings, on neck, below eye, on feathers, and claws. Shield well defined. Traces of mint luster will show.

VERY FINE (*Light to moderate even wear. All major features are sharp.*)

VF-30 (Choice Very Fine)
OBVERSE: Light wear visible on coronet; hair is worn but shows considerable detail. Most stars show details. LIBERTY bold and clear.
REVERSE: Light wear shows on edges and tips of wings. Some detail shows on head and neck feathers. Vertical shield lines complete but some not separated; horizontal lines worn in center.

VF-20 (Very Fine)
OBVERSE: Hair outlined with very little detail. Only a few stars show any details. LIBERTY clear but not bold.
REVERSE: Half of wing feathers visible. Half of lines in shield are clear.

FINE (*Moderate to heavy even wear. Entire design clear and bold.*)

F-12 (Fine)
OBVERSE: Hair and cheek smooth. Stars outlined with no visible details. LIBERTY worn but visible.
REVERSE: Wings show very little detail. Head and one claw outlined only, with no details visible. Neck almost smooth. Most of shield lines merge.

Note: Coins of this type seldom appear in grades lower than Fine. Pieces made at Charlotte, Dahlonega, and New Orleans are frequently found weakly struck. Those from San Francisco often lack feather details.

QUARTER EAGLES—INDIAN HEAD 1908–1929

MINT STATE (*Absolutely no trace of wear.*)

MS-70 (Perfect Uncirculated)
A flawless coin exactly as it was minted, with no trace of wear or injury. Must have full mint luster and brilliance. Any unusual die or planchet traits must be described.

MS-65 (Choice Uncirculated)
No trace of wear; nearly as perfect as MS-70 except for some small blemish. Has full mint luster and brilliance but may show slight discoloration. A few barely noticeable nicks or marks may be present.

MS-60 (Uncirculated)
A strictly Uncirculated coin with no trace of wear, but with blemishes more obvious than for MS-65. May lack full mint luster and brilliance. Check points for signs of abrasion: cheek-

OBVERSE

REVERSE

bone, headdress, headband feathers, shoulder of eagle's left wing.

ABOUT UNCIRCULATED (*Small trace of wear visible on highest points.*)

AU-55 (Choice About Uncirculated)
OBVERSE: There is a trace of wear on cheekbone.
REVERSE: Trace of wear visible on shoulder of eagle's left wing. Three-quarters of the mint luster is still present.

AU-50 (About Uncirculated)
OBVERSE: There is a trace of wear on cheekbone and headdress.
REVERSE: Trace of wear visible on shoulder of wing, head, and breast. Half of the mint luster is still present.

EXTREMELY FINE (*Very light wear on only the highest points.*)

EF-45 (Choice Extremely Fine)
OBVERSE: There is light wear on cheekbone, headdress, and headband.
REVERSE: Light wear shows on upper portion of wing, head, neck, and breast.

EF-40 (Extremely Fine)
OBVERSE: Light wear shows on cheekbone, jaw, and headband. Slight wear visible on feathers of headdress. Stars sharp.
REVERSE: Light wear shows on wing, head, neck, and breast. Leg has full feather detail. Traces of mint luster will show.

VERY FINE (*Light to moderate even wear. All major features are sharp.*)

VF-30 (Choice Very Fine)
OBVERSE: Cheekbone shows flat spot. Small feathers clear; large feathers show some detail. Most of headband detail visible.
REVERSE: Wear shows on wing and neck. Some breast feathers show details. Most of leg feathers visible.

VF-20 (Very Fine)
OBVERSE: Cheekbone worn about halfway. Small feathers

clear but large feathers show a little detail. Hair cord knot is distinct. Headband shows some detail.

REVERSE: Little detail shows on breast and leg feathers. Top of wing and neck worn. Second layer of wing feathers shows.

FINE (*Moderate to heavy even wear. Entire design clear and bold.*)

F-12 (Fine)

OBVERSE: Cheekbone worn; all feathers worn with very little detail visible. Stars outlined, with no details visible. Hair cord knot is worn but visible.

REVERSE: Wing worn, with only partial feathers at bottom visible. All lettering worn but visible.

Note: Coins of this type are seldom collected in grades lower than Fine. Mint marks are often weakly struck.

HALF EAGLES—CORONET HEAD 1839–1908

MINT STATE (*Absolutely no trace of wear.*)

MS-70 (Perfect Uncirculated)

A flawless coin exactly as it was minted, with no trace of wear or injury. Must have full mint luster and brilliance. Any unusual die or planchet traits must be described.

OBVERSE

REVERSE

MS-65 (Choice Uncirculated)
No trace of wear; nearly as perfect as MS-70 except for some small blemishes. Has full mint luster and brilliance but may show slight discoloration. A few barely noticeable bag marks and surface abrasions may be present.

MS-60 (Uncirculated)
A strictly Uncirculated coin with no trace of wear, but with blemishes more obvious than for MS-65. Has full mint luster but may lack brilliance. Surface may be lightly marred by minor bag marks and abrasions. Check points for signs of wear: hair, coronet, wings.

ABOUT UNCIRCULATED (*Small trace of wear visible on highest points.*)

AU-55 (Choice About Uncirculated)
OBVERSE: There is a trace of wear on tip of coronet and hair above eye.
REVERSE: Trace of wear visible on wing tips. Three-quarters of the mint luster is still present.

AU-50 (About Uncirculated)
OBVERSE: There is a trace of wear on coronet, above ear and eye.
REVERSE: Trace of wear visible on wing tips, below eye and on claw. Half of the mint luster is still present.

EXTREMELY FINE (*Light wear on only the highest points.*)

EF-45 (Choice Extremely Fine)
OBVERSE: There is light wear on coronet, and on hair above ear, eye, forelocks, and top of head.
REVERSE: Light wear shows on edges and tips of wings, on neck, below eye, and on claws. Part of the mint luster is still present.

EF-40 (Extremely Fine)
OBVERSE: Light wear shows on coronet, on hair above ear and eye, on the forelock, on top of head, and on cheek. All major details are sharp.
REVERSE: Light wear visible on edges and tips of wings, on neck, below eye, on feathers, and claws. Shield is well defined. Traces of mint luster will show.

VERY FINE (*Light to moderate even wear. All major features are sharp.*)

VF-30 (Choice Very Fine)
OBVERSE: Light wear shows on coronet, hair, and stars but most details are visible. LIBERTY bold.
REVERSE: Light wear visible on edges and tips of wings. Head and neck feathers show some detail. Vertical lines in

shield complete but some not separated; horizontal lines worn in center.

VF-20 (Very Fine)
OBVERSE: Hair worn but major details visible. Top line of coronet broken. Some stars show partial detail. LIBERTY clear but not bold.
REVERSE: Half of wing feathers are visible. Half of lines in shield are clear.

FINE (*Moderate to heavy even wear. Entire design clear and bold.*)

F-12 (Fine)
OBVERSE: Hair and cheekbone smooth. Top line of coronet worn. LIBERTY worn but visible.
REVERSE: Wings show very little detail. Head and one claw outlined only, with no details visible. Neck almost smooth. Most of shield lines merge. (For the 1866 through 1908 group, the motto is worn but readable.)

Note: Coins of this type are seldom collected in grades lower than Fine.

HALF EAGLES—INDIAN HEAD 1908–1929

MINT STATE (*Absolutely no trace of wear.*)

MS-70 (Perfect Uncirculated)
A flawless coin exactly as it was minted, with no trace of wear or injury. Must have full mint luster and brilliance. Any unusual die or planchet traits must be described.

MS-65 (Choice Uncirculated)
No trace of wear; nearly as perfect as MS-70 except for some small blemish. Has full mint luster and brilliance but may show slight discoloration. A few barely noticeable bag marks and surface abrasions may be present.

MS-60 (Uncirculated)
A strictly Uncirculated coin with no trace of wear, but with

OBVERSE   REVERSE

blemishes more obvious than for MS-65. Has full mint luster but may lack brilliance. Surface may be lightly marred by
minor bag marks and abrasions. Check points for signs of
wear: cheekbone, headdress, headband feathers, shoulder
of eagle's left wing.

ABOUT UNCIRCULATED (*Small trace of wear visible on
highest points.*)

AU-55 (Choice About Uncirculated)
OBVERSE: There is a trace of wear on cheekbone.
REVERSE: Trace of wear visible on shoulder of eagle's left
wing. Three-quarters of the mint luster is still present.

AU-50 (About Uncirculated)
OBVERSE: There is a trace of wear on cheekbone and headdress.
REVERSE: Trace of wear visible on shoulder of wing, head,
and breast. Half of the mint luster is still present.

EXTREMELY FINE (*Light wear on only the highest points.*)

EF-45 (Choice Extremely Fine)
OBVERSE: There is light wear on cheekbone, headdress, and
headband.
REVERSE: Light wear shows on upper portion of wing,
head, neck, and breast. Part of mint luster is still present.

EF-40 (Extremely Fine)
OBVERSE: Light wear shows on cheekbone, jaw, and headband. Slight wear visible on feathers of headdress. Stars are
sharp.
REVERSE: Light wear shows on wing, head, neck, and
breast. Leg has full feather detail. Traces of mint luster will
show.

VERY FINE (*Light to moderate even wear. All major features
are sharp.*)

VF-30 (Choice Very Fine)
OBVERSE: Cheekbone worn, shows flat spot. Small feathers
clear; large feathers show some details. Most of headband
detail visible.

REVERSE: Wear shows on wing and neck. Some breast feathers show details. Most of leg feathers visible.

VF-30 (Very Fine)
OBVERSE: Cheekbone worn about halfway. Headdress feathers show some details. Hair cord knot is distinct. Head-band shows only a little detail.
REVERSE: Little detail shows on breast and leg feathers. Top of wing and neck worn. Second layer of wing feathers shows.

FINE (*Moderate to heavy even wear. Entire design clear and bold.*)

F-12 (Fine)
OBVERSE: Cheekbone worn; all feathers worn with very little detail visible. Stars outlined with no details visible. Hair cord knot is worn but visible.
REVERSE: Wing worn, with only partial feathers at bottom visible. All lettering worn but visible.

Note: Coins of this type are seldom collected in grades lower than Fine. Mint marks are often very weakly struck.

EAGLES—CORONET HEAD
1838–1907

MINT STATE (*Absolutely no trace of wear.*)

MS-70 (Perfect Uncirculated)
A flawless coin exactly as it was minted, with no trace of wear or injury. Must have full mint luster and brilliance. Any unusual die or planchet traits must be described.

MS-65 (Choice Uncirculated)
No trace of wear; nearly as perfect as MS-70 except for some small blemishes. Has full mint luster and brilliance but may show slight discoloration. A few barely noticeable bag marks and surface abrasions may be present.

MS-60 (Uncirculated)
A strictly Uncirculated coin with no trace of wear, but with blemishes more obvious than for MS-65. Has full mint luster

OBVERSE

REVERSE

but may lack brilliance. Surface may be lightly marred by minor bag marks and abrasions. Check points for signs of wear: hair, coronet, wings.

ABOUT UNCIRCULATED (*Small trace of wear visible on highest points.*)

AU-55 (Choice About Uncirculated)
OBVERSE: There is a trace of wear on hair above eye and on coronet.
REVERSE: Trace of wear visible on wing tips. Three-quarters of the mint luster is still present.

AU-50 (About Uncirculated)
OBVERSE: There is a trace of wear on hair at ear and above eye, and on coronet.
REVERSE: Trace of wear visible on wing tips, below eye, and on claw. Half of the mint luster is still present.

EXTREMELY FINE (*Light wear on only the highest points.*)

EF-45 (Choice Extremely Fine)
OBVERSE: There is light wear on coronet, and on hair above ear, eye, forelocks, and top of head.
REVERSE: Light wear shows on edges and tips of wings, on neck, below eye, and on claws. Part of the mint luster is still present.

EF-40 (Extremely Fine)
OBVERSE: Light wear shows on coronet, hair, cheek, and stars. All major details sharp.
REVERSE: Light wear visible on wings, head, neck, and claws. Shield is well defined. Traces of mint luster will show.

VERY FINE (*Light to moderate even wear. All major features are sharp.*)

VF-30 (Choice Very Fine)
OBVERSE: There is light wear on coronet, hair, and stars, but most details are visible. There is a break on top line of coronet over two letters in LIBERTY. Cheek worn. LIBERTY bold.
REVERSE: Light wear visible on wings and head but some

details show. Vertical lines in shield complete but some are not separated; horizontal lines worn in center.

VF-20 (Very Fine)
OBVERSE: Hair worn but major details visible. Break on top line of coronet extends over at least three letters in LIBERTY. Cheek well worn. Stars worn but show most details. LIBERTY clear but shows wear.
REVERSE: About half of wing feathers are visible. Very little detail shows in head.

FINE (*Moderate to heavy even wear. Entire design clear and bold.*)

F-12 (Fine)
OBVERSE: Hair and cheekbone smooth. Top line of coronet worn. Some details show in stars. LIBERTY worn but visible.
REVERSE: Wings show very little detail. Head and one claw outlined only, with no details visible. Neck is almost smooth. Most of shield lines merge. (In the 1866 through 1907 group, the motto is worn but readable.)

Note: Coins of this type are seldom collected in grades lower than Fine.

EAGLES—INDIAN HEAD
1907–1933

MINT STATE (*Absolutely no trace of wear.*)

MS-70 (Perfect Uncirculated)
A flawless coin exactly as it was minted, with no trace of wear or injury. Must have full mint luster and brilliance. Any unusual die or planchet traits must be described.

MS-65 (Choice Uncirculated)
No trace of wear; nearly as perfect as MS-70 except for some small blemish. Has full mint luster and brilliance but may show some slight discoloration. A few minute bag marks and surface abrasions may be present.

MS-60 (Uncirculated)
A strictly Uncirculated coin with no trace of wear, but with blemishes more obvious than for MS-65. Has full mint luster but may lack brilliance. Surface may be lightly marred by minor bag marks and abrasions. Check points for signs of wear: above eye, cheek, wing.

ABOUT UNCIRCULATED (*Small trace of wear visible on highest points.*)

AU-55 (Choice About Uncirculated)
OBVERSE: There is a trace of wear above eye.
REVERSE: Trace of wear visible on wing. Three-quarters of the mint luster is still present.

AU-50 (About Uncirculated)
OBVERSE: There is a trace of wear on hair above eye and on forehead.
REVERSE: Trace of wear visible on wing. Half of the mint luster is still present.

EXTREMELY FINE (*Light wear on only the highest points.*)

EF-45 (Choice Extremely Fine)
OBVERSE: There is light wear on hair above eye and on forehead, and on cheekbone.
REVERSE: Light wear shows on wing and head. Part of the mint luster is still present.

EF-40 (Extremely Fine)
OBVERSE: Light wear shows on hair, cheekbone, and feathers.
REVERSE: Light wear visible on wing and head. Traces of mint luster will show.

VERY FINE (*Light to moderate even wear. All major features are sharp.*)

VF-30 (Choice Very Fine)
OBVERSE: There is light wear along forehead, but most detail shows. Moderate wear visible on cheekbone. Light wear shows where feathers meet headband.
REVERSE: Left wing shows more than half the details. Some details in head are visible.

VF-20 (Very Fine)
OBVERSE: About half the hair detail is visible. Moderate wear shows on cheekbone. Some feathers do not touch headband.
REVERSE: There is moderate wear on left wing, which shows only about one-quarter detail. Head almost smooth. All lettering bold.

FINE (*Moderate to heavy even wear. Entire design clear and bold.*)

OBVERSE

REVERSE

F-12 (Fine)
OBVERSE: Hair smooth with no details; cheekbone almost smooth. No feathers touch headband but most feather details visible.
REVERSE: Left wing top and head are worn smooth. Lettering worn but visible.

Note: Coins of this type are seldom collected in grades lower than Fine.

DOUBLE EAGLES—LIBERTY HEAD 1850–1907

MINT STATE (*Absolutely no trace of wear.*)

MS-70 (Perfect Uncirculated)
A flawless coin exactly as it was minted, with no trace of wear or injury. Must have full mint luster and brilliance. Any unusual die or planchet traits must be described.

MS-65 (Choice Uncirculated)
No trace of wear; nearly as perfect as MS-70 except for some small blemishes. Has full mint luster and brilliance but may show slight discoloration. A few minute bag marks and surface abrasions are usually present.

MS-60 (Uncirculated)
A strictly Uncirculated coin with no trace of wear, but with blemishes more obvious than for MS-65. Has full mint luster but may lack brilliance. Surface is usually lightly marred

OBVERSE

REVERSE

by minor bag marks and abrasions. Check points for signs of wear: hair, coronet, eagle's neck and wing, top of shield.

ABOUT UNCIRCULATED (*Small trace of wear visible on highest points.*)

AU-55 (Choice About Uncirculated)
OBVERSE: There is a trace of wear on hair.
REVERSE: Trace of wear visible on wing tips and neck. Three-quarters of the mint luster is still present.

AU-50 (About Uncirculated)
OBVERSE: There is a trace of wear on hair at top and over eye, and on coronet.
REVERSE: Trace of wear visible on wing tips, neck, and at top of shield. Half of the mint luster is still present.

EXTREMELY FINE (*Light wear on only the highest points.*)

EF-45 (Choice Extremely Fine)
OBVERSE: There is light wear on hair and coronet prongs.
REVERSE: Light wear shows on edges and tips of wings, on head and neck, and on horizontal shield lines. Part of the mint luster is still present.

EF-40 (Extremely Fine)
OBVERSE: Light wear shows on hair, coronet prongs, and cheek.
REVERSE: Light wear visible on wings, head, neck, horizontal shield lines, and tail. Traces of mint luster will show.

VERY FINE (*Light to moderate even wear. All major features are sharp.*)

VF-30 (Choice Very Fine)
OBVERSE: About one-quarter of hair detail below coronet visible; half the detail shows above coronet. Cheek and some coronet prongs worn. Stars show wear but all details visible.
REVERSE: Most of wing details visible. Top part of shield shows moderate wear. About half the details in tail visible.

VF-20 (Very Fine)
OBVERSE: Less than half the hair detail above coronet visible.

About half the coronet prongs are considerably worn. Stars are flat but show most details. LIBERTY shows wear but is very clear.
REVERSE: Some wing details visible. Shield shows very little detail at top. Tail is worn with very little detail.

FINE (*Moderate to heavy even wear. Entire design clear and bold.*)

F-12 (Fine)
OBVERSE: All hairlines are well worn with very little detail visible. One-quarter of details within coronet visible. Stars show little detail. LIBERTY readable.
REVERSE: Wings show very little detail. Head and neck smooth. Eye visible. Tail and top of shield smooth.

Note: Coins of this type are seldom collected in grades lower than Fine. The hair curl under the ear is sometimes weakly struck.

In the group between 1866 and 1876, the reverse motto is sometimes weakly struck.

Pieces made at the Carson City Mint are usually found weakly struck and heavily bag marked.

DOUBLE EAGLES— SAINT-GAUDENS 1907–1932

MINT STATE (*Absolutely no trace of wear.*)

MS-70 (Perfect Uncirculated)
A flawless coin exactly as it was minted, with no trace of wear or injury. Must have full mint luster and brilliance. Any unusual die or planchet traits must be described.

MS-65 (Choice Uncirculated)
No trace of wear; nearly as perfect as MS-70 except for some small blemishes. Has full mint luster and brilliance but may show slight discoloration. A few minute bag marks and surface abrasions are usually present.

MS-60 (Uncirculated)
A strictly Uncirculated coin with no trace of wear, but with

blemishes more obvious than for MS-65. Has full mint luster but may lack brilliance. Surface is usually lightly marred by minor bag marks and abrasions. Check points for signs of wear: forehead, breast, knee, nose, eagle's wings and breast.

ABOUT UNCIRCULATED (*Small trace of wear visible on highest points.*)

AU-55 (Choice About Uncirculated)
OBVERSE: There is a trace of wear on left breast and left knee.
REVERSE: Trace of wear visible on high point of wing. Three-quarters of the mint luster is still present.

AU-50 (About Uncirculated)
OBVERSE: There is a trace of wear on nose, breast, and knee.
REVERSE: Trace of wear visible on wings. Half of the mint luster is still present.

EXTREMELY FINE (*Light wear on only the highest points.*)

EF-45 (Choice Extremely Fine)
OBVERSE: There is light wear on forehead, nose, breast, and knee.
REVERSE: Light wear shows on wings and breast, but all feathers are bold. Part of the mint luster is still present.

EF-40 (Extremely Fine)
OBVERSE: Light wear shows on forehead, nose, breast, knee, and just below left knee. Drapery lines on chest visible.
REVERSE: Light wear visible on wings and breast but all feathers bold. Traces of mint luster will show.

VERY FINE (*Light to moderate even wear. All major features are sharp.*)

VF-30 (Choice Very Fine)
OBVERSE: There is light wear on all features, extending above and below left knee and along part of right leg. Some of garment lines on chest are visible.
REVERSE: Light wear visible on left wing and breast; feathers show but some are weak.

OBVERSE

REVERSE

VF-20 (Very Fine)
OBVERSE: Forehead moderately worn. Contours of breast worn. Only a few garment lines on chest are visible. Entire right leg shows moderate wear.
REVERSE: Half of feathers are visible in wings and breast.

FINE (*Moderate to heavy even wear. Entire design clear and bold.*)

F-12 (Fine)
OBVERSE: Forehead and garment smooth; breasts flat. Both legs worn with right bottom missing.
REVERSE: Less than half the wing details are visible. Only a little breast detail is visible.

Note: Coins of this type are seldom found in grades lower than Fine.

COLONIAL COINS, PATTERNS, AND TOKENS

HISTORY

The history of our coinage begins not with the first federal issues but with the coin used earlier by colonists. This period in American coin use, from the exploration of Florida and the first Virginia settlements up to 1792, spans 200 years and is considered one of the most fascinating specialties for collectors. It is rich in types, designs, and methods of production. While a great deal of colonial coinage is rare, some fall into the moderate price range. Here are historical objects of undisputed significance, purchasable in some cases for less than the cost of key-date modern coins. The celebrated Rosa Americana, circulated before George Washington was born, can be had in good condition for less than $100. Even some of the 17th-century "elephant tokens" sell for under $100, though this series also includes rarities of high price. The belief that colonial coinage is only for the wealthy just isn't so.

The story of this nation's beginnings is probably better told by its early money than by any other antiquities. Pilgrim settlers are often pictured as hunters and trappers living off the land. This is partly true, but even in the 1600s there were cities with shops and a real need existed for coinage. When nothing better was available the old barter system was resorted to, as used in ancient times, with goods traded for other goods of similar value. In Massachusetts, iron nails were accepted as legal tender, as well as Indian wampum (shells strung together on cords, each having a set value). As early as the 1640s, twenty years after the *Mayflower,* serious thought was given by the Bay Colony to striking its own money. In 1652 the Massachusetts General Court authorized experimental efforts in this direction, the first attempts being no more than rough metal discs stamped with small symbols. Compared to Europe's elaborate coinage they were meager but proved that this country had the ability to produce a medium of exchange. These were followed by improved domestic efforts as well as importation of coins from abroad, struck expressly for colonial use. These include the Lord Baltimore coins of Maryland and the Colonial Plantation token. By the 17th century's close, a variety of coins and pseudocoins circulated. Some were private or merchant tokens of British or Dutch manufacture. These were largely speculative issues brought to this country in large quantities by persons hoping to acquire vast land parcels. There was little confidence in the integrity of such coinage but it was nevertheless accepted on the basis of weight.

Coins of both England and Spain, brought over by immigrants and traders, circulated pretty freely. Other foreign coins were also met with. Rather than being changed at face value they were, in the early years, valued at metal content, every merchant having a scale to weigh coins brought to him. Spain's dollar or "piece of eight" became the most familiar coin in the colonies, replaced thereafter by the coins of Great Britain. By the time of the Revolution, probably as many as 90% of the coins in American circulation were of British mintage.

Because colonial coins and tokens were not issued by a central government and were produced under challenging conditions, standardization cannot be expected. Sizes, denominations, and quality of workmanship all vary, sometimes to an extreme degree. Included are crude pieces hardly recognizable as coins and works of considerable artistic merit. Some were not milled but hammered, struck by hammering the dies into metal blanks just as the Romans and Greeks made their coins 2,000 years ago. They also vary in scarcity. The collector should not be duped into paying inflated prices for coins merely on the grounds of their being pre-Revolutionary. This in itself is no assurance of rarity. Each issue has its own established value, as shown in the listings section of this book. Allowance must be made for the condition of hammered pieces (whose shape will be somewhat irregular) and for specimens of great rarity, as these are almost impossible to find in the kind of condition one would expect of later coins. On the whole, condition standards are less rigid for colonial than federal issues. On the other hand, the buyer should not accept badly damaged examples in the belief that nothing better can be found.

The most extensively circulated—and faithfully trusted—coin of early colonial America was the Spanish silver dollar or "piece of eight." Introduced to this country by the Spanish explorers and later imported in abundance by traders, it had a value of eight *reals,* each real or "bit" being worth 12½ cents. Thus, the quarter or 25-cent piece came to be known as "two bits."

"Two bits"

"Four bits"

THE SPANISH MILLED DOLLAR
The "Piece of Eight"

The following pages contain descriptions and price valuations for most types of monies used in the American colonies, excluding foreign coins intended to serve currency needs abroad. Most can only be classed as tokens, as they either had no face value or were struck without government sanction. These include merchant pieces and other speculative issues. However, the colonists, being ever-resourceful, attempted from time to time to strike semiofficial or official coinage, and these will be found listed as well. Colonial coinage on the whole is not handsome. It was generally produced under conditions inferior to that of government-issued money, often designed and struck by persons who had little or no prior experience in such work. It is, nevertheless, of great interest from both a numismatic and historical point of view and much of it is extremely rare. As a general rule, the collector should be wary of counterfeits and reproductions, as the majority of these pieces have at one time or other been copied, either as legitimate souvenirs or fraudulently.

SOMMER ISLANDS (BERMUDA)

This so-called "hog money" is thought to be the first coinage of the American colonies. A hog is pictured on one side and a sailing vessel on the other. The workmanship is English. Hogs were not native to the islands but introduced around 1515 by the Spaniard Juan Bermudez, from whom Bermuda takes its name. They apparently increased and multiplied vastly within the next hundred years, serving as an important article of food for the inhabitants. The suggestion that the coins were intended to represent the market value of a hog, just as early Greek coins were sometimes stamped with a likeness of an animal whose price they equaled, is no longer given serious consideration. It was used merely as an emblem. These coins are of lightly silvered brass, inscribed SOMMER ISLANDS. The edges are, as to be expected, irregular, having been produced by the hammering technique rather than milling.

SHILLING

TYPE OF COIN	ABP	G-4 GOOD	EF-40 EX. FINE
☐ Shilling			RARE

SIXPENCE

TYPE OF COIN	ABP	G-4 GOOD	EF-40 EX. FINE
☐ Twopence			RARE
☐ Threepence			RARE
☐ Sixpence			RARE

MASSACHUSETTS–NEW ENGLAND COINAGE

This is the earliest coinage struck on the North American continent. This crude coinage may not be appealing aesthetically but its historical significance is as great, or greater, than any coins subsequently issued in this country. It was produced in limited quantities for local circulation in the Boston area and is extremely rare. When the decision was reached to attempt a native currency, the Massachusetts General Court appointed John Hull "mintmaster." The "mint" was an iron works operated by Joseph Jenks at Saugus, just north of Boston. These coins were made of silver by the ancient process of hammering—beating the designs into them by holding the die against the metal blank and striking it with a mallet. There was, in fact, no design at all. The coins were issued in three denominations—threepence, sixpence, and twelvepence (shilling)—and each carried the letters NE on one side and the value in Roman numerals on the other, most of the surface being blank. Variations in size, shape, and placement of the markings are common. They date to 1652, but no date appears upon them.

NE SHILLING

NE SIXPENCE

NE THREEPENCE

TYPE OF COIN	ABP	G-4 GOOD	EF-40 EX. FINE
☐ NE Shilling			RARE
☐ NE Threepence (less than 3 known)			EXTREMELY RARE
☐ NE Sixpence (less than 8 known)			EXTREMELY RARE

WILLOW TREE COINS

After about four months of circulation of the Massachusetts–New England coinage, it was decided they were unsatisfactory. The legend and numeral of value were so simplistic that anyone possessing smith's tools could reproduce them. There was the further problem—not a new one, as it was faced by English Mints in the Middle Ages—that the large expanses of unstamped metal invited "clipping," a practice in which unscrupulous persons trimmed down the edges and collected quantities of silver while still passing the coins at face value. It was impossible to improve the method of manufacture, there being no milling machines available. But the designs could be improved by the use of more fully engraved dies. This was accomplished with the so-called Willow Tree coinage, introduced in 1653. On the obverse appears a very abstract rendition of a willow tree, surrounded by the place name, with the date and value designation on the reverse (III stood for threepence, VI for sixpence, and XII for shilling). Although struck at odd moments from 1653–60 (there was no regular or continuous production), all specimens are dated 1652.

SHILLING   SIXPENCE

THREEPENCE

TYPE OF COIN	ABP	G-4 GOOD	EF-40 EX. FINE
☐ Willow Tree Shilling			RARE
☐ Willow Tree Threepence		EXTREMELY RARE	
☐ Willow Tree Sixpence			RARE

OAK TREE COINS

Successors to the Willow Tree coins, Oak Tree coins were likewise of Massachusetts origin and, like them, showed a tree on the obverse with the date and numeral of value on the reverse. They were introduced in 1660, the year of the English Restoration (the return of the Stuarts to the throne), an event of no small significance numismatically. While the previous regime, the Protectorate of Oliver Cromwell, was composed of politicians who supported the pilgrim cause, there was genuine fear that the new king—Charles II—might deal harshly with the colonists for being so bold as to strike coins. They attempted to camouflage this activity by retaining the old date, 1652, during the eight years that Oak Tree coins were struck; and, in fact, it remained unaltered for the sixteen years of their successors, Pine Tree coins. In terms of design, these Oak Tree coins were an improvement on their predecessors, being much sharper and bolder. Whether this can be attributed to more deeply engraved dies, more careful hammering, or (a usually overlooked possibility) better annealing or heating of the blanks, is uncertain. The mintmaster was still the same: John Hull. But this much is sure: the Oak Tree coins were turned out in far larger quantities than previous Massachusetts coins.

SHILLING

SIXPENCE   THREEPENCE

TYPE OF COIN	ABP	G-4 GOOD	F-12 FINE	EF-40 EX. FINE
☐ Shilling	390.00	650.00	3000.00	RARE
☐ Twopence	375.00	625.00	2500.00	RARE
☐ Threepence	375.00	625.00	2500.00	RARE
☐ Sixpence	450.00	750.00	3500.00	RARE

PINE TREE COINS

The final version of the Bay Colony "tree" coin, the Pine Tree coin featured a much clearer, if not more botanically accurate, portrait of a tree. Though struck in the same three denominations as the earlier types, there is a Large Planchet and Small Planchet version of the shilling, the Large being slightly rare. Both are of the same weight; the metal was simply hammered thinner on the Large Planchet. It had been demonstrated, by the use of large planchets for the Willow and Oak Tree shillings, that the coin did not stand up well to handling and could be rendered sturdier by reducing its size and thereby increasing the thickness. It was also possible to strike the design more deeply with a thicker planchet. All coins from this series are dated 1652. They were actually struck from 1667–82, during the reign of Britain's Charles II. After 1682 the issuing of coinage was discontinued by the Bay Colony. Many varieties exist in this series.

SHILLING, Large Planchet   SHILLING, Small Planchet

SIXPENCE   THREEPENCE

TYPE OF COIN	ABP	G-4 GOOD	F-12 FINE	EF-40 EX. FINE
☐ Pine Tree Shilling, Small Planchet				
	330.00	550.00	1800.00	RARE
☐ Pine Tree Shilling, Large Planchet				
	390.00	650.00	2500.00	RARE
☐ Pine Tree Threepence	255.00	425.00	1500.00	RARE
☐ Pine Tree Sixpence	270.00	450.00	2000.00	RARE

MARYLAND

Maryland was the second colony, next to Massachusetts, to have coinage of its own. The origins of these coins bear little relation to those of the Bay Colony. While the Massachusetts pieces had been natively designed and struck, Maryland's coins were entirely a foreign product. They date from 1658. At this time Maryland was very sparsely inhabited, its only residents being small colonies of English immigrants, and could not have suffered too seriously from a shortage of coinage. Though not strictly classified as private issues they might well merit that designation. Maryland's first coins were the brainchild of Cecil Calvert, Lord Baltimore (for whom the colony's chief city was named). Calvert did not, as popularly supposed, "own Maryland." He did, however, possess large areas of its land and had the title of Lord Proprietor of Maryland. As an English lord with typical lordly pride, Calvert looked with disdain upon the prospect of Englishmen—his subjects, technically—trading with beads or iron or other objects of barter. So he ordered a batch of English-quality coins to be struck in Britain for use in the colony. They comprised a shilling, sixpence, fourpence or groat, and a penny. The first three were of silver, following the British tradition, the penny in copper. As a result of their production in an established, well-equipped Mint, these coins are considerably more professional in appearance than those of Massachusetts. Lord Calvert placed his own portrait upon them. There was no need to fear censure from the king for this brazen act, as the English Civil War had already swept the king (Charles I) from his throne and Britain was not again to be ruled by a king until 1660. The reverses of the silver pieces carry Calvert's heraldic insignia with the value in Roman numerals. The penny's obverse shows a regal crown surmounted by staffs and banners. There is no numeral of value on the penny but instead the word "denarium," the name of an ancient Roman coin from which the British penny evolved. (To this day the symbol for "penny" in Britain is the letter "d," meaning denarium. The cent sign, ¢, is never used.) Lord Calvert's portrait is a shoulder-length bust without crown, wreath of laurel, or other symbol of rulership. The penny is the scarcest of the denominations, as this is believed to have been a pattern only, not actually placed in use.

FOURPENCE   SHILLING

TYPE OF COIN	ABP	G-4 GOOD	EF-40 EX. FINE
☐ Maryland Shilling	1175.00	1950.00	RARE
☐ Maryland Fourpence	1175.00	1950.00	RARE
☐ Maryland Sixpence	960.00	1600.00	RARE
☐ Maryland Denarium (Penny)		EXTREMELY RARE	

MARK NEWBY OR ST. PATRICK HALFPENCE

The coinage shortage in the early colonies, and the voraciousness with which anything resembling coinage was seized upon as a medium of exchange, is clearly demonstrated by the Newby or St. Patrick halfpence. The coins are really misnamed, as they existed not only in halfpence but farthing denomination (in the British currency system, a farthing or "fourthling" was equal to one-quarter of a penny).

Mark Newby was neither an explorer nor royal governor but apparently a private Irish citizen who came from Dublin and settled in New Jersey in the year 1681. He brought with him a quantity of tokens—they could only very charitably be called coins—which are thought to have been struck at

Dublin about eight years earlier. These were coppers. On the obverse they depict a crowned king kneeling and playing a harp, almost certainly intended as the biblical King David, who is often represented in art as a harpist. St. Patrick, the legendary and patron saint of Ireland, appears on the reverse. On the halfpence he holds a crozier and cross (often mistaken for a clover) while giving benediction to a worshiper; on the farthing he is shown in a similar pose, driving the snakes out of Ireland, one of the many accomplishments with which this saint is credited. The obverse legend is FLOREAT REX, which can be translated as "Prosperity to the King." These are not at all bad-looking pieces and they feature an intriguing detail: The large crown on the obverse was inlaid in brass, to contrast in color with the copper and give the appearance of being golden. It is, however, sometimes lacking. The origin of this St. Patrick money is not clearly known. The possibility that it was struck for circulation in America seems very remote, as (a) there is no record of supportive legislation on either side of the Atlantic, and (b) the coins were apparently not brought to this country until long after striking, which hardly would have been the case had they been designed for use here. In any event, the General Assembly of the New Jersey Province authorized their use as legal tender in May 1682, and for some while thereafter they served as the common currency of New Jersey. The most logical conclusion to be drawn is that Newby was a commercial trader who sought to profit from the shortage of coinage in America, and that he settled in New Jersey because this area was virtually without money of any kind. If so, he would not have been the only colonist to do this. Silver and gold patterns of the farthing were struck, of which the silver is very rare and the gold unique. There may have been similar patterns of the halfpenny, but they have not been discovered. In their normal metal—copper—neither is a coin of extreme scarcity.

ST. PATRICK HALFPENCE   ST. PATRICK FARTHING

TYPE OF COIN	ABP	G-4 GOOD	EF-40 EX. FINE
☐ St. Patrick Halfpence	300.00	500.00	RARE
☐ St. Patrick Farthing (Brass Insert on Obverse)			
	240.00	400.00	RARE
☐ St. Patrick Farthing (Without Brass Insert)			
	240.00	400.00	RARE
☐ St. Patrick Farthing (Silver Pattern)	990.00	1650.00	RARE
☐ St. Patrick Farthing (Gold Pattern)			RARE

COLONIAL PLANTATION TOKEN

The so-called Plantation token was the first coinage authorized for use in the American colonies by the British government. Its history is of great interest. Throughout the middle 17th century it was well known in England that the American provinces, or "plantations" as they were called abroad (largely by persons unaware of the extent of population), suffered from a shortage of coinage. In 1688 an Englishman named John Holt petitioned the king (James II) for a patent or franchise for the striking of coinage for distribution in the colonies. In Britain at this time the system of "patents of exclusivity" was commonplace. Printers would pay a fee to have the exclusive right on putting out Bibles; merchants paid for a franchise to sell a particular product without fear of competition. The fee, which was considerable, had to be paid each year while the franchise was in force. Holt was convinced that the supply of coinage to America would be a very profitable endeavor. The government approved his request for a franchise and shortly thereafter he began to strike his coins, better called tokens. Large in size, they were made of tin and had the face value of one-quarter of a Spanish real or "piece of eight," about fourpence. On their obverse they pictured an equestrian likeness of James II, regal-looking in this design but soon to be driven out of the country into exile. It is important to note that they were not intended for use in any special region but could be exchanged anywhere in the provinces; thus, they carry no place name. The original dies were preserved and restrikes made from them in the late 1820s; their appearance is quite similar to the original and could well be a cause of confusion to beginners. A very rare variety exists, in which the numeral "4" in the value legend on the reverse is positioned vertically instead of horizontally.

PLANTATION TOKEN

TYPE OF COIN	ABP	G-4 GOOD	F-12 FINE	EF-40 EX. FINE	MS-60 UNC.
☐ James II Plantation Token	180.00	300.00	750.00	1500.00	RARE

Restrikes exist that are worth slightly less.

☐ James II Plantation Token, Vertical "4"					RARE

ELEPHANT TOKEN

These extremely popular, intriguing pieces have been the subject of much study and debate. Their origins are only sketchily known. There are three specific types: London token, Carolina token, and New England token. All have the same obverse, a portrait of an elephant without legend or inscription of any kind. These pieces are coppers and were modeled as halfpennies, though they carry no indication of value. The extent to which they circulated in the American colonies is not established. Based on what little information is available, their history may be pieced together as follows.

First in the series was the London token, which on some specimens carries the wording GOD PRESERVE LONDON on the reverse, on others merely LONDON, accompanying a heraldic shield. The belief is that they were struck in 1664 when the population of that city was being decimated by an outbreak of bubonic plague, which apparently is the danger from which preservation was sought. So far this theory makes some historical sense, though it fails to explain the selection of an elephant as the obverse symbol. Could it be that this was a reference to "stamping out" the plague, and that the elephant, as the largest of creatures, would be best equipped to do so? That elephants were well known in London in the 1660s is well established. There were no zoos for the display of wild beasts but elephants and tigers (both from India) were kept in enclosed dungeons in the Tower of London for the amusement of visitors. Natural history drawing was still in an archaic state at that time, which explains why the elephant on Elephant tokens looks rather strange. For a long while thereafter there appears to have been no effort to revive the Elephant token, perhaps because the plague subsided. Then in 1694 it reappeared, in an edition bearing two different reverses: GOD PRESERVE CAROLINA AND THE LORD'S PROPRIETORS and GOD PRESERVE NEW ENGLAND. Just how these pieces came to be, what their intent was, and how they were circulated is totally unknown. It may be presumed that GOD PRESERVE was used merely in the sense of "God Bless," after the fashion of the slogan "God Save the King," not as implication that either Carolina or New England suffered from any specific difficulty.

There is little doubt, based on physical evidence, that they were struck in England, as these tokens are handsomely milled (not hammered) and it is doubtful that such work could have been accomplished in the colonies. It has been said that the London variety was intended for circulation in Tangier, but even if that were so, there is no evidence of it being an official issue. The Carolina and New England pieces could have been entirely speculative. Their distribution may have been local (in England) with no intention of exporting or using them for actual currency in the colonies. This seems the logical answer, especially in view of the extremely small quantities struck. Of the London token there were considerably larger numbers struck, but to classify this as a piece designed for colonial use seems very presumptive. Some specimens undoubtedly reached the colonies at an early date but, if they did, it was only accidentally, in the baggage or pockets of immigrants or traders, just as almost everything else made abroad found its way across the Atlantic.

There are a number of types and varieties. The London token exists in both thin and thick planchet; with interlacing in the central portion of the shield; with sword in the second quarter of the shield (transposed from the first, where it is commonly found); and with the inscription LONDON rather than GOD PRESERVE LONDON. Of these, the transposed sword is the rarest. The chief variety of the Carolina issue is the alteration from PROPRIETERS to the more correct spelling, PROPRIETORS, accomplished not by the introduction of a fresh die but re-engraving the original. If closely inspected, the letter "E," or what remains of it, can be observed.

1694 NEW ENGLAND

1694 PROPRIETORS

1694 PROPRIETERS

1694 GOD PRESERVE LONDON

1694 GOD PRESERVE LONDON (SWORDS)

1694 LONDON

TYPE OF COIN	ABP	G-4 GOOD	EF-40 EX. FINE
☐ 1694 GOD PRESERVE LONDON (thin)	210.00	350.00	RARE
☐ 1694 GOD PRESERVE LONDON (thick)	150.00	250.00	RARE
☐ 1694 GOD PRESERVE LONDON (diag.)	255.00	425.00	RARE
☐ 1694 GOD PRESERVE LONDON (swords)		EXTREMELY RARE	
☐ 1694 LONDON	360.00	600.00	RARE
☐ 1694 NEW ENGLAND			RARE
☐ 1694 PROPRIETORS (overstrike)			RARE
☐ 1694 PROPRIETERS		EXTREMELY RARE	

NEW YORKE TOKEN

The New York colony (referring to the state, not the city) had no coinage of its own in the 17th century. Though settled somewhat later than Massachusetts, New York came close to equaling it in population by the century's close, and the volume of business transacted was at least comparable. It is curious that tiny Maryland and equally tiny New Jersey had coins during the 17th century while New York did not. The closest it came to having one was the New Yorke token, but this can hardly be classed with the Massachusetts, Maryland, or even the New Jersey coinage, as there is no evidence it received official sanction. It was very likely nothing more than a merchant token. This is a smallish piece, roughly equal to our nickel, of which some were struck in brass and others in pewter. On the obverse it carries a rather scrawny eagle with an allegorical design (Cupid is one of the figures) on the reverse. The obverse legend reads NEW YORKE IN AMERICA. Of its origins practically nothing is known. The belief that this coin was struck in Holland is founded more upon assumption, because of New York's extensive Dutch population, than evidence. Its date has been the subject of controversy. The spelling of New York as "New Yorke" suggests a dating in the 17th century, but as this spelling lingered on into the 18th century it is quite possible that the coin or token is not as old as commonly presumed. It is very likely that even in the second quarter of the 18th century a European designing such a piece would have used the "New Yorke" spelling, even if it was no longer current in America. The likelihood that the New Yorke token was struck in Manhattan from dies prepared in Holland is a romantic but not convincing theory.

UNDATED BRASS

TYPE OF COIN	ABP	G-4 GOOD	EF-40 EX. FINE
☐ New Yorke Token, No Date: Brass			RARE
☐ New Yorke Token, No Date: Tin (pewter)			RARE

GLOUCESTER TOKEN

Very few specimens exist of this early amateur token and information about it is likewise scanty. It is apparently the first private token struck on American soil. The composition is brass, leading to the assumption that it might have been a pattern for a silver shilling that was never produced. Whether the brass pieces were intended to circulate is highly doubtful. The Gloucester token is thought to have been the work of Richard Dawson of Gloucester, Virginia. On one side appears a five-pointed star, with a building of modest design on the other. Known specimens are so thoroughly worn that the inscription surrounding this building is unreadable. The best guess is that it was intended to represent the Gloucester County Courthouse or some other public structure. It does not appear to be a place of worship. The Gloucester token dates to 1714.

SHILLING BRASS

TYPE OF COIN	ABP	G-4 GOOD	EF-40 EX. FINE
☐ Gloucester Shilling (brass)			EXTREMELY RARE

ROSA AMERICANA

These extremely handsome coins, thoroughly European in appearance and workmanship, are often referred to as Wood tokens—not from being made of wood (their composition is copper, zinc, and silver) but from William Wood, the Englishman who originated them. Nearly forty years before their appearance, John Holt, another Englishman, had gained a patent from the then-king, James II, to strike coinage for circulation in the American colonies. Upon expiration of the Holt patent or franchise there had been little enthusiasm for its renewal, as Holt's coins—the so-called Plantation tokens—had not proved very successful. As time passed and the population of such cities as Boston, New York, and Philadelphia increased, the prospects for coinage seemed to brighten. William Wood, of whom there is not very much known, obtained a franchise from George I to supply coinage to America, as well as to Ireland. This resulted in the Rosa Americana tokens. These were struck in small denominations only, from a halfpence to twopence. The earliest, which apparently were struck in 1722, carried no date. Later a date was added and these pieces saw fairly large production in the years 1722, 1723, and 1724. After an interval of nearly ten years in which none were produced, a Rosa Americana pattern proof was struck off in 1733. As best as can be ascertained, the Wood patent had fallen into other hands, as Wood died in 1730. His successors probably toyed with the idea of reinstituting the Rosa Americana coins but never got beyond the stage of this single proof.

To judge by the relative commonness of the coin (except for certain varieties, which are rare), they must have been turned out at least in the hundreds and possibly the thousands. The obverses are all alike, picturing George I in profile facing the viewer's right (it was switched to the left on the 1733 trial proof). This is not the king against whom America went to war in the Revolution but the first English monarch of that name, a German who could speak but a few words of English. Surrounding the portrait is, generally, a legend giving the names of the countries over which the king ruled: Great Britain, France, and Hibernia (Ireland). The claim that he ruled France was a purely speculative one, a reference to the victories of Marlborough over Louis XIV's armies, which had ended France's ambition to capture England but in no way gave England rulership over that nation. The reverse shows the rose, sometimes alone, sometimes surmounted by a crown. There is one variation (on the 1724 penny) where the rose is not pictured symbolically but as an actual flower growing up from the ground. These pieces gain their name from the reverse inscription, not present on all, reading ROSA AMERICANA UTILE DULCI, or, roughly, "American Rose, utility and pleasure." The rose had been a symbol of the Tudor kings and queens well before colonization of America. In their extent and variety the Rosa Americana coins are unmatched by any others intended for circulation in America. The opinion held of them today was not shared by colonists, however, who protested that the coins were short-weighted and refused to accept them.

1722 HALFPENNY "DEI GRATIA REX"   1723 PENNY

TYPE OF COIN	ABP	G-4 GOOD	F-12 FINE	EF-40 EX. FINE
☐ Twopence, No Date	105.00	175.00	450.00	1500.00
☐ Twopence, No Date, Motto Sans Label		EXTREMELY RARE		
☐ 1722 Halfpenny, D. G. REX	105.00	175.00	235.00	1400.00
☐ 1722 Halfpenny, DEI GRATIA REX				
	105.00	150.00	235.00	1400.00
☐ 1722 Halfpenny, VTILE DVLCI	290.00	495.00	2200.00	RARE
☐ 1722 Twopence, Period after REX				
	70.00	120.00	350.00	2000.00
☐ 1722 Penny, UTILE DVLCI	60.00	100.00	350.00	2000.00
☐ 1722 Penny, VTILE DVLCI	75.00	125.00	250.00	1600.00
☐ 1722 Penny, GEORGIVS		EXTREMELY RARE		
☐ 1722 Twopence, No Period after REX				
	105.00	175.00	350.00	1400.00
☐ 1723 Twopence	65.00	110.00	300.00	1400.00
☐ 1723 Halfpenny	60.00	100.00	135.00	1200.00
☐ 1723 Halfpenny, Rose Without Crown		EXTREMELY RARE		
☐ 1723 Penny	70.00	120.00	250.00	1100.00

TYPE OF COIN	ABP	G-4 GOOD	F-12 FINE	EF-40 EX. FINE
☐ 1724 Penny (Pattern)			EXTREMELY RARE	
☐ 1724 Penny, No Date, ROSA: SINE: SPINA			EXTREMELY RARE	
☐ 1724 Twopence (Pattern)			EXTREMELY RARE	
☐ 1733 Twopence (Pattern Proof)			EXTREMELY RARE	

WOOD'S COINAGE OR HIBERNIA

These coins, more properly called tokens, were issued under the patent granted to William Wood to strike coinage for America and Ireland (*see* Rosa Americana). *Hibernia* was the Latin name for Ireland. They are included here because these pieces proved unpopular in Ireland—just as did the Rosa Americanas in America—and Wood sought to recover his investment by circulating them in America. History does not record their fate on this side of the Atlantic but it is doubtful that they received a warm reception. They were struck in such enormous numbers, thanks to excessive overconfidence, that most types can be had inexpensively. George I appears on the obverse. There are two reverse types, both picturing a seated female with a harp representing Hibernia, the Irish equivalent of Britannia. There is no need to speculate on the reason for Type I being changed: the figure is portrayed in so ungainly a manner as to appear comical. Type II is only a slight improvement.

1723 OVER 22 HALFPENNY

1723 HALFPENNY

TYPE OF COIN	ABP	G-4 GOOD	F-12 FINE	EF-40 EX. FINE
☐ 1722 Farthing, D.G. REX	95.00	160.00	450.00	3800.00
☐ 1722 Halfpenny, Harp Facing Left	48.00	80.00	150.00	800.00

TYPE OF COIN	ABP	G-4 GOOD	F-12 FINE	EF-40 EX. FINE
☐ 1722 Halfpenny, Harp Facing Right				
	45.00	75.00	150.00	725.00
☐ 1722 Halfpenny, D.G. REX			EXTREMELY RARE	
☐ 1723 Halfpenny	30.00	50.00	150.00	600.00
☐ 1723 Over 22 Halfpenny	45.00	75.00	150.00	775.00
☐ 1723 Halfpenny, Silver (Pattern)			EXTREMELY RARE	
☐ 1723 Farthing, Silver (Pattern)	900.00	1500.00	3000.00	RARE
☐ 1723 Farthing, DEI, GRATIA REX				
	48.00	80.00	125.00	600.00
☐ 1723 Farthing, D.G. REX	50.00	85.00	175.00	700.00
☐ 1724 Halfpenny	48.00	80.00	150.00	1000.00
☐ 1724 Farthing	48.00	80.00	175.00	1400.00

HIGLEY COINAGE

The Higley or Granby tokens were entirely private issues. Had they been imported for circulation from abroad they might be of modest interest at best but these are, in fact, *the first privately produced tokens struck on American soil that actually reached circulation.* All are extremely rare. Dr. Samuel Higley, a Connecticut resident and graduate of Yale University, deplored the coinage shortage in his state and took matters into his own hands. Unsupported by legislation and unsponsored by government funds, Higley engraved his own dies and for coin metal used copper from a mine he owned located near Granby, Connecticut (hence the alternate title of these pieces). Considering their amateur origin, the designs and workmanship are of higher quality than might be expected. On the obverse appears a deer surrounded by inscription. There are two reverse types, one featuring a trio of small hammers, the other a broad-bladed cleaver. As originally issued in 1737 they carried the value of threepence, stated on the obverse legend. Though well received at first, protest was later raised by persons skeptical of their copper content. This inspired the ever-resourceful Higley to add the inscription, I AM GOOD COPPER. When this failed to silence critics, who persisted in their belief that the face value was too high and that Higley was gaining a profit from circulating them, the statement of value was replaced by the not-too-subtle suggestion to VALUE ME AS YOU PLEASE. Even so, the Roman numeral III remained. This placed them in the category of bartering pieces that could be exchanged on the basis of weight. We are told that the local supply was numerous, but this is hardly reflected by their present rarity. It can only be assumed that many individuals hoarded the Higley tokens and melted them. The inscription on the second reverse type (the cleaver) states I CUT MY WAY THROUGH. The "I" is sometimes stated to be a "J," but in fact was intended merely to represent an ornamental "I" with loop at the base.

The collector is cautioned that reproductions of the Higley tokens exist, made by electrotyping and casting, and are of sufficient quality to confuse an inexperienced buyer.

1737 THREEPENCE "CONNECTICVT"

1737 VALUE.ME.AS.YOU.PLEASE
I.AM.GOOD.COPPER

1737 VALUE.ME.AS.YOU.PLEASE
I.CUT.MY.WAY.THROUGH

TYPE OF COIN	ABP	G-4 GOOD	EF-40 EX. FINE
☐ 1737 THE VALUE OF THREEPENCE (3 hammers, CONNECTICVT)			RARE
☐ 1737 THE VALUE OF THREEPENCE (3 hammers, I AM GOOD COPPER)			RARE
☐ 1737 VALUE ME AS YOU PLEASE (3 hammers, I AM GOOD COPPER)			RARE
☐ 1737 VALUE ME AS YOU PLEASE (3 hammers, I AM GOOD COPPER)			EXTREMELY RARE

TYPE OF COIN	ABP	G-4	EF-40
		GOOD	EX. FINE

☐ 1737 VALUE ME AS YOU PLEASE
  (broad axe, I CUT MY WAY THROUGH) — — — RARE
☐ 1739 VALUE ME AS YOU PLEASE
  (broad axe, I CUT MY WAY THROUGH) — — — RARE

VOCE POPULI COINAGE

These impressive pieces are exclusively private issues and not of American origin. They were struck in Dublin, Ireland, in 1760, by a firm whose chief occupation was the making of buttons for military uniforms. Its proprietor was named Roche. The 17th and 18th centuries both witnessed an inordinate quantity of private tokens and pseudomoney struck in Ireland, much of which reached America. It could all logically be included within the realm of Americana but the Voce Populi tokens have become special favorites of collectors, probably on strength of design more than anything else. The obverse features a classical-style portrait profile crowned with laurel wreath. It has traditionally been assumed to be George III but no actual evidence exists to support this belief. The inscription makes no reference to the king but merely carries the words VOCE POPULI, or "Voice of the People." Various interpretations (too lengthy to be discussed here) could be placed upon the use of this common slogan. The reverse pictures a female with harp, a standard Irish symbol, and the word HIBERNIA. This was the Latin name for Ireland. The date is shown in the exergue beneath the figure. It should always be 1760; however, on one occasion a defective die was used for the halfpenny, causing it to read 1700. That the token was actually struck in 1700 can easily be refuted on stylistic as well as other evidence. There is also a variety in which the inscription reads VOOE POPULI.

1760 "VOCE POPULI" HALFPENNY

1760 "VOCE POPULI" FARTHING

TYPE OF COIN	ABP	G-4 GOOD	EF-40 EX. FINE
☐ 1700 Halfpenny (die-cutter's error)		EXTREMELY RARE	
☐ 1760 Halfpenny	60.00	100.00	700.00
☐ 1760 Halfpenny, P Beneath Bust	90.00	150.00	2000.00
☐ 1760 Halfpenny, P Beside Face	150.00	250.00	1800.00
☐ 1760 Halfpenny, VOOE POPULI (die-cutter's error)	150.00	250.00	1000.00
☐ 1760 Farthing	240.00	400.00	3800.00
☐ 1760 Farthing, Small Lettering		RARE	

PITT TOKENS

William Pitt, for whom Pittsburgh is named, is associated with these tokens only to the extent that his portrait appears on them. He apparently was connected in no way with their issuance. Two denominations were struck, or rather pieces in the *sizes* of two denominations (as they bear no value markings): farthing and halfpenny. They carry the date 1766. Just what their purpose was is not clear. The suggestion has been put forward that they were issued in the nature of medals as an honor to Pitt, who, for his stand against the British stamp tax, was held in high regard by agitators for self-government. The long-held popular belief that Pitt tokens were designed by Paul Revere would probably be best relegated to the ranks of numismatic folklore until some firm evidence is discovered. The similarly long-held belief that the engraver was Smithers of Philadelphia is more acceptable. The obverse has Pitt's likeness in profile with the legend NO STAMPS: THE RESTORE OF COMMERCE: 1766. The reverse shows a handsomely rendered sailing ship with the inscription THANKS TO THE FRIENDS OF LIBERTY AND TRADE. Next to the ship is the word AMERICA, which apparently suggests that the vessel is traveling from some foreign port with cargo for this country. "The Restore of Commerce" was a reference to the fact that British-imposed taxes were periling American commerce by rendering goods so costly that the public could not buy nearly as much as it wished to. The halfpenny is known to have been used briefly as coinage. No such use has been established for the farthing, which is much rarer.

1766 HALFPENNY   1766 FARTHING

TYPE OF COIN	ABP	G-4 GOOD	EF-40 EX. FINE
☐ 1766 Halfpenny	330.00	550.00	3500.00
☐ 1766 Farthing			RARE

FRENCH COLONIES IN AMERICA

A number of coins were struck in France for use in that nation's colonies during the 18th century. These were non-geographical pieces that could be exchanged in any French province and carried inscriptions in French and Latin rather than in local languages. It is important to remember in collecting these coins that they were *not* expressly struck for use in America, though they did see use in areas such as Louisiana (named for Louis XIV).

1722 SOU   1767 SOU

COUNTERSTAMPED "RF"   1670 5 SOLS SILVER

TYPE OF COIN	ABP	G-4 GOOD	EF-40 EX. FINE
☐ 1670 5 Sols	375.00	625.00	4800.00
☐ 1670 15 Sols		EXTREMELY RARE	
☐ 1709–1713 30 Deniers, mint mark AA	75.00	125.00	625.00
☐ 1709–1713 30 Deniers, mint mark D	75.00	125.00	625.00
☐ 1710–1713 15 Deniers	75.00	125.00	1200.00
☐ 1738–1748 ½ Sou Marque	90.00	150.00	600.00
☐ 1738–1760 Sou Marque	48.00	80.00	400.00
☐ 1717 6 Deniers		EXTREMELY RARE	
☐ 1720 6 Deniers		EXTREMELY RARE	
☐ 1717 12 Deniers		EXTREMELY RARE	
☐ 1721 Sou, mint mark B for Rouen	168.00	280.00	RARE
☐ 1721 Sou, mint mark H for Rochelle	48.00	80.00	1375.00
☐ 1722 Sou, mint mark H	120.00	200.00	1375.00
☐ 1722 Over 1721	180.00	300.00	1650.00
☐ 1767 Sou	75.00	125.00	1100.00
☐ 1767 Sou, Counterstamped RF	75.00	125.00	500.00

VIRGINIA

Plagued by a coinage shortage, Virginia's colonists petitioned George III for supplies of trading pieces. He responded by authorizing the striking of a copper halfpenny, with his likeness on the obverse and the Virginia seal on its reverse. Proposals were also made for a penny and shilling, or coins which, to judge by the size of the few specimens struck, were intended for these denominations. They never reached circulation and are very rare. The halfpenny was struck in large quantities.

SHILLING

TYPE OF COIN	ABP	G-4 GOOD	EF-40 EX. FINE	MS-60 UNC.
☐ 1773 Halfpenny Period After GEORGIVS				
	60.00	100.00	450.00	1500.00
☐ 1773 Halfpenny No Period After GEORGIVS				
	40.00	65.00	550.00	1600.00
☐ 1773 Penny	PROOF			RARE
☐ 1774 Shilling Silver	PROOF			RARE

STATE OF NEW HAMPSHIRE

New Hampshire has the distinction of being the first state to attempt a local coinage following the Declaration of Independence. In 1776 it authorized William Moulton to produce an experimental batch of copper pieces. The small numbers that have been traced indicate this coin never attained general circulation, though it probably circulated in a small way. The chief type has a tree on the obverse and a harp on the reverse. Other types are known but their status has not been positively established.

1776 PINE TREE   1776 WM COPPER

TYPE OF COIN	VG-8 VERY GOOD
☐ 1776 New Hampshire Copper	RARE
☐ 1776 New Hampshire Copper, WM in center (Pattern Piece)	
	EXTREMELY RARE

STATE OF VERMONT

Vermont's postrevolutionary coinage, probably the best known for its designs of any regional pieces, was struck by Reuben Harmon of Rupert, Vermont, and some by Thomas Machin of Newburgh, New York. This extensive series most often employed portraits of George III but is best known for its "plough money," an obverse design picturing a farm plough in a field against a background of tree-laden mountains. This is sometimes referred to as the most original, creative, and authentically American design to be found on our colonial or federal-era coins. William Coley, a New York goldsmith, was the die cutter for this design.

1785 VERMONTS   1786 VERMONTENSIUM

1787 BRITANNIA

TYPE OF COIN	ABP	G-4 GOOD	EF-40 EX. FINE
☐ 1785 Immune Colombia			RARE
☐ 1785 VERMONTS	216.00	360.00	RARE
☐ 1785 VERMONTIS	270.00	450.00	RARE
☐ 1786 VERMONTENSIUM	126.00	210.00	RARE
☐ 1786 Baby Head	216.00	360.00	RARE
☐ 1786 Bust Faces Left	72.00	120.00	RARE
☐ 1787 Bust Faces Right	95.00	158.00	4000.00
☐ 1787 BRITANNIA reverse; it is thought that the reverse of the Brittania piece was struck from a worn, discarded die for a counterfeit British halfpenny	120.00	200.00	2250.00
☐ 1788 Cent	216.00	360.00	2250.00
☐ 1788 ET LIB INDE	240.00	400.00	RARE

TYPE OF COIN	ABP	G-4 GOOD	EF-40 EX. FINE
☐ 1788 VERMON AUCTORI, Reversed C		EXTREMELY RARE	
☐ 1788 GEORGIVS III REX	390.00	650.00	RARE

STATE OF CONNECTICUT

Connecticut struck more coins in the period from the Revolution to the establishment of a federal currency than any other state. Or, it might be better put, more varieties, as they represent numerous variations of three basic issues. The Mint at which they were struck was established by authority of the state in 1785. It was located at New Haven. The chief die cutters were Abel Buel and James Atlee.

1.
1785 CENT

2.
1785 AFRICAN HEAD

3a.
1786 CENT

4.
1786 CENT

5.
1786 CENT

6.
1786 CENT

7.
1786 CENT

8.
1787 CENT

9.
1787 CENT

10.
1787 CENT

11a.
1787 CENT

12.
1787 CENT

13a.
1787 CENT

14.
1788 CENT

15a.
1788 CENT

16.
1788 CENT

TYPE OF COIN	ABP	G-4 GOOD	EF-40 EX. FINE
☐ 1. 1785 Cent, Bust Right	60.00	100.00	1800.00
☐ 2. 1785 Cent, Bust Right: African Head	75.00	125.00	4050.00
☐ 3. 1785 Cent, Bust Left	120.00	200.00	4050.00
☐ 3a. 1786 Cent, ET LIB INDE	160.00	270.00	3000.00
☐ 4. 1786 Cent, Large Bust Faces Right	150.00	250.00	RARE
☐ 5. 1786 Cent, Mailed Bust Left	60.00	100.00	1500.00
☐ 6. 1786 Cent, Mailed Bust Left (Hercules Head)	108.00	180.00	RARE
☐ 7. 1786 Cent, Draped Bust	75.00	125.00	3200.00
☐ 8. 1787 Cent, Mailed Bust, Small Head Faces Right, ET LIB INDE	96.00	160.00	RARE
☐ 9. 1787 Cent, Mailed Bust Faces Left, INDE ET LIB	96.00	160.00	RARE

TYPE OF COIN	ABP	G-4 GOOD	EF-40 EX. FINE
☐ 10. 1787 Cent, Muttonhead: INDE ET LIB	90.00	150.00	RARE
☐ 11. 1787 Cent, Mailed Bust Faces Left	60.00	100.00	1800.00
☐ 11a. 1787 Cent, Horned Bust	65.00	108.00	2000.00
☐ 12. 1787 Cent, CONNECT	50.00	85.00	2250.00
☐ 13. 1787 Cent, Draped Bust Faces Left	50.00	85.00	1080.00
☐ 13a. 1787 Cent, Bust Left, AUCIORI	65.00	108.00	1350.00
☐ 13b. 1787 Cent, AUCTOPI	65.00	110.00	1980.00
☐ 13c. 1787 Cent, AUCTOBI	65.00	110.00	1980.00
☐ 13d. 1787 Cent, CONNFC	45.00	75.00	1575.00
☐ 13e. 1787 Cent, FNDE	65.00	110.00	1575.00
☐ 13f. 1787 Cent, ETLIR	65.00	110.00	1800.00
☐ 13g. 1787 Cent, ETIIB	65.00	110.00	1800.00
☐ 14. 1788 Cent, Mailed Bust Faces Right	60.00	100.00	1800.00
☐ 14a. 1788 Cent, Small Head	720.00	1200.00	RARE
☐ 15. 1788 Cent, Mailed Bust Faces Left	80.00	135.00	1575.00
☐ 15a. 1788 Cent, Mailed Bust Left, CONNLC	70.00	115.00	2250.00
☐ 16. 1788 Cent, Draped Bust Faces Left	70.00	115.00	1500.00
☐ 16a. Same, CONNLC	160.00	270.00	3150.00
☐ 16b. 1788 Same, INDL ET LIB	110.00	180.00	2700.00

STATE OF NEW JERSEY

No coinage was struck for New Jersey in the colonial period (but *see* Mark Newby halfpence). As the state's population increased, a serious coin shortage was experienced and, on June 1, 1786, its legislature authorized the striking of three million copper pieces, each to weigh "six pennyweight and six grains apiece." The contract for these tokens was awarded to Thomas Goadsby, Walter Mould, and Albion Cox. The full quantity was to be delivered by June 1788, with partial deliveries to be made in quarterly installments of 300,000 each. Soon after work had begun, Goadsby and Cox requested and were granted permission to divide up the quantities and strike them separately, each operating his own facility. Mould set up at Morristown, New Jersey, Cox at Rahway. Goadsby's location is not established but is thought to also have been

Rahway. The obverses of all these tokens show a horse's head and a plough, symbolic of the state's economy being founded largely on agriculture. The legend NOVA CAESAREA is simply New Jersey in Latin. On the reverse is a U.S. shield and E PLURIBUS UNUM. A number of varieties are to be encountered.

1.
1786

3.
1786

8.
1787

11.
1788

12.
1788

TYPE OF COIN	ABP	G-4 GOOD	EF-40 EX. FINE
☐ 1. 1786 Date Under Plough Handle		EXTREMELY RARE	
☐ 2. 1786 Normal Legends (Not illus.)	90.00	150.00	3150.00
☐ 3. 1786 No Colter	120.00	200.00	RARE
☐ 4. 1786 Bridle Variety (Not illus.)	60.00	100.00	3150.00
☐ 5. 1786 Narrow Shield (Not illus.)	60.00	100.00	2520.00
☐ 6. 1786 Wide Shield (Not illus.)	90.00	150.00	2700.00
☐ 7. 1787 Normal Legends (Not illus.)	90.00	150.00	2700.00
☐ 8. 1787 PLURIBS	90.00	150.00	4050.00
☐ 9. 1787 "Serpent Head" (Not illus.)	90.00	150.00	4500.00
☐ 10. 1788 Normal Legends (Not illus.)	60.00	100.00	1500.00
☐ 11. 1788 Horse's Head Faces Right, Running Fox	105.00	175.00	RARE
☐ 12. 1788 Horse's Head Left	240.00	400.00	RARE

STATE OF NEW YORK

The history of New York's local coinage prior to the Revolution reveals only the supposed Dutch merchant token discussed previously and various coins and tokens struck for use elsewhere that, in the ordinary course of trade, found their way to the state. For more than 100 years it was without locally authorized coinage. This void was filled by Dutch, British, French, and, to a lesser extent, Spanish monies, which came to New York through its great port and disseminated throughout the region. Apparently no pressing need was felt for a local coinage because none was officially instituted, even after independence. However, quantities of privately struck money did circulate. Some were the work of Thomas Machin of Newburgh, New York (where Washington had a headquarters during the war), who operated what he surreptitiously called a "hardware manufactory." It was, in fact, a copper mill, whose chief products were tokens. Other New York coins were produced at Rupert, Vermont, by a team of millers (Reuben Harmon and William Coley) who also made coins for Vermont and Connecticut.

There is much yet to be learned about New York's federal-era coinage, but quite a good deal has already been determined. The theory, once popularly maintained, that coins bearing the inscription NOVA EBORAC are of foreign origin is now known to be false. "Nova Eborac" is not some sort of mysterious foreign term. It is simply New York in Latin. (If you wonder how there could be a Latin name for New York, when there are none for railroad and television and other things discovered after the Latin language died, the explanation is quite simple. The Romans did not know of New York but they certainly knew of *old* York in Britain, which they called Eborac. To change this into New York you need only add the Latin word for new—*nova*—and you have Nova Eborac.)

All the New York coins (or tokens) are coppers. They carry various designs, of which the portrait of George Clinton is most famous. There was also an Indian figure (not too impressively portrayed), a New York coat-of-arms, and profile bust pretty confidently believed to be George Washington. Though the designs are not very well drawn, the coins themselves are very professionally struck.

1.
1786

2.
1787

3.
1787

4.
1787

5.
1787

6c.
1787

TYPE OF COIN	ABP	G-4 GOOD	EF-40 EX. FINE
☐ 1. 1786 NON VI VIRTUTE VICI, Thought to be the head of George Washington			RARE
☐ 2. 1787 EXCELSIOR, Eagle on Obverse Faces Left	1200.00	2000.00	RARE
☐ 3. 1787 EXCELSIOR, Eagle on Obverse Faces Right	1200.00	2000.00	RARE
☐ 3a. 1787 EXCELSIOR, Large Eagle on Reverse (Not illus.)			EXTREMELY RARE
☐ 3b. 1787 EXCELSIOR, George Clinton on Reverse (Not illus.)			RARE
☐ 3c. 1787 EXCELSIOR, Indian Standing on Reverse (Not illus.)			EXTREMELY RARE
☐ 3d. 1787 EXCELSIOR, Indian Standing, Eagle on Globe (Not illus.)			EXTREMELY RARE
☐ 4. 1787 LIBERTATEM, Indian Standing, Eagle Faces Right			EXTREMELY RARE
☐ 5. 1787 NOVA EBORAC, Reverse Seated Figure Faces Left	135.00	225.00	3200.00

TYPE OF COIN	ABP	G-4 GOOD	EF-40 EX. FINE
☐ 5a. 1787 NOVA EBORAC, Reverse Seated Figure Faces Right (Not illus.)	120.00	200.00	3250.00
☐ 5b. 1787 NOVA EBORAC, Small Head (Not illus.)	1800.00	3000.00	RARE
☐ 6c. 1787 NOVA EBORAC, Large Head	420.00	700.00	RARE

BRASHER DOUBLOONS

Perhaps the most celebrated, at any rate the most glamorized, U.S. colonial coin is the Brasher doubloon. Though traditionally referred to as colonial it should correctly be termed a federal-era piece, as it was struck after our independence had been gained. This is a private issue. Ephraim Brasher was a goldsmith from New York who became acquainted with George Washington when the latter resided there following the war. To classify this handsome gold piece as a speculative coin would be a mistake. Brasher, artist and patriot, appears to have manufactured it not for purposes of general circulation but as a memorial to the nation's independence and, possibly, a model from which federal coiners could gain inspiration. It dates to 1787, before the introduction of federal coinage but not before much speculation and debate on the matter. The Brasher doubloon, as the name suggests, was modeled after the Spanish coin of that name. It contained 408 grains of gold. As a goldsmith, Brasher would have encountered no difficulty securing the needed bullion for a small quantity of such pieces, but it is doubtful that he had either the resources or intention to strike this coin in large numbers. The obverse pictures the sun rising over a mountain, with the American eagle emblem on the back. The reverse bears the impressed letters E.B., the initials of Brasher's name. Obviously they were not clandestine issues or their origin would not have been so plainly identified. At the time of its issue the Brasher doubloon had a value of about $16. There was also a half doubloon worth $8. All are extremely rare, the variety in which the initials appear on the eagle's breast being preserved in a single specimen only.

EB Punch on Wing

TYPE OF COIN

☐ 1787 (gold) Doubloon, EB Punch on Breast
ALL TYPES EXTREMELY RARE

☐ 1787 (gold) Doubloon, EB Punch on Wing
ALL TYPES EXTREMELY RARE

☐ 1787 (gold) Half Doubloon   ALL TYPES EXTREMELY RARE

STATE OF MASSACHUSETTS

Massachusetts, the first colony to strike its own coins in pre-revolutionary days, also had its own coinage in the period between independence and the establishment of the U.S. Mint. On October 17, 1786, the General Court of that state authorized the setting up of a Mint, "for the coinage of gold, silver, and copper." A stipulation was made that the design for coinage should employ the "figure of an Indian with bow and arrow and a star on one side with the word Common-wealth, on the reverse a spread eagle with the words Mas-sachusetts 1787." The ambitiousness of this project was never fully realized. While coppers were struck in some quantities, a coinage of silver and gold never appeared. In 1789 the Mint was abandoned, having proven costly to operate.

1788 CENT   1788 HALF CENT

TYPE OF COIN	ABP	G-4 GOOD	EF-40 EX. FINE
☐ 1787 Cent, Arrows in Left Talon	120.00	200.00	1620.00
☐ 1787 Cent, Arrows in Right Talon			RARE
☐ 1787 Cent, Horned Eagle (Die Break)	120.00	200.00	1800.00
☐ 1787 Half Cent	105.00	175.00	1620.00
☐ 1788 Cent	72.00	120.00	1575.00
☐ 1788 Half Cent	105.00	175.00	1575.00

MASSACHUSETTS PINE TREE COPPER

The origin of this unique coin is undetermined. Only one specimen is known, undoubtedly a pattern piece, and but for the greatest of good luck it would have been undiscovered. It turned up, buried beneath a Boston street, during an excavation in the 1800s, having probably been entombed nearly a century. Only the sharp eyes of a laborer prevented it from being discarded along with rubbish. Despite this imprisonment its condition is surprisingly good. It shows a pine tree on the obverse, obviously inspired by the Pine Tree coinage of a century earlier, and a figure of Liberty posed as Britannia on the reverse, complete with globe and dog. The date 1776 appears beneath the reverse figure. Whether this was the year of striking or was used merely symbolically to denote our independence from Britain is unknown. The obverse inscription is MASSACHUSETTS STATE while the reverse reads LIBERTY AND VIRTUE. This unique item is owned today by the Massachusetts Historical Society. Reproductions exist.

1776 PINE TREE
(UNIQUE)

MASSACHUSETTS HALFPENNY

This intriguing coin, classical in appearance, is dated 1776 and is often referred to as the Janus Copper or Janus Halfpenny. This is a reference (though not quite historically accurate) to the obverse design, which shows a three-sided head with faces looking forward, left, and right. The mythological god Janus had only two faces, looking right and left (the month of January is named for him; one face looks to the old year, one to the new). On the reverse is a seated representation of Liberty. The Massachusetts Halfpenny is a unique pattern piece. The only known specimen sold for $40,000 in 1979.

MASSACHUSETTS
HALFPENNY

KENTUCKY TOKEN

This novel piece was not of American origin, but struck in England around the year 1792. It is thought to have been occasioned by admission of Kentucky into the Union. On the obverse is a hand holding a petition reading OUR CAUSE IS JUST surrounded by the wording UNANIMITY IS THE STRENGTH OF SOCIETY. The reverse is composed of a star in which are circular ornaments, each bearing the initial letter of a state. As κ for Kentucky appears at the top, this piece is identified with that state. Some specimens have plain edges while others are stamped "Payable at Bedworth," "Payable in Lancaster," etc. It is vital to take note of these markings, as they have a great influence on the value.

1792 TOKEN

TYPE OF COIN	ABP	G-4 GOOD	EF-40 EX. FINE	MS-60 UNC.
☐ 1792 Token, Plain Edge	90.00	150.00	425.00	1350.00
☐ 1792 Token, Engrailed Edge	69.00	115.00	700.00	3780.00
☐ 1792 Token, Lettered Edge, "Payable at I. Fielding," etc.				EXTREMELY RARE
☐ 1792 Token, Lettered Edge, "Payable at Bedworth," etc.				EXTREMELY RARE
☐ 1792 Token, Lettered Edge, "Payable at Lancaster, London, or Bristol"	150.00	250.00	720.00	1575.00

MARYLAND-CHALMERS

The Chalmers tokens were the second group of coins to be struck for circulation in Maryland, preceded by the Lord Baltimore money of a century earlier. Unlike these early pieces, which were of foreign manufacture, the Chalmers coins evolved locally. They were minted at Annapolis in 1783. Apparently they came into being because of the coinage shortage that then existed in Maryland and the hesitancy of that state's legislature to take official action. John Chalmers, their maker, was a goldsmith. He struck them in silver in denominations of threepence, sixpence, and one shilling (twelvepence). Their odd geometrical designs give them an almost cabalistic appearance. All are quite scarce but the majority are obtainable.

LONG WORM   DATE

1783 SHILLING   1783 SIXPENCE   1783 THREEPENCE

TYPE OF COIN	ABP	G-4 GOOD	EF-40 EX. FINE
☐ 1783 Shilling, Short Worm	480.00	800.00	RARE
☐ 1783 Shilling, Long Worm	1080.00	1800.00	RARE
☐ 1783 Shilling, Rings on Reverse		EXTREMELY RARE	
☐ 1783 Sixpence, Small Date	1500.00	2500.00	RARE

TYPE OF COIN	ABP	G-4 GOOD	EF-40 EX. FINE
☐ 1783 Sixpence, Large Date	1500.00	2500.00	RARE
☐ 1783 Threepence	1320.00	2200.00	RARE

BALTIMORE, MARYLAND, OR STANDISH BARRY

Standish Barry was a private citizen of Baltimore who worked at various craft trades including watchmaking and silversmithing. In 1790 he struck, in very limited quantities, a silver threepenny token bearing a portrait on one side and the words THREE PENCE on the other. Due to the low face value and the fact of its being made of silver, the physical size is quite small, about comparable to our dime. Barry's motive is not known with certainty. That he wished to alleviate the shortage of small-denomination coinage in his neighborhood is a possibility, but he produced so few specimens that his goal, if such was his intent, could not have been achieved. A more likely suggestion is that the Barry token was intended chiefly as an advertising piece. This is supported by the appearance of his name, spelled out in full on the reverse, which commonly was done only with tradesmen's tokens. The obverse portrait is thought to have been intended as George Washington, which fails to resemble him only because of artistic inability. Not only the year but the month is stated and the day as well: JULY 4, 90. The whole appearance is crude and amateurish, but collectors treasure it.

TYPE OF COIN	ABP	G-4 GOOD	EF-40 EX. FINE
☐ 1790 Silver Threepence			RARE

RHODE ISLAND TOKEN

The Rhode Island ship token has been variously classified as a coin, token, and medal, and its status is hardly clearer today than when research first began. Struck in 1778 or 1779 (the obverse carries one date, the reverse another), the piece is known in a variety of base metals: copper, brass, tin, and pewter, the composition having little influence on its value. That it was intended as a coin for ordinary circulation and exchange appears remote as it carries no mark of value and would have had to trade on the basis of weight. Being made of different metals, the weight varies and would have resulted in no small measure of confusion. The obverse shows a well-drawn ocean vessel. On the reverse is a complex scene representing the flight of Continental troops from Rhode Island. The inscriptions are in Dutch but the old belief that this production was of Dutch or Dutch-American origin is now given little support. Based upon the reverse theme it could well have been struck in England or by royalists in America. It should be kept in mind that the Revolutionary War had not yet ended in 1778–79 and coins or medals had a certain propaganda value. Reproductions are known to exist.

1778–1779 "VLUGTENDE"   1778–1779 WREATH

TYPE OF COIN	ABP	G-4 GOOD	EF-40 EX. FINE
☐ 1778–79 VLUGTENDE Below Ship			RARE
☐ 1778–79 VLUGTENDE Removed	480.00	800.00	RARE
☐ 1778–79 Wreath Below Ship	480.00	800.00	RARE

1776 CONTINENTAL CURRENCY

The Continental dollar and its affiliates were struck as pattern pieces only, based upon the latest research, and never reached general circulation. They are believed to represent the first attempt at coinage by the Continental Congress, at any rate the first to achieve physical form. Upon declaring its independence from Britain, the United States was cut off from supplies of British currency and anticipated an extreme shortage within the coming months. Actually this shortage did not materialize to the degree feared. Continental currency is crown-size and struck in silver, pewter, and brass. Though the sizes are identical and the coins bear no indication of value, it is presumed the silver pieces were intended as dollars and the base metal varieties as divisions thereof. The exact history of their origin is not recorded, the documentation of it having apparently been swept away in the turbulent times of war. We know that the engraver bore the initials E.G. because he signed his work. An exhaustive search of goldsmiths, silversmiths, and other metalworkers active at that time, having the initials E.G., has led to the conclusion that the 1776 Continental currency was the work of Elisha Gallaudet of Philadelphia. If this is the case, they would undoubtedly have been struck in that city as well. Considering that it was headquarters of the Continental Congress, it seems to fit together historically. The legends include WE ARE ONE and MIND YOUR BUSINESS, the latter not, probably, having been directed toward the British but used merely as a piece of sage advice in the spirit of Ben Franklin. Copies exist, struck at the 1876 Centennial exposition.

1776
CURRENCY
Brass, Pewter,
Silver

1776
CURRENCY
E.G. FECIT
Pewter, Silver

TYPE OF COIN	ABP	G-4 GOOD	EF-40 EX. FINE
☐ 1776 Currency, Brass		EXTREMELY RARE	
☐ 1776 Currency, Pewter		EXTREMELY RARE	
☐ 1776 Currency, Silver		EXTREMELY RARE	

TYPE OF COIN	ABP	G-4 GOOD	EF-40 EX. FINE
☐ 1776 Currency, E.G. FECIT, Pewter			EXTREMELY RARE
☐ 1776 Currency, E.G. FECIT, Silver			EXTREMELY RARE
☐ 1776 Currency, Pewter			EXTREMELY RARE

NOVA CONSTELLATIO SILVERS

These Nova Constellatio silvers are pattern pieces for a federal coinage, the first such pattern pieces of silver struck by the newly born government. They date from 1783, shortly after the War of Independence had been concluded. Supposedly the brainchild of Governor Morris, a signer of the Declaration of Independence and assistant financier of the Confederation, their designer was Benjamin Dudley. At this point the system of cents and dollars, later agreed upon, had not yet evolved; but there was no wish to continue use of the British pound standard. Morris evolved a currency system in which the chief denomination was a mark, consisting of 1,000 units. Division of this coin—also included among the Nova Constellatio patterns—were the quint, equal to 500 units or half a mark, and the bit, with a value of 100 units or a tenth of a mark. Further divisions could then supposedly be made of base metal, in fifty or ten units of whatever seemed practical. If we think of Morris's mark as the equivalent of the dollar (which in reality it was), then the 500 unit piece was the counterpart of 50¢ and the 100 unit piece of 10¢. Morris won little support for his currency proposals and the patterns were never approved for general circulation. Just one specimen is known to exist of each example; however, there are two types (and consequently two known specimens) of the 500-unit piece, one having an inscription on the obverse and the other bearing no inscription.

TYPE OF COIN

☐ 1783 MARK, 1000 Mills, Silver	ALL TYPES EXTREMELY RARE
☐ 1783 QUINT, 500 Mills, Silver	ALL TYPES EXTREMELY RARE
☐ 1783 QUINT, Second Variety, Silver	ALL TYPES EXTREMELY RARE
☐ 1783 Cent, 100 Mills, Silver	ALL TYPES EXTREMELY RARE
☐ 1783 "S" Copper	ALL TYPES EXTREMELY RARE

1783 MARK

1783 QUINT

1783 CENT

SECOND VARIETY

1783 QUINT

NOVA CONSTELLATIO COPPERS

Though their name and design are similar to the Nova Constellatio silver, it is important to note that these coins had quite different origins and purposes. The concept for both was that of Governor Morris, who, in addition to being a legislator, was also a prominent businessman in the late colonial/early federal age. While the silvers were pattern pieces for a proposed federal coinage, these coppers were struck as a personal speculative venture. It is quite likely that their place of origin was not America but Birmingham, England, and that their dies were engraved by an Englishman named Wyon. Upon importation to this country, Morris placed them into circulation as best he could. To judge from the fairly large quantities that exist of most types, their production must have reached the tens of thousands, if not higher.

CONSTELLATIO 1783 BLUNT RAYS

1785 CENT

TYPE OF COIN	ABP	G-4 GOOD	EF-40 EX. FINE
☐ 1783 Cent, CONSTELLATIO, Pointed Rays, Large U.S.	110.00	180.00	1800.00

TYPE OF COIN	ABP	G-4 GOOD	EF-40 EX. FINE
☐ 1783 Cent, CONSTELLATIO, Pointed Rays, Small U.S.	110.00	180.00	1350.00
☐ 1783 Cent, CONSTELLATIO, Blunt Rays	75.00	125.00	1800.00
☐ 1785 Cent, CONSTELLATIO, Blunt Rays	110.00	180.00	1800.00
☐ 1785 Cent, CONSTELLATIO, Pointed Rays	105.00	175.00	1350.00
☐ 1786 Cent, CONSTELLATIO, Pointed Rays		EXTREMELY RARE	

IMMUNE COLUMBIA

It is believed that these tokens, whose obverse designs are in some instances similar to those of the Nova Constellatio coppers, were struck from dies engraved by Thomas Wyon of Birmingham, England. Their history is otherwise shrouded in mystery. That they represent pattern pieces that did not actually circulate seems unquestionable, as they exist in extremely limited quantities. There are several varieties, chiefly in copper, but the piece does exist in silver. A single gold specimen, dated 1785, is included in the government's collection at Washington. It was obtained by trade with the collector Stickney, who accepted a duplicate 1804 silver dollar for it. A later version of the Immune Columbia token, date 1787, was struck from dies by James Atlee. Justice with scales is the reverse theme with a number of different obverses, including a portrait of the then not-too-popular George III.

OBVERSE 1785
IMMUNE COLUMBIA

1785
REVERSE
"NOVA"

IMMUNIS COLUMBIA
1787

TYPE OF COIN	ABP	G-4 GOOD	EF-40 FINE
☐ 1785 Cent, Copper		EXTREMELY RARE	
☐ 1785 Cent, Silver		EXTREMELY RARE	
☐ 1785 Cent, Copper, Extra Star in Reverse		EXTREMELY RARE	

TYPE OF COIN	ABP	G-4 GOOD	EF-40 EX. FINE
☐ 1785 Cent, Copper, CONSTELLATIO, Blunt Rays			EXTREMELY RARE
☐ 1785 Cent, VERMON AUCTORI			EXTREMELY RARE
☐ 1785 Cent, GEORGE III, Obverse			EXTREMELY RARE
☐ 1787 IMMUNIS COLUMBIA			EXTREMELY RARE

CONFEDERATIO

The Confederatio cent, also known as Confederatio copper, is a hybrid coin found with various obverse and reverse designs. Regardless of the designs these are all pattern pieces that never reached circulation and all are extremely rare. Identity of the die cutters is not known but it is believed that at least some were the work of Thomas Wyon of Birmingham, England, and undoubtedly they were struck abroad. One of the obverse motifs features George Washington.

1785 CENT   1785 WASHINGTON

TYPE OF COIN	ABP	EF-40 EX. FINE
☐ 1785 Cent, Stars in Small Circle		EXTREMELY RARE
☐ 1785 Cent, Stars in Large Circle		EXTREMELY RARE
☐ 1785 Cent, George Washington		EXTREMELY RARE

SPECIMEN PATTERNS

A number of copper pattern pieces were struck in or about 1786 for possible use as token currency. Their history is not well established and all are extremely rare. The shield design and E PLURIBUS UNUM inscription on the reverse of some were subsequently used on New Jersey tokens, but the following patterns cannot be classified as belonging to any given locality.

TYPE OF COIN

☐ 1786 IMMUNIS COLUMBIA, Shield Reverse	EXTREMELY RARE
☐ 1786 IMMUNIS COLUMBIA, Eagle Reverse	EXTREMELY RARE
☐ 1786 Eagle on Obverse	EXTREMELY RARE
☐ 1786 Washington/Eagle	EXTREMELY RARE
☐ Undated, Washington Obverse	EXTREMELY RARE

NORTH AMERICAN TOKEN

This is a private piece, one of a number issued following the Revolution, that circulated in this country. Its origin is Irish, having been struck in Dublin. Undoubtedly it represented the effort of an Irish merchant or metalsmith to take advantage of America's coin shortage. The date shown is 1781 but belief is strong that it was actually produced at some later time, possibly in the late 1790s or early 1800s. The United States was experiencing a coin shortage during the presidency of Thomas Jefferson, so it could well date from that era. This situation was well known abroad, as foreigners melting down our coinage were chiefly responsible. On the obverse it pictures a sailing ship with the word COMMERCE and a seated likeness of Hibernia (symbol of Ireland) with her harp on the reverse, inscribed NORTH AMERICAN TOKEN. It may well be that the side of this token traditionally regarded as the obverse was intended as the reverse. Quantities in which the North American token were distributed in the United States are not known. The piece is far from rare. Its size is roughly equivalent to a quarter.

TYPE OF COIN	ABP	G-4 GOOD	EF-40 EX. FINE
☐ 1781 Token	80.00	135.00	1080.00

MACHIN COPPERS

Thomas Machin operated a copper mill at Newburgh, New York. From 1786 to 1789 he was active in the production of tokens, some designed for use in the State of New York (*which see*) and others that were nothing but counterfeits of the British copper halfpenny. He attempted to profit by placing these counterfeits, of lighter than standard weight, into immense circulation. To avoid suspicion he used a variety of dates, going back as far as 1747. But the majority are dated in the early 1770s. The design is always the same: a portrait of the king on the obverse with Britannia on the reverse. As these pieces are not collected by date, their values are constant irrespective of date. They can easily be distinguished from genuine British halfpennies by their cruder die engraving. However, the Machin fakes were not the only ones made of this coin.

TYPE OF COIN	ABP	G-4 GOOD	EF-40 EX. FINE
☐ Halfpenny, various dates	180.00	300.00	4000.00

GEORGIUS TRIUMPHO TOKEN

This controversial coin, dating from 1783, is made of copper. On the obverse is a male portrait in profile with the inscription GEORGIUS TRIUMPHO, which cannot be translated in any other fashion but "George Has Triumphed." Considering that the War for Independence had recently ended with an American victory, the triumphal George should be Washington. But the portrait much more closely resembles George III, the British monarch who sought to preserve American colonization. Just how this George could be regarded to have triumphed at that moment is puzzling. Perhaps the explanation is that Washington was intended but the engraver, being unskilled and having no likeness at hand from which to copy, merely fashioned the portrait after that on English money. A similar situation prevailed at the time among illustrators who designed copperplate portraits for books, the likeness often being guessed at. As photography did not exist and few citizens actually saw celebrities in the flesh, it was not really known if such works were accurate. The reverse pictures Liberty holding an olive branch, and thirteen bars representing the confederation. Its inscription is VOCE POPOLI, an error for "Voce Populi" or "Voice of the People."

TYPE OF COIN	ABP	G-4 GOOD	EF-40 EX. FINE
☐ 1783 GEORGIUS TRIUMPHO	90.00	155.00	1575.00

AUCTORI PLEBIS TOKEN

Not much is known of this copper piece, other than the fact that it closely resembles the early coinage of Connecticut. It is thought to have been struck in England and may never have been intended for American circulation. It has, however, traditionally been included in American colonial and federal-era collections. It bears a date of 1787 and carries a male portrait profile on the obverse with a seated figure of Liberty on the reverse. The workmanship is not especially skilled.

TYPE OF COIN	ABP	G-4 GOOD	EF-40 EX. FINE
☐ 1787 AUCTORI PLEBIS Token	80.00	135.00	2475.00

MOTT TOKEN

An early trade token, this piece had no official sanction nor any legal value as money. Its issuers were William and John Mott, who operated a business on Water Street in the downtown area of Manhattan. Mott Street, now the central boulevard of New York's Chinatown, was named for this family. The Mott token is of copper, picturing on one side the American eagle emblem and (quite unusual) a shelf clock on the other. The clock served an advertising purpose, as the Motts dealt in goldware, silverware, and fancy goods including importations. This token dates from 1789. Of too high a quality for local production, it seems evident they were manufactured in England.

TYPE OF COIN	ABP	G-4 GOOD	EF-40 EX. FINE
☐ 1789 Mott Token, Thick Planchet	75.00	125.00	1350.00
☐ 1789 Mott Token, Thin Planchet	80.00	135.00	1440.00
☐ 1789 Mott Token, Engrailed Edge	185.00	315.00	1980.00

BAR CENT

The Bar cent is a very simply designed coin whose name derives from the fact that its reverse design is composed of a grid containing thirteen bars (one for each state of the confederation). On the obverse are the letters USA in large size, intertwined. Beyond this there is no further ornament or inscription and the origin of this piece has proven a dilemma. It is almost surely a foreign product, made possibly by Wyon (of Nova Constellatio copper fame) of Birmingham, England. Its first public appearance was made in New York in late 1785. It may be presumed that the date of minting was either that year or possibly 1784. Reproductions, against which collectors are cautioned, were produced during the Civil War.

TYPE OF COIN	ABP	G-4 GOOD	EF-40 EX. FINE
☐ Undated, Bar Cent	450.00	765.00	RARE

TALBOT, ALLUM, AND LEE CENTS

These are trade tokens, circulated by a firm of importers known as Talbot, Allum, and Lee, who were headquartered at 241 Pearl Street, New York, in what is now the financial district but then was given over largely to import/export because of its access to the Battery docks. There is no question but that they were struck in England. The corporation's name appears on one side, sometimes with and sometimes without its place of location. The earliest date is 1794 and at this point they carried a value legend of ONE CENT. In 1794 this was removed, possibly out of fear of government protest, and an inscription added to the edge: WE PROMISE TO PAY THE BEARER ONE CENT. There are, however, specimens of the 1795 edition with unlettered edge, which are considerably scarcer. This practice of issuing tokens redeemable at a certain place of business became widespread in the 19th century, especially during the small-change shortage of the Civil War.

1794 NEW YORK   1795 CENT

TYPE OF COIN	ABP	G-4 GOOD	EF-40 EX. FINE
☐ 1794 Cent, With NEW YORK	90.00	150.00	585.00
☐ 1794 Cent, Without NEW YORK	300.00	500.00	RARE
☐ 1795 Cent	105.00	175.00	540.00

GEORGE WASHINGTON PIECES

Following the Revolution, George Washington became a national hero and idol to such a degree that he was virtually worshipped. Books were written on his life, engravers published pictures of him, and his likeness was set into snuff boxes, jewelry cases, and other fancy goods. It is only natural that Washington would also be the subject of numerous tokens and pseudocoins. These were issued beginning in 1783 and (for practical purposes) ceased about 1795, after official federal coinage began circulating. No exact date can be placed on their discontinuance, however, as tokens and medals honoring Washington appeared from time to time thereafter.

Those in the following listing are not strictly classed as commemoratives but might just as well be. They were primarily coppers and contained a cent's worth of that metal. They could, therefore, be used as money, but the extent to which this was done is not known and can be presumed to have been limited, as none were struck in large quantities. The best title for them might be "celebration pieces."

Building a complete collection is outside the realm of possibility because of the extreme scarcity of some issues. A fair assembly of them can, however, be made. Their origins are not well established. Some are believed to have been designed and struck in England. This would seem logical on the basis of workmanship. Those made abroad were surely not designed for circulation there, but for export and distribution within the United States. One of the Washington tokens—in half penny value—declares itself a Welsh product; it carries the inscription NORTH WALES on the reverse. Another was a London tradesman's token. As for their dates, the presumption is that some, at least, were struck subsequent to the year indicated, perhaps in the first decade of the 19th century or even later.

Most have distinctive reverses and are known chiefly by these reverse types. So far as the portraiture is concerned, there is a rich and interesting variety, differing not only in artistic quality but concept. On some, Washington is shown as a Roman-style emperor, wearing a laurel wreath. The majority portray him in military dress. Though a few coins of amateurish design are included in this group there are likewise several of the most skilled and impressive workmanship, which, if executed as sculptures, would be regarded as important works of art. The likelihood that Washington sat for any of the die cutters is remote, but apparently they either had prior experience drawing or sculpting him or worked from some of the better oil pictures, such as those of Stuart. They could not have achieved such faithful portraiture merely from descriptions of his physical appearance.

1.
1783 CENT

2.
1783 CENT

3.
1783 CENT

4.
1783 CENT (DOUBLE HEAD)

6.
1791 CENT

7.
1791 CENT

8.
1791 HALFPENNY

9.
1792 CENT

10.
1792 CENT

11.
1792 HALF DOLLAR

12.
1792 ROMAN HEAD

13.
1792 EAGLE

14.
1793 HALFPENNY

15.
1795 HALFPENNY

16.
1795 PENNY

17.
1795 HALFPENNY

18.
TOKEN

19.
TOKEN

20.
TOKEN

TYPE OF COIN	ABP	G-4 GOOD	EF-40 EX. FINE
☐ 1. 1783 Cent, Large Military Bust	90.00	150.00	540.00
☐ 1a. 1783 Cent, Small Military Bust (Not illus.)	90.00	150.00	540.00
☐ 1b. 1783 Cent, Small Military Bust, Engraved Edge (Not illus.)	90.00	150.00	1080.00
☐ 2. 1783 Cent, Draped Bust	120.00	200.00	1080.00

TYPE OF COIN	ABP	G-4 GOOD	EF-40 EX. FINE
☐ 2a. 1783 Cent, Draped Bust, Button on Cloak (Not illus.)			
	80.00	135.00	990.00
☐ 2b. 1783 Cent, Draped Bust (Not illus.)			
	ALL TYPES EXTREMELY RARE		
☐ 3. 1783 Cent, Draped Bust, UNITY STATES			
	110.00	180.00	585.00
☐ 4. 1783 Cent, Undated, Double Head	110.00	180.00	585.00
☐ 5. 1784 Ugly Head (Not illus.)		EXTREMELY RARE	
☐ 6. 1791 Cent, Small Eagle	135.00	250.00	1260.00
☐ 7. 1791 Cent, Large Eagle	150.00	225.00	1260.00
☐ 8. 1791 Liverpool Halfpenny	420.00	700.00	RARE
☐ 9. 1792 Cent, WASHINGTON PRESIDENT			RARE
☐ 10. 1792 Cent, BORN VIRGINIA	900.00	1500.00	RARE
☐ 11. 1792 Silver		EXTREMELY RARE	
☐ 11a. 1792 Copper		EXTREMELY RARE	
☐ 11b. 1792 Large Eagle		EXTREMELY RARE	
☐ 12. 1792 Roman Head		EXTREMELY RARE	
☐ 13. 1792 Eagle With Stars, Copper		EXTREMELY RARE	
☐ 13a. 1792 Eagle With Stars, Silver		EXTREMELY RARE	
☐ 13b. 1792 Eagle With Stars, Gold		EXTREMELY RARE	
☐ 14. 1793 Ship Halfpenny	240.00	400.00	1000.00
☐ 15. 1795 Halfpenny, Reeded Edge, GRATE, Small Buttons			
	90.00	150.00	650.00
☐ 15a. 1795 Halfpenny, Reeded Edge, GRATE, Large Buttons			
	90.00	150.00	650.00
☐ 15b. 1795 Halfpenny, Lettered Edge, GRATE, Large Buttons			
	216.00	360.00	1080.00
☐ 16. 1795 Penny, Undated, LIBERTY AND SECURITY			
	60.00	100.00	1260.00
☐ 17. 1795 Halfpenny, Dated, LIBERTY AND SECURITY, London			
	90.00	150.00	900.00
☐ 17a. 1795 Halfpenny, LIBERTY AND SECURITY, Birmingham			
	90.00	150.00	900.00
☐ 17b. 1795 Halfpenny, Dated, LIBERTY AND SECURITY, Asylum			
	160.00	270.00	1980.00
☐ 17c. 1795 Halfpenny, Dated, LIBERTY AND SECURITY, Plain Edge			
	110.00	180.00	900.00
☐ 18. Success Token, Small	90.00	150.00	1350.00
☐ 19. 1795 Halfpenny, NORTH WALES	120.00	200.00	800.00
☐ 20. Success Token, Large	120.00	200.00	1080.00

FRANKLIN PRESS TOKEN

This copper token was struck in England as a merchant piece and its use apparently restricted there. Because of its connection with Benjamin Franklin it has interest for collectors of American coinage. The obverse pictures an old-fashioned screw press (driven by jerking a lever), with the words PAYABLE AT THE FRANKLIN PRESS LONDON on the opposite side. It carries a date of 1794. As Franklin died in 1790 he could not have seen this token. Reproductions exist.

TYPE OF COIN	ABP	G-4 GOOD	EF-40 EX. FINE
☐ 1794 Token	110.00	180.00	540.00

CASTORLAND

Royalists who fled France following the revolution's outbreak in 1791 scattered to many parts of the globe. A small colony settled in the New York State farmlands (near Carthage) and called the locality Castorland. The Castorland medal or token is said to be a pattern piece struck in France for a proposed currency. It never reached beyond the experimental stage and both varieties, in silver and copper, are extremely rare. They carry a date of 1796.

TYPE OF COIN

☐ 1796 Silver Original, Reeded Edge   **EXTREMELY RARE**

FUGIO CENTS

The Fugio cents, so called because that word is a component in the obverse inscription, were the first officially sanctioned U.S. federal coinage. It was resolved by Congress in 1787 that a contract be put out with a private miller, James Jarvis, for 300 tons of copper coins. The arrangement was for Jarvis to secure the metal himself and pay all expenses, then sell the coins to the government at face value—his profit arising from the difference between his cost and the total face value. It was a venture of enormous proportions, considering that the United States had not previously authorized any coins. The matter of designing was not left to the contractor. Congress specifically spelled out what these coins should look like: "thirteen circles linked together, a small circle in the middle with the words 'United States' around it, and in the center the words 'We are one'; on the other side of the same piece the following device, viz: a dial with the hours expressed on the face of it; a meridian sun above on one side of which is the word 'Fugio.'" *Fugio* is Latin for "flees." As the obverse carries the saying "Mind Your Business," often attributed to Benjamin Franklin, this is sometimes called the Franklin cent; such terminology is, however, misleading and confusing. The dies were produced by Abel Buel of New Haven, Connecticut, and most of the striking was apparently carried out in that city. Jarvis failed to deliver the agreed-on number of coins, was prosecuted for breach of contract, and imprisoned.

1787 CENT

TYPE OF COIN	ABP	G-4 GOOD	EF-40 EX. FINE
☐ 1787 Cent, Club Rays, Rounded Ends	300.00	500.00	RARE
☐ 1787 Cent, Club Rays, Concave Ends, FUCIO (Not illus.)	1440.00	2400.00	RARE

TYPE OF COIN	ABP	G-4 GOOD	EF-40 EX. FINE
☐ 1787 Cent, Club Rays, Concave Ends, FUGIO	2400.00	4000.00	RARE
☐ 1787 Cent, Club Rays, STATES UNITED			EXTREMELY RARE
☐ 1787 Cent, Pointed Rays, UNITED above, STATES below			EXTREMELY RARE
☐ 1787 Cent, Pointed Rays, UNITED STATES at side of circle (Not illus.)	180.00	300.00	2000.00
☐ 1787 Cent, Pointed Rays, STATES UNITED at side of circle; Cinquefoils	120.00	200.00	2000.00
☐ 1787 Cent, Pointed Rays, STATES UNITED at sides, 8-pointed star on reverse band (Not illus.)	150.00	250.00	3500.00
☐ 1787 Cent, Pointed Rays, STATES UNITED, raised edge on reverse band	120.00	200.00	2500.00
☐ 1787 Cent, Pointed Rays, UNITED STATES, No Cinquefoils	150.00	250.00	RARE
☐ 1787 Cent, Pointed Rays, STATES UNITED, No Cinquefoils	300.00	500.00	RARE
☐ 1787 Cent, AMERICAN CONGRESS, With Rays (Not illus.)			EXTREMELY RARE

NEW HAVEN RESTRIKES

In 1858, C. Wyllys Betts found three sets of dies in New Haven. Restrikes in various metals were made. The restrikes were not made directly from these dies but copies fashioned from them.

1787 CENT

TYPE OF COIN	ABP	G-4 GOOD	EF-40 EX. FINE
☐ Copper	210.00	350.00	1500.00
☐ Silver	225.00	375.00	2800.00
☐ Brass	210.00	350.00	1500.00
☐ Gold			EXTREMELY RARE

FIRST UNITED STATES OF AMERICA MINT ISSUES

1792 BIRCH CENT

The 1792 Birch cent was the first coin to be struck at the newly established U.S. Mint in Philadelphia and the first governmental issue struck by the government as opposed to private contractors. This coin was not circulated but produced as a trial piece only. Along with it were also trial or pattern pieces of half disme, disme, and quarter dollar denominations, all of which are extremely rare. A motion is said to have been made for placing George Washington's likeness on these pieces but that Washington, when informed of this plan, declined to be honored in such a manner. It was then decided to use a portrait of the Goddess of Liberty. The better-known version of the Birch cent is large in size and composed entirely of copper. A smaller cent was also produced, containing a droplet of silver at the center. This was done entirely as an experiment to determine whether a penny coin in small size might be publicly more acceptable than one made exclusively of base metal. The pattern quarter dollar has more the appearance of a medal than a coin. The Birch cent derives its name from Robert Birch, its designer. Birch is thought also to have been among the die cutters for the half disme and disme.

TYPE OF COIN

☐ 1792 Disme (Silver)
☐ 1792 Disme (Copper)
☐ 1792 Half Disme (Silver)
☐ 1792 Birch Cent (Copper)

ALL COINS ARE RARE,
VERY RARE, OR UNIQUE

1792 BIRCH CENT

1792 HALF DISME

1792 HALF DISME

TYPE OF COIN

☐ 1792 Birch Cent (White Metal)   EXTREMELY RARE
☐ 1792 Quarter Dollar (Pattern, Copper)   EXTREMELY RARE
☐ 1792 Quarter Dollar (Pattern, White Metal) EXTREMELY RARE

1792 SILVER CENTER CENT

TYPE OF COIN

☐ 1792 Silver Center Cent   ALL COINS ARE VERY RARE
☐ 1792 Cent, No Silver Center   OR UNIQUE

HALF CENTS, 1793–1857

That the lowly half cent survived into the second half of the 19th century is looked upon as remarkable today by persons not well acquainted with the economic conditions of that time. Despite its minute face value, and the grumblings of many citizens that it did little but clutter their pockets, it served an important function in trade. Many articles in shops were priced fractionally and, without the half cent, difficulty would have been encountered in making change for such purchases. Their availability was, however, frequently abused. Merchants, anxious to rid themselves of half cents, would often give them instead of pennies. As first introduced in 1793, the coin bore a portrait of Liberty facing left on its obverse and a wreathed reverse with the words HALF CENT and UNITED STATES OF AMERICA. The designer was Adam Eckfeldt. The original weight was 6.74 grams and the composition pure copper. The coin has a diameter of 22mm. and is stamped along the edge TWO HUNDRED FOR A DOLLAR. After being struck for a single year it was decided to redesign the coin (coin redesigning occurred frequently in the Mint's early days of operation), the new design being the work of Robert Scot. Liberty was switched round to face right, her features streamlined, and her cap (the "cap of liberty," a reference to caps worn by freed slaves in Roman times) enlarged. The reverse was restyled but not materially altered. Planchets were of the same weight but slightly larger physically, measuring 23.5mm. Another fresh version was placed into use in 1795, this one the work of John S. Gardner; its specifications were the same as its predecessor's. It was later concluded that the weight had been set too high. This ushered in the so-called "thin planchet" half cent, weighing 5.44 grams and still measuring 23.5mm. TWO HUNDRED FOR A DOLLAR was removed from the edge. The varieties of this Liberty Cap half cent are numerous, despite the brief period of its manufacture.

The Liberty Cap half cent was followed in 1800 by introduction of the Draped Bust design, after a period of two years in which coins of this denomination were not minted (they could hardly have been in short supply, as well over 200,000 had been circulated). Liberty's cap was removed and her hairstyle made somewhat more fashionable. The portrait was lengthened somewhat to include a suggestion of shoulders, over which a classical-style garment was placed. The designer was Robert Scot, who had done the 1794 version. Specifications remained the same as before. It was resolved to get these coins into very extensive circulation, resulting in a mintage quantity of more than one million in the year 1804 alone. By the end of 1808, the last year for this design, more than 3 million had been struck. The new half cent was the so-called Classic Head variety, designed by John Reich. Apparently this title was bestowed in the belief that Reich's Liberty more closely approximated Grecian sculpture than had the other types. The face, if stronger, became less physically attractive and more masculine. Stars were set at either side of the portrait and Liberty was given a band round her head with her name imprinted on it. The next design, and the last, was introduced in 1840 but used for proofs only, as the half cent did not return to general circulation until 1849. Christian Gobrecht was the designer and his rendition of Liberty has come to be known as the Braided Hair type. A sharp departure from the Reich approach, it pictured Liberty with a Roman nose and considerable loss of bulk. This could well be considered the most attractive design, portrait-wise, of the half-cent series.

HALF CENTS—LIBERTY CAP, 1793–1797

1793   1794 Pole to Cap

DATE	ABP	G-4 GOOD	F-12 FINE	VF-20 V. FINE
☐ 1793 Facing Left (34,534)				
	1890.00	3150.00	RARE	RARE
☐ 1794 Facing Right (81,600)				
	240.00	400.00	1100.00	RARE
☐ 1795 Plain Edge	240.00	400.00	1000.00	RARE
☐ 1795 Lettered Edge (125,600)				
	240.00	400.00	2000.00	RARE
☐ 1796 With Pole (5,090)			EXTREMELY RARE	
☐ 1796 No Pole			EXTREMELY RARE	
☐ 1797 Plain Edge	360.00	600.00	1200.00	RARE
☐ 1797 Lettered Edge (122,214)				
	720.00	1200.00	RARE	RARE
☐ 1797 1 Above 1	300.00	500.00	1200.00	RARE

HALF CENTS—DRAPED BUST, 1800–1808

1804   Plain **4**   Crosslet **4**   Spiked Chin Variety

DATE	ABP	G-4 GOOD	F-12 FINE	VF-20 V. FINE	EF-40 EX. FINE
☐ 1800 (211,530)					
	39.00	65.00	200.00	400.00	1000.00
☐ 1802 with 1800 Reverse			EXTREMELY RARE		
☐ 1802 (14,366)					
	420.00	700.00			RARE
☐ 1803 (87,900)					
	45.00	75.00	100.00	400.00	1000.00
☐ 1804 Plain 4	45.00	75.00	100.00	175.00	700.00
☐ 1804 Crosslet (1,055,312)					
	50.00	85.00	200.00	350.00	550.00
☐ 1804 Spiked Chin					
	50.00	85.00	200.00	350.00	550.00

DATE	ABP	G-4 GOOD	F-12 FINE	VF-20 V. FINE	EF-40 EX. FINE
☐ 1805 Small 5					
	800.00	1350.00	3500.00		RARE
☐ 1805 Large 5 (814,464)					
	45.00	75.00	175.00	300.00	550.00
☐ 1806 (356,000)					
	45.00	75.00	175.00	225.00	550.00
☐ 1806 Small 6, Stems					
	110.00	185.00	600.00	1400.00	2800.00
☐ 1807 (476,000)					
	40.00	65.00	140.00	225.00	550.00
☐ 1808 (400,000)					
	45.00	75.00	200.00	375.00	700.00
☐ 1808 Over 7	96.00	160.00	525.00	1250.00	RARE

HALF CENTS—TURBAN HEAD, 1809–1837

1837   1837 TOKEN

DATE	ABP	G-4 GOOD	F-12 FINE	VF-20 V. FINE	EF-40 EX. FINE
☐ 1809 (1,154,572)					
	21.00	35.00	100.00	150.00	400.00
☐ 1809 Over 6	27.00	45.00	100.00	150.00	450.00
☐ 1809 Circle Inside O					
	33.00	55.00	135.00	175.00	550.00
☐ 1810 (215,000)					
	45.00	75.00	175.00	375.00	750.00
☐ 1811 (63,140)					
	165.00	275.00	1000.00	2200.00	RARE
☐ 1811 Restrike with 1802 Reverse				EXTREMELY RARE	
☐ 1825 (63,000)					
	36.00	60.00	100.00	150.00	275.00
☐ 1826 (234,000)					
	36.00	60.00	100.00	125.00	275.00

DATE	ABP	G-4 GOOD	F-12 FINE	VF-20 V. FINE	EF-40 EX. FINE
☐ 1828 12 Stars (606,000)					
	45.00	75.00	100.00	175.00	330.00
☐ 1828 13 Stars	45.00	75.00	100.00	100.00	150.00
☐ 1829 (487,000)					
	27.00	45.00	100.00	125.00	200.00
☐ 1831, 8 Known (2,200)					
	Proof Only	Business	Strikes	Original	RARE
☐ 1831 Small Berries	Proof Only	Restrike			RARE
☐ 1831 Large Berries	Proof Only	Restrike			RARE
☐ 1832 (154,000)					
	27.00	45.00	80.00	100.00	125.00
☐ 1833 (120,000)					
	27.00	45.00	80.00	100.00	125.00
☐ 1834 (141,000)					
	27.00	45.00	80.00	100.00	125.00
☐ 1835 (398,000)					
	27.00	45.00	80.00	100.00	135.00
☐ 1836	Proof Only	Original		Restrike	RARE
☐ 1837 Token, Pure Copper					
	27.00	45.00	60.00	150.00	300.00

HALF CENTS—BRAIDED HAIR, 1840–1857

DATE	ABP	PRF-65 PROOF
☐ 1840		Proof Only	RARE
☐ 1841		Proof Only	RARE
☐ 1842	ORIGINAL	Proof Only	RARE
☐ 1843	AND RESTRIKE	Proof Only	RARE
☐ 1844	PROOFS ONLY	Proof Only	RARE

DATE	ABP				PRF-65 PROOF
☐ 1845	1840–49			Proof Only	RARE
☐ 1846	NO MINTAGE			Proof Only	RARE
☐ 1847	RECORDS			Proof Only	RARE
☐ 1848				Proof Only	RARE
☐ 1849				Proof Only	RARE

DATE	ABP	G-4 GOOD	F-12 FINE	VF-20 V. FINE	EF-40 EX. FINE
☐ 1849	(39,864)				
	30.00	50.00	90.00	100.00	200.00
☐ 1850	(39,812)				
	30.00	50.00	90.00	100.00	200.00
☐ 1851	(147,672)				
	27.00	45.00	65.00	100.00	125.00
☐ 1852		Proofs Only—Original and Restrike: RARE			
☐ 1853	(129,964)				
	27.00	45.00	85.00	100.00	125.00
☐ 1854	(55,358)				
	27.00	45.00	85.00	100.00	125.00
☐ 1855	(56,500)				
	27.00	45.00	85.00	100.00	125.00
☐ 1856	(40,430)				
	27.00	45.00	85.00	100.00	125.00
☐ 1857	(35,180)				
	30.00	50.00	100.00	125.00	200.00

LARGE CENTS, 1793–1857

The shrinkage of the cent from its introduction in 1793 to its present size is ample evidence of inflation; the present Lincoln cent weighs only about one-third as much as its distant ancestor. But what the penny has lost in bulk and buying power has been compensated for, at least in part, by its greater convenience. The series began with the Flowing Hair/Chain Reverse type designed by Henry Voight. Its weight was set at 13.48 grams of pure copper, precisely twice that of the half cent. (The government set rigid standards of weight, fearing that without such regulations its coinage would not inspire confidence.) There were no long suspensions of production, as with the half cent. A quantity—varying, of course, in number—was minted each year from the coin's inception until conclusion of the Large Cent in 1857, with the single exception of 1815 because of a metal shortage.

The first design, aptly named Liberty, is shown with billowing hair that appears breeze-blown. Her features are delicate and the overall composition is pleasing. It will be noted that the reverse design bears very close resemblance to the Fugio cent or Franklin cent, struck in 1787. The diameter of this coin varies from 26–27mm. It is consequently not very much smaller than the present fifty-cent piece.

After three months of striking coins from these dies, during which time more than 36,000 were produced, a new design was introduced. The work of Adam Eckfeldt, designer of the first half cent, it retained the Flowing Hair portrait on the obverse but employed a wreath rather than the chained reverse, enclosing the words ONE CENT. Its weight was unchanged but the diameter varies from 26–28mm. or slightly larger than its predecessor. Along the edge is stamped the inscription ONE HUNDRED FOR A DOLLAR.

This design got somewhat further, resulting in a mintage of more than 60,000 pieces, but before the year was out another had taken its place. The Flowing Hair portrait, subjected to criticism in the press (to which the government seems to have been more sensitive than subsequently), was removed in favor of a Liberty Cap type, designed by Joseph Wright. Here the bust of Liberty is positioned somewhat to the right of center; over her left shoulder she balances a staff, on the tip of which rests a conical-shaped cap—the "cap of liberty," symbolic of freedom from slavery in Roman times. This version, too, was assailed, but minters were so weary of making alterations that they continued using it until 1796. The staff and cap looked like an Indian arrow in the opinion of some; others fancied that Liberty was wearing an oversized bow in her hair. The weight was retained but the planchet grew slightly larger, to 29mm.

In 1795, still using the same design, the weight was dropped to 10.89 grams, diameter remained 29mm., and new dies were engraved. The artist was John S. Gardner. His work is often said to be superior to other efforts. The Draped Bust type, first struck in mid-1796, was an effort to render more classicism to the portrait. Designed by Robert Scot, it deleted the much-maligned liberty cap and, while not materially altering Miss Liberty's facial features, gave her the appearance of chubbiness. Specifications remained as previously.

In 1808 the so-called Classic Head made its bow, designed by John Reich. Here Liberty wears a coronet with the word LIBERTY spelled out upon it and the bust is shortened with drapery removed. She grows chubbier still. The reverse is very close to that of a modern "wheat" cent: the words ONE CENT encircled in laurel, surrounded by the legend UNITED STATES OF AMERICA. There are numerous varieties, as enumerated in the listing that follows. The classic head survived until the copper shortage, which followed close upon the heels of the War of 1812, when production of Large Cents was temporarily halted. When resumed in 1816 the design was new. The work of Robert Scot, it was referred to as Matron Head, as Liberty appears to have taken on added years. She, in fact, was growing old with her coinage. A youth in 1792 when the series began, she had now advanced into middle age. The bust is shortened even further; stars now totally encircle it (except for the space containing the date), but the reverse remains the same.

In 1837 the last Large Cent design was put into production. The next two decades yielded many varieties of it, from die re-engravings. This is the Gobrecht version, basically a handsome portrait that returns the youthful goddess image to Liberty and slims her down. The weight was 10.89 grams (the penny was never to return to its old weight-standard), the diameter 27.5mm. Chief variations are the Silly Head and Booby Head, neither of which really merited such ridicule. There was also a Petite Head and Mature Head and ample differences in letter and numeral sizes.

1793 Chain   1793 Wreath

LARGE CENTS—FLOWING HAIR, 1793

DATE	ABP	G-4 GOOD	VG-8 V. GOOD	F-12 FINE	VF-20 V. FINE
☐ 1793 Chain AMERI (36,103)					RARE
☐ 1793 Chain AMERICA					RARE
☐ 1793 Chain Type, Period after Date and LIBERTY					RARE
☐ 1793 Wreath Type, Edge Has Vine and Bars (63,353)	1200.00	2000.00	3000.00		RARE
☐ 1793 Wreath Type, Lettered Edge, 1 Leaf on Edge	1500.00	2500.00	4000.00		RARE
☐ 1793 Wreath Type, Lettered Edge, Double Leaf on Edge					EXTREMELY RARE

LARGE CENTS—LIBERTY CAP, 1793–1796

1793 LIBERTY CAP

1795 JEFFERSON HEAD

ONE CENT
in Center of Wreath

ONE CENT
High in Wreath

DATE	ABP	G-4 GOOD	VG-8 V. GOOD	F-12 FINE	VF-20 V. FINE
☐ 1793	(11,056)				
	2310.00	3850.00			RARE
☐ 1794	(918,521)				
	240.00	400.00	500.00	800.00	2000.00
☐ 1794*	600.00	1000.00	2200.00	3750.00	RARE
☐ 1794**	180.00	300.00	400.00	600.00	1800.00
☐ 1794***	180.00	300.00	500.00	600.00	1800.00
☐ 1794****					RARE

*Head of 1793 **Head of 1795 ***No Fraction Bar ****Stars on Back

☐ 1795 Jefferson Head					
					VERY RARE
☐1795† Lettered Edge*					
	240.00	400.00	600.00	1250.00	2500.00
☐ 1795† Lettered Edge**					
	195.00	325.00	500.00	1000.00	2000.00
☐ 1795†† Plain Edge*					
	180.00	300.00	400.00	700.00	1575.00
☐ 1795†† Plain Edge**					
	180.00	300.00	400.00	700.00	1575.00
☐ 1796††† Liberty Cap					
	231.00	385.00	585.00	1500.00	2700.00

†Total Mintage: 82,000 ††Total Mintage: 456,500 †††Total Mintage: 109,825
*ONE CENT in Center of Wreath **ONE CENT High in Wreath

LARGE CENTS—DRAPED BUST, 1796–1800

Gripped or
Milled Edge
←

LIHERTY 1796 (error)

DATE	ABP	G-4 GOOD	VG-8 V. GOOD	F-12 FINE	VF-20 V. FINE
☐ 1796††	120.00	200.00	350.00	750.00	2500.00
☐ 1796†† LIHERTY (error)	195.00	325.00	750.00	1400.00	4500.00
☐ 1796 † Stems on Wreath	120.00	200.00	400.00	800.00	2500.00
☐ 1797†† Stemless Wreath	120.00	200.00	375.00	650.00	2000.00
☐ 1797†† Stems on Wreath	75.00	125.00	235.00	350.00	850.00
☐ 1797†† Gripped	90.00	150.00	250.00	500.00	900.00
☐ 1797†† Plain Edge	90.00	150.00	325.00	500.00	1000.00
☐ 1798††† over 97	90.00	150.00	300.00	650.00	2500.00
☐ 1798††† Small Date	50.00	85.00	125.00	300.00	750.00
☐ 1798††† Large Date	50.00	85.00	125.00	300.00	500.00
☐ 1798†††*	75.00	125.00	300.00	650.00	1650.00
☐ 1799* over 98	1800.00	3000.00	RARE	RARE	RARE
☐ 1799** Normal Date	1350.00	2250.00	4800.00	RARE	RARE
☐ 1800*** over 1798	45.00	75.00	200.00	300.00	1200.00

†Total Mintage: 363,372 ††Total Mintage: 897,509 †††Total Mintage: 979,700
*Reverse of 96**Single leaf Reverse. Total Mintage: 904,584***Part of 2,822,170

LARGE CENTS—DRAPED BUST, 1800–1801

Normal Date—Normal Die   1800 Over 179

DATE	ABP	G-4 GOOD	VG-8 V. GOOD	F-12 FINE	VF-20 V. FINE
☐ 1800 over 79, Style I Hair	48.00	80.00	175.00	300.00	1250.00
☐ 1800† over 79, Style II Hair	48.00	80.00	175.00	270.00	1000.00
☐ 1800† Unfinished Cyphers	48.00	80.00	175.00	270.00	1000.00
☐ 1800† Normal Date	42.00	70.00	135.00	250.00	600.00
☐ 1801†† Normal Dies, Blunt 1	45.00	75.00	135.00	250.00	600.00
☐ 1801†† First 1 Pointed	42.00	60.00	85.00	200.00	500.00
☐ 1801†† 3 Errors—1/1000, one stem, and UNITED	120.00	200.00	400.00	825.00	2500.00

1802- 1/100   ERROR 1/100   OVER 1/100

DATE	ABP	G-4 GOOD	VG-8 V. GOOD	F-12 FINE	VF-20 V. FINE
☐ 1801†† 1/000	48.00	80.00	150.00	350.00	600.00
☐ 1801†† 1/100 over 1/000	51.00	85.00	150.00	350.00	750.00

†Total Mintage: 2,822,170 ††Total Mintage (all 1801 Varieties) 1,362,837

LARGE CENTS—DRAPED BUST, 1802–1804

DATE	ABP	G-4 GOOD	VG-8 V. GOOD	F-12 FINE	VF-20 V. FINE
☐ 1802††† Normal Dies	45.00	75.00	95.00	200.00	450.00
☐ 1802††† Stemless Wreath	51.00	85.00	150.00	300.00	450.00
☐ 1802††† Fraction 1/000	40.00	80.00	150.00	300.00	550.00
☐ 1803* Small Date, Small Fraction	42.00	70.00	100.00	220.00	450.00
☐ 1803* Small Date, Large Fraction	42.00	72.00	100.00	220.00	450.00
☐ 1803* Large Date, Small Fraction					RARE
☐ 1803* Large Date, Large Fraction	45.00	75.00	200.00	400.00	1400.00

Total Mintage: ††1,362,837 †††3,435,100 *2,471,350

"Mumps" Obverse

"Normal" Obverse

DATE	ABP	G-4 GOOD	VG-8 V. GOOD	F-12 FINE	VF-20 V. FINE
☐ 1803† Mumps Obverse	48.00	80.00	125.00	265.00	525.00
☐ 1803† Stemless Wreath	51.00	85.00	175.00	300.00	575.00
☐ 1803† 1/100 over 1/000	51.00	85.00	175.00	300.00	600.00
☐ 1804 Normal Dies (756,837)	510.00	850.00	1500.00	4000.00	RARE
☐ 1804 Broken Obverse Die	480.00	600.00	1250.00	2000.00	3500.00
☐ 1804 Broken Obverse and Reverse Die	480.00	600.00	1250.00	1850.00	3500.00

†Part of 2,471,350

LARGE CENTS—DRAPED BUST, 1804–1807

1804
Normal Die

1804
Restruck
in 1860

Small Fraction

Large Fraction

Comet Variety, 1807

DATE	ABP	G-4 GOOD	VG-8 V. GOOD	F-12 FINE	VF-20 V. FINE
☐ 1805 Blunt 1 in Date (941,115)					
	42.00	70.00	120.00	175.00	425.00
☐ 1805 Pointed 1 in Date					
	42.00	70.00	120.00	250.00	425.00
☐ 1806 (348,000)					
	45.00	75.00	140.00	250.00	700.00
☐ 1807 over 6 Large 7					
	33.00	55.00	100.00	225.00	450.00
☐ 1807 over 6 Small 7					
	2100.00	3500.00	RARE	RARE	RARE
☐ 1807 Small Fraction (727,000)					
	39.00	65.00	80.00	275.00	500.00
☐ 1807 Large Fraction					
	42.00	70.00	80.00	275.00	400.00
☐ 1807 Comet Variety					
	60.00	100.00	150.00	275.00	800.00

LARGE CENTS—TURBAN HEAD, 1808–1814

DATE	ABP	G-4 GOOD	VG-8 V. GOOD	F-12 FINE	VF-20 V. FINE
☐ 1808, 13 Stars	45.00	75.00	175.00	300.00	650.00
☐ 1808, 12 Stars	(1,109,000)				
	75.00	125.00	250.00	400.00	1000.00
☐ 1809	(222,867)				
	75.00	125.00	275.00	600.00	1500.00
☐ 1810 over 9	36.00	60.00	125.00	325.00	750.00
☐ 1810	(1,458,400)				
	39.00	65.00	120.00	325.00	750.00
☐ 1811 over 10	75.00	125.00	200.00	600.00	1800.00
☐ 1811	(218,025)				
	75.00	125.00	200.00	400.00	1200.00
☐ 1812 Small Date					
	36.00	60.00	125.00	300.00	700.00
☐ 1812 Large Date	(1,075,500)				
	36.00	60.00	125.00	300.00	700.00
☐ 1813 Close Stars					
	39.00	65.00	150.00	325.00	700.00
☐ 1813 Distant Stars	(418,000)				
	36.00	60.00	150.00	325.00	600.00
☐ 1814 Plain 4	39.00	65.00	100.00	300.00	500.00
☐ 1814 Crosslet 4	(357,830)				
	39.00	65.00	100.00	300.00	600.00

LARGE CENTS—CORONET, 1816–1838

DATE	ABP	G-4 GOOD	VG-8 V. GOOD	F-12 FINE	VF-20 V. FINE	MS-60 UNC.
☐ 1816	(2,820,982)					
	15.00	25.00	40.00	75.00	150.00	400.00
☐ 1817 Wide Date						
	18.00	30.00	40.00	65.00	200.00	525.00

1823
Normal

1823
Restrike
Perfect Die

1823
Restrike
Broken Die

DATE	ABP	G-4 GOOD	VG-8 V. GOOD	F-12 FINE	VF-20 V. FINE	MS-60 UNC.
☐ 1817 13 Stars (3,984,400)						
	15.00	25.00	35.00	42.00	75.00	375.00
☐ 1817 15 Stars						
	24.00	40.00	45.00	65.00	175.00	1200.00
☐ 1818 (3,167,000)						
	15.00	25.00	30.00	45.00	80.00	330.00
☐ 1819 over 18						
	18.00	30.00	35.00	45.00	100.00	400.00
☐ 1819 Large Date (2,671,000)						
	18.00	30.00	35.00	45.00	100.00	525.00
☐ 1819 Small Date						
	18.00	30.00	38.00	45.00	100.00	525.00
☐ 1820 over 19						
	18.00	30.00	38.00	50.00	125.00	1200.00
☐ 1820 Small Date (4,407,550)						
	18.00	30.00	38.00	45.00	100.00	700.00
☐ 1820 Large Date						
	18.00	30.00	38.00	45.00	100.00	500.00
☐ 1821 Wide Date (389,000)						
	30.00	50.00	75.00	140.00	525.00	2000.00
☐ 1821 Close Date (389,000)						
	30.00	50.00	75.00	140.00	450.00	1800.00
☐ 1822 Wide Date (2,075,339)						
	15.00	25.00	40.00	65.00	150.00	1500.00
☐ 1822 Close Date						
	15.00	25.00	40.00	65.00	125.00	1250.00
☐ 1823 over 22 (Part of 855,730)						
	42.00	70.00	120.00	300.00	800.00	RARE

DATE	ABP	G-4 GOOD	VG-8 V. GOOD	F-12 FINE	VF-20 V. FINE	MS-60 UNC.
□ 1823 Normal Date						
	50.00	85.00	200.00	400.00	800.00	RARE
□ 1823 Restrike from Broken Obverse Die						
				Uncirculated Only		1500.00
□ 1823 Restrike from Perfect Die (49 Known)					EXTREMELY RARE	
□ 1824 over 22						
	21.00	35.00	45.00	100.00	350.00	RARE
□ 1824 Wide Date	(1,262,090)					
	15.00	25.00	40.00	60.00	200.00	1500.00
□ 1824 Close Date						
	15.00	25.00	40.00	60.00	175.00	1500.00
□ 1825 Small A's	(1,461,000)					
	15.00	25.00	40.00	60.00	125.00	1400.00
□ 1825 Large A's						
	15.00	25.00	40.00	60.00	150.00	1400.00
□ 1826 over 25						
	18.00	30.00	65.00	125.00	250.00	3000.00
□ 1826 Wide Date	(1,517,422)					
	15.00	25.00	35.00	40.00	100.00	1200.00
□ 1826 Close Date						
	15.00	25.00	35.00	40.00	175.00	1200.00
□ 1827	(2,357,733)					
	15.00	25.00	35.00	40.00	150.00	800.00
□ 1828 Small Date	(2,260,625)					
	18.00	30.00	35.00	50.00	125.00	1200.00
□ 1828 Large Date						
	18.00	30.00	35.00	60.00	150.00	1400.00
□ 1829 Small Letters	(1,414,500)					
	18.00	30.00	70.00	175.00	600.00	RARE
□ 1829 Large Letters	(1,414,500)					
	18.00	30.00	35.00	45.00	125.00	625.00
□ 1830 Small Letters						
	15.00	25.00	50.00	150.00	500.00	RARE
□ 1830 Large Letters						
	18.00	30.00	35.00	45.00	150.00	500.00
□ 1831 Small Letters	(3,359,260)					
	18.00	30.00	35.00	50.00	125.00	550.00
□ 1831 Large Letters						
	18.00	30.00	30.00	50.00	100.00	500.00
□ 1832 Small Letters	(2,362,000)					
	15.00	25.00	30.00	50.00	100.00	600.00

DATE	ABP	G-4 GOOD	VG-8 V. GOOD	F-12 FINE	VF-20 V. FINE	MS-60 UNC.
☐ 1832 Large Letters (2,362,000)						
	18.00	30.00	35.00	45.00	125.00	450.00
☐ 1833 Small Letters (2,739,000)						
	15.00	25.00	30.00	40.00	85.00	500.00
☐ 1833 Large Letters						
	15.00	25.00	30.00	40.00	85.00	400.00
☐ 1834*	21.00	35.00	40.00	100.00	300.00	2000.00
☐ 1834** (1,855,110)						
	15.00	25.00	35.00	50.00	65.00	450.00
☐ 1834***	15.00	25.00	35.00	50.00	70.00	450.00
☐ 1835 Small Date, Small Stars						
	15.00	25.00	35.00	40.00	75.00	600.00
☐ 1835 Large Date, Large Stars (3,878,397)						
	15.00	25.00	35.00	40.00	70.00	900.00
☐ 1835 Type of 1836						
	15.00	25.00	35.00	40.00	75.00	425.00
☐ 1836 (2,111,000)						
	18.00	30.00	35.00	45.00	80.00	425.00
☐ 1837 Plain Hair Cord, Small Letters						
	18.00	30.00	35.00	45.00	75.00	500.00
☐ 1837 Plain Hair Cord, Large Letters (5,558,301)						
	18.00	30.00	35.00	45.00	80.00	425.00
☐ 1837 Beaded Hair Cord, Small Letters						
	18.00	30.00	35.00	45.00	80.00	350.00
☐ 1838 (6,370,200)						
	18.00	30.00	35.00	40.00	65.00	400.00
☐ 1838 Line under CENT						
	15.00	25.00	30.00	35.00	60.00	400.00
☐ 1839 Silly Head (All Kinds)						
	18.00	30.00	45.00	75.00	95.00	1000.00
☐ 1839 No Center Dot						
	15.00	25.00	35.00	40.00	85.00	500.00
☐ 1839 Booby Head (3,128,662)						
	18.00	30.00	45.00	50.00	100.00	1000.00
☐ 1839 Petite Head						
	15.00	25.00	30.00	40.00	75.00	350.00
☐ 1839 over 36						
	150.00	250.00	500.00	1000.00	2250.00	RARE

*Large Date—Large Stars—Large Letters Reverse **Small Date—Small Stars—Small Letters Reverse ***Large Date—Small Stars—Small Letters Reverse

LARGE CENTS—BRAIDED HAIR, 1839–1857

Booby Head

1856 Slants

DATE	ABP	G-4 GOOD	VG-8 V. GOOD	F-12 FINE	VF-20 V. FINE	MS-60 UNC.
☐ 1839 Type of 1840						
	15.00	25.00	35.00	45.00	75.00	500.00
☐ 1840 Small Date						
	15.00	25.00	30.00	35.00	65.00	400.00
☐ 1840 Large Date (2,462,700)						
	18.00	30.00	35.00	40.00	65.00	400.00
☐ 1841 (1,597,366)						
	15.00	25.00	30.00	40.00	60.00	500.00
☐ 1842 Small Date						
	15.00	25.00	30.00	40.00	50.00	475.00
☐ 1842 Large Date (2,383,390)						
	15.00	25.00	30.00	40.00	55.00	450.00
☐ 1843 Obverse and Reverse 1842						
	15.00	25.00	30.00	40.00	75.00	500.00
☐ 1843 Obverse 1842 Reverse 1844						
	18.00	30.00	35.00	40.00	50.00	425.00
☐ 1844	15.00	25.00	35.00	40.00	60.00	300.00
☐ 1844 over 81 (2,398,752)						
	21.00	35.00	45.00	75.00	125.00	1500.00
☐ 1845 (3,894,805)						
	15.00	25.00	35.00	40.00	60.00	300.00
☐ 1846 Small Date						
	15.00	25.00	30.00	35.00	50.00	375.00

DATE	ABP	G-4 GOOD	VG-8 V. GOOD	F-12 FINE	VF-20 V. FINE	MS-60 UNC.
☐ 1846 Medium Date	(4,120,800)					
	15.00	25.00	30.00	40.00	50.00	275.00
☐ 1846 Tall Date						
	18.00	30.00	35.00	40.00	50.00	500.00
☐ 1847	15.00	25.00	30.00	35.00	45.00	325.00
☐ 1848	(6,320,680)					
	15.00	25.00	30.00	35.00	45.00	275.00
☐ 1849	(4,260,111)					
	15.00	25.00	30.00	35.00	45.00	300.00
☐ 1850	(4,426,844)					
	15.00	25.00	30.00	35.00	45.00	225.00
☐ 1851	15.00	25.00	30.00	35.00	45.00	225.00
☐ 1851 over 81	(9,899,700)					
	24.00	40.00	45.00	60.00	100.00	625.00
☐ 1852	(5,063,094)					
	15.00	25.00	28.00	35.00	45.00	245.00
☐ 1853	(6,641,131)					
	15.00	25.00	28.00	35.00	45.00	245.00
☐ 1854	(4,236,156)					
	15.00	25.00	28.00	35.00	45.00	245.00
☐ 1855 Upright 5's						
	15.00	25.00	28.00	30.00	65.00	250.00
☐ 1855 Slanting 5's	(1,574,829)					
	15.00	25.00	28.00	30.00	40.00	300.00
☐ 1855 Slanting 5's, Knob on Ear						
	16.80	28.00	35.00	40.00	50.00	400.00
☐ 1856 Upright 5	(2,690,465)					
	16.80	28.00	35.00	40.00	45.00	225.00
☐ 1856 Slanting 5						
	15.00	25.00	28.00	35.00	50.00	225.00
☐ 1857 Small Date	(333,456)					
	39.00	65.00	85.00	150.00	200.00	450.00
☐ 1857 Large Date						
	45.00	75.00	90.00	150.00	200.00	500.00

SMALL CENTS

SMALL CENTS—FLYING EAGLE, 1856–1858

It would be hard to find a coin in the standard U.S. series that proved so unpopular as the Flying Eagle cent—unpopular, that is, orginally. It has since become a favorite of collectors. During 1856, while the Large Cent continued in production, plans were under way to replace it with a smaller coin of the same value. A number of patterns of the Flying Eagle were struck that year at the Philadelphia Mint but were not circulated because the Large Cent was discontinued and minting switched over to this new piece, with a huge output in that one year of nearly 17,500,000 coins. The public balked, charging that the government was forcing the small cent on them. Not only didn't the public care much for that idea, they were also not too fond of the coin. Instead of being struck in pure copper and having the substantial appearance that a cent was supposed to have, its composition was 88% copper and 12% nickel, yielding a coin that was sufficiently pale in color to be called white. (If one wonders about the bickerings over coin sizes, designs, and compositions in the 18th and 19th centuries, it should be realized that far greater attention was focused upon money in those days, when few persons used checks and credit cards were unknown.)

The Flying Eagle cent was designed by James Longacre. Its weight was 4.67 grams and its diameter 19mm. As a designer, Longacre was not unskilled. He proved his abilities with the Indian Head cent, which replaced the Flying Eagle in 1859.

DATE	ABP	G-4 GOOD	F-12 FINE	EF-40 EX. FINE	MS-60 UNC.	PRF-65 PROOF
☐ 1856	(Approx. 1,000)					RARE
☐ 1857	(17,450,000)					
	20.00	35.00	50.00	100.00	400.00	RARE
☐ 1858 Small Letters						
	20.00	35.00	45.00	100.00	400.00	RARE
☐ 1858 Large Letters	(24,600,000)					
	20.00	35.00	45.00	100.00	400.00	RARE

SMALL CENTS—INDIAN HEAD, 1859–1909

Probably the most famous of all U.S. coins (its only challenger for that honor being the Morgan dollar), the Indian Head cent remained in production without change in design for half a century. After the disaster of the Flying Eagle cent, rejected by the public because of its almost white color, the government knew that it must manufacture a cent whose appearance was that of good metal, even if it was not to return to the Large Cent. The question remained: Would a small copper piece be accepted, when Large Cents, containing a much greater quantity of metal, were still widely circulating? The new cent had the same composition as its predecessor, 88% copper and 12% nickel. The first batch of Indian Heads, released in 1859, amounted to 36,400,000 pieces, more than had ever been coined of a single denomination in one year: $364,000 worth of pennies. Beginning in 1864 the copper content was increased to 95%, the nickel removed entirely and replaced with a 5% alloy of tin and zinc. This was so successfully absorbed into the copper that the resulting coin was hardly different in color than if copper alone were used.

Finally the problem was solved, and the Indian Head cent

was on the road to a long successful existence. Its designer was James Longacre. The weight was 4.67 grams and the diameter 19mm., these specifications being the same as the Flying Eagle cent. The portrait is that of an Indian maiden. As first designed, the reverse carried no shield but this was added in 1860, the second year of issue. The Indian Head became the first U.S. coin struck in a quantity of more than 100 million in a year, when 108 million specimens were turned out in 1907. This exceeded the country's population. It is interesting to note that the 1908 and 1909 editions, representing the last two years of this design, are the only dates to be found with mint marks.

The origin of the portrait has been for many years a matter of discussion. It was at one time thought that Longacre had taken it from life, using an Indian girl as his model. This was dismissed when the suggestion was advanced that the profile resembled Longacre's daughter. It is now generally believed that no live model sat for the likeness but that it was based upon classical statuary, of which Longacre was known to be a collector. The Indian Head cent portrait is neither as realistic nor as impressive as that featured on the Buffalo nickel, but this is nevertheless an important coin whose design represented a bold innovation.

1901

1860–1864 Wreath on Shield

DATE	ABP	G-4 GOOD	F-12 FINE	EF-40 EX. FINE	MS-60 UNC.	PRF-65 PROOF
☐ 1859 Copper-Nickel (36,400,000)						
	9.45	15.75	25.00	125.00	300.00	RARE
☐ 1860 Copper-Nickel, Broad Bust (20,566,000)						
	6.00	10.00	21.00	80.00	250.00	3500.00
☐ 1860 Copper-Nickel, Narrow Bust						
	15.00	20.00	38.00	125.00	325.00	RARE
☐ 1861 Copper-Nickel (10,100,000)						
	15.00	20.00	50.00	125.00	300.00	RARE
☐ 1862 Copper-Nickel (28,075,000)						
	8.40	14.00	25.00	60.00	125.00	2400.00
☐ 1863 Copper-Nickel (49,840,000)						
	8.40	14.00	25.00	45.00	125.00	RARE

DATE	ABP	G-4 GOOD	F-12 FINE	EF-40 EX. FINE	MS-60 UNC.	PRF-65 PROOF
☐ 1864 Copper-Nickel (13,740,000)						
	9.60	16.00	40.00	100.00	175.00	3250.00
☐ 1864 Bronze (39,233,714)						
	6.00	10.00	18.00	80.00	175.00	3200.00
☐ 1864 Bronze, L on Ribbon						
	33.00	55.00	175.00	300.00	525.00	RARE
☐ 1865 Bronze (35,429,286)						
	6.00	10.00	22.00	60.00	100.00	800.00
☐ 1866 Bronze (9,826,500)						
	30.00	50.00	100.00	300.00	400.00	4200.00
☐ 1867 Bronze (9,821,000)						
	30.00	50.00	125.00	220.00	325.00	RARE
☐ 1867 Bronze, over 7						
	39.00	65.00	125.00	300.00	1000.00	2200.00
☐ 1868 Bronze (10,266,500)						
	24.00	40.00	100.00	175.00	275.00	RARE
☐ 1869 Bronze (6,420,000)						
	45.00	75.00	250.00	450.00	750.00	3200.00
☐ 1869 Bronze, over 9						
	75.00	125.00	400.00	650.00	1200.00	2450.00
☐ 1870 Bronze (5,275,000)						
	39.00	65.00	200.00	325.00	600.00	2800.00
☐ 1871 Bronze (3,929,500)						
	45.00	75.00	250.00	425.00	575.00	2500.00
☐ 1872 Bronze (4,042,000)						
	51.00	85.00	300.00	550.00	700.00	4400.00
☐ 1873 Bronze, closed 3 (11,676,500)						
	16.80	28.00	75.00	250.00	500.00	2850.00
☐ 1873 Bronze, open 3						
	15.00	25.00	75.00	200.00	275.00	RARE
☐ 1873 Bronze, Doubled Liberty						
	90.00	150.00	700.00	3500.00	RARE	RARE
☐ 1874 Bronze (14,187,500)						
	12.00	20.00	50.00	125.00	300.00	3000.00
☐ 1875 Bronze (13,528,000)						
	12.00	20.00	65.00	150.00	275.00	RARE
☐ 1876 Bronze (7,944,000)						
	18.00	30.00	80.00	225.00	375.00	2550.00
☐ 1877 Bronze (852,500)						
	495.00	825.00	1800.00	3000.00	3200.00	RARE
☐ 1878 Bronze (5,799,850)						
	— 21.00	35.00	85.00	225.00	400.00	1500.00

DATE	ABP	G-4 GOOD	F-12 FINE	EF-40 EX. FINE	MS-60 UNC.	PRF-65 PROOF
☐ 1879 Bronze (16,231,200)						
	6.00	10.00	22.00	75.00	125.00	1350.00
☐ 1880 Bronze (38,964,955)						
	3.60	6.00	10.00	32.50	125.00	1350.00
☐ 1881 Bronze (39,211,575)						
	3.60	6.00	10.00	30.00	85.00	1450.00
☐ 1882 Bronze (38,581,100)						
	3.60	6.00	10.00	30.00	85.00	1600.00
☐ 1883 Bronze (45,598,109)						
	3.60	6.00	10.00	30.00	85.00	1800.00
☐ 1884 Bronze (23,261,742)						
	3.60	6.00	10.00	30.00	100.00	1400.00
☐ 1885 Bronze (11,765,384)						
	6.00	10.00	18.00	75.00	125.00	1600.00
☐ 1886 Bronze (17,654,290), I feather C						
	3.00	5.00	22.00	175.00	250.00	2800.00
☐ 1886 Bronze, C Feather A						
	3.60	7.00	30.00	200.00	500.00	RARE
☐ 1887 Bronze (45,226,483)						
	2.40	4.00	5.50	25.00	75.00	RARE
☐ 1888 Bronze (37,494,414)						
	1.80	3.00	5.50	25.00	50.00	RARE
☐ 1888 Bronze, over 7						
						VERY RARE
☐ 1889 Bronze (48,868,361)						
	2.40	4.00	5.50	20.00	75.00	2100.00
☐ 1890 Bronze (57,182,854)						
	2.40	4.00	5.50	18.00	75.00	2000.00
☐ 1891 Bronze (47,072,350)						
	2.40	4.00	5.50	18.00	75.00	2250.00
☐ 1892 Bronze (37,649,832)						
	2.40	4.00	5.50	24.00	75.00	1500.00
☐ 1893 Bronze (46,642,195)						
	2.40	4.00	5.50	24.00	75.00	1400.00
☐ 1894 Bronze (16,752,132)						
	3.60	6.00	20.00	75.00	100.00	1450.00
☐ 1895 Bronze (38,343,636)						
	2.40	4.00	6.00	18.00	50.00	1250.00
☐ 1896 Bronze (39,057,293)						
	2.40	4.00	6.00	18.00	50.00	2200.00
☐ 1897 Bronze (50,466,330)						
	2.40	4.00	6.00	18.00	50.00	1800.00

DATE	ABP	G-4 GOOD	F-12 FINE	EF-40 EX. FINE	MS-60 UNC.	PRF-65 PROOF
☐ 1898 Bronze (49,923,079)						
	1.50	2.50	5.00	18.00	50.00	1400.00
☐ 1899 Bronze (53,600,031)						
	1.50	2.50	5.00	18.00	50.00	1200.00
☐ 1900 Bronze (66,833,764)						
	1.50	2.50	5.00	15.00	40.00	1400.00
☐ 1901 Bronze (79,611,143)						
	1.50	2.50	5.00	15.00	40.00	1400.00
☐ 1902 Bronze (87,376,722)						
	1.50	2.50	5.00	15.00	40.00	1400.00
☐ 1903 Bronze (85,094,493)						
	1.50	2.50	5.00	15.00	40.00	1200.00
☐ 1904 Bronze (61,328,015)						
	1.50	2.50	5.00	15.00	40.00	1400.00
☐ 1905 Bronze (80,719,163)						
	1.50	2.50	5.00	15.00	45.00	1400.00
☐ 1906 Bronze (96,022,255)						
	1.50	2.50	5.00	15.00	45.00	1400.00
☐ 1907 Bronze (108,138,618)						
	1.50	2.50	5.00	15.00	45.00	2000.00
☐ 1908 Bronze (32,327,987)						
	1.50	2.50	5.00	15.00	45.00	1400.00
☐ 1908S Bronze (1,115,000)						
	60.00	100.00	175.00	250.00	400.00	RARE
☐ 1909 Bronze (14,370,645)						
	15.00	20.00	22.00	32.00	75.00	1400.00
☐ 1909S Bronze (309,000)						
	270.00	450.00	525.00	675.00	950.00	RARE

SMALL CENTS—LINCOLN HEAD, 1909 TO DATE

It is quite likely that, despite having remained in use for fifty years, the Indian Head design would have been retained for the cent beyond 1909 had not President Roosevelt pressed for its removal. The year 1909 marked the 100th anniversary of Abraham Lincoln's birth and Roosevelt (who, not coincidentally, was a member of the same political party) wished to memorialize the anniversary by placing a likeness of Lincoln on the penny. His suggestion was adopted, the result being a design that has survived in continuous use longer than any other in the Mint's history, with no indication that it will soon be replaced. The Indian Head cents were so popular that criticism was risked by their removal. Had they been abandoned in favor of any other design a public outcry might have ensued. But for Lincoln, allowances could be made. This was incidentally the first time an American citizen appeared on coinage of the Mint, as George Washington, though depicted on numerous coins and tokens, was never portrayed on an issue of the federal Mint.

Designer of the Lincoln cent was Victor D. Brenner. Rather than using a close-up profile, Brenner showed Lincoln in quarter-length, with beard, as he appeared in the last few years of his life. It is not known whether the likeness was adapted from a specific photograph, from statuary, or merely from a study of various photos and other artworks. As first struck, the coin carried Brenner's initials and this variety is known as the VDB cent. They were removed midway through production of the 1909 issue and not reinstated until 1918, when they were switched from the reverse to the obverse. Specimens of the 1909 coin with initials, especially those struck at San Francisco, where less than half a million were produced, eventually became favorite collectors' items. At the time little notice was taken of them.

Originally the reverse was composed of the wording ONE CENT—UNITED STATES OF AMERICA enshrouded by wheat sheaves. In 1959 a new reverse was introduced, on the occasion of the 150th anniversary of Lincoln's birth and the 50th of the coin's use. Designed by Frank Gasparro, it pictures the Lincoln Memorial building in Washington, D.C. From 1909–42 the Lincoln cent had a composition of 95% copper and 5% tin and zinc, with a weight of 3.11 grams and a diameter of 19mm.

In 1943 it was made of steel-coated zinc. From 1944–46 what are known as "shell case cents" were made from spent shell casings; their content was 95% copper and 5% tin and zinc, until September of 1962 when the tin was removed from the cent for the last time. The content of the cent from 1962 until 1981 was 95% copper and 5% zinc. Beginning in 1982, the cent has been made of a zinc core with copper coating. Thus, it is now another clad coin, leaving the nickel as the lone nonclad U.S. coin.

1909

No V.D.B.   V.D.B. Restored

DATE	ABP	G-4 GOOD	F-12 FINE	VF-20 V. FINE	EF-40 EX. FINE	MS-60 UNC.	MS-65 UNC.
(1909–1942 COMPOSITION-95% COPPER WITH 5% TIN AND ZINC)
☐ 1909S V.D.B. (484,000)
	405.00	675.00	900.00	1200.00	1500.00	2000.00	RARE
☐ 1909 V.D.B. (27,995,000)
	6.00	10.00	14.00	20.00	25.00	30.00	60.00
☐ 1909 (72,702,618)
	2.40	4.00	5.00	8.00	10.00	20.00	90.00
☐ 1909S (1,825,000)
	60.00	100.00	125.00	175.00	250.00	350.00	800.00
☐ 1909S over S
	60.00	100.00	130.00	190.00	250.00	400.00	925.00
☐ 1910 (146,801,218)
	.30	.50	1.00	1.75	4.00	25.00	140.00
☐ 1910S (6,045,000)
	12.00	20.00	25.00	30.00	38.50	125.00	460.00
☐ 1911 (101,177,787)
	.30	.50	2.00	3.00	5.75	30.00	225.00
☐ 1911D (12,672,000)
	3.90	6.50	9.00	18.00	60.00	100.00	800.00
☐ 1911S (4,026,000)
	12.00	20.00	30.00	38.00	75.00	150.00	1200.00
☐ 1912 (6,853,060)
	1.20	2.00	4.00	8.00	16.00	45.00	260.00
☐ 1912D (10,411,000)
	3.90	6.50	8.25	25.00	65.00	200.00	900.00
☐ 1912S (4,431,000)
	15.00	25.00	30.00	35.00	85.00	200.00	1400.00
☐ 1913 (76,532,352)
	.60	1.00	2.25	5.00	20.00	40.00	260.00
☐ 1913D (15,804,000)
	2.40	4.00	6.00	15.00	50.00	125.00	950.00
☐ 1913S (6,101,000)
	9.00	15.00	18.00	30.00	50.00	175.00	2250.00
☐ 1914 (75,238,432)
	.45	.75	2.25	5.25	18.00	60.00	275.00
☐ 1914D (1,193,000)
	120.00	200.00	350.00	450.00	900.00	3000.00	RARE
☐ 1914S (4,137,000)
	12.00	20.00	28.00	45.00	75.00	400.00	3500.00
☐ 1915 (29,092,120)
	1.20	2.00	5.50	15.00	50.00	125.00	425.00
☐ 1915D (22,050,000)
	1.80	3.00	5.00	10.00	22.00	110.00	400.00

DATE	ABP	G-4 GOOD	F-12 FINE	VF-20 V. FINE	EF-40 EX. FINE	MS-60 UNC.	MS-65 UNC.
☐ 1915S	(4,833,677)						
	10.80	18.00	30.00	35.00	95.00	300.00	2800.00
☐ 1916	(131,838,677)						
	.45	.75	1.00	2.00	6.00	20.00	160.00
☐ 1916D	(35,956,000)						
	.75	1.25	3.50	7.00	18.00	100.00	1000.00
☐ 1916S	(22,510,000)						
	.90	1.50	3.50	8.50	25.00	100.00	1200.00
☐ 1917	(196,429,785)						
	.45	.75	.75	2.00	5.00	20.00	200.00
☐ 1917 Double Die							
	75.00	125.00	250.00	500.00	1200.00	3500.00	RARE
☐ 1917D	(55,120,000)						
	.51	.85	1.50	3.75	25.00	75.00	950.00
☐ 1917S	(32,620,000)						
	.30	.50	1.25	2.25	9.00	75.00	1500.00
☐ 1918	(288,104,634)						
	.30	.50	.75	1.25	5.00	15.00	225.00
☐ 1918D	(47,830,000)						
	.60	1.00	2.25	3.75	12.00	90.00	1400.00
☐ 1918S	(34,680,000)						
	.30	.50	1.50	3.00	10.00	90.00	2000.00
☐ 1919	(392,021,000)						
	.30	.50	.75	1.50	3.00	15.00	125.00
☐ 1919D	(57,154,000)						
	.45	.75	1.50	3.50	9.25	58.00	825.00
☐ 1919S	(139,760,000)						
	.30	.50	1.25	2.50	6.50	45.00	1250.00
☐ 1920	(310,165,000)						
	.30	.50	.75	1.50	5.50	20.00	275.00
☐ 1920D	(49,280,000)						
	.51	.85	2.25	5.00	18.00	75.00	725.00
☐ 1920S	(46,220,000)						
	.30	.50	1.75	2.50	12.00	125.00	RARE
☐ 1921	(39,157,000)						
	.30	.50	1.25	2.50	10.00	45.00	210.00
☐ 1921S	(15,274,000)						
	1.05	1.75	2.75	5.75	38.00	125.00	1200.00
☐ 1922 Missing D, No Mint Mark*							
	315.00	525.00	1000.00	2000.00	4000.00	RARE	RARE
☐ 1922D	(7,160,000)						
	12.00	20.00	25.00	30.00	50.00	100.00	525.00

*Beware of removed mint mark

DATE	ABP	G-4 GOOD	F-12 FINE	VF-20 V. FINE	EF-40 EX. FINE	MS-60 UNC.	MS-65 UNC.
☐ 1923	(74,723,000)						
	.30	.50	.75	1.25	5.25	20.00	200.00
☐ 1923S	(8,700,000)						
	2.10	3.50	5.50	8.75	38.00	275.00	RARE
☐ 1924	(75,178,000)						
	.30	.50	.75	1.00	5.50	28.00	150.00
☐ 1924D	(2,520,000)						
	18.00	30.00	42.00	55.00	100.00	425.00	2000.00
☐ 1924S	(11,696,000)						
	.66	1.10	2.50	4.50	30.00	175.00	2500.00
☐ 1925	(139,949,000)						
	.30	.50	.75	1.00	4.00	12.00	85.00
☐ 1925D	(22,580,000)						
	.60	1.00	2.50	3.75	15.00	85.00	675.00
☐ 1925S	(26,380,000)						
	.60	1.00	2.00	3.25	15.00	100.00	3800.00
☐ 1926	(157,088,000)						
	.18	.30	.65	1.00	3.00	12.00	100.00
☐ 1926D	(28,022,022)						
	.75	1.25	4.00	6.00	16.00	100.00	900.00
☐ 1926S	(4,550,000)						
	6.00	10.00	15.00	20.00	40.00	150.00	RARE
☐ 1927	(144,440,000)						
	.18	.30	.65	1.00	3.00	15.00	75.00
☐ 1927D	(27,170,000)						
	.75	1.25	2.25	3.25	5.25	60.00	600.00
☐ 1927S	(14,276,000)						
	.75	1.25	2.50	5.00	20.00	100.00	2800.00
☐ 1928	(134,116,000)						
	.18	.30	.65	1.00	3.00	12.00	125.00
☐ 1928D	(21,170,000)						
	.60	1.00	2.00	4.00	6.00	40.00	350.00
☐ 1928S	(17,266,000)						
	.60	1.00	3.25	4.50	12.00	100.00	1200.00
☐ 1929	(185,262,000)						
	.18	.30	.65	1.00	3.00	12.00	75.00
☐ 1929D	(41,730,000)						
	.30	.50	1.40	2.50	5.75	28.00	165.00
☐ 1929S	(50,148,000)						
	.45	.75	1.85	2.50	6.00	24.00	125.00
☐ 1930	(157,415,000)						
	.18	.30	.65	1.00	3.00	7.00	75.00

DATE	ABP	G-4 GOOD	F-12 FINE	VF-20 V. FINE	EF-40 EX. FINE	MS-60 UNC.	MS-65 UNC.
☐ 1930D	(40,100,000)						
	.18	.30	.60	1.00	4.00	15.00	75.00
☐ 1930S	(24,286,000)						
	.18	.30	.60	1.00	2.50	15.00	60.00
☐ 1931	(19,396,000)						
	.45	.75	1.25	2.00	5.00	22.00	100.00
☐ 1931D	(4,480,000)						
	3.60	6.00	7.50	10.00	15.00	75.00	425.00
☐ 1931S	(866,000)						
	60.00	100.00	110.00	125.00	130.00	200.00	410.00
☐ 1932	(9,062,000)						
	1.05	1.75	2.25	3.25	6.50	25.00	85.00
☐ 1932D*	(10,500,000)						
	1.05	1.75	2.75	3.00	5.00	20.00	85.00
☐ 1933	(14,360,000)						
	1.20	2.00	3.00	4.00	7.25	25.00	85.00
☐ 1933D	(6,200,000)						
	2.40	4.00	6.00	8.00	15.00	30.00	80.00
☐ 1934	(219,080,000)						
	.07	.12	.28	.50	1.25	12.00	40.00
☐ 1934D	(28,446,000)						
	.15	.25	.60	1.25	3.00	20.00	50.00
☐ 1935	(245,388,000)						
	.15	.25	.30	.35	.60	3.25	30.00
☐ 1935D	(47,000,000)						
	.15	.25	.30	.35	.60	6.00	30.00
☐ 1935S	(38,702,000)						
	.15	.25	.30	.75	3.00	15.00	60.00
☐ 1936	(309,637,569)						
	.15	.25	.30	.75	2.00	6.00	25.00
☐ 1936D	(40,620,000)						
	.15	.25	.35	.60	1.25	5.00	20.00
☐ 1936S	(29,130,000)						
	.15	.25	.45	.65	1.25	5.25	20.00
☐ 1937	(309,179,320)						
	.15	.25	.35	.65	1.10	4.00	18.00
☐ 1937D	(50,430,000)						
	.15	.25	.45	.65	1.10	5.10	18.00

*Note: More than 15,000 specimens of the 1932D cent were included in the Dr. Jerry Buss Collection, sold in 1985. This was the largest quantity ever sold at one time.

DATE	ABP	G-4 GOOD	F-12 FINE	VF-20 V. FINE	EF-40 EX. FINE	MS-60 UNC.	MS-65 UNC
☐ 1937S	(35,500,000)						
	.15	.25	.45	.60	1.10	5.50	18.00
☐ 1938	(156,696,734)						
	.15	.25	.35	.45	1.10	4.25	20.00
☐ 1938D	(20,010,000)						
	.15	.25	.60	.80	1.50	4.25	20.00
☐ 1938S	(15,180,000)						
	.36	.50	.75	.85	1.25	4.25	18.00
☐ 1939	(316,479,520)						
	.15	.25	.35	.45	.65	2.25	18.00
☐ 1939D	(15,160,000)						
	.40	.65	.75	1.00	1.50	5.00	20.00
☐ 1939S	(52,070,000)						
	.21	.35	.55	.85	1.25	4.00	18.00
☐ 1940	(586,825,872)						
	.15	.25	.35	.45	.75	3.00	14.00
☐ 1940D	(83,190,000)						
	.15	.25	.35	.75	1.00	4.00	15.00
☐ 1940S	(112,940,000)						
	.15	.25	.35	.60	1.10	4.00	15.00
☐ 1941	(887,039,100)						
	.15	.25	.35	.50	1.00	3.00	15.00
☐ 1941D	(128,700,000)						
	.15	.25	.35	.65	1.25	4.25	14.00
☐ 1941S	(92,360,000)						
	.15	.25	.50	.75	1.25	4.25	18.00
☐ 1942	(657,828,600)						
	.15	.25	.35	.40	.75	2.00	12.00
☐ 1942D	(206,698,000)						
	.15	.25	.35	.40	.75	2.00	12.00
☐ 1942S	(85,590,000)						
	.18	.30	.50	.90	1.30	5.00	20.00

(1943 WARTIME STEEL COMPOSITION-STEEL COATED WITH ZINC)

DATE	ABP	G-4 GOOD	F-12 FINE	VF-20 V. FINE	EF-40 EX. FINE	MS-60 UNC.	MS-65 UNC
☑ 1943	(684,628,670)						
	.15	.25	.40	.55	.65	2.25	20.00
☐ 1943D	(217,660,000)						
	.24	.40	.50	.55	.65	2.75	15.00
☐ 1943S	(191,550,000)						
	.27	.45	.55	.70	1.00	5.00	30.00

(1944–1946 "SHELL CASE" COPPER COMPOSITION-95% COPPER AND 5% ZINC)

DATE	ABP	G-4 GOOD	F-12 FINE	VF-20 V. FINE	EF-40 EX. FINE	MS-60 UNC.	MS-65 UNC
☐ 1944	(1,435,400,000)						
				.15	.45	.85	8.00

DATE	ABP	VF-20 V. FINE	EF-40 EX. FINE	MS-60 UNC.	MS-65 UNC.
☐ 1944D	(430,578,000)				
	.12	.20	.35	.60	15.00
☐ 1944D/S Variety 1					
	90.00	150.00	250.00	600.00	3800.00
☐ 1944D/S Variety 2					
	51.00	85.00	150.00	265.00	1500.00
☐ 1944S	(282,760,000)				
	.09	.15	.25	.65	7.50
☐ 1945	(1,040,515,000)				
	.06	.10	.25	.65	10.00
☐ 1945D	(226,268,000)				
	.06	.10	.25	.65	7.50
☐ 1945S	(181,770,000)				
	.12	.20	.25	.65	7.50
☐ 1946	(991,655,000)				
	.09	.15	.25	.50	10.00
☐ 1946D	(315,690,000)				
	.09	.15	.25	.50	8.00
☐ 1946S	(198,100,000)				
	.12	.20	.25	.50	10.00
☐ 1946S/D			65.00	200.00	750.00
(1947–1962 COMPOSITION-95% COPPER AND 5% TIN AND ZINC)					
☐ 1947	(190,555,000)				
	.12	.20	.25	.75	12.00
☐ 1947D	(194,750,000)				
	.12	.20	.25	.35	6.00
☐ 1947S	(99,000,000)				
	.15	.25	.30	.75	7.50
☐ 1948	(317,570,000)				
	.12	.20	.25	.60	12.00
☐ 1948D	(172,637,500)				
	.12	.20	.35	.50	7.50
☐ 1948S	(81,735,000)				
	.24	.40	.55	.75	7.50
☐ 1949	(217,490,000)				
	.12	.20	.25	.65	12.00
☐ 1949D	(154,370,500)				
	.12	.20	.25	.65	10.00
☐ 1949S	(64,290,000)				
	.30	.50	.75	1.50	8.00
☐ 1950	(272,686,386)				
	.12	.20	.25	.60	12.00

DATE	ABP	VF-20 V. FINE	EF-40 EX. FINE	MS-60 UNC.	MS-65 UNC.
☐ 1950D	(334,950,000)				
	.09	.15	.25	.35	8.00
☐ 1950S	(118,505,000)				
	.12	.20	.35	.75	7.50
☐ 1951	(294,633,500)				
	.09	.15	.25	.60	12.00
☐ 1951D	(625,355,000)				
	.06	.15	.25	.45	7.50
☐ 1951S	(100,890,000)				
	.12	.30	.35	.65	7.50
☐ 1952	(186,856,980)				
	.09	.15	.25	.75	12.00
☐ 1952D	(746,130,000)				
	.09	.15	.25	.40	7.50
☐ 1952S	(137,800,004)				
	.12	.20	.25	1.00	10.00
☐ 1953	(256,883,800)				
	.09	.15	.25	.15	12.00
☐ 1953D	(700,515,000)				
	.09	.15	.25	.30	7.50
☐ 1953S	(181,835,000)				
	.09	.15	.25	.30	7.50
☐ 1954	(71,873,350)				
	.18	.30	.35	.38	15.00
☐ 1954D	(251,552,500)				
	.09	.15	.25	.30	7.50
☐ 1954S	(96,190,000)				
	.09	.15	.25	.25	7.50
☐ 1955	(330,958,200)				
	.09	.15	.25	.25	7.50
☐ 1955 Doubled Die					
	720.00	1200.00	1600.00	2500.00	RARE
☐ 1955D	(563,257,500)				
	.09	.15	.25	.30	6.00
☐ 1955S	(44,610,000)				
	.15	.25	.40	.75	6.00
☐ 1956	(421,414,384)				
	.09	.15	.25	.25	8.00
☐ 1956D	(1,098,201,100)				
	.09	.15	.25	.25	6.00
☐ 1957	(283,787,952)				
	.09	.15	.25	.25	6.00

DATE	ABP	VF-20 V. FINE	EF-40 EX. FINE	MS-60 UNC.	MS-65 UNC.
☐ 1957D	(1,051,342,000)				
	.09	.15	.25	.20	5.00
☐ 1958	(253,400,652)				
	.09	.15	.25	.20	8.00
☐ 1958D	(800,953,000)				
	.09	.15	.25	.20	6.00

SMALL CENTS—LINCOLN MEMORIAL DESIGN

LINCOLN MEMORIAL

1955 DOUBLED DIE

SMALL DATE

LARGE DATE

DATE	MINTAGE	MS-65 UNC.	PRF-65 PROOF
☐ 1959	610,864,291	.75	5.00
☐ 1959D	1,279,760,000	.75	
☐ 1960 Small Date	588,096,602	6.00	25.00
☐ 1960 Large Date		.50	
☐ 1960D Small Date	1,580,884,000	.50	
☐ 1960D Large Date		.50	
☐ 1961	756,373,244	.50	2.00
☐ 1961D	1,753,266,700	.50	

(SEPTEMBER 1961–1981 COMPOSITION-95% COPPER AND 5% ZINC)

DATE	MINTAGE	MS-65 UNC.	PRF-65 PROOF
☐ 1962	609,263,019	.50	2.00
☐ 1962D	1,793,148,400	.50	
☐ 1963	757,185,645	.50	2.00
☐ 1963D	1,744,020,400	.50	
☐ 1964	2,652,525,762	.50	2.00
☐ 1964D	3,799,071,500	.50	
☐ 1965	1,497,224,900	.75	
☐ 1966	2,188,147,783	.75	
☐ 1967	3,048,667,077	.75	
☐ 1968	1,707,880,965	.75	

DATE	MINTAGE	MS-65 UNC.	PRF-65 PROOF
☐ 1968D	2,886,269,590	.75	
☐ 1968S	261,311,500	.75	2.00
☐ 1969	1,136,910,000	.75	
☐ 1969D	4,002,832,200	.75	
☐ 1969S	547,309,631	.75	2.00
☐ 1970	1,898,315,000	.75	
☐ 1970D	2,891,438,900	.75	
☐ 1970S	693,192,814	.75	
☐ 1970S Small Date		90.00	95.00
☐ 1970S Large Date		.75	2.00
☐ 1971	1,919,490,000	.75	
☐ 1971D	2,911,045,600	.75	
☐ 1971S	528,354,192	.75	3.00
☐ 1972	2,933,255,000	.35	
☐ 1972 Doubled Die		800.00	
☐ 1972D	2,665,071,400	.50	
☐ 1972S	380,200,104	.50	2.00
☐ 1973	3,728,245,000	.50	
☐ 1973D	3,549,576,588	.50	
☐ 1973S	319,937,634	.50	2.00
☐ 1974	4,232,140,523	.50	
☐ 1974D	4,235,098,000	.50	
☐ 1974S	412,039,228	.50	2.00
☐ 1975	4,505,275,300	.50	
☐ 1975D	5,505,275,300	.50	
☐ 1975S Proof Only	2,909,369		4.00
☐ 1976	4,674,292,426	.50	
☐ 1976D	4,221,595,455	.50	
☐ 1976S Proof Only	4,149,945		4.00
☐ 1977	4,469,972,000	.50	
☐ 1977D	4,149,055,800	.50	
☐ 1977S Proof Only	3,250,895		4.00
☐ 1978	5,266,905,000	.50	
☐ 1978D	4,280,233,400	.50	
☐ 1978S Proof Only	3,127,781		4.00
☐ 1979P	6,018,515,201	.50	
☐ 1979D	4,139,357,000	.50	
☐ 1979S Proof Only, Filled S	3,677,200		8.00
☐ 1979S Proof Only, Clear S			10.00
☐ 1980	7,414,705,002	.50	
☐ 1980D	5,140,098,675	.50	
☐ 1980S Proof Only	3,547,130		4.00

DATE	MINTAGE	MS-65 UNC.	PRF-65 PROOF
☐ 1981	7,491,750,500	.50	
☐ 1981D	5,373,235,000	.50	
☐ 1981S Proof Only Type 1	4,065,000		5.00
☐ 1981S Proof Only Type 2			65.00
☐ 1982 Small Date	10,712,525,000	1.50	
☐ 1982 Large Date		1.50	
☐ 1982D Large Date	6,012,979,368	1.50	
(1982 COMPOSITION-COPPER-PLATED ZINC, 97% ZINC, 3% COPPER)			
☐ 1982 Small Date		1.75	
☐ 1982 Large Date		.50	
☐ 1982D Small Date		.50	
☐ 1982D Large Date		.50	
☐ 1982S Proof Only	3,857,480		4.00
☐ 1983	7,752,354,900	.50	
☐ 1983 Double Die Reverse		375.00	
☐ 1983D	6,468,000,000	.50	
☐ 1983S Proof Only	3,228,650		3.50
☐ 1984	8,183,657,000	.50	
☐ 1984D	5,570,000,000	.50	
☐ 1984S Proof Only			4.50
☐ 1985	5,842,628,000	.50	
☐ 1985D	5,329,742,000	.50	
☐ 1985S Proof Only	3,412,110		5.00
☐ 1986	4,622,410,712	.50	
☐ 1986D	4,287,870,420	.50	
☐ 1986S Proof Only	3,211,110		5.75
☐ 1987	4,427,867,241	.50	
☐ 1987D	4,782,420,670	.50	
☐ 1987S Proof Only			3.75
☐ 1988	6,180,720,000	.50	
☐ 1988D	5,151,621,120	.50	
☐ 1988S Proof Only			3.50
☐ 1989	7,321,462,111	.50	
☐ 1989D	5,362,174,181	.50	
☐ 1989S Proof Only			4.50
☐ 1990	6,927,491,004	.50	
☐ 1990D	4,921,800,542	.50	

Note: The 1982 cent was the first U.S. coin struck in a quantity of more than 10 billion.

DATE	MINTAGE	MS-65 UNC.	PRF-65 PROOF
☐ 1990S Proof Only	3,298,540		5.00
☐ 1991	5,165,920,000	.50	
☐ 1991D	4,158,440,218	.50	
☐ 1991S Proof Only	2,866,422		7.00
☐ 1992	4,648,904,000	.50	
☐ 1992D	4,448,672,250	.50	
☐ 1992S Proof Only	4,176,540		6.00
☐ 1993	5,684,705,000	.50	
☐ 1993D	6,426,650,571	.50	
☐ 1993S Proof Only	3,394,792		10.00
☐ 1994	6,500,850,000	.50	
☐ 1994D	7,131,765,000	.50	
☐ 1994S Proof Only	3,269,923		10.00
☐ 1995	6,411,440,000	.50	
☐ 1995 Double Die		52.00	
☐ 1995D	7,128,560,000	.50	
☐ 1995S Proof Only			10.00
☐ 1996	6,612,500,000	.50	
☐ 1996D	6,510,800,000	.50	
☐ 1996S Proof			5.00
☐ 1997	4,622,800,000	.50	
☐ 1997D	4,576,555,000	.50	
☐ 1997S Proof	1,975,000		15.00
☐ 1998	5,032,150,000	.50	
☐ 1998D	5,225,350,000	.50	
☐ 1998S Proof			15.00
☐ 1999	5,237,600,000	.50	
☐ 1999D	6,360,000,000	.50	
☐ 1999S Proof			10.00
☐ 2000	5,503,200,000	.50	
☐ 2000D	8,774,200,000	.50	
☐ 2000S Proof			8.00
☐ 2001	4,959,600,000	.50	
☐ 2001D	5,374,990,000	.50	
☐ 2001S Proof			7.00
☐ 2002P	3,260,800,000	.50	
☐ 2002D	4,028,055,000	.50	
☐ 2002S Proof			6.00
☐ 2003	3,300,000,000	.50	
☐ 2003D	3,548,000,000	.50	
☐ 2003S Proof			5.00

DATE	MINTAGE	MS-65 UNC.	PRF-65 PROOF
☐ 2004	3,379,600,000	.50	
☐ 2004D	3,456,400,000	.50	
☐ 2004S Proof			6.00
☐ 2005	3,935,600,000	.50	
☐ 2005D	3,764,450,500	.50	
☐ 2005S Proof			6.00
☐ 2006	4,387,500,000	.50	
☐ 2006D	4,115,350,000	.50	
☐ 2006S Proof			5.00
☐ 2007	3,855,125,000	.50	
☐ 2007D	3,699,580,000	.50	
☐ 2007S Proof			5.00
☐ 2008		.50	
☐ 2008D		.50	
☐ 2008S Proof			5.00
☐ 2009		.50	
☐ 2009D		.50	
☐ 2009S Proof			5.00
☐ 2010		.50	
☐ 2010D		.50	
☐ 2010S Proof			5.00
☐ 2011		.50	
☐ 2011D		.50	
☐ 2011S Proof			5.00
☐ 2012		.30	
☐ 2012D		.30	
☐ 2012S Proof			5.00

TWO-CENT PIECES (BRONZE), 1864–1873

The two-cent piece was a short-lived coin whose impact upon the world fell far short of its impact on modern numismatists. Small change was growing increasingly scarce during the Civil War, to the point where postage stamps, encased in holders, were being used for money. The government sought to alleviate this by increased production of the penny and introduced the two-cent piece to take the penny's place in areas where it might not be in sufficient supply. Enormous quantities were struck at the outset, approaching 20 million per year, the composition being the same as that of the penny—95% copper to 5% of tin and zinc. The diameter was 23mm. Designer of the two-cent piece was James Longacre, who did most of the Mint's designing at that time.

There is no portrait on the coin; it carries a U.S. shield on one side and a value statement on the other. The lack of portraiture was undoubtedly an effort to prevent this coin from being confused with the penny. Though larger by 4mm. in diameter than the penny, it must be remembered that Large Cents were still found in circulation in 1864—they had been discontinued less than ten years earlier—and one almost needed a scoreboard to keep track of the denominations of coins passing through one's hands. Production totals of the two-cent piece decreased each year of its minting, until only 65,000 were turned out in 1872, and nothing but proofs and restrikes the following year. It died a very silent death.

1864 Small Motto

1864 Large Motto

First Coin to Bear the Motto IN GOD WE TRUST

DATE	ABP	G-4 GOOD	F-12 FINE	EF-40 EX. FINE	MS-60 UNC.	PRF-65 PROOF
☐ 1864 Small Motto (19,847,500)						
	90.00	150.00	350.00	700.00	1400.00	RARE
☐ 1864 Large Motto						
	14.00	20.00	30.00	65.00	125.00	1200.00
☐ 1865 (13,640,000)						
	14.00	20.00	30.00	65.00	125.00	725.00
☐ 1866 (3,177,000)						
	14.00	20.00	30.00	65.00	125.00	725.00
☐ 1867 (3,915,000)						
	14.00	20.00	30.00	65.00	125.00	725.00
☐ 1867 Doubled Die				325.00		
☐ 1868 (3,252,000)						
	14.00	20.00	40.00	60.00	175.00	725.00
☐ 1869 (1,546,500)						
	14.00	20.00	40.00	70.00	200.00	725.00
☐ 1870 (861,250)						
	17.00	25.00	50.00	125.00	300.00	725.00
☐ 1871 (721,250)						
	25.00	35.00	100.00	150.00	325.00	725.00
☐ 1872 (65,000)						
	225.00	275.00	475.00	800.00	1650.00	900.00
☐ 1873 Closed 3, Proofs Only (600)						4000.00
☐ 1873 Open 3 (Restrike), Proofs Only (480)						4200.00

THREE-CENT PIECES

THREE CENT (SILVER), 1851–1873

America's burgeoning population, plus conditions brought about by the California gold strike, resulted in a shortage of small change during the mid 19th century. The decision was made to strike a coin in three-cents denomination and to have its composition of silver, alloyed with 25% copper. Because of its low face value and precious metal content the coin was extremely small physically. Its designer was James Longacre. Rather than portraiture, a symbolic obverse was used, consisting of a six-pointed star and shield. This was done to avoid confusion with the half dime, whose size and color were similar. On the reverse was the Roman numeral III enclosed within an ornamental letter C (for "cents") and surrounded by small stars. The weight was only $4/5$ of a gram—the lightest coin ever struck by the Mint—with a diameter of just 14mm. It was tiny, indeed. Undoubtedly the government expected that this coin, despite serving an important purpose, would not prove popular. It didn't. After striking about 35 million in the first three years of its production, quantities were sharply reduced thereafter. It was subsequently replaced by the "nickel" three-cent piece following the Civil War, which contained no silver whatever.

Though the basic design of the silver three-cent piece was maintained throughout its lifetime—they continued being struck until 1873, though were rarely circulated after 1862—some minor changes were introduced. In 1854 the obverse star was redrawn with a triple border. The final version, put into use in 1859, has a double border. As there are no great rarities among the circulating dates of this series, a complete collection is well within the realm of possibility. In 1854 there was a change of composition to 90% silver/10% copper and the weight was brought down to ¾ of a gram. From then until conclusion of the series all minting was carried out in Philadelphia. Previously the manufacture of this coin had been divided between Philadelphia and New Orleans.

The Mint Mark "O" is on the Reverse to the Right of the III

DATE	ABP	G-4 GOOD	F-12 FINE	EF-40 EX. FINE	MS-60 UNC.	PRF-65 PROOF
☐ 1851 (5,447,400)	18.00	30.00	40.00	75.00	225.00	
☐ 18510 (720,000)	21.00	35.00	60.00	200.00	425.00	
☐ 1852 (18,663,500)	18.00	30.00	50.00	100.00	225.00	
☐ 1853 (11,400,000)	18.00	30.00	50.00	85.00	200.00	
☐ 1854 (671,000)	18.00	30.00	50.00	125.00	400.00	
☐ 1855 (139,000)	24.00	40.00	80.00	235.00	750.00	
☐ 1856 (1,458,000)	18.00	30.00	60.00	150.00	350.00	
☐ 1857 (1,042,000)	18.00	30.00	60.00	150.00	400.00	
☐ 1858 (1,604,000)	18.00	30.00	60.00	125.00	400.00	
☐ 1859 (365,000)	18.00	30.00	60.00	100.00	250.00	2200.00
☐ 1860 (287,000)	18.00	30.00	60.00	100.00	250.00	4100.00
☐ 1861 (498,000)	18.00	30.00	60.00	100.00	250.00	2000.00
☐ 1862 (363,550)	18.00	30.00	60.00	100.00	250.00	1550.00

DATE	ABP	G-4 GOOD	F-12 FINE	EF-40 EX. FINE	MS-60 UNC.	PRF-65 PROOF
☐ 1862, 2 over 1						
	18.00	30.00	60.00	100.00	250.00	RARE
☐ 1863	(21,460)					
	150.00	250.00	325.00	500.00	700.00	1500.00
☐ 1863, 3 over 2, Proofs Only						RARE
☐ 1864	(470)					
	150.00	250.00	400.00	475.00	700.00	1500.00
☐ 1865	(8,500)					
	180.00	300.00	400.00	500.00	700.00	1500.00
☐ 1866	(22,725)					
	150.00	250.00	400.00	475.00	700.00	1500.00
☐ 1867	(4,625)					
	189.00	315.00	400.00	500.00	700.00	1500.00
☐ 1868	(4,100)					
	189.00	315.00	400.00	500.00	700.00	1500.00
☐ 1869	(5,100)					
	189.00	315.00	400.00	500.00	700.00	1500.00
☐ 1870	(4,000)					
	189.00	315.00	400.00	500.00	800.00	1500.00
☐ 1871	(4,260)					
	189.00	315.00	400.00	500.00	800.00	1500.00
☐ 1872	(1,950)					
	189.00	315.00	400.00	500.00	1000.00	1500.00
☐ 1873 Proof Only	(600)					3200.00

THREE CENT (NICKEL), 1865–1889

For all practical purposes, the three-cent piece had been out of circulation during most of the Civil War. Upon the war's conclusion its manufacture was resumed, but no longer was the composition chiefly of silver. In fact, the new version contained no precious metal at all. It was composed of 75% copper and 25% nickel. What the three-cent piece lost metallically it gained physically: its weight more than doubled, rising to 1.94 grams, and its diameter increased to 17mm. It may be wondered why a coin containing 75% copper would be referred to as a "nickel" rather than a "copper." The explanation is that the term "copper" was already in use for the cent. Americans picked up this nickname from the British, who had long been calling their pennies "coppers." As the new three-cent coin represented the greatest use made of nickel by the Mint up to that time, the name "nickel" seemed appropriate. The coin was somewhat better received than its predecessor, as there was not as much danger of confusing it with another denomination. The fact that its life was not particularly long (it was discontinued in 1889) can be attributed more to inflation than any fault of its own. By 1889 there was simply no longer a pressing need for three-cent pieces. At least 20 million were in circulation at that time and this was deemed more than enough to meet whatever demand might exist. The five-cent piece, which began in 1866 to be composed of the same copper-nickel ratio as the three-cent, was adequately filling whatever need the three-cent had earlier satisfied.

The three-cent nickel carried a Liberty head on its obverse and a large Roman numeral III on the reverse. Like the silver version, it was designed by James Longacre. All were struck at Philadelphia. Throughout the quarter-century of production no changes occurred in its design.

In the following listing, note that ABP is for coins in Fine condition or better. Superbly struck, uncirculated coins bring proportionately more than the prices listed.

DATE	ABP	G-4 GOOD	F-12 FINE	EF-40 EX. FINE	MS-60 UNC.	PRF-65 PROOF
☐ 1865	(11,382,000)					
	15.00	25.00	35.00	50.00	165.00	RARE
☐ 1866	(4,801,000)					
	15.00	25.00	35.00	50.00	165.00	1800.00
☐ 1867	(3,915,000)					
	15.00	25.00	35.00	50.00	165.00	1600.00
☐ 1868	(3,252,000)					
	15.00	25.00	35.00	50.00	165.00	1500.00
☐ 1869	(1,604,000)					
	15.00	25.00	35.00	50.00	175.00	1100.00

DATE	ABP	G-4 GOOD	F-12 FINE	EF-40 EX. FINE	MS-60 UNC.	PRF-65 PROOF
☐ 1870	(1,335,000)					
	15.00	25.00	35.00	50.00	175.00	2400.00
☐ 1871	(604,000)					
	15.00	25.00	35.00	50.00	175.00	1200.00
☐ 1872	(862,000)					
	15.00	25.00	35.00	50.00	175.00	1000.00
☐ 1873 Closed 3	(1,173,000)					
	15.00	25.00	35.00	50.00	175.00	1200.00
☐ 1873 Open 3						
	15.00	25.00	35.00	50.00	175.00	RARE
☐ 1874	(790,000)					
	15.00	25.00	35.00	50.00	175.00	1000.00
☐ 1875	(228,000)					
	15.00	25.00	35.00	55.00	200.00	1600.00
☐ 1876	(162,000)					
	15.00	25.00	35.00	55.00	225.00	1600.00
☐ 1877 Proofs Only	(510)					3800.00
☐ 1878 Proofs Only	(2,350)					1200.00
☐ 1879	(41,200)					
	33.00	55.00	100.00	150.00	400.00	700.00
☐ 1880	(24,955)					
	60.00	100.00	120.00	200.00	400.00	750.00
☐ 1881	(1,080,575)					
	12.00	20.00	35.00	50.00	150.00	700.00
☐ 1882	(25,300)					
	60.00	100.00	125.00	300.00	425.00	725.00
☐ 1883	(10,609)					
	90.00	150.00	225.00	400.00	525.00	725.00
☐ 1884	(5,642)					
	180.00	300.00	425.00	625.00	1000.00	725.00
☐ 1885	(4,790)					
	225.00	375.00	525.00	750.00	1200.00	750.00
☐ 1886 Proofs Only	(4,290)					750.00
☐ 1887	(7,961)					
	150.00	250.00	300.00	425.00	600.00	1200.00
☐ 1887 over 6, Proofs Only						1000.00
☐ 1888	(41,083)					
	30.00	55.00	60.00	125.00	335.00	725.00
☐ 1889	(21,561)					
	45.00	75.00	110.00	200.00	335.00	700.00

NICKELS

NICKELS—SHIELD, 1866–1883

Though the silver half dime was still being struck in 1866, its production was too limited to serve as a general circulating coin. This noble old soldier, its origins dating back to the Mint's beginnings, was suffering the effects of general inflation and the bullion shortage of the Civil War, caused in part by a scarcity of laborers for the silver mines. Not knowing what the future might hold, the government had no wish to terminate the silver half dime but it wanted, at the same time, to introduce a coin of proportionate value made of base metal and attempt to popularize it. Thus was born the five-cent nickel or "true nickel," as opposed to the three-cent coin that was also called a nickel.

The five-cent nickel was authorized by Congress on May 16, 1866. It was to have a weight of 5 grams and be composed of three parts copper and one part nickel. The diameter was 20.5mm. James Longacre, chief engraver of the Mint, was called upon to design it and produced a portraitless coin consisting of a shielded obverse with Arabic numeral 5 on the reverse surrounded by stars and rays (or bars). IN GOD WE TRUST appears on the obverse above the shield. Nearly 15,000,000 pieces were struck in the first year of issue. In the following year, 1867, after production had continued briefly, the rays were removed from the reverse, resulting in a rarity of moderate proportions for the "with rays" type.

This is not, however, an expensive coin except in uncirculated condition. It may be asked why the 1867 variety With Rays and the standard 1866 date are valued almost equally, when only 2,019,000 of the former and 14,742,500 of the latter were struck, yielding a scarcity ratio of 7-to-1. The answer is simply that the 1866 would *not* be worth so much if it weren't the first date of its series. There are many collectors buying "first dates" who buy no other coins of the series. For this reason the first year of minting of *any* U.S. coin carries a premium over and above the quantity struck or available in the market. (Compare the 1866 value with that of the 1872, of which fewer than half as many were struck; the former is more common but worth more.)

1866–83

1866–67
With Rays

1867–83
Without Rays

DATE	ABP	G-4 GOOD	F-12 FINE	EF-40 EX. FINE	MS-60 UNC.	MS-65 CH. UNC
☐ 1866 With Rays (14,742,500)						
	15.00	25.00	65.00	200.00	325.00	2200.00
☐ 1867 With Rays (30,908,500)						
	24.00	40.00	80.00	225.00	425.00	4000.00
☐ 1867 No Rays						
	15.00	25.00	35.00	80.00	175.00	900.00
☐ 1868 (28,817,000)						
	15.00	25.00	35.00	80.00	175.00	700.00
☐ 1869 (16,395,000)						
	15.00	25.00	35.00	80.00	175.00	750.00
☐ 1870 (4,806,000)						
	18.00	30.00	75.00	110.00	250.00	1750.00
☐ 1871 (561,000)						
	60.00	100.00	150.00	300.00	525.00	2200.00
☐ 1872 (6,036,000)						
	21.00	35.00	75.00	150.00	275.00	1450.00
☐ 1873 Closed 3 (4,550,000)						
	21.00	35.00	75.00	175.00	400.00	3200.00
☐ 1873 Open 3						
	18.00	30.00	75.00	125.00	275.00	2000.00
☐ 1874 (3,538,000)						
	18.00	30.00	75.00	150.00	300.00	1500.00
☐ 1875 (2,097,000)						
	24.00	40.00	100.00	200.00	325.00	1500.00

DATE	ABP	G-4 GOOD	F-12 FINE	EF-40 EX. FINE	MS-60 UNC.	MS-65 CH. UNC.
☐ 1876	(2,530,000)					
	24.00	40.00	100.00	165.00	300.00	1400.00
☐ 1877 Proofs Only	(500)					RARE
☐ 1878	(2,350)				PROOF—RARE	
☐ 1879	(29,100)					
	240.00	400.00	625.00	800.00	1200.00	2000.00
☐ 1879 9 over 8					EXTREMELY RARE	
☐ 1880	(19,955)					
	240.00	400.00	650.00	1500.00	RARE	RARE
☐ 1881	(72,375)					
	120.00	200.00	400.00	625.00	800.00	2000.00
☐ 1882	(11,476,600)					
	15.00	25.00	30.00	75.00	185.00	700.00
☐ 1883	(1,456,919)					
	15.00	25.00	40.00	75.00	175.00	825.00
☐ 1883 over 2						
	135.00	225.00	450.00	650.00	1500.00	3800.00

NICKEL—LIBERTY HEAD, 1883–1913

When production of the silver half dime picturing Liberty ceased in the 1870s, designers were free to transfer the likeness of this goddess to our nickel five-cent piece. This, however, was not immediately done and, when finally undertaken in 1883, the portrait was not the full figure used for half dimes but a profile bust. The new design was created by Charles E. Barber and gained for this piece the name "Barber nickel," which was once used commonly but seems to have lost popularity. Like its predecessor, it was made of 75% copper and 25% nickel and had a weight of 5 grams. The diameter was slightly larger, measuring 21.2mm., and striking was done at Philadelphia, Denver, and San Francisco.

An embarrassing difficulty occurred with this coin at the outset of production. As first designed, the reverse carried the Roman number V (for 5) without the word CENTS or any sign indicating that cents was intended. Very shortly, unscrupulous persons began gilding the coin with gold wash and passing it to foreigners and other uninformed individuals as a $5 gold piece. The government put a halt to this activity by having the die re-engraved and the word CENTS added.

From then until 1913, when a new design was introduced (the famous Buffalo/Indian), no changes were made in designing. The Liberty Head was struck in great quantities throughout almost its entire run of production, with the total output reaching well into the hundreds of millions. It could still be found in general circulation, though not with much frequency, as late as the 1940s. The 1913 Liberty Head, America's most valuable base-metal coin, has long proved an enigma. The Mint claims not to have struck any Liberty Heads that year, asserting that its production consisted entirely of the Buffalo/Indian. It is certainly believable that no regular production occurred, otherwise the total in existence would not be as small as just five specimens. Even assuming that minting for the year was started with the Liberty Head design and was switched off to the new type after a few days, thousands of coins would by that time have been struck. There seems no logical way in which just five pieces could have been manufactured. The likelihood—though it may slightly tarnish this rarity's appeal—is that 1913 dies were produced, then put aside when the change of design was authorized and used (possibly clandestinely) to strike just a few specimens by a person or persons unknown. This theory is supported by the fact that originally, when first brought to public light, *all five* were owned by the same individual: Colonel Edward H. R. Green of New York, a noted collector of coins, stamps, and art in the World War I era. If struck by the Mint and dispersed, it is almost beyond the realm of possibility that they could have been acquired by one collector within so short a period of time. (Colonel Green, incidentally, is equally noted for being the purchaser of the sheet of 24¢ inverted-center airmail stamps issued in 1918, which he *broke up and sold;* his approach to collecting was rather like that of a dealer or speculator, and one can only wonder at the reason for his association with the 1913 Liberty Head five-cent piece.)

1883

Without CENTS

1887 CENTS

DATE	ABP	G-4 GOOD	F-12 FINE	EF-40 EX. FINE	MS-60 UNC.	MS-65 CH. UNC.
☐ 1883 No CENTS (5,479,519)						
	3.30	5.50	10.00	15.00	45.00	225.00
☐ 1883 With CENTS (16,032,983)						
	12.00	20.00	40.00	110.00	175.00	650.00
☐ 1884 (11,273,942)						
	13.00	22.00	40.00	110.00	225.00	1750.00
☐ 1885 (1,476,490)						
	330.00	550.00	800.00	1500.00	2275.00	RARE
☐ 1886 (3,330,290)						
	135.00	225.00	400.00	750.00	1125.00	RARE
☐ 1887 (15,263,652)						
	9.00	15.00	35.00	100.00	175.00	1100.00
☐ 1888 (10,720,483)						
	16.80	28.00	65.00	210.00	300.00	1550.00
☐ 1889 (15,881,361)						
	9.00	15.00	30.00	100.00	165.00	900.00
☐ 1890 (16,259,272)						
	9.00	15.00	30.00	75.00	175.00	1450.00
☐ 1891 (16,834,350)						
	5.00	10.00	30.00	75.00	175.00	1100.00
☐ 1892 (11,699,642)						
	5.00	8.00	25.00	75.00	165.00	1400.00
☐ 1893 (13,370,195)						
	6.00	8.00	25.00	75.00	160.00	1100.00
☐ 1894 (5,413,132)						
	10.80	18.00	125.00	275.00	380.00	1550.00
☐ 1895 (9,979,884)						
	3.00	5.00	25.00	75.00	175.00	2200.00
☐ 1896 (8,842,920)						
	6.00	10.00	40.00	100.00	200.00	2050.00
☐ 1897 (20,428,735)						
	3.00	5.00	15.00	60.00	125.00	1000.00
☐ 1898 (12,532,087)						
	3.00	5.00	15.00	60.00	150.00	1100.00
☐ 1899 (26,029,031)						
	1.80	3.00	10.00	40.00	120.00	600.00
☐ 1900 (27,255,995)						
	1.35	2.25	10.00	40.00	100.00	700.00
☐ 1901 (26,480,213)						
	1.35	2.25	5.00	40.00	100.00	600.00

DATE	ABP	G-4 GOOD	F-12 FINE	EF-40 EX. FINE	MS-60 UNC.	MS-65 CH. UNC.
☐ 1902	(31,480,579)					
	1.35	2.25	5.50	35.00	100.00	600.00
☐ 1903	(28,006,725)					
	1.35	2.25	5.50	35.00	100.00	600.00
☐ 1904	(21,404,984)					
	1.35	2.25	5.50	35.00	100.00	600.00
☐ 1905	(29,827,276)					
	1.35	2.25	5.50	35.00	100.00	600.00
☐ 1906	(38,613,725)					
	1.35	2.25	5.50	35.00	100.00	735.00
☐ 1907	(39,214,800)					
	1.35	2.25	5.50	35.00	85.00	1100.00
☐ 1908	(22,686,177)					
	1.35	2.25	5.50	35.00	85.00	1100.00
☐ 1909	(11,590,526)					
	1.35	2.25	6.50	35.00	125.00	1100.00
☐ 1910	(30,169,353)					
	1.35	2.25	5.50	35.00	80.00	600.00
☐ 1911	(39,559,372)					
	1.35	2.25	5.50	35.00	80.00	550.00
☐ 1912	(26,236,714)					
	1.35	2.25	5.00	35.00	80.00	600.00
☐ 1912D	(8,474,000)					
	1.35	4.00	12.00	100.00	400.00	2200.00
☐ 1912S	(238,000)					
	135.00	225.00	300.00	1000.00	2000.00	RARE

☐ 1913, Not a Regular Mint Issue, 5 Known—Very rare

NICKELS—BUFFALO OR INDIAN HEAD, 1913–1938

Undoubtedly the most dramatic, artistic, and original set of designs employed for a U.S. coin, the Buffalo/Indian Head nickel went into production in 1913. The composition was 75% copper and 25% nickel, with a weight of five grams. Its diameter was 21.2mm. James E. Fraser, the designer, was not one to go half way. He hired an Indian to sit for the obverse portrait and took his sketching gear to the Bronx Zoo to get a likeness of a buffalo in the flesh. The artwork of this coin is little short of superb: each motif fully fills the planchet ground and is unencumbered by large inscriptions or miscellaneous symbols. Unfortunately the rate of wear in handling was such that few individuals aside from collectors had the opportunity to see the coin at its best. Just like the noble animal it pictured, the American bison, this coin proved to be a rapidly disappearing species. Within only twenty years after its discontinuation in 1938 it had all but vanished from circulation, despite enormous production output.

Critics of the Buffalo/Indian Head nickel were few. Those who spoke against it raised the objection that the buffalo was in danger of extinction. So popular did the bison likeness become that the coin, unlike most others, came to be popularly known by its reverse rather than its obverse.

In 1916 a double die error resulted on some specimens, producing a twin or ghost impression of the date. Of regularly struck pieces, those from the San Francisco Mint in the early and middle 1920s are scarcest.

Mint Mark
is on the
Reverse, Under
FIVE CENTS

1913–1938

1913–
Type I
Buffalo on High Mound

1913
Type 2
Buffalo on Level Ground

DATE	ABP	G-4 GOOD	F-12 FINE	EF-40 EX. FINE	MS-60 UNC.	MS-65 CH. UNC.
☐ 1913 Type 1 (30,993,520)						
	6.00	10.00	15.00	20.00	32.00	200.00
☐ 1913D Type 1 (5,337,000)						
	18.00	20.00	25.00	50.00	100.00	425.00
☐ 1913S Type 1 (2,105,000)						
	30.00	50.00	75.00	100.00	165.00	1000.00
☐ 1913 Type 2 (29,858,700)						
	6.00	10.00	15.00	25.00	50.00	425.00
☐ 1913D Type 2 (4,156,000)						
	60.00	100.00	150.00	250.00	400.00	1800.00
☐ 1913S Type 2 (1,209,000)						
	165.00	275.00	550.00	550.00	1125.00	4200.00

DATE	ABP	G-4 GOOD	F-12 FINE	EF-40 EX. FINE	MS-60 UNC.	MS-65 CH. UNC.
☐ 1914	(20,665,738)					
	12.00	20.00	30.00	40.00	75.00	575.00
☐ 1914 /3						
	99.00	165.00	425.00	1200.00	3325.00	RARE
☐ 1914D	(3,912,000)					
	48.00	80.00	150.00	400.00	475.00	2000.00
☐ 1914S	(3,470,000)					
	15.00	25.00	50.00	100.00	250.00	3000.00
☐ 1915	(20,987,270)					
	3.00	5.00	10.00	32.00	75.00	425.00
☐ 1915D	(7,569,500)					
	12.00	20.00	45.00	135.00	275.00	2800.00
☐ 1915S	(1,505,000)					
	24.00	40.00	125.00	500.00	700.00	3500.00
☐ 1916 Doubled Die Obverse						
						VERY RARE
☐ 1916	(63,498,000)					
	3.00	5.00	10.00	18.00	65.00	425.00
☐ 1916D	(13,333,000)					
	10.80	18.00	25.00	115.00	190.00	2800.00
☐ 1916S	(11,860,000)					
	9.00	15.00	25.00	115.00	200.00	2800.00
☐ 1917	(51,424,029)					
	4.80	8.00	10.00	20.00	80.00	675.00
☐ 1917D	(9,910,800)					
	12.00	20.00	65.00	200.00	400.00	3800.00
☐ 1917S	(4,193,000)					
	15.00	25.00	100.00	225.00	400.00	RARE
☐ 1918	(32,086,314)					
	4.80	8.00	10.00	40.00	150.00	1800.00
☐ 1918D	(8,362,000)					
	15.00	25.00	75.00	250.00	475.00	RARE
☐ 1918D over 17						
						VERY RARE
☐ 1918S	(4,882,000)					
	10.80	18.00	65.00	225.00	575.00	RARE
☐ 1919	(60,868,000)					
	1.80	3.00	5.00	20.00	60.00	750.00
☐ 1919D	(8,006,000)					
	12.00	20.00	100.00	285.00	575.00	RARE

DATE	ABP	G-4 GOOD	F-12 FINE	EF-40 EX. FINE	MS-60 UNC.	MS-65 CH. UNC.
☐ 1919S	(7,521,000)					
	6.00	10.00	65.00	300.00	625.00	RARE
☐ 1920	(63,093,000)					
	1.20	2.00	4.00	18.00	75.00	1000.00
☐ 1920D	(9,418,000)					
	6.00	10.00	40.00	325.00	625.00	RARE
☐ 1920S	(9,689,000)					
	3.00	5.00	35.00	200.00	550.00	RARE
☐ 1921	(10,683,000)					
	3.00	5.00	10.00	65.00	175.00	1000.00
☐ 1921S	(1,557,000)					
	60.00	100.00	300.00	1200.00	1850.00	RARE
☐ 1923	(35,715,000)					
	1.80	3.00	5.00	16.00	85.00	800.00
☐ 1923S	(6,142,000)					
	6.00	10.00	26.00	400.00	550.00	RARE
☐ 1924	(21,620,000)					
	1.20	2.00	8.00	30.00	85.00	1400.00
☐ 1924D	(5,258,000)					
	6.00	10.00	38.00	275.00	425.00	RARE
☐ 1924S	(1,437,000)					
	12.00	20.00	125.00	1225.00	2550.00	RARE
☐ 1925	(35,565,100)					
	3.00	5.00	6.00	18.00	50.00	250.00
☐ 1925D	(4,450,000)					
	7.20	12.00	50.00	215.00	425.00	RARE
☐ 1925S	(6,256,000)					
	4.80	8.00	20.00	210.00	525.00	RARE
☐ 1926	(44,693,000)					
	1.20	2.00	3.25	14.00	38.00	250.00
☐ 1926D	(5,638,000)					
	7.20	12.00	35.00	200.00	400.00	RARE
☐ 1926S	(970,000)					
	15.00	25.00	125.00	1100.00		RARE
☐ 1927	(37,981,000)					
	1.20	2.00	4.00	15.00	42.00	425.00
☐ 1927D	(5,730,000)					
	2.40	4.00	10.00	100.00	225.00	RARE
☐ 1927S	(3,430,000)					
	1.20	2.00	8.00	115.00	600.00	RARE

DATE	ABP	G-4 GOOD	F-12 FINE	EF-40 EX. FINE	MS-60 UNC.	MS-65 CH. UNC.
☐ 1928 (23,411,000)						
	.90	1.50	4.00	15.00	45.00	575.00
☐ 1928D (6,436,000)						
	.90	1.50	6.00	50.00	75.00	1000.00
☐ 1928S (6,936,000)						
	.90	1.50	3.00	30.00	300.00	RARE
☐ 1929 (36,446,000)						
	.90	1.50	3.00	15.00	50.00	525.00
☐ 1929D (8,370,000)						
	.90	1.50	3.00	40.00	80.00	2000.00
☐ 1929S (7,754,000)						
	.90	1.50	3.00	15.00	70.00	600.00
☐ 1930 (22,849,000)						
	.90	1.50	3.00	15.00	45.00	300.00
☐ 1930S (5,435,000)						
	.90	1.50	3.00	18.00	70.00	700.00
☐ 1931S (1,200,000)						
	12.00	20.00	25.00	45.00	70.00	500.00
☐ 1934 (20,313,000)						
	.90	1.50	3.00	12.00	70.00	500.00
☐ 1934D (7,480,000)						
	.90	1.50	6.00	25.00	95.00	1200.00
☐ 1935 (58,264,000)						
	.90	1.50	3.00	5.00	28.00	150.00
☐ 1935 Doubled Die						
	27.00	45.00	125.00	600.00		RARE
☐ 1935D (12,092,000)						
	1.20	2.00	3.00	20.00	75.00	1400.00
☐ 1935S (10,300,000)						
	1.20	2.00	3.00	6.00	60.00	220.00
☐ 1936 (119,001,420)						
	1.20	2.00	3.00	6.00	28.00	165.00
☐ 1936D (24,418,000)						
	1.20	2.00	3.00	6.00	45.00	165.00
☐ 1936S (14,390,000)						
	1.20	2.00	3.00	6.00	45.00	165.00
☐ 1937 (79,485,769)						
	1.20	2.00	3.00	6.00	28.00	75.00
☐ 1937D (17,826,000)						
	1.20	2.00	3.00	6.00	40.00	75.00
☐ 1937D, 3-Legged Buffalo*						
	300.00	500.00	800.00	1500.00	3000.00	RARE

*Beware of altered coins

DATE	ABP	G-4 GOOD	F-12 FINE	EF-40 EX. FINE	MS-60 UNC.	MS-65 CH. UNC.
☐ 1937S	(5,635,000)					
	1.20	2.00	3.00	5.00	35.00	85.00
☐ 1938D	(7,020,000)					
	2.70	4.50	5.00	6.00	25.00 ·	80.00
☐ 1938D over S						
	3.00	5.00	15.00	25.00	65.00	225.00
☐ 1938D over D						
	4.80	8.00	12.00	30.00	40.00	85.00

NICKELS—JEFFERSON, 1938 TO DATE

In 1938 Thomas Jefferson became the third president to be pictured on an American coin (preceded by Lincoln and Washington) when his likeness was installed on the five-cent piece, replacing the Buffalo/Indian Head. When the decision was made to use Jefferson's portrait on this coin, a public competition was instituted to select the best design, accompanied by an award of $1,000. A total of 390 entries was received, the winning one being that of Felix Schlag.

Jefferson is shown in profile facing left on the obverse, with his home at Monticello pictured on the reverse. No alteration has ever been made in the design of this coin but some changes occurred in composition and modeling of the dies. In 1966 Schlag's initials were added, the feeling being that he deserved this honor as much as the designer of the Lincoln cent, whose initials were incorporated into the design.

The coin has always weighed five grams and measured 21.1mm. Originally its content was 75% copper and 25% nickel. Due to a shortage of nickel during World War II because of its use in military production, this metal was entirely removed from the coin in 1942 and substituted with a composition of 56% copper, 35% silver, and 9% manganese. Wartime nickels consequently carry a premium value because of their silver content, though the silver additive was so small that the premium is only minimal. In 1946 the pre-war composition was resumed and has since remained constant. Prior to 1968 the mint mark was on the reverse, to the right of the design. On wartime specimens (1942–45) it is considerably enlarged and placed above Monticello's dome. From 1968 on, it appears on the obverse between the date and portrait.

| Mint Mark from 1968 | Felix Schlag (after 1966) | 1938–1942 1946 to 1968 | | 1942–1945 Silver Content Type with Large Mint Mark over Dome |

DATE	ABP	G-4 GOOD	F-12 FINE	EF-40 EX. FINE	MS-60 UNC.	PRF-65 PROOF
☐ 1938	(19,515,365)					
	.09	.15	.40	2.00	5.00	150.00
☐ 1938D	(5,376,000)					
	.45	.75	1.00	3.00	7.00	
☐ 1938S	(4,105,000)					
	.90	1.50	2.10	3.00	6.00	
☐ 1939	(120,627,535)					
	.09	.15	.25	.75	3.00	150.00
☐ 1939 Doubled Die						
	16.20	27.00	45.00	100.00	225.00	
☐ 1939D	(3,514,000)					
	1.95	3.25	8.00	15.00	75.00	
☐ 1939S	(6,630,000)					
	.45	.75	1.25	3.00	22.00	
☐ 1940	(176,499,158)	.15	.25	.65	1.50	140.00
☐ 1940D	(43,540,000)	.15	.25	.65	3.00	
☐ 1940S	(39,690,000)	.15	.25	.65	3.00	
☐ 1941	(203,283,730)	.15	.25	.40	1.00	125.00
☐ 1941D	(53,432,000)	.15	.25	.65	3.00	
☐ 1941S	(43,445,000)	.15	.25	.65	4.00	
☐ 1942	(49,818,600)	.15	.25	.65	5.00	125.00
☐ 1942D	(13,938,000)					
	.21	.35	.55	2.75	35.00	
☐ 1942D Horizontal D						
	19.00	32.00	50.00	150.00	600.00	
WARTIME SILVER NICKELS						
☐ 1942P	(57,900,600)					
	1.70	—	—	3.00	10.00	265.00
☐ 1942S	(32,900,000)					
	1.70	—	—	3.00	10.00	
☐ 1943P	(271,165,000)					
	1.70	—	—	3.00	7.00	
☐ 1943/2P	21.00	35.00	41.00	125.00	300.00	
☐ 1943 Doubled Eye						
	12.00	20.00	25.00	60.00	125.00	

DATE	ABP	G-4 GOOD	F-12 FINE	EF-40 EX. FINE	MS-60 UNC.	PRF-65 PROOF
☐ 1943D	(15,294,000)					
	1.70	—	—	4.00	8.00	
☐ 1943S	(104,060,000)					
	1.70	—	—	3.00	7.00	
☐ 1944P	(119,150,000)					
	1.70	—	—	3.00	8.00	
☐ 1944D	(32,309,000)					
	1.70	—	—	3.00	8.00	
☐ 1944S	(21,640,000)					
	1.70	—	—	3.00	6.00	
☐ 1945P	(119,408,100)					
	1.70	—	—	3.00	6.00	
☐ 1945P Double Eye						
	12.00	20.00	30.00	40.00	100.00	
☐ 1945D	(37,158,000)					
	1.70	—	—	3.00	6.00	
☐ 1945S	(58,939,000)					
	1.70	—	—	3.00	6.00	
REGULAR PRE-WAR TYPE						
☐ 1946	(161,116,000)		.20	.50	1.00	
☐ 1946D	(45,292,200)		.20	.50	1.00	
☐ 1946D Horizontal D						
	27.00	45.00	75.00	160.00	350.00	
☐ 1946S	(13,560,000)	.15	.30	.65	1.50	
☐ 1947	(95,000,000)	.15	.20	.45	1.10	
☐ 1947D	(37,882,000)	.15	.25	.45	1.10	
☐ 1947S	(24,720,000)	.15	.30	.65	1.50	
☐ 1948	(89,348,000)	.15	.30	.65	2.25	
☐ 1948D	(44,734,000)	.15	.30	.65	2.25	
☐ 1948S	(11,300,000)	.15	.30	.65	2.25	
☐ 1949	(60,652,000)	.15	.30	.65	2.25	
☐ 1949D	(36,498,000)	.15	.30	.65	2.25	
☐ 1949, D over S		.15	30.00	100.00	225.00	
☐ 1949S	(9,716,000)					
	.18	.30	.55	1.00	3.00	
☐ 1950	(9,847,386)					
	.12	.20	.25	.50	3.00	100.00
☐ 1950D	(2,530,000)					
	3.60	6.00	6.50	7.00	18.00	
☐ 1951	(28,689,500)		.20	.50	4.00	85.00
☐ 1951D	(20,460,000)		.20	.50	6.00	
☐ 1951S	(7,776,000)					
	.12	.20	.40	.70	2.00	

Circulated coins of the following dates are not bought by dealers.

DATE	MINTAGE	G-4 GOOD	F-12 FINE	EF-40 EX. FINE	MS-60 UNC.	PRF-65 PROOF
☐ 1952	(64,069,980)		.15	.30	2.00	50.00
☐ 1952D	(30,638,000)		.10	.35	4.25	
☐ 1952S	(20,572,000)	—	.10	.25	1.50	
☐ 1953	(46,772,800)	—	.10	.15	.50	40.00
☐ 1953D	(59,878,600)	—	.10	.16	.50	
☐ 1953S	(19,210,900)	—	.10	.24	1.00	
☐ 1954	(47,917,350)	—	.10	.12	1.00	35.00
☐ 1954D	(117,183,060)	—	.10	.12	1.00	
☐ 1954S	(29,834,000)	—	.10	.12	2.00	
☐ 1954, S over D				20.00	35.00	
☐ 1955	(8,266,200)	.20	.15	.40	1.25	30.00
☐ 1955D	(74,464,110)	.08	.10	.12	.75	
☐ 1955, D over S				25.00	40.00	
☐ 1956	(35,885,374)	—	.10	.18	.75	10.00
☐ 1956D	(67,222,940)	—	.10	.18	.75	
☐ 1957	(39,655,952)	—	.10	.18	.75	6.50
☐ 1957D	(136,828,900)	—	.10	.19	.75	
☐ 1958	(17,963,653)	—	.10	.18	.75	6.50
☐ 1958D	168,249,120				.75	
☐ 1959	28,397,291				.35	5.50
☐ 1959D	160,738,240				.35	
☐ 1960	57,107,602				.35	5.50
☐ 1960D	192,582,180				.35	5.50
☐ 1961	76,668,344				.35	5.50
☐ 1961D	229,342,760				.35	
☐ 1962	100,602,019				.35	5.50
☐ 1962D	280,195,720				.35	
☐ 1963	178,851,645				.35	5.50
☐ 1963D	276,829,460				.35	
☐ 1964	1,028,622,762				.35	5.50
☐ 1964D	1,787,297,160				.35	
☐ 1965	136,131,380				.35	
☐ 1966	156,208,283				.30	
☐ 1967	107,324,750				.30	
☐ 1968D	91,227,800				.30	
☐ 1968S	103,437,510				.30	4.00
☐ 1969D	202,807,500				.30	
☐ 1969S	128,099,631				.30	4.00
☐ 1970D	515,485,380				.30	
☐ 1970S	241,464,814				.30	4.00
☐ 1971	108,884,000				.30	
☐ 1971D	316,144,800				.30	
☐ 1971S Proof Only	3,224,138				.30	5.00
☐ 1972	202,036,000				.30	
☐ 1972D	351,694,600				.30	

DATE	MINTAGE	MS-60 UNC.	PRF-65 PROOF
☐ 1972S Proof Only	3,267,667		6.00
☐ 1973	384,396,000	.30	
☐ 1973D	261,405,400	.30	
☐ 1973S Proof Only	2,769,624		4.00
☐ 1974	601,752,000	.30	
☐ 1974D	277,373,000	.30	
☐ 1974S Proof Only	2,617,350		4.00
☐ 1975	181,772,000	.30	
☐ 1975D	401,875,300	.30	
☐ 1975S Proof Only	2,909,369		4.00
☐ 1976	376,124,000	.30	
☐ 1976D	563,964,147	.30	
☐ 1976S Proof Only	4,149,945		4.00
☐ 1977	585,175,250	.30	
☐ 1977D	297,325,618	.30	
☐ 1977S Proof Only	3,250,095		4.00
☐ 1978	391,308,000	.30	
☐ 1978D	313,092,780	.30	
☐ 1978S Proof Only	3,127,781		4.00
☐ 1979	463,188,123	.30	
☐ 1979D	325,867,600	.30	
☐ 1979S Proof Only, Filled S			5.00
☐ 1979S Proof Only, Open S			5.00
☐ 1980P	593,004,060	.30	
☐ 1980D	502,324,000	.30	
☐ 1980S Proof Only	3,554,800		4.00
☐ 1981P	657,503,295	.30	
☐ 1981D	364,802,000	.30	
☐ 1981S Proof Only, Filled S			4.00
☐ 1981S Proof Only, Open S			4.00
☐ 1982P	292,350,000	.50	
☐ 1982D	373,725,500	.60	
☐ 1982S Proof Only			4.00
☐ 1983P	560,750,000	.60	
☐ 1983D	536,726,000	.60	
☐ 1983S Proof Only	3,228,537		4.00
☐ 1984P	750,000,000	.30	
☐ 1984D	518,000,000	.30	
☐ 1984S Proof Only			6.00
☐ 1985P	676,222,421	.30	
☐ 1985D	463,621,747	.30	
☐ 1985S Proof Only	3,241,412		4.00
☐ 1986P	572,842,600	.30	
☐ 1986D	382,610,212	.30	
☐ 1986S Proof Only	3,101,640		10.00
☐ 1987P	362,111,406	.30	
☐ 1987D	411,690,114	.30	
☐ 1987S Proof Only	39,821,745		4.00
☐ 1988P	770,350,000	.30	

DATE	MINTAGE	MS-60 UNC.	PRF-65 PROOF
☐ 1988D	672,700,640	.30	
☐ 1988S Proof Only	3,116,420		6.00
☐ 1989P	896,764,248	.30	
☐ 1989D	580,862,212	.30	
☐ 1989S Proof Only	3,184,776		5.00
☐ 1990P	652,720,114	.30	
☐ 1990D	646,111,042	.30	
☐ 1990S Proof Only	3,720,411		5.00
☐ 1991P	614,100,000	.30	
☐ 1991D	436,495,570	.30	
☐ 1991S Proof Only	2,867,677		6.00
☐ 1992P	399,550,210	.30	
☐ 1992D	450,568,100	.30	
☐ 1992S Proof Only	4,175,610		5.00
☐ 1993P	412,076,000	.30	
☐ 1993D	406,084,135	.30	
☐ 1993S Proof Only	3,394,792		5.00
☐ 1994P	772,160,000	.30	
☐ 1994P Matte Finish+			125.00
☐ 1994D	715,762,110	.30	
☐ 1994S Proof Only	3,269,923		5.00
☐ 1995P	774,156,000	.30	
☐ 1995D	888,112,000	.30	
☐ 1995S Proof Only			7.00
☐ 1996P	829,332,000	.30	
☐ 1996D	817,736,000	.30	
☐ 1996S Proof Only			4.00
☐ 1997P	470,972,000	.30	
☐ 1997D	466,640,000	.30	
☐ 1997S Proof Only	1,975,000		4.00
☐ 1997P Specimen Frosted Issued in 2-Piece Botanic Gardens + Jefferson $1.00 Sets.			325.00

DATE	MINTAGE	MS-65	PRF-65 PROOF
☐ 1998P	640,776,000	1.75	
☐ 1998D	612,920,000	1.75	
☐ 1998S Proof Only			5.00
☐ 1999P	1,212,000,000	1.75	
☐ 1999D	1,066,720,000	1.75	
☐ 1999S Proof Only			5.00
☐ 2000P	846,220,000	1.75	
☐ 2000D	1,509,520,000	1.75	
☐ 2000S Proof Only			5.00
☐ 2001P	675,740,000	1.75	
☐ 2001D	627,680,000	1.75	
☐ 2001S Proof Only			5.00
☐ 2002P	539,280,000	1.75	
☐ 2002D	691,200,000	1.75	
☐ 2002S Proof Only			5.00
☐ 2003P		1.75	

DATE	MINTAGE	MS-60 UNC.	PRF-65 PROOF
☐ 2003D	441,840,000		.20
☐ 2003S Proof Only	383,040,000		4.00
☐ 2004P Peace Medal	350,000,000	.20	
☐ 2004D Peace Medal	350,000,000	.20	
☐ 2004S Proof Only Peace Medal			15.00
☐ 2004P Keel Boat	350,000,000	.20	
☐ 2004D Keel Boat	350,000,000	.20	
☐ 2004S Proof Only Keel Boat			15.00
☐ 2005P Bison Rev.	420,000,000	.20	
☐ 2005D Bison Rev.	450,000,000	.20	
☐ 2005S Proof Bison Rev.			8.00
☐ 2005P Ocean Rev.	420,000,000	.20	
☐ 2005D Ocean Rev.	450,000,000	.20	
☐ 2005S Proof Ocean Rev.			8.00
☐ 2006P Monticello	671,150,000	.20	
☐ 2006D Monticello	795,330,000	.20	
☐ 2006S Proof Monticello			8.00
☐ 2007P	539,600,000	.20	
☐ 2007D	580,540,000	.20	
☐ 2007S Proof			7.00
☐ 2008P		.20	
☐ 2008D		.20	
☐ 2008S Proof			7.00
☐ 2009P		.20	
☐ 2009D		.20	
☐ 2009S Proof			7.00
☐ 2010P		.20	
☐ 2010D		.20	
☐ 2010S Proof			7.00
☐ 2011P		.20	
☐ 2011D		.20	
☐ 2011S Proof			7.00
☐ 2012P		.20	
☐ 2012D		.20	
☐ 2012S Proof			7.00

HALF DIMES, 1794–1873

The first half dimes did not technically reach manufacture until 1795 but carried a 1794 date, as the dies had been engraved that year and there was no desire to redo this work. The weight was 1.35 grams, the composition consisting of .8924 silver and .1076 copper, or, to speak in rounded figures, nine parts silver to one part copper. After more than forty years of being unchanged compositionally, the silver content was raised to a full nine parts in 1837, which necessitated a weight reduction to 1.34 grams.

The original obverse type was the Flowing Hair Liberty, similar to that of other silver coinage of the time. Its designer was Robert Scot. On the reverse appeared the standing eagle and legend UNITED STATES OF AMERICA. This was replaced by the Draped Bust type with similar reverse in 1796, and the shield eagle reverse in 1800. Beginning in 1829 the Capped Bust was introduced, along with a modified version of the shield eagle (wings downward instead of upturned). The sharpest departure occurred in 1837, with the introduction of a design that was to remain—with modifications—until the series closed out in 1873. This was the Seated Liberty, an attractive bit of classical portraiture but one to which some objection was voiced on the grounds that it closely resembled the figure of Britannia on British coins. The reverse carried the wording HALF DIME within an open wreath, encircled by UNITED STATES OF AMERICA. There was initially no decoration on the obverse beyond the figure of Liberty. In 1838 a series of stars was added as a half-frame to the portrait. Arrows were placed by the date in 1853. The chief revision came in 1860 when the words UNITED STATES OF AMERICA were removed from the reverse and placed on the obverse, supplanting the stars. The reverse wreath was redesigned and made larger and frillier to fill the vacancy.

HALF DIMES—LIBERTY WITH FLOWING HAIR, 1794–1795

DATE	MINTAGE	ABP	G-4 GOOD	F-12 FINE	VF-20 V. FINE
☐ 1794	86,416	1100.00	1750.00	2800.00	4250.00
☐ 1795		900.00	1500.00	2200.00	3500.00

(Both the 1794 and 1795 were struck in 1795)

HALF DIMES—DRAPED BUST, SMALL EAGLE, 1796–1797

DATE	MINTAGE	ABP	G-4 GOOD	F-12 FINE	VF-20 V. FINE
☐ 1796 over 5		1150.00	1850.00	3750.00	5350.00
☐ 1796	10,230	1000.00	1750.00	3500.00	5000.00
☐ 1796 LIKERTY		1000.00	1675.00	3400.00	5150.00
☐ 1797 (13 stars)		1500.00	2250.00	4000.00	6500.00
☐ 1797 (15 stars)	44,527	1000.00	1650.00	3250.00	4650.00
☐ 1797 (16 stars)		1100.00	1750.00	3350.00	4650.00

HALF DIMES—DRAPED BUST, LARGE EAGLE, 1800–1805

DATE	MINTAGE	ABP	G-4 GOOD	F-12 FINE	VF-20 V. FINE
☐ 1800		750.00	1100.00	2000.00	2800.00
☐ 1800 LIBEKTY	24,000	750.00	1100.00	2000.00	2800.00
☐ 1801	33,910	800.00	1200.00	2250.00	3000.00
☐ 1802	13,010				VERY RARE
☐ 1803	37,850	850.00	1250.00	2200.00	3000.00
☐ 1805	15,600	800.00	1200.00	2350.00	3500.00

HALF DIMES—LIBERTY CAP, 1829–1837

DATE	ABP	G-4 GOOD	F-12 FINE	EF-40 EX. FINE	MS-63 UNC.
☐ 1829	(1,230,000)				
	40.00	55.00	90.00	200.00	1000.00
☐ 1830	(1,240,000)				
	40.00	55.00	85.00	165.00	950.00
☐ 1831	(1,242,700)				
	40.00	55.00	85.00	165.00	950.00
☐ 1832	(965,000)				
	40.00	55.00	85.00	165.00	950.00
☐ 1833	(1,370,000)				
	40.00	55.00	85.00	165.00	950.00
☐ 1834	(1,480,000)				
	40.00	55.00	85.00	165.00	950.00
☐ 1835*	(2,760,000)				
	40.00	55.00	85.00	165.00	950.00
☐ 1836	(1,900,000)				
	40.00	55.00	85.00	165.00	950.00
☐ 1837 Large $.05	(2,276,000)				
	40.00	55.00	95.00	185.00	975.00
☐ 1837 Small $.05					
	40.00	65.00	105.00	215.00	2350.00

*Note: 1835 Large Date—Large $.05, Large Date—Small $.05, Same prices;
Small Date—Small $.05, Small Date—Large $.05, Same prices.

HALF DIMES—LIBERTY SEATED, 1837–1859

1837–1838O
No Stars

1838–1859
With Stars

1837–1859
Mint Mark is on the Reverse Under the Value

DATE	ABP	G-4 GOOD	F-12 FINE	EF-40 EX. FINE	MS-60 UNC.	MS-65 CH. UNC.
☐ 1837 Small Date, No Stars						
	30.00	45.00	95.00	250.00	675.00	3750.00
☐ 1837 Large Date, No Stars		(2,250,000)				
	27.00	45.00	95.00	250.00	625.00	3000.00
☐ 1838O No Stars (70,000)						
	60.00	100.00	250.00	950.00	2450.00	RARE
☐ 1838 With Large Stars (2,255,000)						
	12.00	20.00	30.00	90.00	300.00	2150.00
☐ 1838 With Small Stars						
	12.00	20.00	60.00	185.00	600.00	4000.00
☐ 1839 (1,069,150)						
	12.00	20.00	30.00	90.00	285.00	2000.00
☐ 1839O (1,096,550)						
	15.00	25.00	35.00	110.00	550.00	7500.00
☐ 1839O With Large O						
	300.00	500.00	1000.00	3500.00	RARE	RARE
☐ 1840 No Drapery (1,344,085)						
	12.00	20.00	32.00	85.00	300.00	2150.00
☐ 1840O No Drapery						
	15.00	25.00	35.00	95.00	850.00	RARE
☐ 1840 Drapery						
	15.00	25.00	75.00	225.00	450.00	2950.00
☐ 1840O Drapery						
	21.00	35.00	125.00	600.00	3500.00	RARE
☐ 1841 (1,500,000)						
	12.00	20.00	35.00	75.00	210.00	1100.00
☐ 1841O (815,000)						
	14.00	20.00	40.00	125.00	675.00	7000.00
☐ 1842 (815,000)						
	12.00	20.00	35.00	75.00	200.00	1200.00

DATE	ABP	G-4 GOOD	F-12 FINE	EF-40 EX. FINE	MS-60 UNC.	MS-65 CH. UNC.
☐ 1842O	(350,000)					
	21.00	35.00	65.00	525.00	1250.00	15000.00
☐ 1843	(1,165,000)					
	13.00	22.00	30.00	70.00	175.00	1450.00
☐ 1844	(430,000)					
	14.00	22.00	30.00	75.00	190.00	1200.00
☐ 1844O	(220,000)					
	60.00	90.00	225.00	1150.00	5350.00	RARE
☐ 1844O Large O						
	55.00	85.00	210.00	1100.00	5250.00	RARE
☐ 1845	(1,564,000)					
	12.00	20.00	30.00	70.00	175.00	1100.00
☐ 1846	(27,000)					
	300.00	450.00	1150.00	3000.00	13500.00	RARE
☐ 1847	(1,274,000)					
	12.00	18.00	30.00	70.00	215.00	1100.00
☐ 1848 Medium Date	(668,000)					
	14.00	20.00	30.00	75.00	250.00	3000.00
☐ 1848 Large Date						
	16.00	25.00	50.00	160.00	550.00	4250.00
☐ 1848O	(600,000)					
	14.00	20.00	35.00	130.00	475.00	2400.00
☐ 1849	(1,309,000)					
	15.00	22.00	30.00	70.00	210.00	1750.00
☐ 1849 over 46	(1,309,000)					
	15.00	25.00	50.00	125.00	575.00	2850.00
☐ 1849 over 48	(1,309,000)					
	21.00	35.00	65.00	165.00	675.00	3000.00
☐ 1849O	(140,000)					
	21.00	35.00	85.00	450.00	2400.00	RARE
☐ 1850	(955,000)					
	13.00	20.00	35.00	70.00	175.00	1100.00
☐ 1850O	(690,000)					
	15.00	23.00	42.00	125.00	750.00	5000.00
☐ 1851	(781,000)					
	12.00	20.00	30.00	65.00	175.00	1300.00
☐ 1851O	(860,000)					
	13.00	22.00	35.00	115.00	525.00	4250.00
☐ 1852	(1,000,000)					
	12.00	20.00	35.00	70.00	175.00	1100.00
☐ 1852O	(260,000)					
	20.00	30.00	80.00	250.00	825.00	8500.00

DATE	ABP	G-4 GOOD	F-12 FINE	EF-40 EX. FINE	MS-60 UNC.	MS-65 CH. UNC.
☐ 1853 With Arrows (13,210,020)						
	12.00	20.00	28.00	80.00	225.00	1350.00
☐ 1853 No Arrows (135,000)						
	30.00	45.00	100.00	315.00	775.00	2750.00
☐ 1853O With Arrows (2,360,000)						
	15.00	25.00	38.00	85.00	280.00	3650.00
☐ 1853O No Arrows (160,000)						
	150.00	215.00	450.00	1950.00	6000.00	RARE
☐ 1854 With Arrows (5,740,000)						
	12.00	22.00	25.00	65.00	215.00	1500.00
☐ 1854O With Arrows (1,560,000)						
	15.00	25.00	35.00	75.00	250.00	3600.00
☐ 1855 With Arrows (1,750,000)						
	12.00	22.00	25.00	65.00	210.00	2250.00
☐ 1855O With Arrows (600,000)						
	15.00	25.00	38.00	150.00	600.00	4200.00
☐ 1856 (4,880,000)						
	12.00	20.00	25.00	65.00	175.00	1200.00
☐ 1856O (1,100,000)						
	14.00	20.00	28.00	110.00	525.00	2250.00
☐ 1857 (7,280,000)						
	12.00	20.00	25.00	65.00	165.00	950.00
☐ 1857O (1,380,000)						
	14.00	20.00	27.00	70.00	350.00	1600.00
☐ 1858 (3,500,000)						
	12.00	20.00	25.00	65.00	165.00	950.00
☐ 1858 Over Inverted Date						
	24.00	40.00	110.00	200.00	650.00	3500.00
☐ 1858 Double Date						
	18.00	30.00	100.00	265.00	725.00	3750.00
☐ 1858O (1,660,000)						
	12.00	20.00	32.00	90.00	275.00	1500.00
☐ 1859* (340,000)						
	12.00	20.00	32.00	85.00	185.00	1350.00
☐ 1859O (560,000)						
	14.00	22.00	35.00	125.00	275.00	1650.00

*Note: There are two recognized patterns in this series: the transitional pieces of 1859 and 1860. 1859—proof: RARE; 1860—MS-65: RARE.

HALF DIMES—LIBERTY SEATED, 1860–1873 WITH "UNITED STATES OF AMERICA" ON OBVERSE

Mint Marks are Under or Within Wreath on Reverse

DATE	ABP	G-4 GOOD	F-12 FINE	EF-40 EX. FINE	MS-60 UNC.	MS-65 CH. UNC.
☐ 1860	(799,000)					
	12.00	20.00	30.00	60.00	165.00	825.00
☐ 1860O	(1,060,000)					
	13.00	20.00	30.00	60.00	215.00	975.00
☐ 1861	(3,361,000)					
	12.00	20.00	30.00	65.00	175.00	825.00
☐ 1861 over 0						
	21.00	35.00	60.00	300.00	625.00	2750.00
☐ 1862	(1,492,550)					
	15.00	25.00	45.00	75.00	185.00	850.00
☐ 1863	(18,460)					
	115.00	180.00	250.00	525.00	750.00	1500.00
☐ 1863S	(100,000)					
	20.00	30.00	65.00	200.00	800.00	3500.00
☐ 1864	(48,470)					
	235.00	350.00	550.00	1000.00	1250.00	2150.00
☐ 1864S	(90,000)					
	40.00	60.00	125.00	300.00	700.00	3800.00
☐ 1865	(13,500)					
	210.00	325.00	475.00	750.00	875.00	1850.00
☐ 1865S	(120,000)					
	21.00	35.00	65.00	200.00	1000.00	5250.00
☐ 1866	(10,725)					
	200.00	300.00	450.00	675.00	850.00	2750.00
☐ 1866S	(120,000)					
	20.00	32.00	55.00	185.00	475.00	4250.00
☐ 1867	(8,625)					
	325.00	500.00	650.00	800.00	975.00	2150.00
☐ 1867S	(120,000)					
	17.00	25.00	58.00	185.00	550.00	3850.00

DATE	ABP	G-4 GOOD	F-12 FINE	EF-40 EX. FINE	MS-60 UNC.	MS-65 CH. UNC.
☐ 1868	(89,200)					
	40.00	60.00	125.00	350.00	650.00	1900.00
☐ 1868S	(280,000)					
	12.00	20.00	40.00	60.00	350.00	2350.00
☐ 1869	(280,000)					
	12.00	20.00	37.00	60.00	250.00	1150.00
☐ 1869S	(230,000)					
	12.00	20.00	37.00	60.00	325.00	3850.00
☐ 1870*	(536,000)					
	12.00	20.00	32.00	55.00	165.00	850.00
☐ 1871	(1,873,960)					
	12.00	20.00	32.00	55.00	165.00	775.00
☐ 1871S	(161,000)					
	14.00	22.00	40.00	95.00	300.00	2300.00
☐ 1872	(2,947,950)					
	12.00	20.00	32.00	55.00	165.00	800.00
☐ 1872S In Wreath	(837,000)					
	12.00	20.00	32.00	55.00	175.00	750.00
☐ 1872S Below Wreath						
	13.00	20.00	35.00	52.00	175.00	750.00
☐ 1873	(712,600)					
	12.00	20.00	32.00	52.00	165.00	1000.00
☐ 1873S	(324,000)					
	12.00	20.00	32.00	52.00	165.00	750.00

*Note: 1870S is unique; only one known. 2005 sale MS-63 $650,000.00

DIMES

EARLY DIMES, 1796–1891

A coin valued at one-tenth of a dollar was among the first to be authorized by the U.S. Mint, though production did not begin until 1796. Had the dime made its debut even just a year sooner, there is every likelihood it would have carried the Flowing Hair design, but by 1796 there was no longer much enthusiasm for this rendition of Liberty and so the coin got its start with the Draped Bust portrait. This version of Liberty, familiar on other silver pieces, lacks the "cap of liberty" and shows the goddess with a somewhat more fashionable hairdo. On the reverse was the standing eagle, encircled by branches, and the inscription UNITED STATES OF AMERICA. Stars were placed in a circular pattern on the obverse, ranging in number from thirteen to sixteen. The designer was Robert Scot. The weight of this coin was 2.70 grams and its original composition was .8924 silver and .1076 copper, the same as that of the half dime (or, approximately, nine parts of silver to one part of copper). Its diameter was generally 19mm. but slight variations are observed.

In 1798 the standing eagle was replaced by the heraldic or shield eagle on the reverse, over which is a series of stars. Just like the stars on the original obverse, these too can vary in quantity from thirteen to sixteen. In 1809 the portrait was changed to the Capped Bust, whose chief characteristic (aside from Liberty's headgear) is that the profile is switched round to face left instead of right. The reverse type is now the eagle-on-branch, still bearing a shield but with its wings down instead of opened wide. The year 1837 witnessed the most significant alteration up to the time; a likeness of Liberty seated replaced the bust type and the eagle's place on the reverse was taken by the wording ONE DIME within a wreath, surrounded by UNITED STATES OF AMERICA. At first there were no stars on the obverse but these were added in 1838, and arrows were placed at the date in 1853. These, however, were of little duration, as they disappeared in 1856.

DIMES—DRAPED BUST, 1796–1807
EAGLE ON REVERSE

1798–1807

1796–1797
Small Eagle

1798–1807
Large Eagle

DATE	MINTAGE	ABP GOOD	G-4 GOOD	F-12 FINE	VF-20 V. FINE
☐ 1796	22,135	2000.00	2850.00	5250.00	7000.00
☐ 1797 13 Stars		2000.00	2900.00	5750.00	8500.00
☐ 1797 16 Stars	25,261	2000.00	2900.00	5500.00	7250.00
☐ 1798		500.00	750.00	1250.00	2000.00
☐ 1798 over 97 With 13 Stars on Reverse					
		1000.00	1350.00	4500.00	6500.00
☐ 1798 Small 8	27,500	600.00	1000.00	1950.00	3150.00
☐ 1798 over 97 With 16 Stars on Reverse					
		500.00	750.00	1500.00	2400.00
☐ 1800	21,760	500.00	725.00	1500.00	2500.00
☐ 1801	34,640	500.00	725.00	1650.00	4000.00
☐ 1802	10,975	1000.00	1500.00	2750.00	4500.00
☐ 1803	33,040	500.00	725.00	1850.00	2250.00
☐ 1804 With 13 Stars on Reverse					
	8,265	1250.00	1650.00	10000.00	18000.00
☐ 1804 With 14 Stars on Reverse					
	8,265	1350.00	1850.00	11500.00	20000.00
☐ 1805 With 4 Berries	120,780	500.00	725.00	1200.00	1750.00
☐ 1805 With 5 Berries	120,780	500.00	725.00	1200.00	1750.00
☐ 1807	165,000	400.00	650.00	1200.00	1750.00

DIMES—LIBERTY CAP, 1809–1837

DATE	ABP GOOD	G-4 GOOD	F-12 FINE	EF-40 EX. FINE	MS-60 UNC.
☐ 1809 (44,710)					
	100.00	150.00	450.00	1850.00	4000.00
☐ 1811 over 9 (65,180)					
	75.00	125.00	325.00	1750.00	3750.00
☐ 1814 Small Date (421,500)					
	40.00	60.00	125.00	600.00	2500.00
☐ 1814 Large Date					
	30.00	45.00	75.00	450.00	1875.00
☐ 1814 STATES OF AMERICA, No Breaks Between Words: Large Date					
	50.00	75.00	150.00	600.00	2500.00
☐ 1820 Small O					
	30.00	50.00	75.00	625.00	1650.00
☐ 1820 Large O (942,587)					
	30.00	50.00	75.00	425.00	1500.00
☐ 1821 Small Date (1,186,512)					
	30.00	50.00	75.00	500.00	1800.00
☐ 1821 Large Date					
	30.00	50.00	75.00	475.00	1850.00
☐ 1822 (100,000)					
	850.00	1200.00	3000.00	9000.00	17500.00
☐ 1823 over 22, Small E (440,000)					
	30.00	50.00	75.00	475.00	1550.00
☐ 1823 over 22 Large E					
	30.00	50.00	75.00	450.00	1550.00
☐ 1824 over 22	40.00	65.00	185.00	800.00	2350.00
☐ 1825 (Mintage includes 1824) (510,000)					
	30.00	50.00	75.00	450.00	1650.00
☐ 1827 (1,215,000)					
	30.00	50.00	75.00	450.00	1600.00
☐ 1828 Large Date (125,000)					
	36.00	60.00	160.00	700.00	2500.00
☐ 1828 Small Date (125,000) (Reduced Beaded Borders)					
	27.00	45.00	95.00	425.00	1350.00
☐ 1829 Small $.10 (770,000)					
	25.00	38.00	65.00	350.00	1000.00

DATE	ABP GOOD	G-4 GOOD	F-12 FINE	EF-40 EX. FINE	MS-60 UNC.
☐ 1829 Medium Date					
	25.00	38.00	55.00	375.00	1150.00
☐ 1829 Large $.10 (770,000)					
	30.00	45.00	75.00	400.00	1350.00
☐ 1830 Small $.10 (510,000)					
	25.00	38.00	50.00	375.00	1000.00
☐ 1830 Large $.10					
	25.00	38.00	50.00	325.00	950.00
☐ 1830, 30 over 29					
	35.00	55.00	125.00	425.00	1400.00
☐ 1831 (771,350)					
	25.00	38.00	55.00	325.00	950.00
☐ 1832 (522,500)					
	25.00	38.00	55.00	325.00	950.00
☐ 1833 (485,000)					
	25.00	38.00	55.00	325.00	950.00
☐ 1834** Small 4 (635,000)					
	30.00	45.00	60.00	350.00	1050.00
☐ 1834 Large 4					
	30.00	45.00	60.00	350.00	975.00
☐ 1835 (1,410,000)					
	25.00	38.00	55.00	325.00	950.00
☐ 1836 (1,190,000)					
	25.00	38.00	55.00	325.00	950.00
☐ 1837 ALL KINDS (359,500)					
	25.00	38.00	55.00	325.00	950.00

**1834—Small 4, 1834—Large 4: Same Price

DIMES—LIBERTY SEATED, 1837–1860

1837–1838O
No Stars

1837–1891

1838–1860
With Stars

DATE	ABP	G-4 GOOD	F-12 FINE	EF-40 EX. FINE	MS-60 UNC.
☐ 1837 No Stars, Small Date (682,500)					
	33.00	55.00	110.00	550.00	1150.00

DATE	ABP GOOD	G-4 GOOD	F-12 FINE	EF-40 EX. FINE	MS-60 UNC.
☐ 1837 Large Date					
	30.00	50.00	115.00	500.00	1050.00
☐ 1838O No Stars (402,404)					
	40.00	65.00	150.00	750.00	3150.00
☐ 1838 Small Stars No Drapery					
	21.00	35.00	65.00	200.00	675.00
☐ 1838 Large Stars (1,992,500)					
	15.00	25.00	38.00	150.00	425.00
☐ 1838 Partial Drapery					
	21.00	35.00	75.00	275.00	1000.00
☐ 1839 (1,053,115)					
	14.00	22.00	35.00	140.00	525.00
☐ 1839O (1,243,272)					
	18.00	28.00	45.00	165.00	550.00
☐ 1839O Reverse 1838O					
	70.00	105.00	325.00	725.00	RARE
☐ 1840 No Drape (1,358,580)					
	15.00	22.00	35.00	140.00	435.00
☐ 1840O No Drape (1,175,000)					
	18.00	28.00	40.00	225.00	1950.00
☐ 1840 Drapery Added (377,541)					
	25.00	38.00	100.00	325.00	1150.00
☐ 1841 (1,622,500)					
	14.00	22.00	32.00	75.00	350.00
☐ 1841O (2,007,500)					
	18.00	28.00	50.00	115.00	900.00
☐ 1841 Large O Close Bud Reverse					
	500.00	750.00	1500.00	RARE	
☐ 1842 (1,887,500)					
	13.00	21.00	35.00	60.00	375.00
☐ 1842O (2,020,000)					
	20.00	30.00	40.00	285.00	2500.00
☐ 1843 (1,370,000)					
	13.00	23.00	35.00	60.00	385.00
☐ 1843/1843					
	18.00	25.00	45.00	150.00	600.00
☐ 1843O (150,000)					
	60.00	85.00	375.00	1500.00	RARE
☐ 1844 (72,500)					
	150.00	225.00	500.00	1200.00	4500.00

DATE	ABP GOOD	G-4 GOOD	F-12 FINE	EF-40 EX. FINE	MS-60 UNC.	MS-65 CH. UNC.
☐ 1845	(1,755,000)					
	15.00	23.00	29.00	65.00	325.00	2800.00
☐ 1845/1845						
	20.00	28.00	50.00	200.00	800.00	RARE
☐ 18450	(230,000)					
	25.00	35.00	85.00	575.00	4250.00	RARE
☐ 1846	(31,300)					
	100.00	175.00	450.00	1500.00	RARE	RARE
☐ 1847	(245,000)					
	15.00	23.00	40.00	145.00	900.00	RARE
☐ 1848	(451,000)					
	15.00	25.00	38.00	90.00	550.00	6500.00
☐ 1849	(839,000)					
	15.00	25.00	32.00	65.00	400.00	3800.00
☐ 18490	(300,000)					
	18.00	30.00	55.00	285.00	2500.00	RARE
☐ 1850	(1,931,500)					
	15.00	25.00	32.00	60.00	285.00	5750.00
☐ 18500	(510,000)					
	20.00	30.00	42.00	125.00	950.00	6000.00
☐ 1851	(1,026,500)					
	15.00	25.00	32.00	60.00	315.00	4750.00
☐ 18510	(400,000)					
	20.00	30.00	45.00	150.00	2350.00	RARE
☐ 1852	(1,535,500)					
	15.00	23.00	32.00	62.00	315.00	2850.00
☐ 18520	(430,000)					
	21.00	35.00	60.00	285.00	1500.00	RARE
☐ 1853 No Arrows	(95,000)					
	100.00	135.00	275.00	650.00	1000.00	4500.00
☐ 1853 With Arrows	(12,173,010)					
	12.00	18.00	20.00	58.00	325.00	2350.00
☐ 18530	(1,100,000)					
	12.00	20.00	75.00	285.00	1650.00	RARE
☐ 1854	(4,470,000)					
	12.00	18.00	20.00	55.00	350.00	2250.00
☐ 18540	(1,770,000)					
	12.00	18.00	28.00	60.00	300.00	3250.00
☐ 1855	(2,075,000)					
	12.00	18.00	20.00	55.00	325.00	3000.00
☐ 1856 Small Date	(5,780,000)					
	12.00	18.00	21.00	50.00	285.00	4000.00

DATE	ABP GOOD	G-4 GOOD	F-12 FINE	EF-40 EX. FINE	MS-60 UNC.	MS-65 CH. UNC
☐ 1856 Large Date						
	14.00	20.00	23.00	62.00	285.00	4000.00
☐ 1856O (1,180,000)						
	12.00	20.00	25.00	65.00	875.00	6000.00
☐ 1856S (70,000)						
	75.00	125.00	385.00	1200.00	4250.00	RARE
☐ 1857 (5,580,000)						
	11.00	18.00	20.00	60.00	285.00	2350.00
☐ 1857O (1,540,000)						
	12.00	18.00	25.00	75.00	375.00	2350.00
☐ 1858 (1,540,000)						
	12.00	18.00	20.00	55.00	285.00	2650.00
☐ 1858O (290,000)						
	15.00	25.00	40.00	150.00	625.00	7250.00
☐ 1858S (60,000)						
	75.00	115.00	235.00	950.00	3900.00	RARE
☐ 1859* (430,000)						
	13.00	23.00	25.00	58.00	300.00	2500.00
☐ 1859O (480,000)						
	15.00	25.00	28.00	85.00	350.00	2500.00
☐ 1859S (60,000)						
	60.00	110.00	315.00	1300.00	RARE	RARE
☐ 1860S (140,000)						
	25.00	40.00	65.00	425.00	2500.00	13500.00

*Note: There is a recognized pattern in this series—1859 Transitional Pattern

DIMES—LIBERTY SEATED, 1860–1891 WITH "UNITED STATES OF AMERICA" ON OBVERSE

Mint Marks Under or Within Wreath on Reverse

DATE	ABP	G-4 GOOD	F-12 FINE	EF-40 EX. FINE	MS-60 UNC.	MS-65 CH. UNC
☐ 1860 (607,000)						
	12.00	18.00	23.00	42.00	210.00	1300.00

DATE	ABP GOOD	G-4 GOOD	F-12 FINE	EF-40 EX. FINE	MS-60 UNC.	MS-65 CH. UNC.
☐ 1860O	(40,000)					
	250.00	375.00	875.00	4000.00	RARE	RARE
☐ 1861	(1,924,000)					
	12.00	18.00	23.00	40.00	175.00	1350.00
☐ 1861S	(172,500)					
	30.00	45.00	140.00	425.00	2250.00	RARE
☐ 1862	(847,550)					
	14.00	20.00	24.00	50.00	200.00	1275.00
☐ 1862S	(180,750)					
	35.00	50.00	90.00	600.00	1350.00	RARE
☐ 1863	(14,460)					
	250.00	375.00	600.00	950.00	1400.00	4750.00
☐ 1863S	(157,000)					
	30.00	50.00	75.00	350.00	1500.00	RARE
☐ 1864	(39,070)					
	150.00	240.00	475.00	1000.00	1325.00	4350.00
☐ 1864S	(230,000)					
	45.00	70.00	110.00	325.00	1450.00	7500.00
☐ 1865	(10,500)					
	200.00	300.00	600.00	900.00	1375.00	4100.00
☐ 1865S	(175,000)					
	50.00	75.00	240.00	850.00	5500.00	RARE
☐ 1866	(8,725)					
	400.00	600.00	1300.00	2000.00	2500.00	3750.00
☐ 1866S	(135,000)					
	30.00	50.00	90.00	400.00	1200.00	RARE
☐ 1867	(6,625)					
	350.00	525.00	825.00	1250.00	1400.00	3500.00
☐ 1867S	(140,000)					
	25.00	35.00	110.00	450.00	1250.00	7500.00
☐ 1868	(466,250)					
	15.00	20.00	35.00	75.00	350.00	3750.00
☐ 1868S	(260,000)					
	18.00	25.00	40.00	215.00	425.00	5250.00
☐ 1869	(256,600)					
	17.00	23.00	40.00	125.00	385.00	3500.00
☐ 1869S	(450,000)					
	15.00	20.00	27.00	185.00	425.00	3000.00
☐ 1870	(471,500)					
	12.00	20.00	25.00	58.00	275.00	2350.00
☐ 1870S	(50,000)					
	175.00	275.00	425.00	750.00	1750.00	6350.00

DATE	ABP GOOD	G-4 GOOD	F-12 FINE	EF-40 EX. FINE	MS-60 UNC.	MS-65 CH. UNC.
☐ 1871 (753,610)						
	10.00	17.00	20.00	45.00	285.00	1800.00
☐ 1871CC (20,100)						
	2000.00	3000.00	5500.00	RARE	RARE	RARE
☐ 1871S (320,000)						
	18.00	30.00	90.00	225.00	550.00	8500.00
☐ 1872 (2,396,450)						
	10.00	17.00	22.00	35.00	175.00	1300.00
☐ 1872CC (24,000)						
	350.00	450.00	1850.00	RARE	RARE	RARE
☐ 1872S (190,000)						
	18.00	30.00	100.00	265.00	1350.00	RARE
☐ 1873* (2,378,500)						
	15.00	20.00	28.00	175.00	475.00	4350.00
☐ 1873** Open 3 (1,508,600)						
	15.00	25.00	65.00	150.00	525.00	RARE
☐ 1873**Closed 3 (60,000)						
	12.00	20.00	22.00	38.00	165.00	1750.00
☐ 1873CC** (12,400)	UNIQUE—ONLY ONE KNOWN—					
☐ 1873CC* (18,791)						
	2500.00	3750.00	4250.00	RARE	RARE	RARE
☐ 1873S* (455,000)						
	15.00	25.00	40.00	210.00	900.00	RARE
☐ 1874 With Arrows (2,940,000)						
	15.00	25.00	32.00	165.00	525.00	3850.00
☐ 1874CC With Arrows (10,817)						
	2500.00	3350.00	RARE	RARE	RARE	RARE
☐ 1874S With Arrows (240,000)						
	18.00	30.00	80.00	250.00	900.00	9000.00
☐ 1875 (10,350,000)						
	13.20	20.00	22.00	35.00	150.00	1150.00
☐ 1875CC In Wreath						
	20.00	28.00	32.00	85.00	275.00	2350.00
☐ 1875CC Below Wreath (4,645,000)						
	20.00	28.00	32.00	80.00	250.00	2750.00
☐ 1875S In Wreath						
	12.00	20.00	22.00	38.00	150.00	1750.00
☐ 1875S Below Wreath (9,070,000)						
	12.00	20.00	22.00	35.00	150.00	1050.00
☐ 1876 (11,461,150)						
	12.00	17.00	25.00	32.00	150.00	950.00

*With Arrows **No Arrows

DATE	ABP GOOD	G-4 GOOD	F-12 FINE	EF-40 EX. FINE	MS-60 UNC.	MS-65 CH. UNC.
☐ 1876CC	(8,270,000)					
	25.00	40.00	45.00	75.00	250.00	1850.00
☐ 1876CC Double Obverse						
	40.00	65.00	75.00	235.00	500.00	2500.00
☐ 1876S	(10,420,000)					
	12.00	17.00	20.00	32.00	150.00	1700.00
☐ 1877	(7,310,510)					
	12.00	17.00	20.00	32.00	150.00	950.00
☐ 1877CC	(7,700,000)					
	20.00	28.00	35.00	75.00	265.00	2250.00
☐ 1877S	(2,340,000)					
	12.00	17.00	20.00	35.00	150.00	1650.00
☐ 1878	(1,678,300)					
	12.00	17.00	20.00	38.00	150.00	950.00
☐ 1878CC	(200,000)					
	125.00	175.00	265.00	475.00	1250.00	3600.00
☐ 1879	(15,100)					
	150.00	225.00	310.00	525.00	575.00	1150.00
☐ 1880	(37,355)					
	110.00	175.00	265.00	400.00	600.00	1250.00
☐ 1881	(24,975)					
	125.00	185.00	275.00	425.00	550.00	1850.00
☐ 1882	(3,911,100)					
	12.00	17.00	20.00	35.00	150.00	900.00
☐ 1883	(7,675,712)					
	12.00	17.00	20.00	35.00	150.00	900.00
☐ 1884	(3,366,380)					
	12.00	17.00	20.00	35.00	150.00	900.00
☐ 1884S	(564,969)					
	15.00	25.00	35.00	115.00	775.00	4350.00
☐ 1885	(2,533,427)					
	12.00	17.00	20.00	35.00	175.00	900.00
☐ 1885S	(43,690)					
	300.00	450.00	800.00	2650.00	5500.00	RARE
☐ 1886	(6,377,570)					
	12.00	17.00	20.00	35.00	150.00	900.00
☐ 1886S	(206,524)					
	20.00	32.00	60.00	135.00	575.00	5500.00
☐ 1887	(11,283,939)					
	12.00	17.00	20.00	35.00	150.00	900.00
☐ 1887S	(4,454,450)					
	12.00	17.00	20.00	35.00	150.00	1100.00
☐ 1888	(5,496,487)					
	12.00	17.00	20.00	35.00	150.00	900.00

DATE	ABP GOOD	G-4 GOOD	F-12 FINE	EF-40 EX. FINE	MS-60 UNC.	MS-65 CH. UNC.
☐ 1888S	(1,720,000)					
	11.00	17.00	19.00	38.00	300.00	3250.00
☐ 1889	(7,380,711)					
	11.00	17.00	19.00	35.00	165.00	875.00
☐ 1889S	(972,678)					
	14.00	23.00	32.00	70.00	385.00	4350.00
☐ 1890	(9,911,541)					
	11.00	17.00	19.00	35.00	165.00	950.00
☐ 1890S	(1,423,076)					
	12.00	20.00	23.00	75.00	350.00	2250.00
☐ 1890S over S						
	15.00	25.00	40.00	175.00	RARE	RARE
☐ 1891	(15,310,600)					
	11.00	17.00	19.00	38.00	165.00	900.00
☐ 1891O	(4,540,000)					
	12.00	18.00	25.00	60.00	165.00	1650.00
☐ 1891S	(3,196,116)					
	12.00	18.00	20.00	35.00	165.00	1050.00
☐ 1891O With Horizontal O						
	40.00	65.00	135.00	250.00		

DIMES—LIBERTY HEAD OR BARBER, 1892–1916

Mint Mark is Under Wreath on the Reverse

After many years of using a seated figure of Liberty on the dime, it was decided in 1892 to return to a facial portrait. The designer was Charles E. Barber, resulting in the coin coming to be popularly known among collectors as the "Barber dime." Liberty wears a wreath and is encircled by the inscription UNITED STATES OF AMERICA, with the date appearing below the portrait. The reverse is unchanged from that used earlier, the words ONE DIME enclosed in a wreath. This coin's weight was set at 2.5 grams. Its composition was nine parts silver to one part copper and its diameter 17.9mm. It was struck at Philadelphia, Denver, San Francisco, and New Orleans. The very rare 1894 San Francisco minting, of which only twenty-four were produced, is the stellar item of this series. In 1916 the Liberty Head design was replaced by the so-called Mercury Head.

DATE	ABP GOOD	G-4 GOOD	F-12 FINE	EF-40 EX. FINE	MS-60 UNC.	MS-65 CH. UNC.
☐ 1892	(12,121,245)					
	6.00	8.50	18.00	30.00	125.00	675.00
☐ 1892O	(3,841,700)					
	9.00	15.00	35.00	85.00	165.00	1000.00
☐ 1892S	(990,710)					
	45.00	70.00	215.00	275.00	425.00	4150.00
☐ 1893	(3,340,792)					
	6.00	10.00	23.00	47.00	165.00	825.00
☐ 1893, 3 over 2						
	75.00	125.00	175.00	285.00	775.00	5850.00
☐ 1893O	(1,760,000)					
	21.00	35.00	125.00	200.00	350.00	2650.00
☐ 1893S	(2,491,401)					
	10.00	16.00	40.00	100.00	325.00	2850.00
☐ 1894	(1,330,972)					
	18.00	30.00	125.00	185.00	350.00	1150.00
☐ 1894O	(720,000)					
	45.00	75.00	225.00	425.00	1650.00	14000.00
☐ 1894S					EXTREMELY RARE	
☐ 1895	(690,880)					
	60.00	85.00	360.00	550.00	750.00	2350.00
☐ 1895O	(440,000)					
	250.00	350.00	900.00	2375.00	6000.00	22500.00
☐ 1895S	(1,120,000)					
	30.00	45.00	150.00	265.00	525.00	6750.00
☐ 1896	(2,000,672)					
	8.00	12.00	65.00	115.00	185.00	1300.00
☐ 1896O	(610,000)					
	60.00	85.00	325.00	475.00	1000.00	8000.00
☐ 1896S	(575,056)					
	55.00	80.00	300.00	400.00	750.00	3850.00
☐ 1897	(10,869,264)					
	3.00	5.00	9.00	35.00	135.00	650.00
☐ 1897O	(666,000)					
	45.00	75.00	300.00	450.00	975.00	4150.00
☐ 1897S	(1,342,844)					
	12.00	20.00	110.00	185.00	450.00	3500.00

DATE	ABP GOOD	G-4 GOOD	F-12 FINE	EF-40 EX. FINE	MS-60 UNC.	MS-65 CH. UNC.
☐ 1898	(16,320,735)					
	2.40	4.00	8.00	27.00	125.00	650.00
☐ 1898O	(2,130,000)					
	8.50	12.00	100.00	200.00	450.00	3250.00
☐ 1898S	(1,702,507)					
	5.00	8.00	38.00	80.00	350.00	3000.00
☐ 1899	(19,580,846)					
	2.40	4.00	8.00	28.00	125.00	650.00
☐ 1899O	(2,650,000)					
	6.00	10.00	75.00	150.00	400.00	4000.00
☐ 1899S	(1,867,493)					
	5.00	9.00	38.00	50.00	310.00	2850.00
☐ 1900	(17,600,912)					
	2.40	4.00	8.00	28.00	125.00	650.00
☐ 1900O	(2,010,000)					
	12.00	20.00	125.00	215.00	575.00	5000.00
☐ 1900S	(5,168,270)					
	3.50	6.00	13.00	35.00	165.00	1500.00
☐ 1901	(18,860,478)					
	2.40	4.00	8.00	28.00	125.00	650.00
☐ 1901O	(5,620,000)					
	3.00	5.00	20.00	75.00	425.00	4150.00
☐ 1901S	(593,022)					
	55.00	85.00	385.00	475.00	1150.00	5250.00
☐ 1902	(21,380,777)					
	2.40	4.00	7.00	27.00	125.00	675.00
☐ 1902O	(4,500,000)					
	2.70	4.50	18.00	75.00	400.00	4150.00
☐ 1902S	(2,070,000)					
	6.00	10.00	65.00	135.00	375.00	3650.00
☐ 1903	(19,500,755)					
	2.40	4.00	7.00	28.00	125.00	1000.00
☐ 1903O	(8,180,000)					
	3.60	6.00	16.50	57.00	250.00	3750.00
☐ 1903S	(613,300)					
	60.00	90.00	365.00	725.00	1100.00	2650.00
☐ 1904	(14,601,027)					
	2.40	4.00	8.00	28.00	130.00	1250.00
☐ 1904S	(800,000)					
	30.00	50.00	165.00	300.00	750.00	3850.00
☐ 1905	(14,552,350)					
	2.40	4.00	7.00	28.00	125.00	675.00

DATE	ABP GOOD	G-4 GOOD	F-12 FINE	EF-40 EX. FINE	MS-60 UNC.	MS-65 CH. UNC.
☐ 1905O	(3,400,000)					
	3.00	5.00	35.00	100.00	275.00	1250.00
☐ 1905O Micro O						
	16.80	28.00	125.00	240.00	1150.00	RARE
☐ 1905S	(6,855,199)					
	3.00	5.00	10.00	45.00	200.00	900.00
☐ 1906	(19,958,406)					
	2.40	4.00	5.00	25.00	125.00	650.00
☐ 1906D	(4,060,000)					
	3.00	5.00	9.00	35.00	185.00	1650.00
☐ 1906O	(2,610,000)					
	3.60	6.00	50.00	105.00	200.00	1050.00
☐ 1906S	(3,136,640)					
	3.00	5.00	15.00	65.00	225.00	1300.00
☐ 1907	(22,220,575)					
	3.00	5.00	6.00	25.00	125.00	650.00
☐ 1907D	(4,080,000)					
	3.00	5.00	10.00	45.00	275.00	2350.00
☐ 1907O	(5,058,000)					
	3.00	5.00	35.00	75.00	185.00	1150.00
☐ 1907S	(3,178,470)					
	3.00	5.00	18.00	75.00	385.00	2350.00
☐ 1908	(10,600,545)					
	3.00	5.00	6.00	25.00	120.00	650.00
☐ 1908D	(7,490,000)					
	2.50	3.50	6.00	32.00	125.00	875.00
☐ 1908O	(1,789,000)					
	3.90	6.50	45.00	100.00	285.00	1150.00
☐ 1908S	(3,220,000)					
	3.00	5.00	12.50	50.00	310.00	1800.00
☐ 1909	(10,240,650)					
	2.50	3.25	6.00	25.00	125.00	650.00
☐ 1909D	(954,000)					
	6.00	10.00	65.00	135.00	450.00	2650.00
☐ 1909O	(2,287,000)					
	3.00	5.00	15.00	75.00	275.00	1550.00
☐ 1909S	(2,000,000)					
	6.00	10.00	100.00	190.00	525.00	2850.00
☐ 1910	(11,520,551)					
	2.50	3.25	6.00	25.00	125.00	650.00
☐ 1910D	(3,490,000)					
	2.50	3.25	12.00	55.00	225.00	1550.00

DATE	ABP GOOD	G-4 GOOD	F-12 FINE	EF-40 EX. FINE	MS-60 UNC.	MS-65 CH. UNC.
☐ 1910S	(1,240,000)					
	4.00	7.00	55.00	115.00	425.00	2150.00
☐ 1911	(18,870,543)					
	2.50	3.25	6.00	25.00	120.00	650.00
☐ 1911D	(11,209,000)					
	2.50	3.25	6.00	25.00	120.00	650.00
☐ 1911S	(3,530,000)					
	2.50	3.25	10.00	42.00	200.00	975.00
☐ 1912	(19,350,700)					
	2.50	3.25	5.00	25.00	120.00	650.00
☐ 1912D	(11,760,000)					
	2.50	3.25	5.50	25.00	120.00	700.00
☐ 1912S	(3,420,000)					
	2.50	3.25	6.50	32.00	165.00	725.00
☐ 1913	(19,760,000)					
	2.50	3.25	5.00	25.00	125.00	650.00
☐ 1913S	(510,000)					
	23.00	35.00	125.00	250.00	475.00	1250.00
☐ 1914	(17,670,655)					
	2.50	3.25	5.00	25.00	125.00	650.00
☐ 1914D	(11,908,000)					
	2.50	3.25	5.00	25.00	125.00	650.00
☐ 1914S	(2,100,000)					
	2.50	3.25	9.00	38.00	140.00	1150.00
☐ 1915	(5,620,450)					
	2.50	3.25	5.00	25.00	120.00	650.00
☐ 1915S	(960,000)					
	5.00	8.00	38.00	70.00	240.00	1500.00
☐ 1916	(18,490,000)					
	2.50	3.25	5.00	25.00	120.00	650.00
☐ 1916S	(5,820,000)					
	2.50	3.25	5.00	25.00	120.00	650.00

DIMES—MERCURY DIMES, 1916–1945

The Mercury dime is misnamed. The likeness on its obverse is not that of Mercury (a male god) but Liberty, the same mythological figure who had graced dimes since their introduction in 1796. Confusion resulted from the attachment of small wings to Liberty's headdress, which, to students of Greek and Roman folklore, could only represent Mercury, the "quick messenger," whom the gods equipped with wings to better execute his duties. To give Liberty wings was a bit of poetic license; the intended meaning was "liberty of thought," but so vague was this concept that its purpose remained unserved. On the reverse was an object that caused only slightly less confusion—a vertical column of some kind that only the most astute observers could identify. This was designed as a bundle of fasces or sticks with an axe protruding. In Roman times, an imperial or senatorial procession was often accompanied by "fasces bearers" who carried these bundles of wood sticks throughout the streets. Their meaning was supposedly symbolic but they likewise served a practical function: When dusk fell they could be lighted to illuminate the path.

Designer of the Mercury dime was Adolph Weinman. Its specifications are the same as those of the Barber dime. The mint mark appears on the reverse, between the words ONE and DIME, to the left of the fasces. The Mercury dime was composed of 90% silver and 10% copper. It has a weight of 2.5 grams and diameter of 17.9mm.

Mint Mark is on Reverse
at Bottom to Left of Branches

Enlargement Showing
1942 over 41 Dime

DATE	ABP GOOD	G-4 GOOD	F-12 FINE	VF-20 V. FINE	EF-40 EX. FINE	MS-60 UNC.
☐ 1916	(22,180,000)					
	2.50	4.00	7.25	8.50	12.50	35.00
☐ 1916D	(264,000)					
	600.00	875.00	2650.00	4000.00	6250.00	12500.00
☐ 1916S	(10,450,000)					
	3.00	5.00	10.00	15.00	25.00	40.00
☐ 1917	(55,230,000)					
	2.20	3.50	4.00	7.00	9.00	32.00
☐ 1917D	(9,402,000)					
	3.00	5.00	12.00	25.00	55.00	150.00
☐ 1917S	(27,330,000)					
	2.20	3.50	5.00	9.00	15.00	75.00

DATE	ABP GOOD	G-4 GOOD	F-12 FINE	VF-20 V. FINE	EF-40 EX. FINE	MS-60 UNC.
☐ 1918	(26,680,000)					
	2.20	3.50	6.50	12.00	30.00	70.00
☐ 1918D	(22,674,800)					
	2.20	3.50	6.50	13.50	28.00	125.00
☐ 1918S	(19,300,000)					
	2.20	3.50	5.00	11.00	22.00	115.00
☐ 1919	(35,740,000)					
	2.20	3.50	5.00	6.50	12.00	45.00
☐ 1919D	(9,939,000)					
	3.00	5.00	14.00	30.00	42.00	185.00
☐ 1919S	(8,850,000)					
	2.40	4.00	12.00	20.00	45.00	185.00
☐ 1920	(59,030,000)					
	2.20	3.50	4.50	6.00	9.00	35.00
☐ 1920D	(19,171,000)					
	3.00	5.00	6.00	10.00	22.00	125.00
☐ 1920S	(13,820,000)					
	3.00	5.00	6.00	12.00	20.00	135.00
☐ 1921	(1,230,000)					
	40.00	60.00	125.00	275.00	525.00	1250.00
☐ 1921D	(1,080,000)					
	50.00	75.00	200.00	400.00	650.00	1350.00
☐ 1923*	(50,130,000)					
	2.20	3.50	4.25	5.00	8.00	32.00
☐ 1923S	(6,440,000)					
	2.20	3.50	10.00	20.00	72.00	175.00
☐ 1924	(24,010,000)					
	2.20	3.50	4.00	5.00	14.00	43.00
☐ 1924D	(6,810,000)					
	2.40	4.00	8.50	26.00	70.00	185.00
☐ 1924S	(7,120,000)					
	2.40	4.00	7.00	13.50	65.00	235.00
☐ 1925	(25,610,000)					
	2.20	3.50	4.00	5.00	12.00	32.00
☐ 1925D	(5,117,000)					
	2.40	5.00	13.00	47.00	125.00	425.00
☐ 1925S	(5,850,000)					
	2.40	5.00	9.00	20.00	80.00	210.00

*All dimes with 1923D date are counterfeit

DATE	ABP GOOD	G-4 GOOD	F-12 FINE	VF-20 V. FINE	EF-40 EX. FINE	MS-60 UNC.
☐ 1926 (32,160,000)						
	2.20	3.50	5.00	5.50	7.00	28.00
☐ 1926D (6,828,000)						
	2.40	4.00	6.50	12.00	29.00	135.00
☐ 1926S (1,520,000)						
	9.00	15.00	30.00	70.00	260.00	900.00
☐ 1927 (28,080,000)						
	2.20	3.50	4.00	4.75	6.50	28.00
☐ 1927D (4,812,000)						
	2.40	4.00	9.00	30.00	95.00	185.00
☐ 1927S (4,770,000)						
	2.20	3.50	6.00	14.00	32.00	325.00
☐ 1928 (19,480,000)						
	2.20	3.50	4.00	4.50	5.50	28.00
☐ 1928D (4,161,000)						
	3.00	5.00	11.00	25.00	55.00	175.00
☐ 1928S (7,400,000)						
	2.20	3.50	5.00	6.00	20.00	165.00
☐ 1929 (25,970,000)						
	2.20	3.50	4.00	4.50	5.00	23.00
☐ 1929D (5,034,000)						
	2.20	3.50	6.00	8.00	18.00	28.00
☐ 1929S (4,730,000)						
	2.20	3.50	4.50	5.00	10.00	32.00
☐ 1930 (6,770,000)						
	2.20	3.50	4.50	5.00	8.00	28.00
☐ 1930S (1,843,000)						
	2.20	3.50	5.50	7.00	17.50	85.00
☐ 1931 (3,150,000)						
	2.20	3.50	5.00	6.00	15.00	40.00
☐ 1931D (1,260,000)						
	6.00	10.00	15.00	22.00	45.00	110.00
☐ 1931S (1,800,000)						
	3.00	5.00	6.50	12.00	24.00	115.00
☐ 1934 (24,080,000)						
	1.50	2.50	3.00	3.50	4.00	28.00
☐ 1934D (6,772,000)						
	1.50	2.50	3.00	3.50	10.00	50.00
☐ 1935 (58,830,000)						
	1.50	2.50	3.00	3.50	4.00	9.00

DATE	ABP GOOD	G-4 GOOD	F-12 FINE	VF-20 V. FINE	EF-40 EX. FINE	MS-60 UNC.	PRF-65 PROOF
☐ 1935D	(10,477,000)						
	1.50	2.50	2.75	4.00	7.50	40.00	
☐ 1935S	(15,840,000)						
	1.50	2.50	2.75	3.25	5.00	25.00	
☐ 1936	(87,504,130)						
	1.50	2.50	2.75	3.25	4.50	8.50	1400.00
☐ 1936D	(16,132,000)						
	1.50	2.50	2.75	4.00	5.50	28.00	
☐ 1936S	(9,210,000)						
	1.50	2.50	2.75	3.25	3.80	25.00	
☐ 1937	(56,865,756)						
	1.50	2.50	2.75	3.25	4.00	8.50	750.00
☐ 1937D	(14,146,000)						
	1.50	2.50	2.75	3.25	5.00	25.00	
☐ 1937S	(9,740,000)						
	1.50	2.50	2.75	3.25	3.80	25.00	
☐ 1938	(22,198,728)						
	1.50	2.50	2.75	3.25	3.80	12.00	375.00
☐ 1938D	(5,537,000)						
	1.50	2.50	2.75	3.25	6.00	20.00	
☐ 1938S	(8,090,000)						
	1.50	2.50	2.75	3.25	3.80	25.00	
☐ 1939	(67,749,321)						
	1.50	2.50	2.75	3.25	3.80	8.50	310.00
☐ 1939D	(24,394,000)						
	1.50	2.50	2.75	3.25	3.80	8.50	
☐ 1939S	(10,540,000)						
	1.50	2.50	2.75	4.00	4.50	23.00	
☐ 1940	(65,361,827)						
	1.50	2.50	2.75	3.25	3.80	7.00	265.00
☐ 1940D	(21,198,000)						
	1.50	2.50	2.75	3.25	3.80	9.00	
☐ 1940S	(21,560,000)						
	1.50	2.50	2.75	3.25	3.80	9.00	
☐ 1941	(175,106,557)						
	1.50	2.50	2.75	3.25	3.80	7.00	250.00
☐ 1941D	(45,634,000)						
	1.50	2.50	2.75	3.25	3.80	10.00	
☐ 1941S	(43,090,000)						
	1.50	2.50	2.75	3.25	3.80	8.50	

DATE	ABP GOOD	G-4 GOOD	F-12 FINE	VF-20 V. FINE	EF-40 EX. FINE	MS-60 UNC.	PRF-65 PROOF
☐ 1942	(205,432,329)						
	1.50	2.50	2.00	3.25	4.00	7.00	250.00
☐ 1942 Part of Above over 41							
	350.00	450.00	600.00	650.00	800.00	2750.00	
☐ 1942/41D							
	350.00	450.00	600.00	625.00	750.00	2650.00	
☐ 1942D	(60,740,000)						
	1.50	2.50	2.75	3.25	3.50	8.50	
☐ 1942S	(49,300,000)						
	1.50	2.50	2.75	3.25	3.50	11.00	
☐ 1943	(191,710,000)						
	1.50	2.50	2.75	3.25	3.50	7.00	
☐ 1943D	(71,949,000)						
	1.50	2.50	2.75	3.25	3.50	8.50	
☐ 1943S	(60,400,000)						
	1.50	2.50	2.75	3.25	3.50	10.00	
☐ 1944	(231,410,000)						
	1.50	2.50	2.75	3.25	3.50	7.00	
☐ 1944D	(62,224,000)						
	1.50	2.50	2.75	3.25	3.50	8.00	
☐ 1944S	(49,490,000)						
	1.50	2.50	2.75	3.25	3.50	8.00	
☐ 1945	(159,130,000)						
	1.50	2.50	2.75	3.25	3.50	7.00	
☐ 1945D	(40,245,000)						
	1.50	2.50	2.75	3.25	3.50	7.00	
☐ 1945S	(41,920,000)						
	1.50	2.50	2.75	3.25	3.50	10.00	
☐ 1945S Micro S							
	2.00	2.50	2.75	5.00	8.00	28.00	

DIMES—ROOSEVELT, 1946 TO DATE

The Roosevelt dime series is significant for the change made to clad composition in 1965. Upon the death of President Roosevelt in 1945 there was considerable public sentiment to install his likeness on a coin. The penny, nickel, and quarter were not seriously considered, as they already carried portraits of former presidents. As no dollars were being struck, this left only the dime and half dollar, which both carried representations of Liberty, as suitable choices. The dime was selected, probably because of the much wider distribution of this coin. The designer was John Sinnock.

Roosevelt is shown in profile facing left, with the word LIB-ERTY and the inscription IN GOD WE TRUST. The bundle of fasces was retained as the central element for the reverse type, which was redrawn. Originally the mint mark appeared on the reverse, as it had on the Mercury dime, then was switched to the obverse on clad pieces. The weight was 2½ grams. The composition of this coin, originally 90% silver and 10% copper, was altered in 1965 to three parts copper/one part nickel outer covering with an interior of pure copper, yielding a weight of 2.27 grams. The diameter remained 17.9mm.

In the first year of striking the clad dime, more pieces were manufactured than had ever been turned out of a ten-cent piece in the Mint's history, more than 1.6 billion. A serious shortage of dimes had resulted from spectators hoarding the silver coins, and this abundant new supply was intended to replace those lost from circulation. A mintage figure of more than 2 billion was achieved in 1967, or more than $1 worth of dimes for every U.S. citizen.

Mint Mark is on Reverse of Left, Bottom of Torch.

From 1968 Mint Mark at Base of Neck.

DATE	MINTAGE	ABP	MS-60 UNC.	PRF-65 PROOF
☐ 1946	255,250,000	1.50	3.25	
☐ 1946D	61,043,500	1.50	3.25	
☐ 1946S	27,900,000	1.50	3.75	
☐ 1947	121,500,000	1.50	4.00	
☐ 1947D	46,835,000	1.50	5.50	
☐ 1947S	38,840,000	1.50	5.50	
☐ 1948	74,950,000	1.50	3.50	
☐ 1948D	52,841,000	1.50	5.50	
☐ 1948S	35,520,000	1.50	5.00	
☐ 1949	30,940,000	15.00	25.00	
☐ 1949D	26,034,000	6.00	10.00	
☐ 1949S	13,510,000	21.00	35.00	
☐ 1950	50,181,500	2.00	10.00	55.00
☐ 1950D	46,803,000	1.50	5.00	

DATE	MINTAGE	ABP	MS-60 UNC.	PRF-65 PROOF
☐ 1950S	20,440,000	18.00	30.00	
☐ 1951	103,937,602	2.20	3.00	55.00
☐ 1951D	52,191,800	2.20	3.00	
☐ 1951S	31,630,000	6.00	10.00	
☐ 1952	99,122,073	2.20	3.00	42.00
☐ 1952D	122,100,000	2.20	3.00	
☐ 1952S	44,419,500	4.20	7.00	
☐ 1953	53,618,920	2.20	2.75	45.00
☐ 1953D	156,433,000	2.20	2.75	
☐ 1953S	39,180,000	2.20	2.75	
☐ 1954	114,243,503	2.20	2.75	22.00
☐ 1954D	106,397,000	2.20	2.75	
☐ 1954S	22,860,000	2.20	2.75	
☐ 1955	12,828,381	2.20	2.75	20.00
☐ 1955D	13,959,000	2.20	2.75	
☐ 1955S	18,510,000	2.20	2.75	
☐ 1956	109,309,384	2.20	2.75	10.00
☐ 1956D	108,015,100	2.20	2.75	
☐ 1957	161,407,952	2.20	2.75	6.00
☐ 1957D	113,354,330	2.20	2.75	
☐ 1958	32,785,652	2.20	2.75	6.00
☐ 1958D	136,564,600	2.20	2.75	
☐ 1959	86,929,291	2.20	2.75	5.50
☐ 1959D	164,919,790	2.20	2.75	
☐ 1960	72,081,602	2.20	2.75	5.50
☐ 1960D	200,160,400	2.20	2.75	
☐ 1961	96,756,244	2.20	2.75	5.00
☐ 1961D	209,146,550	2.20	2.75	
☐ 1962	75,668,019	2.20	2.75	5.00
☐ 1962D	334,948,380	2.20	2.75	
☐ 1963	126,725,645	2.20	2.75	5.00
☐ 1963D	421,476,530	2.20	2.75	
☐ 1964	933,310,762	2.20	2.75	5.00
☐ 1964D	1,357,517,180	2.20	2.75	
☐ 1965 Clad Coinage Begins	1,652,140,570		.85	
☐ 1966	1,382,734,540		.85	
☐ 1967	2,244,077,300		.85	
☐ 1968	424,470,400		.85	
☐ 1968D	480,748,280		.85	
☐ 1968S Proof Only	3,041,508			2.00

DATE	MINTAGE	MS-60 UNC.	PRF-65 PROOF
☐ 1969	145,790,000	1.10	
☐ 1969D	563,323,870	.85	
☐ 1969S Proof Only	2,934,631		2.00
☐ 1970	345,570,000	.85	
☐ 1970D	754,942,000	.85	
☐ 1970S Proof Only	2,632,810		2.00
☐ 1971	162,690,000	.85	
☐ 1971D	377,914,240	.85	
☐ 1971S Proof Only	3,244,138		2.00
☐ 1972	431,540,000	.85	
☐ 1972D	330,290,000	.85	
☐ 1972S Proof Only	3,267,667		2.00
☐ 1973	315,670,000	.85	
☐ 1973D	455,032,425	.85	
☐ 1973 Proof Only	2,769,624		2.00
☐ 1974	470,248,000	.85	
☐ 1974D	571,083,000	.85	
☐ 1974S Proof Only	2,617,350		2.00
☐ 1975	585,673,900	.85	
☐ 1975D	313,705,250	.85	
☐ 1975S Proof Only	2,909,369		3.00
☐ 1976	568,760,000	.85	
☐ 1976D	695,222,774	.85	
☐ 1976S Proof Only	4,149,945		3.00
☐ 1977	796,900,480	.85	
☐ 1977D	376,610,420	.85	
☐ 1977S Proof Only	3,250,895		2.00
☐ 1978	663,908,000	.85	
☐ 1978D	282,847,540	.85	
☐ 1978S Proof Only	3,127,781		2.00
☐ 1979	315,440,007	.85	
☐ 1979D	390,921,285	.85	
☐ 1979S Proof (I)	3,677,200		8.00
☐ 1979S Proof (II)			12.00
☐ 1980P	735,170,079	.85	
☐ 1980D	719,354,382	.85	
☐ 1980S Proof Only	3,547,130		2.00
☐ 1981P	676,000,000	.85	
☐ 1981D	712,285,000	.85	
☐ 1981S Proof Type I	4,063,080		5.00

DATE		MINTAGE	MS-60 UNC.	PRF-65 PROOF
☐ 1982P*	1981-S Type II	519,474,983	6.00	10.00
☐ 1982D		541,721,064	1.00	
☐ 1982S Proof Only		3,857,000		2.75
☐ 1983P		646,124,004	6.00	
☐ 1983D		730,130,000	1.00	
☐ 1983S Proof Only		3,228,650		2.00
☐ 1984P		856,670,936	.85	
☐ 1984D		704,731,827	.85	
☐ 1984S Proof Only		3,000,210		2.75
☐ 1985P		712,182,461	.85	
☐ 1985D		589,641,000	.85	
☐ 1985S Proof Only		3,121,410		2.00
☐ 1986P		670,210,401	.85	
☐ 1986D		476,420,831	.85	
☐ 1986S Proof Only		3,110,120		4.00
☐ 1987P		774,621,460	.65	
☐ 1987D		676,294,210	.65	
☐ 1987S Proof Only		3,622,101		4.00
☐ 1988P		1,113,410,702	.65	
☐ 1988D		982,001,670	.65	
☐ 1988S Proof Only		3,124,683		4.00
☐ 1989P		1,301,640,121	.65	
☐ 1989D		898,421,711	.65	
☐ 1989S Proof Only		3,200,620		5.00
☐ 1990P		1,130,260,420	.65	
☐ 1990D		876,572,143	.65	
☐ 1990S Proof Only		3,726,456		2.75
☐ 1991P		927,200,110	.65	
☐ 1991D		601,245,110	.65	
☐ 1991S Proof Only		2,867,860		4.00
☐ 1992P		593,550,600	.65	
☐ 1992D		616,273,920	.65	
☐ 1992S Proof Only		2,858,970		5.25
☐ 1992S Silver Proof		1,317,575		8.00
☐ 1993P		766,180,000	.65	

*Note: In 1983, dimes dated 1982 and bearing no mint mark began to be discovered. At first they caused a furor as it was believed they might be great rarities (largely because a whole year had passed before any were noticed). During the first month or two of trading, prices on MS-65 specimens reached as high as $600. At that time it was thought that as few as 300 or 400 might exist. Later it was revealed that a Midwest source owned 4,000 and the existing total is now estimated at around 8,000. Prices on MS-65 specimens are in the $200 to $250 range. Beware of removed mint mark.

DATE	MINTAGE	MS-60 UNC.	PRF-65 PROOF
☐ 1993D	750,110,166	.65	
☐ 1993S Proof Only	2,633,439		7.00
☐ 1993S Silver Proof	761,350		8.00
☐ 1994P	1,189,000,000	.65	
☐ 1994D	1,303,268,110	.65	
☐ 1994S Proof Only	2,484,524		7.00
☐ 1994S Silver Proof	785,325		10.00
☐ 1995P	1,125,500,000	.65	
☐ 1995D	1,274,890,000	.65	
☐ 1995S Proof Only	2,010,284		25.00
☐ 1995S Silver Proof	838,950		35.00
☐ 1996P	1,421,160,000	.65	
☐ 1996D	1,400,300,000	.65	
☐ 1996S Proof Only	1,750,000		3.25
☐ 1996S Silver Proof	775,000		10.00
☐ 1996W	1,457,000	18.00	
☐ 1997P	991,640,000	.65	
☐ 1997D	979,810,000	.65	
☐ 1997S Proof Only	2,000,000		12.00
☐ 1997S Silver Proof	740,000		25.00
☐ 1998	1,163,000,000	.65	
☐ 1998D	1,172,250,000	.65	
☐ 1998S Proof	2,000,000		4.75
☐ 1998S Silver Proof	875,000		8.00
☐ 1999	2,164,000,000	.65	
☐ 1999D	1,397,444,000	.65	
☐ 1999S Proof	2,500,000		4.50
☐ 1999S Silver Proof	800,000		10.00
☐ 2000P	1,842,500,000	.65	
☐ 2000D	1,818,700,000	.65	
☐ 2000S Proof	3,000,000		2.75
☐ 2000S Silver Proof	850,000		4.50
☐ 2001P	1,369,590,000	.65	
☐ 2001D	1,412,800,000	.65	
☐ 2001S Proof	2,250,000		2.75
☐ 2001S Silver Proof	875,000		4.50
☐ 2002P	1,187,500,000	.65	
☐ 2002D	1,379,500,000	.65	
☐ 2002S Proof	2,250,000		2.75
☐ 2002S Silver Proof	875,000		6.75
☐ 2003P	1,085,500,000	.65	
☐ 2003D	986,500,000	.65	
☐ 2003S Proof			2.75
☐ 2003S Silver Proof			4.50

DATE	MINTAGE	MS-60 UNC.	PRF-65 PROOF
☐ 2004P	1,328,000,000	.65	
☐ 2004D	1,159,500,000	.65	
☐ 2004S Proof			2.75
☐ 2004S Silver Proof			4.50
☐ 2005P	1,412,000,000	.65	
☐ 2005D	1,423,500,000	.65	
☐ 2005S Proof			2.75
☐ 2005S Silver Proof			4.50
☐ 2006P	1,295,500,000	.65	
☐ 2006D	1,378,000,000	.65	
☐ 2006S Proof			2.75
☐ 2006S Silver Proof			4.50
☐ 2007P	981,000,000	.65	
☐ 2007D	998,500,000	.65	
☐ 2007S Proof			2.75
☐ 2007S Silver Proof			4.50
☐ 2008P		.65	
☐ 2008D		.65	
☐ 2008S Proof			2.75
☐ 2008S Silver Proof			4.50
☐ 2009P		.65	
☐ 2009D		.65	
☐ 2009S Proof			2.75
☐ 2009S Silver Proof			4.50
☐ 2010P		.65	
☐ 2010D		.65	
☐ 2010S Proof			2.75
☐ 2010S Silver Proof			4.50
☐ 2011P		.65	
☐ 2011D		.65	
☐ 2011S Proof			2.75
☐ 2011S Silver Proof			4.50
☐ 2012P		.65	
☐ 2012D		.65	
☐ 2012S Proof			2.75
☐ 2012S Silver Proof			4.50

TWENTY-CENT PIECES—
LIBERTY SEATED, 1875–1878

The twenty-cent piece was the shortest-lived of any U.S. coin. Authorized by a Congressional Act on March 3, 1875, it was placed into production immediately thereafter, with manufacture divided among the Philadelphia, San Francisco, and Carson City Mints (Mints on the East and West Coasts being employed in hopes the coin would distribute more evenly in circulation than if released exclusively from a single source of production).

Designed by William Barber, it pictured a figure of the goddess Liberty seated on the obverse, framed by stars, with an eagle on the reverse. It was composed of nine-tenths silver and one-tenth copper, with a weight of five grams and a diameter of 22mm. Despite high hopes, the twenty-cent piece never achieved popularity, the chief reason for its rejection being the physical similarity to the quarter. Production was greatly cut back in 1876 and discontinued two years thereafter. All told, less than a million and a half were struck.

DATE		ABP GOOD	G-4 GOOD	F-12 FINE	EF-40 EX. FINE	MS-60 UNC.	PRF-65 PROOF
☐ 1875	(39,700)	120.00	200.00	400.00	500.00	1000.00	RARE
☐ 1875CC	(133,290)	180.00	300.00	500.00	900.00	2175.00	
☐ 1875S	(1,155,000)	60.00	100.00	125.00	300.00	750.00	RARE
☐ 1876	(15,900)	105.00	175.00	300.00	575.00	1000.00	RARE
☐ 1876CC	(10,000)						
				EXTREMELY RARE—AUCTION 2007—RARE			
☐ 1877 Proofs Only	(510)						RARE
☐ 1878 Proofs Only	(600)						RARE

QUARTERS

EARLY QUARTERS, 1796–1866

It became evident from a very early period that the quarter or twenty-five-cent piece would be the most significant division of the dollar in everyday commerce. However, the effect was not fully felt until the 19th century. Striking of the quarter dollar was authorized in 1792 along with other denominations, upon establishment of a national currency. No actual specimens came into circulation until 1796.

The earliest design was the Draped Bust portrait of Liberty, common to other silver coinage, with eagle reverse and the legend UNITED STATES OF AMERICA. Stars appeared alongside Liberty on the obverse and her name was affixed above the portrait, with the date below. The designer was Robert Scot. The original quarter dollar was composed of .8924 silver alloyed with .1076 copper, or roughly a nine-to-one ratio. Its weight was 6.74 grams and the diameter generally 27.5mm., with slight variations to be observed according to the flatness of the planchet. Only 6,146 pieces were struck in 1796 as a trial issue (influenced in some measure by a shortage of silver) and this date has become scarce, even in less than the best condition. Production of quarters was not resumed until 1804, when discontinuation of dollar coins increased the need for them. The Draped Bust type was retained but the reverse changed to the Heraldic or Shield Eagle design.

John Reich designed a new quarter dollar in 1815, identical in composition to its predecessors but having a slightly smaller diameter, 27mm. This was the Capped Bust type, with naturalistic shielded eagle on the reverse. Production got off to a small start but was rapidly expanded. No further change occurred until 1831 when the coin was brought down in size to 24.3mm. and was made a bit thicker, retaining the old weight of 6.74 grams. The designer of this new twenty-five-cent piece was William Kneass (pronounced Niece) and all striking was done at Philadelphia. There is a Small Letters and Large Letters variety of this design, with little influence on value. The portrait is a somewhat streamlined Capped Liberty who appears more noble than previously. This design was of short duration, replaced by the Seated Liberty type in 1838. On the reverse was the shield eagle, beneath which appeared the words QUAR. DOL. (The use of abbreviations did not fully meet the approval of artistic-minded persons.) There was an accompanying change in specifications as well. The silver content was slightly raised, to an even 90%; the copper dropped to an even 10%; and the weight went down to 6.68 grams. The diameter was the same as previously. Designer of this coin was Christian Gobrecht. It was struck at both Philadelphia and New Orleans.

A further reduction in weight was made to 6.22 grams in 1853; arrows were placed at the dates to remind users of the coin that it contained less silver than previously. Compositionally it was unaltered, with nine parts silver to one of copper. On the reverse, sunrays sprang from behind the eagle, an area of the design which previously had been blank. This addition was made for the same reason as the arrows.

QUARTERS—DRAPED BUST, 1796–1807

1796–
1807

1796
Small Eagle

1804–1807
Large Eagle

DATE		ABP GOOD	G-4 GOOD	F-12 FINE	VF-20 V. FINE	MS-60 UNC.
☐ 1796	(5,894)	10000.00	15000.00	19000.00	40000.00	RARE
☐ 1804	(6,738)	2500.00	3750.00	9500.00	14000.00	RARE
☐ 1805	(121,394)	400.00	600.00	1000.00	1850.00	12000.00
☐ 1806	(206,124)	400.00	600.00	1000.00	1850.00	12000.00
☐ 1806 over 5		425.00	600.00	1050.00	2000.00	15000.00
☐ 1807	(220,643)	375.00	575.00	1000.00	1850.00	12000.00

QUARTERS—LIBERTY CAP, 1815–1838

1815–
1838

1815–1828
Motto over Eagle

1831–1838
Without Motto

DATE	ABP GOOD	G-4 GOOD	F-12 FINE	VF-20 V. FINE	MS-60 UNC.
☐ 1815 (89,235)					
	90.00	130.00	450.00	600.00	4250.00
☐ 1818 (361,174)					
	75.00	110.00	215.00	500.00	4000.00
☐ 1818 over 15 (361,174)					
	75.00	115.00	225.00	500.00	4100.00
☐ 1819 Small 9 (144,000)					
	75.00	110.00	250.00	500.00	4000.00
☐ 1819 Large 9					
	75.00	110.00	250.00	500.00	4000.00
☐ 1820 Small O (127,440)					
	75.00	110.00	200.00	500.00	4000.00
☐ 1820 Large O					
	75.00	110.00	250.00	550.00	4000.00
☐ 1821 (216,850)					
	75.00	115.00	200.00	500.00	4000.00
☐ 1822 (64,084)					
	90.00	135.00	265.00	550.00	4500.00
☐ 1822 25 over $.50C					
	900.00	1500.00	7500.00	10000.00	RARE
☐ 1823 over 22 (17,821)					
					VERY RARE
☐ 1824	500.00	800.00	2000.00	3500.00	RARE
☐ 1825 over Dates (168,000)					
	75.00	115.00	200.00	575.00	4350.00
☐ 1827 (original) (4,000)	FEW PIECES KNOWN—EXTREMELY RARE				
☐ 1828 (102,000)					
	75.00	115.00	250.00	500.00	4000.00
☐ 1828 25 over $.50 (102,000)					
	150.00	250.00	650.00	1500.00	9000.00

REDUCED SIZE—NO MOTTO ON REVERSE

Note: 1827 restrike proof 125,000

DATE	ABP GOOD	G-4 GOOD	F-12 FINE	VF-20 V. FINE	MS-60 UNC.
☐ 1831 Small Letters	(398,000)				
	50.00	85.00	135.00	175.00	1850.00
☐ 1831 Large Letters					
	50.00	85.00	135.00	175.00	1850.00
☐ 1832	(320,000)				
	50.00	85.00	135.00	175.00	1850.00
☐ 1833	(156,000)				
	55.00	90.00	135.00	185.00	1950.00
☐ 1834	(286,000)				
	50.00	85.00	135.00	175.00	1750.00
☐ 1835	(1,952,000)				
	50.00	85.00	135.00	175.00	1750.00
☐ 1836	(472,000)				
	50.00	85.00	135.00	175.00	1750.00
☐ 1837	(252,000)				
	50.00	85.00	135.00	175.00	1750.00
☐ 1838	(832,000)				
	50.00	85.00	135.00	175.00	1750.00

QUARTERS—LIBERTY SEATED, 1838–1865
NO MOTTO ABOVE EAGLE

1838–1865

1853
With Rays

Mint Mark is Below Eagle on Reverse 1838–1852 1854–1865 Without Rays

DATE	ABP	G-4 GOOD	F-12 FINE	EF-40 EX. FINE	MS-60 UNC.
☐ 1838*	(832,000)				
	24.00	40.00	65.00	425.00	1750.00
☐ 1839*	(491,146)				
	24.00	40.00	65.00	425.00	1750.00
☐ 1840**	(188,127)				
	20.00	30.00	65.00	425.00	1150.00
☐ 18400*	27.00	45.00	85.00	450.00	1800.00

*No Drapery **Drapery

DATE	ABP GOOD	G-4 GOOD	F-12 FINE	EF-40 EX. FINE	MS-60 UNC.
☐ 18400** (425,200)					
	25.00	38.00	80.00	225.00	1100.00
☐ 1841 (120,000)					
	40.00	65.00	110.00	250.00	900.00
☐ 18410 (452,000)					
	25.00	40.00	65.00	285.00	850.00
☐ 1842 Large Date (88,000)					
	50.00	80.00	165.00	310.00	1350.00
☐ 18420 Small Date					
	200.00	300.00	900.00	4750.00	16000.00
☐ 18420 Large Date (769,000)					
	25.00	38.00	70.00	185.00	1100.00
☐ 1843 (645,000)					
	18.00	30.00	38.00	85.00	500.00
☐ 18430 Small O (968,000)					
	25.00	40.00	95.00	385.00	2100.00
☐ 18430 Large O					
	30.00	45.00	200.00	450.00	1650.00
☐ 1844 (421,000)					
	18.00	28.00	40.00	80.00	500.00
☐ 18440 (740,000)					
	25.00	40.00	55.00	175.00	1100.00
☐ 1845 (922,000)					
	17.00	28.00	40.00	95.00	500.00
☐ 1846 (510,000)					
	17.00	28.00	42.00	100.00	550.00
☐ 1847 (734,000)					
	17.00	28.00	40.00	85.00	525.00
☐ 18470 (368,000)					
	25.00	40.00	75.00	775.00	4250.00
☐ 1848 (146,000)					
	18.00	28.00	75.00	200.00	1100.00
☐ 1849 (340,000)					
	18.00	28.00	50.00	135.00	875.00
☐ 18490 (16,000)					
	275.00	400.00	1000.00	RARE	RARE
☐ 1850 (190,800)					
	20.00	30.00	85.00	150.00	900.00
☐ 18500 (412,000)					
	25.00	40.00	80.00	225.00	1400.00

**Drapery

DATE	ABP GOOD	G-4 GOOD	F-12 FINE	EF-40 EX. FINE	MS-60 UNC.
☐ 1851 (160,000)					
	25.00	38.00	85.00	265.00	900.00
☐ 1851O (88,000)					
	120.00	185.00	500.00	1600.00	6500.00
☐ 1852 (177,060)					
	33.00	55.00	85.00	280.00	650.00
☐ 1852O (96,000)					
	120.00	180.00	425.00	2100.00	8250.00
☐ 1853*** (15,210,020)					
	18.00	30.00	40.00	185.00	1100.00
☐ 1853/4					
	30.00	45.00	135.00	425.00	2500.00
☐ 1853†† (44,200)					
	400.00	600.00	700.00	1450.00	3400.00
☐ 1853O*** (1,332,000)					
	25.00	38.00	55.00	325.00	3000.00
☐ 1854† (12,380,000)					
	18.00	30.00	38.00	85.00	600.00
☐ 1854O† O (1,484,000)					
	25.00	40.00	60.00	100.00	1050.00
☐ 1854O Huge O					
	550.00	750.00	3000.00	RARE	RARE
☐ 1855† (2,857,000)					
	18.00	30.00	40.00	85.00	625.00
☐ 1855O† (176,000)					
	30.00	55.00	110.00	450.00	3350.00
☐ 1855S† (396,400)					
	35.00	65.00	95.00	425.00	2500.00
☐ 1856 No Arrows (7,264,000)					
	18.00	28.00	38.00	85.00	350.00
☐ 1856O (968,000)					
	25.00	40.00	60.00	115.00	1350.00
☐ 1856S	30.00	45.00	90.00	1250.00	6250.00
☐ 1856S Over S (286,000)					
	125.00	175.00	450.00	2250.00	RARE
☐ 1857 (9,644,000)					
	18.00	30.00	38.00	80.00	350.00
☐ 1857O (1,180,000)					
	25.00	38.00	50.00	190.00	950.00

***W/Arrows and Rays †W/Arrows and No Rays ††Over 52, No Arrows

DATE	ABP GOOD	G-4 GOOD	F-12 FINE	EF-40 EX. FINE	MS-60 UNC.
☐ 1857S	(82,000)				
	40.00	65.00	235.00	650.00	3100.00
☐ 1858	(7,368,000)				
	18.00	30.00	35.00	80.00	380.00
☐ 1858O	(520,000)				
	25.00	38.00	45.00	110.00	1400.00
☐ 1858S	(121,000)				
	40.00	65.00	210.00	1850.00	7750.00
☐ 1859	(1,344,000)				
	18.00	30.00	35.00	80.00	400.00
☐ 1859O	(260,000)				
	25.00	38.00	60.00	165.00	1250.00
☐ 1859S	(80,000)				
	75.00	125.00	250.00	3500.00	RARE
☐ 1860	(805,400)				
	18.00	30.00	38.00	85.00	450.00
☐ 1860O	(388,000)				
	25.00	40.00	65.00	100.00	1650.00
☐ 1860S	(56,000)				
	450.00	700.00	1850.00	RARE	RARE
☐ 1861	(4,854,000)				
	18.00	30.00	38.00	85.00	375.00
☐ 1861S	(96,000)				
	100.00	150.00	500.00	3500.00	RARE
☐ 1862	(932,550)				
	20.00	30.00	42.00	90.00	375.00
☐ 1862S	(67,000)				
	45.00	75.00	175.00	800.00	3250.00
☐ 1863	(192,060)				
	27.00	45.00	85.00	200.00	600.00
☐ 1864	(94,070)				
	60.00	100.00	135.00	375.00	650.00
☐ 1864S	(20,000)				
	175.00	235.00	750.00	2500.00	RARE
☐ 1865	(59,300)				
	60.00	100.00	135.00	350.00	725.00
☐ 1865S	(41,000)				
	60.00	100.00	185.00	800.00	3000.00
☐ 1866	ONLY ONE PROOF KNOWN—VERY RARE				

QUARTERS—LIBERTY SEATED, 1866–1891
MOTTO ABOVE EAGLE

In 1866 the words IN GOD WE TRUST were added to the reverse, on a banner between the eagle and the inscription UNITED STATES OF AMERICA. When the weight was changed slightly to 6.25 grams in 1873, the arrows were returned but no further use was made of sunrays on the reverse. The arrows were removed in 1875.

Motto Above Eagle

DATE	ABP GOOD	G-4 GOOD	F-12 FINE	EF-40 EX. FINE	MS-60 UNC.
☐ 1866 (17,525)	250.00	350.00	675.00	1350.00	2350.00
☐ 1866S (28,000)	150.00	250.00	550.00	1850.00	3500.00
☐ 1867 (20,625)	150.00	250.00	450.00	1150.00	1800.00
☐ 1867S (48,000)	125.00	225.00	450.00	2650.00	13500.00
☐ 1868 (30,000)	75.00	125.00	250.00	525.00	1050.00
☐ 1868S (96,000)	60.00	90.00	225.00	750.00	2650.00
☐ 1869 (16,600)	175.00	275.00	450.00	800.00	1675.00
☐ 1869S (76,000)	60.00	100.00	220.00	775.00	2850.00
☐ 1870 (87,400)	45.00	75.00	135.00	285.00	950.00
☐ 1870CC (8,340)		RARE	RARE	RARE	RARE
☐ 1871 (171,232)	25.00	35.00	65.00	310.00	800.00
☐ 1871CC (10,890)	2000.00	3000.00	RARE	RARE	RARE

DATE	ABP GOOD	G-4 GOOD	F-12 FINE	EF-40 EX. FINE	MS-60 UNC.
☐ 1871S (30,900)					
	350.00	500.00	1500.00	3350.00	7500.00
☐ 1872 (182,950)					
	21.00	35.00	75.00	285.00	1150.00
☐ 1872CC (9,100)					
	1000.00	1300.00	2450.00	RARE	RARE
☐ 1872S (103,000)					
	500.00	750.00	1800.00	4750.00	8150.00
☐ 1873* (1,263,700)					
	20.00	30.00	45.00	250.00	1000.00
☐ 1873** Open 3 (220,600)					
	25.00	38.00	75.00	185.00	500.00
☐ 1873** Closed 3					
	75.00	150.00	275.00	1650.00	4750.00
☐ 1873CC* (12,462)					
	3000.00	4500.00	RARE	RARE	RARE
☐ 1873CC** (4,000)					VERY RARE
☐ 1873S* (160,000)					
	25.00	40.00	70.00	300.00	1450.00
☐ 1874* (471,900)					
	18.00	30.00	55.00	215.00	950.00
☐ 1874S** (392,000)					
	25.00	35.00	75.00	225.00	950.00
Arrows Removed Starting 1875					
☐ 1875 (4,293,500)					
	18.00	30.00	35.00	75.00	325.00
☐ 1875CC (140,000)					
	65.00	90.00	215.00	850.00	3500.00
☐ 1875S (680,000)					
	24.00	40.00	85.00	235.00	675.00
☐ 1876 (17,817,150)					
	20.00	30.00	40.00	85.00	325.00
☐ 1876CC (4,944,000)					
	35.00	50.00	80.00	165.00	485.00
☐ 1876S (8,596,000)					
	18.00	30.00	40.00	75.00	325.00
☐ 1877 (10,911,710)					
	18.00	30.00	40.00	75.00	325.00
☐ 1877CC (4,192,000)					
	35.00	50.00	85.00	185.00	425.00

*With Arrows **No Arrows

DATE	ABP GOOD	G-4 GOOD	F-12 FINE	EF-40 EX. FINE	MS-60 UNC.
☐ 1877S (8,996,000)					
	18.00	30.00	35.00	75.00	300.00
☐ 1877S Horizontal S					
	25.00	40.00	90.00	285.00	750.00
☐ 1878 (2,260,000)					
	18.00	30.00	35.00	75.00	325.00
☐ 1878CC (996,000)					
	40.00	60.00	85.00	210.00	650.00
☐ 1878S (140,000)					
	90.00	150.00	325.00	750.00	2150.00
☐ 1879 (14,700)					
	105.00	175.00	250.00	385.00	650.00
☐ 1880 (14,955)					
	90.00	150.00	250.00	385.00	625.00
☐ 1881 (12,975)					
	120.00	200.00	300.00	425.00	650.00
☐ 1882 (16,300)					
	100.00	150.00	250.00	380.00	650.00
☐ 1883 (15,439)					
	100.00	150.00	250.00	415.00	700.00
☐ 1884 (8,875)					
	150.00	250.00	350.00	575.00	750.00
☐ 1885 (14,530)					
	100.00	150.00	250.00	480.00	750.00
☐ 1886 (5,886)					
	200.00	325.00	500.00	750.00	1100.00
☐ 1887 (10,710)					
	150.00	250.00	385.00	550.00	800.00
☐ 1888 (10,833)					
	150.00	250.00	385.00	525.00	750.00
☐ 1888S (1,216,000)					
	20.00	30.00	42.00	80.00	350.00
☐ 1889 (12,711)					
	110.00	160.00	250.00	350.00	600.00
☐ 1890 (80,590)					
	45.00	75.00	115.00	235.00	550.00
☐ 1891 (3,920,600)					
	18.00	30.00	40.00	80.00	325.00
☐ 1891O (68,000)					
	150.00	225.00	625.00	2100.00	4250.00
☐ 1891S (2,216,000)					
	18.00	30.00	40.00	80.00	325.00

QUARTERS—BARBER OR LIBERTY HEAD, 1892–1916

The Barber or Liberty Head quarter, with its classical portrait bust, was introduced in 1892 after a design by Charles E. Barber. Liberty faces right and wears a cap and laurel wreath. On the reverse is a shield eagle holding arrows and branch with (at long last) the words QUARTER DOLLAR spelled out without abbreviation. This was without doubt the handsomest design in the quarter-dollar series and has become extremely popular with collectors. It was struck at Philadelphia, Denver, New Orleans, and San Francisco. The Barber quarter has a composition of 90% silver and 10% copper with a weight of 6.25 grams and a diameter of 24.3mm.

Mint Mark is Below the Eagle on Reverse

DATE	ABP GOOD	G-4 GOOD	F-12 FINE	EF-40 EX. FINE	MS-60 UNC.	MS-65 CH. UNC.
☐ 1892	(8,237,245)					
	8.00	11.00	27.00	80.00	275.00	1350.00
☐ 1892O	(2,640,000)					
	12.00	18.00	45.00	110.00	375.00	1500.00
☐ 1892S	(964,079)					
	25.00	40.00	100.00	190.00	525.00	4350.00
☐ 1893	(5,444,815)					
	8.00	11.00	28.00	85.00	285.00	1750.00
☐ 1893O	(3,396,000)					
	9.00	12.00	38.00	115.00	300.00	1850.00
☐ 1893S	(1,454,535)					
	15.00	23.00	75.00	185.00	475.00	6750.00
☐ 1894	(3,432,972)					
	8.00	11.00	38.00	100.00	285.00	1400.00
☐ 1894O	(2,852,000)					
	8.00	11.00	50.00	160.00	375.00	2150.00
☐ 1894S	(2,648,821)					
	8.00	11.00	45.00	150.00	350.00	2500.00
☐ 1895	(4,440,880)					
	8.00	11.00	40.00	90.00	260.00	1650.00

DATE	ABP GOOD	G-4 GOOD	F-12 FINE	EF-40 EX. FINE	MS-60 UNC.	MS-65 CH. UNC.
☐ 1895O	(2,816,000)					
	9.00	15.00	53.00	155.00	425.00	2850.00
☐ 1895S	(1,764,681)					
	15.00	25.00	85.00	185.00	450.00	3750.00
☐ 1896	(3,874,762)					
	8.00	11.00	28.00	85.00	265.00	1250.00
☐ 1896O	(1,484,000)					
	45.00	65.00	200.00	600.00	1200.00	7250.00
☐ 1896S	(188,039)					
	575.00	750.00	2350.00	5750.00	10500.00	RARE
☐ 1897	(8,140,731)					
	8.00	11.00	25.00	80.00	300.00	1400.00
☐ 1897O	(1,414,800)					
	30.00	55.00	215.00	415.00	950.00	3500.00
☐ 1897S	(542,229)					
	100.00	150.00	325.00	900.00	1650.00	7000.00
☐ 1898	(11,100,735)					
	8.00	11.00	25.00	75.00	260.00	1200.00
☐ 1898O	(1,868,000)					
	12.00	18.00	80.00	275.00	650.00	9000.00
☐ 1898S	(1,020,592)					
	9.00	13.00	60.00	100.00	425.00	8250.00
☐ 1899	(12,624,846)					
	8.00	11.00	23.00	85.00	250.00	1200.00
☐ 1899O	(2,644,000)					
	10.00	13.00	42.00	150.00	450.00	2650.00
☐ 1899S	(708,000)					
	20.00	35.00	110.00	165.00	425.00	3750.00
☐ 1900	(10,016,912)					
	8.00	11.00	25.00	85.00	300.00	1350.00
☐ 1900O	(3,416,000)					
	10.00	15.00	85.00	175.00	550.00	3600.00
☐ 1900S	(1,858,585)					
	8.00	11.00	42.00	90.00	400.00	5500.00
☐ 1901	(8,892,813)					
	25.00	40.00	49.00	100.00	275.00	1500.00
☐ 1901O	(1,612,000)					
	60.00	85.00	215.00	625.00	1050.00	5250.00
☐ 1901S	(72,664)					
	3500.00	4750.00	RARE	RARE	RARE	RARE
☐ 1902	(12,197,744)					
	8.00	11.00	23.00	80.00	250.00	1200.00

DATE	ABP GOOD	G-4 GOOD	F-12 FINE	EF-40 EX. FINE	MS-60 UNC.	MS-65 CH. UNC.
☐ 1902O	(4,748,000)					
	6.00	9.00	60.00	150.00	500.00	3850.00
☐ 1902S	(1,524,612)					
	8.00	12.00	60.00	175.00	525.00	3500.00
☐ 1903	(9,670,064)					
	6.00	9.00	20.00	75.00	260.00	2250.00
☐ 1903O	(3,500,000)					
	8.00	11.00	50.00	135.00	450.00	4650.00
☐ 1903S	(1,036,000)					
	12.00	18.00	55.00	160.00	450.00	2350.00
☐ 1904	(9,588,813)					
	6.00	9.00	20.00	80.00	280.00	1250.00
☐ 1904O	(2,456,000)					
	20.00	32.00	90.00	235.00	875.00	2500.00
☐ 1905	(4,968,250)					
	20.00	32.00	50.00	80.00	250.00	1450.00
☐ 1905O	(1,230,000)					
	30.00	45.00	125.00	275.00	525.00	6250.00
☐ 1905S	(1,884,000)					
	25.00	35.00	80.00	125.00	425.00	3750.00
☐ 1906	(3,656,435)					
	6.00	9.00	20.00	75.00	250.00	1200.00
☐ 1906D	(3,280,000)					
	6.00	9.00	25.00	80.00	260.00	1750.00
☐ 1906O	(2,056,000)					
	8.00	11.00	42.00	115.00	310.00	1300.00
☐ 1907	(7,192,575)					
	6.00	9.00	20.00	70.00	250.00	1200.00
☐ 1907D	(2,484,000)					
	6.00	9.00	27.00	90.00	260.00	2550.00
☐ 1907O	(4,560,000)					
	8.00	11.00	22.00	75.00	250.00	1900.00
☐ 1907S	(1,360,000)					
	8.00	11.00	55.00	140.00	485.00	5850.00
☐ 1908	(4,232,545)					
	6.00	9.00	20.00	75.00	250.00	1200.00
☐ 1908D	(5,788,000)					
	6.00	9.00	20.00	75.00	250.00	1200.00
☐ 1908O	(6,244,000)					
	8.00	11.00	20.00	85.00	250.00	1200.00
☐ 1908S	(784,000)					
	25.00	38.00	135.00	325.00	775.00	4350.00
☐ 1909	(9,268,650)					
	6.00	9.00	20.00	70.00	250.00	1200.00

DATE	ABP GOOD	G-4 GOOD	F-12 FINE	EF-40 EX. FINE	MS-60 UNC.	MS-65 CH. UNC.
☐ 1909D	(5,114,000)					
	6.00	9.00	25.00	90.00	260.00	1250.00
☐ 1909O	(712,000)					
	35.00	55.00	400.00	1500.00	3000.00	8250.00
☐ 1909S	(1,348,000)					
	8.00	11.00	42.00	95.00	325.00	2250.00
☐ 1910	(2,244,551)					
	6.00	9.00	30.00	90.00	300.00	1200.00
☐ 1910D	(1,500,000)					
	6.00	9.00	45.00	130.00	400.00	1850.00
☐ 1911	(3,270,543)					
	6.00	9.00	22.00	80.00	250.00	1200.00
☐ 1911D	(933,600)					
	18.00	32.00	150.00	450.00	950.00	6350.00
☐ 1911S	(988,000)					
	8.00	11.00	60.00	175.00	385.00	1550.00
☐ 1912	(4,400,700)					
	6.00	9.00	20.00	65.00	250.00	1200.00
☐ 1912S	(708,000)					
	20.00	32.00	75.00	125.00	425.00	1750.00
☐ 1913	(484,613)					
	25.00	40.00	110.00	375.00	1000.00	4350.00
☐ 1913D	(1,450,800)					
	9.00	14.00	40.00	90.00	300.00	1200.00
☐ 1913S	(40,000)					
	1250.00	1900.00	5500.00	11000.00	15000.00	35000.00
☐ 1914	(6,244,610)					
	6.00	9.00	18.00	60.00	250.00	1200.00
☐ 1914D	(3,046,000)					
	6.00	9.00	18.00	60.00	250.00	1200.00
☐ 1914S	(264,000)					
	100.00	135.00	425.00	900.00	1350.00	3350.00
☐ 1915	(3,480,450)					
	6.00	9.00	18.00	60.00	250.00	1200.00
☐ 1915D	(3,694,000)					
	6.00	9.00	18.00	60.00	250.00	1200.00
☐ 1915S	(704,000)					
	20.00	32.00	65.00	110.00	250.00	1200.00
☐ 1916	(1,788,000)					
	6.00	9.00	18.00	60.00	250.00	1200.00
☐ 1916D	(6,540,000)					
	6.00	9.00	18.00	60.00	250.00	1200.00

QUARTERS—STANDING LIBERTY, 1916–1930

The Standing Liberty quarter was introduced in 1916 during World War I and its theme was intended to reflect the nation's sentiments at that time. The goddess is portrayed in full length holding a shield with which she, presumably, fends off the defilers of liberty. An eagle in flight is pictured on the reverse, with the words UNITED STATES OF AMERICA and E PLURIBUS UNUM. The designer was Herman A. MacNeil. Specifications are the same as for the Barber quarter.

This design carried so much fine detailing that very moderate handling resulted in obvious wear, making uncirculated specimens more valuable, proportionately, than in the case of most other coins. The chief point of vulnerability was the date, so small in size and positioned in such a way as to receive heavy wear, that many specimens lost their date after only a few years of circulation. The government wished to correct this fault without totally redesigning the obverse and in 1925 hit upon the plan of showing the date in incuse—that is, pressed into the coin rather than raised from its surface. While this did not totally prevent wear it helped keep the dates readable for a longer time.

A series of minor alterations was made in 1917, the second year of issue, including a dressing up of Liberty to satisfy public criticism that the figure was displaying a scandalous amount of flesh. Three stars were added beneath the eagle on the reverse.

Note: Prices listed for MS-60 specimens of Standing Liberty quarters are for ordinary strikes. Exceptional strikes with full head of Liberty in detail are scarcer and sell for higher sums. This is not a question of *wear*, but simply the quality of the coin as originally struck.

1916–30
Mint Mark is to
Left of Date on Obverse

1916–1917
Type I
No Stars Under Eagle

1917–1930
Type II
3 Stars Under Eagle

DATE	ABP GOOD	G-4 GOOD	VG-8 V. GOOD	F-12 FINE	EF-40 EX. FINE	MS-60 UNC.
☐ 1916	(52,000)					
	2000.00	3250.00	6000.00	7000.00	11000.00	13500.00
☐ 1917	(8,792,000)					
	15.00	25.00	55.00	70.00	115.00	275.00
☐ 1917D	(1,509,200)					
	18.00	30.00	75.00	100.00	200.00	325.00
☐ 1917S	(1,952,000)					
	20.00	30.00	80.00	105.00	225.00	375.00

STARS UNDER EAGLE

DATE	ABP GOOD	G-4 GOOD	VG-8 V. GOOD	F-12 FINE	EF-40 EX. FINE	MS-60 UNC.
☐ 1917	(13,880,000)					
	15.00	25.00	40.00	60.00	110.00	225.00
☐ 1917D	(6,224,400)					
	30.00	50.00	50.00	90.00	175.00	285.00
☐ 1917S	(5,552,000)					
	30.00	50.00	55.00	95.00	175.00	275.00
☐ 1918	(12,240,000)					
	12.00	20.00	20.00	32.00	45.00	135.00
☐ 1918D	(7,380,000)					
	18.00	30.00	45.00	75.00	135.00	285.00
☐ 1918S	(11,072,000)					
	12.00	20.00	25.00	38.00	60.00	175.00
☐ 1918S over 7						
	1200.00	1800.00	2350.00	3850.00	7250.00	16500.00
☐ 1919	(11,324,000)					
	22.00	30.00	45.00	70.00	100.00	210.00
☐ 1919D	(1,944,000)					
	60.00	90.00	115.00	220.00	650.00	1100.00
☐ 1919S	(1,836,000)					
	60.00	90.00	110.00	185.00	500.00	1000.00
☐ 1920	(27,860,000)					
	11.00	18.00	22.00	27.00	55.00	150.00
☐ 1920D	(3,586,400)					
	39.00	60.00	70.00	95.00	165.00	420.00
☐ 1920S	(6,380,000)					
	12.00	23.00	28.00	32.00	70.00	250.00
☐ 1921	(1,916,000)					
	125.00	175.00	190.00	400.00	800.00	1750.00
☐ 1923	(9,716,000)					
	12.00	18.00	20.00	35.00	65.00	175.00
☐ 1923S*	(1,360,000)					
	200.00	250.00	350.00	650.00	1500.00	2800.00
☐ 1924	(10,920,000)					
	12.00	20.00	18.00	27.00	50.00	185.00
☐ 1924D	(3,112,000)					
	40.00	60.00	70.00	110.00	210.00	325.00
☐ 1924S	(2,860,000)					
	20.00	30.00	35.00	50.00	135.00	350.00
☐ 1925	(12,280,000)					
	5.75	8.00	9.00	11.00	45.00	160.00

*Note: Check for altered date.

DATE	ABP GOOD	G-4 GOOD	VG-8 V. GOOD	F-12 FINE	EF-40 EX. FINE	MS-60 UNC.
☐ 1926	(11,316,000)					
	5.75	8.00	9.00	11.00	40.00	125.00
☐ 1926D	(1,716,000)					
	5.75	8.00	11.00	25.00	100.00	185.00
☐ 1926S	(2,700,000)					
	5.75	8.00	10.00	12.00	110.00	350.00
☐ 1927	(11,912,000)					
	5.75	8.00	9.00	11.00	35.00	125.00
☐ 1927D	(976,400)					
	10.00	18.00	22.00	32.00	175.00	275.00
☐ 1927S	(396,000)					
	30.00	50.00	60.00	115.00	1150.00	4500.00
☐ 1928	(6,336,000)					
	5.75	8.00	9.00	11.00	35.00	125.00
☐ 1928D	(1,627,600)					
	5.75	8.00	9.00	11.00	45.00	135.00
☐ 1928S	(2,644,000)					
	5.75	8.00	9.00	11.00	42.00	125.00
☐ 1929	(11,140,000)					
	5.75	8.00	9.00	11.00	35.00	125.00
☐ 1929D	(1,358,000)					
	5.75	8.00	9.00	11.00	40.00	125.00
☐ 1929S	(1,764,000)					
	5.75	8.00	9.00	11.00	35.00	125.00
☐ 1930	(5,632,000)					
	5.75	8.00	9.00	11.00	35.00	125.00
☐ 1930S	(1,556,000)					
	5.75	8.00	9.00	11.00	35.00	125.00

QUARTERS—WASHINGTON, 1932 TO DATE

DATE	ABP	G-4 GOOD	F-12 FINE	EF-40 EX. FINE	MS-60 UNC.	MS-65 UNC.
☐ 1932	(5,404,000)					
	5.75	8.00	9.00	11.00	27.00	325.00
☐ 1932D	(436,800)					
	75.00	115.00	155.00	250.00	1200.00	13000.00
☐ 1932S	(408,000)					
	85.00	130.00	175.00	235.00	475.00	5500.00
☐ 1934	(31,912,052)					
	5.75	8.00	9.00	11.00	32.00	130.00
☐ 1934 Doubled Die						
	35.00	50.00	100.00	200.00	365.00	4150.00
☐ 1934D	(3,527,200)					
	5.75	8.00	12.00	32.00	250.00	900.00
☐ 1935	(32,484,000)					
	5.75	7.00	7.50	8.00	21.00	100.00
☐ 1935D	(5,780,000)					
	5.75	7.00	10.00	32.00	265.00	535.00
☐ 1935S	(5,550,000)					
	5.75	7.00	9.00	22.00	110.00	325.00

1932–1967
Mint Mark is
on Reverse
Below Eagle

1968 on—
Mint Mark
to Right of
Hair Ribbon

DATE	MINTAGE	ABP FINE	F-12 FINE	EF-40 EX. FINE	MS-60 UNC.	MS-65 UNC.
☐ 1936	41,303,837	5.00	8.00	9.00	25.00	100.00
☐ 1936D	5,374,000	7.00	10.00	55.00	600.00	1000.00
☐ 1936S	3,828,000	5.00	8.00	15.00	120.00	300.00
☐ 1937	19,701,542	5.00	7.00	10.00	23.00	100.00
☐ 1937D	7,189,600	5.00	8.00	16.00	80.00	160.00
☐ 1937S	1,652,000	5.00	8.50	35.00	175.00	400.00
☐ 1938	9,480,045	5.00	8.00	18.00	95.00	235.00
☐ 1938S	2,832,000	5.00	8.00	23.00	115.00	225.00
☐ 1939	33,548,795	5.00	7.00	8.00	18.00	70.00
☐ 1939D	7,092,000	5.00	7.50	12.00	45.00	125.00
☐ 1939S	2,628,000	5.00	8.00	25.00	100.00	310.00
☐ 1940	35,715,246	5.00	7.00	8.00	17.00	60.00
☐ 1940D	2,797,600	5.00	7.00	25.00	135.00	310.00
☐ 1940S	8,244,000	5.00	7.00	10.00	28.00	55.00
☐ 1941	79,047,287	5.00	7.00	8.00	12.00	40.00
☐ 1941D	16,714,800	5.00	7.00	9.00	35.00	75.00
☐ 1941S	16,080,000	5.00	7.00	8.00	35.00	70.00
☐ 1942	102,117,123	5.00	7.00	8.00	12.00	35.00
☐ 1942D	17,487,200	5.00	7.00	8.00	20.00	40.00
☐ 1942S	19,384,000	5.00	7.00	9.00	75.00	135.00
☐ 1943	99,700,000	5.00	7.00	8.00	10.00	42.00
☐ 1943D	16,095,600	5.00	7.00	8.00	32.00	55.00
☐ 1943S	21,700,000	5.00	7.00	8.00	32.00	60.00
☐ 1943S Doubled Die		18.00	25.00	50.00	210.00	500.00
☐ 1944	104,956,000	5.00	7.00	8.00	10.00	35.00
☐ 1944D	14,600,000	5.00	7.00	8.00	23.00	45.00
☐ 1944S	12,560,000	5.00	7.00	8.00	18.00	32.00
☐ 1945	74,372,000	5.00	7.00	8.00	10.00	37.00
☐ 1945D	12,341,600	5.00	7.00	8.00	18.00	40.00
☐ 1945S	17,004,001	5.00	7.00	8.00	10.00	35.00
☐ 1946	53,436,000	5.00	7.00	8.00	10.00	42.00
☐ 1946D	9,072,800	5.00	7.00	8.00	10.00	45.00
☐ 1946S	4,204,000	5.00	7.00	8.00	10.00	35.00
☐ 1947	22,556,000	5.00	7.00	8.00	13.00	40.00
☐ 1947D	15,338,400	5.00	7.00	8.00	15.00	38.00
☐ 1947S	5,532,000	5.00	7.00	8.00	10.00	30.00
☐ 1948	35,196,000	5.00	7.00	8.00	10.00	32.00
☐ 1948D	16,768,800	5.00	7.00	8.00	13.00	50.00

DATE	MINTAGE	ABP FINE	F-12 FINE	EF-40 EX. FINE	MS-60 UNC.	MS-65 UNC.
☐ 1948S	15,960,000	5.00	6.00	7.00	11.00	45.00
☐ 1949	9,312,000	5.75	6.00	7.00	38.00	75.00
☐ 1949D	10,068,400	5.75	6.00	7.00	18.00	47.00
☐ 1950	24,971,512	4.00	6.00	7.00	10.00	35.00
☐ 1950D	21,075,600	4.00	6.00	7.00	10.00	35.00
☐ 1950D over S		27.00	45.00	150.00	300.00	3500.00
☐ 1950S over D		32.00	60.00	210.00	400.00	900.00
☐ 1950S	10,284,004	4.00	6.00	12.00	40.00	150.00
☐ 1951	43,505,602	4.00	6.00	7.00	10.00	35.00
☐ 1951D	35,354,800	4.00	6.00	7.00	10.00	30.00
☐ 1951S	8,948,000	4.00	6.00	7.00	25.00	55.00
☐ 1952	38,862,073	4.00	6.00	7.00	12.00	30.00
☐ 1952D	49,795,200	4.00	6.00	7.00	10.00	35.00
☐ 1952S	13,707,800	4.00	6.00	7.00	15.00	38.00
☐ 1953	18,664,920	4.00	6.00	7.00	10.00	35.00
☐ 1953D	56,112,400	4.00	6.00	7.00	10.00	28.00
☐ 1953S	14,016,000	4.00	6.00	7.00	10.00	32.00
☐ 1954	54,654,503	4.00	6.00	7.00	8.00	28.00
☐ 1954D	46,305,500	4.00	6.00	7.00	8.00	28.00
☐ 1954S	11,834,722	4.00	6.00	7.00	8.00	27.00
☐ 1955	18,558,381	4.00	6.00	7.00	8.00	30.00
☐ 1955D	3,182,400	4.00	6.00	7.00	8.00	28.00
☐ 1956	44,813,384	4.00	6.00	7.00	8.00	26.00
☐ 1956D	32,334,500	4.00	6.00	7.00	8.00	22.00
☐ 1957	47,779,952	4.00	6.00	7.00	8.00	16.00
☐ 1957D	77,924,160	4.00	6.00	7.00	8.00	18.00
☐ 1958	7,235,652	4.00	6.00	7.00	8.00	16.00
☐ 1958D	78,124,900	4.00	6.00	7.00	8.00	18.00
☐ 1959	25,533,291	4.00	6.00	7.00	8.00	17.00
☐ 1959D	62,054,232	4.00	6.00	7.00	8.00	20.00
☐ 1960	30,855,602	4.00	6.00	7.00	8.00	17.00
☐ 1960D	63,000,324	4.00	6.00	7.00	8.00	17.00
☐ 1961	40,064,244	4.00	6.00	7.00	8.00	17.00
☐ 1961D	83,656,928	4.00	6.00	7.00	8.00	27.00
☐ 1962	39,374,019	4.00	6.00	7.00	8.00	16.00
☐ 1962D	127,554,756	4.00	6.00	7.00	8.00	25.00
☐ 1963	77,391,645	4.00	6.00	7.00	8.00	14.00
☐ 1963D	135,288,184	4.00	6.00	7.00	8.00	16.00
☐ 1964	564,341,347	4.00	6.00	7.00	8.00	14.00
☐ 1964D	704,135,528	4.00	6.00	7.00	8.00	14.00
☐ 1965	1,819,717,540				.75	10.00
☐ 1966	821,101,500				1.10	6.50
☐ 1967	1,524,031,840				.75	10.00
☐ 1968	220,731,500				.75	14.00
☐ 1968D	101,534,000				1.00	7.50

DATE	MINTAGE	MS-60 UNC.	PRF-65 PROOF
☐ 1968S Proof Only	3,041,500		3.00
☐ 1969	176,212,000	2.00	
☐ 1969D	114,372,000	1.65	
☐ 1969S Proof Only	2,934,631		3.00
☐ 1970	136,420,000	.85	
☐ 1970D	417,341,364	.75	
☐ 1970S Proof Only	2,632,810		3.00
☐ 1971	109,284,000	1.00	
☐ 1971D	258,634,428	.80	
☐ 1971S Proof Only	3,224,138		3.00
☐ 1972	215,048,000	.80	
☐ 1972D	311,067,732	.80	
☐ 1972S	3,267,667		3.00
☐ 1973	346,924,000	.80	
☐ 1973D	232,977,400	.80	
☐ 1973S Proof Only	2,796,624		2.50
☐ 1974	801,456,000	.80	
☐ 1974D	363,160,300	.80	
☐ 1974S Proof Only	2,612,568		2.50
☐ 1976 Copper-Nickel Clad	809,780,016	.80	
☐ 1976D Copper-Nickel Clad	860,108,836	.80	
☐ 1976S Copper-Nickel Clad Proof	7,055,099		3.50
☐ 1976S Silver Clad		2.50	
☐ 1976S Silver Clad Proof			5.00
☐ 1977	468,556,900	.80	
☐ 1977D	256,524,078	.80	
☐ 1977S Proof Only	2,090,269		3.00
☐ 1978	521,452,000	.80	
☐ 1978D	287,373,152	.80	
☐ 1978S Proof Only	3,127,781		3.00
☐ 1979	515,709,000	.80	
☐ 1979D	489,790,020	.80	
☐ 1979S Proof, Variety I	3,677,200		3.00
☐ 1979S Proof, Variety II			5.00
☐ 1980P	635,832,101	.80	
☐ 1980D	518,327,444	.80	
☐ 1980S Proof	3,547,130		3.00
☐ 1981P	602,000,000	.80	
☐ 1981D	575,841,732	.80	
☐ 1981S Proof Only, Variety I	4,064,789		3.00
☐ 1981S Proof Only, Variety II			8.00

DATE	MINTAGE	MS-60 UNC.	PRF-65 PROOF
☐ 1982P	500,000,000	4.00	
☐ 1982D	490,665,000	3.00	
☐ 1982S Proof Only	3,856,941		3.00
☐ 1983P	674,000,000	18.00	
☐ 1983D	617,800,000	10.00	
☐ 1983S Proof Only	3,378,125		3.00
☐ 1984P	675,961,834	1.10	
☐ 1984D	550,000,000	1.10	
☐ 1984S Proof Only	3,164,210		3.00
☐ 1985P	780,201,621	1.10	
☐ 1985D	520,888,004	1.10	
☐ 1985S Proof Only	3,260,112		3.00
☐ 1986P	541,643,221	3.00	
☐ 1986D	502,121,106	5.00	
☐ 1986S Proof Only	3,006,420		3.00
☐ 1987P	572,286,210	.80	
☐ 1987D	642,873,921	.80	
☐ 1987S Proof Only	3,821,764		3.00
☐ 1988P	572,741,111	1.00	
☐ 1988D	586,710,461	.80	
☐ 1988S Proof Only	3,272,648		3.00
☐ 1989P	502,768,211	.80	
☐ 1989D	886,461,006	.80	
☐ 1989S Proof Only	3,164,718		3.00
☐ 1990P	632,464,118	.80	
☐ 1990D	964,720,107	.80	
☐ 1990S Proof Only	3,240,766		3.00
☐ 1991P	568,958,210	.80	
☐ 1991D	630,962,680	.80	
☐ 1991S Proof Only	2,867,787		3.00
☐ 1992P	384,760,100	.80	
☐ 1992D	389,764,222	.80	
☐ 1992S Proof Only	2,858,971		3.00
☐ 1992S Silver Proof	1,317,579		8.50
☐ 1993P	639,276,000	.80	
☐ 1993D	645,476,128	.80	
☐ 1993S Proof Only	2,633,439		3.50
☐ 1993S Silver Proof	761,353		8.50
☐ 1994P	825,600,000	.80	
☐ 1994D	880,034,000	.80	
☐ 1994S Proof Only	2,484,594		3.50

DATE	MINTAGE	MS-60 UNC.	PRF-65 PROOF
☐ 1994S Silver Proof	785,329		10.00
☐ 1995P	1,004,336,000	.80	
☐ 1995D	1,103,216,000	.80	
☐ 1995S Proof Only	2,115,500		5.00
☐ 1995S Silver Proof	738,985		10.00
☐ 1996P	925,040,000	.80	
☐ 1996D	908,868,000	.80	
☐ 1996S Proof	1,750,250		4.50
☐ 1996S Silver Proof	775,000		10.00
☐ 1997P	595,740,000	.80	
☐ 1997D	599,680,000	.80	
☐ 1997S Proof Only	2,050,000		6.00
☐ 1997S Silver Proof	740,050		11.00
☐ 1998P	896,268,000	.80	
☐ 1998D	821,000,000	.80	
☐ 1998S Proof Only	2,085,500		6.00
☐ 1998S Silver Proof	875,750		11.00
☐ 1999P DE	373,400,000	1.10	
☐ 1999D DE	401,424,000	1.80	
☐ 1999S DE	3,710,000		4.00
☐ 1999S DE Silver	800,000		15.00
☐ 1999P PA	349,000,000	1.80	
☐ 1999D PA	358,332,000	1.60	
☐ 1999S PA	3,710,000		4.00
☐ 1999S PA Silver	800,000		15.00
☐ 1999P NJ	363,200,000	1.10	
☐ 1999D NJ	299,028,000	1.35	
☐ 1999S NJ	3,710,000		4.00
☐ 1999S NJ Silver	800,000		15.00
☐ 1999P GA	451,188,000	1.00	
☐ 1999D GA	488,744,000	1.25	
☐ 1999S GA	3,710,000		4.00
☐ 1999S GA Silver	800,000		15.00
☐ 1999P CT	688,744,000	.80	
☐ 1999D CT	657,880,000	.80	
☐ 1999S CT	3,710,000		4.00
☐ 1999S CT Silver	800,000		15.00
☐ 2000P MA	628,600,000	.80	
☐ 2000D MA	535,184,000	.80	
☐ 2000S MA	4,020,000		4.00
☐ 2000S MA Silver	850,000		10.00

DATE	MINTAGE	MS-60 UNC.	PRF-65 PROOF
☐ 2000P MD	678,200,000	.80	
☐ 2000D MD	556,532,000	.80	
☐ 2000S MD	4,020,000		4.00
☐ 2000S MD Silver	850,000		10.00
☐ 2000P SC	742,756,000	1.10	
☐ 2000D SC	566,208,000	1.10	
☐ 2000S SC	4,020,000		4.00
☐ 2000S SC Silver	850,000		10.00
☐ 2000P NH	673,040,000	.80	
☐ 2000D NH	495,976,000	.80	
☐ 2000S NH	4,020,000		4.00
☐ 2000S NH Silver	850,000		10.00
☐ 2000P VA	943,000,000	.80	
☐ 2000D VA	651,616,000	.80	
☐ 2000S VA	4,020,000		4.00
☐ 2000S VA Silver	850,000		10.00
☐ 2001P NY	655,400,000	.80	
☐ 2001D NY	619,640,000	.80	
☐ 2001S NY	3,100,000		4.00
☐ 2001S NY Silver	900,000		10.00
☐ 2001P NC	627,600,000	.80	
☐ 2001D NC	427,876,000	.80	
☐ 2001S NC	3,100,000		4.00
☐ 2001S NC Silver	900,000		10.00
☐ 2001P RI	423,000,000	.80	
☐ 2001D RI	447,100,000	.80	
☐ 2001S RI	3,100,000		4.00
☐ 2001S RI Silver	900,000		10.00
☐ 2001P VT	423,400,000	.80	
☐ 2001D VT	459,404,000	.80	
☐ 2001S VT	3,100,000		4.00
☐ 2001S VT Silver	900,000		10.00
☐ 2001P KY	353,000,000	2.00	
☐ 2001D KY	370,564,000	2.00	
☐ 2001S KY	3,100,000		4.00
☐ 2001S KY Silver	900,000		10.00
☐ 2002P TN	361,600,000	2.00	
☐ 2002D TN	286,468,000	2.00	
☐ 2002S TN	3,000,000	1.30	4.00
☐ 2002S TN Silver	900,000		10.00
☐ 2002P OH	217,200,000	.80	

DATE	MINTAGE	MS-60 UNC.	PRF-65 PROOF
☐ 2002D OH	414,832,000	.80	
☐ 2002S OH	3,000,000		4.00
☐ 2002S OH Silver	900,000		10.00
☐ 2002P LA	362,000,000	.80	
☐ 2002D LA	401,804,000	.80	
☐ 2002S LA	3,000,000		4.00
☐ 2002S LA Silver	900,000		10.00
☐ 2002P IN	362,600,000	.80	
☐ 2002D IN	327,200,000	.80	
☐ 2002S IN	3,000,000		4.00
☐ 2002S IN Silver	900,000		10.00
☐ 2002P MS	292,000,000	.80	
☐ 2002D MS	290,000,000	.80	
☐ 2002S MS	3,000,000		4.00
☐ 2002S MS Silver	900,000		10.00
☐ 2003P IL	225,800,000	1.50	
☐ 2003D IL	237,400,000	1.50	
☐ 2003S IL	3,400,000		4.00
☐ 2003S IL Silver	1,125,750		10.00
☐ 2003P AL	225,000,000	.80	
☐ 2003D AL	232,000,000	.80	
☐ 2003S AL	3,400,000		4.00
☐ 2003S AL Silver	1,125,750		10.00
☐ 2003P ME	217,000,000	.80	
☐ 2003D ME	231,000,000	.80	
☐ 2003S ME	3,400,000		4.00
☐ 2003S ME Silver	1,125,750		10.00
☐ 2003P MO	225,000,000	.80	
☐ 2003D MO	228,000,000	.80	
☐ 2003S MO	3,400,000		4.00
☐ 2003S MO Silver	1,125,750		10.00
☐ 2003P AR	226,000,000	.80	
☐ 2003D AR	231,000,000	.80	
☐ 2003S AR	3,400,000		4.00
☐ 2003S AR Silver	1,125,750		10.00
☐ 2004P MICH	233,500,000	.80	
☐ 2004D MICH	225,800,000	.80	
☐ 2004S MICH	2,750,000		4.00
☐ 2004S Silver MICH	1,750,000		12.00
☐ 2004P FLA	240,200,000	.80	
☐ 2004D FLA	241,600,000	.80	

DATE	MINTAGE	MS-60 UNC.	PRF-65 PROOF
☐ 2004S FLA	2,750,000		4.00
☐ 2004S Silver FLA	1,750,000		10.00
☐ 2004P TEX	278,800,000	.80	
☐ 2004D TEX	263,000,000	.80	
☐ 2004S TEX	2,750,000		4.00
☐ 2004S Silver TEX	1,750,000		10.00
☐ 2004P IOWA	213,800,000	.80	
☐ 2004D IOWA	251,800,000	.80	
☐ 2004S IOWA	2,750,000		4.00
☐ 2004S Silver IOWA	1,750,000		10.00
☐ 2004P WI	226,400,000	.80	
☐ 2004D WI	226,800,000	.80	
☐ 2004S WI	2,750,000		4.00
☐ 2004S Silver WI	1,750,000		10.00
☐ 2005P CA	257,200,000	.80	
☐ 2005D CA	263,200,000	.80	
☐ 2005S CA	3,250,000		4.00
☐ 2005S Silver CA	1,675,000		10.00
☐ 2005P MN	239,600,000	.80	
☐ 2005D MN	248,400,000	.80	
☐ 2005S MN	3,250,000		4.00
☐ 2005S Silver MN	1,675,000		10.00
☐ 2005P OR	316,200,000	.80	
☐ 2005D OR	404,000,000	.80	
☐ 2005S OR	3,250,000		4.00
☐ 2005S Silver OR	1,675,000		10.00
☐ 2005P KS	263,400,000	.80	
☐ 2005D KS	300,000,000	.80	
☐ 2005S KS	3,250,000		4.00
☐ 2005S Silver KS	1,675,000		10.00
☐ 2005P WV	360,500,000	.80	
☐ 2005D WV	355,400,000	.80	
☐ 2005S WV	3,250,000		4.00
☐ 2005S Silver WV	1,675,000		10.00
☐ 2006P NEV	276,500,000	.80	
☐ 2006D	315,000,000	.80	
☐ 2006S	2,850,000		4.00
☐ 2006 Silver	1,575,000		10.00
☐ 2006P NEB	320,000,000	.80	
☐ 2006D	275,000,000	.80	
☐ 2006S	2,850,000		4.00

DATE	MINTAGE	MS-60 UNC.	PRF-65 PROOF
☐ 2006 Silver	1,575,000		10.00
☐ 2006P COL	275,000,000	.80	
☐ 2006D	295,500,000	.80	
☐ 2006S	2,850,000		4.00
☐ 2006 Silver	1,575,000		10.00
☐ 2006P S. DAK	305,500,000	.80	
☐ 2006D	355,000,000	.80	
☐ 2006S	2,850,000		4.00
☐ 2006 Silver	1,575,000		10.00
☐ 2006P N. DAK	246,500,000	.80	
☐ 2006D	262,000,000	.80	
☐ 2006S	2,850,000		4.00
☐ 2006 Silver	1,575,000		10.00
☐ 2007P Montana	255,500,000	.80	
☐ 2007D	253,000,000	.80	
☐ 2007S	2,375,000		4.00
☐ 2007 Silver	1,313,000		10.00
☐ 2007P Washington	262,400,000	.80	
☐ 2007D	278,500,000	.80	
☐ 2007S	2,375,000		4.00
☐ 2007 Silver	1,313,000		10.00
☐ 2007P Idaho	293,900,000	.80	
☐ 2007D	288,300,000	.80	
☐ 2007S	2,375,000		4.00
☐ 2007 Silver	1,313,000		10.00
☐ 2007P Wyoming	240,600,000	.80	
☐ 2007D	320,750,000	.80	
☐ 2007S	2,375,000		4.00
☐ 2007 Silver	1,313,000		10.00
☐ 2007P Utah	250,000,000	.80	
☐ 2007D	252,500,000	.80	
☐ 2007S	2,375,000		4.00
☐ 2007 Silver	1,313,000		10.00
☐ 2008 Oklahoma	222,000,000	.65	
☐ 2008D	195,000,000	.65	
☐ 2008S	2,050,000		5.00
☐ 2008S Silver	1,190,000		10.00
☐ 2008P New Mexico	244,000,000	.65	
☐ 2008D	244,000,000	.65	
☐ 2008S	2,050,000		5.00
☐ 2008S Silver	1,190,000		10.00

DATE	MINTAGE	MS-60 UNC.	PRF-65 PROOF
☐ 2008P Arizona	244,000,000	.65	
☐ 2008D	265,000,000	.65	
☐ 2008S	2,050,000		5.00
☐ 2008S Silver	1,190,000		10.00
☐ 2008P Alaska	250,000,000	.65	
☐ 2008D	254,000,000	.65	
☐ 2008S	2,050,000		5.00
☐ 2008S Silver	1,190,000		10.00
☐ 2008P Hawaii	254,000,000	.65	
☐ 2008D	263,500,000	.65	
☐ 2008S	2,050,000		5.00
☐ 2008S Silver	1,190,000		10.00
☐ 2009P D. OFC.	83,500,000	.85	
☐ 2009D	8,750,000	.85	
☐ 2009S	2,100,000		4.00
☐ 2009S Silver	992,500		10.00
☐ 2009P Puerto Rico	53,250,000	.75	
☐ 2009D	85,000,000	.75	
☐ 2009S	2,100,000		4.00
☐ 2009S Silver	992,500		10.00
☐ 2009P Guam	45,000,000	.75	
☐ 2009D	42,500,000	.75	
☐ 2009S	2,100,000		4.00
☐ 2009S Silver	992,500		10.00
☐ 2009P Samoa	42,500,000	.75	
☐ 2009D	39,500,000	.75	
☐ 2009S	2,100,000		4.00
☐ 2009S Silver	992,500		10.00
☐ 2009P Virgin Islands	41,000,000	.75	
☐ 2009D	41,000,000	.75	
☐ 2009S	2,100,000		4.00
☐ 2009S Silver	992,500		10.00
☐ 2009P Mariana Islands	35,000,000	.75	
☐ 2009D	37,500,000	.75	
☐ 2009S	2,100,000		4.00
☐ 2009S Silver	992,500		10.00
☐ 2010P Hot Springs National Park		.75	
☐ 2010D		.75	
☐ 2010S			5.00
☐ 2010S Silver			10.00
☐ 2010P Yellowstone National Park		.75	

DATE	MINTAGE	MS-60 UNC.	PRF-65 PROOF
☐ 2010D		.75	
☐ 2010S			5.00
☐ 2010S Silver			10.00
☐ 2010P Yosemite National Park		.75	
☐ 2010D		.75	
☐ 2010S			5.00
☐ 2010S Silver			10.00
☐ 2010P Grand Canyon National Park		.75	
☐ 2010D		.75	
☐ 2010S			5.00
☐ 2010S Silver			10.00
☐ 2010P Mt. Hood National Park		.75	
☐ 2010D		.75	
☐ 2010S			5.00
☐ 2010S Silver			10.00
☐ 2011P Glacier National Park		.75	
☐ 2011D		.75	
☐ 2011S			5.00
☐ 2011S Silver			10.00
☐ 2011P Olympic National Park		.75	
☐ 2011D		.75	
☐ 2011S			5.00
☐ 2011S Silver			10.00
☐ 2011P Vicksburg National Park		.75	
☐ 2011D		.75	
☐ 2011S			5.00
☐ 2011S Silver			10.00
☐ 2011P Chickasaw National Park		.75	
☐ 2011D		.75	
☐ 2011S			5.00
☐ 2011S Silver			10.00

HALF DOLLARS

EARLY HALF DOLLARS, 1794–1838

As originally conceived, the half dollar was to contain precisely—to the grain—half as much metal as the dollar and was to be struck from metal of the same composition, .8924 silver alloyed with .1076 copper. It weighed 13.48 grams and was slightly larger in diameter than it subsequently became: 32.5mm. Its designer was Robert Scot and its obverse featured a profile portrait of Liberty facing right, the so-called Flowing Hair likeness used on other coins as well, backed by an eagle. Along the edge was stamped its value, as no statement of value appeared within the design (FIFTY CENTS OR HALF A DOLLAR), the words set apart with small ornamental flourishes. Apparently the initial issue in 1794 was struck from just a single set of dies, but in the following year several dies were employed resulting in a number of minor varieties. This was the final appearance of the Flowing Hair fifty-cent piece. The design was replaced in 1796 by the Draped Bust version, to which the shielded eagle reverse was added in 1801.

Because of the trading significance of this coin, an effort was made to place as many half dollars as possible into circulation during its early years. It was temporarily discontinued in 1804 as a result of speculation along with the silver dollar; but unlike the latter, which did not return for more than thirty years, production of the half dollar was resumed in 1805. In that year more than 200,000 were struck, followed by a striking exceeding 800,000 in 1806.

The Capped Bust design was installed on the half dollar in 1807, as it was on other coins. Its designer was a German-

American named John Reich. The Capped Bust is sometimes referred to as Turban Head. The word LIBERTY appears on the cap or turban band. On either side of the portrait is a series of stars, with the date positioned beneath it. The reverse has a modified shielded eagle (or heraldic eagle) with the motto E PLURIBUS UNUM on a banner and 50 C. This coin weighs 13.48 grams and has the same metallic composition as its predecessors. Varieties of the Capped Bust half dollar are so numerous, despite being in use for only about thirty years, that a large collection can be built around this coin. And it is, indeed, an ideal target for specialization, as nearly all specimens fall within the low-to-moderate range of price. Christian Gobrecht redesigned the coin in 1836, retaining the same types but modifying them somewhat. The composition was changed to provide a slightly higher content of silver and a slightly lower content of copper, the ratio now being nine parts silver, one part copper. Its weight was 13.36 grams and the diameter reduced to 30mm. This design was replaced by Liberty Seated in 1839, which remained in use for more than fifty years.

HALF DOLLARS—FLOWING HAIR, 1794–1795

DATE	MINTAGE	ABP GOOD	G-4 GOOD	F-12 FINE	VF-20 V. FINE
☐ 1794	5,300	2000.00	3250.00	11000.00	20000.00
☐ 1795 2 Leaves		800.00	1200.00	3200.00	4250.00
☐ 1795 Recut Date	317,844	800.00	1200.00	3200.00	5500.00
☐ 1795*		1850.00	2600.00	5500.00	9000.00

*3 leaves under each wing

HALF DOLLARS—DRAPED BUST, SMALL EAGLE 1796–1797

DATE	MINTAGE	ABP GOOD	G-4 GOOD	F-12 FINE	VF-20 V. FINE
☐ 1796 15 Stars		25000.00	32500.00	RARE	RARE
☐ 1796 16 Stars		25000.00	33500.00	RARE	RARE
☐ 1797 15 Stars	3,918	25000.00	32500.00	RARE	RARE

HALF DOLLARS—DRAPED BUST, 1801–1807 EAGLE ON REVERSE

DATE	ABP GOOD	G-4 GOOD	VF-20 V. FINE	EF-40 EX. FINE	MS-60 UNC.
☐ 1801 (30,289)	550.00	825.00	3750.00	6500.00	RARE
☐ 1802 (29,890)	600.00	950.00	4000.00	8500.00	RARE
☐ 1803 Large 3	150.00	225.00	800.00	2100.00	12500.00
☐ 1803 Small 3 (188,234)	165.00	265.00	900.00	2500.00	11000.00
☐ 1805	150.00	200.00	725.00	2100.00	5250.00
☐ 1805 over 4 (211,722)	200.00	310.00	1600.00	3200.00	RARE
☐ 1806	150.00	225.00	700.00	2000.00	10000.00
☐ 1806 over 5 (839,576)	150.00	250.00	810.00	2100.00	12500.00
☐ 1806 Inverted over 6	150.00	250.00	1400.00	3850.00	RARE

DATE	ABP GOOD	G-4 GOOD	VF-20 V. FINE	EF-40 EX. FINE	MS-60 UNC.
☐ 1806 Knobbed 6, Large Stars					
	150.00	210.00	700.00	2150.00	9500.00
☐ 1806 Knobbed 6, Stem Not Through Claw			EXTREMELY RARE		
☐ 1807 (301,076)	150.00	210.00	700.00	2100.00	9000.00

HALF DOLLARS—TURBAN HEAD OR "CAPPED BUST," 1807–1836

Motto Above Eagle, Lettered Edge, Large Size

DATE	ABP GOOD	G-4 GOOD	F-12 FINE	EF-40 EX. FINE	MS-60 UNC.
☐ 1807 Small Stars	100.00	135.00	750.00	2000.00	6500.00
☐ 1807 Large Stars (750,500)					
	100.00	135.00	650.00	1700.00	6250.00
☐ 1807 .50 over .20C	100.00	135.00	350.00	1300.00	5500.00
☐ 1808 (1,368,600)	50.00	78.00	110.00	400.00	2600.00
☐ 1808 over 7	58.00	95.00	125.00	480.00	3000.00
☐ 1809 (1,405,810)	50.00	75.00	105.00	350.00	1600.00
☐ 1810 (1,276,276)	50.00	75.00	100.00	310.00	1750.00
☐ 1811 (1,203,644)	50.00	75.00	135.00	350.00	1900.00
☐ 1812 (1,628,059)	50.00	75.00	115.00	300.00	1500.00
☐ 1812 over 11	60.00	100.00	130.00	400.00	2400.00
☐ 1813 (1,241,903)	50.00	75.00	100.00	310.00	2400.00
☐ 1814 (1,039,075)	50.00	75.00	110.00	450.00	1750.00
☐ 1814 over 13	75.00	125.00	165.00	450.00	2650.00
☐ 1815 over 12 (47,150)					
	850.00	1200.00	2400.00	5500.00	17500.00
☐ 1817 (1,215,567)	50.00	75.00	110.00	250.00	1350.00
☐ 1817 over 13	75.00	125.00	300.00	900.00	4000.00
☐ 1818 (1,960,322)	50.00	85.00	125.00	300.00	1400.00
☐ 1818 over 17	70.00	100.00	150.00	350.00	1650.00

DATE	ABP GOOD	G-4 GOOD	F-12 FINE	EF-40 EX. FINE	MS-60 UNC.
☐ 1819 (2,208,000)	45.00	75.00	110.00	210.00	1300.00
☐ 1819 over 18 Large 9	60.00	100.00	120.00	325.00	1600.00
☐ 1820 (751,122)	45.00	75.00	125.00	500.00	1350.00
☐ 1820 over 19	75.00	125.00	150.00	650.00	2500.00
☐ 1821 (1,305,797)	45.00	75.00	100.00	225.00	1500.00
☐ 1822 (1,559,573)	45.00	75.00	100.00	225.00	1300.00
☐ 1822 over 21	60.00	110.00	150.00	400.00	1750.00
☐ 1823 (1,694,200)	45.00	75.00	100.00	200.00	1200.00
☐ 1823 Ugly 3	60.00	100.00	150.00	675.00	3250.00
☐ 1824 (3,504,954)	45.00	75.00	100.00	225.00	1200.00
☐ 1824 over 21 and others					
	55.00	85.00	125.00	325.00	1500.00
☐ 1825 (2,943,166)	45.00	75.00	110.00	200.00	1200.00
☐ 1826 (4,044,180)	45.00	75.00	110.00	200.00	1200.00
☐ 1827* (5,493,400)	45.00	75.00	100.00	200.00	1200.00
☐ 1827 over 6 Curled 2	45.00	75.00	110.00	210.00	1350.00
☐ 1828 (3,075,200)	45.00	75.00	100.00	300.00	1200.00
☐ 1829 (3,712,156)	45.00	75.00	100.00	200.00	1200.00
☐ 1829 over 27	60.00	100.00	125.00	250.00	1300.00
☐ 1830** (4,764,800)	45.00	75.00	100.00	200.00	1200.00
☐ 1831 (5,873,660)	45.00	75.00	100.00	200.00	1200.00
☐ 1832*** (4,797,000)	45.00	75.00	85.00	200.00	1200.00
☐ 1833 (5,206,000)	45.00	75.00	85.00	200.00	1200.00
☐ 1834 (6,412,000)	45.00	75.00	85.00	200.00	1200.00
☐ 1835 (5,352,006)	45.00	75.00	85.00	200.00	1200.00
☐ 1836 All Kinds (6,546,200)					
	45.00	75.00	85.00	175.00	1200.00
☐ 1836 *Lettered edge 50 over 00					
	60.00	100.00	135.00	400.00	1900.00

*Square-Based 2. **Small O, in Date, Large O, in Date: Same Price
***Small Letters, Large Letters: Same Price

HALF DOLLARS—TURBAN HEAD OR "CAPPED BUST," 1836–1839, NO MOTTO ABOVE EAGLE, REEDED EDGE, REDUCED SIZE

DATE	ABP GOOD	G-4 GOOD	F-12 FINE	EF-40 EX. FINE	MS-60 UNC.	PRF-65 PROOF
☐ 1836 Reeded Edge						
	650.00	950.00	1750.00	3250.00	9500.00	

1836–1837 50 CENTS

1838–1839 HALF DOL.

DATE	ABP GOOD	G-4 GOOD	F-12 FINE	EF-40 EX. FINE	MS-60 UNC.	PRF-65 PROOF
☐ 1837	(3,629,820)					
	45.00	75.00	100.00	250.00	1200.00	
☐ 1838	(3,546,000)					
	45.00	75.00	100.00	285.00	1200.00	
☐ 18380	(Approx. 20)				EXTREMELY RARE	
☐ 1839	(3,334,500)					
	45.00	75.00	100.00	300.00	1500.00	
☐ 18390	(179,000)					
	200.00	275.00	750.00	2100.00	4000.00	

HALF DOLLARS—LIBERTY SEATED, 1839–1866 WITHOUT MOTTO ABOVE EAGLE

The Seated Liberty half dollar was based on the now-celebrated design of Christian Gobrecht. The goddess sits looking left, holding a shield on which the word LIBERTY appears and, in the other hand, a staff. The upper portion of the design is encircled by stars. On the reverse is a shield or heraldic eagle holding arrows and branch. Beneath the eagle are the words HALF DOL. After some minor modification of both the obverse and reverse design, the numerals used for giving the date were enlarged in 1846 and a major change occurred in 1853. Because the California gold strikes of 1849 had brought great quantities of this metal into circulation, public confidence in silver was gradually eroding. To inspire greater acceptance of silver coinage their composition was revised to include a higher proportion of bullion. The new ratio—not just for half dollars but silver pieces in general—was nine parts silver to one of copper, the one part of copper being necessary to give this durable metal a fair stability. The weight was 12.44 grams and the diameter 30.6mm. A pair of arrows was placed on the obverse beside the date as warning that the metal content had changed, and—in the event this was overlooked—sunrays were installed on the reverse, radiating from behind the eagle. These were discontinued in 1856.

Beginning in 1866, and probably not coincidentally because the Civil War had recently ended, the motto IN GOD WE TRUST was incorporated into the reverse design on a banner that flies above the eagle's head. When the weight was increased $^{6}/_{20}$ of a gram in 1873, resort was again made to arrows at the date, but no sunrays adorned the reverse. The arrows were removed in 1875. The Seated Liberty half dollar continued to be struck until 1891, though throughout the 1880s its output was very limited.

Mint Mark Is Below Eagle On Reverse

DATE	ABP GOOD	G-4 GOOD	F-12 FINE	EF-40 EX. FINE	MS-60 UNC.	PRF-65 PROOF
☐ 1839 No Drapery from Elbow						
	40.00	60.00	350.00	1250.00	7500.00	RARE
☐ 1839 With Drapery (3,334,560)						
	30.00	45.00	80.00	250.00	850.00	RARE
☐ 1840 Small Letters (1,435,008)						
	40.00	65.00	75.00	200.00	650.00	RARE
☐ 1840 Large Letters						
	85.00	125.00	300.00	800.00	3250.00	NOT MADE
☐ 1840O (855,100)						
	35.00	55.00	100.00	280.00	950.00	NOT MADE
☐ 1841 (310,000)						
	45.00	75.00	110.00	300.00	1300.00	RARE
☐ 1841O (401,000)						
	30.00	42.00	75.00	275.00	775.00	NOT MADE
☐ 1842 Small Date (2,012,764)						
	35.00	55.00	90.00	210.00	1050.00	RARE

DATE	ABP GOOD	G-4 GOOD	F-12 FINE	EF-40 EX. FINE	MS-60 UNC.	PRF-65 PROOF
☐ 1842 Large Date						
	30.00	50.00	75.00	175.00	800.00	NOT MADE
☐ 1842O Small Date						
	345.00	575.00	1400.00	RARE	RARE	NOT MADE
☐ 1842O Large Date						
	35.00	50.00	75.00	210.00	1150.00	NOT MADE
☐ 1843	(3,844,000)					
	40.00	60.00	75.00	185.00	600.00	RARE
☐ 1843O	(2,268,000)					
	50.00	75.00	85.00	200.00	575.00	NOT MADE
☐ 1844	(1,766,000)					
	40.00	60.00	75.00	185.00	625.00	RARE
☐ 1844O	(2,005,000)					
	30.00	45.00	75.00	210.00	650.00	NOT MADE
☐ 1844O Double Date						
	375.00	575.00	1150.00	2750.00	9500.00	NOT MADE
☐ 1845	(589,000)					
	30.00	45.00	85.00	210.00	850.00	RARE
☐ 1845O	(2,094,000)					
	30.00	45.00	70.00	185.00	650.00	NOT MADE
☐ 1846	(2,110,000)					
	30.00	45.00	75.00	175.00	800.00	RARE
☐ 1846 over Horizontal 6						
	100.00	140.00	325.00	700.00	2850.00	NOT MADE
☐ 1846O	(2,304,000)					
	30.00	45.00	70.00	215.00	950.00	NOT MADE
☐ 1847	(1,156,000)					
	40.00	55.00	75.00	175.00	500.00	RARE
☐ 1847 over 6						
	1200.00	1850.00	3500.00	RARE	RARE	RARE
☐ 1847O	(2,584,000)					
	45.00	70.00	80.00	160.00	800.00	NOT MADE
☐ 1848	(580,000)					
	35.00	50.00	115.00	265.00	1000.00	RARE
☐ 1848O	(3,180,000)					
	30.00	50.00	75.00	225.00	900.00	NOT MADE
☐ 1849	(1,252,000)					
	30.00	50.00	80.00	165.00	1000.00	RARE
☐ 1849O	(2,310,000)					
	40.00	65.00	75.00	185.00	950.00	NOT MADE
☐ 1850	(227,000)					
	150.00	215.00	425.00	750.00	1700.00	RARE
☐ 1850O	(2,456,000)					
	30.00	45.00	75.00	215.00	675.00	NOT MADE

DATE	ABP GOOD	G-4 GOOD	F-12 FINE	EF-40 EX. FINE	MS-60 UNC.	PRF-65 PROOF
☐ 1851	(200,750)					
	500.00	750.00	850.00	1250.00	2150.00	RARE
☐ 1851O	(402,000)					
	30.00	45.00	125.00	190.00	700.00	NOT MADE
☐ 1852	(77,130)					
	270.00	450.00	625.00	1000.00	2000.00	RARE
☐ 1852O	(144,000)					
	50.00	80.00	225.00	650.00	2950.00	NOT MADE
☐ 1853**	(3,532,708)					
	30.00	45.00	75.00	300.00	1600.00	RARE
☐ 1853O**	(1,328,000)					
	35.00	40.00	85.00	325.00	2500.00	NOT MADE
☐ 1853O No Arrows						
			3 KNOWN—EXTREMELY RARE—			
☐ 1854***	(2,982,000)					
	30.00	45.00	75.00	165.00	750.00	RARE
☐ 1854O***	(5,240,000)					
	35.00	50.00	75.00	165.00	750.00	NOT MADE
☐ 1855***	(759,500)					
	30.00	45.00	75.00	215.00	800.00	RARE
☐ 1855O	(3,688,000)					
	35.00	50.00	75.00	200.00	775.00	NOT MADE
☐ 1855S***	(129,950)					
	250.00	400.00	875.00	4000.00	RARE	NOT MADE
☐ 1856	(938,000)					
	35.00	50.00	75.00	135.00	575.00	RARE
☐ 1856O	(2,658,000)					
	40.00	60.00	85.00	135.00	475.00	NOT MADE
☐ 1856S	(211,000)					
	60.00	100.00	175.00	650.00	4250.00	NOT MADE
☐ 1857	(1,988,000)					
	32.00	47.00	75.00	135.00	450.00	RARE
☐ 1857O	(818,000)					
	40.00	55.00	75.00	150.00	1050.00	NOT MADE
☐ 1857S	(158,000)					
	60.00	90.00	175.00	750.00	3850.00	NOT MADE
☐ 1858	(4,226,000)					
	30.00	40.00	75.00	135.00	435.00	9000.00
☐ 1858O	(7,294,000)					
	35.00	50.00	75.00	140.00	435.00	NOT MADE

**With Arrows and Rays ***With Arrows

DATE	ABP GOOD	G-4 GOOD	F-12 FINE	EF-40 EX. FINE	MS-60 UNC.	PRF-65 PROOF
☐ 1858S	(476,000)					
	30.00	50.00	75.00	265.00	1100.00	NOT MADE
☐ 1859	(748,000)					
	30.00	50.00	75.00	150.00	550.00	8500.00
☐ 1859O	(2,834,000)					
	30.00	50.00	70.00	150.00	525.00	NOT MADE
☐ 1859S	(566,000)					
	30.00	50.00	75.00	235.00	850.00	NOT MADE
☐ 1860	(303,700)					
	40.00	60.00	75.00	135.00	800.00	7500.00
☐ 1860O	(1,290,000)					
	35.00	55.00	70.00	145.00	525.00	NOT MADE
☐ 1860S	(472,000)					
	35.00	55.00	85.00	175.00	775.00	NOT MADE
☐ 1861	(2,888,400)					
	40.00	60.00	75.00	150.00	525.00	8250.00
☐ 1861O	(330,000)					
	45.00	65.00	75.00	210.00	600.00	NOT MADE
☐ 1861S	(939,500)					
	40.00	60.00	75.00	200.00	850.00	NOT MADE
☐ 1862	(252,350)					
	35.00	50.00	90.00	235.00	650.00	8250.00
☐ 1862S	(1,352,000)					
	40.00	60.00	75.00	150.00	800.00	NOT MADE
☐ 1863	(503,660)					
	35.00	55.00	85.00	225.00	575.00	8250.00
☐ 1863S	(916,000)					
	35.00	55.00	85.00	225.00	650.00	NOT MADE
☐ 1864	(379,570)					
	35.00	55.00	125.00	400.00	1100.00	8250.00
☐ 1864S	(658,000)					
	40.00	60.00	75.00	260.00	900.00	NOT MADE
☐ 1865	(511,900)					
	40.00	60.00	75.00	225.00	1000.00	8000.00
☐ 1865S	(675,000)					
	45.00	65.00	75.00	225.00	850.00	NOT MADE
☐ 1866S*	300.00	500.00	900.00	2400.00	5500.00	NOT MADE

*Note: Part of total mintage: 1,054,000.

HALF DOLLARS—LIBERTY SEATED, 1866–1891
WITH MOTTO ON REVERSE

Arrows at Date   No Arrows at Date   Mint Mark is Below Eagle on Reverse

DATE	ABP GOOD	G-4 GOOD	F-12 FINE	EF-40 EX. FINE	MS-60 UNC.	PRF-65 PROOF
☐ 1866 (745,625)						
	40.00	60.00	80.00	135.00	450.00	4500.00
☐ 1866S*	35.00	55.00	75.00	190.00	600.00	RARE
☐ 1867 (424,325)						
	30.00	50.00	85.00	210.00	425.00	4000.00
☐ 1867S (1,196,000)						
	35.00	55.00	85.00	165.00	475.00	NOT MADE
☐ 1868 (378,000)						
	35.00	55.00	105.00	240.00	525.00	4350.00
☐ 1868S (1,160,000)						
	35.00	55.00	75.00	165.00	475.00	NOT MADE
☐ 1869 (795,900)						
	30.00	45.00	75.00	145.00	435.00	4250.00
☐ 1869S (656,000)						
	40.00	60.00	75.00	185.00	850.00	NOT MADE
☐ 1870 (600,900)						
	30.00	55.00	75.00	175.00	625.00	4350.00
☐ 1870CC (54,617)						
	1000.00	1400.00	3850.00			
☐ 1870S (1,004,000)						
	30.00	55.00	90.00	225.00	1150.00	NOT MADE
☐ 1871 (1,165,360)						
	30.00	55.00	75.00	160.00	600.00	4350.00
☐ 1871CC (139,950)						
	275.00	400.00	800.00	3250.00	RARE	NOT MADE
☐ 1871S (2,178,000)						
	40.00	60.00	75.00	160.00	650.00	NOT MADE

*Part of total mintage: 1,054,000.

DATE	ABP GOOD	G-4 GOOD	F-12 FINE	EF-40 EX. FINE	MS-60 UNC.	PRF-65 PROOF
☐ 1872 (881,550)						
	40.00	60.00	75.00	175.00	550.00	4000.00
☐ 1872CC (272,000)						
	150.00	225.00	400.00	2200.00	RARE	NOT MADE
☐ 1872S (580,000)						
	40.00	60.00	75.00	225.00	1100.00	NOT MADE
☐ 1873 With Arrows (1,815,700)						
	40.00	60.00	75.00	175.00	700.00	RARE
☐ 1873 No Arrows (801,800)						
	30.00	45.00	80.00	235.00	900.00	4000.00
☐ 1873CC With Arrows (214,560)						
	150.00	200.00	400.00	2150.00	8750.00	NOT MADE
☐ 1873CC No Arrows (122,500)						
	200.00	275.00	600.00	2000.00	9500.00	NOT MADE
☐ 1873S With Arrows (288,000)						
	40.00	65.00	185.00	475.00	2400.00	NOT MADE
☐ 1873S No Arrows (5,000)			NONE KNOWN TO EXIST			
☐ 1874 With Arrows (2,360,300)						
	35.00	50.00	75.00	250.00	1050.00	RARE
☐ 1874CC With Arrows (59,000)						
	500.00	750.00	2000.00	5250.00	RARE	NOT MADE
☐ 1874S With Arrows (394,000)						
	30.00	50.00	150.00	400.00	1850.00	NOT MADE
☐ 1875 (6,027,500)						
	30.00	45.00	70.00	130.00	475.00	3500.00
☐ 1875CC (1,008,000)						
	40.00	60.00	125.00	225.00	950.00	NOT MADE
☐ 1875S (3,200,000)						
	30.00	45.00	75.00	135.00	500.00	NOT MADE
☐ 1876 (8,419,150)						
	40.00	60.00	80.00	125.00	500.00	4000.00
☐ 1876CC (1,956,000)						
	45.00	70.00	110.00	225.00	675.00	NOT MADE
☐ 1876S (4,528,000)						
	35.00	50.00	80.00	125.00	450.00	NOT MADE
☐ 1877 (8,304,510)						
	30.00	45.00	80.00	125.00	450.00	4000.00
☐ 1877CC (1,420,000)						
	40.00	60.00	110.00	235.00	675.00	NOT MADE
☐ 1877S (5,356,000)						
	30.00	50.00	70.00	125.00	450.00	NOT MADE

DATE	ABP GOOD	G-4 GOOD	F-12 FINE	EF-40 EX. FINE	MS-60 UNC.	PRF-65 PROOF
☐ 1878	(1,378,400)					
	30.00	42.00	125.00	150.00	475.00	4150.00
☐ 1878CC	(62,000)					
	550.00	750.00	2250.00	3400.00	10000.00	NOT MADE
☐ 1878S	(12,000)					
		RARE	RARE	RARE	RARE	NOT MADE
☐ 1879	(5,900)					
	200.00	285.00	400.00	600.00	800.00	3750.00
☐ 1880	(1,355)					
	180.00	275.00	350.00	600.00	775.00	3600.00
☐ 1881	(10,975)					
	180.00	275.00	375.00	600.00	750.00	3600.00
☐ 1882	(5,500)					
	210.00	325.00	450.00	600.00	800.00	3600.00
☐ 1883	(9,039)					
	210.00	350.00	450.00	600.00	850.00	3600.00
☐ 1884	(5,275)					
	250.00	375.00	475.00	600.00	850.00	3600.00
☐ 1885	(6,130)					
	250.00	375.00	475.00	600.00	850.00	3600.00
☐ 1886	(5,886)					
	275.00	400.00	600.00	650.00	850.00	3600.00
☐ 1887	(5,710)					
	300.00	425.00	625.00	675.00	900.00	3600.00
☐ 1888	(12,833)					
	175.00	300.00	375.00	600.00	800.00	3600.00
☐ 1889	(12,711)					
	200.00	300.00	350.00	600.00	800.00	3600.00
☐ 1890	(12,590)					
	200.00	300.00	375.00	550.00	775.00	3600.00
☐ 1891	(200,600)					
	40.00	60.00	135.00	175.00	475.00	3600.00

HALF DOLLARS—LIBERTY HEAD OR BARBER, 1892–1915

These coins, which resemble the Morgan dollar in portraiture, were prepared from designs by Charles E. Barber and really have no connection with the Morgan dollar aside from the possibility that Barber may have been inspired by it.

The face of Liberty, which faces right, is strong and classical, suggesting the portraiture of Greek coins of ancient time. The weight is somewhat greater than the final version of the Seated Liberty half, 12.5 grams, but its composition is the same, 90% silver and an alloy of 10% copper. The reverse has an attractive eagle with shield and wings spread wide; it holds the traditional arrows and branch. The mint mark appears directly beneath the eagle's tail feathers. Without question this was artistically the finest coin of the half dollar series. It was struck at Philadelphia, New Orleans, Denver, and San Francisco. Not a single rarity is to be found among the Barber halves, with the result that it offers splendid opportunities for completion—even if one wishes to include all the mint marks.

Mint Mark is Below Eagle on Reverse

DATE	ABP GOOD	G-4 GOOD	F-12 FINE	EF-40 EX. FINE	MS-60 UNC.	PRF-65 PROOF
☐ 1892	(935,245)					
	20.00	30.00	75.00	225.00	600.00	3750.00
☐ 1892O	(390,000)					
	210.00	325.00	525.00	675.00	950.00	
☐ 1892S	(1,029,028)					
	175.00	275.00	415.00	650.00	1000.00	
☐ 1893	(1,826,792)					
	15.00	25.00	90.00	265.00	600.00	3650.00
☐ 1893O	(1,389,000)					
	25.00	40.00	135.00	425.00	750.00	
☐ 1893S	(740,000)					
	100.00	200.00	550.00	1000.00	2150.00	
☐ 1894	(1,148,972)					
	25.00	40.00	135.00	325.00	625.00	3850.00
☐ 1894O	(2,138,000)					
	18.00	30.00	125.00	350.00	625.00	
☐ 1894S	(4,048,690)					
	18.00	30.00	90.00	275.00	650.00	

DATE	ABP GOOD	G-4 GOOD	F-12 FINE	EF-40 EX. FINE	MS-60 UNC.	PRF-65 PROOF
☐ 1895	(1,835,218)					
	15.00	23.00	80.00	275.00	600.00	3750.00
☐ 1895O	(1,766,000)					
	30.00	50.00	150.00	310.00	625.00	
☐ 1895S	(1,108,086)					
	25.00	40.00	150.00	325.00	625.00	
☐ 1896	(950,762)					
	18.00	30.00	100.00	285.00	625.00	3650.00
☐ 1896O	(924,000)					
	30.00	50.00	185.00	550.00	1650.00	
☐ 1896S	(1,140,948)					
	75.00	110.00	225.00	525.00	1600.00	
☐ 1897	(2,480,731)					
	10.00	15.00	50.00	235.00	600.00	3650.00
☐ 1897O	(632,000)					
	125.00	175.00	500.00	1100.00	1700.00	
☐ 1897S	(933,900)					
	100.00	140.00	375.00	900.00	2450.00	
☐ 1898	(2,956,735)					
	10.00	15.00	40.00	235.00	600.00	3650.00
☐ 1898O	(874,000)					
	30.00	42.00	250.00	525.00	1250.00	
☐ 1898S	(2,358,550)					
	20.00	35.00	100.00	375.00	900.00	
☐ 1899	(5,538,846)					
	10.00	15.00	45.00	235.00	625.00	3750.00
☐ 1899O	(1,724,000)					
	18.00	30.00	90.00	285.00	725.00	
☐ 1899S	(1,686,411)					
	18.00	30.00	95.00	250.00	650.00	
☐ 1900	(4,762,912)					
	10.00	15.00	50.00	225.00	575.00	3650.00
☐ 1900O	(2,744,000)					
	10.00	15.00	80.00	325.00	875.00	
☐ 1900S	(2,560,322)					
	10.00	15.00	55.00	240.00	700.00	
☐ 1901	(4,268,813)					
	10.00	15.00	50.00	210.00	600.00	3650.00
☐ 1901O	(1,124,000)					
	10.00	15.00	90.00	400.00	1350.00	

DATE	ABP GOOD	G-4 GOOD	F-12 FINE	EF-40 EX. FINE	MS-60 UNC.	PRF-65 PROOF
☐ 1901S	(847,044)					
	25.00	38.00	175.00	725.00	2000.00	
☐ 1902	(4,922,777)					
	10.00	15.00	40.00	210.00	600.00	3650.00
☐ 1902O	(2,526,000)					
	10.00	15.00	65.00	250.00	775.00	
☐ 1902S	(1,460,670)					
	10.00	15.00	75.00	300.00	775.00	
☐ 1903	(2,278,755)					
	10.00	15.00	50.00	225.00	600.00	3850.00
☐ 1903O	(2,100,000)					
	10.00	15.00	65.00	225.00	675.00	
☐ 1903S	(1,920,772)					
	10.00	15.00	70.00	265.00	675.00	
☐ 1904	(2,992,670)					
	10.00	15.00	40.00	225.00	600.00	3850.00
☐ 1904O	(1,117,600)					
	10.00	15.00	90.00	500.00	1400.00	
☐ 1904S	(553,038)					
	30.00	50.00	325.00	1500.00	9750.00	
☐ 1905	(662,727)					
	12.00	18.00	100.00	300.00	625.00	3850.00
☐ 1905O	(505,000)					
	20.00	35.00	125.00	350.00	725.00	
☐ 1905S	(2,494,000)					
	15.00	19.00	65.00	275.00	675.00	
☐ 1906	(1,638,675)					
	10.00	15.00	40.00	240.00	575.00	3750.00
☐ 1906D	(4,028,000)					
	10.00	15.00	40.00	225.00	550.00	
☐ 1906O	(2,446,000)					
	10.00	15.00	40.00	225.00	650.00	
☐ 1906S	(1,740,154)					
	10.00	15.00	65.00	235.00	650.00	
☐ 1907	(2,598,575)					
	10.00	15.00	40.00	225.00	600.00	3750.00
☐ 1907D	(3,856,000)					
	10.00	15.00	40.00	225.00	600.00	
☐ 1907O	(3,946,600)					
	10.00	15.00	40.00	225.00	600.00	

DATE	ABP GOOD	G-4 GOOD	F-12 FINE	EF-40 EX. FINE	MS-60 UNC.	PRF-65 PROOF
☐ 1907S	(3,856,000)					
	10.00	15.00	90.00	385.00	1350.00	
☐ 1908	(1,354,545)					
	10.00	15.00	40.00	225.00	600.00	3650.00
☐ 1908D	(3,280,000)					
	10.00	15.00	40.00	225.00	600.00	
☐ 1908O	(5,360,000)					
	10.00	15.00	40.00	225.00	625.00	
☐ 1908S	(1,644,828)					
	10.00	15.00	85.00	315.00	875.00	
☐ 1909	(2,368,650)					
	10.00	15.00	40.00	225.00	600.00	3650.00
☐ 1909O	(925,400)					
	10.00	15.00	65.00	435.00	1500.00	
☐ 1909S	(1,764,000)					
	10.00	15.00	40.00	250.00	650.00	
☐ 1910	(418,551)					
	12.00	17.00	95.00	375.00	625.00	3650.00
☐ 1910S	(1,948,000)					
	10.00	15.00	50.00	225.00	650.00	
☐ 1911	(1,406,543)					
	10.00	15.00	40.00	225.00	600.00	3650.00
☐ 1911D	(696,080)					
	10.00	15.00	40.00	225.00	600.00	
☐ 1911S	(1,272,000)					
	10.00	15.00	40.00	225.00	600.00	
☐ 1912	(1,550,700)					
	10.00	15.00	40.00	225.00	600.00	3850.00
☐ 1912D	(2,300,800)					
	10.00	15.00	40.00	225.00	600.00	
☐ 1912S	(1,370,000)					
	10.00	15.00	40.00	225.00	625.00	
☐ 1913	(188,627)					
	60.00	95.00	215.00	700.00	1550.00	3850.00
☐ 1913D	(534,000)					
	13.00	18.00	40.00	225.00	600.00	
☐ 1913S	(604,000)					
	13.00	18.00	65.00	275.00	650.00	
☐ 1914	(124,610)					
	125.00	175.00	350.00	850.00	1750.00	3750.00

DATE	ABP GOOD	G-4 GOOD	F-12 FINE	EF-40 EX. FINE	MS-60 UNC.	PRF-65 PROOF
☐ 1914S	(992,000)					
	10.00	15.00	40.00	225.00	600.00	
☐ 1915	(138,450)					
	75.00	135.00	275.00	625.00	1500.00	3850.00
☐ 1915D	(1,170,400)					
	10.00	15.00	40.00	225.00	600.00	
☐ 1915S	(1,604,000)					
	10.00	15.00	40.00	225.00	600.00	

HALF DOLLARS—LIBERTY WALKING, 1916–1947

This attractive design, introduced in 1916, pictured a full-length representation of Liberty on the obverse, dressed in a diaphanous gown and strolling along a field, her right arm upraised as if in acknowledgment of the splendors of nature. In the distance the sun rises (or sets). The designer was A. Weinman, whose initials may be observed—if one has a coin with virtually no wear—on the reverse. His rendition of the eagle on the coin's reverse, a naturalistic type bearing little resemblance to the previously employed shield or heraldic eagle, is a noteworthy piece of art. Sadly, the Liberty Walking half dollar suffered a great deal from rubbing in circulation and much of its delicate linework wore down rapidly, resulting in a shortage of presentable specimens. The collector who wishes to build up a set would be well advised to seek the finest condition obtainable, and be prepared to give a slight premium for coins of the best quality, rather than collect "average" specimens that are, truly, mere shadows of their original selves. The Liberty Walking fifty-cent piece was struck at Philadelphia, San Francisco, and Denver. Its composition is 90% silver and 10% copper with a weight of 12.5 grams and a diameter of 30.6mm.

Note: The sale of Liberty Walking halves as silver bullion should be approached with care. While the majority of common dates in average condition are of no special numismatic value, this series, though modern, does include scarce dates and mint marks that deserve a better fate than the smelter's pot. The silver in these coins amounts to .36169 ounce, or slightly more than one-third of an ounce.

Mint Mark is Under IN
GOD WE TRUST on 1916
and Early 1917. Later Left of "H"
on Reverse

DATE	ABP GOOD	G-4 GOOD	F-12 FINE	EF-40 EX. FINE	MS-60 UNC.	MS-65 UNC.
☐ 1916 (608,000)						
	35.00	50.00	110.00	235.00	350.00	1850.00
☐ 1916D on Obverse (1,014,400)						
	40.00	65.00	95.00	200.00	385.00	2300.00
☐ 1916S on Obverse (508,000)						
	75.00	115.00	300.00	600.00	1000.00	6750.00
☐ 1917 (12,292,000)						
	15.00	20.00	20.00	45.00	125.00	1200.00
☐ 1917D on Obverse (765,400)						
	20.00	30.00	80.00	240.00	625.00	9000.00
☐ 1917D on Reverse (1,940,000)						
	12.00	15.00	50.00	285.00	950.00	18500.00
☐ 1917S on Obverse (952,000)						
	21.00	35.00	160.00	700.00	2500.00	23000.00
☐ 1917S on Reverse (6,554,000)						
	13.00	17.50	20.00	75.00	385.00	14000.00
☐ 1918 (6,634,000)						
	12.00	15.00	20.00	165.00	575.00	3850.00
☐ 1918D (3,853,040)						
	13.00	17.00	50.00	215.00	1350.00	25000.00
☐ 1918S (10,282,000)						
	13.00	17.00	20.00	90.00	485.00	16500.00
☐ 1919 (962,000)						
	20.00	30.00	85.00	525.00	1350.00	9000.00
☐ 1919D (1,165,000)						
	20.00	30.00	110.00	750.00	6500.00	RARE
☐ 1919S (1,552,000)						
	15.00	25.00	90.00	825.00	3500.00	18500.00
☐ 1920 (6,372,000)						
	15.00	18.00	20.00	85.00	350.00	4650.00
☐ 1920D (1,551,000)						
	15.00	18.00	75.00	450.00	1500.00	17500.00

DATE	ABP GOOD	G-4 GOOD	F-12 FINE	EF-40 EX. FINE	MS-60 UNC.	MS-65 UNC.
☐ 1920S	(4,624,000)					
	15.00	18.00	23.00	235.00	875.00	14500.00
☐ 1921	(246,000)					
	125.00	185.00	350.00	2000.00	6500.00	22500.00
☐ 1921D	(208,000)					
	225.00	315.00	575.00	2850.00	9500.00	35000.00
☐ 1921S	(548,000)					
	35.00	55.00	225.00	4250.00	18500.00	RARE
☐ 1923S	(2,178,000)					
	15.00	18.00	30.00	450.00	1650.00	17500.00
☐ 1927S	(2,393,000)					
	12.00	15.00	18.00	175.00	1000.00	9500.00
☐ 1928S	(1,940,000)					
	12.00	15.00	20.00	190.00	1100.00	12000.00
☐ 1929D	(1,001,200)					
	12.00	15.00	20.00	115.00	450.00	3000.00
☐ 1929S	(1,902,000)					
	12.00	15.00	20.00	125.00	475.00	2850.00
☐ 1933S	(1,786,000)					
	13.00	17.00	22.00	75.00	700.00	4000.00
☐ 1934	(6,964,000)					
	8.00	12.00	17.00	20.00	90.00	450.00
☐ 1934D	(2,361,400)					
	8.00	12.00	17.00	32.00	165.00	1450.00
☐ 1934S	(3,652,000)					
	8.00	12.00	17.00	32.00	400.00	3750.00
☐ 1935	(9,162,000)					
	8.00	12.00	17.00	19.00	50.00	285.00
☐ 1935D	(3,003,800)					
	8.00	12.00	17.00	32.00	150.00	2350.00
☐ 1935S	(2,854,000)					
	8.00	12.00	17.00	45.00	300.00	2650.00
☐ 1936	(12,617,901)					
	8.00	12.00	16.00	18.00	40.00	225.00
☐ 1936D	(4,252,400)					
	8.00	12.00	17.00	23.00	85.00	450.00
☐ 1936S	(3,884,000)					
	8.00	12.00	17.00	32.00	150.00	850.00
☐ 1937	(9,527,728)					
	8.00	11.00	16.00	18.00	42.00	210.00

DATE	ABP GOOD	G-4 GOOD	F-12 FINE	EF-40 EX. FINE	MS-60 UNC.	MS-65 UNC.
☐ 1937D (1,760,001)						
	9.00	13.00	18.00	35.00	225.00	675.00
☐ 1937S (2,090,000)						
	9.00	13.00	18.00	27.00	185.00	600.00
☐ 1938 (4,118,152)						
	12.00	16.00	18.00	21.00	75.00	375.00
☐ 1938D (491,600)						
	43.00	62.00	110.00	185.00	500.00	1450.00
☐ 1939 (6,820,808)						
	8.00	11.00	16.00	18.00	45.00	185.00
☐ 1939D (4,267,800)						
	8.00	11.00	16.00	20.00	50.00	165.00
☐ 1939S (2,552,000)						
	10.00	15.00	18.00	25.00	160.00	285.00
☐ 1940 (9,167,279)						
	8.00	11.00	16.00	18.00	35.00	130.00
☐ 1940S (4,550,000)						
	10.00	13.00	17.00	19.00	55.00	350.00
☐ 1941 (24,207,412)						
	8.00	11.00	16.00	18.00	35.00	130.00
☐ 1941D (11,248,400)						
	8.00	11.00	16.00	18.00	42.00	165.00
☐ 1941S (8,098,000)						
	9.00	12.00	17.00	19.00	85.00	800.00
☐ 1942 (47,839,120)						
	8.00	11.00	16.00	18.00	35.00	130.00
☐ 1942D (10,973,800)						
	8.00	11.00	16.00	18.00	38.00	315.00
☐ 1942S (12,708,000)						
	8.00	11.00	16.00	18.00	38.00	525.00
☐ 1943 (53,190,000)						
	8.00	11.00	16.00	18.00	35.00	130.00
☐ 1943D (11,346,000)						
	8.00	11.00	16.00	18.00	45.00	250.00
☐ 1943S (13,450,000)						
	8.00	11.00	16.00	18.00	42.00	325.00
☐ 1944 (28,206,000)						
	8.00	11.00	16.00	18.00	38.00	130.00
☐ 1944D (9,769,000)						
	8.00	11.00	16.00	18.00	38.00	165.00

DATE	ABP GOOD	G-4 GOOD	F-12 FINE	EF-40 EX. FINE	MS-60 UNC.	MS-65 UNC.
☐ 1944S	(8,904,000)					
	8.00	11.00	16.00	18.00	45.00	485.00
☐ 1945	(31,502,000)					
	8.00	11.00	16.00	18.00	35.00	130.00
☐ 1945D	(9,966,500)					
	8.00	11.00	16.00	18.00	38.00	130.00
☐ 1945S	(10,156,000)					
	8.00	11.00	16.00	18.00	42.00	150.00
☐ 1946	(12,118,000)					
	8.00	11.00	16.00	18.00	35.00	175.00
☐ 1946D	(2,151,000)					
	9.00	12.00	17.00	25.00	50.00	135.00
☐ 1946S	(3,724,000)					
	8.00	11.00	16.00	18.00	55.00	175.00
☐ 1947	(4,094,000)					
	8.00	11.00	16.00	18.00	50.00	185.00
☐ 1947D	(3,900,000)					
	8.00	11.00	16.00	18.00	50.00	135.00

HALF DOLLARS—FRANKLIN OR LIBERTY BELL, 1948–1963

The likeness of Benjamin Franklin, which had not previously appeared on a U.S. coin, was installed on the half dollar in 1948. That he was not president can be accounted for by mere circumstance. Had the federal government been formed ten or twenty years sooner, before Franklin had advanced into old age, there is little doubt but that he would have attained the office. Like the Roosevelt dime, introduced two years earlier, this coin was designed by John R. Sinnock. On the reverse is a large representation of the Liberty Bell, adapted from the artwork on the 1926 Sesquicentennial medal celebrating the 150th anniversary of our Declaration of Independence. Franklin is shown in profile facing right. The mint mark is atop the Liberty Bell on the reverse, directly below the words UNITED STATES OF AMERICA. Composition is 90% silver, 10% copper, with a weight of 12.5 grams. The diameter is 30.6mm. It contains .36169 ounces of pure silver, or slightly more than one-third of an ounce.

Mint Mark
is Above
Liberty Bell
on Reverse

DATE	MINTAGE	ABP	F-12 FINE	EF-40 EX. FINE	MS-60 UNC.	MS-65 UNC.
☐ 1948	3,006,184	8.00	10.00	12.00	22.00	75.00
☐ 1948D	4,028,600	8.00	10.00	12.00	22.00	125.00
☐ 1949	5,714,000	9.00	10.00	13.00	40.00	135.00
☐ 1949D	4,120,600	11.00	13.00	20.00	45.00	550.00
☐ 1949S	3,744,000	13.00	14.00	25.00	65.00	135.00
☐ 1950	7,793,509	8.00	10.00	12.00	23.00	100.00
☐ 1950D	8,031,600	8.00	10.00	12.00	21.00	250.00
☐ 1951	16,859,602	8.00	10.00	12.00	18.00	60.00
☐ 1951D	9,475,200	12.00	10.00	12.00	35.00	165.00
☐ 1951S	13,696,000	8.00	10.00	12.00	27.00	70.00
☐ 1952	21,274,074	8.00	10.00	12.00	18.00	65.00
☐ 1952D	25,394,600	8.00	10.00	12.00	18.00	125.00
☐ 1952S	5,526,000	12.00	13.00	14.00	55.00	110.00
☐ 1953	2,796,920	8.00	10.00	12.00	25.00	95.00
☐ 1953D	20,900,400	8.00	10.00	12.00	18.00	100.00
☐ 1953S	4,148,000	12.00	13.00	14.00	30.00	60.00
☐ 1954	13,421,503	8.00	10.00	12.00	17.00	55.00
☐ 1954D	25,445,580	8.00	10.00	12.00	16.00	95.00
☐ 1954S	4,993,400	8.00	10.00	12.00	18.00	38.00
☐ 1955	2,876,381	12.00	13.00	14.00	22.00	47.00
☐ 1956	4,701,384	8.00	10.00	12.00	20.00	35.00
☐ 1957	6,361,952	8.00	10.00	12.00	17.00	38.00
☐ 1957D	19,996,850	8.00	10.00	12.00	17.00	38.00
☐ 1958	4,917,652	8.00	10.00	12.00	17.00	35.00
☐ 1958D	23,962,412	8.00	10.00	12.00	17.00	35.00
☐ 1959	7,349,291	8.00	10.00	12.00	17.00	65.00
☐ 1959D	13,053,750	8.00	10.00	12.00	17.00	90.00
☐ 1960	7,715,602	8.00	10.00	12.00	16.00	95.00
☐ 1960D	18,215,812	8.00	10.00	12.00	16.00	235.00
☐ 1961	11,318,244	8.00	10.00	12.00	16.00	45.00
☐ 1961D	20,276,442	8.00	10.00	12.00	16.00	115.00
☐ 1962	12,932,019	8.00	10.00	12.00	16.00	85.00

DATE	MINTAGE	ABP	F-12 FINE	EF-40 EX. FINE	MS-60 UNC.	MS-65 UNC.
☐ 1962D	35,473,281	8.00	10.00	12.00	16.00	110.00
☐ 1963	25,239,645	8.00	10.00	12.00	15.00	35.00
☐ 1963D	67,069,292	8.00	10.00	12.00	15.00	38.00

HALF DOLLARS—JOHN F. KENNEDY
1964 TO DATE

Following the death of President Kennedy in 1963 there was considerable public sentiment for honoring his memory on coinage. As all coins except the half dollar already carried portraits of presidents, it was decided to install his likeness on this coin, even though its design had been changed as recently as 1948.

The portrait was designed by Gilroy Roberts and Frank Gasparro, the reverse featuring a shield eagle surrounded by stars. As introduced in 1964, the coin was of regular silver composition (90% silver, 10% copper, .36169 ounces of silver by weight) but was altered in 1965 to the clad standard, consisting of a 21% silver/79% copper interior covered with 80% silver/20% copper, total weight of silver being .14792 ounces. Its weight was 11.5 grams, down from 12.5. In 1971 the silver was removed from its core and a new composition used for the exterior, comprising three parts copper to one of nickel. The silver had been entirely replaced and the weight fell to 11.34 grams. The only alteration in design occurred in 1976 when a figure of Independence Hall in Philadelphia was added to the reverse, supplanting the eagle, as part of the Bicentennial program. On the obverse the date appeared as 1776–1976. In the following year the normal reverse was readopted. A quantity of silver-clad pieces were struck in 1976, the first (and last) in this series since 1970.

This has been termed a difficult coin on which to find the mint mark. As first issued, it may be observed on the reverse, above the L and F in the word HALF. In 1968 it was brought to the obverse, beneath the portrait and above the date.

The scarcest Kennedy half dollar is the 1993S silver proof, not minted for general circulation. The Kennedy half dollar has a diameter of 30.6mm.

Mint Mark 1964–1967   Mint Mark 1968 on

DATE	MINTAGE	ABP EX. FINE	EF-40 EX. FINE	MS-60 UNC.	PRF-65 PROOF
☐ 1964	277,254,766	8.00	10.00	11.00	22.00
☐ 1964D	156,205,446	8.00	10.00	11.00	
CLAD COINAGE					
☐ 1965	65,879,366			5.00	
☐ 1966	108,984,933			5.00	
☐ 1967	295,045,968			5.00	
☐ 1968D	246,951,930			5.00	
☐ 1968S Proof Only	3,041,508				6.50
☐ 1969D	129,881,800			5.00	
☐ 1969S Proof Only	2,934,631				6.50
☐ 1970D	2,150,000			16.50	
☐ 1970S Proof Only	2,632,810				9.00
☐ 1971	155,164,000			1.00	
☐ 1971D	302,097,424			1.00	
☐ 1971S Proof Only	3,224,138				4.00
☐ 1972	153,180,000			1.00	
☐ 1972D	141,890,000			1.00	
☐ 1972S Proof Only	3,224,138				4.00
☐ 1973	64,964,000			1.00	
☐ 1973D	83,171,400			1.00	
☐ 1973S Proof Only	2,769,624				4.00
☐ 1974	201,588,250			1.00	
☐ 1974D	79,088,210			1.00	
☐ 1974D Doubled Die		30.00		45.00	
☐ 1974S Proof Only	2,617,350				4.00
☐ 1976 Copper-Nickel Clad	234,318,200			1.00	
☐ 1976D Copper-Nickel Clad	287,565,290			1.00	
☐ 1976S Copper-Nickel Clad Proof Only	7,123,300				4.00
☐ 1976S Silver Clad	4,250,000			6.00	
☐ 1976S Silver Clad Proof	3,215,730				10.00
☐ 1977	43,569,000			1.00	
☐ 1977D	31,450,250			1.00	

DATE	MINTAGE	MS-60 UNC.	PRF-65 PROOF
☐ 1977S Proof Only	3,450,895		5.00
☐ 1978	14,350,000	2.00	
☐ 1978D	13,765,799	3.00	
☐ 1978S Proof Only	3,127,781		5.00
☐ 1979	68,311,400	1.50	
☐ 1979D	15,815,400	1.50	
☐ 1979S Proof Only (I)	3,677,200		5.00
☐ 1979S Proof Only (II)			20.00
☐ 1980P	29,500,000	1.50	
☐ 1980D	33,456,450	1.50	
☐ 1980S Proof Only	3,555,000		5.00
☐ 1981P	29,544,206	1.50	
☐ 1981D	27,839,525	1.50	
☐ 1981S Proof Only (I)	4,063,000		5.00
☐ 1981S Proof Only (II)			15.00
☐ 1982P	10,920,700	2.50	
☐ 1982D	13,150,000	2.50	
☐ 1982S Proof Only (I)	3,229,000		5.00
☐ 1983P	34,100,000	5.00	
☐ 1983D	32,475,000	5.00	
☐ 1983S Proof Only	3,228,621		5.00
☐ 1984P	26,031,084	1.75	
☐ 1984D	26,275,000	1.75	
☐ 1984S Proof Only			5.00
☐ 1985P	18,922,112	4.00	
☐ 1985D	19,911,760	3.50	
☐ 1985S Proof Only	3,372,220		5.00
☐ 1986P	12,110,530	6.00	
☐ 1986D	15,463,220	6.00	
☐ 1986S Proof Only	3,111,000		6.00
☐ 1987P	2,926,121	4.25	
☐ 1987D	2,926,121	4.25	
☐ 1987S Proof Only	3,820,764		5.00
☐ 1988P	12,979,642	4.25	
☐ 1988D	12,121,420	4.25	
☐ 1988S Proof Only	3,100,100		5.00
☐ 1989P	25,100,420	3.00	
☐ 1989D	23,006,111	3.00	
☐ 1989S Proof Only	3,115,720		5.00
☐ 1990P	22,368,400	3.00	
☐ 1990D	20,192,044	3.00	
☐ 1990S Proof Only	3,008,029		5.00
☐ 1991P	14,860,240	2.00	
☐ 1991D	15,156,667	4.00	
☐ 1991S Proof Only	2,877,789		5.00
☐ 1992P	17,658,310	1.50	
☐ 1992D	16,000,110	2.50	

DATE	MINTAGE	MS-60 UNC.	PRF-65 PROOF
☐ 1992S Proof Only	2,858,882		6.00
☐ 1992S Silver Proof Only	1,317,579		16.00
☐ 1993P	15,510,000	2.00	
☐ 1993D	15,000,000	2.50	
☐ 1993S Proof Only	2,633,439		8.00
☐ 1993S Silver Proof	761,353		30.00
☐ 1994P	23,718,000	1.50	
☐ 1994D	23,828,110	1.50	
☐ 1994S Proof Only	2,484,594		10.00
☐ 1994S Silver Proof	785,329		30.00
☐ 1995P	26,496,000	1.50	
☐ 1995D	26,288,000	1.50	
☐ 1995S Proof Only	2,010,000		20.00
☐ 1995S Silver Proof	838,950		45.00
☐ 1996P	24,442,000	1.50	
☐ 1996D	24,744,000	1.50	
☐ 1996S Proof Only	1,750,000		8.00
☐ 1996S Silver Proof	775,000		30.00
☐ 1997P	20,882,000	1.50	
☐ 1997D	19,876,000	2.00	
☐ 1997S Proof Only	2,050,000		15.00
☐ 1997 Silver Proof	742,000		32.00
☐ 1998P	15,646,000	1.50	
☐ 1998D	15,064,000	1.50	
☐ 1998S Proof Only	2,075,000		12.00
☐ 1998S Silver Proof	875,000		27.00
☐ 1998S Silver Matte Finish	106,000	350.00	
☐ 1999P	8,900,000	1.50	
☐ 1999D	10,358,000	2.00	
☐ 1999S Proof	2,540,000		12.00
☐ 1999S Silver Proof	800,000		32.00
☐ 2000P	22,600,000	1.65	
☐ 2000D	19,466,000	1.65	
☐ 2000S Proof	3,100,000		8.00
☐ 2000S Silver Proof	850,000		20.00
☐ 2001P	21,200,000	1.50	
☐ 2001D	19,504,000	1.50	
☐ 2001S Proof	2,300,000		8.00
☐ 2001S Silver Proof	890,000		22.00
☐ 2002P Not Made for Circulation	3,100,000	3.50	
☐ 2002D Not Made for Circulation	2,500,000	4.00	
☐ 2002S Proof	2,275,000		8.00
☐ 2002S Silver Proof	761,500		18.00
☐ 2003P	2,500,000	2.00	
☐ 2003D	2,500,000	2.00	
☐ 2003S Clad Proof	2,172,500		7.00
☐ 2003S Silver Proof	1,125,750		15.00

DATE	MINTAGE	MS-60 UNC.	PRF-65 PROOF
☐ 2004P	2,900,000	1.50	
☐ 2004D	2,900,000	1.50	
☐ 2004S Clad Proof	1,789,500		10.00
☐ 2004S Silver Proof	1,175,950		20.00
☐ 2005P	3,800,000	1.50	
☐ 2005D	3,500,000	1.50	
☐ 2005S Clad Proof	2,275,000		8.00
☐ 2005S Silver Proof	1,069,750		17.00
☐ 2006P	2,400,000	1.50	
☐ 2006D	2,000,000	1.50	
☐ 2006S Clad Proof	2,000,500		8.00
☐ 2006S Silver Proof	1,050,000		17.00
☐ 2007P	2,400,000	1.50	
☐ 2007D	2,400,000	1.50	
☐ 2007S Clad Proof	1,700,000		8.00
☐ 2007S Silver Proof	875,000		17.00
☐ 2008P	1,700,000	1.50	
☐ 2008D	1,700,000	1.50	
☐ 2008S Clad Proof			8.00
☐ 2008S Silver Proof			20.00
☐ 2009P	1,900,000	1.50	
☐ 2009D	1,900,000	1.50	
☐ 2009S Clad Proof			8.00
☐ 2009S Silver Proof			18.00
☐ 2010P	1,800,000	1.50	
☐ 2010D	1,700,000	1.50	
☐ 2010S Clad Proof			8.00
☐ 2010S Silver Proof			20.00
☐ 2011P		1.50	
☐ 2011D		1.50	
☐ 2011S Clad Proof			8.00
☐ 2011S Silver Proof			20.00
☐ 2012P		1.50	
☐ 2012D		1.50	
☐ 2012S Clad Proof			8.00
☐ 2012S Silver Proof			20.00

SILVER DOLLARS

EARLY, 1794–1804; PATTERNS, 1836–1839; REGULAR ISSUE, 1840–1873

The silver dollar, probably the most significant U.S. coin of the 19th century, was authorized on April 2, 1792, and was intended as the chief currency piece or standard for other silver coinage. However, striking was not begun until 1794. The word "dollar" is a corruption of Taler or Thaler, a large silver coin widely distributed in Europe and well known to Colonial America. Prior to use of this term in domestic coinage it had become common to refer to Spain's "pieces of eight" as dollars, so it was natural that this crownlike silver piece should likewise be called a dollar.

The first design, the Flowing Hair variety, was executed by Robert Scot and may be observed on other coinage of that era. Its reverse was an eagle surrounded by the words UNITED STATES OF AMERICA. The composition was .8924 silver and .1076 copper, the addition of this roughly one-tenth part of base metal being needed to provide ruggedness. It weighed 26.96 grams and was the heaviest U.S. silver coin excepting the Trade dollar of much later vintage. Its diameter varies between 39 and 40mm. Along the edge is impressed the words HUNDRED CENTS ONE DOLLAR OR UNIT, interspersed with typographical ornament.

There was very limited striking of dollars in the initial year of their appearance, less than 2,000 being turned out. The following year, 1795, witnessed greatly increased production, but because of the surface softness of these coins and the extensive handling to which they were subjected, it is not easy finding specimens in the best grades of condition. "Average" examples can be had rather easily.

There are two reverse varieties of the 1795 Flowing Hair dollar, one in which three leaves appear beneath the eagle's wings on either side, another with two leaves. Toward the end of 1795 the Flowing Hair obverse was replaced by the Draped Bust, with the so-called "small eagle" reverse (the eagle's wings and body in general being scaled smaller than previously). The Draped Bust obverse is found with dates in small or large numerals, and with the legend UNITED STATES OF AMERICA in small or large letters on the reverse. There are also differences in the number of stars on the obverse. In 1798 the shield eagle reverse was introduced, still with the Draped Bust portrait. These types were continued until 1803 when the striking of silver dollars was suspended.

It was at one time believed that the Mint coined a few dollars in 1804 but it has now been established beyond reasonable doubt that silver dollars dated 1804 were struck in the 1830s for inclusion in proof sets. Apparently the die for an 1804 coin was prepared before any decision was reached to discontinue production and it was stored away at the Mint for those thirty years. In any case, the 1804 dollar is an extremely rare piece whose popularity (and price) has not suffered in the least by results of research into its origins. A handful of restrikes were later made in 1859. There is scarcely any difference in rarity or value between the 1830s proofs and the 1859 restrikes. Of all 1804 silver dollars (both types), fifteen exist.

In 1836 Christian Gobrecht prepared designs for a new silver dollar, which at first was struck in limited numbers to test public response. A seated figure of Liberty appeared on the obverse with a flying eagle reverse. The obverse carried no wording whatever. On the reverse were the words UNITED STATES OF AMERICA and ONE DOLLAR, the eagle set within a ground of stars. There are some varieties of this reverse containing no stars. Full-scale output of silver dollars was not resumed until 1840. For this issue, and for many years following, the shield or heraldic eagle was used for the reverse and the face value was abbreviated into ONE DOL. In 1866 the motto IN GOD WE TRUST was added to the reverse, on a banner flowing above the eagle. The mint mark is located below the eagle and above the statement of value. Striking of dollars in this design ceased in 1873.

SILVER DOLLARS—LIBERTY WITH
FLOWING HAIR, 1794–1795

DATE	MINTAGE	ABP	G-4 GOOD	F-12 FINE	VF-20 V. FINE	MS-60 UNC.
☐ 1794	1,758	2013—Gem Mint State Coin sold for $10,000,000				
☐ 1795*	160,295	1400.00	2000.00	4750.00	6500.00	75000.00

*Includes both 2-Leaf and 3-Leaf Varieties

SILVER DOLLARS—DRAPED BUST, 1795–1798
SMALL EAGLE ON REVERSE

DATE	MINTAGE	ABP	G-4 GOOD	F-12 FINE	VF-20 V. FINE	MS-60 UNC.
☐ 1795	42,738	1300.00	1900.00	4000.00	5250.00	
☐ 1796	72,920	1300.00	1900.00	4200.00	6000.00	
☐ 1796 Small Letters, Small Date						
		1300.00	1900.00	4750.00	8000.00	
☐ 1796 Large Letters, Small Date						
	7,776	1300.00	1900.00	4000.00	6250.00	
☐ 1797 9 Stars Left, 7 Right, Small Letters						
		1350.00	2000.00	5500.00	9000.00	RARE
☐ 1797 9 Stars Left, 7 Right, Large Letters						
		1300.00	1900.00	4200.00	5750.00	RARE
☐ 1797 10 Stars Left, 6 Right						
		1300.00	1900.00	4000.00	5250.00	RARE
☐ 1798 13 Stars						
	327,536	1300.00	1900.00	4200.00	5350.00	RARE

SILVER DOLLARS—DRAPED BUST, 1798–1804
LARGE EAGLE ON REVERSE

DATE	MINTAGE	ABP	G-4 GOOD	F-12 FINE	VF-20 V. FINE	MS-60 UNC.
☐ 1798		700.00	1000.00	1800.00	3000.00	23000.00
☐ 1799*	423,515	725.00	1000.00	2000.00	3000.00	23000.00
☐ 1800*	220,920	700.00	1000.00	2000.00	3150.00	28000.00
☐ 1801*	54,454	750.00	1000.00	2150.00	3500.00	35000.00
☐ 1802*	41,650	850.00	1150.00	2150.00	3500.00	35000.00
☐ 1802 over 1*		850.00	1150.00	2150.00	3500.00	35000.00
☐ 1803*	66,064	875.00	1250.00	2150.00	3650.00	32500.00

☐ 1804 One of the most valued coins in the world—less than 15 known. Three varieties were struck—class 1 PF-68 sold for $4,000,000, class 1 PRF-65 for $1,800,000 and class 3 PRF-58 for $875,000.

*Includes all types

SILVER DOLLARS—LIBERTY SEATED
(GOBRECHT), 1836–1839
WITH FLYING EAGLE ON REVERSE

DATE	MINTAGE	VF-20 V. FINE	EF-40 EX. FINE	PRF-65 PROOF
☐ 1836	approx. 1,025	12500.00	17500.00	90000.00
☐ 1838	approx. 31		Proof Only	135000.00
☐ 1839	approx. 303		Proof Only	90000.00

SILVER DOLLARS—LIBERTY SEATED, 1840–1865
NO MOTTO OVER EAGLE

Mint Mark
is Below Eagle
on Reverse

DATE	ABP	G-4 GOOD	F-12 FINE	VF-20 V. FINE	MS-60 UNC.
☐ 1840	(61,005)				
	200.00	285.00	375.00	450.00	4000.00
☐ 1841	(173,000)				
	200.00	275.00	350.00	450.00	3000.00
☐ 1842	(184,618)				
	200.00	265.00	325.00	450.00	2750.00
☐ 1843	(165,100)				
	200.00	265.00	325.00	450.00	2750.00
☐ 1844	(20,000)				
	250.00	325.00	450.00	550.00	7500.00
☐ 1845	(24,500)				
	225.00	300.00	425.00	525.00	11000.00
☐ 1846	(110,600)				
	200.00	265.00	350.00	475.00	2850.00
☐ 1846O	(59,000)				
	200.00	265.00	400.00	500.00	8250.00
☐ 1847	(140,750)				
	200.00	265.00	350.00	450.00	3000.00
☐ 1848	(15,000)				
	225.00	325.00	550.00	700.00	6250.00
☐ 1849	(62,600)				
	200.00	265.00	350.00	450.00	3000.00
☐ 1850	(7,500)				
	270.00	450.00	700.00	1100.00	8000.00
☐ 1850O	(40,000)				
	225.00	325.00	525.00	850.00	12500.00
☐ 1851	(1,300)				
					45000.00
☐ 1852	(1,100)				
					42500.00

DATE	ABP	G-4 GOOD	F-12 FINE	VF-20 V. FINE	MS-60 UNC.
☐ 1853	(46,110)				
	200.00	325.00	500.00	700.00	4000.00
☐ 1854	(33,140)				
	750.00	1250.00	2850.00	3250.00	9500.00
☐ 1855	(26,000)				
	600.00	950.00	1600.00	2100.00	10000.00
☐ 1856	(63,500)				
	250.00	385.00	600.00	800.00	4750.00
☐ 1857	(94,000)				
	285.00	440.00	600.00	800.00	3500.00
☐ 1858 Proofs Only (80)				Proof 63—17500.00	
☐ 1859	(256,500)				
	200.00	285.00	450.00	600.00	3000.00
☐ 1859O	(360,000)				
	200.00	265.00	325.00	400.00	2250.00
☐ 1859S	(20,000)				
	225.00	350.00	525.00	700.00	14000.00
☐ 1860	(218,930)				
	200.00	265.00	400.00	500.00	2650.00
☐ 1860O	(515,000)				
	200.00	265.00	325.00	400.00	2200.00
☐ 1861	(78,500)				
	400.00	650.00	900.00	1000.00	3350.00
☐ 1862	(12,090)				
	350.00	575.00	900.00	1250.00	5250.00
☐ 1863	(27,660)				
	350.00	550.00	1150.00	1300.00	3500.00
☐ 1864	(31,170)				
	225.00	350.00	500.00	600.00	3500.00
☐ 1865	(47,000)				
	225.00	325.00	450.00	600.00	4500.00
☐ 1866 No Motto, 2 Known				Proof—VERY RARE	

SILVER DOLLARS—LIBERTY SEATED, 1866–1873
MOTTO "IN GOD WE TRUST" ADDED

DATE	ABP	G-4 GOOD	F-12 FINE	EF-40 EX. FINE	MS-60 UNC.
☐ 1866	(49,625)				
	225.00	325.00	400.00	725.00	2500.00
☐ 1867	(47,525)				
	225.00	325.00	375.00	725.00	2500.00
☐ 1868	(162,700)				
	200.00	275.00	365.00	675.00	3000.00
☐ 1869	(424,300)				
	200.00	300.00	365.00	625.00	2500.00
☐ 1870	(416,000)				
	200.00	300.00	350.00	575.00	2250.00
☐ 1870CC	(12,462)				
	350.00	550.00	1000.00	3500.00	32500.00
☐ 1870S				EXTREMELY RARE	
☐ 1871	(1,074,760)				
	200.00	275.00	325.00	575.00	2500.00
☐ 1871CC	(1,376)				
	1000.00	1900.00	4750.00	15000.00	RARE
☐ 1872	(1,106,450)				
	200.00	265.00	325.00	550.00	2200.00
☐ 1872CC	(3,150)				
	700.00	1000.00	3850.00	9000.00	28500.00
☐ 1872S	(9,000)				
	250.00	375.00	500.00	2000.00	11000.00
☐ 1873	(193,600)				
	200.00	285.00	325.00	575.00	2250.00
☐ 1873CC	(2,300)				
	5000.00	8500.00			RARE
☐ 1873S	(700)		UNKNOWN IN ANY COLLECTION		

SILVER DOLLARS—TRADE, 1873–1885

In the early 1870s there was mounting pressure to increase the silver dollar's weight, as American commerce with Japan was being hindered by the fact that our silver dollar was somewhat smaller than European crowns. It was decided to strike a special coin, known as the "Trade dollar," to weigh 27.22 grains and be composed of nine parts silver to one part copper. Much agitation to retain the silver dollar as a domestic circulating coin resulted in the government authorizing this new enlarged version to pass as legal tender (for its $1 face value) in transactions of $5 or less. This caused confusion and dissatisfaction, and in 1878 striking of a separate domestic silver dollar, based upon the pre–Trade dollar standard, was resumed. For a while they were issued simultaneously until the Trade dollar died a gradual death, its final year of striking being 1885. The last year in which they were struck in numbers that could be termed sufficient for free circulation was 1878.

The Trade dollar has sometimes been called one of the handsomest U.S. coins of that denomination. True enough, the design is well drawn, but striking of circulating specimens was in such low relief that the slightest handling all but obliterated the more attractive detailing. Only when seen in proof state can the Trade dollar's beauty be recognized. The designer was William Barber. On the obverse is a seated figure of Liberty, with an eagle reverse. The wording TRADE DOLLAR appears at the foot of the reverse. This is the only U.S. coin to proclaim its composition; the reverse is inscribed 420 GRAINS, 900 FINE meaning, of course, .900 silver to .100 base metal.

Beginning in 1876 the Trade dollar was no longer legal for domestic use. The Treasury Department (assailed from all sides in those days) left itself open to sharp criticism by not offering to redeem Trade dollars until 1887, eleven years later. In diameter the Trade dollar was no larger than the normal issues, 38.1mm., but somewhat thicker. It was the heaviest U.S. silver coin ever minted. Only recently has it come into what might be termed popularity among collectors. In terms of mintage totals vs. regular dollars it is still rather underpriced.

In the following listing, note that superbly struck pieces bring proportionately more than the prices shown.

Mint Mark
is Below Eagle
in Reverse

DATE	ABP	G-4 GOOD	F-12 FINE	EF-40 EX. FINE	MS-60 UNC.
☐ 1873 (397,500)					
	75.00	110.00	175.00	300.00	1200.00
☐ 1873CC (124,500)					
	175.00	250.00	350.00	775.00	10000.00
☐ 1873S (703,000)					
	75.00	110.00	175.00	275.00	1500.00
☐ 1874 (987,800)					
	75.00	115.00	165.00	275.00	1150.00
☐ 1874CC (1,373,200)					
	175.00	250.00	350.00	650.00	3400.00
☐ 1874S (2,549,000)					
	75.00	110.00	165.00	265.00	1050.00
☐ 1875 (218,000)					
	100.00	150.00	325.00	525.00	2600.00
☐ 1875CC (1,573,700)					
	175.00	235.00	325.00	550.00	2750.00
☐ 1875S (4,487,000)					
	75.00	100.00	155.00	265.00	950.00
☐ 1875S over CC (155,000)					
	150.00	225.00	440.00	1000.00	5500.00
☐ 1876 (456,150)					
	75.00	110.00	160.00	265.00	1000.00
☐ 1876CC (509,000)					
	200.00	275.00	425.00	700.00	9000.00
☐ 1876S (5,227,000)					
	75.00	105.00	155.00	250.00	950.00
☐ 1877 (3,039,710)					
	75.00	105.00	155.00	245.00	975.00
☐ 1877CC (534,000)					
	175.00	230.00	375.00	700.00	2500.00

DATE	ABP	G-4 GOOD	F-12 FINE	EF-40 EX. FINE	MS-60 UNC.	PRF-63 PROOF
☐ 1877S (9,519,000)						
	75.00	100.00	150.00	250.00	1000.00	
☐ 1878 Proofs Only (900)						3500.00
☐ 1878CC (97,000)						
	300.00	425.00	1100.00	3750.00	13500.00	
☐ 1878S (4,162,000)						
	75.00	100.00	150.00	250.00	1000.00	
☐ 1879 Proofs Only (1,541)						3500.00
☐ 1880 Proofs Only (1,987)						3500.00
☐ 1881 Proofs Only (960)						3650.00
☐ 1882 Proofs Only (1,097)						3650.00
☐ 1883 Proofs Only (979)						3650.00
☐ 1884 Proofs Only (10)					EXTREMELY RARE	
☐ 1885 Proofs Only (5)					EXTREMELY RARE	

SILVER DOLLARS—LIBERTY HEAD OR MORGAN, 1878–1904 and 1921

For the resumption of the standard silver dollar series a new design was chosen. The work of George T. Morgan, and thereby popularly called the Morgan dollar, it showed a profile head of Liberty backed with an eagle holding arrows and branch. The motto IN GOD WE TRUST was installed above the eagle in Old English Gothic lettering. On the obverse appeared the slogan E PLURIBUS UNUM. For many years the Morgan dollar was the best known and probably most respected silver "crown" in the world. Artistically the work is superb, rendered all the more impressive by the fact that its detailing did not become easily effaced with use. Morgan's goal was to fashion for this country a coin that, if it did not carry the financial power of ancient Greek silver pieces, might be regarded as their equal in design.

The Morgan dollar remained unchanged in weight and composition throughout its history. It was composed of nine parts silver to one part copper and weighed 412.5 grains. The diameter is 38.1mm. After having been struck in large quantities for two and a half decades, production sometimes exceeding 30 million pieces annually, it was suspended in 1904 because of a shortage of silver. Striking was resumed in 1921, but only briefly, as the new Peace dollar was introduced that same year. However there were more Morgan dollars coined in 1921—over 80 million—than in any previous year. The mint mark is placed below the eagle on the reverse. The Morgan dollar contains .77344 ounces of silver, or slightly more than three-quarters of an ounce.

In the following listing, note that superbly struck specimens with few bag marks bring substantially more than the prices listed.

Mint Mark is Below Eagle on Reverse

DATE	ABP	F-12 FINE	EF-40 EX. FINE	MS-60 UNC.	MS-65 UNC.
☐ 1878, 8 Tail Feathers	(750,000)				
	40.00	48.00	55.00	175.00	1550.00
☐ 1878, 7 Tail Feathers	(416,000)				
	35.00	42.00	50.00	85.00	1150.00
☐ 1878, 1879 Reverse					
	35.00	42.00	50.00	100.00	2150.00
☐ 1878, 7 over 8 Tail Feathers					
	37.00	50.00	53.00	185.00	2400.00
☐ 1878CC	(2,212,000)				
	85.00	105.00	140.00	300.00	1750.00
☐ 1878S	(9,774,000)				
	35.00	42.00	50.00	70.00	335.00
☐ 1879	(14,807,100)				
	25.00	30.00	38.00	55.00	900.00
☐ 1879CC	(756,000)				
	125.00	155.00	700.00	4400.00	30000.00
☐ 1879CC over CC					
	140.00	175.00	625.00	4100.00	32000.00
☐ 1879O	(2,887,000)				
	32.00	37.00	42.00	90.00	4150.00
☐ 1879S, 1878 Reverse	(9,110,000)				
	32.00	42.00	50.00	185.00	6000.00
☐ 1879S, 1879 Reverse					
	23.00	28.00	38.00	53.00	175.00

DATE	ABP	F-12 FINE	EF-40 EX. FINE	MS-60 UNC.	MS-65 UNC.
☐ 1880 (12,601,355)					
	28.00	33.00	40.00	50.00	800.00
☐ 1880CC (591,000)					
	150.00	185.00	250.00	525.00	1250.00
☐ 1880CC,1878 Reverse					
	160.00	200.00	265.00	525.00	2250.00
☐ 1880 over 79CC					
	165.00	215.00	300.00	650.00	2850.00
☐ 1880O (5,305,000)					
	30.00	35.00	40.00	90.00	RARE
☐ 1880S (8,900,000)					
	23.00	28.00	40.00	53.00	185.00
☐ 1881 (9,163,975)					
	23.00	28.00	40.00	50.00	750.00
☐ 1881CC (206,000)					
	275.00	350.00	425.00	525.00	925.00
☐ 1881O (5,708,000)					
	30.00	35.00	40.00	55.00	1350.00
☐ 1881S (12,760,000)					
	23.00	28.00	40.00	53.00	185.00
☐ 1882 (11,101,000)					
	23.00	28.00	40.00	53.00	575.00
☐ 1882CC (1,133,000)					
	75.00	95.00	125.00	210.00	525.00
☐ 1882O (6,090,000)					
	30.00	35.00	40.00	55.00	1300.00
☐ 1882O, O over S					
	35.00	42.00	70.00	260.00	RARE
☐ 1882S (9,250,000)					
	23.00	28.00	40.00	53.00	185.00
☐ 1883 (12,191,039)					
	23.00	28.00	40.00	53.00	250.00
☐ 1883CC (1,204,000)					
	75.00	95.00	115.00	215.00	510.00
☐ 1883O (8,725,000)					
	25.00	33.00	42.00	50.00	220.00
☐ 1883S (6,250,000)					
	23.00	28.00	50.00	775.00	RARE
☐ 1884 (14,070,875)					
	23.00	28.00	40.00	55.00	350.00
☐ 1884CC (1,136,000)					
	100.00	125.00	160.00	215.00	525.00
☐ 1884O (9,730,000)					
	23.00	28.00	40.00	50.00	185.00
☐ 1884S (3,200,000)					
	23.00	28.00	50.00	8000.00	RARE
☐ 1885 (17,787,767)					
	23.00	28.00	40.00	50.00	185.00

DATE	ABP	F-12 FINE	EF-40 EX. FINE	MS-60 UNC.	MS-65 UNC.
☐ 1885CC	(228,000)				
	450.00	550.00	600.00	725.00	1250.00
☐ 1885O	(9,185,000)				
	30.00	35.00	40.00	50.00	185.00
☐ 1885S	(1,497,000)				
	23.00	28.00	65.00	285.00	2300.00
☐ 1886	(19,963,886)				
	23.00	28.00	40.00	50.00	185.00
☐ 1886O	(10,710,000)				
	32.00	37.00	45.00	950.00	RARE
☐ 1886S	(750,000)				
	45.00	58.00	115.00	375.00	3150.00
☐ 1887	(20,290,710)				
	23.00	28.00	40.00	50.00	185.00
☐ 1887 over 6					
	40.00	50.00	55.00	410.00	2675.00
☐ 1887O	(11,550,000)				
	23.00	28.00	40.00	75.00	2750.00
☐ 1887O over 6					
	40.00	50.00	67.00	485.00	28500.00
☐ 1887S	(1,771,000)				
	25.00	30.00	42.00	155.00	2650.00
☐ 1888	(19,183,833)				
	27.00	32.00	40.00	52.00	250.00
☐ 1888O	(12,150,000)				
	30.00	35.00	40.00	55.00	650.00
☐ 1888S	(657,000)				
	135.00	175.00	190.00	350.00	3250.00
☐ 1889	(21,726,811)				
	23.00	28.00	38.00	50.00	385.00
☐ 1889CC	(350,000)				
	750.00	1000.00	3000.00	25000.00	RARE
☐ 1889O	(11,875,000)				
	23.00	28.00	40.00	200.00	8250.00
☐ 1889S	(700,000)				
	45.00	60.00	80.00	285.00	2300.00
☐ 1890	(16,802,590)				
	23.00	28.00	40.00	50.00	2150.00
☐ 1890CC	(2,309,041)				
	75.00	105.00	140.00	500.00	5750.00
☐ 1890O	(10,701,000)				
	23.00	28.00	40.00	90.00	2250.00
☐ 1890S	(8,230,373)				
	23.00	28.00	40.00	70.00	1250.00

DATE	ABP	F-12 FINE	EF-40 EX. FINE	MS-60 UNC.	MS-65 UNC.
☐ 1891	(8,694,206)				
	23.00	28.00	40.00	75.00	8500.00
☐ 1891CC	(1,618,000)				
	75.00	100.00	150.00	465.00	5250.00
☐ 1891O	(7,954,529)				
	23.00	28.00	40.00	210.00	8250.00
☐ 1891S	(5,296,000)				
	23.00	28.00	40.00	70.00	1750.00
☐ 1892	(1,037,245)				
	35.00	47.00	53.00	315.00	5500.00
☐ 1892CC	(1,352,000)				
	160.00	210.00	515.00	1500.00	9500.00
☐ 1892O	(2,744,000)				
	24.00	29.00	43.00	285.00	8000.00
☐ 1892S	(1,200,000)				
	45.00	60.00	335.00	RARE	RARE
☐ 1893	(378,792)				
	175.00	210.00	310.00	800.00	9250.00
☐ 1893CC	(667,000)				
	240.00	325.00	1500.00	4500.00	RARE
☐ 1893O	(300,000)				
	175.00	260.00	575.00	3000.00	RARE
☐ 1893S	(100,000)				
	3000.00	4000.00	9500.00	RARE	RARE
☐ 1894	(110,972)				
	950.00	1350.00	1500.00	3850.00	35000.00
☐ 1894O	(1,723,000)				
	40.00	57.00	115.00	950.00	RARE
☐ 1894S	(1,260,000)				
	50.00	65.00	160.00	900.00	8250.00
☐ 1895*	(12,880)				
	22500.00	28000.00	32500.00	45000.00	75000.00
☐ 1895O	(450,000)				
	255.00	375.00	625.00	15000.00	RARE
☐ 1895S	(400,000)				
	375.00	525.00	1275.00	4000.00	28500.00
☐ 1896	(9,976,762)				
	23.00	28.00	40.00	50.00	250.00
☐ 1896O	(4,900,000)				
	30.00	37.00	48.00	1500.00	RARE
☐ 1896S	(5,000,000)				
	35.00	43.00	235.00	2350.00	19000.00
☐ 1897	(2,822,731)				
	23.00	28.00	40.00	50.00	350.00

*Check carefully for removed mint mark.

DATE	ABP	F-12 FINE	EF-40 EX. FINE	MS-60 UNC.	MS-65 UNC.
☐ 1897O	(4,004,000)				
	22.00	28.00	45.00	900.00	RARE
☐ 1897S	(5,825,000)				
	22.00	28.00	40.00	90.00	675.00
☐ 1898	(5,884,725)				
	22.00	28.00	40.00	52.00	285.00
☐ 1898O	(4,440,000)				
	22.00	28.00	40.00	55.00	185.00
☐ 1898S	(4,102,000)				
	32.00	39.00	55.00	285.00	2350.00
☐ 1899	(330,846)				
	125.00	175.00	200.00	275.00	950.00
☐ 1899O	(12,290,000)				
	22.00	28.00	40.00	52.00	185.00
☐ 1899S	(2,562,000)				
	32.00	40.00	60.00	410.00	2300.00
☐ 1900	(8,830,912)				
	22.00	28.00	42.00	50.00	185.00
☐ 1900O	(12,590,000)				
	22.00	28.00	42.00	52.00	185.00
☐ 1900O over CC					
	40.00	55.00	110.00	350.00	1900.00
☐ 1900S	(3,540,000)				
	33.00	38.00	50.00	350.00	1850.00
☐ 1901	(6,962,813)				
	40.00	48.00	125.00	2850.00	RARE
☐ 1901O	(13,320,000)				
	30.00	35.00	42.00	52.00	200.00
☐ 1901S	(2,284,000)				
	30.00	35.00	55.00	500.00	3500.00
☐ 1902	(7,994,777)				
	30.00	35.00	47.00	65.00	500.00
☐ 1902O	(8,636,000)				
	30.00	35.00	40.00	55.00	190.00
☐ 1902S	(1,530,000)				
	80.00	110.00	200.00	415.00	3000.00
☐ 1903	(4,652,755)				
	38.00	48.00	60.00	80.00	375.00
☐ 1903O	(4,450,000)				
	250.00	325.00	375.00	435.00	750.00
☐ 1903S	(1,241,000)				
	90.00	125.00	350.00	4000.00	11000.00

DATE	ABP	F-12 FINE	EF-40 EX. FINE	MS-60 UNC.	MS-65 UNC.
☐ 1904	(2,788,650)				
	25.00	33.00	45.00	110.00	2750.00
☐ 1904O	(3,720,000)				
	35.00	42.00	50.00	60.00	185.00
☐ 1904S	(2,304,000)				
	40.00	55.00	225.00	2000.00	11000.00
☐ 1921	(44,690,000)				
	20.00	24.00	33.00	45.00	185.00
☐ 1921D	(20,345,000)				
	20.00	24.00	34.00	50.00	400.00
☐ 1921S	(21,695,000)				
	20.00	24.00	34.00	50.00	1750.00

SILVER DOLLARS—PEACE, 1921–1935; 1964

It was decided, following the Armistice of 1918, to issue a coin commemorating world peace, and to make this a circulating coin rather than a limited issue. As production of silver dollars was being resumed in 1921, this was the logical denomination. This coin, known as the Peace dollar, was designed by Anthony DeFrancisci, who had some reputation as a designer of medals. Its obverse pictured a profile head of Liberty, quite different in character from those on other coins, and a standing eagle (perched on a mound) on its reverse. The word "Peace" was incorporated into the reverse.

As originally engraved, the dies were similar in nature to those of a medal, intended to strike in high relief. The following year modified dies were introduced. Coining of silver dollars was halted in 1935 and never resumed, the subsequent Ike and Anthony dollars being of a different metallic composition. Mint mark appears beneath the word ONE in ONE DOLLAR on the reverse. The Peace dollar is composed of 90% silver and 10% copper and has a weight of 412.5 grains. The diameter is 38.1mm. and the silver content is .77344 of an ounce.

Note: In 1964 it was decided to resume striking silver dollars after a nearly 30-year lapse. The Peace design was used and production was at the Denver Mint. Before the coins reached circulation, the "silver controversy" of the year culminated in the Mint's decision to switch to clad coinage.

Production of the 1964D silver dollar was halted and the unreleased total of 316,000 was ordered melted. In the intervening years a number of rumors have circulated about specimens that escaped melting, but there is no proven evidence of any in existence. Technically this coin, if it did exist, would be illegal to own and subject to confiscation.

Mint Mark—Below ONE and to Left of Wing Tip

DATE	MINTAGE	ABP	F-12 FINE	EF-40 EX. FINE	MS-60 UNC.	MS 65 UNC.
☐ 1921	1,006,473	90.00	130.00	145.00	300.00	2100.00
☐ 1922	51,737,000	20.00	24.00	33.00	42.00	150.00
☐ 1922D	15,063,000	20.00	24.00	33.00	55.00	650.00
☐ 1922S	17,475,000	20.00	24.00	33.00	52.00	2500.00
☐ 1923	30,800,000	20.00	24.00	33.00	42.00	150.00
☐ 1923D	6,811,000	20.00	24.00	33.00	70.00	1300.00
☐ 1923S	19,020,000	20.00	24.00	33.00	52.00	6500.00
☐ 1924	11,811,000	20.00	24.00	33.00	43.00	175.00
☐ 1924S	1,728,000	20.00	25.00	33.00	235.00	9500.00
☐ 1925	10,198,000	20.00	24.00	33.00	43.00	165.00
☐ 1925S	1,610,000	20.00	24.00	33.00	105.00	23000.00
☐ 1926	1,939,000	20.00	24.00	33.00	58.00	575.00
☐ 1926D	2,348,700	20.00	24.00	33.00	90.00	1000.00
☐ 1926S	6,980,000	20.00	24.00	34.00	60.00	1100.00
☐ 1927	848,000	30.00	35.00	40.00	90.00	3000.00
☐ 1927D	1,268,900	30.00	35.00	40.00	210.00	5000.00
☐ 1927S	866,000	30.00	36.00	40.00	210.00	10000.00
☐ 1928	360,649	275.00	375.00	385.00	525.00	4750.00
☐ 1928S	1,632,000	30.00	38.00	50.00	180.00	21000.00
☐ 1934	954,057	35.00	43.00	50.00	125.00	800.00
☐ 1934D	1,569,500	35.00	43.00	52.00	165.00	2000.00
☐ 1934S	1,011,000	42.00	56.00	180.00	2100.00	8750.00
☐ 1935	1,576,000	35.00	43.00	50.00	85.00	800.00
☐ 1935S	1,964,000	35.00	43.00	52.00	300.00	1700.00
☐ 1964D	316,000			NONE KNOWN TO EXIST		

DOLLARS

DOLLARS—EISENHOWER, 1971–1978

In 1971, following the death of President Eisenhower, a dollar piece with his likeness on the obverse, backed by an adaptation of the Apollo 11 insignia, was placed into circulation. Our astronauts had landed on the moon just two years earlier and this was commemorated by the reverse. Frank Gasparro, chief engraver of the Mint, was its designer. Due to the greatly increased price of silver bullion it was not possible to mint this coin as a "silver dollar." Its size was equivalent to that of earlier silver dollars but the composition bore little resemblance to the old standard. Two versions were struck: a collector's edition with an 80% silver content and ordinary circulating coins with an outer layer of three parts copper and one part nickel enclosing an interior of pure copper. The former had a weight of 24.68 grams. Both have a 38.1mm. diameter. In 1976 a special reverse design was applied, featuring a representation of the Liberty Bell superimposed against the moon, in connection with the Bicentennial. The obverse carried a double date, "1776–1976." Some silver-clad specimens were struck, their specifications the same as stated above. In the following year the original reverse was reinstated. The final year of production was 1978.

DATE	MINTAGE	MS-60 UNC.	PRF-65 PROOF
☐ 1971 Copper-Nickel Clad	47,799,000	9.50	
☐ 1971D Copper-Nickel Clad	68,587,424	7.75	
☐ 1971S Silver Clad	11,133,764	15.00	18.00
☐ 1972 Copper-Nickel Clad	75,390,000	20.00	

| Mint Mark Below Head on Obverse | | Bicentennial 1776–1976 Reverse |

DATE	MINTAGE	MS-60 UNC.	PRF-65 PROOF
☐ 1972D Copper-Nickel Clad	92,548,511	8.75	
☐ 1972S Silver Clad	4,004,657	14.50	16.00
☐ 1973 Copper-Nickel Clad	2,000,056	11.50	
☐ 1973D Copper-Nickel Clad	2,000,000	11.50	
☐ 1973S Copper-Nickel Clad	2,760,339		12.00
☐ 1973S Silver Clad	1,883,140	15.00	50.00
☐ 1974 Copper-Nickel Clad	27,366,000	14.50	
☐ 1974D Copper-Nickel Clad	45,520,175	7.25	
☐ 1974S Copper-Nickel Clad	2,617,350		12.00
☐ 1974S Silver Clad	3,216,420	11.25	16.00
☐ 1976 Copper-Nickel Clad Variety I	4,021,250	11.50	
☐ 1976 Copper-Nickel Clad Variety II	113,325,000	7.75	
☐ 1976D Copper-Nickel Clad Variety I	21,048,650	7.25	
☐ 1976D Copper-Nickel Clad Variety II	82,179,355	5.75	
☐ 1976S Copper-Nickel Clad Variety I	2,845,390		15.00
☐ 1976S Copper-Nickel Clad Variety II	4,149,675		15.00
☐ 1976S Silver Clad (40%)	4,239,460	20.00	30.00
☐ 1977 Copper-Nickel Clad	12,598,220	5.50	
☐ 1977D Copper-Nickel Clad	32,985,000	5.50	
☐ 1977S Copper-Nickel Clad	3,250,895		12.00
☐ 1978 Copper-Nickel Clad	25,702,000	5.50	
☐ 1978D Copper-Nickel Clad	33,012,890	5.50	
☐ 1978S Copper-Nickel Clad	3,127,781		12.00

DOLLARS—SUSAN B. ANTHONY, 1979–1981; 1999

In 1979 the Eisenhower dollar was replaced by one picturing Susan B. Anthony, agitator for female suffrage in the earlier part of the 20th century. The new coin, the target of much controversy, had the distinction of a number of "firsts":

• First general issue U.S. coin to picture a female (excluding mythological and symbolic types)
• First nongold dollar coin of small size
• First general issue U.S. coin with noncircular edge

The Anthony dollar measures 26.5mm., or about the size of a quarter. To avoid its confusion with coins of that denomination, the edge was not made circular but squared out into sections. Its composition is: exterior, three parts copper to one part nickel; interior, pure copper. The weight is 8.1 grams. On the reverse appears the Apollo 11 insignia used for the Eisenhower dollar. Public dissatisfaction with the coin has placed its future in doubt. The designer was Frank Gasparro.

DATE	MINTAGE	MS-60 UNC.	PRF-65 PROOF
☐ 1979P Copper-Nickel Clad	360,222,000	2.25	
☐ 1979D Copper-Nickel Clad	287,000,000	2.25	
☐ 1979S Copper-Nickel Clad Variety I	110,000,000	2.25	7.00
☐ 1979S Copper-Nickel Clad Variety II Proof Only	3,677,000		60.00
☐ 1980P	27,600,000	2.25	
☐ 1980D	41,595,000	2.25	
☐ 1980S	20,425,000	2.25	6.00
☐ 1981P	2,995,000	5.00	
☐ 1981D	3,237,631	5.00	
☐ 1981S Variety I	3,500,000	4.50	6.00
☐ 1981S Variety II			225.00
☐ 1999P	29,592,000	4.00	25.00
☐ 1999D	11,766,000	4.00	

DOLLARS—SACAGAWEA, 2000–2008

The golden dollar's front has Sacagawea portrayed in three-quarter profile. On her back, Sacagawea carries Jean

Baptiste, her infant son. Six months pregnant when she joined the Lewis and Clark expedition, Sacagawea gave birth to Jean Baptiste early in the journey.

In rendering Sacagawea, Goodacre included the large, dark eyes attributed to her in Shoshone legends. Goodacre also used a present-day Shoshone college student as her model.

DATE	MINTAGE	MS-60 UNC.	PRF-65 PROOF
☐ 2000P	768,120,000	2.00	
☐ 2000D	518,916,000	2.00	
☐ 2000S	3,075,000		8.00
☐ 2001P	62,460,000	3.00	
☐ 2001D	70,940,000	3.00	
☐ 2001S	2,300,000		15.00
☐ 2002P Not Made for General Circulation	3,875,000	4.00	
☐ 2002D Not Made for General Circulation	3,700,000	4.00	
☐ 2002S	2,319,000		10.00
☐ 2003P	3,080,000	5.00	
☐ 2003D	3,080,000	5.00	
☐ 2003S			8.00
☐ 2004P	2,660,000	3.00	
☐ 2004D	2,660,000	2.50	
☐ 2004S			8.00
☐ 2005P	2,520,000	3.00	
☐ 2005D	2,520,000	3.00	
☐ 2005S			8.00
☐ 2006P		3.00	
☐ 2006D		3.00	
☐ 2006S			8.00
☐ 2007P		3.00	
☐ 2007D		3.00	
☐ 2007S			8.00
☐ 2008P		3.00	
☐ 2008D		3.00	
☐ 2008S			8.00

GOLD DOLLARS, 1849–1889

No gold dollars were struck in the Mint's early years. It was felt (logically enough, based upon conditions that existed then) that silver would serve adequately for this denomination and that gold should be restricted to coins of a higher face value. However, a series of events occurred, following the California gold strikes of 1849, that rendered gold dollars a necessity. Chief among them was the growing practice of citizens, especially in the West, to trade with bullion rather than coinage. So in 1849 a gold dollar was introduced.

Designed by James Longacre, the gold dollar carried a Liberty head on the obverse and was backed by a simple reverse featuring a wreath and the numeral 1 in Arabic. A series of stars encircled the obverse portrait. As this coin was, by necessity, of diminutive size, elaborate designing was not possible. The Liberty gold dollar weighed 1.672 grams and was composed of 90% gold and 10% copper. It had a diameter of 13mm. The mint mark appears below the wreath. In 1854 the obverse was given over to an Indian Head and the coin made flatter, its diameter increased to 15mm. The weight was unaltered. There was a further change in 1856 when a new die was cast for the obverse, showing the Indian Head a bit larger. This was the final variety for the gold dollar, whose last year of coining was 1889. The gold content by weight for all three types was .04837 of an ounce.

PLEASE NOTE: THE PRICES THAT ARE LISTED REFLECT A GOLD SPOT PRICE OF $1250.00 PER OUNCE.

GOLD DOLLARS—LIBERTY HEAD WITH CORONET, SMALL SIZE, 1849–1854

DATE	MINTAGE	ABP IN F-12	F-12 FINE	EF-40 EX. FINE	MS-60 UNC.
☐ 1849 (4 Varieties)	688,600	140.00	175.00	275.00	750.00
☐ 1849C Closed Wreath	11,634	550.00	750.00	1600.00	RARE
☐ 1849C Open Wreath	4 Known			EXTREMELY RARE	
☐ 1849D	21,588	750.00	1000.00	2000.00	RARE
☐ 1849O	215,000	125.00	175.00	350.00	900.00
☐ 1850	481,953	120.00	170.00	275.00	500.00
☐ 1850C	6,966	600.00	950.00	1450.00	RARE
☐ 1850D	8,382	750.00	1100.00	1800.00	RARE
☐ 1850O	14,000	145.00	240.00	500.00	3000.00
☐ 1851	3,317,671	120.00	170.00	275.00	500.00
☐ 1851C	41,267	600.00	900.00	1450.00	3500.00
☐ 1851D	9,832	750.00	1050.00	1850.00	RARE
☐ 1851O	290,000	130.00	175.00	300.00	800.00
☐ 1852	2,045,351	120.00	170.00	275.00	550.00
☐ 1852C	9,434	650.00	950.00	1400.00	RARE
☐ 1852D	6,360	1000.00	1250.00	1800.00	RARE
☐ 1852O	140,000	125.00	175.00	350.00	1350.00
☐ 1853	4,076,051	120.00	170.00	275.00	500.00
☐ 1853C	11,515	650.00	1000.00	1500.00	RARE
☐ 1853D	6,583	850.00	1250.00	1850.00	RARE
☐ 1853O	290,000	130.00	175.00	285.00	750.00
☐ 1854	855,502	130.00	180.00	290.00	650.00
☐ 1854D	2,935	850.00	1250.00	2350.00	RARE
☐ 1854S	14,635	225.00	325.00	550.00	2650.00

GOLD DOLLARS—SMALL INDIAN HEAD, FEATHER HEADDRESS, LARGE SIZE, 1854–1856

Mint Mark Below Wreath on Reverse

DATE	MINTAGE	ABP IN F-12	F-12 FINE	EF-40 EX. FINE	MS-60	PROOF-65 UNC.
☐ 1854	783,943	185.00	250.00	450.00	2000.00	RARE
☐ 1855	758,269	185.00	250.00	450.00	2000.00	RARE
☐ 1855C	8,903	750.00	1250.00	6500.00	RARE	
☐ 1855D	1,811	2700.00	4500.00	RARE	RARE	
☐ 1855O	55,000	275.00	400.00	800.00	RARE	
☐ 1856S	24,600	450.00	675.00	1600.00	RARE	

GOLD DOLLARS—LARGE LIBERTY HEAD, FEATHER HEADDRESS, LARGE SIZE, 1856–1889

Mint Mark Below Wreath on Reverse

DATE	ABP IN F-12	F-12 FINE	EF-40 EX. FINE	MS-60 UNC.
☐ 1856 Upright 5 (1,762,936)				
	135.00	210.00	325.00	585.00
☐ 1856 Slant 5 (1,762,936)				
	135.00	210.00	300.00	450.00
☐ 1856D (1,460)				
	1700.00	2500.00	RARE	RARE
☐ 1857 (774,789)				
	135.00	210.00	275.00	450.00
☐ 1857C (13,280)				
	625.00	975.00	1600.00	RARE
☐ 1857D (3,533)				
	700.00	1100.00	2250.00	RARE
☐ 1857S (10,000)				
	150.00	235.00	750.00	RARE
☐ 1858 (117,995)				
	120.00	190.00	275.00	475.00
☐ 1858D (3,477)				
	750.00	1150.00	1650.00	RARE
☐ 1858S (10,000)				
	200.00	275.00	600.00	RARE

DATE	ABP IN F-12	F-12 FINE	EF-40 EX. FINE	MS-60 UNC.	PRF-65 PROOF
☐ 1859	(168,244)				
	135.00	200.00	285.00	450.00	RARE
☐ 1859C	(5,235)				
	700.00	1050.00	1850.00	RARE	
☐ 1859D	(4,952)				
	750.00	1100.00	1875.00	RARE	
☐ 1859S	(15,000)				
	150.00	235.00	575.00	RARE	
☐ 1860	(36,688)				
	130.00	200.00	285.00	500.00	RARE
☐ 1860D	(1,566)				
	1500.00	2250.00	RARE	RARE	
☐ 1860S	(13,000)				
	200.00	285.00	525.00	2800.00	
☐ 1861	(527,499)				
	125.00	200.00	300.00	485.00	RARE
☐ 1861D		RARE	RARE	RARE	
☐ 1862	(1,326,865)				
	130.00	210.00	285.00	500.00	RARE
☐ 1863	(6,250)				
	425.00	675.00	1500.00	RARE	RARE
☐ 1864	(5,950)				
	225.00	350.00	575.00	1500.00	RARE
☐ 1865	(3,725)				
	225.00	350.00	550.00	1500.00	RARE
☐ 1866	(7,180)				
	210.00	285.00	500.00	1000.00	RARE
☐ 1867	(5,250)				
	225.00	350.00	600.00	1050.00	RARE
☐ 1868	(10,525)				
	180.00	235.00	375.00	900.00	RARE
☐ 1869	(5,925)				
	175.00	350.00	525.00	1150.00	RARE
☐ 1870	(6,335)				
	185.00	250.00	500.00	900.00	RARE
☐ 1870S	(3,000)				
	225.00	325.00	850.00	2500.00	
☐ 1871	(3,930)				
	185.00	265.00	450.00	825.00	RARE
☐ 1872	(3,530)				
	185.00	250.00	450.00	1150.00	RARE

DATE	ABP IN F-12	F-12 FINE	EF-40 EX. FINE	MS-60 UNC.	PRF-65 PROOF
☐ 1873 Open 3 (125,125)					
	125.00	185.00	275.00	500.00	
☐ 1873 Closed 3					
	225.00	300.00	800.00	1650.00	RARE
☐ 1874 (198,820)					
	125.00	185.00	275.00	500.00	RARE
☐ 1875 (420)					
	1200.00	2000.00	4000.00	RARE	RARE
☐ 1876 (3,245)					
	185.00	265.00	400.00	750.00	RARE
☐ 1877 (3,920)					
	135.00	225.00	400.00	850.00	RARE
☐ 1878 (3,020)					
	150.00	235.00	400.00	725.00	RARE
☐ 1879 (3,030)					
	150.00	225.00	350.00	650.00	RARE
☐ 1880 (1,636)					
	130.00	200.00	285.00	550.00	RARE
☐ 1881 (7,660)					
	130.00	200.00	285.00	550.00	RARE
☐ 1882 (5,040)					
	135.00	200.00	310.00	575.00	RARE
☐ 1883 (10,840)					
	130.00	200.00	310.00	500.00	RARE
☐ 1884 (6,206)					
	130.00	200.00	310.00	500.00	RARE
☐ 1885 (12,205)					
	130.00	200.00	310.00	500.00	RARE
☐ 1886 (6,016)					
	130.00	200.00	310.00	500.00	RARE
☐ 1887 (8,543)					
	130.00	200.00	310.00	500.00	RARE
☐ 1888 (16,080)					
	130.00	185.00	285.00	475.00	RARE
☐ 1889 (30,729)					
	120.00	175.00	265.00	465.00	RARE

Note: Many gold dollars in the 1880s were hoarded and appear in gem, proof-like condition. Beware of these pieces being sold as proofs.

QUARTER EAGLES—
$2.50 GOLD PIECES

The $2.50 gold piece, authorized on April 2, 1792, was known as a "Quarter Eagle" (i.e., the quarter part of an Eagle or $10 gold piece). Striking was not begun until 1796. As early production was extremely limited—in no year were as many as 10,000 struck until 1834—these are scarce and valuable coins. Designed by Robert Scot, the original type featured a capped Liberty on the obverse and shield eagle reverse. The portrait is quite different from that used on silver coinage and in general the engraving may be said to be somewhat superior. No wording other than LIBERTY adorns the obverse, with UNITED STATES OF AMERICA on the reverse. The composition was .9167 gold to .0833 copper, or more than nine-tenths gold, with a weight of 4.37 grams and a diameter that varied slightly but normally was about 20mm.

There are two obverse types, one with and one without a circular border of stars. In 1808 the portrait, while retaining the cap, was entirely redesigned. It was shifted around to face left instead of right, the cap was deemphasized, Liberty's features were redrawn in an effort at greater femininity, her hair was made curlier, and the eagle was likewise refurbished. John Reich was the designer. From 1809 to 1820 no quarter eagles were minted. When the series was resumed in 1821 it was with modified obverse and reverse types and the diameter had shrunk to 18.5mm. However, the coin contained fully as much gold as previously and the decreased diameter was compensated for by a slight increase in thickness.

The obverse was changed in 1834 to the so-called Classic Head type, a more stylish rendition of Liberty, designed by the Mint's chief designer, William Kneass (pronounced Niece). The weight was reduced to 4.18 grams and the composition altered to contain less than nine-tenths gold: .8992 to .1008 copper. The diameter was 18.2mm. Christian Gobrecht made some alterations to this design in 1840 but it was not materially changed. However, the gold content was increased to an even .900 and the diameter brought down to 18mm. Total gold content by weight was .12094. This design remained in use for sixty-seven years, surpassed for longevity only by the Lincoln penny (1909–present).

An interesting variation occurred in 1848, the so-called California Quarter Eagle. In that year Colonel Mason, the Military Governor of California, shipped about 230 ounces of gold to Secretary of War Marcy in Washington, D.C. Marcy had the bullion melted down and struck into Quarter Eagles, distinguished by the abbreviation CAL. above the eagle's head on the reverse. This was not an integral part of the design but was stamped separately. As little more than 1,000 specimens were struck, it became a choice collector's item. Purchasers should be on guard against fakes. The Gobrecht Quarter Eagle was discontinued in 1907. Specimens dated after 1900, and some earlier ones, are valued primarily for their bullion content.

PLEASE NOTE: THE PRICES THAT ARE LISTED REFLECT A GOLD SPOT PRICE OF $1250.00 PER OUNCE.

QUARTER EAGLES—LIBERTY CAP, 1796–1807

1796
No Stars

1797–1807
With Stars

1796–1807

DATE	MINTAGE	ABP IN F-12	F-12 FINE	EF-40 EX. FINE	MS-60 UNC.
☐ 1796 No Stars	963			VERY RARE	
☐ 1796 With Stars	432			VERY RARE	
☐ 1797	427			VERY RARE	
☐ 1798	1,094	4250.00	6000.00	17500.00	RARE
☐ 1802 over 1	3,033	4250.00	6000.00	17500.00	RARE
☐ 1804, 14 Star Reverse					
	3,327	4250.00	6250.00	18000.00	RARE
☐ 1804, 13 Star Reverse				VERY RARE	

DATE	MINTAGE	ABP IN F-12	F-12 FINE	EF-40 EX. FINE	MS-60 UNC.
☐ 1805	1,781	3750.00	6250.00	17500.00	RARE
☐ 1806 over 4	1,616	4000.00	7000.00	18000.00	RARE
☐ 1806 over 5		5000.00	8500.00	20000.00	
☐ 1807	6,812	3500.00	5750.00	16750.00	RARE

QUARTER EAGLES—BUST TYPE, TURBAN HEAD, 1808–1834

1808
Draped
Bust
Round Cap

1821–1834
Undraped
Liberty
Round Cap

1808–1834
Motto
Over Eagle

DATE	MINTAGE	ABP IN F-12	F-12 FINE	EF-40 EX. FINE	MS-60 UNC.
☐ 1808	2,710	17500.00	24000.00	VERY RARE	
REDUCED SIZE (18.5mm. dia.)					
☐ 1821	6,448	5000.00	6500.00	RARE	RARE
☐ 1824 over 21	2,600	6000.00	7500.00	RARE	RARE
☐ 1825	4,434	5250.00	6750.00	RARE	RARE
☐ 1826 over 25	760	6000.00	8000.00	RARE	RARE
☐ 1827	2,800	5500.00	7500.00	RARE	RARE
☐ 1829	3,403	4000.00	6000.00	11000.00	RARE
☐ 1830	4,540	4000.00	6000.00	11000.00	RARE
☐ 1831	4,520	4000.00	6000.00	11000.00	RARE
☐ 1832	4,400	4000.00	6000.00	11000.00	RARE
☐ 1833	4,160	4000.00	6000.00	11500.00	RARE
☐ 1834 Motto	4,000	—	RARE	RARE	RARE

QUARTER EAGLES—LIBERTY HEAD WITH RIBBONS, 1834–1839 NO MOTTO OVER EAGLE

Mint Mark is Above Date on Obverse

DATE	MINTAGE	ABP IN F-12	F-12 FINE	EF-40 EX. FINE	MS-60 UNC.
☐ 1834 No Motto	112,234	250.00	375.00	825.00	3850.00
☐ 1835	131,402	250.00	375.00	825.00	3850.00
☐ 1836	547,986	235.00	350.00	825.00	3850.00
☐ 1837	45,080	400.00	550.00	1200.00	4500.00
☐ 1838	47,030	250.00	375.00	875.00	4350.00
☐ 1838C	7,908	725.00	1100.00	3850.00	RARE
☐ 1839	27,021	500.00	650.00	1750.00	RARE
☐ 1839C	18,173	800.00	1200.00	3500.00	RARE
☐ 1839D	13,674	1100.00	1450.00	5250.00	RARE
☐ 18390	17,781	350.00	450.00	1750.00	RARE

QUARTER EAGLES—LIBERTY HEAD WITH CORONET, 1840–1907

Mint Mark is Below Eagle on Reverse

DATE	MINTAGE	ABP IN F-12	F-12 FINE	EF-40 EX. FINE	MS-60 UNC.
☐ 1840	18,859	200.00	285.00	950.00	6350.00
☐ 1840C	12,838	900.00	1300.00	2700.00	RARE
☐ 1840D	3,532	1750.00	2350.00	RARE	RARE
☐ 18400	26,200	250.00	375.00	900.00	RARE
☐ 1841			PROOF—EXTREMELY RARE		
☐ 1841C	10,297	850.00	1100.00	2500.00	RARE
☐ 1841D	4,164	1000.00	1400.00	5000.00	RARE

DATE	MINTAGE	ABP IN F-12	F-12 FINE	EF-40 EX. FINE	MS-60 UNC.
☐ 1842	2,823	750.00	1100.00	3100.00	RARE
☐ 1842C	6,737	1000.00	1350.00	3400.00	RARE
☐ 1842D	4,643	1050.00	1350.00	4150.00	RARE
☐ 1842O	19,800	250.00	385.00	1150.00	RARE
☐ 1843	100,546	225.00	280.00	500.00	2850.00
☐ 1843C Small Date	26,096	1200.00	1500.00	RARE	RARE
☐ 1843C Large Date	26,096	800.00	1000.00	2500.00	RARE
☐ 1843D	36,209	850.00	1100.00	2250.00	RARE
☐ 1843O Small Date	368,002	225.00	280.00	525.00	1900.00
☐ 1843O Large Date	368,002	250.00	350.00	850.00	RARE
☐ 1844	6,784	275.00	400.00	1000.00	RARE
☐ 1844C	11,622	750.00	950.00	3000.00	RARE
☐ 1844D	17,332	800.00	1000.00	2500.00	RARE
☐ 1845	91,051	225.00	280.00	450.00	1250.00
☐ 1845D	19,460	800.00	1100.00	2650.00	RARE
☐ 1845O	4,000	550.00	850.00	2500.00	RARE
☐ 1846	21,598	225.00	310.00	575.00	RARE
☐ 1846C	4,808	850.00	1150.00	2850.00	RARE
☐ 1846D	19,303	850.00	1200.00	2650.00	RARE
☐ 1846O	66,000	225.00	325.00	575.00	RARE
☐ 1847	29,814	225.00	300.00	475.00	3250.00
☐ 1847C	23,226	700.00	950.00	2250.00	RARE
☐ 1847D	15,784	750.00	1000.00	2650.00	RARE
☐ 1847O	124,000	250.00	325.00	500.00	RARE
☐ 1848	8,886	300.00	400.00	950.00	RARE
☐ 1848 CAL. above Eagle					
	1,389		32500.00	40000.00	RARE
☐ 1848C	16,788	800.00	1050.00	2150.00	RARE
☐ 1848D	13,771	900.00	1150.00	2400.00	RARE
☐ 1849	23,294	250.00	325.00	550.00	2650.00
☐ 1849C	10,220	850.00	1100.00	2300.00	RARE
☐ 1849D	10,945	850.00	1100.00	2100.00	RARE
☐ 1850	252,923	225.00	275.00	450.00	1000.00
☐ 1850C	9,148	800.00	1100.00	2150.00	RARE
☐ 1850D	12,148	850.00	1150.00	2250.00	RARE
☐ 1850O	84,000	240.00	325.00	550.00	RARE
☐ 1851	1,372,748	225.00	280.00	400.00	525.00
☐ 1851C	14,923	750.00	1050.00	2500.00	RARE
☐ 1851D	11,264	850.00	1150.00	2350.00	RARE
☐ 1851O	148,000	240.00	350.00	450.00	3500.00

DATE	MINTAGE	ABP IN F-12	F-12 FINE	EF-40 EX. FINE	MS-60 UNC.
☐ 1852	1,159,681	225.00	310.00	425.00	600.00
☐ 1852C	9,772	750.00	925.00	2350.00	RARE
☐ 1852D	4,078	800.00	1200.00	2750.00	RARE

DATE	ABP IN F-12	F-12 FINE	EF-40 EX. FINE	MS-60 UNC.	PRF-63 PROOF
☐ 1852O (140,000)	225.00	325.00	400.00	4150.00	
☐ 1853 (1,404,668)	225.00	300.00	400.00	575.00	
☐ 1853D (3,178)	1000.00	1250.00	3500.00	RARE	
☐ 1854 (596,258)	225.00	300.00	400.00	525.00	
☐ 1854C (7,295)	900.00	1200.00	2350.00	RARE	
☐ 1854D (1,760)	1500.00	2150.00	RARE	RARE	
☐ 1854O (153,000)	225.00	325.00	500.00	1750.00	
☐ 1854S (246)	EXTREMELY RARE				
☐ 1855 (235,480)	225.00	300.00	425.00	575.00	
☐ 1855C (3,677)	900.00	1225.00	3250.00	RARE	
☐ 1855D (1,123)	2250.00	2850.00	RARE	RARE	
☐ 1856 (384,240)	225.00	315.00	425.00	575.00	RARE
☐ 1856C (7,913)	850.00	1150.00	2850.00	RARE	
☐ 1856D (874)		RARE	RARE	RARE	
☐ 1856O (21,100)	225.00	325.00	800.00	RARE	
☐ 1856S (71,120)	225.00	325.00	450.00	4250.00	
☐ 1857 (214,130)	225.00	315.00	400.00	500.00	RARE
☐ 1857D (2,364)	900.00	1250.00	3000.00	RARE	

DATE	ABP IN F-12	F-12 FINE	EF-40 EX. FINE	MS-60 UNC.	PRF-63 PROOF
☐ 1857O (34,000)					
	225.00	350.00	500.00	4150.00	
☐ 1857S (68,000)					
	225.00	350.00	500.00	5250.00	
☐ 1858 (47,377)					
	225.00	320.00	400.00	1350.00	RARE
☐ 1858C (9,056)					
	750.00	1000.00	2350.00	RARE	
☐ 1859 Reverse of 1858					
	225.00	350.00	600.00	2750.00	
☐ 1859 (39,464)					
	225.00	300.00	425.00	1250.00	22500.00
☐ 1859D (2,244)					
	900.00	1500.00	3500.00	RARE	
☐ 1859S (15,200)					
	240.00	400.00	1200.00	RARE	
☐ 1860 Reverse of 1858					
	800.00	1000.00	2250.00	RARE	
☐ 1860 (22,675)					
	225.00	300.00	400.00	1150.00	21500.00
☐ 1860C (7,469)					
	950.00	1150.00	2500.00	RARE	
☐ 1860S (35,600)					
	250.00	350.00	625.00	3750.00	
☐ 1861 Reverse of 1858					
	400.00	600.00	1200.00	4250.00	
☐ 1861 (1,272,518)					
	250.00	350.00	400.00	750.00	20000.00
☐ 1861S (24,000)					
	265.00	365.00	900.00	RARE	
☐ 1862 (112,353)					
	240.00	350.00	800.00	4500.00	17500.00
☐ 1862 2 over 1					
	500.00	675.00	1850.00	RARE	
☐ 1862S (8,000)					
	550.00	800.00	2250.00	RARE	
☐ 1863 VERY RARE	PROOF ONLY				55000.00
☐ 1863S (10,800)					
	350.00	550.00	1650.00	RARE	
☐ 1864 (2,874)					
	2750.00	4000.00	RARE	RARE	17000.00
☐ 1865 (1,545)					
	2250.00	3000.00	RARE	RARE	18500.00

DATE	ABP IN F-12	F-12 FINE	EF-40 EX. FINE	MS-60 UNC.	PRF-63 PROOF
☐ 1865S	(23,376)				
	275.00	375.00	750.00	5000.00	
☐ 1866	(3,110)				
	650.00	900.00	3150.00	RARE	14000.00
☐ 1866S	(38,461)				
	250.00	350.00	775.00	6500.00	
☐ 1867	(3,250)				
	275.00	365.00	725.00	4500.00	14000.00
☐ 1867S	(28,000)				
	275.00	365.00	675.00	3850.00	
☐ 1868	(3,625)				
	250.00	350.00	450.00	2150.00	15000.00
☐ 1868S	(34,000)				
	265.00	385.00	500.00	3500.00	
☐ 1869	(4,343)				
	250.00	325.00	475.00	3000.00	13000.00
☐ 1869S	(29,500)				
	275.00	350.00	525.00	3650.00	
☐ 1870	(4,555)				
	240.00	300.00	475.00	4000.00	12500.00
☐ 1870S	(16,000)				
	240.00	300.00	465.00	4000.00	
☐ 1871	(5,350)				
	250.00	325.00	450.00	2250.00	11500.00
☐ 1871S	(22,000)				
	225.00	300.00	400.00	2150.00	
☐ 1872	(3,030)				
	225.00	325.00	800.00	4650.00	11500.00
☐ 1872S	(18,000)				
	225.00	275.00	525.00	4150.00	
☐ 1873 Open 3	(178,025)				
	225.00	280.00	400.00	650.00	
☐ 1873 Closed 3					
	225.00	280.00	400.00	700.00	11000.00
☐ 1873S	(27,000)				
	225.00	300.00	475.00	2850.00	
☐ 1874	(3,940)				
	225.00	300.00	450.00	2350.00	13500.00
☐ 1875	(420)				
	1750.00	2500.00	RARE	RARE	15000.00
☐ 1875S	(11,600)				
	225.00	300.00	450.00	3750.00	
☐ 1876	(4,221)				
	275.00	350.00	750.00	3500.00	10500.00

DATE	ABP IN F-12	F-12 FINE	EF-40 EX. FINE	MS-60 UNC.	PRF-63 PROOF
☐ 1876S	(5,000)				
	225.00	320.00	550.00	2850.00	
☐ 1877	(1,652)				
	265.00	350.00	800.00	3150.00	11500.00
☐ 1877S	(35,000)				
	225.00	280.00	400.00	650.00	
☐ 1878	(286,260)				
	225.00	280.00	400.00	500.00	15000.00
☐ 1878S	(55,000)				
	225.00	280.00	400.00	550.00	
☐ 1879	(88,900)				
	225.00	280.00	400.00	525.00	10000.00
☐ 1879S	(43,500)				
	225.00	280.00	400.00	2150.00	
☐ 1880	(2,996)				
	225.00	280.00	400.00	1800.00	10000.00
☐ 1881	(680)				
	900.00	1250.00	3500.00	9500.00	11000.00
☐ 1882	(4,040)				
	225.00	280.00	400.00	1000.00	9500.00
☐ 1883	(1,960)				
	225.00	280.00	525.00	2500.00	9500.00
☐ 1884	(1,993)				
	225.00	280.00	525.00	1600.00	9500.00
☐ 1885	(887)				
	450.00	650.00	1950.00	5500.00	10000.00
☐ 1886	(4,088)				
	225.00	280.00	450.00	1000.00	8500.00
☐ 1887	(6,282)				
	225.00	280.00	450.00	850.00	8000.00
☐ 1888	(16,098)				
	225.00	280.00	400.00	525.00	8000.00
☐ 1889	(17,648)				
	225.00	280.00	400.00	525.00	8500.00
☐ 1890	(8,813)				
	225.00	280.00	400.00	550.00	8000.00
☐ 1891	(11,040)				
	225.00	280.00	425.00	525.00	7500.00
☐ 1892	(2,545)				
	225.00	280.00	400.00	850.00	7500.00
☐ 1893	(30,106)				
	225.00	280.00	400.00	600.00	7500.00

DATE	ABP IN F-12	F-12 FINE	EF-40 EX. FINE	MS-60 UNC.	PRF-63 PROOF
☐ 1894	(4,122)				
	240.00	280.00	400.00	900.00	7000.00
☐ 1895	(6,119)				
	225.00	265.00	375.00	500.00	5500.00
☐ 1896	(19,202)				
	225.00	265.00	375.00	500.00	5500.00
☐ 1897	(28,551)				
	225.00	265.00	375.00	500.00	5500.00
☐ 1898	(24,165)				
	225.00	265.00	375.00	500.00	5500.00
☐ 1899	(27,350)				
	225.00	265.00	375.00	500.00	5500.00
☐ 1900	(67,205)				
	225.00	265.00	375.00	500.00	5500.00
☐ 1901	(91,323)				
	225.00	265.00	375.00	500.00	5500.00
☐ 1902	(133,733)				
	225.00	265.00	375.00	500.00	5500.00
☐ 1903	(201,257)				
	225.00	265.00	375.00	500.00	5500.00
☐ 1904	(160,960)				
	225.00	265.00	375.00	500.00	5500.00
☐ 1905	(217,944)				
	225.00	265.00	375.00	500.00	5500.00
☐ 1906	(179,490)				
	225.00	265.00	375.00	500.00	5500.00
☐ 1907	(336,448)				
	225.00	265.00	375.00	500.00	5500.00

Note: Specimens dated 1905S are counterfeits, made either by die striking or applying a false mint mark to a genuine 1905.

QUARTER EAGLES—INDIAN HEAD, 1908–1929

The Quarter Eagle was redesigned in 1908 by Bela Lyon Pratt. Liberty was removed from its obverse and replaced by a portrait of an Indian wearing a warbonnet. A standing eagle adorned the reverse. The coin has no raised edge and the designs plus inscriptions are stamped in incuse, or recessed beneath the surface, rather than being shown in high relief. The composition is .900 gold, .100 copper, with a weight of 4.18 grams. Its diameter is 18mm. with total gold content by weight remaining at .12094 ounces. Quarter Eagles were last struck in 1929, the year of this nation's financial difficulties.

Mint Mark is to Left of Value on Reverse

DATE	ABP IN VF-20	VF-20 V. FINE	EF-40 EX. FINE	MS-60 UNC.	PRF-65 PROOF
☐ 1908	(565,057)				
	225.00	275.00	300.00	425.00	25000.00
☐ 1909	(441,899)				
	225.00	275.00	300.00	425.00	25000.00
☐ 1910	(492,682)				
	225.00	275.00	300.00	425.00	24000.00
☐ 1911	(404,191)				
	225.00	275.00	300.00	425.00	25000.00
☐ 1911D	(55,680)				
	2500.00	3200.00	4150.00	RARE	
☐ 1912	(616,197)				
	225.00	275.00	300.00	425.00	25000.00
☐ 1913	(722,165)				
	225.00	275.00	300.00	425.00	25000.00
☐ 1914	(240,117)				
	265.00	315.00	375.00	675.00	26000.00
☐ 1914D	(448,000)				
	225.00	275.00	300.00	425.00	
☐ 1915	(606,100)				
	225.00	275.00	300.00	425.00	30000.00
☐ 1925D	(578,000)				
	225.00	275.00	300.00	425.00	
☐ 1926	(446,000)				
	225.00	275.00	300.00	425.00	
☐ 1927	(388,000)				
	225.00	275.00	300.00	425.00	
☐ 1928	(416,000)				
	225.00	275.00	300.00	425.00	
☐ 1929	(532,000)				
	225.00	275.00	300.00	425.00	

$3.00 GOLD PIECES

LIBERTY HEAD WITH FEATHER HEADDRESS, 1854–1889

Introduction and apparent public acceptance of the gold dollar in 1849 led to speculation on the possible usefulness of gold coinage in other denominations. The $3 gold piece, composed of nine-tenths gold with an alloy of one-tenth copper, was introduced in 1854. It carried an Indian head on the obverse and a wreathed reverse. Its diameter was 20.5mm. and the weight 5.015 grams. Though the $3 gold piece continued to be struck until 1889 it had become obvious as early as pre–Civil War years that no great demand or popularity was enjoyed by this coin. The designer was James Longacre. In 1854 the word DOLLARS was set in smaller characters than subsequently. Total gold content by weight was .14512 ounces.

PLEASE NOTE: THE PRICES THAT ARE LISTED RE-FLECT A GOLD SPOT PRICE OF $1250.00 PER OUNCE.

 Mint Mark is Below Wreath on Reverse

DATE	ABP IN VF-20	VF-20 V. FINE	EF-40 EX. FINE	MS-60 UNC.	PRF-65 PROOF
☐ 1854	(136,618)				
	600.00	800.00	1200.00	RARE	RARE
☐ 1854D	(1,120)				
		RARE	RARE	RARE	
☐ 1854O	(24,000)				
	1000.00	2150.00	3000.00	RARE	

DATE	ABP IN VF-20	VF-20 V. FINE	EF-40 EX. FINE	MS-60 UNC.	PRF-65 PROOF
☐ 1855	(50,555)				
	650.00	900.00	1250.00	RARE	RARE
☐ 1855S	(6,000)				
	850.00	1150.00	2850.00	RARE	
☐ 1856	(26,010)				
	650.00	800.00	1250.00	3250.00	RARE
☐ 1856S*	(34,500)				
	675.00	950.00	1850.00	RARE	
☐ 1857	(20,891)				
	650.00	825.00	1250.00	3650.00	RARE
☐ 1857S	(14,000)				
	750.00	1350.00	2850.00	RARE	
☐ 1858	(2,133)				
	750.00	1100.00	2150.00	RARE	RARE
☐ 1859	(15,638)				
	650.00	900.00	1450.00	RARE	RARE
☐ 1860	(7,155)				
	650.00	950.00	1850.00	RARE	RARE
☐ 1860S	(7,000)				
	900.00	1350.00	3000.00	RARE	
☐ 1861	(6,072)				
	700.00	1050.00	2200.00	RARE	RARE
☐ 1862	(5,785)				
	700.00	1150.00	2200.00	RARE	RARE
☐ 1863	(5,039)				
	700.00	1150.00	2200.00	RARE	RARE
☐ 1864	(2,680)				
	700.00	1150.00	2200.00	RARE	RARE
☐ 1865	(1,165)				
	1150.00	1850.00	3200.00	RARE	RARE
☐ 1866	(4,030)				
	700.00	1100.00	1650.00	RARE	RARE
☐ 1867	(2,650)				
	710.00	1150.00	1850.00	RARE	RARE
☐ 1868	(4,875)				
	675.00	1000.00	1400.00	RARE	RARE
☐ 1869	(2,525)				
	700.00	1150.00	1650.00	RARE	RARE
☐ 1870	(3,535)				
	675.00	1050.00	1750.00	RARE	RARE

*Note: Found in Small, Medium, and Large "S" Varieties.

DATE	ABP IN VF-20	VF-20 V. FINE	EF-40 EX. FINE	MS-60 UNC.	PRF-65 PROOF
☐ 1870S	EXTREMELY RARE				
(2) The other piece is in the cornerstone of the San Francisco Mint.					
☐ 1871 (1,330)					
	725.00	975.00	1650.00	RARE	RARE
☐ 1872 (2,030)					
	700.00	975.00	1650.00	RARE	RARE
☐ 1873 Open 3 (25)	PROOF ONLY—VERY RARE				
☐ 1873 Closed 3 Restrike				VERY RARE	
☐ 1874 (41,820)					
	675.00	900.00	1250.00	2650.00	RARE
☐ 1875 Proofs Only (20)	VERY RARE				
☐ 1876 Proofs Only (45)	VERY RARE				
☐ 1877 (1,488)					
	1500.00	2200.00	RARE	RARE	RARE
☐ 1878 (82,324)					
	600.00	875.00	1150.00	2750.00	RARE
☐ 1879 (3,030)					
	625.00	900.00	1350.00	3650.00	RARE
☐ 1880 (1,036)					
	625.00	1000.00	2150.00	4750.00	40000.00
☐ 1881 (550)					
	1050.00	1500.00	3250.00	RARE	38500.00
☐ 1882 (1,540)					
	700.00	1000.00	1650.00	4000.00	37500.00
☐ 1883 (940)					
	700.00	1000.00	2000.00	4500.00	35000.00
☐ 1884 (1,106)					
	950.00	1250.00	2250.00	4500.00	35000.00
☐ 1885 (910)					
	900.00	1200.00	2500.00	5750.00	32500.00
☐ 1886 (1,142)					
	850.00	1100.00	1900.00	5250.00	30000.00
☐ 1887 (6,160)					
	725.00	1000.00	1600.00	4250.00	30000.00
☐ 1888 (5,291)					
	650.00	1000.00	1500.00	4250.00	30000.00
☐ 1889 (2,429)					
	650.00	975.00	1450.00	4250.00	30000.00

Note: Beware of deceiving counterfeits with the following dates: 1855, 1857, 1878, 1882, and 1888.

STELLA—$4.00 GOLD PIECES

LIBERTY HEAD WITH FLOWING OR COILED HAIR, 1879–1880

In 1879 and 1880 proofs were struck, in limited quantities, of a $4 gold coin that never reached circulation. It was called Stella and was coined not only in gold but also in various other metals. The gold specimens are extremely valuable. There are two obverse types, one designed by Barber and the other by Morgan.

PLEASE NOTE: THE PRICES THAT ARE LISTED REFLECT A GOLD SPOT PRICE OF $1250.00 PER OUNCE.

Flowing Hair   Coiled Hair

DATE	MINTAGE	ABP IN PRF-65	PRF-65 PROOF
☐ 1879 Flowing Hair Proofs Only	415		225000.00
☐ 1879 Coiled Hair Proofs Only	10		VERY RARE
☐ 1880 Flowing Hair Proofs Only	15		VERY RARE
☐ 1880 Coiled Hair Proofs Only	10		VERY RARE

HALF EAGLES—$5.00 GOLD PIECES, 1795–1929

The Half Eagle or $5 gold piece was authorized on April 2, 1792, and first struck in 1795. It has the distinction of being the first gold coin struck by the U.S. Mint. Production was limited in the early years. Its designer was Robert Scot. The composition was .9167 gold to .0833 copper alloy, yielding a weight of 8.75 grams and a diameter of (generally) 25mm. A capped portrait of Liberty facing right adorned the obverse, with stars and date appearing below the portrait; on the reverse is a spread-winged eagle holding in its beak a wreath, surrounded by the wording UNITED STATES OF AMERICA. Some alterations in the number of stars and size of figures in the date will be observed. These should be taken into close account, as they can have a considerable bearing on value.

In 1807 John Reich redesigned the Half Eagle. The bust, now "capped and draped," was turned around to face left and the eagle modified. A shortened bust was introduced in 1813. A further modification was made in 1829 but with the same basic design retained. By this time the Half Eagle had become an important circulating as well as banking piece, whose significance was to later increase. The year 1834 brought a revised design known as the Classic Head, the work of William Kneass. The weight of this new coin was 8.36 grams and its composition .8992 gold to .1008 copper, with a diameter of 22.5mm. The slogan IN GOD WE TRUST, previously used on the reverse, was dropped, probably because of a shortage of space. This was followed by Gobrecht's Coronet head in 1839, used until 1908. Its gold content was raised slightly to nine-tenths and the copper reduced to one-tenth. Gold content by weight was .24187 ounces. There are small- and large-date varieties of this coin.

In 1866, following the Civil War, IN GOD WE TRUST was added to the rather cramped space between the eagle's head and the legend UNITED STATES OF AMERICA. Composition was as before but the weight was changed to 8.359 grams and the diameter reduced to 21.6mm. One of the longest lived of coin designs, it remained in use a full seventy years, to be replaced by Pratt's Indian Head in 1908.

PLEASE NOTE: THE PRICES THAT ARE LISTED RE-FLECT A GOLD SPOT PRICE OF $1250.00 PER OUNCE.

HALF EAGLES—LIBERTY HEAD, 1795–1807 EAGLE ON REVERSE

Head Right
1795–1807

1795–1798
Small Eagle

1795–1807
Large Eagle

DATE	MINTAGE	ABP IN F-12	F-12 FINE	EF-40 EX. FINE	MS-60 UNC.
☐ 1795 Small Eagle	8,707	15000.00	18000.00	30000.00	RARE
☐ 1795 Large Eagle		7500.00	10000.00	RARE	RARE
☐ 1796 over 95 Small Eagle					
	3,399	15000.00	18500.00	40000.00	RARE
☐ 1797 over 95 Large Eagle					
	6,406	6000.00	8750.00	21000.00	RARE
☐ 1798 Small Eagle	6 Known			EXTREMELY	RARE
☐ 1798 Large Eagle, All Types	3000.00	4000.00	9500.00	RARE	
	24,867				
☐ 1799	7,451	3000.00	4000.00	9000.00	RARE
☐ 1800	37,620	3000.00	3850.00	8500.00	RARE
☐ 1802 over 1	53,176	3000.00	3850.00	8500.00	RARE
☐ 1803 over 2	33,506	3000.00	4000.00	8750.00	RARE
☐ 1804 Small and Large 8					
	30,475	2750.00	3850.00	8500.00	RARE
☐ 1805	33,183	2750.00	3850.00	8500.00	RARE
☐ 1806 Round and Pointed Top 6					
	64,093	2850.00	3850.00	8500.00	RARE
☐ 1807 Head Right	33,496	2750.00	3750.00	8250.00	RARE

HALF EAGLES—DRAPED BUST, 1807–1812, VALUE 5D ON REVERSE

HEAD
LEFT

"Round Cap"

DATE	MINTAGE	ABP IN F-12	F-12 FINE	EF-40 EX. FINE	MS-60 UNC.
☐ 1807	50,597	2250.00	3250.00	6000.00	RARE
☐ 1808	55,578	2250.00	3250.00	6250.00	RARE
☐ 1809/8	33,875	2250.00	3250.00	7000.00	RARE
☐ 1810 (4 varieties)	100,287	2250.00	3250.00	6500.00	RARE
☐ 1811	99,581	2250.00	3250.00	6000.00	RARE
☐ 1812	58,087	2250.00	3250.00	6000.00	RARE

HALF EAGLES—LIBERTY HEAD, ROUND CAP, 1813–1834 MOTTO OVER EAGLE

DATE	MINTAGE	ABP IN F-12	F-12 FINE	EF-40 EX. FINE	MS-60 UNC.
☐ 1813	95,428	2500.00	3500.00	8000.00	RARE
☐ 1814 over 13	15,454	4000.00	5500.00	8500.00	RARE
☐ 1815	635	22500.00	28500.00	EXTREMELY RARE	
☐ 1818	48,588	3000.00	4250.00	RARE	RARE
☐ 1819	51,723	6000.00	8500.00	VERY RARE	
☐ 1820	263,806	3500.00	4750.00	13500.00	RARE
☐ 1821	34,641		RARE	RARE	
☐ 1822		Only 3 Known—EXTREMELY RARE			
☐ 1823	14,485	3500.00	4900.00	16000.00	RARE

DATE	MINTAGE	ABP IN F-12	F-12 FINE	EF-40 EX. FINE	MS-60 UNC.
☐ 1824	17,340	3250.00	4750.00	RARE	RARE
☐ 1825 over 21	29,060	3500.00	5000.00	RARE	RARE
☐ 1825 over 24				EXTREMELY RARE	
☐ 1826	18,069	3500.00	5000.00	RARE	50000.00
☐ 1827	24,913	4000.00	5500.00	RARE	60000.00
☐ 1828	28,029	4250.00	5750.00	RARE	RARE
☐ 1828 over 27				EXTREMELY RARE	
☐ 1829 Small Date	57,442	25000.00	35000.00		VERY RARE
☐ 1829 Large Date		9500.00	13000.00		VERY RARE
☐ 1830	126,351	10000.00	15000.00	RARE	RARE
☐ 1831	140,594	10000.00	15000.00	RARE	RARE
☐ 1832*	157,487	10000.00	15000.00	RARE	RARE
☐ 1833	193,630	10000.00	15000.00	RARE	RARE
☐ 1834**	50,141	10000.00	15000.00	RARE	RARE

*1832 Square Based 2, 13 Stars   **1834 Crosslet 4: MS-60 $100000.00

HALF EAGLES—LIBERTY HEAD WITH RIBBON, 1834–1838 NO MOTTO OVER EAGLE

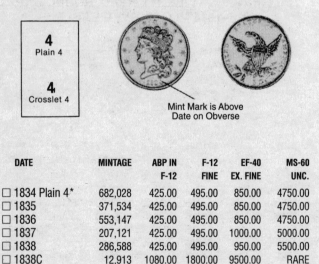

4 Plain 4

4 Crosslet 4

Mint Mark is Above Date on Obverse

DATE	MINTAGE	ABP IN F-12	F-12 FINE	EF-40 EX. FINE	MS-60 UNC.
☐ 1834 Plain 4*	682,028	425.00	495.00	850.00	4750.00
☐ 1835	371,534	425.00	495.00	850.00	4750.00
☐ 1836	553,147	425.00	495.00	850.00	4750.00
☐ 1837	207,121	425.00	495.00	1000.00	5000.00
☐ 1838	286,588	425.00	495.00	950.00	5500.00
☐ 1838C	12,913	1080.00	1800.00	9500.00	RARE
☐ 1838D	20,583	1080.00	1800.00	6500.00	RARE

*1834 Crosslet 4 worth more: MS-60 Unc. $30000.00

HALF EAGLES—LIBERTY HEAD WITH CORONET, 1839–1908

1839–1908

1839–66
No Motto

1866–1908
With Motto

DATE	ABP IN F-12	F-12 FINE	EF-40 EX. FINE	MS-60 UNC.	PRF-65 PROOF
☐ 1839 (118,143)					
	400.00	475.00	625.00	3800.00	
☐ 1839C (23,467)					
	1000.00	1250.00	3500.00	18000.00	
☐ 1839D (18,939)					
	950.00	1200.00	3850.00	22500.00	
☐ 1840 (137,382)					
	400.00	500.00	750.00	3800.00	
☐ 1840C (19,028)					
	950.00	1250.00	3000.00	19500.00	
☐ 1840D (22,896)					
	1000.00	1300.00	3600.00	13000.00	
☐ 1840O (30,400)					
	425.00	575.00	825.00	9500.00	
☐ 1841 (15,833)					
	400.00	550.00	825.00	4150.00	
☐ 1841C (21,511)					
	1000.00	1250.00	2350.00	12000.00	
☐ 1841D (30,495)					
	1000.00	1300.00	2400.00	13000.00	
☐ 1841O (50)	UNKNOWN				
☐ 1842 (27,578)					
	400.00	525.00	1150.00	11000.00	
☐ 1842C Large Date (27,480)					
	900.00	1200.00	2350.00	RARE	
☐ 1842D Small Date (59,608)					
	1000.00	1350.00	2500.00	RARE	
☐ 1842O (16,400)					
	550.00	750.00	3500.00	RARE	

DATE	ABP IN F-12	F-12 FINE	EF-40 EX. FINE	MS-60 UNC.	PRF-65 PROOF
☐ 1843	(611,205)				
	400.00	450.00	600.00	1900.00	
☐ 1843C	(44,353)				
	950.00	1250.00	2500.00	10000.00	
☐ 1843D	(98,452)				
	1100.00	1500.00	2500.00	10500.00	
☐ 1843O	(101,075)				
	450.00	525.00	1350.00	10000.00	
☐ 1844	(340,330)				
	400.00	485.00	575.00	2250.00	
☐ 1844C	(23,631)				
	1100.00	1450.00	2850.00	RARE	
☐ 1844D	(88,982)				
	1050.00	1400.00	2600.00	RARE	
☐ 1844O	(364,600)				
	425.00	485.00	625.00	4500.00	
☐ 1845	(417,099)				
	400.00	475.00	575.00	2150.00	
☐ 1845D	(90,629)				
	1000.00	1350.00	2150.00	RARE	
☐ 1845O	(41,000)				
	425.00	575.00	850.00	9000.00	
☐ 1846	(395,942)				
	400.00	475.00	600.00	2350.00	
☐ 1846C	(12,995)				
	1000.00	1300.00	2250.00	RARE	
☐ 1846D	(80,294)				
	1050.00	1450.00	2350.00	10500.00	
☐ 1846O	(58,000)				
	425.00	500.00	950.00	9500.00	
☐ 1847	(915,981)				
	425.00	475.00	550.00	1850.00	
☐ 1847 Impression of extra 7					
	500.00	600.00	875.00	3200.00	
☐ 1847C	(84,151)				
	1000.00	1450.00	2500.00	RARE	
☐ 1847D	(64,405)				
	1100.00	1500.00	2650.00	RARE	
☐ 1847O	(12,000)				
	1000.00	1400.00	4350.00	RARE	
☐ 1848	(260,775)				
	400.00	475.00	550.00	1950.00	

DATE	ABP IN F-12	F-12 FINE	EF-40 EX. FINE	MS-60 UNC.	PRF-65 PROOF
☐ 1848C (64,472)					
	1100.00	1400.00	2350.00	RARE	
☐ 1848D (47,465)					
	1100.00	1400.00	2500.00	RARE	
☐ 1849 (133,070)					
	400.00	475.00	550.00	2450.00	
☐ 1849C (64,823)					
	1100.00	1400.00	2450.00	RARE	
☐ 1849D (39,036)					
	1150.00	1450.00	2750.00	RARE	
☐ 1850 (64,941)					
	400.00	475.00	625.00	3100.00	
☐ 1850C (63,591)					
	1000.00	1400.00	2150.00	RARE	
☐ 1850D (53,950)					
	1100.00	1500.00	2750.00	RARE	
☐ 1851 (377,505)					
	400.00	465.00	550.00	2500.00	
☐ 1851C (49,176)					
	1000.00	1400.00	2350.00	RARE	
☐ 1851D (62,710)					
	1100.00	1500.00	2400.00	RARE	
☐ 1851O (41,000)					
	450.00	550.00	1500.00	RARE	
☐ 1852 (573,901)					
	400.00	450.00	525.00	1750.00	
☐ 1852C (72,574)					
	1100.00	1400.00	2100.00	RARE	
☐ 1852D (91,452)					
	1250.00	1550.00	2650.00	RARE	
☐ 1853 (305,770)					
	400.00	450.00	525.00	1750.00	
☐ 1853C (65,571)					
	1050.00	1400.00	2350.00	RARE	
☐ 1853D (89,687)					
	1150.00	1500.00	2500.00	RARE	
☐ 1854 (160,675)					
	400.00	450.00	550.00	2000.00	
☐ 1854C (39,291)					
	1200.00	1500.00	2350.00	RARE	

DATE	ABP IN F-12	F-12 FINE	EF-40 EX. FINE	MS-60 UNC.	PRF-65 PROOF
☐ 1854D	(56,413)				
	1200.00	1600.00	2650.00	RARE	
☐ 1854O	(46,000)				
	475.00	550.00	675.00	7000.00	
☐ 1854S	(268) EXTREMELY RARE				
☐ 1855	(117,098)				
	425.00	475.00	525.00	2000.00	
☐ 1855C	(39,788)				
	1100.00	1400.00	2400.00	RARE	
☐ 1855D	(22,432)				
	1150.00	1500.00	2500.00	RARE	
☐ 1855O	(11,100)				
	500.00	650.00	2400.00	RARE	
☐ 1855S	(61,000)				
	450.00	525.00	950.00	RARE	
☐ 1856	(197,990)				
	400.00	450.00	550.00	2250.00	
☐ 1856C	(28,457)				
	1100.00	1500.00	2100.00	RARE	
☐ 1856D	(19,786)				
	1200.00	1500.00	2250.00	RARE	
☐ 1856O	(10,000)				
	475.00	625.00	1650.00	RARE	
☐ 1856S	(105,100)				
	400.00	450.00	725.00	7500.00	
☐ 1857	(98,188)				
	400.00	450.00	550.00	1850.00	
☐ 1857C	(31,360)				
	1100.00	1400.00	2150.00	RARE	
☐ 1857D	(17,046)				
	1100.00	1500.00	2350.00	RARE	
☐ 1857O	(13,000)				
	475.00	625.00	1250.00	RARE	
☐ 1857S	(87,000)				
	425.00	475.00	625.00	8000.00	
☐ 1858	(15,136)				
	425.00	465.00	600.00	3500.00	
☐ 1858C	(38,856)				
	1100.00	1400.00	2150.00	RARE	
☐ 1858D	(15,362)				
	1200.00	1500.00	2500.00	RARE	

DATE	ABP IN F-12	F-12 FINE	EF-40 EX. FINE	MS-60 UNC.	PRF-65 PROOF
☐ 1858S	(18,600)				
	550.00	750.00	2650.00	RARE	
☐ 1859	(16,814)				
	400.00	450.00	575.00	6000.00	
☐ 1859C	(31,487)				
	1100.00	1400.00	2100.00	RARE	
☐ 1859D	(10,366)				
	1200.00	1500.00	2300.00	RARE	
☐ 1859S	(13,220)				
	900.00	1150.00	3500.00	RARE	
☐ 1860	(19,825)				
	425.00	450.00	700.00	3800.00	
☐ 1860C	(14,813)				
	1250.00	1500.00	2500.00	RARE	
☐ 1860D	(14,635)				
	1300.00	1600.00	3000.00	RARE	
☐ 1860S	(21,200)				
	550.00	775.00	2150.00	RARE	
☐ 1861	(639,950)				
	425.00	450.00	550.00	1900.00	
☐ 1861C	(6,879)				
	1400.00	1800.00	4200.00	RARE	
☐ 1861D	(1,597)				
	4500.00	6000.00	17500.00	RARE	
☐ 1861S	(9,500)				
	700.00	900.00	3900.00	RARE	
☐ 1862	(4,465)				
	525.00	750.00	3150.00	RARE	
☐ 1862S	(9,500)				
	1500.00	2000.00	RARE	RARE	
☐ 1863	(2,472)				
	1000.00	1400.00	6500.00	RARE	
☐ 1863S	(17,000)				
	900.00	1250.00	4000.00	RARE	
☐ 1864	(4,220)				
	500.00	750.00	2350.00	RARE	
☐ 1864S	(3,888)				
	4500.00	7500.00	RARE	RARE	
☐ 1865	(1,295)				
	1000.00	1200.00	7500.00	RARE	

DATE	ABP IN F-12	F-12 FINE	EF-40 EX. FINE	MS-60 UNC.	PRF-65 PROOF
☐ 1865S (27,612)					
	850.00	1200.00	3000.00	RARE	
☐ 1866S No Motto (43,020)					
	1200.00	1500.00	4200.00	RARE	
☐ 1866S With Motto* (43,020)					
	750.00	825.00	2500.00	RARE	
☐ 1866 (6,720)					
	500.00	650.00	1400.00	RARE	
☐ 1867 (6,920)					
	475.00	575.00	1500.00	11500.00	
☐ 1867S (29,000)					
	750.00	950.00	2350.00	RARE	
☐ 1868 (5,725)					
	450.00	550.00	950.00	10500.00	
☐ 1868S (52,000)					
	425.00	525.00	1500.00	RARE	
☐ 1869 (1,785)					
	550.00	750.00	2100.00	RARE	
☐ 1869S (31,000)					
	425.00	500.00	1650.00	RARE	
☐ 1870 (4,035)					
	525.00	675.00	1850.00	RARE	
☐ 1870CC (7,675) VERY RARE					
☐ 1870S (17,000)					
	550.00	750.00	2500.00	RARE	
☐ 1871 (3,230)					
	600.00	850.00	1750.00	11000.00	
☐ 1871CC (20,770)					
	1300.00	1750.00	4000.00	RARE	
☐ 1871S (25,000)					
	375.00	475.00	900.00	RARE	
☐ 1872 (1,690)					
	575.00	725.00	1800.00	RARE	
☐ 1872CC (16,980)					
	1350.00	1650.00	4250.00	RARE	
☐ 1872S (36,400)					
	375.00	450.00	875.00	11000.00	
☐ 1873 (112,505)					
	350.00	425.00	550.00	1000.00	

*Note: From 1866 to 1908 all have motto "In God We Trust" over eagle on reverse.

DATE	ABP IN F-12	F-12 FINE	EF-40 EX. FINE	MS-60 UNC.	PRF-65 PROOF
☐ 1873CC (7,416)					
	2250.00	2850.00	12500.00	RARE	
☐ 1873S (31,000)					
	425.00	550.00	1500.00	RARE	
☐ 1874 (3,508)					
	425.00	550.00	1400.00	RARE	
☐ 1874CC (21,198)					
	850.00	1100.00	2650.00	RARE	
☐ 1874S (16,000)					
	450.00	625.00	2000.00	RARE	
☐ 1875 (220) VERY RARE					
☐ 1875CC (11,828)					
	1050.00	1500.00	4250.00	RARE	
☐ 1875S (9,000)					
	450.00	575.00	1800.00	RARE	
☐ 1876 (1,477)					
	900.00	1100.00	3150.00	RARE	
☐ 1876CC (6,887)					
	1100.00	1400.00	4000.00	RARE	
☐ 1876S (4,000)					
	1000.00	1400.00	3400.00	RARE	
☐ 1877 (1,152)					
	550.00	750.00	2600.00	RARE	
☐ 1877CC (8,680)					
	900.00	1200.00	4000.00	RARE	
☐ 1877S (26,700)					
	450.00	575.00	675.00	RARE	
☐ 1878 (131,740)					
	325.00	425.00	525.00	625.00	
☐ 1878CC (9,054)					
	1650.00	2250.00	RARE	RARE	
☐ 1878S (144,700)					
	325.00	400.00	475.00	750.00	
☐ 1879 (301,950)					
	325.00	400.00	450.00	625.00	
☐ 1879CC (17,281)					
	700.00	925.00	2000.00	RARE	
☐ 1879S (426,200)					
	325.00	400.00	450.00	850.00	

*Note: Only 20 proofs struck in 1875.

DATE	ABP IN F-12	F-12 FINE	EF-40 EX. FINE	MS-60 UNC.	PRF-65 PROOF
☐ 1880 (3,166,436)	325.00	385.00	435.00	550.00	
☐ 1880CC (51,017)	475.00	600.00	1050.00	RARE	
☐ 1880S (1,348,900)	325.00	385.00	435.00	550.00	
☐ 1881 (5,708,800)	325.00	385.00	435.00	550.00	
☐ 1881CC (13,886)	475.00	700.00	2150.00	RARE	
☐ 1881S (969,000)	325.00	385.00	435.00	550.00	
☐ 1882 (21,514,560)	325.00	385.00	435.00	550.00	
☐ 1882CC (82,817)	500.00	625.00	950.00	9500.00	
☐ 1882S (969,000)	325.00	385.00	435.00	550.00	
☐ 1883 (233,440)	325.00	385.00	435.00	550.00	
☐ 1883CC (12,958)	475.00	650.00	1500.00	RARE	
☐ 1883S (83,200)	325.00	395.00	450.00	950.00	
☐ 1884 (191,048)	325.00	385.00	435.00	600.00	
☐ 1884CC (16,402)	475.00	700.00	1250.00	RARE	
☐ 1884S (177,000)	325.00	385.00	435.00	550.00	
☐ 1885 (601,506)	325.00	385.00	435.00	550.00	
☐ 1885S (1,211,500)	325.00	385.00	435.00	550.00	
☐ 1886 (388,432)	325.00	385.00	435.00	550.00	
☐ 1886S (3,268,000)	325.00	385.00	435.00	550.00	
☐ 1887 (87) Proof Only		VERY RARE			
☐ 1887S (1,912,000)	325.00	385.00	435.00	550.00	

DATE	ABP IN F-12	F-12 FINE	EF-40 EX. FINE	MS-60 UNC.	PRF-65 PROOF
☐ 1888	(18,296)				
	350.00	400.00	450.00	650.00	
☐ 1888S	(293,900)				
	325.00	385.00	435.00	1100.00	
☐ 1889	(7,565)				
	350.00	450.00	500.00	1100.00	
☐ 1890	(4,328)				
	350.00	425.00	500.00	1800.00	
☐ 1890CC	(53,800)				
	475.00	600.00	700.00	1750.00	
☐ 1891	(61,413)				
	325.00	385.00	435.00	575.00	
☐ 1891CC	(208,000)				
	475.00	600.00	800.00	1650.00	
☐ 1892	(753,572)				
	325.00	385.00	435.00	575.00	
☐ 1892CC	(82,968)				
	475.00	650.00	700.00	1650.00	
☐ 1892O	(10,000)				
	475.00	650.00	900.00	3150.00	
☐ 1892S	(298,400)				
	325.00	385.00	435.00	550.00	
☐ 1893	(1,528,197)				
	325.00	385.00	435.00	550.00	
☐ 1893CC	(60,000)				
	500.00	625.00	750.00	1650.00	
☐ 1893O	(110,000)				
	350.00	400.00	450.00	950.00	
☐ 1893S	(224,000)				
	325.00	385.00	435.00	550.00	
☐ 1894	(957,955)				
	325.00	400.00	450.00	575.00	
☐ 1894O	(16,660)				
	350.00	450.00	575.00	1500.00	
☐ 1894S	(55,900)				
	350.00	450.00	550.00	2650.00	
☐ 1895	(1,345,936)				
	325.00	385.00	435.00	575.00	
☐ 1895S	(112,000)				
	350.00	465.00	575.00	2650.00	

DATE	ABP IN F-12	F-12 FINE	EF-40 EX. FINE	MS-60 UNC.	PRF-65 PROOF
□ 1896 (59,063)					
	325.00	385.00	435.00	550.00	
□ 1896S (115,400)					
	325.00	385.00	435.00	1150.00	
□ 1897 (867,883)					
	325.00	385.00	435.00	625.00	
□ 1897S (345,000)					
	325.00	385.00	435.00	800.00	
□ 1898 (633,495)					
	325.00	385.00	435.00	550.00	
□ 1898S (1,397,400)					
	325.00	385.00	435.00	550.00	
□ 1899 (1,710,729)					
	325.00	385.00	435.00	550.00	
□ 1899S (1,545,000)					
	325.00	385.00	435.00	550.00	
□ 1900 (1,405,730)					
	325.00	385.00	435.00	550.00	
□ 1900S (329,000)					
	325.00	385.00	435.00	550.00	
□ 1901 (616,040)					
	325.00	385.00	435.00	550.00	
□ 1901S (3,648,000)					
	325.00	385.00	435.00	550.00	
□ 1901S 1 over 0					
	475.00	575.00	650.00	750.00	
□ 1902 (172,562)					
	325.00	385.00	435.00	550.00	
□ 1902S (939,000)					
	325.00	385.00	435.00	550.00	
□ 1903 (227,024)					
	325.00	385.00	435.00	550.00	
□ 1903S (1,885,000)					
	325.00	385.00	435.00	550.00	
□ 1904 (392,136)					
	325.00	385.00	435.00	550.00	
□ 1904S (97,000)					
	325.00	400.00	475.00	850.00	
□ 1905 (302,308)					
	325.00	385.00	435.00	550.00	
□ 1905S (880,700)					
	325.00	385.00	435.00	550.00	

DATE	ABP IN F-12	F-12 FINE	EF-40 EX. FINE	MS-60 UNC.	PRF-65 PROOF
☐ 1906	(348,820)				
	325.00	385.00	435.00	550.00	28000.00
☐ 1906D	(320,000)				
	325.00	385.00	435.00	550.00	
☐ 1906S	(598,000)				
	325.00	385.00	435.00	625.00	
☐ 1907	(626,192)				
	325.00	385.00	435.00	550.00	28000.00
☐ 1907D	(888,000)				
	325.00	385.00	435.00	550.00	
☐ 1908	(421,874)				
	325.00	385.00	435.00	550.00	

HALF EAGLES—INDIAN HEAD, 1908–1929

Bela Lyon Pratt's Indian Head design replaced the Liberty Head Half Eagle in 1908. Like the Quarter Eagle these coins are uniquely without raised edges and have designs stamped in incuse or recess rather than raised from the surface. A standing eagle adorns the reverse, with mint mark to the left of the value. These Half Eagles contained 90% gold and 10% copper with a weight of 8.359 grams. The diameter is 21.6mm. and the gold content by weight is .24167 ounces each. Striking of Half Eagles was suspended during World War I and not resumed until 1929, their final year of production.

Mint Mark is to Left of Value on Reverse

DATE	ABP IN VF-20	VF-20 V. FINE	EF-40 EX. FINE	MS-60 UNC.	PRF-65 PROOF
☐ 1908 (578,012)	325.00	375.00	400.00	575.00	37500.00
☐ 1908D (148,000)	325.00	375.00	400.00	575.00	
☐ 1908S (82,000)	425.00	525.00	1000.00	2350.00	
☐ 1909 (627,138)	325.00	375.00	410.00	625.00	47500.00
☐ 1909D (3,423,560)	325.00	375.00	400.00	575.00	
☐ 1909O* (34,200)	3000.00	3850.00	6250.00	32000.00	
☐ 1909S (297,200)	425.00	475.00	550.00	1500.00	
☐ 1910 (604,250)	325.00	375.00	400.00	575.00	40000.00
☐ 1910D (193,600)	325.00	375.00	400.00	575.00	
☐ 1910S (770,200)	325.00	375.00	400.00	1100.00	
☐ 1911 (915,139)	325.00	375.00	400.00	575.00	40000.00
☐ 1911D (72,500)	550.00	675.00	850.00	8250.00	
☐ 1911S (1,416,000)	350.00	400.00	425.00	800.00	
☐ 1912 (790,144)	325.00	375.00	400.00	600.00	40000.00
☐ 1912S (392,000)	425.00	475.00	550.00	1750.00	
☐ 1913 (916,099)	325.00	375.00	400.00	575.00	38500.00
☐ 1913S (408,000)	425.00	475.00	565.00	2150.00	
☐ 1914 (247,125)	325.00	375.00	400.00	575.00	38500.00
☐ 1914D (247,000)	325.00	375.00	400.00	575.00	
☐ 1914S (263,000)	325.00	375.00	400.00	1500.00	

*Some "O" mint marks are false.

DATE	ABP IN VF-20	VF-20 V. FINE	EF-40 EX. FINE	MS-60 UNC.	PRF-65 PROOF
☐ 1915*	(588,075)				
	325.00	375.00	400.00	600.00	47500.00
☐ 1915S	(164,000)				
	350.00	400.00	475.00	1900.00	
☐ 1916S	(240,000)				
	350.00	400.00	475.00	900.00	
☐ 1929	(662,000)				
	8500.00	11500.00	13500.00	32500.00	

*Coins marked 1915D are not authentic.

EAGLES—$10.00 GOLD PIECES, 1795–1907

Gold pieces valued at $10 were released for general circulation in 1795. Despite the large face value and the super-large buying power ($10 in the 1790s was equivalent to about $200 in present-day money), this coin was struck in substantial numbers, chiefly as a banking piece. Though bullion shortages, speculation, and world economic conditions made the Eagle's career far from sedate, it retained great influence throughout most of its history. The first design, conceived by Robert Scot, comprised a capped bust of Liberty facing right with the so-called Small Eagle reverse, depicting an eagle holding a wreath in its beak. The Shield or Heraldic Eagle replaced this type in 1797 and production was stepped up, output reaching more than 37,000 in 1799. The content was .9167 gold to .0833 copper, with a weight of 17.5 grams and diameter generally of 33mm. From 1805 to 1837 no Eagles were struck.

When production resumed in 1838 the portrait of Liberty had undergone a thorough alteration at the hands of Christian Gobrecht. This was the Coronet type, with modified shielded eagle on the reverse. It weighed 16.718 grams with a 9-to-1 gold content (alloyed with copper) and diameter of 27mm. The gold content by weight was .48375 ounces. The slogan E PLURIBUS UNUM, previously used on the reverse, was dropped. For many years no motto appeared on the reverse until the installation, in 1866, of IN GOD WE TRUST. The composition and other specifications remained unaltered. No change was made until 1907 when the Indian Head obverse, designed by Augustus Saint-Gaudens, was introduced.

PLEASE NOTE: THE PRICES THAT ARE LISTED REFLECT A GOLD SPOT PRICE OF $1250.00 PER OUNCE.

EAGLES—LIBERTY HEAD, SMALL EAGLE, 1795–1797

DATE	MINTAGE	ABP IN F-12	F-12 FINE	EF-40 EX. FINE	MS-60 UNC.
☐ 1795* 9 Leaves	5,583	22000.00	34000.00		VERY RARE
☐ 1796	4,146	21000.00	32500.00		VERY RARE
☐ 1797 Part of Liberty Head, Small Eagle					
	3,615	23500.00	35000.00		VERY RARE

EAGLES—LIBERTY HEAD, LARGE EAGLE, 1797–1804

4 Stars Right   6 Stars Right   Large Eagle

DATE	MINTAGE	ABP IN F-12	F-12 FINE	EF-40 EX. FINE	MS-60 UNC.
☐ 1797 Large Eagle	10,940	6500.00	9000.00	22500.00	RARE
☐ 1798 over 97, 9 Stars Left, 4 Right					
	900	9000.00	12500.00	RARE	RARE
☐ 1798 over 97, 7 Stars Left, 6 Right					
	842	20000.00	30000.00		VERY RARE
☐ 1799	37,449	6000.00	8500.00	16500.00	37500.00
☐ 1800	5,999	6500.00	9000.00	17000.00	37500.00
☐ 1801	44,344	6500.00	9000.00	16500.00	37500.00
☐ 1803	15,017	6500.00	9000.00	16500.00	37500.00
☐ 1804	3,757	12000.00	16000.00	32500.00	RARE

*Note: 1795 13 Leaves EF-40 $50000.00.

EAGLES—LIBERTY HEAD WITH CORONET, 1838–1907

1862

1838–1866
No Motto
Mint Mark is Below Eagle on Reverse

1866–1907
With Motto

DATE	ABP IN F-12	F-12 FINE	EF-40 EX. FINE	MS-60 UNC.	PRF-65 PROOF
☐ 1838 Large Letters	(7,200)				
	1500.00	2000.00	8750.00	RARE	
☐ 1839 Large Letters	(25,800)				
	800.00	900.00	3000.00	RARE	
☐ 1839 Small Letters	(12,447)				
	1100.00	1500.00	4850.00	RARE	
☐ 1840	(47,338)				
	800.00	900.00	1300.00	10000.00	
☐ 1841	(63,131)				
	800.00	900.00	1150.00	9500.00	
☐ 1841O	(2,500)				
	1850.00	2500.00	RARE	RARE	
☐ 1842	(81,507)				
	800.00	900.00	1100.00	RARE	
☐ 1842O	(27,400)				
	800.00	900.00	1300.00	RARE	
☐ 1843	(75,462)				
	800.00	900.00	1050.00	RARE	
☐ 1843O	(175,162)				
	800.00	900.00	1150.00	13500.00	
☐ 1844	(6,361)				
	900.00	1050.00	3500.00	RARE	
☐ 1844O	(118,700)				
	800.00	900.00	1300.00	12500.00	
☐ 1845	(26,153)				
	800.00	900.00	1150.00	RARE	
☐ 1845O	(47,500)				
	800.00	900.00	1250.00	RARE	

DATE	ABP IN F-12	F-12 FINE	EF-40 EX. FINE	MS-60 UNC.	PRF-65 PROOF
☐ 1846	(20,095)				
	800.00	900.00	1250.00	RARE	
☐ 1846O	(81,780)				
	800.00	900.00	1400.00	RARE	
☐ 1847	(862,258)				
	800.00	900.00	1000.00	3450.00	
☐ 1847O	(417,099)				
	800.00	900.00	1000.00	5500.00	
☐ 1848	(145,484)				
	800.00	900.00	1100.00	5000.00	
☐ 1848O	(35,850)				
	800.00	900.00	1500.00	RARE	
☐ 1849	(653,618)				
	800.00	900.00	1100.00	3250.00	
☐ 1849O	(23,900)				
	800.00	950.00	2250.00	RARE	
☐ 1850*	(291,451)				
	800.00	900.00	1000.00	3750.00	
☐ 1850O	(57,500)				
	800.00	900.00	1250.00	RARE	
☐ 1851	(176,328)				
	800.00	900.00	1100.00	4350.00	
☐ 1851O	(263,000)				
	800.00	900.00	1200.00	6500.00	
☐ 1852	(263,106)				
	800.00	900.00	1100.00	5000.00	
☐ 1852O	(18,000)				
	850.00	1000.00	1750.00	RARE	
☐ 1853	(201,253)				
	800.00	900.00	1100.00	3650.00	
☐ 1853O	(51,000)				
	800.00	950.00	1150.00	RARE	
☐ 1854	(54,250)				
	800.00	900.00	1100.00	6000.00	
☐ 1854O	(52,500)				
	800.00	900.00	1100.00	RARE	
☐ 1854S	(123,826)				
	800.00	900.00	1150.00	RARE	
☐ 1855	(121,701)				
	800.00	900.00	1150.00	4350.00	

*Note: Small Date more—MS-60 $6,000.

DATE	ABP IN F-12	F-12 FINE	EF-40 EX. FINE	MS-60 UNC.	PRF-65 PROOF
☐ 1855O	(18,000)				
	850.00	1000.00	2250.00	RARE	
☐ 1855S	(9,000)				
	1250.00	1650.00	3000.00	RARE	
☐ 1856	(60,490)				
	800.00	900.00	1100.00	3500.00	
☐ 1856O	(14,500)				
	850.00	1000.00	2000.00	RARE	
☐ 1856S	(26,000)				
	800.00	900.00	1100.00	RARE	
☐ 1857	(16,606)				
	800.00	900.00	1000.00	RARE	
☐ 1857O	(5,500)				
	850.00	1050.00	2400.00	RARE	
☐ 1857S	(26,000)				
	800.00	900.00	1250.00	RARE	
☐ 1858*	(2,521)				
	2750.00	3500.00	7000.00	RARE	
☐ 1858O	(20,000)				
	800.00	900.00	1250.00	RARE	
☐ 1858S	(11,800)				
	1000.00	1250.00	3100.00	RARE	
☐ 1859	(16,093)				
	800.00	900.00	1050.00	RARE	
☐ 1859O	(2,300)				
	2250.00	2850.00	RARE	RARE	
☐ 1859S	(7,007)				
	1500.00	2150.00	RARE	RARE	
☐ 1860	(11,783)				
	800.00	900.00	1050.00	RARE	RARE
☐ 1860O	(11,100)				
	800.00	900.00	1150.00	RARE	
☐ 1860S	(5,500)				
	1650.00	2500.00	RARE	RARE	
☐ 1861	(113,233)				
	800.00	900.00	1100.00	6000.00	RARE
☐ 1861S	(15,500)				
	1000.00	1300.00	4750.00	RARE	
☐ 1862	(10,995)				
	850.00	1000.00	1400.00	RARE	RARE

*Check for removed mint mark.

DATE	ABP IN F-12	F-12 FINE	EF-40 EX. FINE	MS-60 UNC.	PRF-65 PROOF
☐ 1862S (12,500)					
	1100.00	1350.00	3500.00	RARE	
☐ 1863 (1,248)					
	2250.00	3600.00	RARE	RARE	RARE
☐ 1863S (10,000)					
	900.00	1200.00	4000.00	RARE	
☐ 1864 (3,580)					
	1100.00	1400.00	RARE	RARE	RARE
☐ 1864S (2,500)					
	7000.00	9500.00	RARE	RARE	
☐ 1865 (4,005)					
	1200.00	1500.00	RARE	RARE	RARE
☐ 1865S (16,700)					
	2250.00	2750.00	RARE	RARE	
☐ 1866 With Motto (3,780)					
	850.00	1000.00	2350.00	RARE	RARE
☐ 1866S No Motto (8,500)					
	1500.00	2250.00	8500.00	RARE	
☐ 1866S With Motto (11,500)					
	900.00	1100.00	3600.00	RARE	
☐ 1867 (3,140)					
	1000.00	1250.00	2800.00	RARE	RARE
☐ 1867S (9,000)					
	1200.00	1800.00	RARE	RARE	
☐ 1868 (10,655)					
	700.00	825.00	1000.00	RARE	RARE
☐ 1868S (13,500)					
	900.00	1100.00	2250.00	RARE	
☐ 1869 (1,855)					
	1100.00	1400.00	3000.00	RARE	RARE
☐ 1869S (6,430)					
	950.00	1250.00	2350.00	RARE	
☐ 1870 (2,535)					
	850.00	1050.00	1500.00	RARE	RARE
☐ 1870CC (5,908)					
		RARE	RARE	RARE	
☐ 1870S (8,000)					
	900.00	1250.00	2500.00	RARE	
☐ 1871 (1,780)					
	950.00	1300.00	3000.00	RARE	RARE

DATE	ABP IN F-12	F-12 FINE	EF-40 EX. FINE	MS-60 UNC.	PRF-65 PROOF
☐ 1871CC (7,185)	1500.00	2250.00	6750.00	RARE	
☐ 1871S (16,500)	900.00	1250.00	2350.00	RARE	
☐ 1872 (1,650)	1350.00	1850.00	4000.00	RARE	RARE
☐ 1872CC (5,500)	2500.00	3500.00	RARE	RARE	
☐ 1872S (17,300)	800.00	850.00	1200.00	RARE	
☐ 1873 (825)	3000.00	3850.00	RARE	RARE	RARE
☐ 1873CC (4,543)	3000.00	3700.00	RARE	RARE	
☐ 1873S (12,000)	825.00	900.00	2300.00	RARE	
☐ 1874 (53,160)	650.00	850.00	875.00	1850.00	RARE
☐ 1874CC (16,767)	1500.00	2500.00	4250.00	RARE	
☐ 1874S (10,000)	850.00	1050.00	2750.00	RARE	
☐ 1875 (120) PROOF—VERY RARE					
☐ 1875CC (7,715)	2500.00	3250.00	7500.00	RARE	
☐ 1876 (732)	1750.00	2350.00	7250.00	RARE	RARE
☐ 1876CC (4,696)	1750.00	2350.00	RARE	RARE	
☐ 1876S (5,000)	900.00	1100.00	3500.00	RARE	
☐ 1877 (817)	—	2800.00	RARE	RARE	RARE
☐ 1877CC (3,332)	2150.00	2850.00	RARE	RARE	
☐ 1877S (17,000)	650.00	825.00	950.00	RARE	
☐ 1878 (73,800)	650.00	775.00	825.00	1200.00	RARE
☐ 1878CC (3,244)	2000.00	2500.00	RARE	RARE	

DATE	ABP IN F-12	F-12 FINE	EF-40 EX. FINE	MS-60 UNC.	PRF-65 PROOF
☐ 1878S (26,100)					
	750.00	850.00	1000.00	RARE	
☐ 1879 (384,770)					
	650.00	750.00	850.00	1200.00	RARE
☐ 1879CC (1,762)					
	—	RARE	RARE	RARE	
☐ 1879O (1,500)					
	1550.00	1900.00	RARE	RARE	
☐ 1879S (224,000)					
	650.00	750.00	850.00	1100.00	
☐ 1880 (1,644,876)					
	650.00	750.00	850.00	950.00	RARE
☐ 1880CC (11,192)					
	700.00	900.00	1000.00	RARE	
☐ 1880O (9,500)					
	650.00	750.00	850.00	RARE	
☐ 1880S (506,205)					
	650.00	750.00	850.00	950.00	
☐ 1881 (3,877,260)					
	650.00	750.00	850.00	950.00	RARE
☐ 1881CC (24,015)					
	650.00	775.00	1300.00	RARE	
☐ 1881O (8,350)					
	650.00	750.00	1100.00	RARE	
☐ 1881S (970,000)					
	650.00	750.00	850.00	1100.00	
☐ 1882 (2,324,480)					
	650.00	750.00	850.00	950.00	RARE
☐ 1882CC (6,764)					
	950.00	1150.00	1900.00	RARE	
☐ 1882O (10,280)					
	650.00	750.00	850.00	11000.00	
☐ 1882S (132,000)					
	650.00	750.00	850.00	900.00	
☐ 1883 (208,740)					
	650.00	750.00	850.00	925.00	RARE
☐ 1883CC (12,000)					
	700.00	800.00	1400.00	RARE	
☐ 1883O (800)					
	3000.00	4750.00	RARE	RARE	

DATE	ABP IN F-12	F-12 FINE	EF-40 EX. FINE	MS-60 UNC.	PRF-65 PROOF
☐ 1883S (38,000)					
	650.00	750.00	850.00	1450.00	
☐ 1884 (76,017)					
	650.00	750.00	850.00	1050.00	RARE
☐ 1884CC (9,925)					
	850.00	1050.00	1500.00	RARE	
☐ 1884S (124,250)					
	650.00	750.00	850.00	1000.00	
☐ 1885 (124,527)					
	650.00	750.00	850.00	950.00	RARE
☐ 1885S (228,000)					
	650.00	750.00	850.00	950.00	
☐ 1886 (236,160)					
	650.00	750.00	850.00	950.00	
☐ 1886S (826,000)					
	650.00	750.00	850.00	950.00	
☐ 1887 (53,680)					
	650.00	750.00	850.00	1000.00	RARE
☐ 1887S (817,000)					
	650.00	750.00	850.00	950.00	
☐ 1888 (132,996)					
	650.00	750.00	850.00	950.00	RARE
☐ 1888O (21,335)					
	650.00	750.00	850.00	950.00	
☐ 1888S (648,700)					
	650.00	750.00	850.00	950.00	
☐ 1889 (4,485)					
	650.00	750.00	850.00	3250.00	RARE
☐ 1889S (425,400)					
	650.00	750.00	850.00	950.00	
☐ 1890 (58,043)					
	650.00	750.00	850.00	950.00	
☐ 1890CC (17,500)					
	850.00	1100.00	1200.00	3000.00	
☐ 1891 (91,868)					
	650.00	750.00	850.00	950.00	RARE
☐ 1891CC (103,732)					
	850.00	1100.00	1100.00	1650.00	
☐ 1892 (797,552)					
	650.00	750.00	850.00	950.00	

DATE	ABP IN F-12	F-12 FINE	EF-40 EX. FINE	MS-60 UNC.	PRF-65 PROOF
☐ 1892CC (40,000)	850.00	1000.00	1250.00	4000.00	
☐ 1892O (28,688)	700.00	800.00	875.00	1000.00	
☐ 1892S (115,500)	650.00	750.00	850.00	950.00	
☐ 1893 (1,840,895)	650.00	750.00	850.00	950.00	40000.00
☐ 1893CC (14,000)	850.00	1000.00	1250.00	RARE	
☐ 1893O (17,000)	700.00	800.00	900.00	1450.00	
☐ 1893S (141,350)	650.00	750.00	850.00	950.00	
☐ 1894 (2,470,782)	650.00	750.00	850.00	950.00	40000.00
☐ 1894O (197,500)	675.00	775.00	875.00	1150.00	
☐ 1894S (25,000)	650.00	750.00	850.00	3250.00	
☐ 1895 (567,826)	650.00	750.00	850.00	950.00	40000.00
☐ 1895O (98,000)	650.00	750.00	850.00	950.00	
☐ 1895S (49,000)	650.00	750.00	850.00	2500.00	
☐ 1896 (76,348)	650.00	750.00	850.00	950.00	40000.00
☐ 1896S (123,750)	650.00	750.00	850.00	2350.00	
☐ 1897 (1,000,159)	650.00	750.00	850.00	950.00	40000.00
☐ 1897O (42,500)	650.00	750.00	850.00	950.00	
☐ 1897S (234,750)	650.00	750.00	850.00	950.00	
☐ 1898 (812,197)	650.00	750.00	850.00	950.00	40000.00
☐ 1898S (473,600)	650.00	750.00	850.00	950.00	

DATE	ABP IN F-12	F-12 FINE	EF-40 EX. FINE	MS-60 UNC.	PRF-65 PROOF
☐ 1899	(1,262,305)				
	650.00	750.00	850.00	950.00	38500.00
☐ 1899O	(37,047)				
	650.00	750.00	850.00	1125.00	
☐ 1899S	(841,000)				
	650.00	750.00	850.00	1000.00	
☐ 1900	(293,960)				
	650.00	750.00	850.00	950.00	37500.00
☐ 1900S	(81,000)				
	650.00	750.00	850.00	950.00	
☐ 1901	(1,718,825)				
	650.00	750.00	850.00	950.00	37500.00
☐ 1901O	(72,041)				
	650.00	750.00	850.00	975.00	
☐ 1901S	(2,812,750)				
	650.00	750.00	850.00	950.00	
☐ 1902	(82,513)				
	650.00	750.00	850.00	950.00	37500.00
☐ 1902S	(469,500)				
	650.00	750.00	850.00	950.00	
☐ 1903	(125,926)				
	650.00	750.00	850.00	950.00	37500.00
☐ 1903O	(112,771)				
	650.00	750.00	850.00	1075.00	
☐ 1903S	(518,620)				
	650.00	750.00	850.00	950.00	
☐ 1904	(162,038)				
	650.00	750.00	850.00	950.00	40000.00
☐ 1904O	(108,950)				
	650.00	750.00	850.00	1075.00	
☐ 1905	(201,078)				
	650.00	750.00	850.00	950.00	37500.00
☐ 1905S	(369,250)				
	650.00	750.00	850.00	1125.00	
☐ 1906	(165,496)				
	650.00	750.00	850.00	950.00	37500.00
☐ 1906D	(981,000)				
	650.00	750.00	850.00	950.00	
☐ 1906O	(86,895)				
	650.00	750.00	850.00	1000.00	

DATE	ABP IN F-12	F-12 FINE	EF-40 EX. FINE	MS-60 UNC.	PRF-65 PROOF
☐ 1906S	(457,000)				
	650.00	750.00	850.00	950.00	
☐ 1907	(1,203,973)				
	650.00	750.00	850.00	950.00	40000.00
☐ 1907D	(1,020,000)				
	650.00	750.00	850.00	950.00	
☐ 1907S	(210,000)				
	650.00	750.00	850.00	950.00	

EAGLES—INDIAN HEAD, 1907–1933

Augustus Saint-Gaudens, a noted sculptor and really the first artist of international repute to design an American coin, strove to inject a touch of creative feeling in coin design. True to the artistic spirit of the times he sacrificed such supposedly old-fashioned qualities as balance to achieve imagination of line and composition. His eagle, on the reverse, is totally stylized, its strength and symmetry purposely overemphasized. At first the motto IN GOD WE TRUST was omitted, owing to President Theodore Roosevelt's opinion that the name of God was not suitable for use on coinage in any context. He was overruled by Congress in 1908 and the motto appeared shortly thereafter. Striking of Eagles, which had reached as high as nearly 4½ million pieces in a single year ($45,000,000 face value), was discontinued in 1933. The Saint-Gaudens Eagle contained 90% gold and 10% copper, with a diameter of 27mm. and a weight of 16.718 grams. The bullion weight is .48375 of an ounce.

1907–1908 Without Motto

1907–1933

1908–1933 With Motto

Mint Mark is Left of Value on Reverse

DATE	ABP IN VERY FINE	VF-20 V. FINE	EF-40 EX. FINE	MS-60 UNC.	PRF-65 PROOF
☐ 1907 Without Periods (239,406)					
	675.00	735.00	800.00	1100.00	
☐ 1907 Wire Rim With Periods Before and After U.S.A. (500)					
	15000.00			23000.00	
☐ 1907 Rolled Rim, Periods (42)				RARE	
☐ 1908 No Motto (33,500)					
	675.00	735.00	800.00	1250.00	
☐ 1908 With Motto (341,486)					
	800.00	850.00	900.00	1000.00	55000.00
☐ 1908D No Motto (210,000)					
	675.00	735.00	800.00	1200.00	
☐ 1908D (386,500)					
	675.00	735.00	900.00	1150.00	
☐ 1908S (59,850)					
	825.00	875.00	1100.00	2750.00	
☐ 1909 (184,863)					
	675.00	735.00	800.00	950.00	80000.00
☐ 1909D (121,540)					
	675.00	735.00	800.00	1200.00	
☐ 1909S (292,350)					
	675.00	750.00	950.00	1300.00	
☐ 1910 (318,704)					
	675.00	735.00	825.00	950.00	70000.00
☐ 1910D (2,356,640)					
	675.00	735.00	800.00	950.00	
☐ 1910S (811,000)					
	675.00	735.00	850.00	1400.00	
☐ 1911 (505,595)					
	675.00	735.00	800.00	925.00	55000.00
☐ 1911D (30,100)					
	950.00	1100.00	2150.00	12000.00	
☐ 1911S (51,000)					
	850.00	1000.00	1150.00	2400.00	
☐ 1912 (405,083)					
	675.00	735.00	825.00	950.00	55000.00
☐ 1912S (300,000)					
	675.00	735.00	825.00	1400.00	
☐ 1913 (442,071).					
	675.00	735.00	825.00	950.00	55000.00

DATE	ABP IN VERY FINE	VF-20 V. FINE	EF-40 EX. FINE	MS-60 UNC.	PRF-65 PROOF
☐ 1913S	(66,000)				
	850.00	1050.00	1200.00	7750.00	
☐ 1914	(151,050)				
	675.00	735.00	850.00	900.00	55000.00
☐ 1914D	(343,500)				
	675.00	735.00	850.00	900.00	
☐ 1914S	(208,000)				
	850.00	1000.00	1100.00	1500.00	
☐ 1915	(351,075)				
	675.00	735.00	850.00	900.00	55000.00
☐ 1915S	(59,000)				
	850.00	1050.00	1100.00	4500.00	
☐ 1916S	(138,500)				
	675.00	735.00	850.00	1300.00	
☐ 1920S	(126,500)				
	12500.00	15000.00	19000.00	RARE	
☐ 1926	(1,014,000)				
	675.00	735.00	850.00	900.00	
☐ 1930S	(96,000)				
	8500.00	10500.00	15000.00	27000.00	
☐ 1932	(1,463,000)				
	675.00	735.00	850.00	900.00	
☐ 1933	(312,500)			VERY RARE	

Note: The rare dates of this series are heavily counterfeited. Be sure that you buy from a reputable dealer.

DOUBLE EAGLES—
$20.00 GOLD PIECES

The Double Eagle or $20 gold piece was the largest denomination coin issued for regular use by the U.S. Mint. It was introduced in 1849, as a direct result of the California gold strikes. Discovery of gold at Sutter's Mill had not only made vast new supplies available to the government, but also focused increased attention on gold as a medium of exchange. Necessity for a $20 face value coin was further prompted by the fact that the Treasury Department was not yet issuing paper currency.

These coins are known as Double Eagles, as a result of being twice the size of Eagles or $10 gold pieces. Their composition was exactly the same as the lower denomination gold coins, .900 fine, or nine parts of 24K gold alloyed with one part copper. The Double Eagle contained .96750 of an ounce of pure gold, or just a slight fraction under one full ounce. With the copper content added, the coin's weight was more than an ounce, making it not only our highest denomination coin but the heaviest physically. However, it was smaller in diameter than the silver $1, at 34mm.

The first Double Eagles carried a portrait of Liberty facing left, by James B. Longacre, with a heraldic eagle on the reverse. Two significant changes were made during the use of this design, which was removed in 1907. In 1866 the motto IN GOD WE TRUST was added above the eagle, and in 1877 the statement of value (on the reverse) was changed from TWENTY D. to TWENTY DOLLARS.

PLEASE NOTE: THE PRICES THAT ARE LISTED REFLECT A GOLD SPOT PRICE OF $1250.00 PER OUNCE.

DOUBLE EAGLES—LIBERTY HEAD, 1849–1866

Mint Mark is Below Eagle on Reverse

DATE	ABP IN VF-20	VF-20 V. FINE	EF-40 EX. FINE	MS-60 UNC.	PRF-65 PROOF
☐ 1849	UNIQUE—Only 1 Known in U.S. Mint Collection				
☐ 1850	(1,170,261)				
	1625.00	1850.00	2250.00	12500.00	
☐ 1850O	(141,000)				
	1650.00	2000.00	4350.00	RARE	
☐ 1851	(2,087,155)				
	1625.00	1950.00	2100.00	8500.00	
☐ 1851O	(315,000)				
	1650.00	2100.00	3750.00	RARE	
☐ 1852	(2,053,026)				
	1625.00	1850.00	2150.00	4850.00	
☐ 1852O	(190,000)				
	1700.00	2000.00	3500.00	RARE	
☐ 1853	(1,261,326)				
	1625.00	1850.00	2150.00	5150.00	
☐ 1853O	(71,000)				
	1750.00	2100.00	3600.00	RARE	
☐ 1854	(757,899)				
	1625.00	1850.00	2150.00	8500.00	
☐ 1854O	(3,250)		VERY RARE		
☐ 1854S	(141,469)				
	1625.00	1850.00	3250.00	RARE	
☐ 1855	(364,666)				
	1625.00	1850.00	2150.00	9500.00	
☐ 1855O	(8,000)				
	7500.00	11000.00	RARE	RARE	
☐ 1855S	(879,675)				
	1625.00	1875.00	2150.00	7750.00	
☐ 1856	(329,878)				
	1625.00	1850.00	2150.00	8250.00	

DATE	ABP IN VF-20	VF-20 V. FINE	EF-40 EX. FINE	MS-60 UNC.	PRF-65 PROOF
☐ 1856O	(2,250) EXTREMELY RARE				
☐ 1856S	(1,189,750)				
	1700.00	2000.00	2150.00	6250.00	
☐ 1857	(439,375)				
	1625.00	1850.00	2100.00	4000.00	
☐ 1857O	(30,000)				
	1750.00	2000.00	4000.00	RARE	
☐ 1857S	(970,500)				
	1625.00	1850.00	2100.00	5500.00	
☐ 1858	(211,714)				
	1625.00	1850.00	2100.00	6750.00	
☐ 1858O	(35,250)				
	1900.00	2650.00	4750.00	RARE	
☐ 1858S	(846,710)				
	1625.00	1850.00	2100.00	8250.00	
☐ 1859	(43,597)				
	1750.00	2000.00	2600.00	RARE	
☐ 1859S	(636,445)				
	1625.00	1850.00	2100.00	9250.00	
☐ 1859O	(9,100)				
	4500.00	6500.00	RARE	RARE	
☐ 1860	(577,670)				
	1625.00	1850.00	2100.00	6000.00	RARE
☐ 1860O	(6,600)				
		RARE	RARE	RARE	
☐ 1860S	(544,950)				
	1625.00	1850.00	2100.00	7500.00	
☐ 1861	(2,976,453)				
	1625.00	1850.00	2150.00	6250.00	
☐ 1861O	(5,000)				
	—	RARE	RARE	RARE	
☐ 1861S	(768,000)				
	1625.00	1850.00	2250.00	12500.00	
☐ 1862	(92,133)				
	2000.00	2400.00	5500.00	RARE	RARE
☐ 1862S	(854,173)				
	1625.00	1900.00	2200.00	RARE	
☐ 1863	(142,790)				
	1850.00	2100.00	3250.00	RARE	RARE
☐ 1863S	(966,570)				
	1625.00	1950.00	2400.00	7500.00	

DATE	ABP IN VF-20	VF-20 V. FINE	EF-40 EX. FINE	MS-60 UNC.	PRF-65 PROOF
☐ 1864	(204,285)				
	1700.00	2000.00	2400.00	RARE	
☐ 1864S	(793,660)				
	1625.00	1875.00	2250.00	10000.00	
☐ 1865	(351,200)				
	1625.00	2000.00	2250.00	7250.00	
☐ 1865S	(1,042,500)				
	1625.00	2000.00	2250.00	6000.00	
☐ 1866S	(842,250)				
		RARE	RARE	RARE	

DOUBLE EAGLES—LIBERTY HEAD, 1866–1876, WITH MOTTO AND "TWENTY D" ON REVERSE

Mint Mark is Below Eagle on Reverse

DATE	ABP IN VF-20	VF-20 V. FINE	EF-40 EX. FINE	MS-60 UNC.	PRF-65 PROOF
☐ 1866	(698,775)				
	1450.00	1650.00	1800.00	RARE	RARE
☐ 1866S	(842,250)				
	1450.00	1650.00	1800.00	RARE	
☐ 1867	(238,760)				
	1450.00	1650.00	1750.00	4500.00	
☐ 1867S	(920,250)				
	1450.00	1650.00	2000.00	RARE	
☐ 1868	(98,600)				
	1500.00	1800.00	2100.00	RARE	RARE
☐ 1868S	(837,500)				
	1475.00	1700.00	2000.00	RARE	
☐ 1869	(175,155)				
	1450.00	1650.00	1800.00	7500.00	RARE

DATE	ABP IN VF-20	VF-20 V. FINE	EF-40 EX. FINE	MS-60 UNC.	PRF-65 PROOF
☐ 1869S	(686,750)				
	1450.00	1650.00	1750.00	8250.00	
☐ 1870	(155,185)				
	1450.00	1650.00	1750.00	RARE	RARE
☐ 1870CC	(3,789)		VERY RARE		
☐ 1870S	(982,000)				
	1450.00	1650.00	1750.00	6750.00	
☐ 1871	(80,150)				
	1450.00	1650.00	1800.00	9000.00	RARE
☐ 1871CC	(14,687)				
		RARE	RARE	RARE	
☐ 1871S	(928,000)				
	1450.00	1650.00	1750.00	5500.00	
☐ 1872	(251,880)				
	1450.00	1650.00	1750.00	5000.00	RARE
☐ 1872CC	(29,650)				
	1900.00	2650.00	5750.00	RARE	
☐ 1872S	(780,000)				
	1400.00	1600.00	1750.00	3500.00	
☐ 1873	(1,709,825)				
	1400.00	1600.00	1700.00	2400.00	RARE
☐ 1873CC	(22,410)				
	2250.00	3000.00	RARE	RARE	
☐ 1873S	(1,040,600)				
	1400.00	1600.00	1700.00	2250.00	
☐ 1874	(366,800)				
	1400.00	1600.00	1700.00	2500.00	
☐ 1874CC	(115,085)				
	1750.00	2050.00	2850.00	RARE	
☐ 1874S	(1,241,000)				
	1400.00	1600.00	1700.00	2500.00	
☐ 1875	(295,740)				
	1400.00	1600.00	1700.00	2150.00	
☐ 1875CC	(111,151)				
	1550.00	1900.00	2350.00	8000.00	
☐ 1875S	(1,230,000)				
	1400.00	1600.00	1700.00	2150.00	
☐ 1876	(583,905)				
	1400.00	1600.00	1700.00	2350.00	
☐ 1876CC	(138,441)				
	1550.00	1900.00	2500.00	11500.00	

DATE	ABP IN VF-20	VF-20 V. FINE	EF-40 EX. FINE	MS-60 UNC.	PRF-65 PROOF
☐ 1876S	(1,597,000)				
	1450.00	1600.00	1700.00	2150.00	

Note: 1861 and 1861S both with A. C. Paquet Reverse; 61-5 Rare; 61 Ex. Rare

DOUBLE EAGLES—LIBERTY, 1877–1907, WITH MOTTO AND "TWENTY DOLLARS" ON REVERSE

Mint Mark is Below Eagle on Reverse

DATE	ABP IN VF-20	VF-20 V. FINE	EF-40 EX. FINE	MS-60 UNC.	PRF-65 PROOF
☐ 1877	(397,670)				
	1325.00	1500.00	1600.00	1850.00	RARE
☐ 1877CC	(42,565)				
	1750.00	2050.00	2350.00	RARE	
☐ 1877S	(1,735,000)				
	1325.00	1500.00	1600.00	1850.00	
☐ 1878	(534,645)				
	1325.00	1600.00	1700.00	1850.00	RARE
☐ 1878CC	(13,180)				
	1900.00	2400.00	4750.00	RARE	
☐ 1878S	(1,739,000)				
	1300.00	1500.00	1600.00	1850.00	
☐ 1879	(2,075,630)				
	1300.00	1500.00	1550.00	1800.00	
☐ 1879CC	(10,708)				
	2500.00	3250.00	5750.00	RARE	
☐ 1879O	(2,325)				
		RARE	RARE	RARE	
☐ 1879S	(1,223,800)				
	1300.00	1500.00	1550.00	1750.00	

DATE	ABP IN VF-20	VF-20 V. FINE	EF-40 EX. FINE	MS-60 UNC.	PRF-65 PROOF
☐ 1880 (51,456)					
	1400.00	1600.00	1700.00	5250.00	RARE
☐ 1880S (836,000)					
	1300.00	1500.00	1550.00	1700.00	
☐ 1881 (2,260)					
		RARE	RARE	RARE	
☐ 1881S (727,000)					
	1300.00	1500.00	1550.00	1700.00	
☐ 1882 (630)					
		RARE	RARE	RARE	
☐ 1882CC (39,140)					
	1700.00	2000.00	2750.00	RARE	
☐ 1882S (1,125,000)					
	1300.00	1500.00	1550.00	1750.00	
☐ 1883 Proofs Only (40)	EXTREMELY RARE				
☐ 1883CC (59,962)					
	1700.00	2000.00	2600.00	9750.00	
☐ 1883S (1,189,000)					
	1650.00	1950.00	2050.00	2200.00	
☐ 1884 Proofs Only (71)					VERY RARE
☐ 1884CC (81,139)					
	1600.00	1800.00	2350.00	7250.00	
☐ 1884S (916,000)					
	1300.00	1500.00	1550.00	1750.00	
☐ 1885 (828)					
		RARE	RARE	RARE	
☐ 1885CC (9,450)					
	1900.00	2300.00	5750.00	RARE	
☐ 1885S (683,500)					
	1300.00	1500.00	1550.00	1750.00	
☐ 1886 (1,106)					
		RARE	RARE	RARE	
☐ 1887 Proofs Only (121)					VERY RARE
☐ 1887S (283,000)					
	1300.00	1500.00	1550.00	1750.00	
☐ 1888 (226,266)					
	1300.00	1500.00	1550.00	1750.00	
☐ 1888S (859,600)					
	1300.00	1500.00	1550.00	1750.00	
☐ 1889 (44,111)					
	1300.00	1500.00	1550.00	1850.00	

DATE	ABP IN VF-20	VF-20 V. FINE	EF-40 EX. FINE	MS-60 UNC.	PRF-65 PROOF
☐ 1889CC	(30,945)				
	1650.00	1900.00	2250.00	8000.00	
☐ 1889S	(774,700)				
	1300.00	1350.00	1375.00		
☐ 1890	(75,995)				
	1300.00	1350.00	1375.00	160.00	85000.00
☐ 1890CC	(91,209)				
	1650.00	1900.00	2100.00	5250.00	
☐ 1890S	(802,750)				
	1300.00	1350.00	1400.00	2200.00	
☐ 1891	(1,442)				
	5000.00	6500.00	15000.00	RARE	90000.00
☐ 1891CC	(5,000)				
	3000.00	4250.00	10000.00	RARE	
☐ 1891S	(1,288,125)				
	1300.00	1350.00	1375.00	1600.00	
☐ 1892	(4,523)				
	1625.00	1850.00	3250.00	15500.00	85000.00
☐ 1892CC	(27,265)				
	1650.00	1900.00	2250.00	8000.00	
☐ 1892S	(930,150)				
	1300.00	1350.00	1375.00	1600.00	
☐ 1893	(344,399)				
	1350.00	1425.00	1475.00	1700.00	85000.00
☐ 1893CC	(18,402)				
	1650.00	1900.00	2350.00	7750.00	
☐ 1893S	(996,175)				
	1300.00	1350.00	1375.00	1600.00	
☐ 1894	(1,368,990)				
	1325.00	1375.00	1400.00	1650.00	85000.00
☐ 1894S	(1,048,550)				
	1300.00	1350.00	1375.00	1600.00	
☐ 1895	(1,114,656)				
	1300.00	1350.00	1375.00	1600.00	85000.00
☐ 1895S	(1,143,500)				
	1300.00	1350.00	1375.00	1600,00	
☐ 1896	(792,663)				
	1300.00	1350.00	1375.00	1600.00	85000.00
☐ 1896S	(1,403,925)				
	1300.00	1350.00	1375.00	1600.00	

DATE	ABP IN VF-20	VF-20 V. FINE	EF-40 EX. FINE	MS-60 UNC.	PRF-65 PROOF
☐ 1897	(1,383,261)				
	1300.00	1350.00	1375.00	1600.00	85000.00
☐ 1897S	(1,470,250)				
	1300.00	1350.00	1375.00	1600.00	
☐ 1898	(170,470)				
	1300.00	1350.00	1375.00	1600.00	85000.00
☐ 1898S	(2,575,175)				
	1300.00	1350.00	1375.00	1600.00	
☐ 1899	(1,669,384)				
	1300.00	1350.00	1375.00	1600.00	85000.00
☐ 1899S	(2,010,300)				
	1300.00	1350.00	1375.00	1600.00	
☐ 1900	(1,874,584)				
	1300.00	1350.00	1375.00	1600.00	85000.00
☐ 1900S	(2,459,500)				
	1300.00	1350.00	1375.00	1600.00	
☐ 1901	(111,526)				
	1300.00	1350.00	1375.00	1600.00	85000.00
☐ 1901S	(1,596,000)				
	1300.00	1350.00	1375.00	1600.00	
☐ 1902	(31,254)				
	1300.00	1350.00	1375.00	1600.00	85000.00
☐ 1902S	(1,753,625)				
	1300.00	1350.00	1375.00	1600.00	NOT MADE
☐ 1903	(287,428)				
	1300.00	1350.00	1375.00	1600.00	85000.00
☐ 1903S	(954,000)				
	1300.00	1350.00	1375.00	1600.00	
☐ 1904	(6,256,797)				
	1300.00	1350.00	1375.00	1600.00	85000.00
☐ 1904S	(5,134,175)				
	1300.00	1350.00	1375.00	1600.00	
☐ 1905	(59,011)				
	1300.00	1350.00	1375.00	1600.00	85000.00
☐ 1905S	(1,813,000)				
	1300.00	1350.00	1375.00	1600.00	
☐ 1906	(69,690)				
	1300.00	1350.00	1375.00	1600.00	85000.00
☐ 1906D	(620,250)				
	1300.00	1350.00	1375.00	1600.00	

DATE	ABP IN VF-20	VF-20 V. FINE	EF-40 EX. FINE	MS-60 UNC.	PRF-65 PROOF
☐ 1906S	(2,065,750)				
	1300.00	1350.00	1375.00	1600.00	
☐ 1907	(1,451,864)				
	1300.00	1350.00	1375.00	1600.00	8500.00
☐ 1907D	(842,250)				
	1300.00	1350.00	1375.00	1600.00	
☐ 1907S	(2,165,800)				
	1300.00	1350.00	1375.00	1600.00	

DOUBLE EAGLES—$20.00 GOLD PIECES, 1907–1933

The Longacre Liberty design was replaced by the Saint-Gaudens in 1907, featuring a striding figure of Liberty holding a torch on the obverse and an eagle in flight on the reverse. A fact seldom mentioned is that this, of all representations of Liberty on our coins, was the only full-face likeness, the others being profiles or semiprofiles. Composition and weight remained as previously. The motto IN GOD WE TRUST, at first omitted on request of Theodore Roosevelt, was added by an Act of Congress in 1908. Striking of Double Eagles ceased in 1933. This final version of the mighty coin had a 90% gold/10% copper composition, with a weight of 33.436 grams (of which .96750 of an ounce was pure gold—almost a full ounce). Its diameter was 34mm.

As a speculative item for gold investors, the Double Eagle has enjoyed greater popularity and media publicity in recent months than ever in its history. This should not be surprising, as it contains very nearly an exact ounce of gold and its worth as bullion can be figured easily based upon daily gold quotations.

DOUBLE EAGLE LIBERTY STANDING "ST. GAUDENS" ROMAN NUMERALS MCMVII

Roman Numeral High Relief, Wire Rim,
Plain Edge, 14 Rays over Capitol.
Three Folds on Liberty's Skirt

DATE	ABP IN VF-20	VF-20 V. FINE	EF-40 EX. FINE	MS-60 UNC.	PRF-65 CH. PROOF
☐ 1907-MCMVII Ex. High Relief—Lettered Edge					VERY RARE
☐ 1907-MCMVII Ex. High Relief—Plain Edge					VERY RARE
☐ 1907 Flat Rim*	6250.00	7750.00	9000.00	15000.00	
☐ 1907 Wire Rim* (11,250)	6000.00	7500.00	8750.00	14500.00	

*Note: Separate mintage figures were not kept on the 1907 flat rim and wire rim varieties.

DOUBLE EAGLES—LIBERTY STANDING "ST. GAUDENS," 1907–1908 DATE IN ARABIC NUMERALS, NO MOTTO ON REVERSE

Mint Mark is Out on Obverse

DATE	MINTAGE	ABP IN VF-20	VF-20 V. FINE	EF-40 EX. FINE	MS-60 UNC.
☐ 1907*	361,667	1300.00	1500.00	1550.00	1650.00
☐ 1908	4,271,551	1300.00	1500.00	1550.00	1650.00

*Note: Small Letters on Edge, Large Letter on Edge—Unique.

DOUBLE EAGLES—LIBERTY STANDING
"ST. GAUDENS," 1908–1933
WITH MOTTO ON REVERSE

Motto
IN GOD
WE TRUST

Mint Mark is Out on Obverse

DATE	ABP IN VF-20	VF-20 V. FINE	EF-40 EX. FINE	MS-60 UNC.	PRF-65 PROOF
☐ 1908DNM	(663,750)				
	1300.00	1500.00	1550.00	1600.00	
☐ 1908WM	(156,359)				
	1300.00	1500.00	1550.00	1600.00	
☐ 1908DWM	(349,500)				
	1300.00	1500.00	1550.00	1600.00	
☐ 1908SWM	(22,000)				
	2350.00	2850.00	3150.00	11000.00	
☐ 1909	(161,282)				
	1300.00	1500.00	1600.00	1625.00	90000.00
☐ 1909 over 8					
	1750.00	1900.00	2100.00	2350.00	
☐ 1909D	(52,500)				
	1300.00	1500.00	1550.00	3250.00	
☐ 1909S	(2,774,925)				
	1300.00	1500.00	1550.00	1600.00	
☐ 1910	(482,167)				
	1300.00	1500.00	1550.00	1600.00	85000.00
☐ 1910D	(429,000)				
	1300.00	1500.00	1550.00	1600.00	
☐ 1910S	(2,128,250)				
	1300.00	1500.00	1550.00	1600.00	
☐ 1911	(197,350)				
	1300.00	1500.00	1550.00	1600.00	85000.00
☐ 1911D	(846,500)				
	1300.00	1500.00	1550.00	1600.00	
☐ 1911S	(775,750)				
	1300.00	1500.00	1550.00	1600.00	

DATE	ABP IN VF-20	VF-20 V. FINE	EF-40 EX. FINE	MS-60 UNC.	PRF-65 PROOF
☐ 1912	(149,824)				
	1300.00	1500.00	1550.00	1600.00	90000.00
☐ 1913	(168,838)				
	1300.00	1500.00	1550.00	1600.00	90000.00
☐ 1913D	(393,500)				
	1300.00	1500.00	1550.00	1600.00	
☐ 1913S	(34,000)				
	1300.00	1500.00	1550.00	2600.00	
☐ 1914	(95,320)				
	1300.00	1500.00	1600.00	1650.00	90000.00
☐ 1914D	(453,000)				
	1300.00	1525.00	1575.00	1625.00	
☐ 1914S	(1,498,000)				
	1300.00	1500.00	1550.00	1600.00	
☐ 1915	(152,050)				
	1300.00	1500.00	1550.00	1600.00	90000.00
☐ 1915S	(567,500)				
	1300.00	1500.00	1550.00	1600.00	
☐ 1916S	(796,000)				
	1300.00	1500.00	1550.00	1600.00	
☐ 1920	(228,250)				
	1300.00	1500.00	1550.00	1600.00	
☐ 1920S	(558,000)				
	12500.00	16000.00	18000.00	50000.00	
☐ 1921	(528,500)				
	27500.00	35000.00	RARE	RARE	
☐ 1922	(1,375,500)				
	1300.00	1500.00	1550.00	1600.00	
☐ 1922S	(2,658,000)				
	1300.00	1500.00	1550.00	2500.00	
☐ 1923	(566,000)				
	1300.00	1500.00	1550.00	1600.00	
☐ 1923D	(1,702,000)				
	1300.00	1500.00	1550.00	1600.00	
☐ 1924	(4,323,500)				
	1300.00	1500.00	1550.00	1600.00	
☐ 1924D	(3,049,500)				
	1325.00	1525.00	1600.00	4200.00	
☐ 1924S	(2,927,500)				
	1325.00	1550.00	1700.00	4250.00	

DATE	ABP IN VF-20	VF-20 V. FINE	EF-40 EX. FINE	MS-60 UNC.	NONE ADD AFTER 1915
☐ 1925	(2,831,750)				
	1300.00	1500.00	1550.00	1600.00	
☐ 1925D	(2,938,500)				
	1650.00	1900.00	2750.00	4750.00	
☐ 1925S	(2,776,500)				
	1850.00	2250.00	4000.00	10000.00	
☐ 1926	(816,750)				
	1300.00	1500.00	1550.00	1600.00	
☐ 1926D	(481,000)				
	13000.00	16500.00	18000.00	23000.00	
☐ 1926S	(2,041,500)				
	1650.00	1800.00	1950.00	3400.00	
☐ 1927	(2,946,750)				
	1300.00	1500.00	1525.00	1575.00	
☐ 1927D	(180,000)			VERY RARE	
☐ 1927S	(3,107,000)				
	6500.00	8000.00	9500.00	25000.00	
☐ 1928	(8,816,000)				
	1300.00	1500.00	1525.00	1575.00	
☐ 1929	(1,779,750)				
	9000.00	12000.00	13500.00	23000.00	
☐ 1930S	(74,000.00)				
		RARE	RARE	RARE	
☐ 1931	(2,938,250)				
	10000.00	12500.00	14000.00	35000.00	
☐ 1931D	(106,500)				
	9000.00	11000.00	12500.00	42500.00	
☐ 1932	(1,101,750)				
	11000.00	15000.00	16000.00	32500.00	
☐ 1933*	(445,525)			7,500,000.00	

*Note: Never placed in circulation because of gold recall legislation. 1 coin legalized.

COMMEMORATIVE COINAGE

Commemorative coinage—that is, coins whose designs present a departure from the normal types for their denomination—was first struck in the ancient world. Roman emperors delighted in issuing coins portraying members of the family or topical events; they served an important propaganda purpose. Commemorative coins must be distinguished from medals, as the former have a stated face value and can be spent as money while the latter serve a decorative function only. During the Mint's first century it coined no commemoratives whatever. Its first was the Columbian half dollar of 1892, issued in connection with the Columbia Exposition. To date the total has reached 158 pieces, of which one is a silver dollar; one a silver quarter; 143 are half dollars (comprising 48 major types); two are $2.50 gold pieces; two are $50 gold pieces; and nine are $1 gold pieces. There is some objection to including the $50 Quintuple Eagles as commemorative *coins*, as regular coins of this denomination were never issued. They do, however, bear a statement of face value and are spendable.

Commemorative coins are issued by a special Act of Congress and overseen by a committee established for the purpose. Sale of commemoratives is made to the public (and coin dealers) at an advance in price over the face value, this advance being excused on grounds that specimens supplied as choice and uncirculated have, presumably, sufficient collector appeal to be worth more than their stated denomination. While commemoratives have certainly not all advanced in price at a comparable pace, all have shown very healthy increases and proved excellent investments for their original or early purchasers.

A pair of medals is traditionally collected in conjunction with commemorative silver coins and careful note should be taken of them: the Octagonal North American Centennial, 1828–1925, designed by Opus Fraser, struck on thick and thin planchets in a total issue of 40,000 (the latter are scarcer); and the Wilson dollar, designed by George T. Morgan of Morgan dollar fame in connection with the opening of the Philippine Mint. The 2 Kroner commemoratives of 1936 issued by Sweden are also frequently collected with our commemoratives, though small in size and quite plentiful, as they relate to the Delaware Tercentenary, or 300th anniversary.

The extent to which commemorative coins have been used as money is not precisely determined but is thought to be very limited. As the original owners paid a premium for these coins it is not likely that many—except in time of dire need—would have cared to exchange them merely at face value. It should not automatically be presumed that specimens in less than Uncirculated condition were indeed used as money and passed through many hands. Their substandard preservation could well be the result of injury, ill-advised cleaning or mounting procedures, or wear received from handling in traveling from collection to collection. Nevertheless, discriminating buyers expect commemoratives to be in Uncirculated state and anything inferior is worth much less (the discount being sharper than for a circulating coin).

The existence of proofs among the commemorative series has aroused much debate. Commemoratives are occasionally seen as proofs, notably the Columbian and Isabella quarters, but this is no evidence that all or even a majority of commemoratives were available in proof state. It is easy to be confused on this point, as well-struck Uncirculated specimens occasionally have a prooflike appearance.

The gold commemorative series began not long after the silver, in 1903. Far fewer gold commemoratives were issued, as the large physical size necessary for impressive designing resulted in a coin of very high face value. Experiments were made with $1 gold commemoratives, which some critics called puny, and goliaths of $50 denomination, which were indeed eye-catching but well beyond the budget of most citizens in those days. The value of these pieces in Extremely Fine condition is about one-third the price for Uncirculated—ample proof that most buying activity originates with numismatists rather than bullion speculators.

EARLY COMMEMORATIVE COINS, 1892–1954
COLUMBIAN EXPOSITION (Silver $.25)

Comparatively little notice was at first taken of this handsome commemorative, because the Columbian Exposition (at which it was issued) had already produced a commemorative and a larger one, in fifty-cent denomination. The Isabella quarter dollar, originally sold at the exposition for $1, soon became a popular favorite of collectors. Agitation for it was made by the fair's Board of Lady Managers, which may explain why it portrays a female on the obverse—Isabella of Spain, who helped finance Columbus's voyage round the world—and a symbol of "female industry" on its reverse. The coin was designed by C. E. Barber and struck in 1893.

DATE	MINTAGE	ABP IN MS-60	MS-60 UNC.	MS-65 UNC.
☐ 1893	24,214	375.00	475.00	2350.00

COLUMBIAN EXPOSITION (Silver $.50)

DATE	MINTAGE	ABP IN MS-60	MS-60 UNC.	MS-65 UNC.
☐ 1892	950,000	20.00	28.00	425.00
☐ 1893	1,550,405	20.00	27.00	400.00

LAFAYETTE MONUMENT (Silver $1.00)

The celebrated Lafayette dollar holds a special rank among commemoratives, being the first $1 denomination coin of its sort and the first to portray an American president. On its obverse is a profile bust of General Lafayette (the French officer so instrumental to our efforts in ending colonial domination) over which a profile of Washington is superimposed. The reverse carries a fine equestrian likeness of Lafayette, adapted from a statue put up in Paris as a gift from the American people. This coin was designed by C. E. Barber and struck in 1900. It was sold originally at twice the face value, with proceeds going to the Lafayette Memorial Commission.

DATE	MINTAGE	ABP IN MS-60	MS-60 UNC.	MS-65 UNC.
☐ 1900	36,026	675.00	875.00	10000.00

LOUISIANA PURCHASE EXPOSITION
(Gold $1.00)

1903–Jefferson   1903–McKinley

DATE	MINTAGE	ABP IN MS-60	MS-60 UNC.	MS-65 UNC.
☐ 1903 Jefferson	17,500	450.00	650.00	1700.00
☐ 1903 McKinley	17,500	450.00	650.00	1650.00

LEWIS AND CLARK EXPOSITION (Gold $1.00)

DATE	MINTAGE	ABP IN MS-60	MS-60 UNC.	MS-65 UNC.
☐ 1904	10,025	800.00	1100.00	6750.00
☐ 1905	10,041	1100.00	1350.00	12500.00

PANAMA-PACIFIC EXPOSITION (Silver $.50)

DATE	MINTAGE	ABP IN MS-60	MS-60 UNC.	MS-65 UNC.
☐ 1915S	27,134	375.00	525.00	1650.00

PANAMA-PACIFIC EXPOSITION (Gold $1.00)

Panama-Pacific

DATE	MINTAGE	ABP IN MS-60	MS-60 UNC.	MS-65 UNC.
☐ 1915S	15,000	450.00	625.00	1500.00

PANAMA-PACIFIC EXPOSITION (Gold $2.50)

DATE	MINTAGE	ABP IN MS-60	MS-60 UNC.	MS-65 UNC.
☐ 1915S	6,766	1500.00	2000.00	6500.00

PANAMA-PACIFIC EXPOSITION (Gold $50.00)

This huge coin, containing nearly 2½ ounces of gold, was not the world's largest gold piece but by far the most substantial coin of that metal struck by the U.S. government. (To give some indication of changes in the market from 1915, the date of issue, until today, $50 worth of gold today is about one-sixth of an ounce.) It was issued for the Panama-Pacific Exposition and was struck in two varieties, one with round and one with octagonal edge, the former being somewhat scarcer and more valuable. Minerva is pictured on the obverse and the Athenian state symbol, the owl, representative of wisdom, on the reverse. The place of issue was San Francisco and the designer Robert Aitken. This is definitely not a piece for bullion speculators as its value is many times that of the gold content and under no circumstances would a $50 Panama-Pacific—or any U.S. gold commemorative—be melted down.

ROUND

DATE	MINTAGE	ABP IN MS-60	MS-60 UNC.	MS-65 UNC.
☐ 1915S	483	47500.00	65000.00	160000.00

OCTAGONAL

DATE	MINTAGE	ABP IN MS-60	MS-60 UNC.	MS-65 UNC.
☐ 1915S	645	46500.00	62500.00	150000.00

Note: The double sets were authorized Mint issues. They consisted of two specimens of each coin, mounted so that both sides could be seen. The original price in 1915 was $400.

McKINLEY MEMORIAL (Gold $1.00)

DATE	MINTAGE	ABP IN MS-60	MS-60 UNC.	MS-65 UNC.
☐ 1916	10,003	400.00	575.00	1500.00
☐ 1917	8,004	525.00	700.00	1850.00

ILLINOIS CENTENNIAL (Silver $.50)

DATE	MINTAGE	ABP IN MS-60	MS-60 UNC.	MS-65 UNC.
☐ 1918	100,058	110.00	135.00	450.00

MAINE CENTENNIAL (Silver $.50)

DATE	MINTAGE	ABP IN MS-60	MS-60 UNC.	MS-65 UNC.
☐ 1920	50,028	115.00	160.00	425.00

PILGRIM TERCENTENARY (Silver $.50)

DATE	MINTAGE	ABP IN MS-60	MS-60 UNC.	MS-65 UNC.
☐ 1920	152,112	75.00	100.00	235.00
☐ 1921	20,053	125.00	195.00	350.00

MISSOURI CENTENNIAL (Silver $.50)

DATE	MINTAGE	ABP IN MS-60	MS-60 UNC.	MS-65 UNC.
☐ 1921	15,428	400.00	600.00	3000.00
☐ 1921 Same with 2 × 4 (Above 1821)	5,000	550.00	700.00	2900.00

ALABAMA CENTENNIAL (Silver $.50)

DATE	MINTAGE	ABP IN MS-60	MS-60 UNC.	MS-65 UNC.
☐ 1921	59,038	150.00	210.00	1400.00
☐ 1921 Same with 2 × 2 on Obverse				
	6,006	240.00	350.00	1450.00

GRANT MEMORIAL (Silver $.50)

DATE	MINTAGE	ABP IN MS-60	MS-60 UNC.	MS-65 UNC.
☐ 1922	67,405	90.00	125.00	625.00
☐ 1922 Same with Star on Obverse				
	4,256	950.00	1300.00	7250.00

GRANT MEMORIAL (Gold $1.00)

1922–Grant

DATE	MINTAGE	ABP IN MS-60	MS-60 UNC.	MS-65 UNC.
☐ 1922	5,016	1150.00	1500.00	2500.00
☐ 1922 Same with Star	5,000	1250.00	1600.00	2600.00

MONROE DOCTRINE CENTENNIAL (Silver $.50)

DATE	MINTAGE	ABP IN MS-60	MS-60 UNC.	MS-65 UNC.
☐ 1923S	274,077	50.00	75.00	1600.00

HUGUENOT-WALLOON TERCENTENARY
(Silver $.50)

DATE	MINTAGE	ABP IN MS-60	MS-60 UNC.	MS-65 UNC.
☐ 1924	142,080	100.00	135.00	300.00

LEXINGTON-CONCORD SESQUICENTENNIAL
(Silver $.50)

DATE	MINTAGE	ABP IN MS-60	MS-60 UNC.	MS-65 UNC.
☐ 1925	162,013	75.00	105.00	400.00

STONE MOUNTAIN MEMORIAL (Silver $.50)

DATE	MINTAGE	ABP IN MS-60	MS-60 UNC.	MS-65 UNC.
☐ 1925	1,314,709	50.00	70.00	200.00

CALIFORNIA DIAMOND JUBILEE (Silver $.50)

DATE	MINTAGE	ABP IN MS-60	MS-60 UNC.	MS-65 UNC.
☐ 1925S	86,594	165.00	215.00	725.00

FORT VANCOUVER CENTENNIAL (Silver $.50)

DATE	MINTAGE	ABP IN MS-60	MS-60 UNC.	MS-65 UNC.
☐ 1925	14,944	275.00	375.00	850.00

AMERICAN INDEPENDENCE
SESQUICENTENNIAL (Silver $.50)

DATE	MINTAGE	ABP IN MS-60	MS-60 UNC.	MS-65 UNC.
☐ 1926	141,120	75.00	105.00	2150.00

AMERICAN INDEPENDENCE
SESQUICENTENNIAL (Gold $2.50)

Philadelphia

DATE	MINTAGE	ABP IN MS-60	MS-60 UNC.	MS-65 UNC.
☐ 1926	46,019	350.00	475.00	3150.00

OREGON TRAIL MEMORIAL (Silver $.50)

DATE	MINTAGE	ABP IN MS-60	MS-60 UNC.	MS-65 UNC.
☐ 1926	47,955	125.00	165.00	265.00
☐ 1926S	83,055	125.00	165.00	275.00
☐ 1928	6,028	175.00	235.00	325.00
☐ 1933D	5,008	300.00	375.00	425.00

DATE	MINTAGE	ABP IN MS-60	MS-60 UNC.	MS-65 UNC.
☐ 1934D	7,006	150.00	200.00	275.00
☐ 1936	10,006	140.00	175.00	285.00
☐ 1936S	5,006	140.00	185.00	325.00
☐ 1937D	12,008	150.00	200.00	300.00
☐ 1938 Set PDS	6,005	350.00	500.00	1000.00
☐ 1939 Set PDS	3,004	1250.00	1650.00	1950.00

VERMONT-BENNINGTON SESQUICENTENNIAL
(Silver $.50)

DATE	MINTAGE	ABP IN MS-60	MS-60 UNC.	MS-65 UNC.
☐ 1927	28,162	200.00	265.00	575.00

HAWAII DISCOVERY SESQUICENTENNIAL
(Silver $.50)

DATE	MINTAGE	ABP IN MS-60	MS-60 UNC.	MS-65 UNC.
☐ 1928	9,958	2000.00	2500.00	4500.00

MARYLAND TERCENTENARY (Silver $.50)

DATE	MINTAGE	ABP IN MS-60	MS-60 UNC.	MS-65 UNC.
☐ 1934	25,015	115.00	160.00	235.00

TEXAS INDEPENDENCE CENTENNIAL (Silver $.50)

DATE	MINTAGE	ABP IN MS-60	MS-60 UNC.	MS-65 UNC.
☐ 1934	61,413	100.00	135.00	225.00
☐ 1935 Set PDS	10,007	300.00	450.00	875.00
☐ 1936 Set PDS	9,039	300.00	450.00	875.00
☐ 1937 Set PDS	6,605	325.00	475.00	900.00
☐ 1938 Set PDS	3,775	550.00	725.00	1250.00

DANIEL BOONE BICENTENNIAL (Silver $.50)

DATE	MINTAGE	ABP IN MS-60	MS-60 UNC.	MS-65 UNC.
☐ 1934	10,007	100.00	130.00	260.00
☐ 1935 Set PDS	5,005	285.00	400.00	775.00

DATE	MINTAGE	ABP IN MS-60	MS-60 UNC.	MS-65 UNC.
☐ 1935 Set (1934 Reverse)				
	2,003	700.00	875.00	1850.00
☐ 1936 Set PDS	5,006	285.00	400.00	775.00
☐ 1937 Set PDS	2,506	650.00	875.00	1250.00
☐ 1938 Set PDS	2,100	825.00	1100.00	1600.00

CONNECTICUT TERCENTENARY (Silver $.50)

DATE	MINTAGE	ABP IN MS-60	MS-60 UNC.	MS-65 UNC.
☐ 1935	25,018	200.00	265.00	400.00

ARKANSAS CENTENNIAL (Silver $.50)

DATE	MINTAGE	ABP IN MS-60	MS-60 UNC.	MS-65 UNC.
☐ 1936 Single Coin		75.00	100.00	160.00
☐ 1935 Set PDS	5,505	225.00	325.00	675.00
☐ 1936 Set PDS	9,660	225.00	325.00	675.00
☐ 1937 Set PDS	5,505	250.00	350.00	750.00
☐ 1938 Set PDS	3,155	400.00	525.00	1750.00
☐ 1939 Set PDS	2,104	800.00	1050.00	2850.00

ARKANSAS-ROBINSON (Silver $.50)

DATE	MINTAGE	ABP IN MS-60	MS-60 UNC.	MS-65 UNC.
☐ 1936	25,265	110.00	150.00	260.00

HUDSON, NEW YORK, SESQUICENTENNIAL (Silver $.50)

DATE	MINTAGE	ABP IN MS-60	MS-60 UNC.	MS-65 UNC.
☐ 1935	10,008	600.00	825.00	1350.00

CALIFORNIA-PACIFIC EXPOSITION, SAN DIEGO (Silver $.50)

DATE	MINTAGE	ABP IN MS-60	MS-60 UNC.	MS-65 UNC.
☐ 1935S	70,132	70.00	95.00	135.00
☐ 1936D	30,082	85.00	110.00	160.00

OLD SPANISH TRAIL (Silver $.50)

DATE	MINTAGE	ABP IN MS-60	MS-60 UNC.	MS-65 UNC.
☐ 1935	10,008	1000.00	1250.00	1450.00

PROVIDENCE, RHODE ISLAND, TERCENTENARY (Silver $.50)

DATE	MINTAGE	ABP IN MS-60	MS-60 UNC.	MS-65 UNC.
☐ 1936		70.00	90.00	145.00
☐ 1936 Set	15,010	225.00	300.00	625.00

CLEVELAND CENTENNIAL AND GREAT LAKES EXPOSITION (Silver $.50)

DATE	MINTAGE	ABP IN MS-60	MS-60 UNC.	MS-65 UNC.
☐ 1936	50,030	80.00	110.00	145.00

WISCONSIN TERRITORIAL CENTENNIAL
(Silver $.50)

DATE	MINTAGE	ABP IN MS-60	MS-60 UNC.	MS-65 UNC.
☐ 1936	25,015	150.00	200.00	235.00

CINCINNATI MUSIC CENTER (Silver $.50)

DATE	MINTAGE	ABP IN MS-60	MS-60 UNC.	MS-65 UNC.
☐ 1936		225.00	275.00	450.00
☐ 1936 Set PDS	5,005	700.00	900.00	1750.00

LONG ISLAND TERCENTENARY (Silver $.50)

DATE	MINTAGE	ABP IN MS-60	MS-60 UNC.	MS-65 UNC.
☐ 1936	81,826	65.00	90.00	185.00

YORK COUNTY, MAINE, TERCENTENARY
(Silver $.50)

DATE	MINTAGE	ABP IN MS-60	MS-60 UNC.	MS-65 UNC.
☐ 1936	25,015	150.00	200.00	250.00

BRIDGEPORT, CONNECTICUT, CENTENNIAL
(Silver $.50)

DATE	MINTAGE	ABP IN MS-60	MS-60 UNC.	MS-65 UNC.
☐ 1936	25,015	100.00	135.00	195.00

LYNCHBURG, VIRGINIA, SESQUICENTENNIAL
(Silver $.50)

DATE	MINTAGE	ABP IN MS-60	MS-60 UNC.	MS-65 UNC.
☐ 1936	20,013	180.00	225.00	285.00

ALBANY, NEW YORK, CHARTER 250TH ANNIVERSARY (Silver $.50)

DATE	MINTAGE	ABP IN MS-60	MS-60 UNC.	MS-65 UNC.
☐ 1936	17,671	225.00	265.00	300.00

ELGIN, ILLINOIS, PIONEER MEMORIAL (Silver $.50)

DATE	MINTAGE	ABP IN MS-60	MS-60 UNC.	MS-65 UNC.
☐ 1936	20,015	150.00	200.00	240.00

SAN FRANCISCO–OAKLAND BAY BRIDGE (Silver $.50)

DATE	MINTAGE	ABP IN MS-60	MS-60 UNC.	MS-65 UNC.
☐ 1936	71,424	115.00	150.00	200.00

COLUMBIA, SOUTH CAROLINA, SESQUICENTENNIAL (Silver $.50)

DATE	MINTAGE	ABP IN MS-60	MS-60 UNC.	MS-65 UNC.
☐ 1936		175.00	215.00	250.00
☐ 1936 Set PDS	8,009	550.00	700.00	800.00

DELAWARE TERCENTENARY (Silver $.50)

DATE	MINTAGE	ABP IN MS-60	MS-60 UNC.	MS-65 UNC.
☐ 1936	20,993	200.00	250.00	285.00

BATTLE OF GETTYSBURG 75TH ANNIVERSARY (Silver $.50)

DATE	MINTAGE	ABP IN MS-60	MS-60 UNC.	MS-65 UNC.
☐ 1936	26,030	350.00	450.00	800.00

NORFOLK, VIRGINIA, BICENTENNIAL AND TERCENTENARY (Silver $.50)

DATE	MINTAGE	ABP IN MS-60	MS-60 UNC.	MS-65 UNC.
☐ 1936	16,936	275.00	350.00	400.00

ROANOKE COLONIZATION 350TH ANNIVERSARY (Silver $.50)

DATE	MINTAGE	ABP IN MS-60	MS-60 UNC.	MS-65 UNC.
☐ 1937	29,030	150.00	200.00	240.00

BATTLE OF ANTIETAM 75TH ANNIVERSARY (Silver $.50)

DATE	MINTAGE	ABP IN MS-60	MS-60 UNC.	MS-65 UNC.
☐ 1937	18,028	550.00	675.00	750.00

NEW ROCHELLE, NEW YORK, 250TH ANNIVERSARY (Silver $.50)

DATE	MINTAGE	ABP IN MS-60	MS-60 UNC.	MS-65 UNC.
☐ 1938	15,226	275.00	350.00	400.00

IOWA STATEHOOD CENTENNIAL (Silver $.50)

DATE	MINTAGE	ABP IN MS-60	MS-60 UNC.	MS-65 UNC.
☐ 1946	100,057	70.00	95.00	130.00

BOOKER T. WASHINGTON MEMORIAL ($.50)

DATE	MINTAGE	ABP IN MS-60	MS-60 UNC.	MS-65 UNC.
☐ 1946		15.00	23.00	60.00
☐ 1946 Set PDS	200,113	50.00	70.00	175.00
☐ 1947 Set PDS	100,017	90.00	125.00	250.00
☐ 1948 Set PDS	8,005	135.00	185.00	240.00
☐ 1949 Set PDS	6,004	185.00	240.00	325.00
☐ 1950 Set PDS	6,004	110.00	160.00	225.00
☐ 1951 Set PDS	7,004	110.00	160.00	210.00

BOOKER T. WASHINGTON–
GEORGE WASHINGTON CARVER (Silver $.50)

DATE	MINTAGE	ABP IN MS-60	MS-60 UNC.	MS-65 UNC.
☐ 1951		18.00	23.00	75.00
☐ 1951 Set PDS	10,004	95.00	135.00	500.00
☐ 1952 Set PDS	8,006	95.00	135.00	385.00
☐ 1953 Set PDS	8,003	95.00	135.00	535.00
☐ 1954 Set PDS	12,006	95.00	135.00	400.00

MODERN COMMEMORATIVE COINS, 1982 TO DATE

Note: Regarding ABP prices, dealers will usually discount for coins that are not in the original packaging.

GEORGE WASHINGTON'S BIRTHDAY 250TH ANNIVERSARY (Silver $.50)

The U.S. resumed its commemorative coin program with this silver half dollar in 1982, after a lapse of twenty-eight years. The reason for its long suspension was that the value of silver far exceeded the traditional face values of commemorative coins. However, since commemoratives are issued for collectors and not for circulation, it was finally decided that the public would not object to low face values. The year 1982 marked the 250th anniversary of George Washington's birth. This was considered an appropriate occasion for resumption of the commemorative series. This coin is .900 silver and has the same specifications as earlier silver commemorative half dollars, and likewise the same as circulating half dollars up to 1964. The obverse carries an equestrian portrait of Washington looking left, with a view of Mount Vernon on the reverse. The artistic style was designed to conform, at least generally, to that of the majority of earlier commemorative halves.

DATE	MINTAGE	ABP	MS-65 UNC.	PRF-65 PROOF
☐ 1982S Proofs Only	4,894,044	8.00		12.00
☐ 1982D	2,210,458	8.00	12.00	

OLYMPIAD GAMES XXIII, LOS ANGELES
(Silver $1.00)

The set of two commemorative silver dollars issued in 1983 and 1984 for the Los Angeles Olympic Games marked the first $1 silver commemoratives in more than eighty years. Enormous publicity and controversy surrounded these coins, concerning their designs, face values, and the method of distributing them to the public. The first coin, dated 1983, pictures a discus thrower on the obverse with a profile bust of an eagle on the reverse. The second, dated 1984, shows the entrance to the Los Angeles Coliseum (site of the 1984 Games) on the obverse, and a full-length eagle on the reverse. These coins have the same specifications as the standard U.S. silver dollar, last struck in 1935, and contain approximately three-fourths of an ounce of .999+ silver. Debate arose over whether or not they should show a face value and, if so, the amount. It was decided that they should have a $1 face value, in spite of the fact that they contain several times that value in silver. This virtually ensured that they—unlike some commemoratives of the past—will never end up in circulation. Yet they are legal tender, and could be passed at $1 if an owner desired.

DATE	MINTAGE	ABP	MS-65 UNC.	PRF-65 PROOF
☐ 1983P	294,543	26.00	35.00	
☐ 1983S	1,751,039	23.00		32.00
☐ 1983D	174,014	26.00	35.00	
☐ 1984P	217,954	26.00	35.00	
☐ 1984S	1,917,885	32.00		46.00
☐ 1984D	116,675	25.00	35.00	

OLYMPIAD GAMES XXIII, LOS ANGELES
(Gold $10.00)

This $10 gold commemorative, carrying the date 1984, marked U.S. re-entry into commemorative gold—which many forecasters claimed would never occur. Issuance of a gold commemorative under modern circumstances called for a drastic change in approach. Traditionally (prior to the Gold Recall Act of 1933), our gold commemoratives contained slightly less than their face value in gold, just as did our gold circulating coins. With today's much higher gold prices, the Los Angeles XXIII Olympiad $10 gold commemorative contains about twenty times its face value in gold. They were distributed to the public at prices that took this factor into account, as well as including a handling fee (which many persons in the numismatic community charged to be exorbitant). A pair of torch bearers is shown on the obverse, symbolizing the ceremony of "lighting the Olympic flame" to open the

Games. The American eagle symbol with stars, arrows, and branches is pictured on the reverse. This coin has the same specifications used in striking circulating $10 gold pieces, prior to their discontinuance.

DATE	MINTAGE	ABP	MS-65 UNC.	PRF-65 PROOF
☐ 1984P	33,309	600.00		675.00
☐ 1984D	34,533	600.00		675.00
☐ 1984S	48,551	600.00		675.00
☐ 1984W*	456,971	600.00	675.00	675.00

*Note: "W" mint mark indicates West Point, New York.

STATUE OF LIBERTY–ELLIS ISLAND CENTENNIAL (Clad $.50)

The U.S. Statue of Liberty Coin Program honored the centennial of the Statue of Liberty and Ellis Island. It was the most successful commemorative coin program in the history of the Mint. More than 15 million gold, silver, and clad Liberty coins were sold, raising more than $83 million in surcharges used to renovate the Statue of Liberty and Ellis Island.

DATE	MINTAGE	ABP	MS-65 UNC.	PRF-65 PROOF
☐ 1986D	928,008	2.00	4.00	
☐ 1986S	6,925,627	2.00		4.00

STATUE OF LIBERTY–ELLIS ISLAND CENTENNIAL (Silver $1.00)

The Statue of Liberty commemorative silver dollar, .900 Fine: This beautiful coin commemorates and celebrates the Statue of Liberty. The obverse portrays a classic likeness of our Lady of Liberty standing on Ellis Island. The reverse shows the Torch of Liberty with the famous inscription inviting all of those who love and look for freedom.

DATE	MINTAGE	ABP	MS-65 UNC.	PRF-65 PROOF
☐ 1986P	723,635	22.00	28.00	
☐ 1986S	6,414,638	20.00		27.00

STATUE OF LIBERTY–ELLIS ISLAND CENTENNIAL (Gold Half Eagle)

The Statue of Liberty $5 gold commemorative: The obverse depicts the head of the Statue of Liberty and the date. The reverse is a version of a flying eagle.

DATE	MINTAGE	ABP	MS-65 UNC.	PRF-65 PROOF
☐ 1986W	499,261	300.00	375.00	350.00

CONSTITUTION BICENTENNIAL (Silver $1.00)

The U.S. Constitution Coin Program commemorated the bicentennial of the Constitution. More than $52.6 million in surcharges was raised from the sale of more than 4 million gold and silver coins. All surcharges went to reduce the national debt.

The Constitution silver dollar commemorative, .900 Fine: The obverse shows a quill pen and the words WE THE PEOPLE superimposed over the Constitution document. The reverse depicts a group of "We the People."

DATE	MINTAGE	ABP	MS-65 UNC.	PRF-65 PROOF
☐ 1987P	451,629	20.00	27.00	
☐ 1987S	2,747,116	19.00		25.00

CONSTITUTION BICENTENNIAL (Gold Half Eagle)

The Constitution $5 gold commemorative: The obverse depicts a flying eagle with a superimposed quill pen. The reverse again shows the quill pen over which is superimposed WE THE PEOPLE.

DATE	MINTAGE	ABP	MS-65 UNC.	PRF-65 PROOF
☐ 1987W	865,884	300.00	350.00	350.00

OLYMPIAD GAMES XXIV, CALGARY, SEOUL (Silver $1.00)

The 1988 U.S. Olympic Coin Program was created to raise money for the U.S. Olympic Committee to fund Olympic and amateur training programs. More than $22.9 million, generated by the sale of the 1.9 million Olympic gold and silver coins, was contributed to the U.S. Olympic Committee.

DATE	MINTAGE	ABP	MS-65 UNC.	PRF-65 PROOF
☐ 1988D	191,368	25.00	35.00	
☐ 1988S	1,359,366	20.00		27.00

OLYMPIAD GAMES XXIV, CALGARY, SEOUL
(Gold Half Eagle)

DATE	MINTAGE	ABP	MS-65 UNC.	PRF-65 PROOF
☐ 1988W	344,378	300.00	350.00	350.00

BICENTENNIAL OF CONGRESS (Clad Half Dollar)

This coin program commemorated the bicentennial of the U.S. Congress. More than $14.6 million in surcharges was raised from the sale of more than 2 million gold, silver, and clad Congressional coins to restore and preserve public areas of the U.S. Capitol.

DATE	MINTAGE	ABP	MS-65 UNC.	PRF-65 PROOF
☐ 1989D	163,753	5.00	7.50	
☐ 1989S	767,897	5.00		7.00

BICENTENNIAL OF CONGRESS (Silver $1.00)

DATE	MINTAGE	ABP	MS-65 UNC.	PRF-65 PROOF
☐ 1989D	135,203	25.00	35.00	
☐ 1989S	762,198	24.00		33.00

BICENTENNIAL OF CONGRESS
(Gold Half Eagle)

DATE	MINTAGE	ABP	MS-65 UNC.	PRF-65 PROOF
☐ 1989W	211,589	300.00	350.00	350.00

EISENHOWER BIRTHDAY CENTENNIAL
(Silver $1.00)

The 1990 Dwight David Eisenhower commemorative coin celebrated the 100th anniversary of the birth of the 34th president of the United States, and honored his military career and peacetime leadership. More than 1.3 million Eisenhower centennial silver dollar coins were sold, generating more than $9.7 million in surcharges to reduce the national debt.

DATE	ABP	MS-65 UNC.	PRF-65 PROOF
☐ 1990P	20.00		27.00
☐ 1990W	20.00	28.00	

MOUNT RUSHMORE 50TH ANNIVERSARY
(Clad Half Dollar)

The Mount Rushmore anniversary coins commemorated the 50th anniversary of the completion of the historic Mount Rushmore National Monument. Approximately $12 million in surcharges raised from the sale of these coins has been paid to the Mount Rushmore National Memorial Society to assist in efforts to improve, enlarge, and renovate the Memorial.

DATE	ABP	MS-65 UNC.	PRF-65 PROOF
☐ 1991D	10.00	17.00	
☐ 1991S	8.00		13.00

MOUNT RUSHMORE 50TH ANNIVERSARY
(Silver $1.00)

DATE	ABP	MS-65 UNC.	PRF-65 PROOF
☐ 1991P	35.00	45.00	
☐ 1991S	30.00		40.00

MOUNT RUSHMORE 50TH ANNIVERSARY
(Gold Half Eagle)

DATE	ABP	MS-65 UNC.	PRF-65 PROOF
☐ 1991W	300.00	365.00	375.00

KOREAN WAR 38TH ANNIVERSARY
(Silver $1.00)

The Korean War Memorial coin commemorated the 38th anniversary of the end of the Korean War. A surcharge of $7 per coin sold was designated to assist in the construction of the Korean War Veterans Memorial to be built in Washington, D.C. More than $5.8 million was raised from the sale of more than 830,000 coins. President George H. W. Bush participated in the groundbreaking ceremony for the Memorial on June 14, 1992 (Flag Day).

DATE	ABP	MS-65 UNC.	PRF-65 PROOF
☐ 1991D	25.00	35.00	
☐ 1991S	20.00		27.00

UNITED SERVICE ORGANIZATION'S 50TH ANNIVERSARY (Silver $1.00)

The United Services Organization coin commemorated the 50th anniversary of the USO and honored its continuing commitment to serve the needs of America's Armed Forces at home and abroad. Sales of the silver dollar resulted in more than $3.1 million in surcharges divided equally between the USO (to fund the organization's many programs worldwide for the members of the United States military and their families) and the Treasury Department (to reduce the national debt).

DATE	ABP	MS-65 UNC.	PRF-65 PROOF
☐ 1991D	27.00	35.00	
☐ 1991S	21.00		28.00

OLYMPIAD GAMES XXV, ALBERTVILLE, BARCELONA (Clad $.50)

Designs for the 1992 U.S. Olympic gold $5, silver $1, and clad $.50 coins were selected after an open coin design competition held by the U.S. Mint. Surcharges included in the price of each coin were paid to the United States Olympic Committee to train and finance U.S. Olympic athletes. More than 1.4 million coins were sold, resulting in more than $9 million in contributions to the U.S. Olympic Committee.

DATE	ABP	MS-65 UNC.	PRF-65 PROOF
☐ 1992P	5.00	8.00	
☐ 1992S	5.00		8.00

OLYMPIAD GAMES XXV, ALBERTVILLE, BARCELONA (Silver $1.00)

DATE	ABP	MS-65 UNC.	PRF-65 PROOF
☐ 1992D	33.00	45.00	
☐ 1992S	33.00		45.00

OLYMPIAD GAMES XXV, ALBERTVILLE, BARCELONA (Gold Half Eagle)

DATE	ABP	MS-65 UNC.	PRF-65 PROOF
☐ 1992W	300.00	350.00	350.00

WHITE HOUSE BICENTENNIAL (Silver $1.00)

The Silver Dollar Coin Program commemorated the 200th anniversary of the laying of the White House cornerstone. The authorized mintage of 500,000 coins, with a surcharge of $10 per coin, sold out within the pre-issue period. Surcharges of $5 million went to the White House Endowment Fund to maintain the historic public rooms of the White House and to support the White House collection of fine art and historic furnishings.

OBVERSE   REVERSE

DATE	ABP	MS-65 UNC.	PRF-65 PROOF
☐ 1992D	20.00	28.00	
☐ 1992W	27.00		39.00

COLUMBUS DISCOVERY QUINCENTENNIAL
(Clad $.50)

The Columbus Quincentenary Coin Program celebrated the 500th anniversary of the discovery of America by Christopher Columbus. Sales of the coins raised more than $7.6 million in surcharges to endow the Christopher Columbus Fellowship Foundation. The Foundation awards fellowships to promote "new discoveries in all fields of endeavor for the benefit of mankind."

OBVERSE   REVERSE

DATE	ABP	MS-65 UNC.	PRF-65 PROOF
☐ 1992D	8.00	12.00	
☐ 1992S	6.00		8.50

COLUMBUS DISCOVERY QUINCENTENNIAL
(Silver $1.00)

OBVERSE

REVERSE

DATE	ABP	MS-65 UNC.	PRF-65 PROOF
☐ 1992P	25.00		33.00
☐ 1992D	35.00	45.00	

COLUMBUS DISCOVERY QUINCENTENNIAL
(Gold Half Eagle)

OBVERSE

REVERSE

DATE	ABP	MS-65 UNC.	PRF-65 PROOF
☐ 1992W	300.00	350.00	350.00

BILL OF RIGHTS—JAMES MADISON (Clad $.50)

The gold $5, silver $1, and silver $.50 coins commemorate the first ten amendments to the Constitution of the United States, known as the Bill of Rights, and the role that James Madison, the fourth president of the United States, played in supporting their adoption. Sales of the coins raised more than $9 million in surcharges for the James Madison Memorial Fellowship Trust Fund to encourage teaching and graduate study of the Constitution of the United States.

OBVERSE   REVERSE

DATE	ABP	MS-65 UNC.	PRF-65 PROOF
☐ 1993S	12.00		18.50
☐ 1993W	16.00	23.00	

BILL OF RIGHTS—JAMES MADISON
(Silver $1.00)

OBVERSE   REVERSE

DATE	ABP	MS-65 UNC.	PRF-65 PROOF
☐ 1993D	35.00	45.00	
☐ 1993S	30.00		39.00

BILL OF RIGHTS—JAMES MADISON
(Gold Half Eagle)

OBVERSE   REVERSE

DATE	ABP	MS-65 UNC.	PRF-65 PROOF
☐ 1993W	300.00	350.00	350.00

WW II 50TH ANNIVERSARY
(Clad $.50)

The gold $5, silver $1, and clad $.50 coins commemorate the involvement of the United States in World War II. Sales of the coins raised more than $7 million in surcharges to help fund the construction of a memorial in Washington, D.C., to honor members of the Armed Forces of the United States who served in World War II, and to create a United States D-Day and Battle of Normandy Memorial in Normandy, France.

OBVERSE

REVERSE

DATE	ABP	MS-65 UNC.	PRF-65 PROOF
☐ 1993P	10.00	15.00	16.50

WW II 50TH ANNIVERSARY
(Silver $1.00)

OBVERSE

REVERSE

DATE	ABP	MS-65 UNC.	PRF-65 PROOF
☐ 1993D	33.00	42.00	
☐ 1993W	32.00		39.00

WW II 50TH ANNIVERSARY
(Gold Half Eagle)

OBVERSE   REVERSE

DATE	ABP	MS-65 UNC.	PRF-65 PROOF
☐ 1993W	300.00	350.00	350.00

WORLD CUP SOCCER (Clad $.50)

Obverse (L) and Reverse (R) of 1994 World Cup Cupro-Nickel Half Dollar

The World Cup commemorative coins, established by Public Law 102-281, authorized the Mint to produce gold $5, silver $1, and clad $.50 coins to celebrate the World Cup, which was staged for the first time ever in the United States. Surcharges included in the price of each coin were paid to World Cup USA 1994, Inc. for organizing and staging the 1994 World Cup, and to fund scholarships through the United States Soccer Federation Foundation. The World Cup coins were available individually, in sets, and in special Host City venue editions featuring the nine sites where the World Cup games were played.

DATE	ABP	MS-65 UNC.	PRF-65 PROOF
☐ 1994D	7.00	11.00	
☐ 1994P	7.00		12.00

WORLD CUP SOCCER
(Silver $1.00)

Obverse (L) and Reverse (R) of 1994 World Cup Silver Dollar Coin

DATE	ABP	MS-65 UNC.	PRF-65 PROOF
☐ 1994D	32.00	40.00	
☐ 1994S	28.00		35.00

WORLD CUP SOCCER
(Gold Half Eagle)

Obverse (L) and Reverse (R) of 1994 World Cup Gold Five Dollar Coin

DATE	ABP	MS-65 UNC.	PRF-65 PROOF
☐ 1994W	325.00	385.00	385.00

THOMAS JEFFERSON BIRTHDAY 250TH ANNIVERSARY (Silver $1.00)

OBVERSE   REVERSE

Public Law 103-186 signed by President Clinton on December 14, 1993, authorized the Mint to produce silver dollars to commemorate the 250th anniversary of the birth of Thomas Jefferson on April 13, 1743. The Thomas Jefferson Coin and Currency Set provided a brief history of Jefferson's role in establishing America's decimal coinage system, from his earliest thoughts on the subject to Congressional approval of Jefferson's plan, and his role in establishing the first U.S. Mint. Surcharges included in the price of each coin were paid to the Thomas Jefferson Memorial Foundation to help fund educational programs and restoration of Monticello, Jefferson's primary residence, and to the Corporation for Jefferson's Poplar Forest to help fund restoration of Jefferson's retreat home. This program sold out during the pre-issue period with surcharges paid as follows: The Thomas Jefferson Memorial Foundation had received $5 million and Jefferson's Poplar Forest had received $714,630 as of June 27, 1994.

DATE	ABP	MS-65 CH. UNC.	PRF-65 CH. PROOF
☐ 1993P	25.00	35.00	
☐ 1993S	20.00		29.00

WOMEN IN MILITARY SERVICE FOR AMERICA MEMORIAL (Silver $1.00)

Authorized by Congress in 1986, The Women in Military Service for America Memorial will document the history of American servicewomen. The memorial will provide an unprecedented tribute to military women, at the same time encouraging Americans of all ages to learn about the women who have defended America throughout history.

The Women in Military Service for America Memorial Foundation (WIMSA) has taken on the task of raising the funds required to build the memorial, which according to legislation must be built without federal funds. To date, WIMSA has nearly $11 million available for the memorial, but an additional $5 million is needed before construction can begin. The memorial is to be built at the gateway to Arlington National Cemetery.

- The exterior will incorporate the existing 1930s neo-classical hemicycle, which serves as the ornamental gateway to Arlington National Cemetery. Restoration and adaptation will allow for a memorial structure above ground and an educational center below.
- The terrace will feature an arc of glass "pages" inscribed with quotations about or from servicewomen. Acting as skylights, the glass panels will dramatically reflect the quotations on the walls of the gallery below.
- The Court of Honor will center on a waterfall and reflecting pool. A continuous stream of water will gather to form a waterfall, and from there flow into a narrow channel leading to a circular reflecting pool. The flow of water will symbolize the "singular voices" of American servicewomen coming together as a "chorus of voices."
- Visitors will be able to access a computer register that will feature the name and picture of each registered servicewoman with service details and their most memorable experience. To date 100,000 women have registered and WIMSA expects to register an additional 400,000 by the time the memorial is dedicated.

Surcharges from the 500,000 Women in Military Service for America Memorial commemorative silver dollars will contribute a maximum of $5 million toward construction. Regarding the coins themselves, each weighs 26.730 grams and is 1.5 inches in diameter. Composition is 90% silver (0.76) and 10% copper. Mintage consists of 500,000 maximum of each coin, as authorized by Congress.

Both Proof and Uncirculated versions of the WIMSA silver dollars were minted and sold individually or in a three-coin set. Coins were available at discounted prices during the pre-issue period of July 29–September 9, 1994. In accordance with congressional legislation, once mintage levels of 500,000 were sold, no more coins were issued, and no coins were minted after April 30, 1995.

The Proof version of the coins was minted at the U.S. Mint in Philadelphia, Pennsylvania. Uncirculated coins were minted at the U.S. Mint in West Point, New York.

Designed by Mint engraver T. James Ferrell, the obverse of the coin profiles servicewomen and represents the five branches of the U.S. military. The coin's reverse was designed by Thomas D. Rogers, Sr., and portrays the approved design for the Women in Military Service for America Memorial.

DATE	ABP	MS-65 UNC.	PRF-65 PROOF
☐ 1994P	28.00		35.00
☐ 1994W	32.00	42.00	

VIETNAM VETERANS MEMORIAL (Silver $1.00)

Since the Vietnam Veterans Memorial was completed over two decades ago, it has been visited by more than 2.5 million people per year, making it one of the most frequented memorials in the nation's capital. It is estimated that 80 percent of the visitors to The Wall are moved to touch the names on its polished black surface.

The Memorial, truly unique in its exposed, accessible design, is susceptible to a unique set of conservation problems. The Vietnam Veterans Memorial Fund (VVMF) is currently involved in an extensive effort to provide funds for reparations, long-term maintenance, and ensuring that the record of names continues to be updated.

- Cracks have appeared in a number of the black granite panels. Extensive research is needed in order to confirm the cause of the cracks and to recommend action to remedy any damage and deterioration. To date, theories about the cracks conflict. Possible causes range from pressure exerted by the ground behind the Memorial to the condition and placement of the support anchors.
- New names to The Wall are being added as appropriate. The additions record those individuals who have died as a direct result of war injuries incurred in Vietnam. Changes in status from missing in action to killed in action are made as remains are returned from the war zone.
- Additional granite panels will be purchased to allow for the replacement of damaged or vandalized sections. The panels need to be stored in special frames enabling them to weather consistently with the existing Memorial. The granite is mined in Bangalore, India, and fabricated and cut to size in Barre, Vermont.
- Repairs to the cobblestone walkways and lighting system are continually needed due to extensive foot traffic.
- Funding for the Memorial's reparations and additions is not available through the U.S. Park Service due to budget limitations and must be raised entirely from private sources.

Surcharges raised from 500,000 Vietnam Veterans Memorial commemorative silver dollars contributed a maximum of $5 million to the repair and long-term maintenance of the Memorial. Each coin weighs 26.730 grams and the diameter is 1.5 inches. Composition is 90% silver (0.76) and 10% copper, and 500,000 maximum of each coin were minted, as authorized by Congress.

Both Proof and Uncirculated versions of the U.S. Veterans commemorative silver dollars were minted and were sold individually or in a three-coin set. Coins were available at discounted prices, during the pre-issue period of July 29–September 9, 1994. In accordance with congressional legislation, once mintage levels of 500,000 were sold, no more coins were issued, and no coins were minted after April 30, 1995.

The Proof version of the coins was minted at the U.S. Mint in Philadelphia, Pennsylvania. Uncirculated coins were minted at the U.S. Mint in West Point, New York.

The obverse of the coin, designed by Mint engraver John Mercanti, features a section of the Vietnam Veterans Memorial Wall, with an outstretched hand touching a name. Thomas D. Rogers, Sr., also a U.S. Mint engraver, designed the coin's reverse, which depicts three medals awarded during the Vietnam War.

DATE	ABP	MS-65 UNC.	PRF-65 PROOF
☐ 1994P	48.00		65.00
☐ 1994W	65.00	85.00	

NATIONAL PRISONER OF WAR MUSEUM
(Silver $1.00)

The National Prisoner of War Museum, to be built in Andersonville, Georgia, aims to communicate the prisoner of war (POW) experience regardless of when, where, why, or how the individual was captured or imprisoned. For the first time, hundreds of POW artifacts and documents will be used to help visitors understand the horrors, stress, and suffering of those denied their freedom during periods of war. The museum will provide a long-awaited tribute to American POWs from the American Revolution to the recent Somalian peace-keeping efforts.

The American Ex-Prisoners of War and the National Park Service have joined together to make the museum a reality. Funds raised since 1984 enabled groundbreaking and paid for the installation of utilities in the summer of 1994, while the state of Georgia is funding access roads and signage.

- The museum's location will be the grounds of the largest prisoner of war camp operated during the Civil War, where nearly 13,000 of the 45,000 imprisoned soldiers died during fourteen months of operation.
- The exhibits have been designed to take visitors on a journey through the life of the POW, from the trauma of initial capture to the time of liberation or repatriation. The different aspects of the POW's existence to be highlighted are: Capture, Physical Environment, Living Conditions, Communications, Privation, Morale and

Friendships, and, finally, Freedom. A special section entitled "Those Who Wait" will convey the devotion and suffering of family members and friends.

- Visitors will exit through the Commemorative Courtyard, allowing them to reflect on the experience and history just witnessed. Fresh water, a highly valued commodity for all POWs, will run through the courtyard featuring a bronze statue, which is symbolic of all POWs attempting to drink from the stream.

Proceeds from the Prisoner of War commemorative silver dollar will contribute significantly to the millions needed for the National POW Museum. The first $3 million raised is designated for the museum's construction; the next million will create an endowment fund for maintenance; and the final one million will go to maintaining national Veterans Administration cemeteries. Each silver dollar weighs 26.730 grams and the diameter is 1.5 inches. Composition is 90% silver (0.76) and 10% copper, and mintage is 500,000 maximum of each coin, as authorized by Congress.

Both Proof and Uncirculated versions of the U.S. Veterans commemorative silver dollars were minted and were sold individually or in a three-coin set. Coins were available at discounted prices, during the pre-issue period of July 29–September 9, 1994. In accordance with congressional legislation, once mintage levels of 500,000 were sold, no more coins were issued, and no coins were minted after April 30, 1995.

The Proof version of the coins was minted at the U.S. Mint in Philadelphia, Pennsylvania. Uncirculated coins were minted at the U.S. Mint in West Point, New York.

The obverse of the coin was designed by Department of Veterans Affairs employee Tom Nielsen and engraved by Alfred Maletsky. A chained eagle breaks free through a ring of barbed wire. "Freedom," also breaking through the barbed wire, is inscribed to the right of the eagle's wing. The coin's reverse was designed by Edgar Z. Steever IV and portrays the proposed design for the National Prisoner of War Museum.

DATE	ABP	MS-65 UNC.	PRF-65 PROOF
☐ 1994P	32.00		42.00
☐ 1994W	55.00	85.00	

UNITED STATES CAPITOL BICENTENNIAL
(Silver $1.00)

The U.S. Capitol commemorative silver dollar weighs 26.730 grams and its diameter is 1.5 inches. Its composition is 90% silver and 10% copper. Mintage consisted of 500,000 coins, as authorized by Congress. An Architectural History package chronicles the development of the Capitol's architecture, and features a Proof coin.

Both Proof and Uncirculated versions of the U.S. Capitol commemorative silver dollar were minted. Coins were available at discounted prices, during the pre-issue period of September 9–October 21, 1994. In accordance with Congressional legislation, once mintage levels of 500,000 were reached, no more coins were issued, and no coins were minted after April 30, 1995.

The Proof version of the coins was minted at the U.S. Mint in San Francisco, California. Uncirculated coins were minted at the U.S. Mint in Denver, Colorado.

The obverse of the coin, designed by Mint Sculptor/Engraver William C. Cousins, features a view of the Capitol dome. A ring of thirteen stars, representing the original states, encircles the statue of Freedom. LIBERTY and IN GOD WE TRUST are inscribed to the left of the dome. An eagle, shield, and American flags are portrayed on the reverse of the coin, as they appear in one of four stained glass windows installed in the grand stairways of the House and Senate wings. The intricate design was executed by Mint Sculptor/Engraver John Mercanti. The words UNITED STATES OF AMERICA and ONE DOLLAR decorate the border of the coin.

DATE	ABP	MS-65 UNC.	PRF-65 PROOF
☐ 1994D	32.00	42.00	
☐ 1994S	30.00		38.00

CIVIL WAR BATTLEFIELDS
(Clad $.50)

OBVERSE

REVERSE

The clad half dollar weighs 11.340 grams, ± 0.454 gram. Its diameter is 30.61mm. (1.205 in.), ± 0.08mm. (± 0.003 in.), and composition is 92% copper and 8% nickel. The maximum mintage as authorized by Congress was 2,000,000.

Both Proof and Uncirculated versions of the clad half dollar were struck at the U.S. Mint in San Francisco, California.

The obverse of the clad half dollar, designed by Don Troiani, is a tribute to the Civil War drummer boys. The reverse, designed by T. James Ferrell, depicts a battlefield scene and has the inscription ENRICHING OUR FUTURE BY PRESERVING OUR PAST.

DATE	ABP	MS-65 UNC.	PRF-65 PROOF
☐ 1995S	25.00	35.00	
☐ 1995S	22.00		32.00

CIVIL WAR BATTLEFIELDS
(Silver $1.00)

OBVERSE   REVERSE

The silver dollar in this series weighs 26.730 grams, ± 0.400 grams. Diameter is 38.10mm. (1.5 in.), ± 0.08mm. (± 0.003 in.), and its composition is 90% silver and 10% copper. The maximum mintage as authorized by Congress was 1,000,000.

The Proof version of the coin was struck at the U.S. Mint in San Francisco, California, and the Uncirculated version was struck at the U.S. Mint in Philadelphia, Pennsylvania.

The obverse of the silver dollar, designed by Don Troiani, shows an infantryman raising a canteen to the lips of a wounded foe. The reverse, designed by John Mercanti, displays a quotation from Joshua Chamberlain, the college teacher from Maine who became one of the heroes of Gettysburg.

DATE	ABP	MS-65 UNC.	PRF-65 PROOF
☐ 1995P	45.00	55.00	
☐ 1995S	37.00		45.00

CIVIL WAR BATTLEFIELDS
(Gold Half Eagle)

OBVERSE   REVERSE

The gold $5 weighs 8.359 grams ± 0.042 grams, and its diameter is 21.59mm. (0.850 in.) ± 0.08mm. (± 0.003 in.). Composition consists of 90% gold, 6% silver, and 4% copper. The maximum mintage as authorized by Congress was 300,000.

Both Proof and Uncirculated versions of the coin were struck at the U.S. Mint in West Point, New York.

The obverse of the gold $5 coin, designed by Don Troiani, shows a Civil War bugler on horseback sounding a call to the troops. The reverse, designed by Alfred Maletsky, carries the image of a bald eagle, symbol of American strength.

DATE	ABP	MS-65 UNC.	PRF-65 PROOF
☐ 1995W	450.00	600.00	425.00

SPECIAL OLYMPICS WORLD GAMES
(Silver $1.00)

DATE	ABP	MS-65 UNC.	PRF-65 PROOF
☐ 1995P	30.00		38.00
☐ 1995W	33.00	42.00	

OLYMPIAD GAMES XXVI, ATLANTA, GEORGIA
(Clad $.50)

Each clad commemorative coin weighs 11.34 grams and its diameter is 1.21 inches. (30.61mm.). Composition consists of 92% copper and 8% nickel. The maximum mintage as authorized by Congress is as follows: 1995—2,000,000 each of two clad coins; 1996—3,000,000 each of two clad coins.

The Proof version of the clad coins was struck at the San Francisco Mint and the Uncirculated at the Denver Mint.

Regarding the obverse of the 1995 coins, there were two types: a Basketball obverse, designed by Clint Hansen, and a Baseball obverse, designed by Edgar Steever. There was a common 1995 reverse showing a globe, designed by T. James Ferrell.

For the 1996 coins, there was a Swimming obverse, designed by William Krawczewicz, and a Soccer obverse, designed by Clint Hansen. Atlanta Centennial Olympic Games Logo was the common 1996 reverse, designed by Malcolm Farley.

DATE	ABP	MS-65 UNC.	PRF-65 PROOF
☐ 1995S Basketball	11.00	17.00	16.00

DATE	ABP	MS-65 UNC.	PRF-65 PROOF
☐ 1995S Baseball	13.00	20.00	18.00

DATE	ABP	MS-65 UNC.	PRF-65 PROOF
☐ 1996S Swimming	110.00	140.00	32.00

DATE	ABP	MS-65 UNC.	PRF-65 PROOF
☐ 1996S Soccer	100.00	130.00	85.00

OLYMPIAD GAMES XXVI, ATLANTA, GEORGIA
(Silver $1.00)

The silver $1 commemorative coin weighs 26.73 grams and its diameter is 1.5 inches. (38.10mm.). Composition is 90% silver and 10% copper. Maximum mintage as authorized by Congress was: 1995—750,000 each of four silver coins, and 1996—1,000,000 each of four silver coins.

The Proof version of the silver dollars was struck at the Philadelphia Mint and the Uncirculated coins at the Denver Mint.

Regarding the 1995 coins, there appeared a Gymnastics obverse (designed by Jim Sharpe), Paralympics—Blind Runner obverse (designed by Jim Sharpe), Athletics (Track & Field) obverse (designed by John Mercanti), and a Cycling obverse (designed by John Mercanti). Clasped Hands was the common 1995 reverse (designed by William Krawczewicz).

For 1996, there was a Tennis obverse (designed by Jim Sharpe), Paralympics—Wheelchair Athlete obverse (designed by Jim Sharpe), Rowing obverse (designed by Bart Forbes), and Athletics (High Jump) obverse (designed by Calvin Massey). Atlanta Centennial Olympic Games Logo was the common 1996 reverse (designed by Thomas D. Rogers, Sr.).

DATE	ABP	MS-65 UNC.	PRF-65 PROOF
☐ 1995P Gymnastics	27.00		37.00
☐ 1995D Gymnastics	35.00	45.00	

DATE	ABP	MS-65 UNC.	PRF-65 PROOF
☐ 1995P Cycling	32.00		42.00
☐ 1995D Cycling	100.00	135.00	

DATE	ABP	MS-65 UNC.	PRF-65 PROOF
☐ 1995P Track & Field	30.00		38.00
☐ 1995D Track & Field	55.00	75.00	

DATE	ABP	MS-65 UNC.	PRF-65 PROOF
☐ 1995P Paralympic	32.00		39.00
☐ 1995D Paralympic	50.00	70.00	

DATE	ABP	MS-65 UNC.	PRF-65 PROOF
☐ 1996P Tennis	55.00		72.00
☐ 1996D Tennis	185.00	235.00	

DATE	ABP	MS-65 UNC.	PRF-65 PROOF
☐ 1996P Rowing	52.00		65.00
☐ 1996D Rowing	180.00	240.00	

DATE	ABP	MS-65 UNC.	PRF-65 PROOF
☐ 1996P High Jump	32.00		42.00
☐ 1996D High Jump	210.00	285.00	

DATE	ABP	MS-65 UNC.	PRF-65 PROOF
☐ 1996P Paralympic	50.00		68.00
☐ 1996D Paralympic	200.00	275.00	

OLYMPIAD GAMES XXVI, ATLANTA, GEORGIA
(Gold Half Eagle)

The $5 gold commemorative coin weighs 8.359 grams and its diameter is .850 inches. (21.59mm.). Composition is 90% gold and 10% alloy. The maximum mintage as authorized by Congress was: 1995—175,000 each of two gold coins; 1996—300,000 each of two gold coins.

The Proof and Uncirculated versions of the gold coins were struck at the West Point Mint, New York.

The 1995 coins carry a Torch Runner obverse, designed by Frank Gasparro, and an Olympic Stadium obverse, designed by Marcel Jovine. An eagle is the common 1995 reverse, designed by Frank Gasparro.

For 1996, there is a Flag Bearer obverse, designed by Patricia L. Verani, and a Cauldron obverse, designed by Frank Gasparro. Atlanta Centennial Olympic Games Logo with Wreath is the common 1996 reverse, designed by William Krawczewicz.

DATE	ABP	MS-65 UNC.	PRF-65 PROOF
☐ 1995W Torch Runner	525.00	675.00	365.00

DATE	ABP	MS-65 UNC.	PRF-65 PROOF
☐ 1995W Atlanta Stadium	1850.00	2350.00	365.00

DATE	ABP	MS-65 UNC.	PRF-65 PROOF
☐ 1996W Olympic Flame	2000.00	2500.00	365.00

DATE	ABP	MS-65 UNC.	PRF-65 PROOF
☐ 1996W Flag Bearer	2000.00	2500.00	365.00

SMITHSONIAN INSTITUTION 150TH ANNIVERSARY (SILVER $1.00)

The Smithsonian Institution was founded in 1846 with proceeds from the estate of James Smithson, a noted British chemist and mineralogist who discovered the zinc ore now known as "Smithsonite." In his will, Smithson bequeathed his entire estate, in excess of $500,000 in British gold sovereigns, to "the United States of America to found at Washington, under the name of the Smithsonian Institution, an establishment for the increase and diffusion of knowledge."

The obverse of the silver dollar, with limited mintage of 650,000 is by U.S. Mint Sculptor/Engraver Thomas D. Rogers, Sr. Rogers's design features the Smithsonian Institution building known as "the Castle," bordered by laurel leaves on each side and below by the inscription "Smithsonian" and the dates "1846–1996," recognizing the sesquicentennial of the Congressional Act establishing the Institution.

The reverse of the silver dollar, by Mint Sculptor/Engraver John Mercanti, depicts an allegorical figure atop the world, carrying the torch of knowledge and a scroll inscribed, "art, history, and science"—the major disciplines for which the Smithsonian is known. At the right are inscribed Smithson's words, "For the increase and diffusion of knowledge."

The obverse of the gold $5 coin, with a limited mintage of 100,000, is by Mint Sculptor/Engraver Al Maletsky. It features a bust of James Smithson in the classical style popular in the early 1800s and the sesquicentennial dates. The reverse, by Sculptor/Engraver T. James Ferrell, features the widely recognized Smithsonian sunburst symbol.

DATE	ABP	MS-65 UNC.	PRF-65 PROOF
☐ 1996P	34.00		42.00
☐ 1996D	80.00	110.00	

SMITHSONIAN INSTITUTION 150TH ANNIVERSARY (GOLD $5.00)

DATE	ABP	MS-65 UNC.	PRF-65 PROOF
☐ 1996W	525.00	650.00	365.00

NATIONAL COMMUNITY SERVICE SILVER DOLLAR

This limited edition commemorative silver dollar, produced at the San Francisco Mint, honors the millions of Americans who give generously of their time and energy volunteering at schools and youth service programs, helping with the elderly, and contributing to other community service projects.

Surcharges included in the price of the coin will go to the National Community Service Trust, a nonprofit organization formed to support and encourage the development of innovative community service programs and courses at educational institutions and in communities across the nation.

The coin's obverse, designed by U.S. Mint sculptor/engraver Thomas D. Rogers, Sr., features a standing figure of Liberty, inspired by an original design by renowned sculptor Augustus Saint-Gaudens for the 1905 Women's Auxiliary of the Massachusetts Civil Service Reform Association. With her right hand, Liberty extends a lamp, shedding light over a book, symbolizing learning and discovery. Her left hand holds a shield. In the background, the sun encircles the flame of the lamp, symbolizing the light of knowledge. Saint-Gaudens is widely acknowledged as America's foremost sculptor and engraver of the 20th century.

The reverse of the coin, by U.S. Mint sculptor/engraver William C. Cousins, bears the inscription "Service for America" at center, encircled by a laurel wreath.

DATE	ABP	MS-65 UNC.	PRF-65 PROOF
☐ 1996S	80.00	115.00	47.00

U.S. BOTANIC GARDEN
Silver ($1.00)

The U.S. Botanic Garden silver dollar celebrates the vision of our founding fathers, including George Washington, Thomas Jefferson, and James Madison, realized when President James Monroe signed legislation in 1820 that led to the creation of what is now the oldest continually operating botanic garden in the nation.

The silver dollar's obverse design, by Edgar Z. Steever, IV, depicts the garden's multiarched French facade—reminiscent of early renderings of Monticello and the Lincoln Memorial. The silver dollar's reverse design, by William C. Cousins, presents a timeless rendition of America's national flower—the rose—beneath a remarkably detailed rose garland.

Public Law 103-328, signed by President Clinton on September 29, 1994, calls for minting of not more than 500,000 90% silver coins. A portion of the proceeds from the sale of the coins go to the National Fund for the U.S. Botanic Garden to fund the National Garden in Washington, D.C.

Of special interest to collectors, the U.S. Botanic Garden commemorative silver dollar is included in the last Prestige

Set that the U.S. Mint will offer, with a limited edition of 80,000 sets. The Prestige Set series includes the Proof U.S. Botanic Garden silver dollar and Proof versions of the 1997 Kennedy half dollar, Washington quarter, Roosevelt dime, Jefferson nickel, and Lincoln cent.

The Mint offers a limited edition of 25,000 sets. The U.S. Botanic Garden Coinage and Currency Set is available by mail order only. This set features an Uncirculated 1997 U.S. Botanic Garden silver dollar, an Uncirculated 1997 Jefferson nickel, and a current Uncirculated George Washington one-dollar note with a Virginia Federal Reserve bank seal.

DATE	ABP	MS-65 UNC.	PRF-65 PROOF
☐ 1997P	23.00	33.00	38.00

FRANKLIN D. ROOSEVELT
Gold ($5.00)

The design for the obverse of the FDR Gold $5 Coin, by U.S. Mint Sculptor/Engraver T. James Ferrell, is based on one of President Roosevelt's favorite photographs: a portrait of the commander-in-chief reviewing the U.S. fleet in San Francisco Bay. The reverse design, by U.S. Mint Graphic Designer James Peed, bears a rendering of the presidential seal as displayed at FDR's 1933 inauguration.

Legislation sponsored by Representative Norman Y. Mineta (D-CA) and signed into law on October 20, 1996, by President Clinton as part of P.L. 104-329 authorizes the Mint to produce no more than 100,000 of the FDR Commemorative gold coin.

DATE	ABP	MS-65 UNC.	PRF-65 PROOF
☐ 1997W	550.00	700.00	425.00

LAW ENFORCEMENT OFFICERS MEMORIAL
Silver ($1.00)

Established in 1792, the U.S. Mint Police are one of the older law enforcement agencies in the nation. Having set the standard "as secure as Fort Knox," U.S. Mint police officers continue to meet that standard every day protecting over 2,000 Mint employees, hundreds of thousands of yearly visitors, and $100 billion of America's gold, silver, platinum, and coins.

The nearly 500 U.S. Mint police officers protect Fort Knox, the four U.S. Mint production facilities in West Point, NY; Philadelphia, PA; Denver, CO; San Francisco, CA; Lanham, MD, and the headquarters in Washington, D.C., and provide protection advice and assistance to other federal law enforcement agencies and foreign governments.

Legislation authorizing the National Law Enforcement Officers Memorial to be built was enacted into law in October 1984. The memorial was dedicated on October 15, 1991, and its mission is to generate increased public support for the law enforcement profession by permanently recording and appropriately commemorating the service and sacrifice of law enforcement officers and to provide information that will help promote law enforcement safety.

DATE	ABP	MS-65 UNC.	PRF-65 PROOF
☐ 1997P	80.00	110.00	70.00

JACKIE ROBINSON
Silver ($1.00)
Gold ($5.00)

One hundred thousand gold coins are being struck at the West Point Mint, and 200,000 silver dollars at the San Francisco Mint. A portion of the proceeds from sales of the coins will benefit the Jackie Robinson Foundation, which supports educational and leadership programs to encourage, train, and motivate minority youth.

The obverse of the silver dollar coin, by Mint Sculptor Al Maletsky, depicts Robinson stealing home plate, as he did during a 1955 World Series game between the New York Yankees and the Brooklyn Dodgers. The silver reverse, by Mint Sculptor/Engraver T. James Ferrell, features the 50th anniversary logo of the Jackie Robinson Foundation, surrounded by inscriptions highlighting two of Robinson's achievements: "Rookie of the Year 1947," and "Hall of Fame 1962." An identical commemorative patch was worn by all Major League Baseball players during the 1997 season.

The obverse of the gold $5 coin, by Mint Sculptor/Engraver William Cousins, depicts Robinson in his later years as a civil rights leader and political activist. The reverse, by Mint Graphic Designer Jim Peed, is a baseball design with the years of Robinson's life, 1919–1972, and the inscription "Legacy of Courage" in the center.

DATE	ABP	MS-65 UNC.	PRF-65 PROOF
☐ 1997S	55.00	75.00	62.00

DATE	ABP	MS-65 UNC.	PRF-65 PROOF
☐ 1997W	2150.00	2650.00	550.00

THE BLACK REVOLUTIONARY WAR PATRIOTS
Silver ($1.00)

According to law, the U.S. Mint is authorized to produce up to 500,000 silver dollars to commemorate Black Revolutionary Patriots and the 275th anniversary of the birth of Crispus Attucks. A portion of the proceeds from sales of the coins will support the construction of the Black Patriots Memorial on the National Mall in Washington, D.C. near the Lincoln Memorial and the Vietnam Veterans Memorial.

The obverse of the silver dollar, designed by Mint Sculptor/Engraver John Mercanti, is a portrait of Crispus Attucks, the first patriot killed in the infamous Boston Massacre in 1770, the event that many historians believe triggered the Revolutionary War.

The reverse design, by Ed Dwight, depicting a black patriot family, is also the design of the sculpture for the Black Patriots Memorial, honoring not only the black soldiers who fought for freedom, but also the families who supported them. Dwight, the first African American to be trained as an astronaut, has created more than 55 monuments and memorials to honor notable African Americans, and his art appears in private collections, in major museums, and at the Smithsonian Institution.

DATE	ABP	MS-65 UNC.	PRF-65 PROOF
☐ 1998S	70.00	95.00	52.00

ROBERT F. KENNEDY
Silver ($1.00)

The portrait of Robert F. Kennedy on the coin's obverse is one of the most realistic ever. The sculptor/engraver worked with Kennedy's widow, Ethel, who instructed the artist on her late husband's features. The reverse shows the seal of the Department of Justice, where Kennedy worked as attorney general to advance civil rights for all Americans, and the seal of the United States Senate, where he was serving when he was assassinated.

Thomas D. Rogers, who designed the coin's obverse, wanted the coin to reflect Kennedy's compassion and character, as well his intensity and thoughtful concern. In addition to sculpting the plaster sculpture used for the obverse, Rogers sculpted the plaster for the intricate design on the reverse.

Rogers designed and sculpted the reverses of the Columbus Quincentenary silver dollar and gold five dollar; the obverse and reverse of the World War II Military silver dollar, Vietnam Veterans, Special Olympics, and 1996 Olympic silver dollars. He designed and sculpted the obverses of the Smithsonian and Community Service commemorative silver dollars as well as the reverse of the Franklin D. Roosevelt gold five dollar.

James Peed sketched the reverse of this coin as a collage

of the United States Senate seal with the United States Attorney General's seal. Peed has been credited with the original concept for the obverse of the 1984 Olympic gold ten dollar, designed and sculpted the 1992 Olympic gold five dollar reverse and the Jackie Robinson gold five dollar reverse, and won a national competition for the 1986 Vietnam Veterans Medal reverse.

DATE	ABP	MS-65 UNC.	PRF-65 PROOF
☐ 1998S	28.00	39.00	55.00

GEORGE WASHINGTON
Gold ($5.00)

"Officially, this coin commemorates the 200th anniversary of our first president's death," said U.S. Mint Director Philip N. Diehl. "But to my mind it also commemorates what has survived of his life and the life of our republic for two centuries, and ensures that this place will remain for all time ready to receive everyone who comes here."

The George Washington Commemorative $5 coin marks the inaugural striking of Laura Gardin Fraser's award-winning design, one of the most popular designs submitted in the 1931 design competition for a special new quarter dollar commemorating the birth of George Washington. Fraser's stunning portrait is modeled on the famed life-mask bust of Washington by noted French sculptor Jean Antoine Houdon. Fraser's reverse design depicts a powerful bald eagle with exquisitely detailed overlapping planes of rough feathers.

A portion of the proceeds from sales of the coin are authorized to be used by the Mount Vernon Ladies' Association for preservation of George Washington's Mount Vernon and to educate the American people about this great man and his incomparable gifts to his nation.

DATE	ABP	MS-65 UNC.	PRF-65 PROOF
☐ 1999W	335.00	425.00	410.00

YELLOWSTONE NATIONAL PARK
Silver ($1.00)

"We are honored to be part of a program promoting the conservation and preservation of our nation's most precious national treasures, the natural wonders and wilderness of Yellowstone and America's other national parks," said U.S. Mint Associate Director for Numismatics David Pickens. Pickens was joined by Michael Finley, superintendent of Yellowstone National Park, and Jim Maddy, president of the National Park Foundation, at the Interior Museum of the Department of the Interior for the official launch of the program.

The obverse design, by Mint Sculptor/Engraver Edgar Z. Steever, depicts one of Yellowstone Park's famous geysers with the park's tree-lined landscape in the background. The reverse, by Mint Sculptor/Engraver William C. Cousins, portrays an American buffalo on the plains with a brilliant sun rising above the mountains in the background and is intended to be reminiscent of the seal of the Department of the Interior.

In 1872, Ulysses S. Grant signed Yellowstone Park into law, inaugurating the beginning of the nation's National Park System. Yellowstone is now recognized around the world as a universal symbol of American conservation, wilderness, and natural beauty. A portion of the proceeds from the sales of each coin are authorized to help support Yellowstone National Park, as well as other national parks through the National Park Foundation. With a maximum mintage of 500,000 coins, both the Uncirculated and Proof versions of the Yellowstone National Park silver dollar have been minted at the Philadelphia Mint and bear the P mint mark.

DATE	ABP	MS-65 UNC.	PRF-65 PROOF
☐ 1999P	35.00	45.00	48.00

DOLLEY MADISON
Silver ($1.00)

As first lady during her husband's two presidential terms, and serving as hostess during the first Jefferson administration, Dolley Madison brought competing factions together in a social setting, using her natural diplomatic talents to ease political tensions and pave the way for civil debate in the young republic. She is credited with defining the role of first lady by establishing a style of ceremonial etiquette that did not yet exist. In addition, the first lady of the nation's fourth president, James Madison, was instrumental in organizing the rescue of important government papers, including Gilbert Stuart's portrait of George Washington, as the British burned the capital in 1814.

The obverse side of the coin carries a portrait of the young Dolley Madison, with her image framed by her favorite Cape Jasmine flowers and the Ice House Temple, which still stands on the grounds of her home at Montpelier today. The reverse side of the coin depicts a pastoral perspective of the mansion at Montpelier.

DATE	ABP	MS-65 UNC.	PRF-65 PROOF
☐ 1999P	21.00	30.00	35.00

LIBRARY OF CONGRESS
Silver ($1.00)
Bimetallic ($10.00)

These two commemorative coins are considered to be "The Coins of Many Firsts" because they represent the first gold and platinum bimetallic coin struck by the U.S. Mint, the first U.S. Mint commemorative coins of this century and millennium, and the first U.S. Mint Commemorative Coins honoring a library.

The commemorative silver dollar's obverse, designed by Mint Engraver/Sculptor Thomas D. Rogers, Sr., is an open book superimposed over the torch of learning, which personifies the vast knowledge provided by the Library. The reverse, designed by Mint Engraver/Sculptor John Mercanti, is an architectural rendering of the dome on the Library's Jefferson Building.

The stunning Library of Congress commemorative bimetallic coin contains precious metal combining an inner core of platinum encircled by an outer ring of gold. The outer ring is stamped from a sheet of gold, and then a solid core of platinum is placed within the ring. The gold ring and platinum core is then simultaneously coined forming an annular bead where the two precious metals meet.

The bimetallic coin's obverse, designed by Mint Engraver/Sculptor John Mercanti, features the hand of Minerva raising the torch of learning over the dome of the magnificent Jefferson Building. The coin's reverse, designed by Mint Engraver/Sculptor Thomas D. Rogers, Sr., contains the logo of the Library of Congress encircled by a laurel wreath.

The Library of Congress, founded in 1800, comprises the world's most comprehensive record of human creativity. Its three massive structures, the Jefferson, Adams, and Madison Buildings, contain nearly 119 million items on approximately 530 miles of bookshelves. The collection includes more than 18 million cataloged books, 2 million recordings, 12 million photographs, 4 million maps, and 53 million manuscripts.

President Thomas Jefferson played a pivotal role in the Mint's and the Library's development. Jefferson proposed the decimal coinage system we use today and was a leading advocate for founding a national mint on American soil. An avid learner and lifelong collector of books, Jefferson sold his personal library of 6,487 books to Congress for $23,950 after the British burned the new Capitol and Library in 1814.

DATE	ABP	MS-65 UNC.	PRF-65 PROOF
☐ 2000P Silver Dollar	25.00	33.00	35.00

DATE	ABP	MS-65 UNC.	PRF-65 PROOF
☐ 2000W Bimetallic $10	2750.00	3500.00	1275.00

LEIF ERICSON MILLENNIUM
Silver ($1.00)

"This jointly issued coin set magnificently symbolizes a shared history and friendship with the Republic of Iceland that dates back through the last millennium," said U.S. Mint Director Jay W. Johnson. "What a beautiful way to celebrate the 1,000 years since the discovery of the New World by Leif Ericson, by issuing a first of its kind U.S./foreign commemorative coin set." "The Leif Ericson commemorative coin is really the perfect millennium collectible," said David Pickens, associate director for numismatics, "commemorating a 1,000-year anniversary in the year 2000."

The two beautifully detailed coins, designed respectively by the United States and the Republic of Iceland, are minted by the United States Mint. Both coins are legal tender and are struck from 26.73 grams of 90 percent silver. The United States Proof silver and Uncirculated silver coins display a heroic portrait of the intrepid explorer, Leif Ericson, on the obverse, designed by Mint Engraver/Sculptor John Mercanti, and a depiction of his Viking ship under full sail on the reverse, designed by Mint Engraver/Sculptor James Ferrell.

The Icelandic Proof silver coin's obverse features an image of Stirling Calder's famous sculpture of Leif Ericson, presented to Iceland by the United States in 1930. The reverse of the coin depicts the eagle, the dragon, the bull, and the giant from the Icelandic Coat of Arms. The designer of the coin is Icelandic artist Throstur Magnusson.

DATE	ABP	MS-65 UNC.	PRF-65 PROOF
☐ 2000P	50.00	70.00	65.00

AMERICAN BUFFALO
Silver ($1.00)

The American Buffalo commemorative silver dollar recreates James Earle Fraser's famous Buffalo nickel design that circulated from 1913 to 1938. The obverse depicts a profile of a Native American. The reverse features an American buffalo—an important symbol for many Native Americans.

The American Buffalo commemorative coin is available as a Proof silver dollar coin, as an Uncirculated silver dollar coin, as a two-coin set, or in the American Buffalo Coinage & Currency Set. The Proof coins will bear the Philadelphia mint mark; the Uncirculated coins will feature the Denver mint mark.

DATE	ABP	MS-65 UNC.	PRF-65 PROOF
☐ 2001D	125.00	175.00	
☐ 2001P	150.00		185.00

THE U.S. CAPITOL VISITOR CENTER
Clad (50¢)
Silver ($1.00)
Gold ($5.00)

Celebrate the first meeting of Congress in the U.S. Capitol and be part of history in the making by helping build the first ever Visitor Center for the U.S. Capitol. Congress has authorized three commemorative coins to celebrate the bicentennial of the first meeting of Congress at the U.S. Capitol building in Washington, D.C. A portion of the proceeds from the sale of each coin—$35 for gold, $10 for silver, $3 for clad—is authorized to be paid to the Capitol Preservation Fund for the purpose of aiding the construction, maintenance, and preservation of a new Capitol Visitor Center. The Visitor Center will offer modern facilities, free educational movies, and exhibits and will eliminate long waits outside.

The gold $5 coin is the design of Elizabeth Jones, the only woman to hold the position of U.S. Mint chief sculptor/engraver. The obverse of this coin includes an intricate carving of a single Corinthian column, the type found on the Capitol building. The coin's reverse is adorned with an image of the original structure, beautifully portraying the edifice where the first congressional session was held in the U.S. Capitol.

The silver dollar obverse is a creation of artist Marika Somogy. The obverse portrays the original U.S. Capitol superimposed on the image of today's Capitol building. The contrasting images illustrate how we have grown as a nation. The reverse is the design of Mint Sculptor/Engraver

John Mercanti and portrays a bald eagle cloaked in a banner inscribed "U.S. Capitol Visitor Center."

Dean McMullen designed the clad half-dollar obverse. It features the original U.S. Capitol building within an outline of the present day Capitol. The reverse is a combination of designs by artists Marcel Jovine and Alex Shagin. It portrays 16 stars and the inscription "32 SENATORS; 106 HOUSE MEMBERS." The stars represent the number of states and the inscription reflects the number of members in the 6th Congress—the first Congress to meet in the new Capitol in 1800.

DATE	ABP	MS-65 UNC.	PRF-65 PROOF
☐ 2001P	12.00	17.50	16.00

DATE	ABP	MS-65 UNC.	PRF-65 PROOF
☐ 2001P	32.00	42.00	42.00

DATE	ABP	MS-65 UNC.	PRF-65 PROOF
☐ 2001W	1750.00	2250.00	350.00

2002 OLYMPIC WINTER GAMES
Silver ($1.00)
Gold ($5.00)

The world's greatest athletes gather every four years to test their skills and determination. They have trained for a lifetime—untold hours of struggle, pain, frustration, and disappointment endured for the hope of one glorious moment. The Olympics have never been about sport alone; they are a showcase for the greatest qualities of the human spirit—courage, sacrifice, perseverance, and determination. The Olympics tell the story of the dignity of mankind.

In February of 2002, the world gathered in Salt Lake City to celebrate the power of the human spirit—the forum, the Olympic Winter Games. For seventeen days the world was once again united in heart-stopping competition and joyous celebration. Stories of hope, optimism, and inspiration were etched into the hearts of men and women and history books.

The Olympics and the human spirit they exhibit inspire every man, woman, and child to strive for greatness. They "Light the Fire Within" us all. These great traits that, once kindled, spread throughout the world create a better place for all humanity.

As a testament to the courage of the human spirit, and as a world symbol of peace, the message of the Olympics endures. The Olympic Winter Games of 2002 continued this legacy.

ABOUT THE COINS

Authorized by Congress under Public Law 106-435, the U.S. Mint issued two commemorative coins to support the 2002 Salt Lake Olympic Winter Games. A portion of the proceeds from the sale of each coin—$35 for gold and $10 for silver—was authorized to help support the 2002 Salt Lake Olympic Winter Games.

The gold $5 is the design of U.S. Mint Sculptor/ Engraver Donna Weaver. The obverse of this coin features the 2002 Salt Lake Olympic Winter Games Crystal Emblem superimposed on top of the Games' secondary identity mark entitled: "Rhythm of the Land." The reverse portrays the Olympic flame in relief atop a cauldron.

The silver dollar obverse is the design of U.S. Mint Sculptor/ Engraver John Mercanti. It features the Crystal Emblem of the 2002 Olympic Winter Games, Olympic Rings, and the

Games' secondary identity mark entitled: "Rhythm of the Land." The designer of the reverse is U.S. Mint Sculptor/Engraver Donna Weaver. It portrays the Salt Lake City skyline with the Rocky Mountains in the background.

DATE	ABP	MS-65 UNC.	PRF-65 PROOF
☐ 2002P SLC Olympics	32.00	42.00	42.00
☐ 2002W SLC Olympics	300.00	365.00	350.00
☐ 2002W West Point Bicentennial	20.00	27.00	32.00
☐ 2003P First Flight Dollar	33.00	42.00	48.00
☐ 2003P First Flight Half Dollar	10.00	14.00	17.00
☐ 2003W First Flight Gold $10	825.00	1050.00	895.00
☐ 2004P Thomas Edison $1	23.00	32.00	38.00
☐ 2004P Lewis & Clark $1	32.00	42.00	43.00
☐ 2005P Justice John Marshall $1	32.00	42.00	40.00
☐ 2005P Marine Corps $1	35.00	47.00	45.00
☐ 2005P Ben Franklin—Scientist $1	28.00	37.00	48.00
☐ 2005P Ben Franklin—Founding Father $1	25.00	35.00	33.00
☐ 2006S San Francisco Mint $1	32.00	42.00	30.00
☐ 2006S San Francisco Mint Gold $5	300.00	365.00	350.00
☐ 2007P Jamestown $1	27.00	35.00	33.00
☐ 2007W Jamestown Gold $5	300.00	365.00	300.00
☐ 2007P Little Rock Desegregation $1	23.00	30.00	40.00
☐ 2008P Bald Eagle $1	23.00	32.00	42.00
☐ 2008P Bald Eagle .50	10.00	14.00	15.00
☐ 2008W Bald Eagle Gold $5	300.00	365.00	350.00
☐ 2009P Louis Braille $1	23.00	32.00	32.00
☐ 2009P Abraham Lincoln $1	23.00	33.00	40.00
☐ 2010P American Veterans $1	28.00	35.00	32.00
☐ 2010P Boy Scouts $1	25.00	33.00	43.00
☐ 2011P US Army $1 (S-Proof)	42.00	55.00	45.00
☐ 2011P Medal of Honor $1 (S-Proof)	38.00	48.00	52.00
☐ 2011P US Army 50¢ (S-Proof)	45.00	60.00	35.00
☐ 2011P US Army $5.00	425.00	550.00	450.00
☐ 2011 Medal of Honor $5	450.00	575.00	475.00
☐ 2012 Infantry Soldier $1	32.00	42.00	50.00
☐ 2012 Star-Spangled Banner $1	35.00	45.00	50.00
☐ 2012 Star-Spangled Banner $5	450.00	575.00	450.00

U.S. TERRITORIAL COINAGE

PHILIPPINE COINAGE

The United States held sovereignty over the Philippines after paying $20 million to Spain at the end of the Spanish-American War and issued their coinage from 1903 to 1945. Proof coins were struck in Philadelphia from 1903 to 1908, while business strikes were minted in San Francisco. By 1920 the United States had opened a branch mint in Manila, and Philippine coinage was struck there. During WWII, production shifted back to the U.S. mainland.

For more information on Philippine coinage, please refer to *The Official Price Guide to World Coins.*

	ABP	F-12 FINE	EF-40 EX. FINE	MS-60 UNC.	MS-63 UNC.
PHIL ½ CENT					
☐ 1903	1.50	2.00	3.50	40.00	75.00
☐ 1903 Proof	50.00			65.00	120.00
☐ 1904	2.00	3.00	4.00	60.00	90.00
☐ 1904 Proof	50.00			75.00	125.00
☐ 1905 PF	150.00			225.00	375.00
☐ 1906 PF	125.00			175.00	300.00
☐ 1908 PF	125.00			175.00	300.00
PHIL ONE CENT					
☐ 1903	.75	2.00	4.00	25.00	50.00
☐ 1903 PF	60.00			75.00	125.00
☐ 1904	1.00	2.00	4.00	25.00	50.00
☐ 1904 PF	65.00			80.00	150.00
☐ 1905	1.00	2.00	4.00	30.00	55.00

	ABP	F-12 FINE	EF-40 EX. FINE	MS-60 UNC.	MS-63 UNC.
☐ 1905 PF	150.00			200.00	350.00
☐ 1906 PF	125.00			165.00	325.00
☐ 1908 PF	125.00			150.00	300.00
☐ 1908 S	2.00	4.00	12.00	45.00	100.00
☐ 1908 S/S Horned S					
	25.00	32.00	50.00	165.00	310.00
☐ 1908 S/S/S	25.00	32.00	60.00	200.00	350.00
☐ 1909 S	10.00	15.00	30.00	90.00	175.00
☐ 1910 S	4.00	6.00	12.00	35.00	90.00
☐ 1911 S	4.00	6.00	12.00	32.00	85.00
☐ 1911 S over S	25.00	35.00	85.00	125.00	300.00
☐ 1912 S	7.00	10.00	20.00	45.00	165.00
☐ 1912 S over S	20.00	25.00	60.00	120.00	225.00
☐ 1913 S	2.00	4.00	10.00	30.00	90.00
☐ 1914 S	3.00	4.00	15.00	45.00	125.00
☐ 1914 S over S	20.00	28.00	50.00	125.00	275.00
☐ 1915 S	35.00	45.00	85.00	600.00	1500.00
☐ 1916 S	8.00	12.00	30.00	125.00	215.00
☐ 1916 S over S	22.00	30.00	50.00	200.00	400.00
☐ 1917 S	3.50	6.00	12.00	65.00	110.00
☐ 1917/6S	100.00	125.00	165.00	800.00	1950.00
☐ 1918 S	4.00	6.00	12.00	50.00	95.00
☐ 1918 Med S	15.00	18.00	25.00	110.00	185.00
☐ 1918 Large S	350.00	425.00	700.00	1400.00	2650.00
☐ 1919 S	4.00	6.00	10.00	50.00	125.00
☐ 1920	5.00	7.50	12.50	60.00	135.00
☐ 1920 S	15.00	20.00	35.00	175.00	410.00
☐ 1921	1.00	4.00	6.25	40.00	80.00
☐ 1922	1.00	4.00	6.25	40.00	95.00
☐ 1925	1.00	4.00	5.00	25.00	60.00
☐ 1926	1.00	4.00	5.00	22.00	50.00
☐ 1927 M	1.00	4.00	5.00	38.00	55.00
☐ 1928 M	.75	1.00	5.00	35.00	55.00
☐ 1929 M	.75	1.00	5.00	40.00	60.00
☐ 1930 M	.75	1.00	5.00	25.00	50.00
☐ 1930 M/M	8.00	12.00	25.00	100.00	250.00
☐ 1931 M	.75	1.00	5.00	28.00	50.00
☐ 1932 M	.75	1.00	5.00	25.00	55.00
☐ 1933 M	.75	1.00	5.00	25.00	45.00
☐ 1934 M	.75	1.00	5.00	25.00	48.00
☐ 1936 M	.75	1.00	5.00	22.00	40.00
☐ 1937 M	.75	1.00	5.00	22.00	40.00

	ABP	F-12 FINE	EF-40 EX. FINE	MS-60 UNC.	MS-63 UNC.
☐ 1938 M	1.00	1.50	4.00	24.00	40.00
☐ 1939 M	1.00	1.50	4.00	24.00	45.00
☐ 1940 M	1.00	1.50	4.00	17.00	28.00
☐ 1941 M	1.25	2.00	4.00	26.00	55.00
☐ 1944 S	.25	.50	1.00	5.00	9.00
☐ 1944 S Doubled					
	2.00	4.00	8.00	40.00	75.00
5 CENT					
☐ 1903	1.00	4.00	6.00	20.00	45.00
☐ 1903 PF	50.00			70.00	125.00
☐ 1904	2.00	4.00	10.00	35.00	45.00
☐ 1904 PF	55.00			80.00	150.00
☐ 1905 PF	150.00			165.00	325.00
☐ 1906 PF	110.00			150.00	300.00
☐ 1908 PF	115.00			155.00	300.00
☐ 1916 S	32.00	45.00	100.00	600.00	1400.00
☐ 1917 S	4.00	6.50	15.00	90.00	285.00
☐ 1918 S	4.00	6.50	15.00	100.00	300.00
☐ 1918 S Mule	450.00	550.00	1650.00	7500.00	14000.00
☐ 1919 S	4.00	7.50	17.00	90.00	400.00
☐ 1920	4.00	7.50	14.00	100.00	325.00
☐ 1921	4.00	7.50	14.00	100.00	250.00
☐ 1925	7.00	10.00	26.00	140.00	275.00
☐ 1926	5.00	7.50	16.00	150.00	225.00
☐ 1927	5.00	7.50	16.00	120.00	165.00
☐ 1928	4.00	5.00	12.00	95.00	150.00
☐ 1930	2.00	5.00	8.00	55.00	140.00
☐ 1931	2.00	5.00	8.00	55.00	140.00
☐ 1932	2.00	5.00	8.00	60.00	140.00
☐ 1934	2.00	5.00	8.00	100.00	150.00
☐ 1934 Doubled MM					
	7.00	12.00	25.00	120.00	285.00
☐ 1935	1.00	2.00	5.00	100.00	165.00
☐ 1937	.70	1.50	4.00	36.00	85.00
☐ 1938	.70	2.00	4.00	28.00	50.00
☐ 1941	1.00	2.00	5.00	30.00	50.00
☐ 1944 P	.70	1.00	2.00	4.00	7.50
☐ 1944 S	.75	1.00	2.00	4.00	7.50
☐ 1945 S	.75	1.00	2.00	4.00	7.50
10 CENT					
☐ 1903-S	10.00	15.00	42.00	600.00	1400.00
☐ 1903	2.00	3.50	6.00	40.00	100.00

	ABP	F-12 FINE	EF-40 EX. FINE	MS-60 UNC.	MS-63 UNC.
☐ 1903 PF	80.00			105.00	175.00
☐ 1904	20.00	25.00	45.00	70.00	165.00
☐ 1904 S	3.00	4.00	12.00	55.00	125.00
☐ 1904 PF	80.00			105.00	175.00
☐ 1905 PF	175.00			210.00	375.00
☐ 1906 PF	125.00			165.00	325.00
☐ 1907	2.00	4.00	6.00	50.00	120.00
☐ 1907 S	2.00	4.00	6.00	55.00	135.00
☐ 1908 PF	150.00			190.00	350.00
☐ 1908 S	2.00	2.75	6.00	75.00	125.00
☐ 1909 S	10.00	15.00	35.00	550.00	1600.00
☐ 1911 S	3.00	8.00	20.00	115.00	400.00
☐ 1912 S	3.00	8.00	18.00	100.00	275.00
☐ 1912 S/S	28.00	35.00	55.00	400.00	750.00
☐ 1913 S	3.00	5.00	18.00	150.00	375.00
☐ 1914 S Long Cross Bar					
	12.00	17.00	35.00	325.00	700.00
☐ 1914 S	7.00	10.00	22.00	225.00	500.00
☐ 1915 S	12.00	17.00	30.00	450.00	1200.00
☐ 1917 S	2.00	3.00	5.00	45.00	100.00
☐ 1918 S	2.00	3.00	5.00	40.00	80.00
☐ 1919 S	2.00	3.00	5.00	45.00	110.00
☐ 1920 M	2.75	3.75	10.00	135.00	265.00
☐ 1921	2.00	3.00	4.00	23.00	55.00
☐ 1929	2.00	3.00	4.00	23.00	50.00
☐ 1935	2.00	3.00	4.00	20.00	50.00
☐ 1937	2.00	2.75	2.00	15.00	35.00
☐ 1938	2.00	2.75	2.00	15.00	35.00
☐ 1941	2.00	3.00	4.00	15.00	30.00
☐ 1944 D	2.00	2.60	3.00	4.00	8.00
☐ 1945 D	2.00	2.60	3.00	4.00	8.00
☐ 1945 D/D	8.00	12.00	20.00	55.00	115.00
TWENTY CENT					
☐ 1903	5.00	6.00	10.00	55.00	135.00
☐ 1903 S	15.00	22.00	60.00	750.00	2250.00
☐ 1903 PF	110.00			150.00	225.00
☐ 1904	25.00	32.00	45.00	120.00	225.00
☐ 1904 S	5.00	6.00	12.00	85.00	190.00
☐ 1904 PF	110.00			150.00	220.00
☐ 1905 S	15.00	20.00	50.00	600.00	1500.00
☐ 1905 PF	225.00			285.00	450.00
☐ 1906 PF	200.00			275.00	400.00

	ABP	F-12 FINE	EF-40 EX. FINE	MS-60 UNC.	MS-63 UNC.
☐ 1907	4.00	5.00	12.00	150.00	525.00
☐ 1907 S	4.00	5.00	10.00	75.00	350.00
☐ 1908 S	4.00	5.00	12.00	400.00	1000.00
☐ 1908 PF	225.00			275.00	450.00
☐ 1909 S	12.00	25.00	45.00	400.00	1400.00
☐ 1910 S	15.00	22.00	50.00	450.00	1700.00
☐ 1911 S	12.00	19.00	45.00	325.00	1400.00
☐ 1912 S	8.00	15.00	24.00	185.00	525.00
☐ 1913 S	7.00	15.00	24.00	200.00	400.00
☐ 1914 S	10.00	15.00	32.00	225.00	1400.00
☐ 1915 S	15.00	22.00	45.00	650.00	1750.00
☐ 1916 S	7.00	18.00	30.00	225.00	450.00
☐ 1917 S	4.00	5.00	12.00	85.00	185.00
☐ 1918 S	4.00	5.00	10.00	85.00	175.00
☐ 1919 S	4.00	5.00	8.00	150.00	300.00
☐ 1920 M	5.00	8.00	10.00	185.00	350.00
☐ 1921	4.00	5.00	7.00	60.00	125.00
☐ 1928/7 Mule	20.00	35.00	125.00	1000.00	2250.00
☐ 1929 Repunch Date					
	15.00	25.00	60.00	85.00	135.00
☐ 1929	4.00	5.00	9.00	40.00	65.00
☐ 1937	4.00	5.00	6.00	20.00	35.00
☐ 1938	4.00	5.00	6.00	20.00	35.00
☐ 1941	4.00	5.00	5.75	28.00	56.00
☐ 1944 D	4.45	5.00	5.25	6.00	7.00
☐ 1944 D/S	18.00	25.00	50.00	115.00	230.00
☐ 1945 D	4.45	5.00	5.25	6.00	7.00
FIFTY CENT					
☐ 1903	15.00	18.00	20.00	100.00	175.00
☐ 1903S					80000.00
☐ 1903 PF	100.00			135.00	225.00
☐ 1904	25.00	35.00	75.00	175.00	300.00
☐ 1904-S	15.00	20.00	25.00	165.00	265.00
☐ 1904 PF	115.00			165.00	275.00
☐ 1905 S	22.00	30.00	50.00	575.00	2650.00
☐ 1905 PF	290.00			365.00	575.00
☐ 1906 PF	250.00			300.00	475.00
☐ 1907	10.00	12.00	18.00	200.00	500.00
☐ 1907-S	10.00	12.00	32.00	225.00	375.00
☐ 1908-S	10.00	12.00	55.00	500.00	1600.00
☐ 1908 PF	250.00			325.00	450.00
☐ 1909 S	12.00	15.00	30.00	400.00	1300.00
☐ 1917 S	10.00	12.00	25.00	200.00	550.00

	ABP	F-12 FINE	EF-40 EX. FINE	MS-60 UNC.	MS-63 UNC.
☐ 1917 S Broken 7					
	15.00	22.00	45.00	500.00	1500.00
☐ 1918 S	10.00	12.00	17.00	115.00	228.00
☐ 1918 Inverted S					
	35.00	45.00	95.00	250.00	525.00
☐ 1919 S	10.00	14.00	15.00	150.00	225.00
☐ 1920	10.00	14.00	15.00	65.00	125.00
☐ 1921	10.00	12.00	14.00	50.00	100.00
☐ 1944 S	10.00	12.00	12.50	15.00	18.00
☐ 1944 S/S	25.00	35.00	55.00	120.00	175.00
☐ 1945 S	10.00	12.00	12.50	15.00	18.00
☐ 1945 S/S	35.00	50.00	70.00	120.00	200.00
PESO					
☐ 1903	30.00	35.00	40.00	200.00	750.00
☐ 1903 S	30.00	35.00	40.00	150.00	500.00
☐ 1903 PF	200.00			275.00	550.00
☐ 1904	60.00	80.00	125.00	250.00	550.00
☐ 1904-S	30.00	35.00	42.00	175.00	375.00
☐ 1904 PF	200.00			285.00	585.00
☐ 1905-S	32.00	39.00	45.00	300.00	950.00
☐ 1905-S Straight Serif					
	50.00	65.00	80.00	700.00	3250.00
☐ 1905 PF	575.00			900.00	1750.00
☐ 1906 S	1750.00	2500.00	4000.00	25000.00	45000.00
☐ 1906 PF	600.00			800.00	1500.00
☐ 1907 S	25.00	30.00	32.00	100.00	300.00
☐ 1908 S	25.00	30.00	35.00	100.00	275.00
☐ 1908 S/S	50.00	70.00	135.00	450.00	1250.00
☐ 1908 S Double Diz & Inverted MM					
	100.00	125.00	185.00	485.00	875.00
☐ 1908 PF	550.00			675.00	1275.00
☐ 1909 S	25.00	35.00	20.00	100.00	350.00
☐ 1909 S/S	35.00	45.00	65.00	175.00	750.00
☐ 1909 S/S/S	100.00	150.00	200.00	500.00	1500.00
☐ 1910 S	25.00	35.00	40.00	235.00	500.00
☐ 1911 S	30.00	40.00	80.00	2000.00	10000.00
☐ 1912 S	30.00	50.00	100.00	2500.00	11500.00
COMMEMORATIVE					
☐ 1936 50 C	40.00	50.00	75.00	125.00	215.00
☐ 1936 Murphy Quezon					
	70.00	85.00	120.00	200.00	375.00
☐ 1936 Roosevelt Quezon					
	70.00	85.00	125.00	225.00	425.00

GOLD AND SILVER BULLION COINS

PLEASE NOTE: THE PRICES THAT ARE LISTED REFLECT A GOLD SPOT PRICE OF $1250.00 PER OUNCE AND A SILVER SPOT PRICE OF $20.00 PER OUNCE.

AMERICAN EAGLE BULLION GOLD

The American Eagle bullion coins are minted in $5: weight 52.4 grains, contains one-tenth ounce pure gold; $10: weight 130.9 grains, contains one-quarter ounce pure gold; $25: weight 261.8 grains, contains one-half ounce pure gold; $50: weight 523.6 grains, contains 1 ounce pure gold. The obverse design is similar to the St. Gaudens $20 gold piece, 1907–1933 design. The coin date appears in Roman numerals. The reverse shows a group of American eagles.

DATE	MINTAGE	ABP	MS-65 UNC.	PRF-65 PROOF
☐ 1986 $5.00	912,609	140.00	160.00	
☐ 1986 $10.00	726,031	375.00	450.00	
☐ 1986 $25.00	599,566	900.00	1000.00	
☐ 1986 $50.00	1,362,650	1300.00	1350.00	
☐ 1986W $50.00	446,290	1475.00		1650.00
☐ 1986 Set (2 coins)				1700.00
☐ 1987 $5.00	580,266	140.00	160.00	
☐ 1987 $10.00	269,255	375.00	450.00	
☐ 1987 $25.00	131,255	925.00	1025.00	
☐ 1987P $25.00	143,398	800.00	900.00	
☐ 1987 $50.00	1,045,506	1300.00	1350.00	
☐ 1987W $50.00	147,498	1475.00		1650.00

DATE	MINTAGE	ABP	MS-65 UNC.	PRF-65 PROOF
☐ 1987 Set (2 coins)		2200.00		2650.00
☐ 1988 $5.00	159,500	140.00	160.00	
☐ 1988P $5.00	143,881	150.00		175.00
☐ 1988 $10.00	49,000	450.00	550.00	
☐ 1988P $10.00	98,028	375.00		450.00
☐ 1988 $25.00	45,000	1400.00	1650.00	
☐ 1988P $25.00	76,528	750.00		900.00
☐ 1988 $50.00	465,500	1275.00	1375.00	
☐ 1988W $50.00	87,133	1500.00		1800.00
☐ 1988 Set (4 coins)		2850.00		3250.00
☐ 1989 $5.00	264,790	140.00	160.00	
☐ 1989P $5.00	84,647	150.00		175.00
☐ 1989 $10.00	81,789	450.00	550.00	
☐ 1989P $10.00	54,170	375.00		450.00
☐ 1989 $25.00	44,820	1500.00	1750.00	
☐ 1989P $25.00	44,798	750.00		900.00
☐ 1989 $50.00	415,790	1275.00	1375.00	
☐ 1989W $50.00	54,570	1600.00		1900.00
☐ 1989 Set (4 coins)		3000.00		3450.00
☐ 1990 $5.00	208,760	140.00	160.00	
☐ 1990P $5.00	90,120	155.00		180.00
☐ 1990 $10.00	40,000	475.00	575.00	
☐ 1990P $10.00	60,790	400.00		450.00
☐ 1990 $25.00	30,000	1750.00	2000.00	
☐ 1990P $25.00	50,000	775.00		925.00
☐ 1990 $50.00	36,500	1275.00	1375.00	
☐ 1990W $50.00	61,000	1550.00		1700.00
☐ 1990 Set (4 coins)		2750.00		3250.00
☐ 1991 $5.00	33,000	175.00	225.00	
☐ 1991P $5.00	85,000	150.00		175.00
☐ 1991 $10.00	30,000	475.00	575.00	
☐ 1991P $10.00	56,000	375.00		450.00
☐ 1991 $25.00	24,000	2500.00	2900.00	
☐ 1991P $25.00	51,000	750.00		850.00
☐ 1991 $50.00	233,000	1275.00	1375.00	
☐ 1991W $50.00	64,000	1450.00		1650.00
☐ 1991 Set (4 coins)		2750.00		3250.00
☐ 1992 $5.00	209,000	130.00	150.00	
☐ 1992P $5.00	65,000	150.00		175.00
☐ 1992 $10.00	59,500	375.00	450.00	
☐ 1992P $10.00	46,000	375.00		450.00
☐ 1992 $25.00	54,000	1050.00	1200.00	
☐ 1992P $25.00	41,000	750.00		850.00
☐ 1992 $50.00	27,500	1275.00	1375.00	
☐ 1992W $50.00	45,000	1450.00		1650.00

DATE	MINTAGE	ABP	MS-65 UNC.	PRF-65 PROOF
☐ 1992 Set (4 coins)		2750.00		3250.00
☐ 1993 $5.00	210,709	150.00	190.00	
☐ 1993P $5.00	58,649	150.00		190.00
☐ 1993 $10.00	71,864	375.00	450.00	
☐ 1993P $10.00	46,464	375.00		450.00
☐ 1993 $25.00	73,324	875.00	975.00	
☐ 1993P $25.00	43,319	775.00		875.00
☐ 1993 $50.00	480,192	1275.00	1375.00	
☐ 1993P $50.00	34,389	1500.00		1650.00
☐ 1993 Set (4 coins)		2750.00		3250.00
☐ 1994 $5.00	206,380	130.00	150.00	
☐ 1994W $5.00	62,850	150.00		175.00
☐ 1994 $10.00	72,650	375.00	450.00	
☐ 1994W $10.00	48,175	350.00		425.00
☐ 1994 $25.00	62,400	900.00	1000.00	
☐ 1994W $25.00	44,500	725.00		825.00
☐ 1994 $50.00	221,633	1275.00	1375.00	
☐ 1994W $50.00	46,500	1450.00		1600.00
☐ 1994 Set (4 coins)		2750.00		3250.00
☐ 1995 $5	223,025	160.00	190.00	
☐ 1995W $5	62,665	150.00		175.00
☐ 1995 $10	83,752	375.00	450.00	
☐ 1995W $10	47,525	350.00		425.00
☐ 1995 $25	53,474	1200.00	1400.00	
☐ 1995W $25	45,375	725.00		825.00
☐ 1995 $50	200,636	1275.00	1375.00	
☐ 1995W $50	46,375	1450.00		1600.00
☐ 1995 Set (4 coins)		2750.00		3250.00
☐ 1995 10th Anniversary (W) Silver Eagle		3500.00		4500.00
☐ 1996 $5	402,000	130.00	150.00	
☐ 1996W $5	57,500	150.00		175.00
☐ 1996 $10	60,318	425.00	475.00	
☐ 1996 $10 Proof	38,219	350.00		425.00
☐ 1996 $25	39,287	1250.00	1450.00	
☐ 1996 $25 Proof	35,000	725.00		825.00
☐ 1996 $50	189,150	1275.00	1375.00	
☐ 1996 $50 Proof	36,150	1450.00		1600.00
☐ 1996 (4-Piece Proof Set)		2650.00		3150.00
☐ 1997 $5	528,250	150.00	185.00	
☐ 1997W $5	35,000	150.00		180.00
☐ 1997 $10	108,800	325.00	375.00	
☐ 1997 $10 Proof	29,800	350.00		425.00
☐ 1997 $25	79,600	875.00	975.00	
☐ 1997 $25 Proof	26,344	725.00		825.00
☐ 1997 $50	664,500	1275.00	1375.00	

DATE	MINTAGE	ABP	MS-65 UNC.	PRF-65 PROOF
☐ 1997W $50	33,000	1450.00		1600.00
☐ 1997 (4-Piece Proof Set)		2650.00		3150.00
☐ 1998 $5	1,344,500	130.00	150.00	
☐ 1998 $5 Proof	39,400	150.00		180.00
☐ 1998 $10	309,829	325.00	375.00	
☐ 1998 $10 Proof	29,500	350.00		425.00
☐ 1998 $25	169,025	635.00	700.00	
☐ 1998 $25 Proof	25,374	725.00		800.00
☐ 1998 $50	1,468,500	1275.00	1375.00	
☐ 1998W $50	25,886	1450.00		1600.00
☐ 1998 (4-Piece Proof Set)		2650.00		3150.00
☐ 1999 $5	2,750,250	130.00	150.00	
☐ 1999 $5 Proof	48,500	150.00		180.00
☐ 1999 $10	564,250	325.00	375.00	
☐ 1999 $10 Proof	34,417	350.00		400.00
☐ 1999 $25	263,010	650.00	710.00	
☐ 1999 $25 Proof	30,425	725.00		800.00
☐ 1999 $50	1,505,025	1275.00	1375.00	
☐ 1999W $50	31,500	1450.00		1600.00
☐ 1999 (4-Piece Proof Set)		2650.00		3150.00
☐ 2000 $5	569,150	130.00	150.00	
☐ 2000 $5 Proof	50,000	150.00		180.00
☐ 2000 $10	128,950	325.00	375.00	
☐ 2000 $10 Proof	36,025	350.00		400.00
☐ 2000 $25	79,287	900.00	1000.00	
☐ 2000 $25 Proof	32,025	725.00		825.00
☐ 2000 $50	433,319	1275.00	1375.00	
☐ 2000W $50	33,000	1450.00		1600.00
☐ 2000 (4-Piece Proof Set)		2650.00		3150.00
☐ 2001 $5	269,147	150.00	180.00	
☐ 2001 $5 Proof	37,500	150.00		180.00
☐ 2001 $10	71,250	375.00	450.00	
☐ 2001 $10 Proof	25,600	350.00		400.00
☐ 2001 $25	48,050	1050.00	1200.00	
☐ 2001 $25 Proof	23,250	725.00		800.00
☐ 2001 $50	143,605	1275.00	1375.00	
☐ 2001W $50	24,500	1450.00		1600.00
☐ 2001 (4-Piece Proof Set)		2650.00		3150.00
☐ 2002 $5	230,025	175.00	215.00	
☐ 2002 $5 Proof	40,850	150.00		180.00
☐ 2002 $10	62,025	375.00	450.00	
☐ 2002 $10 Proof	29,250	350.00		400.00
☐ 2002 $25	70,025	925.00	1050.00	
☐ 2002 $25 Proof	26,646	725.00		800.00
☐ 2002 $50	222,025	1275.00	1375.00	

DATE	MINTAGE	ABP	MS-65 UNC.	PRF-65 PROOF
☐ 2002W $50	27,500	1450.00		1600.00
☐ 2002 (4-Piece Proof Set)		2650.00		3150.00
☐ 2003 $5	245,025	150.00	180.00	
☐ 2003 $5 Proof	40,025	150.00		185.00
☐ 2003 $10	74,025	335.00	385.00	
☐ 2003 $10 Proof	30,275	375.00		450.00
☐ 2003 $25	79,025	650.00	725.00	
☐ 2003 $25 Proof	28,250	775.00		875.00
☐ 2003 $50	416,032	1275.00	1375.00	
☐ 2003W $50	28,344	1550.00		1750.00
☐ 2003 (4-Piece Proof Set)		2850.00		3350.00
☐ 2004 $5	250,010	150.00	180.00	
☐ 2004 $5 Proof	35,125	150.00		185.00
☐ 2004 $10	72,010	335.00	385.00	
☐ 2004 $10 Proof	28,825	350.00		425.00
☐ 2004 $25	98,050	650.00	725.00	
☐ 2004 $25 Proof	27,330	725.00		825.00
☐ 2004 $50	417,019	1275.00	1375.00	
☐ 2004W $50	28,200	1450.00		1600.00
☐ 2004 (4-Piece Proof Set)		2650.00		3150.00
☐ 2005 $5	300,050	150.00	180.00	
☐ 2005 $5 Proof	49,250	150.00		185.00
☐ 2005 $10	72,000	335.00	385.00	
☐ 2005 $10 Proof	37,200	375.00		475.00
☐ 2005 $25	80,025	650.00	725.00	
☐ 2005 $25 Proof	34,300	725.00		800.00
☐ 2005 $50	356,550	1275.00	1375.00	
☐ 2005W $50	35,250	1450.00		1600.00
☐ 2005 (4-Piece Proof Set)		2650.00		3150.00
☐ 2006 $5	285,000	150.00	180.00	
☐ 2006 $5 Proof	47,250	150.00		185.00
☐ 2006 $10	60,000	335.00	385.00	
☐ 2006 $10 Proof	36,125	375.00		450.00
☐ 2006 $25	66,000	650.00	725.00	
☐ 2006 $25 Proof	34,325	725.00		800.00
☐ 2006 $50	237,510	1275.00	1375.00	
☐ 2006W $50	47,100	1450.00		1600.00
☐ 2006 (4-Piece Proof Set)		2650.00		3150.00
☐ 2007 $5	190,000	155.00	185.00	
☐ 2007 $5 Proof	58,500	150.00		185.00
☐ 2007 $10	34,000	375.00	450.00	
☐ 2007 $10 Proof	46,190	375.00		450.00
☐ 2007 $25	47,000	950.00	1100.00	
☐ 2007 $25 Proof	44,025	725.00		800.00
☐ 2007 $50	140,000	1275.00	1375.00	
☐ 2007W $50	51,810	1450.00		1600.00

DATE	MINTAGE	ABP	MS-65 UNC.	PRF-65 PROOF
☐ 2007 (4-Piece Proof Set)		2650.00		3100.00
☐ 2008 $5	305,000	130.00	150.00	
☐ 2008 $5 Proof	28,125	150.00		185.00
☐ 2008 $10	70,000	335.00	385.00	
☐ 2008 $10 Proof	18,875	450.00		525.00
☐ 2008 $25	61,000	650.00	725.00	
☐ 2008 $25 Proof	22,600	850.00		1000.00
☐ 2008 $50	710,000	1275.00	1375.00	
☐ 2008W $50	30,235	1800.00		2000.00
☐ 2008 (4-Piece Proof Set)		3000.00		3500.00
☐ 2009 $5	275,000	130.00	150.00	
☐ 2009 $5 Proof	Not Made			
☐ 2009 $10	110,000	335.00	385.00	
☐ 2009 $10 Proof	Not Made			
☐ 2009 $25	110,000	650.00	725.00	
☐ 2009 $25 Proof	Not Made			
☐ 2009 $50	1,493,000	1275.00	1375.00	
☐ 2009 $50 Proof	Not Made			
☐ 2009 (4-Piece Proof Set)	Not Made			
☐ 2010 $5	380,000	130.00	150.00	
☐ 2010 $5 Proof		150.00		185.00
☐ 2010 $10	58,000	335.00	385.00	
☐ 2010 $10 Proof		350.00		425.00
☐ 2010 $25	40,000	650.00	725.00	
☐ 2010 $25 Proof		725.00		800.00
☐ 2010 $50	988,500	1275.00	1375.00	
☐ 2010 $50 Proof		1450.00		1600.00
☐ 2010 (4-Piece Proof Set)		2650.00		3000.00
☐ 2011 $5		150.00	180.00	
☐ 2011 $5 Proof		150.00		185.00
☐ 2011 $10		335.00	385.00	
☐ 2011 $10 Proof		375.00		450.00
☐ 2011 $25		650.00	725.00	
☐ 2011 $25 Proof		725.00		800.00
☐ 2011 $50		1275.00	1375.00	
☐ 2011 $50 Proof		1450.00		1600.00
☐ 2011 (4-Piece Proof Set)		2650.00		300.00
☐ 2012 $5		130.00	150.00	
☐ 2012 $5 Proof		150.00	185.00	
☐ 2012 $10		335.00	375.00	
☐ 2012 $10 Proof		350.00	425.00	
☐ 2012 $25		635.00	685.00	
☐ 2012 $25 Proof		725.00	800.00	
☐ 2012 $50		1275.00	1375.00	
☐ 2012 $50 Proof		1450.00	1600.00	
☐ 2012 (4-Piece Proof Set)		2650.00		3000.00

AMERICAN SILVER DOLLAR EAGLE BULLION

The American Silver Dollar Eagle bullion coin is minted in 99.93 fine silver; weight, 479.9 grains; contains 1 ounce pure silver. The obverse design was taken from the famous Walking Liberty half-dollar coin. The reverse shows an American eagle with breasted shield.

DATE	MINTAGE	ABP	MS-65 UNC.	PRF-65 PROOF
☐ 1986P	5,393,005	35.00	42.00	
☐ 1986S	1,446,778	65.00		75.00
☐ 1987P	11,442,335	33.00	39.00	
☐ 1987S	904,732	60.00		75.00
☐ 1988P	5,004,646	33.00	39.00	
☐ 1988S	557,370	60.00		75.00
☐ 1989P	5,203,327	33.00	39.00	
☐ 1989S	617,694	60.00		75.00
☐ 1990P	5,840,200	35.00	40.00	
☐ 1990S	695,500	60.00		75.00
☐ 1991P	7,191,000	34.00	39.00	
☐ 1991S	511,925	60.00		75.00
☐ 1992P	5,540,00	35.00	40.00	
☐ 1992S	498,000	60.00		75.00
☐ 1993	6,763,762	34.00	40.00	
☐ 1993P	405,913	65.00		80.00
☐ 1994	4,227,319	37.00	45.00	
☐ 1994P	372,168	80.00		100.00
☐ 1995	4,672,051	37.00	45.00	
☐ 1995P	438,511	70.00		90.00
☐ 1995 10th Anniversary (W) Proof	30,125	2850.00		3500.00
☐ 1996	3,603,386	50.00	70.00	
☐ 1996P	500,000	65.00		80.00
☐ 1997	4,295,004	35.00	40.00	

DATE	MINTAGE	ABP	MS-65 UNC.	PRF-65 PROOF
☐ 1997P	435,368	60.00		75.00
☐ 1998	4,847,549	35.00	40.00	
☐ 1998P	450,000	55.00		70.00
☐ 1999	7,408,640	35.00	40.00	
☐ 1999P	549,769	55.00		70.00
☐ 2000	9,239,132	33.00	38.00	
☐ 2000P	600,000	55.00		70.00
☐ 2001	9,001,711	33.00	38.00	
☐ 2001P	746,398	55.00		70.00
☐ 2002	10,539,026	33.00	38.00	
☐ 2002P	647,342	55.00		70.00
☐ 2003	8,500,000	33.00	38.00	
☐ 2003P	747,830	55.00		70.00
☐ 2004	8,882,500	33.00	38.00	
☐ 2004P	801,500	60.00		75.00
☐ 2005	8,891,000	33.00	38.00	
☐ 2005P	816,663	55.00		70.00
☐ 2006	10,675,000	33.00	38.00	
☐ 2006P	1,092,500	55.00		70.00
☐ 2007	9,025,000	33.00	38.00	
☐ 2007P	821,750	55.00		70.00
☐ 2008	20,580,000	33.00	38.00	
☐ 2008P	701,000	55.00		70.00
☐ 2009	30,459,000	33.00	38.00	
☐ 2010	29,110,000	33.00	38.00	
☐ 2010P		55.00		70.00
☐ 2011		33.00	38.00	
☐ 2011P		55.00		70.00
☐ 2012		34.00	39.00	
☐ 2012P		65.00		80.00

COMMEMORATIVE MEDALS

NORTH AMERICAN CENTENNIAL

DATE	MINTAGE	ABP IN MS-60	MS-60 UNC.	MS-65 UNC.
☐ 1925 Thin	12,000	225.00	285.00	650.00
☐ 1925 Thick	40,000	135.00	185.00	375.00

SO-CALLED WILSON DOLLAR

DATE	MINTAGE	ABP IN MS-60	MS-60 UNC.	MS-65 UNC.
☐ 1920 Silver	2,200	750.00	1100.00	3750.00
☐ 1920 Copper	3,700	850.00	1250.00	4000.00

2 KRONER, SWEDEN

DATE	MINTAGE	ABP IN MS-60	MS-60 UNC.	MS-65 UNC.
☐ 1936 2 Kroner Delaware Swedish Tercentennial				
	500,000	20.00	30.00	70.00

U.S. PROOF SETS, 1936 TO DATE

The technical definition of a proof is a coin made for presentation or collector purposes. Beginning in the second half of the 19th century, the Mint struck proofs of many of its coins; some, but not a great number, appeared previously. A proof is not made from a specially manufactured die but rather an ordinary die set aside exclusively for use in proofs. The dies are cleaned and polished more frequently than those used for ordinary circulating coins. When any sign of wear or imperfection appears, the die is scrapped. This is why proofs have a somewhat higher surface relief (bas-relief) than uncirculated specimens, leading to the conclusion—mistakenly—that more deeply engraved dies are employed. After coming from the press, proofs are not touched except with gloves or special tongs made for the purpose, and are inspected for uniformity. Any exhibiting flaws of any nature are rejected. Proofs that pass inspection are housed in holders, so that nothing may interfere with their finish.

Frosted proofs were not produced for forty years (from 1936 until 1978), when selected issues started once again to be produced. These have a lustrous shining ground but the design and lettering are nonreflective or frosted. So-called matte proofs have a granular finish. These, too, are a thing of the past. Brilliant proofs, those struck from 1936 to date, are mirrorlike over the entire surface, not only the ground but also design and lettering. It is well to keep in mind (for beginners) that a coin found in circulation is never a proof, regardless of the brilliance of its luster or perfection of its condition. It is simply a "prooflike" coin.

Proof sets have been struck by the Mint since 1936, though none were issued in the years 1943–49. Beginning in 1968 they were issued in stiff plastic holders rather than pliable vinyl. Proof sets are now struck only at the San Francisco Mint and all coins carry the "S" mint mark. **Note:** Prestige and Premier sets contain commemorative coins.

DATE	MINTAGE	MS-65 PROOF
☐ 1936	3,837	7250.00
☐ 1937	5,542	4000.00
☐ 1938	8,045	1750.00
☐ 1939	8,795	1650.00
☐ 1940	11,246	1400.00
☐ 1941	15,287	1350.00
☐ 1942 1 Nickel		1250.00
☐ 1942 2 Nickels	21,120	1400.00
☐ 1950	51,386	550.00
☐ 1951	57,500	575.00
☐ 1952	81,980	225.00
☐ 1953	128,800	210.00
☐ 1954	233,300	110.00
☐ 1955	378,200	120.00
☐ 1956	699,384	55.00
☐ 1957	1,247,952	30.00
☐ 1958	875,652	38.00
☐ 1959	1,149,291	32.00
☐ 1960 Small Date	1,691,500	35.00
☐ 1960 Large Date	1,691,500	30.00
☐ 1961	3,028,244	27.00
☐ 1962	3,218,019	27.00
☐ 1963	3,075,645	27.00
☐ 1964	3,949,634	26.00
☐ 1968S	3,041,508	8.00
☐ 1968S Without S 10¢		15,500.00
☐ 1969S	2,360,000	7.50
☐ 1970S	2,600,000	10.00
☐ 1970S Small Date, ¢		75.00
☐ 1970S Without S, 10¢	2,200	850.00
☐ 1971S	3,244,138	4.50
☐ 1971S Without S, 5¢	1,655	1325.00
☐ 1972S	3,267,667	4.50
☐ 1973S	2,769,624	8.50
☐ 1974S	2,617,350	10.00
☐ 1975S	2,850,715	10.00
☐ 1976S 40%, 3 pieces	4,000,000	28.00
☐ 1976S	4,150,210	9.00
☐ 1977S	3,251,125	8.50
☐ 1978S	3,127,781	8.00
☐ 1979S Solid S	3,677,175	9.50
☐ 1979S Open S		70.00
☐ 1980S	3,547,130	6.50
☐ 1981S Solid S	4,110,000	7.00
☐ 1981S Open S		265.00

DATE	MINTAGE	MS-65 PROOF
☐ 1982S	3,857,479	4.50
☐ 1983S	3,139,000	4.50
☐ 1983S Prestige	130,000	47.00
☐ 1984S	1,850,110	5.50
☐ 1984S Prestige	300,000	30.00
☐ 1985S	3,460,210	4.00
☐ 1986S	2,391,100	6.50
☐ 1986S Prestige	600,000	32.00
☐ 1987S	3,462,200	4.00
☐ 1987S Prestige	425,000	29.00
☐ 1988S	3,164,125	6.50
☐ 1988S Prestige	225,000	32.00
☐ 1989S	3,100,002	4.50
☐ 1989S Prestige	215,000	37.00
☐ 1990S	2,793,500	6.50
☐ 1990S Prestige	505,000	29.00
☐ 1990 No "S" Cent		4850.00
☐ 1991S	2,610,000	5.50
☐ 1991S Prestige	255,000	44.00
☐ 1992S	2,650,000	5.50
☐ 1992S Prestige	182,000	43.00
☐ 1992S Silver	1,009,500	23.00
☐ 1992S Silver Premier	210,000	26.00
☐ 1993S	2,400,000	5.00
☐ 1993S Silver	570,210	32.00
☐ 1993S Silver Premier	175,000	35.00
☐ 1993S Prestige	225,000	55.00
☐ 1994S	2,308,750	5.00
☐ 1994S Prestige	215,000	50.00
☐ 1994S Silver	636,000	25.00
☐ 1994S Silver Premier	150,000	30.00
☐ 1995S	2,010,250	12.00
☐ 1995S Prestige	107,000	77.00
☐ 1995S Silver	549,750	45.00
☐ 1995S Silver Premier	130,000	58.00
☐ 1996S	1,700,000	8.00
☐ 1996S Prestige	60,000	315.00
☐ 1996S Silver	620,500	32.00
☐ 1996S Silver Premier	150,000	34.00
☐ 1997S	1,975,000	11.00
☐ 1997S Prestige	80,000	62.00
☐ 1997S Silver	605,500	29.00
☐ 1997S Silver Premier	135,000	38.00
☐ 1998S	2,085,000	11.00

DATE	MINTAGE	MS-65 PROOF
☐ 1998S Silver	640,000	27.00
☐ 1998S Silver Premier	240,650	29.00
☐ 1999S (9 coins)	2,543,000	12.00
☐ 1999S (5 Quarters)	804,500	7.00
☐ 2000S	3,082,500	7.00
☐ 2000S Silver	965,420	45.00
☐ 2001S	2,294,000	15.00
☐ 2001S Silver	889,700	55.00
☐ 2002S	2,317,000	8.00
☐ 2002S Silver	892,225	50.00
☐ 2003S	2,172,650	8.00
☐ 2003S Silver	1,125,750	42.00
☐ 2004S	1,789,500	10.00
☐ 2004S Silver	951,175	42.00
☐ 2005S	2,275,000	7.00
☐ 2005S Silver	1,069,500	42.00
☐ 2006S	2,000,500	9.50
☐ 2006S Silver	1,050,000	42.00
☐ 2007S	1,700,000	19.00
☐ 2007S Silver	875,000	52.50
☐ 2008S	1,405,000	75.00
☐ 2008S Silver	765,000	62.00
☐ 2009S	1,300,000	32.00
☐ 2009S Silver	695,000	65.00
☐ 2010S		57.00
☐ 2010S Silver		65.00
☐ 2011S		49.00
☐ 2011S Silver		87.00
☐ 2012S		100.00
☐ 2012S Silver		185.00
☐ 2013S		40.00
☐ 2013S Silver		59.00

Note: Some mintage totals for Proof Sets represent estimates based upon best available information.

U.S. MINT SETS, 1947 TO DATE

Beginning collectors habitually confuse the terms "proof set" and "mint set." It is important to recognize the distinction between them, especially as the values are quite different. The buyer who thinks he has a bargain on a proof set, when in fact he has bought a mint set, may have paid too much.

Mint sets originated well after the selling of special proof sets had become established. Manufacture of proof sets was suspended during World War II. Following conclusion of the war (1945), the Mint chose not to immediately resume proof sets, but instead to sell mint sets as a substitute. They were introduced in 1947, sold well, and continued to be produced after proof sets were reinstated in 1950.

Mint sets contain the same coins as proof sets (one of each denomination, from each Mint, for that year), but the coins are not proofs. They are standard "business strikes," just like coins released into general circulation. Naturally they are uncirculated, as the Mint takes specimens from its assembly lines that have not gone into circulation. In terms of specific grade, this is really a matter of luck. Some coins in mint sets are flawless and merit a full MS-70 rating. The vast majority are not quite so fine, and would grade between MS-60 and MS-65. In buying a mint set from a dealer, you can be certain that all the coins will be uncirculated, but a condition grade higher than MS-60 should not be anticipated for any of them. In offering mint sets, dealers do not mention condition grade, as it can vary from coin to coin within a set.

To carry the values indicated, sets must be in the original sealed holders in which they were sold. In the years 1965, 1966, and 1967, when no proof sets were struck, mint sets were placed in rigid plastic holders and called "Special Mint Sets," in hopes they would appeal to the regular buyers of proof sets. The standard packaging for mint sets was originally a cardboard holder, which was abandoned in favor of plastic envelopes in 1959.

Mintage figures are not recorded for mint sets, as the coins involved are not specially produced for that purpose.

DATE	MS-60 OR BETTER
☐ 1947 Double Set	1700.00
☐ 1948 Double Set	975.00
☐ 1949 Double Set	1400.00
☐ 1950*	NOT ISSUED
☐ 1951 Double Set	1150.00
☐ 1952 Double Set	1050.00
☐ 1953 Double Set	775.00
☐ 1954 Double Set	385.00
☐ 1955 Double Set	285.00
☐ 1956 Double Set	285.00
☐ 1957 Double Set	350.00
☐ 1958 Double Set	265.00
☐ 1959	55.00
☐ 1960	47.00
☐ 1961	47.00
☐ 1962	47.00
☐ 1963	42.00
☐ 1964	42.00
☐ 1965 Special Mint Set	12.00
☐ 1966 Special Mint Set	11.00
☐ 1967 Special Mint Set	12.00
☐ 1968 P-D-S	7.50

*Note: No mint sets were sold this year, only proof sets. Many mint sets were, however, assembled by dealers and placed in packaging similar to that of the Mint's. In cases where the coins in these privately assembled mint sets are strictly uncirculated, they will have a slight premium value.

DATE	MS-60 OR BETTER
☐ 1969 P-D-S	8.00
☐ 1970 P-D-S	20.00
☐ 1971 P-D-S	4.50
☐ 1972 P-D-S	3.50
☐ 1973 P-D-S	12.50
☐ 1974 P-D-S	7.25
☐ 1975	7.50
☐ 1976	8.00
☐ 1976S (25¢, 50¢, $1 only—40% Silver)	20.00
☐ 1977	7.50
☐ 1978	8.50
☐ 1979	6.50
☐ 1980	6.75
☐ 1981	11.00
☐ 1982 Non-Government Set	65.00
☐ 1983 Non-Government Set	75.00
☐ 1984	4.00
☐ 1985	4.25
☐ 1986	8.00
☐ 1987	5.00
☐ 1988	6.00
☐ 1989	4.00
☐ 1990	4.00
☐ 1991	5.00
☐ 1992	4.50
☐ 1993	6.00
☐ 1994	4.00
☐ 1995	5.50
☐ 1996	20.00
☐ 1997	7.00
☐ 1998	4.50
☐ 1999	8.00
☐ 1999 SBA	9.50
☐ 2000	8.00

DATE	MS-60 OR BETTER
☐ 2001	10.00
☐ 2002	10.00
☐ 2003	9.00
☐ 2004	12.00
☐ 2005	10.00
☐ 2006	11.00
☐ 2007	30.00
☐ 2008	62.00
☐ 2009	29.00
☐ 2010	29.00
☐ 2011	35.00
☐ 2012	80.00
☐ 2013	40.00

BU ROLLS

BU rolls are now among the most talked about and heavily traded of all numismatic items. The total quantity of coins sold in rolls far exceeds all other coin sales combined. They have become the favorite numismatic investment among thousands of investors. To a lesser extent they are also bought by collectors, though sales to collectors have not appreciably increased.

What is a BU roll? The term BU, which has been used in coin collecting for more than two generations, stands for *Brilliant Uncirculated*. Some define it as Best Uncirculated or Bright Uncirculated. Regardless of the way one interprets it, the important point about a BU coin is that it is uncirculated. Its condition grade is a minimum of MS-60 on the ANA grading scale. It may be higher than MS-60 but in buying rolls advertised only as BU, with no grade specified, do not expect any of the coins to grade higher than MS-60. It is possible to get BU rolls in MS-63 and MS-65 but, of course, the price is higher.

A roll comprises coins of the same denomination and, almost always, the same type. If Indian Head and Lincoln cents were mixed in the same roll, this would be advertised as a "mixed roll." Most BU roll trading occurs in *solid date rolls.* A solid date roll is one in which all the coins are of the same date and same place of manufacture: 1946D, 1948S, 1982P, etc. The number of coins in a roll varies by denomination: cents, fifty coins; nickels, forty; dimes, fifty; quarters, forty; half dollars, twenty. The roll may be wrapped in bank paper or contained in a lucite holder.

All rolls passing through the coin market are "assembled rolls." They were not put together at the Mint but by coin dealers, collectors, and investors. The possibility always exists that a circulated coin might have slipped in, so it is advisable to examine all the coins in a roll.

Because new rolls are constantly being made up and old ones broken, the scarcity factor is difficult to determine. While the vast majority of BU rolls are of 20th-century coins, they are also available for most of the common-date coins of the late 19th century as well. Generally they are not available for scarce coins of the 19th century, nor even for some scarce dates of the 20th. If the coin is very common, with a mintage of 100 million or more, there will be literally thousands of BU rolls passing through the market. It may seem paradoxical, but the common coins are often preferred by investors, who feel that their low prices make them an ideal speculation. Some rolls can be had for less than $1, such as late-date Lincolns, and these too are bought by investors. At the other end of the spectrum are rolls bringing $3,600 or more, such as the 1941S Walking Liberty half dollar. Rolls, like single coins, come in all price ranges.

It is important to note that the price of a BU roll does not necessarily reflect the value of the same coin when sold singly. You cannot multiply the single coin price to arrive at the roll price. BU rolls find their own value levels in trading, and the price can sometimes be quite far out of line with that of the individual coin. There are various reasons for this, chiefly tied to supply and demand. At any given time there may be a huge surplus of certain BU rolls on the market, or such an extreme shortage that dealers cannot buy them fast enough to fill orders. The availability of any coin in BU rolls may be a very different story than its availability as a single specimen. Also, investors will frequently "bandwagon" a group of coins in BU rolls, all buying the same rolls. They do not buy the single specimens, so the shortage of supply is not reflected in single specimens. This is becoming more pronounced in today's coin market, now that BU rolls have become so popular with investors. Of course, the dealers also influence the prices. When a dealer is buying common to medium-scarce coins for his stock, he prefers to buy in rolls, regardless of whether he intends to sell the coins in rolls or individually. It is more convenient for him and, in many cases, more economical.

The following prices for BU rolls were current at the time of going to press.

Lincoln Cents

1934	$625.00	1950S	$60.00
1334D	$3000.00	1951	$145.00
1935	$950.00	1951D	$25.00
1935D	$825.00	1951S	$60.00
1935S	$2800.00	1952	$130.00
1936	$300.00	1952D	$27.00
1936D	$450.00	1952S	$165.00
1936S	$925.00	1953	$35.00
1937	$275.00	1953D	$25.00
1937D	$275.00	1953S	$35.00
1937S	$350.00	1954	$35.00
1938	$575.00	1954D	$23.00
1938D	$750.00	1954S	$20.00
1938S	$425.00	1955	$22.00
1939	$140.00	1955D	$18.00
1939D	$525.00	1955S	$28.00
1939S	$215.00	1956	$12.00
1940	$165.00	1956D	$12.50
1940D	$285.00	1957	$12.00
1940S	$225.00	1957D	$12.00
1941	$130.00	1958	$12.00
1941D	$275.00	1958D	$12.00
1941S	$300.00	1959	$2.75
1942	$100.00	1959D	$3.00
1942D	$135.00	1960	$2.00
1942S	$500.00	1960D	$2.00
1943	$75.00	1960 Small Date	$125.00
1943D	$190.00	1960D Small Date	$7.50
1943S	$285.00	1961	$2.00
1944	$35.00	1961D	$2.00
1944D	$43.00	1962	$2.75
1944S	$95.00	1962D	$2.25
1945	$90.00	1963	$1.50
1945D	$55.00	1963D	$1.75
1945S	$52.00	1964	$1.25
1946	$45.00	1964D	$1.50
1946D	$35.00	1965	$2.00
1946S	$240.00	1966	$4.00
1947	$235.00	1967	$5.50
1947D	$45.00	1968	$2.00
1947S	$40.00	1968D	$2.00
1948	$75.00	1968S	$2.00
1948D	$140.00	1969	$7.00
1948S	$150.00	1969D	$1.75
1949	$185.00	1969S	$6.50
1949D	$130.00	1970	$1.75
1949S	$125.00	1970D	$2.75
1950	$125.00	1970S	$5.00
1950D	$45.00	1971	$12.00
		1971D	$3.50

1971S	$11.00	1992	$3.50
1972	$4.00	1992D	$5.50
1972D	$6.00	1993	$3.50
1972S	$4.00	1993D	$17.50
1973	$2.00	1994	$2.25
1973D	$2.00	1994D	$2.25
1973S	$6.00	1995	$2.25
1974	$2.00	1995D	$5.00
1974D	$2.00	1996	$4.00
1974S	$10.00	1996D	$6.50
1975	$3.00	1997	$3.50
1975D	$2.00	1997D	$4.00
1976	$2.00	1998	$2.50
1976D	$2.50	1998D	$3.50
1977	$2.50	1999	$2.60
1977D	$3.50	1999D	$2.50
1978	$3.50	2000	$2.75
1978D	$8.50	2000D	$3.00
1979	$3.00	2001	$4.50
1979D	$3.00	2001D	$2.25
1980	$2.50	2002	$2.25
1980D	$2.50	2002D	$3.50
1981	$2.00	2003	$4.00
1981D	$2.00	2003D	$2.25
1982	$2.50	2004	$2.00
1982D	$2.00	2004D	$4.50
1982 Small Date (zinc)	$25.00	2005	$2.00
1982 Large Date (zinc)	$12.00	2005D	$3.00
1983	$4.00	2006	$4.50
1983D	$9.50	2006D	$2.00
1984	$10.00	2007	$2.00
1984D	$16.00	2007D	$2.00
1985	$7.50	2008	$2.00
1985D	$18.00	2008D	$2.00
1986	$20.00	2009	$2.25
1986D	$28.00	2009D	$2.50
1987	$7.00	2010	$2.50
1987D	$15.00	2010D	$2.50
1988	$7.00	2011	$2.50
1988D	$12.50	2011D	$2.50
1989	$4.00	2012P	$2.50
1989D	$6.00	2012D	$2.50
1990	$5.00		
1990D	$7.00	**Buffalo Nickels**	
1991	$6.50	1934	$2800.00
1991D	$18.50	1934D	$4200.00
		1935	$1500.00
		1935D	$3000.00
		1935S	$2400.00
		1936	$1600.00
		1936D	$1500.00
		1936S	$1650.00

1937	$1200.00	1953	$24.00
1937D	$1250.00	1953D	$18.00
1937S	$1300.00	1953S	$35.00
1938D	$1200.00	1954	$55.00
		1954D	$23.00
Jefferson Nickels		1954S	$22.00
1938	$450.00	1955	$21.00
1938D	$325.00	1955D	$12.00
1938S	$350.00	1956	$9.00
1939	$160.00	1956D	$12.00
1939D	$3250.00	1957	$15.00
1939S	$2750.00	1957D	$6.50
1940	$150.00	1958	$6.00
1940D	$120.00	1958D	$6.00
1940S	$300.00	1959	$6.00
1941	$190.00	1959D	$6.00
1941D	$310.00	1960	$4.00
1941S	$350.00	1960D	$6.00
1942	$325.00	1961	$6.00
1942D	$1875.00	1961D	$5.50
1942S	$475.00	1962	$7.00
1943	$285.00	1962D	$6.00
1943D	$165.00	1963	$4.00
1943S	$295.00	1963D	$4.50
1944	$700.00	1964	$4.00
1944D	$725.00	1964D	$4.00
1944S	$550.00	1965	$9.50
1945	$325.00	1966	$6.00
1945D	$275.00	1967	$12.00
1945S	$200.00	1968 D	$5.00
1946	$82.00	1968 S	$5.00
1946D	$82.00	1969D	$6.00
1946S	$47.00	1969S	$6.00
1947	$65.00	1970D	$4.00
1947D	$62.00	1970S	$4.00
1947S	$65.00	1971	$27.00
1948	$53.00	1971D	$7.00
1948D	$175.00	1972	$7.00
1948S	$95.00	1972D	$6.00
1949	$310.00	1973	$6.00
1949D	$215.00	1973D	$6.00
1949S	$140.00	1974	$4.00
1950	$100.00	1974D	$4.00
1950D	$350.00	1975	$12.00
1951	$225.00	1975D	$6.00
1951D	$250.00	1976	$12.00
1951S	$285.00	1976D	$12.00
1952	$125.00	1977	$6.00
1952D	$225.00	1977D	$6.00
1952S	$42.00	1978	$4.00

1978D	$5.50	2003D	$4.00
1979	$4.00	2004	$4.00
1979D	$5.00	2004D	$4.00
1980	$4.00	2005	$4.00
1980D	$5.00	2005D	$4.00
1981	$4.00	2006	$3.50
1981D	$5.00	2006D	$3.50
1982	$275.00	2007	$4.00
1982D	$95.00	2007D	$5.00
1983	$125.00	2008	$4.00
1983D	$115.00	2008D	$6.00
1984	$22.00	2009	$55.00
1984D	$6.50	2009D	$20.00
1985	$10.00	2010	$4.00
1985D	$8.00	2010D	$4.00
1986	$9.00	2011	$4.00
1986D	$25.00	2011D	$4.00
1987	$5.00	2012	$4.00
1987D	$4.50	2012D	$4.00
1988	$4.50		
1988D	$10.00	**Mercury Dimes**	
1989	$5.00	1934	$1500.00
1989D	$8.00	1934D	$2300.00
1990	$12.00	1935	$950.00
1990D	$10.00	1935D	$2600.00
1991	$11.00	1935S	$1650.00
1991D	$12.00	1936	$700.00
1992	$45.00	1936D	$2000.00
1992D	$6.00	1936S	$1600.00
1993	$14.00	1937	$675.00
1993D	$20.00	1937D	$1300.00
1994	$8.00	1937S	$1600.00
1994D	$8.00	1938	$1100.00
1995	$11.00	1938D	$1300.00
1995D	$25.00	1938S	$1275.00
1996	$9.00	1939	$650.00
1996D	$8.50	1939D	$625.00
1997	$16.00	1939S	$1650.00
1997D	$60.00	1940	$600.00
1998	$19.00	1940D	$800.00
1998D	$19.00	1940S	$625.00
1999	$8.50	1941	$400.00
1999D	$8.00	1941D	$725.00
2000	$8.00	1941S	$550.00
2000D	$6.00	1942	$450.00
2001	$12.00	1942D	$725.00
2001D	$10.00	1942S	$1050.00
2002	$5.00	1943	$460.00
2002D	$5.00	1943D	$650.00
2003	$9.00	1943S	$675.00

1944	$425.00	1962	$95.00
1944D	$625.00	1962D	$95.00
1944S	$700.00	1963	$95.00
1945	$375.00	1963D	$95.00
1945D	$475.00	1964	$95.00
1945S	$575.00	1964D	$95.00
		1965	$10.00
Roosevelt Dimes		None Minted	
1946	$170.00	1966	$10.00
1946D	$175.00	1967	$8.50
1946S	$200.00	1968	$8.50
1947	$185.00	1968D	$9.00
1947D	$250.00	1969	$37.00
1947S	$210.00	1969D	$18.00
1948	$225.00	1970	$9.00
1948D	$300.00	1970D	$9.00
1948S	$225.00	1971	$14.00
1949	$1100.00	1971D	$9.00
1949D	$550.00	1972	$8.50
1949S	$2000.00	1972D	$8.50
1950	$450.00	1973	$10.00
1950D	$235.00	1973D	$9.00
1950S	$1350.00	1974	$8.00
1951	$210.00	1974D	$8.00
1951D	$210.00	1975	$9.00
1951S	$725.00	1975D	$15.00
1952	$175.00	1976	$23.00
1952D	$215.00	1976D	$15.00
1952S	$265.00	1977	$9.00
1953	$200.00	1977D	$8.50
1953D	$175.00	1978	$8.00
1953S	$160.00	1978D	$8.50
1954	$150.00	1979	$8.00
1954D	$150.00	1979D	$8.00
1954S	$110.00	1980	$8.00
1955	$110.00	1980D	$8.00
1955D	$110.00	1981	$8.00
1955S	$110.00	1981D	$8.00
1956	$130.00	1982	$375.00
1956D	$105.00	1982D	$115.00
1957	$105.00	1983	$260.00
1957D	$185.00	1983D	$110.00
1958	$130.00	1984	$8.00
1958D	$160.00	1984D	$15.00
1959	$105.00	1985	$12.00
1959D	$105.00	1985D	$11.00
1960	$95.00	1986	$24.00
1960D	$95.00	1986D	$22.00
1961	$95.00	1987	$8.00
1961D	$95.00	1987D	$9.00

		Washington Quarters	
1988	$10.00	**Washington Quarters**	
1988D	$10.00	1934	$1350.00
1989	$10.00	1934D	$8250.00
1989D	$13.00	1935	$1300.00
1990	$14.00	1935D	$8000.00
1990D	$8.00	1935S	$4500.00
1991	$10.00	1936	$1400.00
1991D	$10.00	1936S	$4750.00
1992	$8.00	1937	$1150.00
1992D	$8.00	1937D	$3250.00
1993	$9.50	1937S	$5350.00
1993D	$14.00	1938	$2800.00
1994	$12.50	1938S	$3250.00
1994D	$12.50	1939	$1000.00
1995	$18.00	1939D	$1600.00
1995D	$23.00	1939S	$2950.00
1996	$13.00	1940	$1500.00
1996D	$14.00	1940D	$4650.00
1997	$28.00	1940S	$1100.00
1997D	$10.00	1941	$425.00
1998	$10.00	1941D	$2500.00
1998D	$17.00	1941S	$2000.00
1999	$9.00	1942	$450.00
1999D	$9.00	1942D	$950.00
2000	$8.00	1942S	$4350.00
2000D	$8.00	1943	$385.00
2001	$8.00	1943D	$1650.00
2001D	$9.00	1943S	$1900.00
2002	$9.00	1944	$375.00
2002D	$10.00	1944D	$625.00
2003	$9.00	1944S	$950.00
2003D	$8.00	1945	$400.00
2004	$8.00	1945D	$950.00
2004D	$8.00	1945S	$550.00
2005	$8.00	1946	$400.00
2005D	$8.00	1946D	$385.00
2006	$9.00	1946S	$385.00
2006D	$8.00	1947	$700.00
2007	$9.00	1947D	$450.00
2007D	$8.00	1947S	$465.00
2008	$10.00	1948	$400.00
2008	$8.00	1948D	$625.00
2009	$27.00	1948S	$435.00
2009D	$15.00	1949	$1800.00
2010	$8.00	1949D	$1250.00
2010D	$8.00	1950	$385.00
2011	$8.00	1950D	$415.00
2011D	$8.00	1950S	$800.00
2012	$8.00	1951	$315.00
2012D	$8.00	1951D	$400.00

1951S	$1200.00	1976S 40%	
1952	$400.00	Proof Silver	$150.00
1952D	$410.00	1976D	$18.00
1952S	$450.00	1977	$17.00
1953	$500.00	1977D	$17.00
1953D	$325.00	1978	$17.00
1953S	$325.00	1978D	$17.00
1954	$300.00	1979	$15.00
1954D	$285.00	1979D	$15.00
1954S	$265.00	1980	$15.00
1955	$275.00	1980D	$15.00
1955D	$275.00	1981	$15.00
1956	$325.00	1981D	$16.00
1956D	$200.00	1982	$300.00
1957	$190.00	1982D	$200.00
1957D	$190.00	1983	$700.00
1958	$190.00	1983D	$400.00
1958D	$275.00	1984	$17.00
1959	$185.00	1984D	$23.00
1959D	$185.00	1985	$32.00
1960	$185.00	1985D	$23.00
1960D	$250.00	1986	$75.00
1961	$180.00	1986D	$185.00
1961D	$180.00	1987	$15.00
1962	$180.00	1987D	$15.00
1962D	$180.00	1988	$35.00
1963	$180.00	1988D	$20.00
1963D	$180.00	1989	$20.00
1964	$180.00	1989D	$15.00
1964D	$180.00	1990	$20.00
1965	$90.00	1990D	$25.00
None Minted		1991	$25.00
1966	$50.00	1991D	$30.00
1967	$45.00	1992	$40.00
1968	$25.00	1992D	$25.00
1968D	$35.00	1993	$40.00
1969	$35.00	1993D	$37.00
1969D	$45.00	1994	$42.00
1970	$25.00	1994D	$50.00
1970D	$18.00	1995	$48.00
1971	$42.00	1995D	$55.00
1971D	$19.00	1996	$21.00
1972	$19.00	1996D	$28.00
1972D	$19.00	1997	$25.00
1973	$22.00	1997D	$38.00
1973D	$24.00	1998	$18.00
1974	$18.00	1998D	$18.00
1974D	$18.00		
1976	$19.00	**State Quarters**	
1976S 40% Silver	$135.00	1999	$17.00
		1999D	$18.00

2000	$15.00	1943S	$1200.00
2000D	$15.00	1944	$725.00
2001	$14.00	1944D	$1150.00
2001D	$14.00	1944S	$1200.00
2002	$14.00	1945	$725.00
2002D	$14.00	1945D	$1050.00
2003	$14.00	1945S	$1000.00
2003D	$14.00	1946	$1050.00
2004	$14.00	1946D	$1000.00
2004D	$14.00	1946S	$1050.00
2005	$14.00	1947	$1000.00
2005D	$14.00	1947D	$1000.00
2006	$14.00		
2006D	$14.00	**Franklin Halves**	
2007	$14.00	1948	$435.00
2007D	$14.00	1948D	$435.00
2008	$14.00	1949	$1150.00
2008D	$14.00	1949D	$1400.00
2009	$15.00	1949S	$1900.00
2009D	$17.00	1950	$675.00
2010	$14.00	1950D	$850.00
2010D	$15.00	1951	$375.00
2011	$14.00	1951D	$750.00
2011D	$15.00	1951S	$650.00
		1952	$400.00
Walking Liberty Halves		1952D	$385.00
1934	$2150.00	1952S	$1500.00
1935	$1650.00	1953	$575.00
1935D	$5000.00	1953D	$400.00
1935S	$6750.00	1953S	$700.00
1936	$1150.00	1954	$375.00
1936D	$2200.00	1954D	$385.00
1936S	$3600.00	1954S	$350.00
1937	$1100.00	1955	$375.00
1937D	$4500.00	1956	$385.00
1937S	$3400.00	1957	$335.00
1938	$1950.00	1957D	$335.00
1939	$1300.00	1958	$315.00
1939D	$2100.00	1958D	$300.00
1939S	$2400.00	1959	$325.00
1940	$1100.00	1959D	$350.00
1940S	$1250.00	1960	$325.00
1941	$800.00	1960D	$350.00
1941D	$1150.00	1961	$315.00
1941S	$3250.00	1961D	$325.00
1942	$700.00	1962	$320.00
1942D	$1300.00	1962D	$290.00
1942S	$1350.00	1963	$265.00
1943	$710.00	1963D	$265.00
1943D	$1650.00		

Kennedy Halves

1964	$225.00	1990D	$42.00
1964D	$230.00	1991	$40.00
1965	$75.00	1991D	$35.00
None Minted		1992	$25.00
1966	$80.00	1992D	$38.00
1967	$75.00	1993	$60.00
1968D	$75.00	1993D	$25.00
1969D	$75.00	1994	$20.00
1970D	$325.00	1994D	$20.00
1971	$23.00	1995	$20.00
1971D	$21.00	1995D	$35.00
1972	$25.00	1996	$23.00
1972D	$20.00	1996D	$25.00
1973	$20.00	1997	$28.00
1973D	$20.00	1997D	$23.00
1974	$20.00	1998	$27.00
1974D	$23.00	1998D	$32.00
1976	$19.00	1999	$32.00
1976S 40% Silver	$140.00	1999D	$43.00
1976S 40% Silver Proof	$155.00	2000	$37.00
1976D	$19.00	2000D	$48.00
1977	$24.00	2001	$30.00
1977D	$20.00	2001D	$30.00
1978	$23.00	2002	$30.00
1978D	$27.00	2002D	$30.00
1979	$20.00	2003	$30.00
1979D	$23.00	2003D	$30.00
1980	$19.00	2004	$30.00
1980D	$19.00	2004D	$30.00
1981	$19.00	2005	$30.00
1981D	$19.00	2005D	$30.00
1982	$135.00	2006	$32.00
1982D	$110.00	2006D	$35.00
1983	$90.00	2007	$30.00
1983D	$140.00	2007D	$30.00
1984	$26.00	2008	$30.00
1984D	$29.00	2008D	$30.00
1985	$60.00	2009	$30.00
1985D	$35.00	2009D	$32.00
1986	$62.00	2010	$30.00
1986D	$60.00	2010D	$30.00
1987	$40.00	2011	$30.00
1987D	$40.00	2011D	$32.00
1988	$62.00	2012	$22.00
1988D	$35.00	2012D	$22.00
1989	$29.00		
1989D	$25.00		
1990	$32.00		

PRIMARY METALS

COPPER

Copper has the distinction of use in more U.S. coins than any other metal. In fact, there has been only one coin in U.S. history—the 1943 cent—that did not contain copper. Copper was used in its pure state for the early half cent and large cent; alloyed into bronze for the later small cent; alloyed with nickel for the five-cent piece; and, usually in a 1-to-9 ratio, used as an alloy metal for all our silver and gold coins from the 18th to 20th centuries. The most notable use of copper for our coins was in the Half Cent and Large Cent. As these coins were entirely unalloyed, they show the true beauty of pure copper, many specimens having toned to remarkable shades of red, yellow, burgundy, violet, orange, and virtually every known color. A brief copper shortage during World War II, when it became a vital material in war production, resulted in the noncopper 1943 cent, as well as a reduction in the copper content of five-cent pieces for several years. Inflation and the heavy industrial demand for copper made it necessary, in 1982, for the cent's composition to be changed to zinc with a copper coating.

SILVER

From the earliest days of the Mint, silver was regarded as the chief metal for coins in general circulation. It was used in coins having face values from 1¢ to $1, those of higher value being struck in gold. Problems arose during the administration of Thomas Jefferson, when silver bullion carried a higher value abroad than in the U.S. Huge quantities of our silver coins were exported by speculators, for the purpose of melting. This brought about a long suspension of the silver $1. Then, in 1965, the rising market price of silver in both the United States and Europe prompted its removal from the 10¢ and 25¢. It remained in the 50¢ in reduced quantity, but was later removed from that coin, too.

GOLD

The most glamorous of the metals used in U.S. coinage, gold was employed by the Mint in striking coins of $1, $2.50, $3, $4, $5, $10, and $20 denominations as well as a commemorative coin with $50 face value. The $10 gold piece, struck for more than 100 years, was called an Eagle, and its subdivisions were similarly named: Quarter Eagle ($2.50) and Half Eagle ($5), with the $20 termed Double Eagle. The standard fineness for all these coins, during most of their years of manufacture, was .900 with an alloying of .100 copper to give stability. Though all gold denominations were available for general circulation, their actual use in circulation became limited after the Civil War, when paper currency was introduced. The Great Depression of this century caused President Roosevelt to halt all striking of gold coins and to "call in" all gold coins for redemption (Gold Recall Act of 1933). Prohibition against private ownership of gold was removed in the presidency of Gerald Ford, resulting in its widespread purchase by investors and others.

SILVER COIN VALUE CHART*
Prices Reflect Melt Value of Individual Coins

SILVER PRICE PER OUNCE	AMOUNT OF PURE SILVER	5.00	7.50	10.00	15.00	20.00	25.00	30.00	35.00	40.00	45.00	50.00	55.00	60.00	CHANGE IN VALUE PER DOLLAR
1942–45 5¢ U.S.	.05626 oz.	.28	.42	.56	.85	1.13	1.41	1.69	1.97	2.25	2.54	2.82	3.10	3.38	.056
1965–70 U.S. 50¢ (40%)	.14792 oz.	.74	1.11	1.48	2.22	2.96	3.70	4.44	5.18	5.92	6.66	7.40	8.14	8.88	.148
1964 & Earlier U.S. 10¢	.07232 oz.	.36	.54	.72	1.09	1.45	1.81	2.17	2.54	2.90	3.26	3.62	3.98	4.34	.072
1964 & Earlier U.S. 25¢	.18084 oz.	.90	1.35	1.80	2.72	3.62	4.53	5.43	6.33	7.24	8.14	9.05	9.95	10.85	.18
1964 & Earlier U.S. 50¢	.36169 oz.	1.81	2.71	3.62	5.43	7.24	9.05	10.85	12.66	14.47	16.28	18.09	19.90	21.71	.362
1935 & Earlier U.S. $1	.77344 oz.	3.87	5.80	7.73	11.61	15.47	19.34	23.21	27.07	30.94	34.81	38.68	42.54	46.41	.772

*Note: Dealers who purchase silver coins to be melted normally pay 15–25% under melt value in order to cover their cost of handling.

GOLD COIN VALUE CHART*
Prices Reflect Melt Value of Individual Coins

GOLD PRICE PER OUNCE	AMOUNT OF PURE GOLD	1000.00	1100.00	1200.00	1300.00	1400.00	1500.00	1600.00	1700.00	1800.00	1900.00	2000.00	2100.00	2200.00
U.S. $1.00	.04837 oz.	48.37	52.80	57.60	62.40	67.20	72.56	77.39	82.23	87.07	91.90	96.74	101.58	106.41
U.S. $2.50	.12094 oz.	120.94	133.10	145.20	157.30	169.40	181.41	193.50	205.60	217.69	229.79	241.88	253.97	266.07
U.S. $3.00	.14512 oz.	145.12	159.50	174.00	188.50	203.00	217.68	232.19	246.70	261.22	275.73	290.24	304.75	319.26
U.S. $5.00	.24187 oz.	241.87	266.20	290.40	314.60	338.80	362.81	386.99	411.18	435.37	459.55	483.74	507.93	532.11
U.S. $10.00	.48375 oz.	483.75	532.40	580.80	629.20	677.60	725.63	774.00	822.38	870.75	919.13	967.50	1015.88	1064.25
U.S. $20.00	.96750 oz.	967.50	1063.70	1160.40	1257.10	1353.80	1451.25	1548.00	1644.75	1741.50	1838.25	1935.00	2031.75	2128.50

*Note: Dealers normally purchase U.S. gold coins for a premium over melt.

U.S. COINS WEIGHTS & MEASURES

COIN/DATES OF ISSUE	GRAMS WGT.	TOL.	GRAINS WGT.	TOL.	DIAMETER (mm)	COMPOSITION	SPECIFIC GRAVITY
HALF CENT							
1793-1795	6.739		104.000		23.50*	Pure Copper	8.92
1795-1836	5.443		84.000		23.50*	Pure Copper	8.92
1840-1857	5.443	0.227	84.000	3.50	23.50*	Pure Copper	8.92
LARGE CENT							
1793-1795	13.478		208.000		28.50*	Pure Copper	8.92
1795-1837	10.886		168.000		28.50*	Pure Copper	8.92
1837-1857	10.886	0.454	168.000	7.00	28.50*	Pure Copper	8.92
SMALL CENT							
1856-1864	4.666	0.259	72.000	4.00	19.30*	88 Cu, 12 Ni	8.92
1864-1873	3.110	0.259	48.000	4.00	19.05	95 Cu, 5 Zn & Sn	8.84
1873-1942	3.110	0.130	48.000	2.00	19.05	95 Cu, 5 Zn & Sn	8.84
1943	2.689/2.754	0.130	41.500/	2.00	19.05	Zinc coated steel	7.80
			42.500***				
1944-1946	3.110	0.130	48.000	2.00	19.05	95 Cu, 5 Zn	8.86
1947-1962	3.110	0.130	48.000	2.00	19.05	95 Cu, 5 Zn & Sn	8.84
1962-1982	3.110	0.130	48.000	2.00	19.05	95 Cu, 5 Zn & Sn	8.86
1982	2.500	0.100	38.581	1.54	19.05	97.5 Zn, 2.5 Cu****	7.17
TWO CENTS							
1864-1873	6.221	0.259	96.000	4.00	23.00*	95 Cu, 5 Zn &. Sn	8.84
THREE CENTS (Cu-Ni)							
1865-1873	1.944	0.259	30.000	4.00	17.90*	75 Cu, 25 Ni	8.92
1873-1889	1.944	0.130	30.000	2.00	17.90*	75 Cu, 25 Ni	8.92
FIVE CENTS							
1866-1873	5.000	0.130	77.162	2.00	20.50*	75 Cu, 25 Ni	8.92
1873-1883	5.000	0.194	77.162	3.00	20.50*	75 Cu, 25 Ni	8.92

COIN/DATES OF ISSUE	GRAMS WGT.	TOL.	GRAINS WGT.	TOL.	DIAMETER (mm)	COMPOSITION	SPECIFIC GRAVITY
1883-1942	5.000	0.194	77.162	3.00	21.21	75 Cu, 25 Ni	8.92
1942-1945	5.000	0.194	77.162	3.00	21.21	56 Cu, 35 Ag, 9 Mn	9.25*
1946-	5.000	0.194	77.162	3.00	21.21	75 Cu, 25 Ni	8.92
TRIME (Silver)							
1851-1853	0.802	0.032	12.375	0.50	14.00*	750 Ag, 250 Cu	10.11
1854-1873	0.746	0.032	11.520	0.50	14.00*	900 Ag, 100 Cu	10.34
HALF DIME							
1794-1795	1.348		20.800		16.50*	892.427 + Ag, 107.572 Cu	10.32
1795-1805	1.348		20.800		16.50*	892.427 + Ag, 107.572 Cu	10.32
1829-1837	1.348		20.800		15.50*	892.427 + Ag, 107.572 Cu	10.32
1837-1853	1.336	0.032	20.625	0.50	15.50*	900 Ag, 100 Cu	10.34
1853-1873	1.244	0.032	19.200	0.50	15.50*	900 Ag, 100 Cu	10.34
DIME							
1796-1828	2.696		41.600		18.80*	892.427 + Ag, 107.572 Cu	10.32
1828-1837	2.696		41.600		17.90*	892.427 + Ag, 107.572 Cu	10.32
1837-1853	2.673	0.032	41.250	0.50	17.90*	900 Ag, 100 Cu	10.34
1853-1873	2.488	0.032	38.400	0.50	17.90*	900 Ag, 100 Cu	10.34
1873-1964	2.500	0.097	35.581	1.50	17.91	900 Ag, 100 Cu	10.34
1965	2.268	0.091†	35.000	1.40†	17.91	75 Cu, 25 Ni on pure Cu	8.92
TWENTY CENTS							
1875-1878	5.000	0.097	77.162	1.50	22.50*	900 Ag, 100 Cu	10.34
QUARTER DOLLAR							
1796-1828	6.739		104.000		27.00*	892.427 + Ag, 107.572 Cu	10.32
1831-1837	6.739		104.000		24.26*	892.427 + Ag, 107.572 Cu	10.32
1837-1853	6.682	0.065	103.125	1.00	24.26*	900 Ag, 100 Cu	10.34
1853-1873	6.221	0.065	96.000	1.00	24.26*	900 Ag, 100 Cu	10.34
1873-1947	6.250	0.097	96.452	1.50	24.26	900 Ag, 100 Cu	10.34
1947-1964	6.250	0.194	96.452	3.00	24.26*	900 Ag, 100 Cu	10.34

COIN/DATES OF ISSUE	GRAMS WGT.	TOL.	GRAINS WGT.	TOL.	DIAMETER (mm)	COMPOSITION	SPECIFIC GRAVITY
1965	5.670	0.227†	87.500	3.50†	24.26	75 Cu, 25 Ni on pure Cu	8.92
1976	5.750†	0.200†	88.736†	3.09†	24.26	40% silver clad**	9.53
HALF DOLLAR							
1794-1795	13.478		208.000		32.50*	892.427 + Ag, 107.572 Cu	10.32
1796-1836	13.478		208.000		32.50*	892.427 + Ag, 107.572 Cu	10.32
1836-1853	13.365	0.097	206.250	1.50	30.61*	900 Ag, 100 Cu	10.34
1853-1873	12.441	0.097	192.000	1.50	30.61*	900 Ag, 100 Cu	10.34
1873-1947	12.500	0.097	192.904	1.50	30.61	900 Ag, 100 Cu	10.34
1947-1964	12.500	0.250	192.904	4.00	30.61	900 Ag, 100 Cu	10.34
1965-1970	11.500	0.400†	177.472	6.17†	30.61	40% silver clad**	9.53
1971-	11.340	0.454†	175.000	7.00†	30.61	75 Cu, 25 Ni on pure Cu	8.92
1976	11.500	0.400†	177.472	6.17†	30.61	40% silver clad**	9.53
1982	12.500	0.400†	192.904	6.17†	30.56	900 Ag, 100 Cu	10.34
DOLLAR							
1794-1795	26.956		416.000		39.50*	892.427 + Ag, 107.572 Cu	10.32
1796-1803	26.956		416.000		39.50*	892.427 + Ag, 107.572 Cu	10.32
1840-1935	26.730	0.097	412.500	1.50	38.10	900 Ag, 100 Cu	10.34
1971-1978	22.680	0.907†	350.000	14.00†	38.10	75 Cu, 25 Ni on pure Cu	8.92
1971-1976	24.592	0.984†	379.512	15.18†	38.10	40% silver clad**	9.53
1979-1981	8.100	0.300†	125.000	5.00†	26.50	75 Cu, 25 Ni on pure Cu	8.92
1983-1988	26.730	0.400	412.500	6.17	38.10	90 Ag, 10 Cu	10.34
TRADE DOLLAR							
1873-1888	27.216	0.097	420.000	1.50	38.10	900 Ag, 100 Cu	10.34
GOLD DOLLAR							
1849-1854	1.672	0.016	25.800	0.25	13.00*	900 Au, 100 Cu & Ag	17.16
1854-1873	1.672	0.016	25.800	0.25	14.86*	900 Au, 100 Cu & Ag	17.16
1873-1922	1.672	0.016	25.800	0.25	14.86*	900 Au, 100 Cu & Ag	17.16

COIN/DATES OF ISSUE	GRAMS WGT.	TOL.	GRAINS WGT.	TOL.	DIAMETER (mm)	COMPOSITION	SPECIFIC GRAVITY
QUARTER EAGLE							
1795-1808	4.374		67.500		20.00*	916.667 Au, 83.333 Cu & Ag	17.45
1821-1827	4.374		67.500		18.50*	916.667 Au, 83.333 Cu & Ag	17.45
1829-1834	4.374		67.500		18.20*	916.667 Au, 83.333 Cu & Ag	17.45
1834-1836	4.180	0.008	64.500	0.13	18.20*	899.225 Au, 100.775 Cu & Ag	17.14
1837-1839	4.180	0.016	64.500	0.25	18.20*	900 Au, 100 Cu & Ag	17.16
1840-1873	4.180	0.016	64.500	0.25	17.78*	900 Au, 100 Cu	17.16
1873-1929	4.180	0.016	64.500	0.25	17.78*	900 Au, 100 Cu	17.16
THREE DOLLARS							
1854-1873	5.015		77.400		20.53*	900 Au, 100 Cu & Ag	17.16
1873-1889	5.015	0.016	77.400	0.25	20.53*	900 Au, 100 Cu	17.16
FOUR DOLLARS (Pattern issue)							
1879-1880	7.000*		108.026*		21.59	857 Au, 43 Ag, 100 Cu*	16.67*
HALF EAGLE							
1795-1829	8.748		135.000		25.00*	916.667 Au, 83.333 Cu & Ag	17.45
1829-1834	8.748		135.000		22.50*	916.667 Au, 83.333 Cu & Ag	17.45
1834-1836	8.359	0.017	129.000	0.26	22.50*	899.225 Au, 100.775 Cu & Ag	17.14
1837-1840	8.359	0.016	129.000	0.25	22.50*	900 Au, 100 Cu & Ag	17.16
1840-1849	8.359	0.016	129.000	0.25	21.54*	900 Au, 100 Cu & Ag	17.16
1849-1873	8.359	0.032	129.000	0.50	21.54*	900 Au, 100 Cu & Ag	17.16
1873-1929	8.359	0.016	129.000	0.25	21.54*	900 Au, 100 Cu	17.16
1986-1988	8.359	0.042	129.000	0.65	21.59	900 Au, 60 Ag, 40 Cu	17.60
EAGLE							
1795-1804	17.496		270.000		33.00*	916.667 Au, 83.333 Cu & Ag	17.45
1838-1849	16.718	0.016	258.000	0.25	27.00*	900 Au, 100 Cu & Ag	17.16
1849-1873	16.718	0.032	258.000	0.50	27.00*	900 Au, 100 Cu & Ag	17.16
1873-1933	16.718	0.032	258.000	0.50	27.00*	900 Au, 100 Cu	17.16

COIN/DATES OF ISSUE	GRAMS WGT.	TOL.	GRAINS WGT.	TOL.	DIAMETER (mm)	COMPOSITION	SPECIFIC GRAVITY
1984	16.718	0.088	258.000	1.36	27.00	900 Au, 100 Cu	17.30
DOUBLE EAGLE							
1850-1873	33.436	0.032	516.000	0.50	34.29	900 Au, 100 Cu & Ag	17.16
1873-1933	33.436	0.032	516.000	0.50	34.29	900 Au, 100 Cu	17.16
AMERICAN EAGLE BULLION COINS 1986-							
Dollar	31.103	min	479.993	min	40.60	999.3 Ag	10.49
$5	3.393	0.028	52.362	0.43	16.50	916.7 Au, 30 Ag, 53.3 Cu	17.78
$10	8.483	0.050	130.913	0.77	22.00	916.7 Au, 30 Ag, 53.3 Cu	17.78
$25	16.966	0.085	261.825	1.31	27.00	916.7 Au, 30 Ag, 53.3 Cu	17.78
$50	33.931	min	523.635	min	32.70	916.7 Au, 30 Ag, 53.3 Cu	17.78

* -Unofficial data.

** -Consists of layers of 800 Ag, 200 Cu bonded to a core of 209 Ag, 781 Cu

*** -Cents struck on steel planchets produced in 1942 weighed 41.5 grains, while those struck on planchets produced later in 1943 weighed 42.5 grains.

**** -Consists of a planchet composed of 99 .2 percent Zn and 0.8 percent Cu, the whole plated with pure copper.

† -Not specified by law, established instead by the Director of the Mint.

Au = Gold; Ag = Silver; Cu = Copper; Mn = Manganese; Ni =Nickel; Sn =Tin; Zn =Zinc

Reprinted by permission from *Counterfeit Detection: A Reprint from The Numismatist, Volume II* (1988), published by the American Numismatic Association, 818 North Cascade Avenue, Colorado Springs, CO 80903-3279

TROY WEIGHT
(PRECIOUS METALS, JEWELS, ETC.)

3.068 grains (gr.)	⇌ 1 carat (car.)	⇌ 200 mg.
24 grains	⇌ 1 pennyweight (dwt.)	⇌ 1.555 g.
20 pennyweights	⇌ 1 ounce (oz. t.)	⇌ 31.1035 g.
12 ounces or 5760 grains	⇌ 1 pound (lb. t.)	⇌ 373.24 g. or 0.3732 kg.
1 lb. avoirdupois	⇌ 14.58 troy ozs.	
1 troy oz.	⇌ 480 grains	
1 gram	⇌ 15.432 grains	

Metric Equivalents: 1 grain ⇌ 0.0648 gram; in weighing pearls, etc., a grain ⇌ ¼ carat (0.77 troy grains) or 50 mg.

REFERENCE CHART FOR METAL CHARACTERS

METAL		MELTING POINT (FAHRENHEIT)	HARDNESS (KILOGRAMS PER SQUARE MILLIMETER)	SPECIFIC GRAVITY
Platinum	(Pt.)	3,171°	50	21.5
Gold	(Au)	1,945°	18	19.3
Silver	(Ag)	1,762°	25	10.1
Nickel	(Ni)	2,651°	80	8.9
Copper	(Cu)	1,983°	50	8.9
Iron	(Fe)	2,368°	60	7.8
Aluminum	(Al)	1,216°	18	2.6
Tin	(Sn)	449°	8	7.3
Lead	(Pb)	620°	4	11.4
Zinc	(Zn)	786°	35	7.0

A quick glance will show nickel is the hardest, lead the softest, and platinum the heaviest and most resistant to heat.

CIVIL WAR TOKENS

Dale H. Cade

These tokens, among others, have also been known as "emergency money" or as "necessity money." Prior to and during the Civil War, the government-issued paper money was generally looked upon suspiciously by the common person, and the "hard currency," or government coinage, was preferred. This, in turn, resulted in the "hard currency" being hoarded and disappearing from the marketplace, first in the larger denominations, and then even the one-cent pieces. This shortage of small coinage made life very difficult for merchants trying to make change for their customers. Earlier attempts at alleviating this shortage of small change involved the use of postage stamps, encased postage, and fractional currency. The stamps, being inherently quite fragile, had a very limited useful life, and proved unsuitable as a medium of commercial exchange. An enterprising inventor came up with the idea of encasing stamps in a thin brass shell with a mica "window" so that the denomination of the stamp could be seen. These encased postage stamps provided the durability that the unencased stamps did not, but their cost—more than the value of the stamp within—was a primary deterrent to their use. The fractional currency, although more durable than the unencased postage stamp, was also paper money, and suffered the same lack of general acceptance as the government-issued currency. Specimens of the encased postage stamps and the fractional currency can still be obtained, and in a broad sense, if issued during the 1860–1864 period, are also Civil War tokens. However, the civil war tokens most generally accepted and collected are to follow.

With the relegation of the stamps, cased and uncased, and the fractional currency to the "I thought it was a good idea" category, the merchants revived an older practice of issuing metallic tokens advertising their establishment, and used them to make change, in lieu of the vanished "hard currency" of the government, to carry on commerce. Since these tokens were the size and color of the small cent coin issued by the government, and looked like the small cent, at least superficially, they were traded at the value of one cent. While other denominations are known, the one-cent valuation was by far the most common, accounting for well over 95 percent of the tokens issued.

These tokens would, generally, contain the merchant's name and address, the store name, and the product(s) sold on the obverse side of the tokens. The reverse side of the token would usually contain a patriotic slogan or device. These reverse designs could, and did, exhibit a wide range of diversity of design and thought. Some of the more popular designs included the American flag, the American eagle, a bust of Lincoln or Washington or other dignitaries of the day, the American Indian head patterned after the Indian head coinage of the day, and the legend "one cent," with variations. The photos to follow are typical of the store card product. The attribution used is the Fuld system, and a more comprehensive discussion of this system will follow later in this chapter.

OBV	REV	OBV	REV
	IL150J-5a		PA13E-8a

These tokens were a good deal for the merchants financially, as well as providing a medium of change for their customers. The merchants would contract with a token producer to purchase a quantity of them bearing their advertisement at a price significantly lower than what they would redeem them for in merchandise or give out as change. As an example, if a merchant purchased 5,000 tokens at a price of ten dollars, his cost per token would be two-tenths of a cent. He would then redeem or exchange them at a valuation of one cent, realizing a net profit of 400 percent on the deal. Not a bad little money maker for the merchant! In addition to the monetary advantage, the merchant was receiving valuable advertising for his place of business by virtue of his name, address, and profession or merchandise appearing on the obverse, a constant reminder to the holder of the token. You may well ask why these tokens were valued at only one cent. Besides the similarities mentioned earlier, it must be remembered that at the time of the Civil War, one cent purchased considerably more than it does today.

What makes Civil War tokens unique is that unlike most private issue tokens that are redeemable only at the issuer's place of business, these tokens were accepted by other merchants in lieu of government-issued hard currency, at the nominal value of one cent. It has been estimated that over one million of these tokens are existent today, and that at the height of their popularity, over 25 million tokens were issued. No other token has had the distinction of having the tacit approval of the government to replace their coinage with private mintage coinage. While the government may not have publicly approved their use, neither did it strongly object to it. That the merchants themselves were not completely at ease with the legality of what they were doing is evident by some of the reverse designs that say "not one cent," with the "not" appearing either in very small letters or very large letters, and in some cases of circulated pieces, the "not" has been scratched out or defaced with scratches.

Collectors of Civil War tokens are in general agreement that to qualify as a Civil War token, the token should have been made and issued during the period 1860–1864, mainly in the Northern states, and mainly east of the Mississippi River. Currently, 21 states are recognized as having issued merchants tokens within their boundaries during the Civil War years. There are over 8,500 known store card varieties from over 400 towns and cities, and some 1,500 merchants. There are also another 75 or so cards that can be attributed to Sutlers (merchants to the military). In addition, there are over 1,800 varieties of patriotic Civil War tokens that are unattributable to any specific merchant, but use the store card reverse dies, plus others. While there were issuers in Southern and border states, and some west of the Mississippi River, the preponderance of issuers lie within the boundaries previously described. There is evidence that these tokens enjoyed a wide circulation for the period of issue. Unlisted varieties of both store cards and patriotics are still being located and reported.

All went well until early in 1864, when a New York City merchant, the Third Avenue Railroad, requested another New York City merchant, Gustavus Lindenmuller, to redeem a large quantity of his tokens, which they had accepted in the course of business. When Lindenmuller laughingly refused to redeem his tokens, the railroad had no redress, and incidents such as these forced the hand of the government. In April and June of 1864, the Congress passed acts that made it illegal to use privately minted tokens or money in lieu of government-issued money. Thus ended the era of the Civil War token as a "hard money" replacement. The government action, however, did not forbid the use of these tokens if their usage was confined to business dealings solely with the issuer. This practice continues to this day in some stores under the euphemism of "credit check," "good for," "wooden nickel," etc. These present-day tokens are redeemable only at the issuer's place of business, and only for merchandise, no cash refunds or cash values.

Civil War tokens are generally the size of the small copper-nickel Indian Head cent of 1860 (19mm.), as previously mentioned. Although there are a few specimens of other sizes, notably 23mm. and 26mm. in diameter, this size is by far the most common, accounting for over 98 percent of the tokens issued, both store cards and patriotics. Their thickness was generally between 1.25mm. and 1.50mm., although specimens are known outside this range. By comparison, the copper-nickel cent is approximately 1.75mm. thick. The most commonly used materials for these tokens are copper and brass, which together account for some 95 percent of all known Civil War tokens. In addition, other materials used include two varieties of "lead" (one is lead-based, the other tin-based), white metal (shown to be primarily zinc), hard rubber, German silver (also known in Civil War collecting circles as "nickel" prior to non-destructive testing that revealed them to be German silver), copper-nickel (nearly always a re-stamped government-issued copper-nickel cent), tin, silver (almost always struck over a government-issued dime), and plated varieties including silver-plated copper and brass pieces, gold or gilt-plated copper and brass pieces, copper-plated lead, and tin-plated copper and brass. (The tin plating and base material had been thought to be zinc until electron microprobe and X-ray diffraction testing proved them to be tin.) It is generally accepted that the lead, white metal, hard rubber, German silver, and, perhaps, the copper-nickel pieces, in addition to the copper and brass pieces, were intended for use in the world of commerce, whereas the silver and plated pieces were more likely specially made for private collectors. The reasoning behind this conclusion is that the cost of producing these "vanity pieces" or "show ponies," as they have sometimes been called, exceeds by several times the exchange value in the marketplace. Also supporting this conclusion is that these pieces are seldom found in the lower grades, indicating very little, if any, usage, and that, probably by accident. These pieces are generally of high rarity, compared to the copper and brass pieces, which also supports the conclusion that there were not many pieces made, a position that also supports the idea of special collector pieces. In today's collecting world, the analogy can be made that these "vanity pieces" roughly correspond to the mint and proof sets on today's market versus the coin strikes intended for the commercial world. The term "off metal" is frequently used to designate token materials other than copper or brass.

Early collectors of Civil War tokens devised a rarity scale to denote the relative abundance of one variety over another. The scale was derived, in part, from the noted frequency of appearance on the market of a given variety, and also, in part, by their frequency of appearance in large collections, both private and in public museums. To this end, the rarity scale must be considered to be a guide only (educated guess), and not an absolute value.

Rarity	10	1 only (unique)
	9	2 to 4 pieces (very rare)
	8	5 to 10 pieces (rare)
	7	11 to 20 pieces
	6	21 to 75 pieces
	5	76 to 200 pieces
	4	201 to 500 pieces
	3	501 to 2,000 pieces
	2	2,001 to 5,000 pieces (common)
	1	over 5,000 pieces (very common)

Civil War tokens fall into three classifications: 1) merchant store cards (fixed location for place of business); 2) patriotics (no merchant attribution); and 3) Sutlers (nonlocal merchants that served the armed services exclusively). The store cards are those that have enough information on the obverse side of the token to establish the issuing merchant's name, the address of his place of business, and the nature of his business. The reverse of the token usually carries a patriotic slogan or symbol, but sometimes will carry additional information about the business (see photos below, left). There are a few specimens where the reverse of the token carries another merchant's message (see photos below, right). This latter type of token is referred to as a dual merchant token. Some dual merchant tokens are for merchants in different cities or towns, and sometimes in different states.

OBV	REV	OBV	REV
OH765E-1a		MI225CN-3a	
Same Merchant		Different Merchants	

Until fairly recently, the attribution of these Civil War tokens was rather unwieldy, requiring nearly a complete description of both obverse and reverse to correctly identify the token. One of the earliest attempts to bring order into the attribution part of this collecting field was done by Joseph Barnett. A bit later, Hetrich and Guttag established a numbering system for Civil War tokens, both store cards and patriotics. Their efforts were published in a book, *Civil War Tokens and Tradesmen's Cards,* by Hetrich and Guttag, published by Alfred D. Hoch in 1924. The basis for the "H & G" system, as it was called, was to first group the known reverse dies by theme or design, then assign sequential numbers to them, starting with number 1. A listing of known die combinations was made starting with die number 1 as the obverse, and listing all reverse dies in combination with die number 1 in numerical sequence, then all material varieties of a given obverse/reverse pairing. After assembling this list, each entry was assigned a number beginning with 1. Gaps were left in the number assignment sequence for later additions. In the H & G book, Joseph Barnett added a list of corrections/additions in the 3rd Edition (1968), which had been previously published in the *Numismatist* in 1943 and 1944.

In similar fashion, Hetrich and Guttag assigned "H & G" numbers to the Civil War store cards, arranging them alphabetically, first by state, then by city or town within a state, then by merchant within a town or city, and lastly, by variety (reverse die number), and by token material. Joseph Barnett also contributed corrections/additions to the store card section of the 3rd Edition. The first store card H & G number used is 2001, to separate this series from the patriotic series, which ended with number 1305. As in the patriotic system, open numbers were left for future additions.

While the H & G numbering system was a great advance when introduced, being essentially a closed-end system, it became unwieldy as more varieties tried to find a place within. In the early 1960s, Melvin and George Fuld published their "black book" pamphlets (Whitman Publishing Company, now out of print) that were the forerunners of references 1), 2), and 3), and in which they introduced a new numbering system (the Fuld numbering system) for attributing Civil War tokens, both store cards and patriotics. The Fulds took the closed-end H & G system and, following the same arranging sequences utilized by Hetrich and Guttag, created an open-ended system. In the Fuld system, each state was assigned a two-letter abbreviation, each city or town within the state had its own number (with lots of space for new additions), each merchant in a town or city was assigned a letter identification, each variety of the merchant (obverse or reverse variation) was assigned a number, and lastly, the token material was assigned a lower-case letter designator. The Fulds separated the reverse dies into two lists—those appearing on patriotic tokens being assigned numbers from 1 through 999, and the reverses appearing on store cards being assigned number 1,000 and higher. The effect of this was to have dual die identities in some instances where a reverse die appeared on both store cards and patriotic tokens.

To see how this system works for store cards, take, for example, a Civil War store card token with this attribution:

MI225AR-4d (ref 1)

This translates as follows:

MI	state of Michigan
225	City of Detroit
AR	Merchant P. N. Kneeland
4	Variety containing a 1047 reverse
d	Token material is copper-nickel

Thus, using the Fuld attribution system, the complete pedigree of the token can be expressed by a simple short code. As mentioned earlier, this system is open ended and adaptable to the inclusion of new varieties as they become known.

Patriotic Civil War tokens can be thought of as having store card reverses for both obverse and reverse designs, although this is not completely true as there are some patriotic dies that have no store card counterpart. When the Fulds introduced their patriotic attribution system in the "black book," the material designator was omitted. The problem was that for some die combinations there are several token materials, and this code did not differentiate between them. To remedy this shortcoming, the listings were augmented in reference 3) to include the same material designator codes used for the store cards. For example, a typical patriotic attribution using Fuld and augmented Fuld could read:

112/396 (ref 2)

112/396fp (copper) (ref 3)

This translates to

112	die used on obverse side of token
396	die used on reverse of token
fp	material is silver plated
(copper)	base metal of token is copper

It can be readily seen that the addition of the material code provides an effective material discriminator that completes the attribution without having to resort to other sources to finish the attribution. The two photo illustrations following demonstrate the use of this system.

OBV   REV
214/416a

OBV   REV
231/352Ba

It is readily apparent that by using these two similar but differing systems, not only can the token be immediately classified as store card or patriotic Civil War token, but its attribution is also defined. As with the store card attribution, the lower-case letter(s) at the end of the die designators identify the token material. In the case of plated or "struck over" pieces, an additional parenthetical expression is required to define the base material or understrike.

The third, and last, classification of Civil War tokens are the Sutler pieces. As alluded to earlier, the Sutlers were merchants who attached themselves to regimental units, and were the unit's Post Exchange, to use a present-day equivalent. Since they had no fixed base of operations like the local merchants, their tokens carried a military association rather than a city or town and street address. They have also been known as "nonlocal" merchants, an apt term, since they went where their regiment went. Their "store" was a horse- or mule-drawn wagon that supplied the needs and "luxuries" not supplied by the Army. David Schenkman (ref 4) has established an attribution code for these Sutlers that provides a short form of identification. Take, for example, the following Sutler attribution (Schenkman):

AN25B (ref 4)

This code breaks down as follows:	Sutler attached to an Ohio Regiment (noted on token)
AN	William Jamison (also on token)
25	Good for 25 cents in goods
B	token material is brass

Sutler tokens departed from the customary valuation of one cent used by the fixed-base merchants. The lowest denomination on Sutler tokens is 5 cents, and other denominations include 10-, 15-, 25-, and 50-cent tokens. These tokens generally had a patriotic motif on the reverse, although some carried additional information for the merchant on the reverse.

OBV   REV
C25C George McAlpen 11th Pennsylvania Cavalry Sutler

For the collector who likes error pieces, the Civil War token area is a personal gold mine! Because of the apparent laxity of final inspection before token delivery to the purchaser, a large proportion of error pieces found their way into the marketplace. These errors fall into three distinct groupings: 1) planchet errors, 2) die errors (die sinking errors), and 3) striking errors. The first, planchet errors, consist primarily of planchet punching errors from the planchet strip. These errors are known as clips, and may be curved, straight, or irregular. They occur when the punch overlaps a previously punched hole in the strip, when the punch hangs over the side of the strip, and when the punch overhangs the end of the strip, respectively. Other examples of planchet errors include rough and/or porous surface planchets made from poorly prepared planchet strips, an occasional cracked planchet, and also an occasional partially delaminated planchet, also due to poor strip preparation. These last three errors are rarely, if ever, seen on U.S. mintage. Since the planchets are made from mixtures of materials, both remelts and new materials, and since quality control was virtually nonexistent, it is not uncommon to find tokens that appear to be copper on one side and brass on the other side (bimetallic), but are, in reality, the result of poor material mixing and distribution when the original planchet strip was made.

The second error grouping, die errors, consists primarily of spelling errors in the cutting-in (sinking) of the die. There are specimens that exhibit misspelled street and city names, sometimes the wrong state, sometimes the merchant's name or stock in trade is misspelled (e.g., "GROCKERY" for "CROCKERY," "QJEENSLAND" FOR "QUEENSLAND" in reference to a line of fine chinaware, "SEGAR" for "CIGAR," etc). There are also transpositions of letters in a name, and some backward letters, notably "N"s. Another source of die errors is incomplete cover-ups of spelling errors, wherein the original error spelling is visible along with the corrected spelling. Sometimes the die sinker would fill in the offending error and re-cut the die in part. If this filling comes out during die use in the press, the resulting "hole" in the die will produce a "cud" or "blob" of material on the surface of the struck token. Of interest, also, are the few specimens that appear to be a case of the wrong size die and design. The "standard" size of a Civil War token is 19mm., or the size of the small cent. There are Civil War tokens that are larger (23mm. and 26mm.) that carry a nearly identical design to their 19mm. brothers, and one can only wonder if this was deliberate or an accident. If the latter, were tokens struck from this incorrect die size merely to recoup any losses from fabricating the incorrect die size for the order? There are many mysteries and inconsistencies to be found on the Civil War tokens, and that only adds to their mystique.

The third grouping, striking errors, is the most noticeable, after the planchet errors. The most common of these errors involves die cracks that produce raised lines on the struck token. These lines (die cracks) start out small and progress into larger (wider and deeper) cracks and ultimately into a spiderweb-like pattern of raised lines and sometimes adjacent cuds if the die starts to crumble along the break. At this stage, the die is termed "shattered," and its useful life is at an end. In U.S. coinage, dies are not permitted to approach this stage, but are taken out of service after just a few small die cracks are evident.

Another striking error occurs when the wrong diameter planchet is struck. For example, a 19mm. die impresses a 26mm. planchet resulting in a broad, flat "rim" and normal die impression within. This product would almost certainly be "broadstruck" as well, or struck without the normal strike collar in place. If the retaining strike collar slips during the striking, the resulting piece can have a "railroad rim," so named because of its resemblance to a railroad car's flanged wheel, or some other strange appearance.

Another striking error occurs when the upper and lower dies are not properly aligned, a very common error on Civil War tokens, and lastly, an "off center" strike occurs when the planchet is not correctly positioned at the time of the striking. Civil War token specimens are known where the amount of "off center" approaches 75 to 80 percent, but mostly, the percentage is smaller, about 10 to 20 percent.

These errors receive a mixed review, with some collectors wanting no part of them, and other collectors prizing them over non-error pieces. This is typical of what makes collecting Civil War tokens interesting. They are not rigidly structured like U.S. coinage, and may be collected in numerous ways. Some of the more popular collecting approaches are: by subject (Indian head, Liberty head, Washington, Lincoln, eagle, etc.); by profession (druggist, dentist, dry goods merchant, product, etc.); and by state, city, or merchant sets. The ways to collect Civil War tokens are limited only by your imagination and your pocketbook.

Because of the many designs present on Civil War tokens, grading of these pieces can be more of a problem than with U.S. coinage. In reference 2, there is a chapter on pricing and grading of Civil War tokens. The grading does not involve the cosmetics of the token, but only the relationship of its present state to that when it was issued. The grading is presented both pictorially and in written form, and is based on the grading descriptions of small cents of the Civil War era, as described in Brown and Dunn, *A Guide to the Grading of United States Coins.* As a general rule, grades below fine (F) are not collectible except where the piece is of high rarity (R9 or R10). The grade is usually expressed using the letter grading system (UNC., AU, XF, VF, F, etc.), although some dealers prefer to combine the letter grade with the numerical grade of the Sheldon system. This combining of systems yields grades that read: UNC-60, AU-50 or 55, XF-40 or 45, VF-20 or 30, F-12, VG-8, G-4, and AG-3. In all cases, the second number represents the "grade $+$" rating, or better than the base grade, but not good enough for the next higher grade. A "grade $-$" is not normally used.

Pricing of these Civil War tokens is dependent on four factors: 1) the attribution of the token; 2) the token grading; 3) the token rarity; and 4) the cosmetic appearance of the token. The first three factors have been discussed earlier. By cosmetic appearance, I am referring to the "eye appeal" of the token, and this involves the presence or absence of things such as residues, stains, minor or major damage such as nicks, gouges, deep scratches, etc., and of course, the previously mentioned errors. Cleaning of tokens is generally discouraged, and a negative factor, but some collectors do not mind that the token has been cleaned. It is purely a matter of personal choice. Prices for "off metal" pieces command a premium over the prices for copper or brass pieces of the same die pairings. Also, keep in mind that a 130-÷-year-old circulated token is bound to pick up a few bruises along the way. To this end, small gouges ("bag marks," the effects of other coins/tokens rubbing while carried in a pocket or purse, etc.) and minor scratches are considered "normal" for these tokens, and have been factored into the pricing guide to follow.

Because of the volatility of prices in the token market, any attempts to quote prices, including this attempt, *must be considered as a guide only.* Prices for a given piece will vary from seller to seller, and from coast to coast. The examples to follow are for a Civil War token in extra fine (XF) grade with "normal" wear and tear no major problems, and no extenuating circumstances such as the only issue of a merchant, city, state, etc.

RARITY	PRICE
1 or 2	$25.00–$35.00
3 or 4	$35.00–$40.00
5 or 6	$50.00–$60.00
7 or 8	$75.00–$90.00
9 or 10	$125.00–$200.00+

"Off metal" pieces command an additional 30 to 50 percent of the base price. I must emphasize again that *the foregoing "prices" must be treated as a guide only, and that particular pieces may cost more or less than the table would indicate.* For tokens grading less than XF, prices should be reduced by 10 to 20 percent per grade. For grades above XF, prices should be increased by 20 to 30 percent for AU, and double or more for Uncirculated pieces. For pieces that are virtually free of "normal" wear and tear, a premium of 10 to 15 percent should be expected. For minor damage (rim nicks, prominent gouges or deep scratches, interior damage areas, etc.), a bigger price reduction of 25 to 50 percent could be expected. There are some Civil War tokens that command higher prices by virtue of being the only card issued by a merchant, a town, or a state; a prized error piece; a card common to both the Civil War era and to another collecting field (for example, a transportation token, a pharmacy, a saloon, a brewery, etc.); and others.

The Civil War Token Society is a national nonprofit organization founded in 1967 for the purpose of stimulating interest and research in the field of Civil War token collecting as a hobby. Society activities include the publishing of a quarterly journal containing articles of general interest to Civil War token collectors, the conducting of quarterly auctions for the benefit of the Society membership, maintaining a library for the use of the membership, providing an attribution service for members, and establishing local chapters and conducting regional meetings. We hold an annual business meeting in conjunction with the American Numismatic Association (ANA) meeting in the summer of each year. The library has a number of Civil War token slide shows that are available on a loan basis for members to present at local meetings. The annual membership dues are $15. For additional information on the Society and membership please visit their website at www.cwstsociety .com or email them at cwtpal@aol.com. The references 1), 2), and 3) are products of the Civil War Token Society efforts, and are accepted as the definitive texts in the Civil War token collecting field. Likewise, reference 4) was authored by one of our Society members, and it, too, is considered to be one of the definitive texts in the Sutler collecting field.

References:
1) FULD, *U.S. Civil War Store Cards,* 2nd Edition, 1975 (Quarterman Pubs).
2) FULD, *Patriotic Civil War Tokens,* 4th Edition, 1982 (Krause Pubs).
3) CIVIL WAR TOKEN SOCIETY, *Die Photos and Fuld/ Moore Listings Update of Patriotic Civil War Tokens,* 4th Edition, 1993 (CWTS Pubs).
4) SCHENKMAN, *Civil War Sutlers Tokens and Cardboard Scrip,* 1983 (Jade House Pubs).

CONFEDERATE COINAGE

Following its secession from the Union in 1861, the Confederate government of Louisiana took control of the federal Mint at New Orleans (the only Mint operating in Southern territory), along with its materials and machinery. Jefferson Davis, president of the C.S.A., appointed C. G. Memminger his secretary of the Treasury and authorized production of a Confederate half dollar. This was presumably manufactured by taking ordinary half dollars and removing their reverse motif, to which was added a shield with seven stars (one for each state that had joined the C.S.A.), a Liberty cap, a wreath of sugarcane and cotton, and the wording CONFEDERATE STATES OF AMERICA HALF DOL. No serious effort was made to circulate this coin, only four specimens being struck. Restrikes were later made. J. W. Scott somehow got hold of the original reverse die and, having keen business aptitude, struck off 500 examples for sale to souvenir hunters. He used his own obverse, consisting of wording without portraiture or other design.

CONFEDERATE HALF DOLLAR

1861
HALF DOL.

DATE	ABP IN MS-60	VF-20 V. FINE	MS-60 UNC.	MS-65 UNC.
☐ 1861 Half Dollar (4)	—	—	—	UNKNOWN
☐ 1861 Half Dollar Restrike (500)				
	—	—	—	10000.00
☐ 1861 Scott Token Obverse, Confederate Reverse (500)				
	—	—	—	7500.00

CONFEDERATE CENT

This was the only Confederate coin intended for general circulation—and it never got that far. Robert Lovett of Philadelphia was commissioned by agents of the C.S.A. to prepare coins in the denomination of one cent in 1861. He was to design the coin, engrave their dies, and do the actual striking as well. After producing a certain quantity, of which only twelve have been discovered, Lovett ceased operations and hid both the coins and the dies from which they were struck, fearing, as a resident of the North, arrest by authorities on grounds of complicity with the enemy. Restrikes were subsequently made, in gold, silver, and copper, by John Haseltine. The figures given here for mintages of the restrikes are based on best available information. Haseltine, in his memoirs of the affair, states that the die broke on the fifty-ninth coin. There are nevertheless believed to be seventy-two restrikes in existence. Haseltine made a point of striking no reproductions in nickel for fear they might be taken for originals.

ORIGINAL	RESTRIKE

DATE	MINTAGE	ABP IN MS-60	MS-60 UNC.	MS-65 CH. UNC.
☐ 1861 Cent (original)	12	—		35,000.00
☐ 1861 Restrike, Silver, Proof	12 4000.00	—		18,000.00
☐ 1861 Restrike, Copper	55	—		15,000.00

THE CIVIL WAR TOKEN SOCIETY

Founded in 1967, the Civil War Token Society is a national, non-profit organization dedicated to help stimulate interest and research in the field of Civil War token collecting. Activities include publishing a journal (The Civil War Token Journal), conducting auctions, maintaining a reference library, providing an attribution service for a nominal fee, establishing State chapters and conducting regional meetings. There are currently over 1,000 active members.

CWTS Membership Application

Name _____
Address _____
City State _____ ZIP_____
email _____ Phone_____

Membership Categories and Dues Amounts

Regular	$15.00 per year
Life Member	$300.00 total
Associate Member*	$7.50 per year
Junior Member**	$7.50 per year

*Resides with a Regular or Life Member, no Journal included
**Under 18 years of age, date of birth: _____

Please make your check or money order payable to CWTS and mail to: John Ostendorf, CWTS Sec., 523 Hiawasee Rd, Waxahachie, TX 75165.

Payments also may be made via Pay Pal at www.CWTSociety.com

For more information email cwtpal@aol.com

GLOSSARY

Coin collecting, like any hobby, has a language of its own spoken by its practitioners and students. New collectors unfamiliar with terms like obverse, reverse, mint mark, and Double Eagle may feel confused by a bewildering lexicon. But the language need not be confusing.

The terms defined here are those that may be commonly encountered during the normal course of coin collecting. Many terms mentioned within the definition for another term are often defined individually as well.

Alloy. Mixture of more than one metal.

Altered. A coin that has been deliberately changed to make it resemble a rare or more valuable piece.

American Eagle. A legal tender bullion coin struck and issued by the U.S. Mint beginning in 1986. The Mint strikes four .9167 fine gold coins and a .999 fine silver coin.

Bag marks. *See* Contact marks.

Bicentennial coins. Quarter dollar, half dollar, and dollar struck in 1975–76 with special reverse designs commemorating the 200th anniversary of the signing of the Declaration of Independence.

Blank. An unstruck disc of metal that when fully processed becomes a planchet, which is later turned into a coin. Simply put, a blank is a planchet that has not been through the entire planchet-making process. *See* Planchet.

Buffalo nickel. Nickname given the Indian Head 5-cent coin. Nickname is commonly used; most U.S. coins are named after their obverse design; the creature on the reverse is a bison, not a buffalo; and no U.S. coin denomination is legally designated a "nickel."

Clad. Composite coinage metal strip composed of a core, usually of a base metal such as copper, and surface layers of more valuable metal like copper-nickel. The U.S. dimes, quarter dollars, and half dollars struck since 1965 are a clad coinage.

Coin. Usually a piece of metal, marked with a device, issued by a governing authority and intended to be used as money.

Colonial coins. Coins struck by one of the thirteen British colonies prior to the American Revolution. Few of the colonial coins were struck with the authority of the British throne, which legally had all coinage rights in Great Britain and the colonies.

Commemorative coin. A coin struck to celebrate a specific individual, event, or group, often on an anniversary date. Commemoratives can be struck for sale to collectors, such as those struck to commemorate the 1996 Olympic Games in Atlanta, or for circulation, such as the 1976 Bicentennial coins.

Contact marks. Surface abrasions found on U.S. coins as a result of coins striking the surfaces of other coins during bagging and shipping procedures.

Coronet. A style of Liberty Head used on U.S. copper and gold coins for much of the 19th century. Liberty wears a coronet (usually marked with the word LIBERTY).

Date. The date on a coin generally, though not always, represents the year a coin was struck. For example, most coins dated 1996 were actually struck in 1996. However, during the coinage shortage that hit the United States in the mid-1960s, 1964- and 1965-dated coins were struck into 1966 in an attempt to prevent hoarding.

Denomination. The face value of a coin; the amount of money it is worth as legal tender.

Device. The principal design element, such as a portrait, shield, or heraldic emblem, on the obverse or reverse of a coin.

Die. A hardened metal punch, the face of which carries an incuse mirror-image to be impressed on one side of a planchet.

Disme. Original spelling of "dime." Believed to have been pronounced to rhyme with "team" or possibly with a silent "s," to sound the same as the modern "dime."

Double Eagle. A $20 gold coin of the United States.

Eagle. A $10 gold coin of the United States.

Edge. Often termed the third side of a coin, it is the surface perpendicular to the obverse and reverse, not to be confused with the rim. Edges can be plain, reeded, lettered, or otherwise ornamented.

Fantasy. An object having the physical characteristics of a coin, issued by an agency other than a governing authority (or without official sanction), yet purporting to be issued by a real or imagined governing authority as a coin.

Field. The flat part of a surface of a coin surrounding and between the head, legend, or other designs.

Flow lines. Microscopic striations in a coin's surface caused by the movement of metal under striking pressures.

Frost. Effect caused by striking a coin with sandblasted dies, often used in reference to Proof coins.

German silver. An alloy of copper, nickel, and zinc, but no silver. Also called American silver, Feuchtwanger's composition, and nickel-silver.

Grading. The process of determining a coin's condition or level of preservation. A coin's grade represents the amount of wear and tear it has received since it was struck. The less wear, the higher the grade and the higher the value. A popular grading scale in use today uses a 1-70 scale, with 70 representing rarely seen perfection and 1 representing a coin so worn that it can barely be identified as to date and design.

Half cent. The smallest denomination issued by the United States. Struck between 1793 and 1857.

Half dimes, half dismes. A silver 5-cent coin of the United States. The Mint Act of April 2, 1792, authorized "half dismes." *See* Disme for pronunciation guidelines.

Half Eagle. A $5 gold coin of the United States.

Hub. A right-reading, positive punch used to impress wrong-reading, mirror-image dies.

Incuse. The opposite of bas-relief; design is recessed rather than raised. Used when referring to coins, medals, and tokens.

Indian Head 5-cent coin. Seven denominations of U.S. coin have borne an Indian Head design; 1-cent, 5-cent coin, gold dollar, $2.50 quarter Eagle, $3 gold coin, $5 Half Eagle, and $10 Eagle. *See also* Buffalo nickel.

Intrinsic. As applied to value, the net metallic value as distinguished from face and collector value.

Jugate. Accolated, conjoined. As related to coins, it refers to a design featuring overlapping portraits, such as on the 1900 Lafayette-Washington commemorative silver dollar.

Krugerrand. A gold bullion coin of South Africa. It is composed of .9167 fine gold and is available in several weights.

Large Cent. Refers to the U.S. cents of 1793–1857, with diameters between 26 and 29mm., depending on the year a particular coin was struck.

Legal tender. Currency (coins or paper money) explicitly determined by a government to be acceptable in the discharge of debts.

Lettered edge. An incused or raised inscription on the edge of a coin. The last U.S. coin to have a lettered edge was the 1992 Olympic Games silver dollar.

Minor coin. For U.S. coins, a silver coin of less than $1 face value, or any coin struck in base metal.

Mint mark. A letter or other symbol indicating the Mint of origin.

Money. A medium of exchange.

Nickel. A silver-white metal widely used for coinage. It is factually incorrect to use "nickel" for the copper-nickel 5-cent coin. In the mid-19th century, copper-nickel cents and 3-cent coins were also nicknamed "nickel," like the modern 5-cent coin. The U.S. Mint has never struck a coin officially called a "nickel."

Numismatics. The science, study, or collecting of coins, medals, paper money, tokens, orders and decorations, and similar objects.

Numismatist. A person knowledgeable in numismatics, who conducts serious, frequently original research.

Obverse. The side of a coin that bears the principal design or device, often as prescribed by the issuing authority. In informal English, the "heads."

Pattern. Coinlike piece designed to test coin designs, mottoes, or denominations proposed for adoption as a regular issue and struck in the metal to be issued for circulation, but which were not adopted, at least in year of pattern issue. The 1856 Flying Eagle cent is a pattern; the coin was not struck for circulation or authorized until 1857.

Penny. The nickname given the 1-cent coin. The U.S. Mint has never struck a penny for use in the United States. The nickname derives from the country's English origins; England still uses a denomination called a penny.

Pioneer gold. Gold coins, often privately produced, struck in areas of the United States to meet the demands of a shortage of coins, generally in traditional U.S. coin denominations. Often called "private gold," which is correct for many but not all of the issues, and "territorial gold," which is incorrect since none of the coins were struck by a territorial government.

Planchet. The disc of metal that, when placed between the dies and struck, becomes a coin. A planchet differs from a blank in that it has been fully processed and is ready for striking into a coin. *See* Blank. Also called flan, generally in reference to ancient coins.

Proof. A coin struck especially for collectors, using special techniques that impart special surfaces to a coin. A set of Proof coins is called a Proof set. The U.S. Mint offers collectors Proof versions of its circulating coinage, American Eagle bullion coins, and commemorative coins.

Quarter dollar. A 25-cent coin of the United States.

Quarter Eagle. A $2.50 gold coin of the United States last struck in 1929.

Restrike. A numismatic item produced from original dies at a later date. In the case of a coin, the restrike usually occurs to fulfill a collector demand and not a monetary requirement.

Reverse. The side opposite the obverse, usually but not always the side with the denomination. The side opposite the side containing the principal design. Informally, the "tails."

Series. Related coinage of the same denomination, design, and type, including modifications and varieties.

Slab. A rigid plastic, permanently sealed holder, usually rectangular, especially those used by third-party grading services.

Three-dollar gold. The United States issued a $3 gold coin from 1854 through 1889.

Type. A basic coin design, regardless of minor modifications. The Indian Head and Jefferson 5-cent coins are different types.

Uncirculated Mint set. A set of Uncirculated coins sold by the U.S. Mint. It generally contains an example of each coin struck for circulation that year. However, some sets contain a coin or coins not being struck for circulation that year.

Unique. Extant in only one known specimen. Very often misused, as in "semiunique."

Variety. The difference between individual dies or hubs of the same basic design or type. For example, the dies used by the U.S. Mint in the 18th and 19th centuries featured many design elements, such as letters, numerals, and stars, that were punched in by hand individually on each die. Thus the date on one coin might be positioned slightly differently than the date on a coin from another die. The differences between the two dies represent different varieties.

Vignette. A pictorial element on a piece of paper money, such as the image of the Lincoln Memorial on the back of the $5 bill.

Want list. A list given by a collector to a dealer listing coins wanted for the collector's collection.

Whizzing. The severe polishing of a coin in an attempt to improve its appearance and salability to the uninformed. A form of alteration considered misleading by the coin collecting community, and which actually lowers the value of a coin.

Wire Rim. Slight flange on coins or medals caused by heavy striking pressure, often characteristic of Proof coins.

Year set. A set of coins of a given year, generally privately or individually produced.

Zinc cent. A nickname applied to the current Lincoln cent. The composition was changed in 1982 from brass (95% copper, 5% zinc) to copper-plated zinc in order to reduce the cost of producing the cent.

FAST-FIND COIN
REFERENCE INDEX

The Blackbooks!

Where Heritage Counts

Through the Boy Scouts of America, millions of young men have enjoyed coin collecting—a hobby passed along by generations of fathers and sons. The BSA is proud to offer Coin Collecting, one of its 120 merit badges.

The revised edition of the BSA's *Coin Collecting* merit badge pamphlet teaches Scouts the basics of coin collecting, including how to understand mint marks, the meaning of collecting and grading terms, and how to use reference catalogs. The pamphlet is invaluable in a Scout's journey toward earning the merit badge.

By becoming a merit badge counselor, the seasoned coin collector can help Scouts achieve their goals. Contact your BSA local council to volunteer.

BOY SCOUTS OF AMERICA®

COIN COLLECTING

BOY SCOUTS OF AMERICA
MERIT BADGE SERIES

Order by calling
1-800-323-0732
or visit your local Scouting retailer.